Examining Colonial Wars and Their Impact on Contemporary Military History

Miguel Madueño
Rey Juan Carlos University, Spain

Alberto Guerrero
Universidad de Granada, Spain

IGI Global
PUBLISHER of TIMELY KNOWLEDGE

A volume in the Advances in Public Policy and
Administration (APPA) Book Series

Published in the United States of America by
IGI Global
Information Science Reference (an imprint of IGI Global)
701 E. Chocolate Avenue
Hershey PA, USA 17033
Tel: 717-533-8845
Fax: 717-533-8661
E-mail: cust@igi-global.com
Web site: http://www.igi-global.com

Library of Congress Cataloging-in-Publication Data

Names: Madueño, Miguel, 1978- editor. | Guerrero, Alberto, 1977- editor.
Title: Examining colonial wars and their Impact on contemporary military
   history / edited by Miguel Madueño, Alberto Guerrero.
Description: Hershey, PA : Information Science Reference, [2023] | Includes
   bibliographical references and index. | Summary: "This book aims to
   approach the phenomenon of colonial wars with the intention of
   understanding our most immediate past in order to analyse the
   contemporary and current scenario with new tools. It is a book that will
   contribute to the dissemination of contents without neglecting the
   considerations of the social sciences and history, with a compilation
   and at the same time analytical character"-- Provided by publisher.
Identifiers: LCCN 2022053582 (print) | LCCN 2022053583 (ebook) | ISBN
   9781668470404 (hardcover) | ISBN 9781668470411 (paperback) | ISBN
   9781668470428 (ebook)
Subjects: LCSH: Military history, Modern--20th century. |
   Decolonization--Colonies--History--20th century. | Imperialism.
Classification: LCC U42.5 E93 2023 (print) | LCC U42.5 (ebook) | DDC
   355.02--dc23/eng/20221122
LC record available at https://lccn.loc.gov/2022053582
LC ebook record available at https://lccn.loc.gov/2022053583

This book is published in the IGI Global book series Advances in Public Policy and Administration (APPA) (ISSN: 2475-6644; eISSN: 2475-6652)

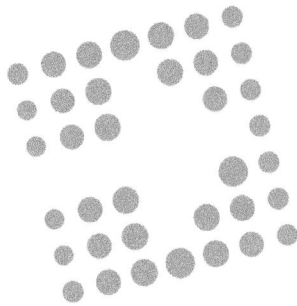

Advances in Public Policy and Administration (APPA) Book Series

ISSN:2475-6644
EISSN:2475-6652

Mission

Proper management of the public sphere is necessary in order to maintain order in modern society. Research developments in the field of public policy and administration can assist in uncovering the latest tools, practices, and methodologies for governing societies around the world.

The **Advances in Public Policy and Administration (APPA) Book Series** aims to publish scholarly publications focused on topics pertaining to the governance of the public domain. APPA's focus on timely topics relating to government, public funding, politics, public safety, policy, and law enforcement is particularly relevant to academicians, government officials, and upper-level students seeking the most up-to-date research in their field.

Coverage

- Government
- Law Enforcement
- Political Economy
- Politics
- Public Administration
- Public Funding
- Public Policy
- Resource Allocation
- Urban Planning

IGI Global is currently accepting manuscripts for publication within this series. To submit a proposal for a volume in this series, please contact our Acquisition Editors at Acquisitions@igi-global.com or visit: http://www.igi-global.com/publish/.

Titles in this Series

For a list of additional titles in this series, please visit: http://www.igi-global.com/book-series/advances-public-policy-administration/97862

Acceleration of the Biopsychosocial Model in Public Health
Simon George Taukeni (University of Namibia, Namibia)
Medical Information Science Reference • © 2023 • 347pp • H/C (ISBN: 9781668464960) • US $325.00

Handbook of Research on the Regulation of the Modern Global Migration and Economic Crisis
Emilia Alaverdov (Georgian Technical University, Georgia) and Muhammad Waseem Bari (Government College University, Faisalabad, Pakistan)
Information Science Reference • © 2023 • 393pp • H/C (ISBN: 9781668463345) • US $285.00

Maintaining International Relations Through Digital Public Diplomacy Policies and Discourses
Türker Elitaş (Hatay Mustafa Kemal University, Turkey)
Information Science Reference • © 2023 • 270pp • H/C (ISBN: 9781668458228) • US $240.00

Handbook of Research on Transforming Government, Nonprofits, and Healthcare in a Post-Pandemic Era
Joanne E. Howard (Illinois Institute of Technology, USA)
Information Science Reference • © 2023 • 590pp • H/C (ISBN: 9781668423141) • US $270.00

Minding the Gap Between Restorative Justice, Therapeutic Jurisprudence, and Global Indigenous Wisdom
Marta Vides Saade (Ramapo College of New Jersey, USA) and Debarati Halder (Parul Institute of Law, Parul University, India)
Information Science Reference • © 2023 • 260pp • H/C (ISBN: 9781668441121) • US $215.00

Societal Transformations and Resilience in Times of Crisis
Ghazala Shoukat (University of Sindh, Jamshoro, Pakistan) and Muhammad Nawaz Tunio (Mohammad Ali Jinnah University, Karachi, Pakistan)
Information Science Reference • © 2023 • 252pp • H/C (ISBN: 9781668453261) • US $215.00

African Policy Innovation and the Political Economy of Public-Private Policy Partnerships
Fred Olayele (Sprott School of Business, Carleton University, Canada)
Information Science Reference • © 2022 • 297pp • H/C (ISBN: 9781799873839) • US $215.00

IGI Global
PUBLISHER of TIMELY KNOWLEDGE

701 East Chocolate Avenue, Hershey, PA 17033, USA
Tel: 717-533-8845 x100 • Fax: 717-533-8661
E-Mail: cust@igi-global.com • www.igi-global.com

Table of Contents

Detailed Table of Contents

Chapter 1
Alfonso Bermúdez Mombiela, Universitat Pompeu Fabra, Spain

The aim of this chapter will be to analyse how the main colonial powers deployed, at the end of the 19th century and the beginning of the 20th, different propaganda strategies with the aim of convincing their populations that the colonial adventure was the solution to their internal problems. In addition, it is intended to deepen the knowledge, on the one hand of the forms and methods used by the different European states to transmit colonial values and disseminate their colonial discourse and, on the other, to analyse how the different populations of the metropolises reacted to the fact that his country had colonies in overseas territories, in his various responses of consent, protest, or resigned acceptance, as well as the attempts to carry out anti-colonial actions by some European leftist parties.

Chapter 2
Natalija Shikova, International Balkan University, North Macedonia

Self-determination has been defined as the right of people to freely determine their political status and pursue their economic, social, and cultural development. During decolonization, the right aimed towards the establishment of the self-government for the peoples – inhabitants of nonself-governed colonial territories. Over the last half century, the process of decolonization resulted in a successful attainment of formal sovereignty for the former colonies. However, the liberation movements reached self-determination externally but failed to reach it internally. Since the process of decolonization is formally over, there is a change in a right holder and the mode for practicing self-determination. Except for an aggregate population – people within the state that can practice an external form of self – determination, as a process internal self-determination can be granted to different subnational groups. The ones that reached external self-determination should accept legal norms that grant forms of internal self-determination.

Chapter 3

María Gajate Bajo, University of Salamanca, Spain

In the construction of the collective remembrance of any war, literary, journalistic, and soldier' chronicles have become very significant and this evidence has been clearly exposed in recent researches on cultural warfare studies. From this statement, the purpose of this chapter is to examine an individual testimony to increase our understanding of the complex Spanish-Moroccan War (1859-1860). Rather than delving into its military dynamics, the main goal of this contribution will consist of providing a profound comprehension of this struggle, its extensive international implications and legacy thanks to a detailed analysis of The Spanish Campaign in Morocco. This is an interesting compilation of the previous reports written by Frederick Hardman, an unknown (at least among Spaniards) foreign correspondent whose words can be extremely enlightening insofar as it will be applied the analytic tool of British informal imperialism as basis for the study of the multidimensional Spanish-Moroccan relationships.

Chapter 4

César García Andrés, Valladolid University, Spain
Pablo Arconada Ledesma, Valladolid University, Spain

This research delves into the colonial conflicts in one of the most confrontational regions of the continent: The Horn of Africa. The geostrategic importance of this area meant that during the first decades of colonisation, several European countries set their sights on these territories, which are currently occupied by Eritrea, Somalia, Djibouti, and Ethiopia. However, the arrival of Europeans in the Horn of Africa was opposed by the local population living in these territories. This resistance to the European invasion is one of the main studies in this analysis, along with the mark it left on the Ethiopian Empire to initiate its expansionism. The object of study is interdisciplinary in nature, but history is undoubtedly the basis of all our argumentation. However, history must be connected to other fields of study, mainly international relations and African studies. The resources that have been used to carry out this research are a list of a wide bibliography on the subject, together with official documents, newspaper, and resources from geographical societies.

Chapter 5

Alberto Guerrero Martín, University of Granada, Spain

The aim of this work is to study how the Spanish army developed the counter-insurgency struggle against the Cuban insurgents, what measures were taken, and whether or not they worked, focusing above all on one of the most successful counter-guerrilla units of this war: the Cazadores de Valmaseda (Valmaseda Hunters). The main sources used for this purpose are the operational reports of the Valmaseda Hunters and the memoirs of some of the protagonists of the campaign, as well as the historiography on this conflict and the available bibliography on irregular warfare during the 19th century.

During the second half of 1896, taking advantage of the cruelty of the insurrection of the Revolutionary forces in the district of Cuba, the Philippine Revolutionary society called Katipunan, which had been founded in July 1892 to promote the insurgency against Spanish sovereignty, took up arms in a truly disturbing way on the island of Luzon. After several violent incidents, the situation became extremely worrying and the Spanish government finally listened to the request made by the Governor General of the district to send troops from the Peninsula. Thus, in record time, fifteen expeditionary light infantry battalions were created by the Spanish Army in addition to other small artillery and cavalry expeditionary units for their military deployment in the Philippine archipelago to put down this new and violent insurrection up.

In recent decades, international studies have been the subject of exciting debates encouraged from critical perspectives, especially from constructivist approaches. Among these debates, the present text intends to pay attention to the revisionism of the narrative around the genealogy of the scientific study of international relations in the first third of the 20th century and the vindication of imperialism in the genesis of international studies. In Spain, the permeability to such historiographical views has not penetrated too much in the review of the genealogy of international studies and even less in the role of imperialism. A question certainly present in the studies on the foreign policy of the period but absent in the analysis of the academic and institutional habitat of international studies in Spain.

The German army's campaigns against the Herero and Nama peoples between 1904 and 1907 were the result of the sum of several dynamics that defined their development: Western military culture, the emergence of Total War, German military doctrine, and biological racism linked to the cultural revolution that took place in Europe in the last decades of the 19th century. However, the defining factor in its development was the international position of the German Empire at the beginning of the 20th century. The result was not only the defeat of two indigenous peoples, but also the first genocide of the 20th century. However, this genocide was not a planned action but the result of the German military's inability to defeat the indigenous warriors. After the victory of the Kaiser's soldiers, the imperial general staff was unable to draw any lessons from this colonial war, despite the limitations of the concept of the decisive battle, the cornerstone of its military doctrine.

This article explores the links between China and Spain since the establishment of formal diplomatic relations in 1864 until the fall of the Qing Dynasty in 1912. To this aim, the authors investigate documents kept by the Ministry of Qing Foreign Affairs at The First Historical Archives of China, in Beijing. Specifically, the authors examine 809 documents of diplomatic communications between the Qing central government and the Spanish institutions in Chinese, French, Spanish, and English. Based on these documents, a database was designed that allowed a full quantitative, diachronic, and thematic analysis of their content. Once the four main topics were defined (diplomatic agreements, protocol, economic and minority issues), each one was independently presented and analyzed. The chapter finds that Spain's relations with late Qing China were characterized by the search for mutual diplomatic support, but lacked an economic or strategic background to cement them. As the authors argue, the documents of the Waiwubu demonstrate how Spain was a friendly but irrelevant nation for the Chinese Qing administration.

This chapter attempts to explain the historical process by which Japan succeeded in becoming a leading colonial power in the Far East. It will analyze the dramatic changes that took place in Japanese foreign policy and international relations from the mid-nineteenth century onwards. Changes that enabled a country with a feudal-type structure to build a national and centralist state and to achieve an unprecedented expansion in the Pacific Ocean and continental Asia. In short, it will describe the process by which Tokyo created in a few decades one of the largest and most ephemeral colonial empires in the history of mankind, supported by rampant nationalism and militarism.

The decolonization of the Spanish-French Protectorate of Morocco initiated after the dethronement of Sultan Mohammed V on August 20, 1953 was a process that was accelerated as a result of the action of terrorism. The way in which the French protectorate administration managed this event unilaterally, without the favor of either Spain or the international community, ended up precipitating that over the next three years the Protectorate of Morocco was plunged into a climate of strong socio-political instability capitalized by the action of terrorism sponsored by the nationalist elements as an instrument to achieve the emancipation of the Alaouite country. The colonial conflict in the Protectorate could only be quelled when France finally agreed to hold diplomatic negotiations with the Moroccan nationalist movements and the legitimate sultan, culminating in the recognition of Morocco's independence in March 1956.

The case of Yugoslavia is paradigmatic in the light of its traumatic decomposition, through a war resulting from religious tensions, nationalism, and revanchism. However, in the decades following the end of the Second World War, Yugoslavia was one of the major protagonists of the historical period known as the Cold War. From a position of theoretical independence from the two opposing blocs, Yugoslavia led the Non-Aligned Movement, and from this organisation it was, as a state, an active defender of the processes of decolonisation and on numerous occasions the main supporter of the new states that were gaining independence from their metropolises. The case of Algeria was significant in the relationship between Yugoslavia and anti-colonialism, for never before had Yugoslav involvement been so intense as in this French colony in North Africa.

The present paper analyzes the occupation of Santo Domingo in 1965 which was the largest US military operation directed against a Latin American country, not only during the Cold War, but in the entire century. In a global Cold War framework, on the one hand, by the détente between the superpowers after the Cuban missile crisis and, on the other, by the force of the Third World and Third World internationalism, the authors explain the impact of the events that occurred on this Caribbean Island had on post-colonial construction, as well as defining a global anti-imperialist struggle. Finally, and according to the review of historical archives from North America, France, and Latin America, among others, which are the primary and secondary sources that accompany the analysis of the proposed research, these conclusions will be delivered in accordance with this historical research.

Based on critical geopolitics, and more specifically on the possibilities offered by practical geopolitics, the following chapter aims to analyse the essence of the discourse of the Portuguese state authorities in relation to Portugal's status as a colonial power, especially after the beginning of the decolonization process, from the early 1960s onwards. Specifically, the period covered by this paper runs from 1955, the year of Portugal's accession to the United Nations, until the end of the dictatorship in 1974. For this purpose, the primary sources used are the parliamentary sessions held in the Portuguese National Assembly and the public speeches delivered by the head of state, António de Oliveira Salazar. The paper thus shows how the foundations of the country's foreign policy were evolving at a particularly convulsive moment in its history, when the legitimization/threat binomial held a central position in terms of discourse.

Miguel Madueño Álvarez, Rey Juan Carlos University, Spain
Julio Alfonso Gonzalez, National University of Distance Education, Spain

The Rhodesian War (1965-1980), known to Anglo-Saxons as The Bush War and to Zimbabweans as the Second Chimurenga conflict or War of Liberation, was the conflict that pitted Ian Smith's unilateral white minority government against pro-independence Zimbabwean guerrillas supported by various communist countries. The nature of the conflict, which was characterized for the small number of combatants, the isolation of the Rhodesian regime, the presence of guerrillas, and the difficulties in obtaining materials, led to the mechanisms of counter-insurgency warfare being set in motion. In this text, the different characteristic elements of this type of warfare have been analysed in terms of combat tactics and military operations, the kind of troops, and the weaponry used as an example of a counterinsurgency conflict.

Felipe Rodolfo Debasa Navalpotro, Rey Juan Carlos University, Spain
Yuliia Andriichenko, Taras Shevchenko National University of Kyiv, Ukraine
Nataliia Popova, Taras Shevchenko National University of Kyiv, Ukraine
Iryna Sytdykova, Taras Shevchenko National University of Kyiv, Ukraine

This chapter raises the problems of colonial wars in the modern world. According to the generally accepted point of view, the elimination of the colonial system had been completed by the end of the twentieth century, as a result of which 90 independent new states arose. But in practice, colonialism has not ceased to exist, but rather continues developing, though in new hybrid forms. Despite numerous international legal norms which were adopted to combat colonialism, more developed countries have repeatedly resorted to armed intervention to restore their interests on the territories they once controlled, including the establishment of a political regime loyal to them, since the end of the last century.

Preface

The contemporary era brought with it a new conception of the art of war that manifested itself in more complex tactics and strategies that honoured different natures. Thus, while the two world wars were the main protagonists of the war scene during the 20th century and have attracted the most attention from researchers and military historians, other contemporary episodes have been largely forgotten.

The complexity of colonial wars was due to the different forms of colonisation exercised by the metropolises for almost a hundred years, with their particular technological development and the numerous ethnic amalgamations that settled in the conquered territories, making their definition and study a complicated task. As a general rule, a power or metropolis conquered by force a territory with a lower level of development, establishing a relationship of acculturation manifested in the economic, social, political and cultural spheres.

On other occasions it came about as a result of a request for help from a native leader who needed the intervention of a metropolis to guarantee the stability of his territory, in colonial systems of shared sovereignty known as protectorates. Finally, in other cases there were real conflicts when the metropolis imposed its brute force in the face of resistance from the indigenous population, which usually ended dramatically for the colonised and could lead to reprisals or very severe colonial systems. To this must be added the reciprocal effect, i.e. the phenomenon of decolonisation that affected the former colonies and protectorates in Asia and Africa during the second half of the 20th century and which brought with it a number of prominent liberation and independence conflicts.

The aim of this book is to recover some of the most relevant episodes of the colonial wars in order to highlight their historical value both for the metropolises and for the territories affected by globalisation. The heterogeneity of the processes of colonisation and decolonisation led to an equally disparate series of conflicts among which it is difficult to identify a common denominator. However, by focusing on a chronology between 1885 and 1980, which covers almost one hundred years, we aim to review the most important milestones of colonialism and its war perspective.

The book begins with a paper by Alfonso Bermúdez that analyses how the main colonial powers deployed different propaganda strategies in the late 19th and early 20th centuries to convince their populations that the colonial adventure was the solution to their internal problems. Natalija Shivova discusses decolonisation and the right to self-determination of peoples to freely determine their political status and to pursue their economic, social and cultural development. The third chapter is by María Gajate, who focuses her analysis on the Spanish-Moroccan war (1859-1860) and draws on the reports of correspondent Frederick Hardman, demonstrating how literary, journalistic and soldiers' chronicles have become highly relevant today, especially in cultural studies of the war. And without leaving the African continent, César García delves into the colonial conflicts in one of the regions of the Horn of

Africa, whose geostrategic importance led several European countries to set their sights on the region, which also provoked strong local resistance to the arrival of the Europeans.

Focusing on purely military aspects, Alberto Guerrero studies the organisation and functioning of the Spanish army in Cuba during the captaincy generalship of Valeriano Weyler (1896-1897). Weyler, an expert in counter-insurgency tactics, managed to reverse the situation and would most likely have ended up dominating the rebellion had he not been dismissed. Continuing with the Spanish army, but this time in the Philippines, Miguel Ángel López de la Asunción presents a study of the expeditionary battalions that were created in 1896 to confront the Philippine insurgency represented by the revolutionary society known as the Katipunan. In the first third of the twentieth century, José Luis Neila approaches the revisionist narrative on the genealogy of the scientific study of international relations and the vindication of imperialism in the genesis of international studies. Roberto Muñoz Bolaños also moves in these early years of this century, dealing with the German operations against the Hereros and the Nama (1904-1908), highlighting not only the defeat of these peoples, but also the first genocide of the century. The chapter by Raúl Ramírez and Guanjie Niu, who study the links between China and Spain from the establishment of formal diplomatic relations in 1864 until the fall of the Qing dynasty in 1912, is suggestive for its infrequency. And it was in the 1960s when the Meiji Restoration took place and a historical process took place whereby Japan managed to become a leading colonial power in the Far East, which is the subject of Pedro Panera's analysis in his chapter.

After the Second World War, the first decolonisation movements took place, such as that of the Spanish-French protectorate of Morocco (1953-1956), analysed by José Manuel Azcona and José Carlos Aránguez, who point out that it was a process that was accelerated by the action of terrorism. The independence of neighbouring Algeria and the role of Yugoslavia during its war of independence will be addressed by Luis Illanas, looking at the Balkan country's intense involvement in this event. The next chapter is by Pedro Martínez Lillo and Javier Castro Arcos, who present an analysis of the US occupation of Santo Domingo in 1965, the largest US operation on the continent. In the context of the Portuguese colonial wars, Mariano García de las Heras and Jerónimo Ríos analyse the essence of the discourse of the Portuguese state authorities in relation to Portugal's status as a colonial power, especially after the beginning of the decolonisation process in the early 1960s. The Rhodesian war (1965-1980), analysed by Miguel Madueño and Julio Alberto Alfonso, focuses on the counter-insurgency tactics and military operations carried out to put an end to guerrilla warfare. The book closes with a chapter by Felipe Rodolfo Debasa, Yuliia Andriichenko, Natalia Popova and Iryna Sytdykova, who delve into the current century to analyse the Russian-Ukrainian war from the point of view of colonial conflicts, since for these authors the most developed countries have repeatedly resorted since the end of the last century to armed intervention to restore their interests in the territories they controlled.

We hope that readers will enjoy and learn from this book as much as the authors, who are keen to promote the study of colonial wars.

Miguel Madueño Álvarez
Rey Juan Carlos University, Spain

Alberto Guerrero Martín
Universidad de Granada, Spain

Chapter 1
Colonial Wars and Public Opinion in a Comparative Perspective

Alfonso Bermúdez Mombiela
Universitat Pompeu Fabra, Spain

ABSTRACT

The aim of this chapter will be to analyse how the main colonial powers deployed, at the end of the 19th century and the beginning of the 20th, different propaganda strategies with the aim of convincing their populations that the colonial adventure was the solution to their internal problems. In addition, it is intended to deepen the knowledge, on the one hand of the forms and methods used by the different European states to transmit colonial values and disseminate their colonial discourse and, on the other, to analyse how the different populations of the metropolises reacted to the fact that his country had colonies in overseas territories, in his various responses of consent, protest, or resigned acceptance, as well as the attempts to carry out anti-colonial actions by some European leftist parties.

INTRODUCTION

It is commonly accepted that colonialism is an indispensable part of the history not only of the colonised countries but also of the colonising countries themselves. In fact, it is argued that the two histories are interconnected, as the expansion of Europeans into the then so-called "underdeveloped" continents would not only change these territories forever but would have fundamental consequences within the metropolises themselves. Thus, this book chapter is conceived from a transnational perspective, based on the premise that all European colonial powers faced similar problems in carrying out their overseas expansion and receiving the consent of the population of their metropolises. Also, the chapter starts from the conception that colonialism had a fundamental impact on the development and configuration of European history, not only at economic or geopolitical levels, but also ideologically. Given the many similarities between the various European colonialisms, some authors have suggested that it might be

DOI: 10.4018/978-1-6684-7040-4.ch001

useful to contemplate the possibility of a European colonial culture, since imperialism was a shared experience that transgressed national perspectives (Stanard, 2011).

Methodologically, to carry out this chapter, the main historiographical contributions on this subject in recent years will be taken as the object of study, especially those referring to the reactions of European populations to the colonialist dynamic. Thus, through an analysis of the historiography of the four major colonial powers, United Kingdom, France, Germany and Italy (others such as Belgium, the Netherlands, Portugal, Spain, etc. have been left out of the study for logistical and academic reasons) an attempt will be made to construct a study that reflects on the main mechanisms of dissemination of the colonial discourse, as well as a brief outline of the possible consequences of this propagandistic bombardment. This book chapter will argue that the process was common to all countries and was particularly personalised in the figure of the geographical and exploratory societies, the newspapers as well as the colonial exhibitions that toured Europe in the first third of the 20th century. Likewise, this chapter will try to deepen the knowledge of the real impact on European public opinion, as well as the anti-colonial responses in several of the countries studied. In this way, this book chapter will attempt to approach the complicated concept of "public opinion" through a two-way analysis, from above and from below, referring, on the one hand, to the discourses emanating from the political and economic elites and, on the other, to the possible responses and reactions of the populations of the metropolises. However, this author is aware that approaching public opinion is complicated, and that knowledge of this subject requires more in-depth analyses, some of which are suggested at the end of the chapter.

BACKGROUND

In the archaeological site that is British society in the nineteenth and early twentieth centuries there are, of course, thousands of imperial shards to be found. Dug out and piled up at the side, they can be made to look overwhelming. Studied in situ, however, one gets a different impression. They appear widely scattered and concentrated in certain layers and at particular spots. One misses an awful lot if one is not aware of where, exactly, they have been found. Some of them lie close to the remains of other structures or artefacts in a way that suggests that they may have broken off from them, and not from 'imperialism' at all. Between them there are also great expanses of nothing: of earth or rock whose barrenness may be as significant as the presence elsewhere of the shards themselves. This is where knowledge of the context is vital. (Porter, 2004).

These words, which Bernard Porter dedicated to the study of the impact of imperialism on the European populations of the late 19th and early 20th centuries, illustrate the historian's complicated task of trying to assess how the inhabitants of the metropolises might have been affected by the fact that their country occupied overseas territories and subjugated other peoples. The quantity of finds may seem overwhelming, as a thorough analysis will be able to find thousands of vestiges that, if analysed simply quantitatively, piling them on top of each other, may lead to hasty or reductionist conclusions. In fact, if these fragments are not studied in their proper context, bearing in mind that they may be linked to other concepts, the overall perspective may be lost.

In view of these difficulties, how can the historian measure the public reaction to colonialism? From a methodological perspective, this is a problem that researchers have faced for decades. It is possible to know how the nations tried to sell the colonial discourse to their population, but it is always an enigma what the real impact of this propaganda was, whether it was internalised by the people or not. The mechanisms used by the states and the private initiative to sell the colonial discourse can be traced, but it is much more difficult to know the real impact of this discourse, especially due to the lack of sources.

Historiographically, for many years the study of the impact of colonialism on the metropolises was largely ignored. Other aspects, such as the causes of colonial expansion, power structures or the processes of decolonisation meant that historians rarely asked what the colonies had meant for public opinion. What the British call the *repatriation* of the Empire was virtually overlooked for many years, which is undoubtedly a serious historiographical hole. Fortunately, for some decades now, this situation has been gradually reversed, and works such as those included in the *Studies in Imperialism* series, led by John M. Mackenzie and his school in Manchester, have been appearing, which have focused on the study of what is known as "popular imperialism", and have developed interesting theories in this respect. What Mackenzie and his disciples have mainly tried to show was how empire marked the lives of what they call "ordinary people", imperialism being for them not a minority issue, but a core ideology in British society from the 1880s to the late 1950s. This school of thought has come into conflict with the theories of Bernard Porter, for whom British imperial expansion during the New Imperialist era had little effect on the lower classes in the UK. The British Empire being an institution run almost entirely by members of an upper- and middle-class minority, there was no need for mass engagement with the Empire in the metropole (2004). Between these two positions we can find intermediate hypothesis; Peter Marshall, for example, accepts that Britain's history and its empire cannot be separated, but sees the impact of empire as complementary rather than decisive, its role being to reinforce existing trends in the UK (1996).

Moving to France, historians have long wondered whether the French reacted positively or negatively to colonial propaganda policy. For many years, the most widespread view was that empire was never a popular enterprise in France (Ageron, 1978), a country too attached to its metropolitan territory and traditional agrarian values to worry about foreign possessions. However, more recent studies have demonstrated the validity of more social or cultural approaches to the impact of the colonies in France. For example, Tony Chafer and Amanda Sackur argued that empire was crucial to popular culture, and played a pivotal role in shaping post-1870 French society and culture (2002). Other works have tended to attempt to demonstrate the validity of a French "popular imperialism" (Evans, 2004), or they affirm that it is necessary to differentiate between "deep" France, which was not colonialist, but neither was it anti-colonialist and the population was divided between a majority that approved, or at least did not oppose imperial policy, and two minorities, one of imperialists that did support it fervently, and another of anti-colonialists who criticized it, depending on the situation (Biondi, 1993).

For its part, in Germany, a long historiographical tradition has ignored the role of the colonies in the history of the Second Reich and the Weimar Republic, considering German colonialism as a footnote in history. Fortunately, in recent years a new historiographical impulse has emerged and has tried to bring Germany's colonial performance out of oblivion, arguing that colonialism was not so irrelevant to German society. In fact, interesting questions and debates have been raised, such as the relationship that could exist between imperialism and the development of National Socialism, especially regarding the massacres of the Herero and Nama at the beginning of the 20th century (Kundrus, 2011). Contributions have also been made in various fields where colonialism affected, such as cinema, social sciences, medicine, or advertising (Simons & Honold, 2002; Zantop, 1997; Schöning, 1997; Eckart, 1997). All these contributions reveal that colonialism was part of a broad spectrum of thoughts and experiences within German society that should not be neglected, and that there was indeed a considerable push from

German elites, especially from private or semi-private initiatives, which its objective was to influence the population in a favourable way to German colonization.

Regarding Italy, until the latter part of the 20th century, Italy's colonial past was a largely neglected subject in historical scholarship. Before that, only a handful of historians, among them the most prominent Angelo del Boca and Nicola Labanca, who began to postulate the existence of a "social imperialism" that implied an extremely close relationship between colonialism and the construction of a national identity (1994), had shown some interest. However, at the beginning of the 21st century, colonial studies experienced a resurgence, producing remarkable progress in the quantity and quality of research. Later, interesting advances have been made, especially several collective volumes that have finally achieved or come close to finally catching up with Italian historiography and augurs a positive panorama in this sense (Ben-Ghiat & Fuller, 2005; Bertella & Dau Novelli, 2015; Srivastava, 2018).

MAIN FOCUS OF THE CHAPTER

Colonies from Above: Geographical Societies, Press, Colonial Exhibitions and *Völkerschauen*

To begin with, it should be noted that, throughout the 19th century, advances in technology, science and industrialisation provided the "tools of empire" (steamships, railways, telegraphs, medicine, and armaments) that made the world accessible to Europeans; between 1871 and 1914 a combination of great diplomatic tension, the formation of alliances and an arms race occurred, in which is traditionally called "Armed Peace" (Wesseling, 1981). Meanwhile, the idea of "race" allowed the distribution of superiority and inferiority throughout the world along the axes of culture, biology, and nation. In fact, Europeans defined their world in terms of hierarchies of civilisation, generally assuming that the civilised had the right and duty to intervene in the affairs of the less civilised (Bowersow, 2010). Thus, the imperialism of the 1860s and 1880s provoked a real surge of interest in overseas territories, which led to the founding of more than eighty geographical societies in the major cities of Europe. These organisations were composed of different groups with different priorities: from scientists and amateurs with academic interests, to social, political, and economic elites with commercial and geopolitical interests in the colonies. In short, privileged groups with financial or political interests abroad constituted these societies as powerful lobbies (Atkinson, 2005).

Therefore, the second half of the 19th century saw the growth of a whole series of propagandist leagues and societies that promoted the colonial agenda, pushing policies such as emigration, naval supremacy, and tariff reform, all with the aim of extolling the virtues and values of the colonies. By doing so, imperialism was legitimised by geography and other academic disciplines, which attributed racial difference to climate and environment, or justified spatial expansionism with geopolitical theories. It is undeniable that the development of scientific disciplines like geography allowed the practical construction of the colonial territories. This process was common to all countries and was particularly represented by the geographical and exploratory societies, such as the British *Navy League*, the French *instituts coloniaux*, the German *Deutsche Kolonialgesellschaft* (DKG) and *Flottenverein*, or the Italian *Società geográfica*. All of them meant that, from that time onwards, the colonial spaces, hitherto unreachable, were delimited and ordered according to European guidelines. The policies deployed by these societies took all kinds of forms, which, although they varied from country to country, had common denominators.

In Britain, empire was embedded in the fabric of everyday British life. It was in the food, the clothes, the newspapers, the books, the music... in short, empire was part of British lives, in a cross-class way, moreover. From lecture tours by prominent colonial politicians or advocates of imperialism, the design of school textbooks or the creation of popular festivals, such as Empire Day in 1902 in Britain, to the propagation of all sorts of paraphernalia related to empire and the colonies, and even seemingly minor details. For example, it was at this time that maps of the world in Britain's school classrooms began to appear with British possessions coloured in red, at the initiative of the Navy League. The hope of politicians like Joseph Chamberlain, Alfred Milner or George Curzon was to get the population to assimilate a set of values linked to imperialism, to create an efficient alternative to the rapid development and advance of socialism and communism. The British worker had to internalise the idea that the fact that Britain had an empire was economically profitable for him as a private individual, provided jobs, was a source of national glory and therefore a source of self-satisfaction.

In this way, the gradual emergence of colonial lobbies was driving the extension of colonial values in all the countries in a methodical way. In France, too, the supporters of colonial expansion soon realised that, in order to be able to continue with it, they first had to convince the French population of the benefits of the expansionist policy, in order to create a certain *état d'esprit* among the population, and so they began to organise themselves into what would later become known as the *Parti Colonial*, a group whose members, of various political affiliations, shared a common interest in France's colonial expansion. The first club of politicians, intellectuals, and officials, the *Comité de l'Afrique Française*, was created in 1890, and in 1892 a group of pro-imperial deputies was founded in the National Assembly (Sèbe, 2013). The launch of the *Union Coloniale* in 1895 was the last step towards the creation of an efficient network of colonial supporters.

The members of these small but powerful groups, which were closely intertwined and enjoyed privileged connections with the geographical societies, intended to influence the government and raise public awareness of the colonies, or at least reduce public opposition to colonial expansion. Thus, the geographical societies in Paris and the provinces actively promoted better awareness of the empire. Colonial advocates, whether politicians, writers, or journalists, made extensive use of the concept of "civilising mission" to justify their expansionist agenda, which gradually became an integral part of the ideals of the French Third Republic. This colonial agenda included several key assumptions, most important of which was that the colonies should serve France by providing economic gains and raw materials, and attracting French investment (Aldrich, 1996). After the First World War, the successor to the *Parti Colonial* was the *Ligue Maritime et Coloniale Française*, which took shape in June 1920, backed by the prestigious *Académie Française*, with the merger of two imperialist lobbies, the *Ligue Française Maritime* and the *Ligue Coloniale Française* (Thomas, 2005).

Moving to Germany, from the end of the 19th century onwards, supporters of colonial expansion began to organise themselves through various initiatives. According to Hans-Ulrich Wehler, the ruling elites used social imperialism as the glue to hold together a fractured society and to maintain popular support for the social status quo, avoiding the internal threat of social revolution, shifting tensions to the periphery (1969). First, in 1887, the *Deutsche Kolonialgesellschaft* (DKG), emerged as the main colonialist lobby. Formed from the merger of the *Deutscher Kolonialverein*, established in 1882 and the *Gesellschaft für Deutsche Kolonialisation*, established in 1884, with an important presence of aristocrats and members of the Reichstag, this society was born with the aim of promoting German colonialism through various initiatives and policies, being the German government's think tank on overseas matters and developing advisory commissions for the government itself and private companies (Demhardt, 2002). Later, the

DKG was joined by the *Deutsche Flottenverein*, founded in April 1898 by representatives of various economic sectors, such as the Krupp heavy industries, shipyards, and banks, as well as politicians and military professionals such as Admiral Alfred von Tirpitz (Rüger, 2009). In this way, German society began to receive extensive amounts of imperial propaganda from both the DKG and the *Flottenverein*. Thus, ideas such as the need for colonial possessions as a means of securing German foreign trade interests, the promotion of the creation and development of a German navy, or the desirability of establishing settlement colonies abroad as a destination for German emigrant labour were conveyed (Eley, 1991).

Regarding Italy, a growing political and social movement also began to develop at the end of the 19th century, seeking to push for the expansion of its areas of influence in Africa, in the heat of a world scenario in which other powers were taking position while Italy remained stagnant both economically and geopolitically (Tripodi, 1999). In the last quarter of the 19th century, Italian elites saw colonial expansion not only in economic terms, but also as an instrument to iron out differences among Italians. Angelo Del Boca argued in fact that the Italian ruling class sought to divert attention from internal problems due to its inability to solve them rather than because it was firmly convinced that the colonies were an absolute necessity for the country (1992). Christopher Duggan argues that what inspired politicians to bring Italy into colonial politics was the desire to give the *Risorgimento* a necessary component of popular participation, which must be understood within the framework of the complicated nationalization process of the recasting of Italy after the unification (2001). As early as 1869, taking advantage of the recent opening of the Suez Canal, the Rubattino Trading Company began to turn its attention to the strategic Bay of Assab. In the same year, the *Società Geografica Italiana* carried out its first exploratory expedition to Africa, with a mission to Eritrea led by the explorer Orazio Antinori. Subsequently, in 1879, the *Società di Esplorazione Commerciale*, to which several Italian industrial groups belonged, established itself in Africa, the same year in which the African Club was created in Italy, which three years later became the *Società Africana d'Italia*. Later, institutions such as the *Istituto Coloniale Italiano* in Rome in 1906 and the *Istituto Agricolo Coloniale Italiano* in Florence in 1909 were founded. The first, founded by a group of politicians, explorers, diplomats, and university professors, had the objective of being the unofficial spokesman of the Italian government to inform the population about both state and private colonial action, develop the economy of the colonies, promote and encourage the diffusion of colonial culture and technical preparation for colonial initiatives. The second, founded by a group of Italian agronomists and tropicalists, had the objective of promoting the study of the environment and tropical agriculture, in addition to carrying out a task of training agricultural specialists (Atkinson, 2005).

Therefore, it can be seen how, in all studied countries, a network of organisations, private, public, or even semi-public (given the origins of their members), was woven, deploying a set of strategies designed to foster a sense of belonging within an empire as opposed to a much more local or national frame of reference. In conjunction with the expansion of these geographical and commercial societies, it is vital to consider the role of the press in the circulation of ideas and opinions among the public, at a time when the introduction of technical advances such as the telegraph, the expansion of the railways and the decline in illiteracy meant that newspapers were consumed on an increasingly massive scale. For example, by the turn of the century, virtually all British newspapers printed daily news directly or indirectly related to Britain's overseas possessions. Many of the journalists, editors and newspaper owners were genuine enthusiasts of the empire, which affected the editorial line of the newspapers, and undoubtedly motivated several of the most significant press campaigns and events of the time, such as the follow-up to the Boer War in the late 19th century or the holding of the Imperial Press Conference in June 1909. Also, by the late nineteenth century, an embryonic imperial press system had emerged, (including *The Times*, the

Daily Mail, and the *National Review*) based on strong similarities and links between the press in Britain and the Dominions (Potter, 2003). In France, the illustrated supplements of major newspapers, such as *Le Petit Journal* from 1884 or *Le Petit Parisien* from 1889, often featured an evocative colour engraving depicting scenes of colonial conquest on their front pages. Likewise, the bulletin of the *Ligue Maritime et Coloniale Française*, media articles, books, documentaries, and academic lecture series emphasised the centrality of the empire to France's prosperity and power (Thomas, 2005).

In Germany, the clearest example is the use of the new media of photography and film, which played a generally vital role in popularising imperial themes and values. For example, between 1905 and 1908, the DKG provided its local branches with short films to arouse support and interest in the German colonies; this action was complemented by collaborations with the *Flottenverein* and school parties followed by evening screenings for adults, used to increase the popular appeal of early colonial films (Gissibl, 2011). Another connection between the German population and the colonials was related to the consumption of new products from foreign lands, as during the 20th century, the consumption of colonial products (*Kolonialwaren*) such as sugar, cocoa, coffee, or spices became accessible to wider strata of society (Perraudin & Zimmerer, 2010).

In Italy, too, a major effort was made to popularise African colonialism, especially after the Dogali and Adowa disasters, using the book peddlers, known as the *Pontremolesi*, who remained in the late 19th century a rudimentary but essential and effective way of distributing written culture. Through this and other formulas, novels were widely available, such as those of publisher Edoardo Perino, who published Giuseppe Piccinini's bestselling *La Guerra d'Africa* between 1887-1888 by instalments, a method that would become a hugely successful tradition in Italian book publishing up to the present day (Finaldi, 2011). Later, the advent of fascism brought with it a renewed discursive effort aimed at legitimising Italian colonial expansion in Africa, which also benefited from the latest advances in propaganda, such as cinema, radio, and the mass press. The strategy deployed by the Fascist regime to win the support of the Italian population for the colonial project was in fact systematised. From the beginning of the Duce's regime, for example, the propaganda that accompanied the birth of an authentic colonial literature was managed directly by the Ministry of the Colonies, with the creation in 1926 of the monthly publication *Esotica. Mensile di letteratura coloniale*, which two years later became *L'Oltremare*, the organ of the Fascist Colonial Institute (Boddi, 2012). Later, the propaganda campaign that accompanied the launch of the Ethiopian invasion in 1935 was truly overwhelming. The fascist regime used all the means at its disposal, including the cinema, newsreels, mass-produced books and newspapers, publicity, and radio, deploying, according to Adolfo Mignemi, a painstaking strategy to ensure that the Ethiopian campaign of 1935- 36 had massive support (1984).

It should also be mentioned that imperial propaganda transformed the perception of the military among the population of the metropolis. Until the early 19th century, the population's impression of the troops was very negative; they were basically savage and brutalised groups of men who were forced to be kept at home in times of war or revolt. However, through constant imperial propaganda, a more favourable and acceptable face of the soldier was spread, supported by illustrated magazines, plays, postcards or merchandising. Thus, according to J. M. Mackenzie, at least for the British case (and probably, according to this author, it can be applied to the rest of the powers) colonial warfare played a vital role in transforming the reputation of the military, as it fitted perfectly into a number of cultural and literary traditions: the enthusiasm for chivalric virtues, the tradition of adventure based on high moral values, a fascination with individual heroic action in the service of the state, and the increasing predominance of martial values in music, illustrations and youth literature (1992).

On the other hand, the expansion of imperial images and propagandistic themes cannot be understood without considering the growing importance of colonial exhibitions. In Britain, from the Colonial and Indian Exhibition of 1886, exhibitions were entirely empire-centred, peaking with the Wembley Empire Exhibition in London in 1924-1925 and continuing until the Glasgow Empire Exhibition in 1938. In France, colonial aspects already appeared in the *expositions universelles* in Paris in 1889 and 1900, and especially in the specifically colonial exhibition held for the first time in Lyon in 1894. Later, there were specific colonial exhibitions in 1906 in Marseilles and 1907 in Paris; and, of course, the great Colonial Exhibition of Vincennes in 1931. In Germany, in turn, one of the most widespread ways of transmitting and reinforcing imperial values was through the cultural displacement of indigenous peoples for commercial spectacles in the form of travelling exhibitions, known as *Völkerschauen*, which would be understood as "people's exhibitions" or even "human zoos". These shows accompanied the heyday of European imperialism between the 1870s and 1930s and were massive events. For example, a group of Nubians presented by Carl Hagenbeck at the Berlin Zoological Garden in 1878 attracted 62,000 visitors on a single Sunday, while the Ceylonese exhibition that toured Europe in 1886 was visited by more than a million people during the ten weeks it was held in Paris. Subsequently, between 1896 and 1940, around forty colonial exhibitions propagated the colonial idea, connecting the empire abroad with cities all over Germany, and were a particularly popular instrument after 1918 to keep the memory of the colonies alive (Dreesbach, 2005).

All these spectacles, both the colonial exhibitions and the hugely popularly attended *Völkerschauen*, offered the opportunity for Europeans to, supposedly, learn about ethnography, indigenous traditions, crafts, and art, but, in fact, helped to reinforce the patterns of imperialist domination and subordination. Moreover, the itinerant nature of many of these exhibitions undoubtedly encouraged the extension and reaffirmation of these values transnationally. However, these spectacles were not a real image of the peoples represented and their ways of life, but rather a construction of the clichés that Europeans had towards foreigners, created by storybooks, images and histories. Especially, human zoos contributed very significantly to the solidification of racist attitudes and were often a humiliating representation of foreign cultures. Nevertheless, these exhibits were praised by the scientific community, so that the construction of racial difference received scientific validation from the intellectual authorities.

To recap, it can be seen how the expansion of geographical societies, press, and colonial expositions, had the purpose, with all the deployment of resources, to prevent colonial expansion from arousing growing opposition, to avoid the perception that the costs of empire outweighed the benefits, or perhaps even worse: that the public opinion would come to the conclusion that the benefits of colonialism were monopolised by the privileged classes, while the negative aspects, such as the sending of troops or economic setbacks, were borne by the rest of society. At the same time, a fundamental strategy in carrying out the process of conquest was fulfilled: the production of an irreconcilable difference between Europe and the colonies, in which the former was considered synonymous with civilisation and the latter with backwardness, lacking reason and incapable of moral sense or rational thought. This artificial opposition between the European "us" and the indigenous "them" was crucial for the European self-conception, as it not only dehumanised the natives, but also created the necessary conditions to legitimise their enslavement and the colonisation of the continent. Thus, the racialisation and naturalisation of difference was reflected in concepts drawn from Darwinian social language, such as the "survival of the fittest", the "civilising mission" or the European construction of Africa as the so-called Dark Continent, and sought to construct what Frederick Cooper and Ann Stoler have called "grammars of difference" to describe the hierarchies established in the colonial discourse that would protect the image of the moral and cultural superiority of the colonising nation (1997). In fact, the theory of evolution was a powerful weapon in the debate of the differences between races and peoples (Wesseling 2013).Therefore, the project of conquest was organised around a paradigm of difference and a hierarchy of values in which Europe had the right and duty to bring civilisation to these backward territories. This racist and pseudo-scientific belief formed the context in which colonial states sought to remake colonial spaces, on unequal terms, and often through the instrument of violence (Brioni and Bonsa Gulema, 2018).

Colonies From Below: Political Parties, and Anti-colonial Responses

Another aspect that has received little historiographical attention has been the study of those sectors critical of the empire and the colonies. Those who, at some point, questioned expansionist policies and have been lumped, perhaps erroneously, into the category of "anti-imperialists". Perhaps wrongly, because it is worth reflecting on whether at some point in the history of several countries there was anything like an anti-imperialist current.

For example, in Britain, except on rare occasions, such as in the context of the Boer War, there was never any explicit criticism of colonial policy. Politically, in fact, no party expressing outright opposition to empire ever gained much support in the British political landscape. There are even historians who consider that the amount of attention these displays of dissatisfaction with empire have received is disproportionate to their actual historical significance (Thompson, 2014). Studies of anti-imperialism in Britain conclude that the moments when any political or economic group opposed colonial expansion were, at best, limited and context-specific, and that at no time was anyone in favour of dismantling the empire or abandoning the colonies. At most, there was opposition to the acquisition of new territories or questioning of the performance of the British colonial administration (Cain, 2002).

Overall opposition to Empire was thus fragmentary and diffuse. The anti-imperialism of figures such as Richard Cobden or John Bright reflected a variety of points ranging from hostility to the acquisition of new territories, which did not necessarily imply the abandonment of existing possessions, to a desire to introduce representative government in the white-settled colonies, to generic assertions that Empire was unprofitable and perpetuated the power of Britain's aristocracy. Proclamations for decolonisation were rare, and when they were made, they were never based on appeals to universalist principles of democracy or self-determination. It is quite likely that even the main leftist party, the Labour Party, consciously avoided taking a stand on an issue on which it felt unable to construct a strong discourse against mainstream opinion (Prior, 2010). Looking at the thought and work of two of its most important founders, Keir Hardie and Ramsay MacDonald, the approaches that set the tone for the Labour Party revolved around moral outrage at exploitation in the colonies, but with very little attempt to trace the causes of such evils or to propose strategies for their elimination (Howe, 1998). Thus, apart from a diffuse ideological impact, British anti-imperialism never took a militant form, as it did in France or Italy for example, as it shall be seen below.

In fact, in France, anti-colonial movements did play a more prominent role, especially after the First World War, and were largely led by workers' parties. However, the leadership of anti-colonial protest will change over time, as the positions of the parties changed as the twentieth century progressed. The clearest example is French socialism, embodied in the SFIO (*Section Française de l'Internationale Ouvrière*), which will begin the 20th century opposing all colonial expansion, following the dictates of the Stuttgart Congress of the Second International in 1907. However, from the 1920s onwards it will nuance its position. In practice, French socialism was in favour of what might be called a pragmatic or even accidentalist colonialism, in which the right of the French, as a superior race, to possess colonies was assumed, but the aim was to fight the abuses of colonialism, without questioning the system itself. The measures advocated by socialist colonial policy were the increase of self-government in the colonies, economic development, gradual participation of the natives in politics, the attempted repression of mistreatment of the natives, restrictions on exploitative commercial activity, and the promotion of education, medical care, and other benefits for non-Europeans. Thus, they were inclined to favour assimilationist policies that would gradually integrate colonial populations with metropolitan France (Aldrich, 1996).

Therefore, since the French socialists were not opposed to having an empire, it was the French communists, who split from the SFIO to found the French Communist Party (*Parti Communiste Français*, PCF) in 1920, who were to spearhead the anti-colonialist movement. Hence, the PCF included anti-colonialism in its political programme and developed initiatives to try to undermine the French government, such as the establishment in 1924 of the Committee against the Rif War, the first formal anti-colonialist association, supporting the struggle of Abd el-Krim, or the organisation of a 24-hour general strike in October 1925 that brought together nearly one million participants across France (Bermúdez, 2016). However, it should not be ruled out that these protests arose from a context in which the French government was in trouble, after the defeat in the Uarga valley in 1925. Moreover, the hypothesis that the PCF mobilised the population to take advantage of a moment of government weakness cannot be discarded. And of course, the distant role of the Soviet Union in the impetus for these protest mobilisations should not be disregarded.

As for the Second German Reich, the colonies were rarely seen by Reichstag debates or political party proclamations. Colonial events only had any impact on Germans at certain key moments, such as during the "Boxer War", or the "Hottentottenwahlen" or "Hottentot elections" in January 1907 (Lü, 2010). In 1906, due to the persistence of the colonial campaigns, at a high cost for Germany, a political crisis occurred when the German government asked for a supplementary budget of 29 million marks for the war in southwestern Africa. This led to a marked division between the political parties, finding on the one hand those in favour of granting credit, such as the *Deutschkonservative Partei* or the *Nationalliberale Partei*, and on the other those opposed to credit, such as the Catholics of the *Zentrum* and especially the SPD (*Sozialdemokratische Partei Deutschlands*). For the party that was most vehemently opposed to the colonial war, the SPD, these elections were a real blow since, although the Social Democrats were the party with the most votes, they lost almost half of their seats.

In fact, the SPD's position on colonial expansion has given rise to interesting debates. Traditionally, it has been considered that the SPD was the only German political option that raised criticism of colonialism, considering that the previously seen criticisms of the *Zentrum* of the 1906 budgets were caused by economic conditions. Hans-Ulrich Wehler postulated that only the SPD, unlike all other political parties, had a critical opinion on colonialism (1969), a position shared by David Blackbourn and Geoff Eley (1989). The truth is that the SPD's position on colonialism is still under dispute. From historians who deny its relevance in German politics, or affirm that the party assumed colonialist and racist postulates before the First World War (Fischer, 2007; Smith, 1998; El-Tayeb, 2001; Hyrkkänen, 1986; Conrad, 2006), to new interpretations, such as Jens-Uwe Guettel, who argues that, first of all, very different ideological tendencies coexisted in the SPD, some in favour of colonialism, others against it and others half way, and, secondly, that the official position of the party remained against colonialism until the First World War (2012). This does not mean, of course, that all members of the SPD shared anti-colonial views. In fact, the main intellectuals of the party were divided on the question of colonialism for a long time. On the one hand, some like Bernstein, Bloch and Schippel directly approved colonial expansion, or at least accepted the fact of having colonies in a pragmatic way, as Gustav Noske. On the other, figures like Henke, Ledebour, Kautsky, or Rosa Luxemburg publicly proclaimed their opposition to all anti-colonial policies. In any case, it can be said that anti-colonialism was used by the SPD to attack the different governments of the II Reich until months before the outbreak of the First World War, and that later the loss of all the German colonies in favour of the other powers would eliminate this issue from their agenda politics.

It remains to be asked what role, if any, played the anti-colonialist movements in Italy. The reality is that apart from specific moments of explosion of popular anger against the colonial defeats, such as those of Dogali and Adowa, in 1887 and 1896, Italian anti-colonialism was represented, spasmodically, only by the Italian Socialist Party (PSI) in the first place, and later by the *Partito Comunista d'Italia* (PCd'I), which would indeed be capable of deploying a powerful campaign of opposition to the Ethiopian War from exile in the 1930s, and also had one of the most important Marxist intellectuals outstanding of the 20th century, Antonio Grasmci, who elaborated a brilliant theoretical opposition to colonialism. Unfortunately, it is difficult to find specific works that have dealt with the opposition to colonialism in Italy before the Ethiopian War. In this sense, the best-known work was made by Maurizio Degl'Innocenti on the Socialist Party and the war in Libya, in which he states that Filippo Turati and the other socialist leaders underestimated Italy's participation in the war, relying on an anti-imperialism that it never became as strong as they believed (1976). Italians, except in the aftermath of the Adowa disaster, appear to have supported, or at least not vehemently opposed, their country's expansion into Africa, and there are indications that the Socialist Party genuinely feared that the popularity of the war in Africa was a vector of patriotism that helped to strengthen the relationship between the state and the Italian population (Finaldi, 2011).

The relationship of Italian socialism with colonialism was therefore complex. It is even known that, within the Party itself, the colonial conflicts caused an internal division. For example, the conquest of Libya was supported by such prominent figures of the Italian left as Angelo Olivetti, Arturo Labriola, or Ivanoe Bonomi (curiously, one of the Italian socialist figures who most opposed the Libyan campaign was a young Benito Mussolini). Therefore, colonialism caused important divisions within Italian socialism, which moved between absolute rejection and pragmatic acceptance of it, in a case like the German and French ones. In fact, a resounding and unified opposition could not be seen in an Italian workers' party until the *Tesi di Lione* of the *Partito Comunista d'Italia* of 1926, written by Antonio Gramsci. According to this author, colonialism came from internal hegemonies that subjected the subaltern classes within the nation to economic and political exploitation. Likewise, Gramsci compared the exploitation to which the Eritreans and Libyans were being subjected to the exploitation suffered by the Italian south by the industrial north. Among all the anti-colonial actions that the Italians could carry out, it must be highlighted what would become one of the most outstanding anti-colonial actions in the history of opposition to colonialism, during the Italian invasion of Ethiopia in 1935-36, which it even surpassed the demonstrations against the Rif War carried out by the French communists in 1925.

In 1935-36, the *Partito Comunista d'Italia* promoted a radical anti-colonial campaign against the Italian invasion of Ethiopia, hoping that this costly war would prove so unpopular with the Italian working classes that it could serve to overthrow the fascist regime. This campaign would be motivated, according to authors such as Neelam Srivastava, by the fact that the Communist Party knew from its internal sources that many Italians were very disillusioned with this adventure into which Mussolini had dragged the nation (2018). The communists' strategy was to publish a series of pamphlets and manifestos condemning the fascist aggression against Ethiopia, asking the Italians to revolt against the regime. Not only that, but the party also organized a joint congress with the PSI in France, which was attended by numerous anti-fascist groups, including the two communist internationals and some 100,000 Italian workers living abroad. However, despite the great reception of this campaign, it does not seem that within Italy itself the communist proclamations had much echo, much less that it was possible to carry out any type of colonial opposition action within the framework of a regime as repressive as the fascist.

To recap, about the strategies used by different groups to oppose their governments' invasion of colonised territories, it should be said that, in most of the cases, the answers that could be cautiously call "anticolonial" came from the left-wing sectors. When these actions came from the central or right-wing sectors, as in the German case of the *Zentrum* during the "Hottentottenwahlen" or the British politicians of both parties that criticised the Boer War, were a result of economic or political reasons. Although it is possible to find examples of anticolonial protests among the bourgeois parties and the left-wing politics, such as the discourses of George Clemenceau against Jules Ferry in 1885, they should be understood as a relevant political tactic rather than as an ideological complaint against colonialism.

Hence, if there were any critiques related to the European invasion of Africa, Asia, and Oceania, they came inevitably from the workers' parties, where a wide variety of criteria and approaches to such critiques can be found. This array of possibilities goes from the English Labour Party representative Ramsay Macdonald's shy opposition (never turned into mobilisations) to the enormous divisions created by colonialism in the German SPD, or to the violent opposition of the French and Italian communist parties. Regarding the latter, it is not clear yet if this opposition was originated by an internal influence or if, on the other hand, it responded to exogenous reasons like the Soviet Union's willingness to destabilise the bourgeois regimes of western Europe.

Even considering the most aggressive types of protests, like the French PCF's mobilisations in October 1925 or the Italian PCI's campaign against the Ethiopia War developed from exile, it must be said that the reasons behind these actions were not so clearly related to feelings of solidarity towards the colonised people. On the contrary, they mostly tended to be preestablished opposing tactics against the bourgeois governments based on the criticism of the waste of resources and men that the overseas campaigns entailed. Although it is true that the workers' parties rapidly established a dogmatic opposition theory of the exploitation of men by men in the Stuttgart Conference of 1907, it can be assumed that if the European socialist and communist parties opposed colonialism, it was mostly because their main motivations were closely associated with political strategies instead of an ideological position that could be called humanitarian.

In any case, if one must try to sketch what Europeans thought about their countries' colonial expansion, it can be said that there is no homogeneous response, and that the historian must do the analysis on a case-by-case basis. Mostly, population moved between a habitual indifference and a spasmodic response at key moments. It seems that most people were generally indifferent to the empire, and even knew little about it. This does not mean that they did not care, especially when there was a crisis, but it would be more of a mild, vague concern, in a broad sense, and often more an extension of a generic patriotism.

In the British case, the only thing that could be said is that the British consented to the empire. There was a sufficient level of support, or acquiescence, and there was not overtly critical or antagonistic majority opinion towards the empire. Consent was broken on occasion, such as during the great Iraqi revolt of 1920, when Britain tried to take control of Iraq with conscript soldiers from World War I, who in several cases mutinied. Thus, it seems that if it did not cost lives or money, the empire was tolerated by the population, that most of the population adhered to the imperial status quo, and a minority pointedly opposed imperialist policy.

The French case would be like the British case, with the difference that in France there was a much more defined and militant anti-colonialist movement following the uprisings in Morocco and Syria in the 1920s, led by French communists. However, the motivations of the protests against the Rif War in 1925 were too much conditioned by the Uarga Disaster, so they should be understood more as a reaction to a specific episode than for structural reasons, and it cannot be discarded that the virulence of the French Communist Party's protests was more an opportunist strategy than a real opposition to French colonialism.

In the German case, the impact of empire on German social, cultural, and political life should not be disregarded, despite the short period of formal colonial rule. At the very least, there is evidence of significant efforts by political and especially economic groups to arouse colonialist opinions in broad layers of German society. Nevertheless, the evidence suggests that German society only took an interest in its empire at certain key moments, such as during the Boxer rebellion or the 1907 elections, and that in the remaining periods the empire remained an entity apart from the lives of ordinary Germans. The SPD's position is also unclear, although fortunately, historiography is making good progress on this issue.

And finally, in the Italian case, although there were times when the Italian population took a strong interest in the colonial campaigns, the real impetus for territorial expansion was always in the hands of very marked elites, and colonialism never became a fully-fledged instrument of nationalisation. It can therefore be concluded that, apart from the occasional anger during the defeats of 1887 and 1896, and the momentary euphoria of the victories in 1912 and 1936, the Italian empire never became a daily preoccupation for the population of the metropolis. Moreover, the attempts to provoke anti-colonial responses were unsuccessful, either because of Italian indifference or the harsh repression of Mussolini's fascist regime.

SOLUTIONS AND RECOMMENDATIONS

Throughout this book chapter, there has been one methodological problem that remains unanswered, and that revolves around the question of the real impact of colonialism on European public opinion. It is relatively straightforward to measure the colonial stimuli to which Europeans were subjected, but it is much more complicated to know what they really thought about them. The real meaning of what the colonies meant to the people cannot be read solely from a newspaper printout, the lyrics of a song, an exhibition catalogue, or a film script. The historian must flee from the assumption that what appeared in the newspapers or in the cinema was assumed as the absolute truth by public opinion, an affirmation that is based on widespread illiteracy. Social history has been demonstrating for many years that the fact that a person does not know how to read or write, or has not received a school education, does not prevent them from having a political education. So, these sources can tell us a lot about the different types of imperial propaganda, but nothing about their reception. Moreover, it should be considered that the target audience addressed by this propaganda was in its majority the working class, a social class who probably did not have either the time or money for leisure time outside their home. It is easy to exaggerate the effects of popular culture elements; therefore, the historian should be cautious before drawing any hurried conclusions. Likewise, an analysis that would be limited to reproducing what the different newspapers thought about the colonies, although it will be very useful to find out what the media thought about the subject, it will not be able to delve into what the Europeans really thought about their colonies. In any case, it will be possible to carry out a stacking by a flood of opinions with an official character, which will sometimes criticize the different governments, but which in any case will reflect the feelings of some minorities.

Taking the British case as an example, it was difficult to find out whether people attending the Empire Day parades on a large scale did it because they have assimilated some imperialist values or simply because of the well-known British devotion to the monarchy. Similarly, this happens with the massive attendance to the German *Völkerschauen* or the Colonial Exposition of Vincennes in 1931. It is even harder to know in the contexts lacking freedom, such as the Italian parades after the victory of the Ethiopian War in the 1930s. It is extremely complicated to find out whether the people who attended these celebrations did it to show their favour to the regime as real supporters of the Ethiopian territory colonial invasion, or just out of obligation.

Hence, from these examples, the historian should be very cautious during the analysis of the moments when it seemed that the populations massively supported the colonial campaigns with a large-scale attendance to certain events, or with a newspaper's report about a celebration. These moments should be analysed critically rather than being considered as an irrefutable source documenting massive support to colonial politics. Similarly, nor should the reactions of the workers' parties to colonialism be taken as the expression of public opinion. While it is true that European left parties tended to reflect the yearnings and aspirations of the lower classes, it should not be disregarded their political objectives, which could sometimes be aligned with criticising bourgeois regimes for political gain. The position of these parties towards colonialism should therefore be taken with caution, and it should never be assumed that they strictly reflected most of the public opinion.

Therefore, this author believes that studying public opinion should move away from a monolithic conception, which can in no case be a set of issues confusedly piled up, but rather something like a game of Russian dolls, with its many overlapping facets. This author also believes that public opinion must be based on the study of the relations between the rulers and the ruled, it must also rely on the forms of expression and reply of the latter, and on the channels and elements that make up the political dialogue. To try to overcome this barrier between public opinion and published opinion, this author considers essential to reflect on the sources that show popular opinions and feelings, such as personal testimonials and letters from individuals, a field of study that is already being developed by some authors and that can bring interesting results to the field.

FUTURE RESEARCH DIRECTIONS

As a final reflection, it should be highlighted that the comparative study of the European colonial historiography has pointed at some limitations of our discipline. Although historiography has been developing fruitfully in the last years, especially thanks to a new generation of young researchers interested in new theoretical approaches, and significant progress has been made in the knowledge of the great trends of opinion from culturalist approaches, there are yet significant limitations that should be addressed.

According to this author's opinion, a fundamental change in colonial historiography is needed. Traditional topics like the narration of military campaigns, or the vision that political parties and social movements had of colonialism should be relegated to a secondary position in favour of a new history, marked by the cultural shift, and moving towards an interest in daily life experiences, where topics such as identity, mindsets, ideologies, or women should hold a central position in the discipline. For instance, some methodological difficulties could be overcome by means of looking at the conscription system documentation, which can familiarise the researcher with the different attitudes that young men adopted when forced into the army because of the mandatory military service. Doing so can reveal that the main responsible agents in the popular protests conscription were the soldiers' mothers and girlfriends, and that anti-colonial responses were often initiated by popular sectors, and exploited by political opportunists, who took their lead.

Another future direction for research using the comparative perspective, could be about the theory that nations with colonies tended to import hostile attitudes and values for the development of modern democracy. It seems that the imperial vision injected a powerful feeling of hierarchy and militarism, a "frontier mentality", and values attached to aggressive masculinity, whereas the metropolis political forces headed in an opposite direction towards values such as egalitarianism, popular democracy, feminism, and women rights.

Furthermore, there should be more studies about the deploying of brutal methods to submit and "civilise" the so-called underdeveloped people. In today's world, those actions would be considered as genocides or crimes against humanity, but at that moment it was accepted because they were carried out against indigenous people, and therefore, savages. For instance, consider the extermination of the Herero and Nama people by the Germans in 1905, the brutal tactics employed by the British in the Boer War, the ethnic cleansing by the Italians in Libya, or the use of chemical weapons in Ethiopia in these last 30 years.

Through this renovation of research paradigms, the academic field of colonial studies needs to be revived and energised by a new wave of studies who would aim to explore new approaches that broaden the current limitations of the field, to shed light on the contradictions of a colonial past that the collective consciousness has neglected or rejected too frequently.

CONCLUSION

In conclusion, this book chapter has taken a two-way approach, reflecting on the one hand on how state and private bodies, especially geographical societies, transmitted colonial values to the European population, through various channels such as press, literature, and cinema, and on the other hand, from below, what reactions, both supportive and protesting, and even indifference, they provoked in the European population.

This book chapter has also analysed the importance of the transmission of colonial values through international exhibitions, such as the Wembley Empire Exhibition in London in 1924-1925, the great Colonial Exhibition in Vincennes in 1931 and, of course, the numerous *Völkerschauen*. The analysis of these exhibitions reveals that Europeans constructed an image of the colonies that did not resemble reality, but rather the very mental, ideological, and racist construction that Europeans wanted to reflect of the peoples then known as "uncivilised".

There are still many mysteries concerning the real influence of the colonies in the metropolitan society and culture. This book chapter has attempted to gain an understanding of the real impact of colonialism on European public opinion, which is very difficult to measure. In this respect, it has been concluded that there was never a homogeneous response, and that public opinion generally adopted a majority indifference towards the colonies, apart from key moments, such as colonial crises or defeats in overseas wars. These responses were occasionally used by European left-wing parties, especially the Italian and French communist parties, to try to destabilise European regimes.

ACKNOWLEDGMENT

This work has been supported by the funding of the Spanish Ministry of Science and Innovation through the "Subprograma Juan de la Cierva-Formación", convocatoria 2021, programme MCIN/AEI/10.13039/501100011033 and the European Union "NextGenerationEU"/PRTR.

REFERENCES

Ageron, Ch.-R. (1978). *France coloniale ou parti colonial? [Colonial France or colonial party?]* Presses Universitaires de France.

Aldrich, R. (1996). *Greater France. A History of French Overseas Expansion*. Palgrave Macmillan.

Atkinson, D. (2005). Constructing Italian Africa: Geography and Geopolitics. In R. Ben-Ghiat & M. Fuller (Eds.), *Italian Colonialism* (pp. 15–27). Palgrave Macmillan. doi:10.1007/978-1-4039-8158-5_2

Ben-Ghiat, R., & Fuller, M. (2005). *Italian Colonialism*. Palgrave Macmillan. doi:10.1007/978-1-4039-8158-5

Bermúdez, A. (2016). Movilizaciones contra la Guerra Del Rif en Francia (1925). [Mobilizations against the Rif War in France (1925).] In P. Hernández (Ed.), *Las Violencias y la Historia [Violence and History]* (pp. 667–686). Hergar Ediciones Antema.

Bertella, P., & Dau Novelli, C. (2015). *Colonialism and National Identity*. Cambridge Scholars Publishing.

Biondi, J. P. (1993). *Les Anticolonialistes (1881-1962) [The Anticolonialists (1881-1962).]*. Hachette Littératures.

Blackbourn, D., & Eley, G. (1984). *The Peculiarities of German History*. Oxford University Press. doi:10.1093/acprof:oso/9780198730583.001.0001

Boddi, M. (2012). *Letteratura dell'Impero e romanzi coloniali (1922-1935) [Empire literature and colonial novels (1922-1935).]*. Caramanica.

Bowersow, J. (2010). Boy's and Girl's Own Empires. Gender and the Uses of the Colonial World in Kaiserreich Youth Magazines. In M. Perraudin & J. Zimmerer (Eds.), *German Colonialism and National Identity* (pp. 57–69). Routledge.

Brioni, S., & Bonsa Gulema, S. (2018). *The Horn of Africa and Italy. Colonial, Postcolonial and Transnational Cultural Encounters*. Peter Lang.

Cain, P. (2002). *Hobson and Imperialism: Radicalism, New Liberalism, and Finance 1887-1938*. Oxford University Press. doi:10.1093/acprof:oso/9780198203902.001.0001

Chafer, T., & Sackur, A. (2002). *Promoting the Colonial idea: Propaganda and Visions of Empire in France*. Palgrave Macmillan. doi:10.1057/9781403919427

Conrad, S. (2006). *Globalisierung und Nation im Deutschen Kaiserreich*. C. H. Beck.

Cooper, F., & Stoler, A. L. (1997). *Tensions of Empire. Colonial Cultures in a Bourgeois World*. University of California Press.

Degl'innocenti, M. (1976). *Il socialismo italiano e la guerra di Libia [Italian socialism and the war in Libya*.]. Editori Riuniti.

Del Boca, A. (1992). *Gli Italiani in Africa Orientale I, dall' Unita alla Marcia su Rome [The Italians in East Africa I, from the United to the March on Rome.*]. Mondadori.

Demhardt, I. J. (2002). *Deutsche Kolonialgesellschaft 1888-1918. Ein Beitrag zur Organisationsgeschichte der deutschen Kolonialbewegung [German Colonial Society 1888-1918. A contribution to the organizational history of the German colonial movement.*]. Selbstverlag.

Dreesbach, A. (2005). *Gezähmte Wilde: die Zurschaustellung «exotischer» Menschen in Deutschland 1870-1940 [Tamed savages: the display of "exotic" people in Germany 1870-1940.*]. Campus.

Duggan, C. (2001). *Creare la nazione: vita di Francesco Crispi [Creating the nation: life of Francesco Crispi.*]. Laterza.

Eckart, W. U. (1997). *Medizin und Kolonialimperialismus: Deutschland 1884-1945. [Medicine and Colonial Imperialism: Germany 1884-1945.*] Schöningh Verlag.

El-Tayeb, F. (2001). *Schwarze Deutsche. Der Diskurs um 'Rasse' und Nationalität 1890–1933 [Black Germans. Der Diskurs um 'Rasse' und Staatsangehörig 1890–1933.*]. Campus.

Eley, G. (1991). *Reshaping the German Right: Radical Nationalism and Political Change after Bismarck*. University of Michigan Press. doi:10.3998/mpub.8157

Evans, M. (2004). *Empire and culture: the French experience, 1830-1940*. Palgrave Macmillan. doi:10.1057/9780230000681

Finaldi, G. (2011). The peasants did not think of Africa: empire and the Italian state's pursuit of legitimacy, 1871-1945. In Mackenzie J. M. (Ed.), European empires and the people: popular responses to imperialism in France, Britain, the Netherlands, Belgium, Germany and Italy (pp. 195-228). Manchester University Press.

Fisher, L. (2007). *The Socialist Response to Antisemitism in Imperial Germany*. Cambridge University Press. doi:10.1017/CBO9780511511783

Gissibl, B. (2011). Imaginaton and beyond: cultures and geographies of imperialism in Germany, 1848-1918. In Mackenzie J. M. (Ed.), European empires and the people: popular responses to imperialism in France, Britain, the Netherlands, Belgium, Germany and Italy (pp. 158-194). Manchester University Press.

Guettel, J.-U. (2012). The Myth of the Pro-Colonialist SPD: German Social Democracy and Imperialism before World War I. *Central European History*, 45(3), 452–484. doi:10.1017/S0008938912000350

Howe, S. (1998). *Anti-Colonialism in British Politics: The Left and the End of Empire, 1918-1964*. Oxford University Press.

Hyrkkänen, M. (1986), *Sozialistische Kolonialpolitik. Eduard Bernsteins Stellung zur Kolonialpolitik und zum Imperialismus 1882-1914.* [*Socialist Colonial Policy. Eduard Bernstein's position on colonial politics and imperialism 1882-1914.*] Ein Beitrag zur Geschichte des Revisionismus. SHS.

Kundrus, B. (2011). From the Periphery to the Center: On the Significance of Colonialism for the German Empire. In S. O. Müller & C. Torp (Eds.), *Imperial Germany Revisited: Continuing Debates and New Perspectives* (pp. 253–266). Berghahn Books.

Labanca, N. (1994). *Storia dell'Italia coloniale.* [*History of colonial Italy.*] Fenice 2000.

Lü, Y. (2010). The War That Scarcely Was. The Berliner Morgenpost and the Boxer Uprising. In M. Perraudin & J. Zimmerer (Eds.), *German Colonialism and National Identity* (pp. 45–57). Routledge.

Mackenzie, J. M. (1986). *Propaganda and Empire. The Manipulation of British Public Opinion, 1880-1960.* Manchester University Press.

Mackenzie, J. M. (1992). *Popular imperialism, and the military, 1850-1950.* Manchester University Press.

Marshall, P. (1996). *The Cambridge Illustrated History of the British Empire.* Cambridge University Press.

Migenmi, A. (1984). *Immagine coordinata per un impero.* [*Coordinated image for an empire.*] *Etiopía 1935-1936,* Gruppo editoriale Forma.

Perraudin, M., & Zimmerer, J. (2010). *German Colonialism and National Identity.* Routledge. doi:10.4324/9780203852590

Porter, B. (2004). *The Absent-Minded Imperialists. Empire, Society, and Culture in Britain.* Oxford University Press.

Potter, S. J. (2003). *News and the British World: The Emergence of an Imperial Press System 1876-1922.* Oxford University Press. doi:10.1093/acprof:oso/9780199265121.001.0001

Prior, C. (2010). Empire before Labour: The 'Scramble for Africa' and the Media. In Frank, B. Horner, C. & Stewart, D. (eds.). The British Labour Movement and Imperialism (pp. 23-40). Cambridge Scholars Publishing.

Rüger, J. (2009). *The Great Naval Game: Britain and Germany in the Age of Empire (Studies in the Social and Cultural History of Modern Warfare).* Cambridge University Press.

Schöning, J. (1997). *Triviale tropen: exotische reise- und Abenteuerfilme aus Deutschland, 1919-1939.* [*Trivial tropics: exotic travel and adventure films from Germany, 1919-1939.*] Kritik.

Sèbe, B. (2013). *Heroic imperialists in Africa. The promotion of British and French colonial heroes, 1870-1939.* Manchester University Press.

Simons, O., & Honold, A. (2002). *Kolonialismus als Kultur. Literatur, Medien, Wissenschaften in der deutschen Gründerzeit des Fremden* [Colonialism as a culture. Literature, media, science in the German early days of the foreign.]. Francke Verlag.

Smith, H. W. (1998). The Talk of Genocide, the Rhetoric of Miscegenation: Notes on the Debates in the German Reichstag Concerning Southwest Africa, 1904-14. In S. Friedrischmeyer, S. Lennox, & S. Zantop (Eds.), *The Imperialist Imagination: German Colonialism and Its Legacy* (pp. 107–123). University of Michigan Press.

Srivastava, N. (2018). *Italian Colonialism and Resistances to Empire, 1930-1970*. Palgrave Macmillan. doi:10.1057/978-1-137-46584-9

Stanard, M. (2011). Afterword. In Mackenzie J. M. (Ed.), European empires and the people: popular responses to imperialism in France, Britain, the Netherlands, Belgium, Germany and Italy (pp. 229-233). Manchester University Press.

Thomas, M. (2005). *The French Empire between the Wars*. Manchester University Press.

Thompson, A. (2014). *Imperial Britain: The Empire in British Politics, 1880-1932*. Routledge. doi:10.4324/9781315840321

Tripodi, P. (1999). *L'eredità coloniale in Somalia* [*The colonial legacy in Somalia.*]. St. Martin Press. doi:10.1057/9780333982907

Wehler, H.-U. (1969). *Bismarck und der Imperialismus*. [Bismarck and imperialism.] Kiepenheuer u. Witsch.

Wesseling, H. L. (1981). Colonial Wars and Armed Peace, 1870–1914: A Reconnaissance. *Itinerario*, 5(5), 53–73. doi:10.1017/S0165115300007142

Wesseling, H. L. (2013). *The European Colonial Empires, 1815–1919*. Routledge.

Zantop, S. (1997). *Colonial Fantasies: Conquest, Family, and Nation in Precolonial Germany, 1770-1870*. Duke University Press.

Chapter 2
Decolonization and the Right to Self-Determination

Natalija Shikova

 https://orcid.org/0000-0003-3885-7870

International Balkan University, North Macedonia

ABSTRACT

Self-determination has been defined as the right of people to freely determine their political status and pursue their economic, social, and cultural development. During decolonization, the right aimed towards the establishment of the self-government for the peoples – inhabitants of nonself-governed colonial territories. Over the last half century, the process of decolonization resulted in a successful attainment of formal sovereignty for the former colonies. However, the liberation movements reached self-determination externally but failed to reach it internally. Since the process of decolonization is formally over, there is a change in a right holder and the mode for practicing self-determination. Except for an aggregate population – people within the state that can practice an external form of self – determination, as a process internal self-determination can be granted to different subnational groups. The ones that reached external self-determination should accept legal norms that grant forms of internal self-determination.

INTRODUCTION

The right to self-determination is much called and less understood right within international law. Since its proclamation as a political principle, the idea about self-determination has passed several historical phases (Shehadi, 1993), and its evolution has continued within the United Nations system. The most significant was its transformation from a principle of international law to right to all peoples. Additionally, most widely applied during the context of decolonization, it reached another qualitative change where its focus shifted from its external application in the sense of creating an independent state to an emphasis on its internal dimension (Franck, 1992) related to the participatory rights of different ethnic, religious or minority groups or indigenous peoples into a decision-making process (Henrard, 2000). During the historical period of decolonization, the right to self – determination aimed towards the establishment of self-government for the peoples –, i.e., inhabitants of nonself-governed colonial territories. After the

DOI: 10.4018/978-1-6684-7040-4.ch002

period of decolonization, the vagueness remained: who are the "peoples" with the right to self – determination? Because the answer often depended on the political context, the application of the right was marked with a lack of practical and contextual consistency, making it still an open issue subject to numerous influences and different interpretations within historical, legal, economic, and political debates.

Historically, the legal framework that gave impetus to the process of decolonization was firmly established upon several instruments that later assist in shaping the form of right to self – determination as part of international customary, as well as treaty law. Namely, The General Assembly Resolution 1514, "Declaration on the Granting of Independence to Colonial Countries and Peoples" (1960), set the legal ground for the process of decolonization; Resolution 1541, "Principles which should guide Members in determining whether or not an obligation exists to transmit the information called for under Article 73e of the Charter" (1960), established methods for achieving self-government for the nonself-governing territories, and the most controversial one – the General Assembly Resolution 2625, "Declaration on Principles of International Law concerning Friendly Relations and Co-operation among States in accordance with the Charter of the United Nations" (1970), arguably extended the meaning of the right by introducing an internal dimension in the form of a representative government and (for some) a possibility for secession if that representativeness is lacking (Buchheit, 1978; Cassese, 1995). These documents, supported by treaties such as the Charter of UN (1945) and two international human rights covenants - International Covenant for Civil and Political Right (ICCPR) (1966) and International Covenant for Economic Social and Cultural Rights (ICSCR) (1966), placed self-determination as a right to all peoples and created legal obligations for states to respect it.

The legal documents provided an opportunity for realization of the right to self-determination but at the same time prohibited violation of state integrity. However, it was considered that the self-determination of the colonies did not violate territorial integrity, meaning that international law gave them a separate and distinct status. Nonself-governing territories were defined as territories that are geographically separated from the administrator country and have a different ethnicity or culture (Resolution 2625, 1970). Geographically separated, in practice, meant separated by the ocean, a condition that was called "a saltwater thesis." According to these international instruments, a secession was prohibited, but decolonization was not.

For theorists, the colonial population became a "people" with the right to self-determination by developing a collective awareness of its subordination and exploitation by imperial powers, as well as through its common struggle for liberation. Hence, the identification marker was whether the people were part of the territory that was under strife or not (Knop, 2002) and had an identity other than the identity of the administrators. The right to self-determination was defined exclusively on a territorial basis, and from a legal point of view, ethnicity, culture and other social characteristics had nothing to do with the right to self-determination (Hanauer, 1995).

In the abovementioned clarifications of the right and its right holder, even with caution, a significant role played the International Court of Justice (ICJ). Although quite late since the principle gained a prominent position within the UN Charter, the ICJ made a reference in its Advisory opinion for Namibia in 1971 (Opinion, 1971). The given statements were vague, but the Court accepted self-determination as one of the essential principles of contemporary international law. Nevertheless, in its Advisory opinion for Western Sahara (1975), the Court didn't clarify who is the right holder, or what is meant by the term "peoples." That clearly shows that the application of the right to self – determination was not an easy task and in most of the cases it was balanced with others principles of international law, such as the principles of territorial integrity, state sovereignty and, *uti possidetis juris* (Summers, 2007; Halperin at all, 1992; Buchanan, 2003). The establishment of these balances was additionally influenced by the general political circumstances and national practice of constructing and shaping ideas about "peoples."

The chapter examines the concept, interpretation and application of the right to self-determination during decolonization and possibilities for its further developments. After all, the main difficulties in the implementation as right to all (stated in a Charter of UN and international human rights instruments) remained the clarification of a legal category, or who can exercise the right? As a way forwards and a last occurrence, apart from colonial peoples or the peoples that were inhabiting nonself-governing territories (former colonies), indigenous populations were recently accepted in international law as another category of rights holders. To them, the right to self-determination is granted in its internal aspect, and it is related to participation in the decision-making process in society they live, connected with the measures for protection of their separate identity. Likewise, the internal aspect of self-determination can be applied to various ethnic, linguistic and religious minorities and can serve as a model for accommodating the diversity, and with that can help in diminishing the quest for separate statehood. Internal self-determination can function within a democratic frame, and although it cannot possibly solve all the secession conflicts, the solutions that are part of it are worth trying.

BACKGROUND

If history would have been a chronicle of voluntary association and dissociation of human groupings, then probably there would be no need for the doctrine of self-determination. Without conquests, forced annexations, dynasty unions, and colonial subjugations, the peoples of the world, presumably, would have been organized into freely selected political units. However, the social organization of humanity is no result of a peaceful evolution and thus in the 20th century caused the emergence of the principle of self-determination - a primary expression of disagreement against all forms of forced political association (Buchheit, 1978). Despite the attempts to give legal shape to the concept of self-determination, the right that drives out from this principle continues to create controversy related to its unclearness and inconsistency in the application.

As a first challenge, international lawyers are attempting to define its substance, and in general, its substance is clear. That can be easily seen from the instruments that are establishing it. Namely, Resolution 1514 (1960), which initiated the dynamics of colonization, gave content to the right to self-determination, although the right to self-determination only meant the achievement of sovereign independence and the formation of a separate state (Henrard, 2000). Resolution 1541 (1960) gave options for how the right to self-determination can be realized except by achieving sovereign independence, such as establishing a free association with an independent state or through integration with an independent state. The Declaration 2625 (1970) stressed the need for representation. Additionally, self-determination was established as a collective right, although set into individual human rights instruments, and proclaimed as a right and a basis for the enjoyment of all other rights. Consequently, the right to self-determination is complex and encompasses many connected rights. The right involves the right of people to freely define their political status, and civil and political rights, the right of people to freely exercise their economic development, permanent sovereignty over natural resources, the right of people to freely practice their social development, and the right of people to freely determine their cultural development (Cristescu, 1981).

Unlike the substance, its application is still vague and inconsistent, and that in general is related to the legal specification of its right holder, or the "peoples" to whom the right to the self – determination is granted (Castelino, 2014). A legal observation and historical analysis will show that the understanding of the term "people" was never clear and even more – it continues to change (Castelino, 2000a). Following that argument, we can see that during decolonization, the people were considered to be colonial countries and people or people under foreign domination or occupation. The colonial population was normatively united as a "people" by the fact that it collectively suffered from the injury of colonialism. Therefore, the main idea of the right of self-determination was to ensure corrective justice for those exposed to historical suffering (Bhalla, 1991; Brilmayer, 1991; Duursma, 1996). As a result, upon the set resolutions and other legal instruments, since 1946, over seventy territories and former colonies have been decolonized, and a great number of them have become sovereign states and UN members.

Despite the formal success, the application of the right to self-determination faced many difficulties. In those endeavors, the ICJ attempted to clear the conceptual and legal fog. However, in defining the right holder, the interpretation practice of the ICJ was tightly related to other doctrines and among them to the doctrines of *uti possidetis juris* and *terra nulius*.

Currently, since the decolonization process is over, we have to take into account another meaning of the term "people." Considering most of the theoretics of international law, in contemporary meaning, the people are considered to be the whole people, the entirety of a nation, considering the need for representation stressed in the 2625 Declaration (1970). This means that in general, the legal title of the right to self-determination is vested in the aggregate population of the existing state, not in the substitute groups (Kuokkanen, 2019). An addition to those changes related to the understanding of the legitimate right holder, indigenous peoples, or those whose territory was occupied by outside settlers and lived as quasi-colonial subjects on their lands, is recognized as a new category within international law (Castelino, 2014). Regarding practicing, the emerging idea is that the right of self-determination should be practiced within its internal aspect. The internal aspect of the right to self – determination (which is as well applicable to the national, ethnic, religious, and linguistic minorities and indigenous peoples) – is understood as a frame that encompasses a wide and flexible range of options that are addressing, protecting, and promoting diversity within the existing state (Halperin at all, 1992; Hannum, 1990; Cassese, 1995; Castellino 2000; Falk, 2002; Summers, 2007).

MAIN FOCUS OF THE CHAPTER

The most problematic issue is defining the legitimate right holder of self – determination. In the beginning, the right was narrowly set within the frame of the "saltwater" thesis, or it was applied only to the colonized peoples that lived in geographically separated territories from the imperial country. The right was applied only to the external colonies, while the internal colonies were excluded from its application (Tully, 2000). Apart from it, there was another restriction – the right to self-determination was applied within uti possidetis boundaries or the boundaries established by the colonial powers (Weller, 2009). In establishing the standards ICJ interpretations and advisory opinions gave certain, although not always clear guidelines. That led to inconstant practice and attempts to restrict the right only within the period of decolonization. However, the meaning of the right, the ways for practicing it, and the ideas about the right holder had changed, and as an outcome and recently indigenous populations could practice internal – self-determination.

Colonial Peoples

For the colonial population, gaining the status of a right holder was a process that passed through different political periods and legal changes until it was recognized as such. Historically, the colonial powers legitimized their acquisition of overseas territories and "legally" established their influence by signing treaties with the local chiefs and other indigenous rulers as a way of a trade by which they obliged themselves that would grant colonial peoples security in exchange for exclusive economic rights over their resources. That acquisition was confirmed at the Congress of Berlin (1884). The signed treaties marked the spheres of influence among the European states. The colonial people were treated as subjects of international law, but the European states among themselves could change that particular land acquisition without obtaining their further consent (Hanauer, 1995). Legally, that meant that the majority of the territories that got under the European colonial powers were regarded as they were acquired by cession (Shaw, 2008).

Within the League of Nations, although proclaimed as a principle for liberation and equality, self-determination was not accepted as a part of international law. Various Ligue of Nations instruments were very specific in scope; they restricted the application of self-determination and never placed it as a general right to all (Henrard, 2000). However, the Covenant of the Ligue of Nations established a Mandate system and made a change in the treatment of the colonies. As a result, mandatory powers were obliged to grant freedom of religion, prohibit the slave trade and ensure the well-being of the people inhabiting the colonies. In some sense, the Mandate system initiated the development of the law of decolonization (Hanauer, 1995), which at its core has the establishment of the right to self-determination.

The Atlantic Charter (1941) set the basis for a modern international system that is not accepting territorial changes that do not respect the wishes of the people and their right to choose the form of government under which they will live, but self-determination was related only to the European states and not to the colonies. After the Second World War, both the USA and the USSR favored decolonization, and respectfully, the principle of self-determination was incorporated within the UN Charter (1945). UN Charter Chapters XI and XII address the decolonization of nonself-governing territories and international trusteeships. However, the main tendency was to freeze the border disputes, and therefore, its applicability was limited only to these territories and to the people within those territorial units (Shehadi, 1993). In comparison to the League of Nations, the UN system made a drastic change concerning the colonies, their position within international law, and the right to self-determination gradually shifted from principle to right to all.

The UN Charter in articles 1 and 55 recognizes the right to self-determination, although sets a vague definition for those entitled to the right. For some, the Charter refers to states, or the nations, as entities capable of signing the Charter. However, the term nation over time was interpreted more broadly, and the Coordination Committee of the UN Secretariat within the word "nation" involved colonies, mandates, protectorates, and quasi-states, as well as states and nations in the sense of political entities, and to peoples as groups of human beings that may or may not comprise a state or a nation. Based on that self – determination as a principle governed the relations among states and non-self-governing peoples, or the peoples that have not yet attained a full measure of self-government. As a right to all self – determination become recognized in article 1 of the major human rights covenants (ICCPR and ICESCR), but still, at that time, the debates were linked only to the context of decolonization (Hanauer, 1995).

The right to self-determination was related to territory or to the piece of land, a nongoverning unit whose people have a right to self-determination, and territory become a critical marker in defining the "peoples" (Hanauer, 1995). Consequently, "self" other than the ones of the territorial entities under the colonial rule of trusteeship territories was not recognized as a potential legitimate right holder, and no other form of self-determination came to exist, except obtaining an independent statehood (Shehadi, 1993). The right to self-determination was assigned to the people inhabiting former colonies, but the ethnic composition of those colonies was irrelevant. The doctrine of *uti possidetis juris* firmly protected the existing political order by stressing the need that the established borders need to be upheld, although in the first place they were artificially constructed by the colonial powers (Hanauer, 1995).

The Doctrine of *Uti Possidetis Juris* and *Terra Nullius*

The broadly mentioned doctrine related to the decolonization - *uti possidetis juris*, legally drives from the Roman Law norm *uti possidetis, ita possidetis* (meaning as you possess, so you possess) - as a possessory interdict that praetor was using to prevent the disturbance of immovable possession from another individual; intended to maintain general order and to protect *status quo* (Castellino, 2008). According to this procedural principle of jus civile, the burden of proof was on the side that does not possess the immovable thing, meaning the possession was awarded to the concrete possessor, or to the one that in fact had the land (Borkowski & du Plessis, 1994). In its extended interpretation, the doctrine granted the rights of the existing stakeholders to the land, and as a result of this interpretation, new states during decolonization become independent of the same boundaries of the administrative units of the territory of the colonial power, or the metropolitan state. The influence of this principle was seen in Latin America in constructing the boundaries of newly independent successor states of the Spanish Empire in South America. Its application should have helped in excluding sovereignty gaps, preventing hostilities, and discouraging foreign intervention. However, it was more accurately applied in the practice related to the decolonization of the African states (Shaw, 2008). The principle tends to protect the existing order, and its additional implementation, such as in the case of the dissolution of former socialistic federations (USSR; SFRY), sends a clear message that the creation of small secessionist states within the international system is not acceptable or desirable (Ratner, 1996).

Ideally, the states have governments that base their legitimacy on the consent of the governed. This was not a case related to the decolonization. The realization of self-determination, which was based on territoriality, as the sole objective factor in the determination of the people's identity and limited to the principle of *uti possidetis juris*, was simply a way in which colonizers transferred their power over the forces that emerged on the ground, without taking into account the will of the people governed. The doctrine took as a sole identity marker the territory within the administrative borders established by the colonial powers. As such, it preserved the existing artificiality. Instead of stability and order, led to general instability because it was difficult to accommodate the created artificial identities within the newly emerged countries (Ratner, 1996). The application of the doctrine did not always give satisfactory solutions since the administrative boundaries in the first place were frequently ill-defined, or were difficult to prove. They were established without any consideration of the ethnic composition of the population. That led to the inclusion of opposed groups within the new state and the unwillingness of the international community to consider any other options (Brownlie & Crawford, 2012). The neglected territorial issues raised dissatisfaction and initiated a new round of interstate conflicts and attempts for secession (Ylönen, 2017).

After gaining independence, the newly emerging states demarcated their borders as international ones and brought constitutions that confirmed them, believing that they could extend their title to the parts of the territory that was not under their effective control, but it was still considered an integral part of the new state. This leads to further misinterpretation among *de jure* and *de facto uti possidetis juris*. As a clarification, the element of "a critical date" became a milestone that indicated a moment from when *de jure possession* was recognized. That is most cases was a day when colonizers departed, even without the new government being *de facto* capable of establishing effective control over territory. The element of a "critical date" become a central point of dispute among the new states, and although arbitrary, it became a determining factor in forming statehood (Castellino, 2008). Hence, the concept became especially relevant in defining the new borders, although relative in meaning and dependable on the circumstances of the case (Shaw 2008).[1]

Unlike the concept of *uti possidetis juris*, the concept of *terra nulluis* derives from *jus gentium* or the law for the people who in Ancient Rome did not have the status of Roman citizens and were considered peregrines (foreigners). It is related to occupation as an original mode for gaining possession over vacant, uninhabited land of territory - *terra nullius*. The principle got prominence during the European expansion towards the Americas and was used to legitimize the acquisition of lands in the IXX and early XX centuries that belong to indigenous people or communities. Indigenous people inhabiting those lands were not organized within (for that time) recognizable social and political forms, and their land was considered to be vacant or uninhabited. The tribes were considered uncivilized, and despite their presence on it, the land that was inhabited was regarded as *terra nullius*. Once the land *terra nulluis* was acquired by the settler, or by the colonial power, the boundaries were set to demark the possession among the settlers. However, to be effective, the occupation requires possession and administration, or occupying state can establish sovereign power if it establishes an administration over that particular territory. Nevertheless, the colonial powers did not always manage to have effective control over the whole territory or over its inhabitants. Although that makes questionable their acquisition of land by occupation and even an eventual possibility of gaining a legal title over the land, those established boundaries during the decolonization were transformed into international borders of independent states, further protected by the doctrine of *uti possidetis juris* (Castellino, 2008).

The principle of uti possidetis juris received great importance with its acceptance by the International Court of Justice (ICJ) in the case of Burkina Faso vs. the Republic of Mali (1986) and the Western Sahara case (1975), together with the doctrine of occupation and terra nullius (Duncan, Patton, & Sanders (2000). Except within the UN and ICJ practice, the same principle was accepted and confirmed by the Organization of African Unity (O.A.U.) in its attempts to make the decolonization process as peaceful as possible, declaring that colonial borders existing from the date of independence are a tangible reality, and all O.A.U. member states should respect such borders (Shaw, 2008). It was declared that it is of interest to all Africans to uphold the borders, although those practices often led to separatist, irredentist or revanchist actions. Moreover, the UN and O.A.U. harmonized themself in rejecting ethnic and historical claims to the right to self-determination and firmly adhered to this territorial interpretation (Castellino, 2008).

The Practice of the International Court of Justice

In its Advisory opinion for Namibia in 1971, the Court accepted self-determination as one of the essential principles of contemporary international law, applicable to all nonself-governing territories, as enshrined in the Charter of the United Nations. According to the ICJ, this concept of sacred trust was confirmed and expanded to all territories whose peoples have not yet attained a full measure of self-government and that embrace the territories under a colonial régime (Opinion, 1971). In its decisions, the ICJ frequently used the doctrine of territoriality with the clear intention of maintaining the *status quo* and restricting conflicts. Those questions were discussed by an ICJ Chamber in the case of Burkina Faso *vs.* the Republic of Mali (1986), a dispute over the border. The Court was deciding about the delimitation of part of the land frontier between the two states, following grave incidents between the armed forces of the two countries. Both parties submitted parallel requests to the Chamber for the indication of interim measures of protection, based on a special agreement. The Court specified that the settlement of the dispute should be based on the principle that sets the intangibility of the borders inherited from colonialism (Opinion, 1986). In this frontier dispute, the ICJ stated that the principle should secure the borders existing in the moment when independence was achieved. With the application of the *uti possidetis juris*, the administrative borders were transformed into international ones. Even though in this case there was an entity that could be identified and could not be seen to correspond to that particular colonial border, the ICJ gave priority to nation-building and the stability of the new states (Summers, 2007). The Court considered that the principle obtained a status of customary law; it is applied generally, connected with the phenomenon of independence, whenever it occurs, unaffected by the emergence of the people's right to self-determination. In this border dispute, the Court balanced the right to self-determination with other legal principles and stood in defense of the existing polity to prevent fratricidal struggles after the withdrawal of the administrative powers (Shaw, 2008)

The ICJ refers to the self – determination as a right of peoples (nations). Nations and peoples are usually defined as groups that share certain common characteristics, such as language, culture, and a sense of mutual identity. However, they are not the only groups that have such characteristics. Can the people be made up of different tribes? - these questions were posted to the International Court of Justice (ICJ) in 1975 to bring an advisory opinion to the Western Sahara case. Namely, Court was asked if Western Sahara was in the time of colonization by Spain *terra nullius*; if the answer to this question was negative, what were the legal ties between this territory and the Kingdom of Morocco and the Mauritanian entity?

The Court found that Western Sahara was not *terra nullius* before the colonization by Spain (taking into account the critical date – the arrival of the colonizers, around 1890s). Western Sahara was inhabited by people who were politically organized in tribes and have chiefs as representatives (Brownlie & Crawford, 2012). ICJ tried to strike a balance between three positions (Spanish, Moroccan, and Mauritanian) and concluded that there were links between Western Sahara, Morocco, and Mauritania but that they were cultural and social links that were not as important as the principle of territorial sovereignty and could not affect the application of Resolution 1514 (1960). ICJ concluded that despite Western Sahara's historic links with Mauritania and Morocco, the people of Western Sahara have a right to self-determination (Opinion, 1975). However, the Court did not refer to "the people" but to "the peoples" and limited the legal consequences of their opinion by saying that this opinion did not affect Western Sahara's right to self-determination. Therefore, the Court set the self-determination of Western Sahara as an empty concept, leaving its case, the procedures, and the outcome open to the parties (Cassese, 1995; Knop, 2002; Epstein, 2009). However, apart from it, in its opinion, ICJ explained the concept of *terra nullius* as a land that no one ever claimed and it is open for grabs. In contrast, in this case, the Court found that the land has a population on it, it belongs to that population and it is not open for grabs –, i.e., the Court found that Saharans were distant people who historically populated that land and their territories were not *terra nullius* (Knop, 2002).

The abovementioned cases represent landmark cases when dealing with self-determination and decolonization. Despite the flows, upon those premises, except Western Sahara, all nonself-governing territories already achieved self-determination (Knop, 2002). However, the ICJ can only examine interstate claims. In that sense, there is little or no possibility that the case will be raised on behalf of the indigenous people or other nonstate claimants to the territory. Although some states may be willing to sponsor some of those quests, the Court has the procedure of admissibility, and most of them will not fall under Court jurisdiction. Since these instruments have limited applicability, they put groups in a position to seek the protection of their rights within existing state structures (Castellino, 2008).

Indigenous Peoples

Indigenous peoples are the third and most recent category of rights holders of self-determination recognized by international law. That is, despite the reservations of states about the affirmation of indigenous self-determination, or their questioning of the extension of the right to self-determination outside the colonial context. However, it becomes prominent that indigenous people are a separate legal category that should not be subjugated to minorities or guaranteed minority rights. They do not perceive themselves as minorities, and according to them (and according to many theorists of international law), they are the "original peoples", the first ones occupying the territory, previously self-governed nations, and their rights are undoubtedly linked to the memories of the displacement from the land to which they belonged and with which they have a strong connection (Moore, 2003; Levy 2003). They have historical continuity with precolonial and preinvasion societies that have developed in their territories and are regarded as distinct from other sectors of society that now dominate on those territories, or from parts of them. Indigenous peoples are determined to protect, develop and pass on to future generations their ancestral territories and their ethnic identity as a basis for their continued existence as people following their cultural models, social institutions, and legal systems (Martínez Cobo, 1981). The foundations for indigenous self-determination are nondiscrimination, respect for cultural integrity, control over land and resources, social justice and development, and self-government (Anaya, 1996; Anaya & Puig, 2018).

The UN General Working Group on Indigenous Peoples, established in 1982 by the Subcommittee on Prevention of Discrimination and the Protection of Minorities, provided the general impetus for determining the legal character of indigenous peoples. In 1994, it submitted to the UN Commission on Human Rights a Draft Declaration of the Rights of Indigenous Peoples in which the indigenous peoples were placed in the category of peoples entitled to self-determination in accordance with international law, subject to the same criteria and restrictions as applied to other peoples in compliance with the UN Charter (Wilson, 1996). In this regard, the UN Declaration on the Rights of Indigenous Peoples (2007) contains several articles that affirm the principle of internal self-determination for indigenous peoples through establishing and controlling educational institutions in their mother tongue; territorial and non-territorial autonomy; control over natural resources; and promoting and maintaining institutional structures, customs, procedures, and practices under internationally recognized human rights standards. These rights of indigenous peoples illustrate a broad doctrine of the rights of the peoples, but in another sense represent a dramatic expansion of this doctrine. For the first time since decolonization, the right to self-determination was granted to a subnational group within an existing state, and that for many extended the boundaries of international law (Wilson, 1996).

SOLUTIONS AND RECOMMENDATIONS

The obligations imposed on the administrative powers of nonself-governing and trust territories are now almost completely outdated since nearly all colonial people achieved independence. In essence, self-determination gives an ability to the "people" to determine their own "future." However, the concept of people differs significantly when self-determination is seen as a process, not as an end. In its internal dimension, the people are a source of state sovereignty, and as a process implies, they have a democratic form of government. The current understanding contradicts the previous notion about the people as inhabitants of mandated and trusted territories, that could practice self-determination only once, as a single occurrence, and strictly during the process of decolonization. In that process, the achievement of independence was the final step in exercising the right, and the international community focused on the external form of self-determination (Shehadi, 1993). Considering the postcolonial countries, the historical and colonial borders that have failed to take into account ethnic and historical realities can be seen as a cause both for the collapse of states and the continuation of conflict in many states (Dugard, 2003). The principle of *uti possidetis juris* was not able to resolve all territorial boundary disputes. However, according to international law, the boundaries defined in treaties are achieving permanence; they must be respected and can only be changed with the consent of the states that are directly concerned with that particular change (Shaw, 2008).

In further developments, after the post-Cold War environment, theoretically and practically the focus shifted towards the internal aspect of the right to self-determination and to tendencies for preserving peoples' cultural ethnic, and historical identity, while simultaneously providing chances to influence political order under which they live. Unlike changing the international identity as an outcome of external self-determination, internal self-determination can be reached within existing state borders where people can effectively participate in decision-making processes (Kolonder, 1994). Hence, internal self-determination assumes the right to authentic government and the right for people to freely choose the political and economic regime, while external self-determination is related to the international status of the people and territory they live (Cassese, 1995). Internal self-determination requires necessary participation in the decision-making process, and participatory rights coming from it are closely related to the participatory meaning of the term "people" (Henrard, 2000). Part of the internal – self-determination can be territorial or nonterritorial autonomy and self–government for the various population/ethnic groups since the principle of territorial integrity remains a paramount principle in international law. That protects the existing borders and is supported by international law and practice. Within those limitations, minorities and indigenous people can practice internal self-determination by granting a form of autonomy within state structures, inclusion in democratic processes, and protection of minority rights. This frame ranges from special rights for certain groups to power-sharing arrangements, consociationalism, multiculturalism, minority rights, polytechnic rights, linguistic rights, and various measures aimed to protect separate identities and ensure power balances.

FUTURE RESEARCH DIRECTIONS

Self-determination can be considered a political and legal process through which people gain and maintain control over culture, society, and the economy. Within the UN system, it evolved into a right, and in essence, the UN were consistent in formulating its characteristics and elements in line with the attempts for preserving territorial integrity. Consequently, the right to self-determination was granted only to dependent, colonial people and was defined on territorial rather than on ethnic criteria. The UN General Assembly resolutions and ICJ advisory opinions created an *opinio juris* that contributed to the formation of a customary law related to self-determination as a general principle accepted by law (Statute ICJ). The right to self-determination was developed to promote moral and political values that brought an end to colonialism and imperialism and gave a chance to traditionally exploited people to control their societies. However, the right to self-determination needs to evolve to changing circumstances of the international system (Cassese, 1995). The secession is not supported by the international community; consequently, self-determination should reside on recognized social, cultural, and political rights and the possibilities to achieve greater autonomy or other forms of participation and representation for the people who have that legal fortune to exist as minorities or separate groups within existing states (Hanauer, 1995).

Initially, the right was limited to the ex-colonial population as a whole and not to its constituent ethnic groups, aiming to support decolonization without posing a threat to the stability and unity of postcolonial states. The African states that emerged from decolonization established a limitation of the definition of peoples and wanted to preserve their sovereignty, refusing substate interpretation of the right to self-determination. In that process, the new governments of the former colonies regarded self-determination as a unique event, occurring in a moment of independence of the colony, that could not empower people once decolonization was completed (Franck, 1992). Decolonization spread the concept of the nation-state to territories that did not have essential conditions for their emergence, or for their existence on the territories where they were created. They established themselves as sovereign states due to their recognition and support by the international community. If not main, that was one of the reasons why their independence was marked by the rise of secessionist movements and interethnic conflicts (Miillerson, 2003).

Nonetheless, in the middle of the last century, the idea about the people got a new shape, and the people became the ones within the democratic constructed society - a people within the state (Turp, 2001). They can as a collective practice external self – determination, while all the subgroups can be entitled to internal – self-determination. From that point, if we accept internal self – determination as a way to the realization of an authentic form of government and participation in it, as a part of a possible solution for secessionist demands and conflicts, the international community should support the internal – self-determination claims and help in addressing them before they are transformed into quests for external – self-determination (Kolonder, 1994). This should be in line with efforts to create standards for the democratic government (Kolonder, 1994; Franck, 2000; Murphy, 2000) since internal self-determination can only exist in a democratic frame. Initially, during decolonization, the UN was reluctant to intervene in the internal affairs of the new states (Archibugi, 2003). In the time of being, values of democracy were not universally shared as they are not now, but with historical distance, perhaps it is plausible to say that at least in some form, they can be bear today.

CONCLUSION

The vague interpretations of the concepts and inconsistent practice raised the doubts that in the case of decolonization, the right to self-determination was implemented in a very provisional way, without taking into account the will of the people who were governed and without creating the necessary democratic institutions. In many cases, territoriality was taken as the sole objective factor that determined the identity of the people, and it was considered more important than other factors, such as race, tribe, and language. That was established as practice, without taking into account that in the first place, the territorial borders were artificially created by the colonial settlers, disregarding the history and ethnic structure of the colonial countries. Once applied, the right to self – determination got singular application - as soon as the colony became a state, it started to defend its territorial integrity, preventing any further exercise of external self – determination, while its internal aspect (such as representation, political rights and alike for different subgroups) was often out of reach. To add to this, in many cases, it is argued that the doctrine of *uti possidetis juris* was wrongly applied or particular entity(ies) was/ were wrongfully incorporated into a newly independent state. These inequalities and shortcomings lead to practical consequences (Weller, 2009). Characteristically, self-determination has been defined as the right of people freely to determine their political status and pursue their economic, social, and cultural development. Although colonialism practically no longer exists, and many constructs accepted in the past have disappeared (such as colonialism, protectorates, mandates, UN trusteeships, etc.), the doctrine of self-determination cannot stay stuck in the colonial bottle. It has already been transformed from the principle of exclusion to a principle of inclusion – a right to participate (Franck, 1992). Recently, the inclusion of the indigenous people within the scope of international law challenged state-oriented versions of self-determination by extending it with novel forms of nonterritorial self-governance (Shikova, 2020), which illustrates a legal extension of the term peoples to a subnational group. Over the last half-century, the process of decolonization came a long way marked by the success of the attainment of formal sovereignty of the Third World states. The liberation movements reached self-determination externally but failed to reach it internally. Today, from a historical distance, the process can be critically observed, and we can conclude that right to self-determination was unable to solve the issues related to internal self-determination. To reach that objective, in the hope of a better future, seemingly, now the same peoples who achieved self-determination should accept legal norms that set and grant forms for internal self-determination. Those ideas in essence are based on the ideas about democracy and introducing democratic parameters in conflicting societies. Although democracy is not a norm of international law, some democratic aspects, such as having a representative government or participation in the decision-making process, can be universally shared, and UN institutions should put forth efforts to support those endeavors.

REFERENCES

Advisory Opinion, I. C. J. (1971). Legal consequences for states of the continued presence of South Africa in Namibia (South West Africa) notwithstanding. *Security Council Resolution 276* (1970). https://www.icj-cij.org/en/case/53/advisory-opinions

Anaya, J. (1996). *Indigenous peoples in international law*. Oxford University Press.

Anaya, J., & Puig, S. (2017). Mitigating state sovereignty: The duty to consult with indigenous peoples. *University of Toronto Law Journal, 67*(4), 435–464. doi:10.3138/utlj.67.1

Archibugi, D. (2003). A critical analysis of the self – determination of peoples: A cosmopolitan perspective. *Constellations (Oxford, England), 10*(4), 488–505. doi:10.1046/j.1351-0487.2003.00349.x

Bhalla, R. S. (1991). The right of self-determination in international law. In W. Twining (Ed.), *Issues of self-determination* (pp. 91–101). Aberdeen University Press.

Borkowski, A., & du Plessis, P. (1994). *Textbook on Roman Law*. Oxford University Press.

Brilmayer, L. (1991). Secession and self-determination: A territorial interpretation. *Yale J. Int'l L.*, (16), 177–202.

Brownlie, I., & Crawford, J. (2012). *Brownlie's Principles of Public International Law*. Oxford University Press.

Buchanan, A. (2003). The Quebec secession issue: democracy, minority rights and the rule of law. In S. Macedo & A. Buchanan (Eds.), *Secession and self–determination* (pp. 238–272). Nomos XLV.

Buchheit, L. C. (1978). *Secession, the legitimacy of self-determination*. Yale University Press.

Cassese, A. (1995). *Self- determination of the peoples, a legal reappraisal*. Cambridge University Press.

Castellino, J. (2000). *International law and self- determination*. Kluwer Law International. doi:10.1163/9789004480896

Castellino, J. (2000a). *International law & self-determination: the interplay of the politics of territorial possession with formulations of post colonial national identity*. Martinus Nijhoff. doi:10.1163/9789004480896

Castellino, J. (2008). Territorial integrity and the "right" to self- determination: An examination of the conceptual tools. *Brooklyn Journal of International Law*, *33*(2), 499–564.

Castellino, J. (2014). International law and self-determination: peoples, indigenous peoples, and minorities. In Christian, W, von Ungern-Sternberg, A., & Abushov, K. (Eds.), Self-determination and secession in international law (pp. 27-45). Oxford University Press.

Cobo Martínez, J. (1986). *Study on the problem of discrimination against indigenous populations*. UN Doc E/CN.4/Sub.2/1986/Add.4.

Cristescu, A. (1981). *The right to self-determination, historical and current development on the basis of United Nations instruments*. United Nations.

Dugard, J. (2003). A legal basis for secession - relevant principles and rules. In J. Dahliz (Ed.), *Conflict avoidance and - regional appraisals* (pp. 89–97). Asser press. doi:10.1007/978-90-6704-699-2_7

Duncan, I., Patton, P., & Sanders, W. (2000). Introduction. In Duncan, I., Patton, P., & Sanders, W. (Eds.), Political theory and the rights of indigenous peoples (pp.1- 25). Cambridge University Press.

Duursma, J. S. (1997). Fragmentation and the international relations of micro-states: Self-determination and statehood. *Leiden Journal of International Law*, *10*, 579–586.

Epstein, P. (2009). Behind closed doors:"autonomous colonization" in post United Nations era- the case of Western Sahara. *Annual Survey of International and Comparative Law*, *15*(1), 107–143.

Falk, R. (2002). Self-determination under international law: the coherence of doctrine versus the incoherence of experience. In Danspeckgruber, W. (Ed.), Self – determination of peoples, community, nation and state in an interdependent world (pp.31- 67). Lynne Rienner Publishers.

Franck, T. M. (1992). The emerging right to democratic governance. *Am. J. Int'l L.*, *86*(1), 46–91. doi:10.2307/2203138

Franck, T. M. (2000). Legitimacy and democratic entitlement. In G. H. Fox & B. R. Roth (Eds.), *Democratic governance and international law* (pp. 25–47). Cambridge University Press. doi:10.1017/CBO9780511522307.002

Halperin, M. H., Scheffer, D. J., & Small, P. L. (1992). *Self – determination in the new world order.* Carnegie Endowment for International Peace.

Hanauer, L. (1995). The irrelevance of self – determination law to ethno- national conflicts: A new look at the Western Sahara case. *Emory International Law Review*, *9*(1), 133–178.

Hannum, H. (1990). *Autonomy, sovereignty, and self-determination, the accommodation of conflict rights*. University of Pennsylvania Press.

Henrard, K. (2000). *Devising an adequate system of minority protection*. Kluwer Law International. doi:10.1163/9789004482500

ICJ. (1975). *Reports of judgments, advisory opinions and orders*. Western Sahara, advisory opinion. https://www.icj-cij.org/public/files/case-related/61/061-19751016-ADV-01-00-EN.pdf

ICJ. (1986). *Frontier Disputes (Burkina Faso/Republic of Mali)*. ICJ. https://www.icj-cij.org/en/case/69

Knop, K. (2002). *Diversity and self- determination in the international law*. Cambridge University Press. doi:10.1017/CBO9780511494024

Kolonder, E. (1994). The future of the right to self – determination. *Connecticut Journal of International Law*, *10*, 153–168.

Kuokkanen, R. (2019). *Restructuring relations, restructuring relations: indigenous self-determination, governance, and gender*. Oxford University Press. doi:10.1093/oso/9780190913281.001.0001

Levy, J. T. (2003). Indigenous self- government, secession and self- determination. In Macedo, S. and A. Buchanan, Secession and self- determination, (pp. 119-136). Nomos XLV.

Miillerson, R. (2003). Sovereignty and secession: then and now, here and there. In J. Dahlitz (Ed.), *Secession and international law, conflict avoidance and regional appraisals* (pp. 125–167). Asser press. doi:10.1007/978-90-6704-699-2_10

Moore, M. (2003). An historical argument for indigenous self- determination. In Macedo, S. and A. Buchanan, Secession and self- determination, pp. 89–118. Nomos XLV.

Murphy, S. (2000). Democratic legitimacy and the recognition of states and governments. In G. H. Fox & B. R. Roth (Eds.), *Democratic governance and international law* (pp. 123–154). Cambridge University Press. doi:10.1017/CBO9780511522307.005

Ratner, S. (1996). Drawing a better line: Uti possidetis and the borders of new states. *AJIL*, *90*(4), 590–624. doi:10.2307/2203988

Shaw, M. (2008). *International law*. Cambridge university press. doi:10.1017/CBO9780511841637

Shehadi, K. S. (1993). *Ethnic self-determination and the break-up of states*. The Adelphi Papers. doi:10.1080/05679329308449209

Shikova, N. (2020). The possibilities and limits of non-territorial autonomy in securing indigenous self-determination. *Philosophy and Society*, *31*(3), 277–444. doi:10.2298/FID2003363S

Statute of the International Court of Justice. (n.d.). *Statute*. ICJ. https://www.icj-cij.org/en/statute

Summers, J. (2007). *Peoples and international law, how nationalism and self-determination shape a contemporary law of nations*. doi:10.1163/ej.9789004154919.i-468

Tully, J. (2000). The Struggles of Indigenous Peoples for and of Freedom. In Duncan, I., Patton, P., & Sanders, W. (Eds.), Political theory and the rights of indigenous peoples (pp. 36-60). Cambridge University Press.

Turp, D. (2001). *Qubecs Right to Secessionist Self-determination: The colliding paths of Canadas Clarity Act and Qubecs Fundamental Rights Act*. Unpublished paper.

Weller, M. (2009). Settling self-determination conflicts: Recent developments. *European Journal of International Law*, *20*(1), 111–165. doi:10.1093/ejil/chn078

Wilson, J. (1996). Ethnic groups and the right to self- determination. *Conn. J. Int'l L.*, *11*(3), 433–486.

Ylönen, A. (2017). Confronting the 'Arab North': Interpretations of slavery and religion in Southern Sudanese Separatist Resistance. In Taylor, I., João Ramos, M. & Kaarsholm, P. (Eds.) Fluid networks and hegemonic powers in the Western Indian Ocean (pp. 104-129). ISCTE-IUL. .

ENDNOTES

[1] Within the international order the state is a generally accepted and recognized form of political public administration on the territory concerned. Territorially is one of the elements of statehood, set within the Montevideo Convention on rights and the duties of states (1933), where the acquisition of defined and fixed territory is fundamental and it is a precondition for recognition of statehood. However, this notion of territoriality remains contested in international law in respect of the right to self – determination. To determine the fixed territory international law applies the doctrine tools uti possidetis juris, tetra nullius as well as the principle of effectiveness, or having effective control over the concerned territory.

Chapter 3
"¿Cosas de España?":
Frederick Hardman and the Spanish–Moroccan War (1859–1860)

María Gajate Bajo
University of Salamanca, Spain

ABSTRACT

In the construction of the collective remembrance of any war, literary, journalistic, and soldier' chronicles have become very significant and this evidence has been clearly exposed in recent researches on cultural warfare studies. From this statement, the purpose of this chapter is to examine an individual testimony to increase our understanding of the complex Spanish-Moroccan War (1859-1860). Rather than delving into its military dynamics, the main goal of this contribution will consist of providing a profound comprehension of this struggle, its extensive international implications and legacy thanks to a detailed analysis of The Spanish Campaign in Morocco. This is an interesting compilation of the previous reports written by Frederick Hardman, an unknown (at least among Spaniards) foreign correspondent whose words can be extremely enlightening insofar as it will be applied the analytic tool of—British—informal imperialism as basis for the study of the multidimensional Spanish-Moroccan relationships.

INTRODUCTION

There is a centuries-old relationship connecting the Iberian Peninsula and the Islamic Maghreb. Situated at the intersection of Europe and Africa, the Middle East and the Atlantic world, the Strait of Gibraltar constitutes the key of this link as well as the core of several clashes throughout History. The first armed conflict between Spain and Morocco in the Modern Age began in 1859, when troops –45.000 men[1]– sent by Marshall Leopoldo O'Donnell (leader of the pragmatist Liberal Union) crushed a revolt by kabylies against Ceuta, a Spanish presidio since 1578. It is not necessary to say that this entire episode took place under the attentive British eye.

This first Spanish-Moroccan war, also known as the War of Africa, exploded at a critical moment for Morocco, which was plunged into a severe crisis of authority. Although some historians have misinterpreted this problem as a sign of division, the existence of a Moroccan identity, based on Islam and Arab

DOI: 10.4018/978-1-6684-7040-4.ch003

culture, was not debatable (Villalobos, 2004, pp. 31-38). On the contrary, perhaps this was the reason of the long Sultanate resistance to the European attacks. In any case, the great powers of the Old World saw in this internal Moroccan disorder the opportunity to satiate their imperialist appetites and Spain, committed to the defence of Ceuta and Melilla from a weaker position, did not remain oblivious to this competition either (La Porte, 2022, pp. 695-698).

The armistice signed on 26 April 1860, the Treaty of Wad Ras, was partially positive for Madrid's diplomacy. On the one hand, it legitimised the perpetual extension of the Spanish presence in Ceuta and Melilla, the end of the assaults on these cities, the recognition of Spanish sovereignty over the Chafarinas Islands, the retrocession of Santa Cruz de la Mar Pequeña to establish a fishing post, permission for missionaries to stablish a Christian church in Tetouan, and Spanish administration over the later city until reparations of 20.000.000 *duros* were paid. Moreover, once Morocco paid this compensation, partly with money borrowed from the British, O'Donnell had to withdraw his soldiers from Tetouan. Great Britain, eager to preserve the *status quo* in the Strait of Gibraltar, played an essential role in constraining Spain's advancement in Morocco and Frederick Hardman's chronicles will contribute to understand the real difficulty of these bilateral relations and the motives of that so-called *small peace,*- obviously, for Spaniards (Pedraz Marcos, 2000, pp. 60-61)-, with a vague recall as well as the nature of British informal imperialism in the nineteenth century.

BACKGROUND

The War of Africa has received considerable historiographical attention in Spain and Morocco (Zarouk, 2007). As the United Kingdom was also a major player in the conflict (although its priority at the time was to dominate the Chinese market), British academics have also undertaken its study, albeit to a lesser extent. The questions raised by both sides have been many, feeding fruitful and, above all, challenging debates. It is also very appealing to see how this shared history changes depending on who is telling it. This shows how important it is to analyse any war episode from different angles and how difficult it is for the researcher to avoid the influences of so-called banal nationalism (Billig, 2014). It is precisely at this significant point, in the healthy ambition to identify certain prejudices of this nature, that our interest in Frederick Hardman's testimony lies.

This chapter is based on some earlier research. Firstly, and although today it may be considered a settled question, the aims of the Spanish-Moroccan War have been much discussed. For a long time, it was argued that O'Donnell needed a policy of prestige, which would guarantee greater internal stability and international recognition. Lécuyer and Serrano referred, for example, to a last romantic war (1976: 116): conceived as an instrument of national regeneration, alien to the materialistic logic of the industrial century. Similarly, Madariaga noted the unusualness of the high-handed language adopted by a second-rate power, Elizabethan Spain, and emphasized the God-given character of the conflict: "It was presented to public opinion as the sacred duty of washing away the outraged national honour" (Madariaga, 2009, p.20).

However, overemphasizing the domestic aspect as the trigger for the War of Africa has had its risks: it ignored the growing concern that the different political forces showed for Spain's international role. All the military operations of this period, in Cochinchina, Mexico, etc., far from being "quixotic, unconnected and without defined objectives" (Inarejos, 2009, p.2), revealed more premeditation than one might think. It is a fact that, by backing aggression against Morocco, the different parties and factions damaged their own interests by avoiding doing their opposition work. It is therefore conceivable that, beneath this conformism that appealed to the spirit of the Crusade, the civilising principle or Canovist providentialism (Velasco, 2013: 99-100), there were other more spurious objectives: the defence of Ceuta and its port at a time when the Strait of Gibraltar was being revalued in parallel to the construction of the Suez Canal; the search for new markets; and even the strengthening of the Canary Islands. These were the logical concerns of a new colonial dynamic in which O'Donnell was participating to compensate for the disintegration of the squalid overseas empire and to keep the army under his control. The British, sceptical of abstractions such as honour since the Jenkins' Ear episode, were instantly aware of the ambitions of the Liberal Union, which explains their reluctance towards Spanish action.

In a second place, the war of 1859-1860 has been studied extensively in relation to the difficult Spanish nationalization process. In this sense, many historians have recognized the intense wave of patriotism it generated (García Balañá, 2012, pp. 95-103). The media and also literature −a paradigmatic example was *El Cañón Rayado*, tirelessly demonising Spain's traditional enemy, the Moor− magnified the hypothetical benefits of the war and fuelled popular fervour by encouraging xenophobic sentiments (Romero, 2014: 641). Thus, they contributed to the spread throughout the country of initiatives to help the combatants, knowing that the calamities to which the soldiers were subjected were many. Isabella II, for example, offered her jewels, while several sainetes, zarzuelas and romances were performed to raise funds (Collado, 2019, 608-611). For the neo-Catholic faction, the War of Africa was a new Crusade and an instrument to commemorate the Reconquista; from the progressive and democratic positions, on the other hand, the need to introduce civilisation into Morocco was argued. In the end, a stammering Africanism that defended a secular mission entrusted to Spain prevailed: due to geographical and historical imperatives and, combined with a certain inferiority complex, the struggle had therapeutic effects for the homeland (Serralloga, 1998, p. 158; Martin-Márquez, 2011, p. 67).

The panacea, however, proved to be ephemeral. For this reason, Iglesias Amorín has recently scrutinized how the campaign was transmitted to the population to the point of concluding that this unanimity must be questioned. Against a traditional memory, plagued by war propaganda lies because it represents the triumph of the 'from above' perspective, there will be the 'from below' remembrance, shaped by cholera victims and by those who resist to military service, even by self-mutilating. According to his opinion, an increasing 'nation consumption' does not necessarily meant an increasing nationalized masses: the economic motivation of the Catalonian Volunteers, for instance, was stronger than their patriotic feelings and nationalist subscriptions were not as natural as we usually consider them to be (Iglesias Amorín, 2020, pp. 293-296). Similarly, it could be argued that during the War of Africa, the demagogic attitude of some newspapers, obedient to the recommendations of the warmongering Posada Herrera, Minister of the Interior, was reprehensible (Albi, 2018, p.31); and it is also true that many acts of individual resistance to conscription were detected. Nevertheless, the effort to dissociate these behaviours from this grandiloquent Spanish nationalism does not imply that they can be associated with alternative abstractions, such as a premature anti-colonialism. Therefore, this debate remains open to the extent that it is impossible to "weigh" patriotism, and it is up to the researcher to continue to track reactions of all sorts. As for sub-state nationalisms, there does seem to be a greater historiographical consensus in accepting that Catalanism and Basque nationalism looked favourably on this war for its usefulness in publicising regional myths and symbols that did not clash with Spanish ones (García Balañá, 2002; Kühne, 2017). Unlike what happened in 1859-1860, the Rif War (1909-1927) would be used as a weapon against Madrid's policy.

Finally, in addition to considering its objectives and links to nationalization processes, the War of Africa has been examined in light of its international implications. The denunciation of the historiographical vacuum in the study of nineteenth-century Spain's foreign policy has been a commonplace among scholars, which is fortunately being filled (Inarejos, 2009, p.2; Blanco, 2012, p.19). Although Spain had the approval of the United Kingdom and France, London sought to dissuade O'Donnell from his offensive. It knew that a Moroccan victory was in its advantage, but considering it unlikely, it opposed the conflict. Nonetheless, Madrid's will eventually prevailed, as Galdós explained: "The Spaniards went to war because they needed *gallear* (strut around) a little before Europe [...] General O'Donnell showed great sagacity [...] An imitator of Napoleon III, he sought in military glory a means of integrating nationality" (2004, p.132).

The United Kingdom apparently accepted the official argument, that of avenging a grievance. In the parliamentary session of 22 October, O'Donnell asserted that "we are not driven by a spirit of conquest, we are not going to Africa to attack the interests of Europe". In fact, he reiterated this idea in the circulars of 24 September and 29 October, sent to diplomatic representatives abroad. In practice, however, Spain was imposing limitations on itself which, as we know, were a response to previous British demarches. They were aimed at obtaining a written commitment to renounce the occupation of certain enclaves. For the British, who had already become involved in Spanish domestic affairs, taking advantage of delays in the payment of public debt, Morocco was synonymous with Tangier (the main supplier of meat to the Rock). If any power seized this city, Gibraltar's geostrategic value would disappear. Queen Victoria, therefore, did not want any alteration of the status quo in the area: she sought to maintain good relations with Mohammed IV because the commercial treaty of 1856, which granted preferential treatment in Morocco for goods from Gibraltar, brought her enormous profits (Barbe, 2016, p.20). Though, John Drummond-Hay, his strongman in Tangier, could not avoid this war2. He tried to bring the positions of Blanco del Valle and El-Jetib closer together (much more complex, admittedly, was his dealings with the Anyerinos themselves) and also cajoled Calderón Collantes, Minister of State, for further assurances on Tangier. In the end, however, the consul had to surrender to the evidence that Spain did not want any British mediation. Thus, the Admiralty, resigned but threatening, opted to send ships to Gibraltar. In the words of Foreign Secretary Lord Russell: "If Spain has a whim to make war, it must be condescended to" (Ben-Srhir, 2005, p.93).

MAIN FOCUS OF THE CHAPTER

This chapter will be intended as a contribution to two interrelated scholarly realms. Firstly, to the study of Spanish colonialism, in which Spanish Africa have received little attention in comparison to the America and the Philippines. Secondly, to Hispano-Moroccan studies, which have focused more on Al-Andalus than on the post-1492 interactions or on the influence of third actors.

The research is based on the hypothesis that the complex nature of the War of Africa, the first milestone of Spain's contemporary colonial presence in Africa, can be appreciated accurately by studying its international implications. Since British action was decisive in understanding the limited territorial objectives that O'Donnell publicly set for himself, the journalistic testimony of Frederick Hardman will be analysed. His book *The Spanish Campaign in Morocco*, which has a wide resonance among the Anglo-Saxon audiences, will be used to explore the successes and weaknesses of the United Kingdom's controversial informal imperialism over Spain. In particular, much attention will be paid to the journalist's comments on the behaviour of Spanish troops in the campaign and the genesis of the Treaty of Wad Ras. Of course, his references to the poisoned Anglo-Spanish relations, which show the class between different national feelings, will also merit close scrutiny.

Much has been written on the practice of informal imperialism in the United Kingdom, less so in Spain (Sharman, 2021: 4). For the former, it could be all summarised in one axiom: "Trade with informal control if possible; trade with rule where necessary"[3]; the latter, on the other hand, seems to have exhausted its energies, resisting this soft economic and geopolitical interventionism, always nourished by a good dose of Darwinism. In Spanish historiography, only Martín Corrales has echoed this concept to highlight that Madrid also tried to emulate London, using the Sultanate as its "testing ground". But the effort proved so unsuccessful that in the end arms prevailed in Margallo's and 1909 campaigns (Martín Corrales, 2004, p.26). As an analytical category, informal imperialism has been questioned for its vagueness —in drawing the line between the usual asymmetry in any bilateral relationship and this form of interference— and also for its imprecision in explaining the decision-making process or, if one prefers, in identifying the promoters. Thus, it will be argued here that the United Kingdom and Spain were in fact engaged in a conflict of colonial competition in the Sultanate. London diplomacy, convinced of the existence of a pact between Pyrenean neighbours, was concerned about the Gallic advance on Algeria and sought to intimidate France by challenging the weak element in the alliance. Hardman's writings will help us to better understand these Anglo-Hispanic relations and their impact on the development of the Spanish-Moroccan war.

Frederick Hardman and His Encounter with Spain

The War of Africa was a campaign full of chiaroscuros: improvised, but popular; with hardly any naval means, although hundreds of soldiers that were involved in several skirmishes and some battles. Al of them, besides, without a clear purpose and suffering indescribably from cholera. The chroniclers and also the Arabists, who since 1840 had been indiscreetly promoting Spanish intervention in Morocco to stop France (Martin-Márquez, 2011: 65), finally saw their dream come true: journalism experienced a truly unusual boom coinciding with the outbreak of hostilities.

While the Spanish press has been sufficiently analysed, especially if we think of the testimony of Pedro Antonio de Alarcón or Núñez de Arce (Santiáñez, 2007; Sánchez Mejía, 2013; Gajate Bajo, 2021), studies on foreign chroniclers are scarce. Obviously, it is imperative to look at the contributions of external historiography to make progress in this direction. As Britain was the great imperialist power of the 19th century, it is understandable that there is an abundance of works analysing its imperial experience as a historical phenomenon[4]. The approaches have been diverse: from the classic studies focused on the examination of its causes, international implications, through the examination of military operations, to the more recent socio-cultural approaches, based on the study of imaginaries, identities, the repercussions of the imperialist phenomenon in the metropolises, anti-imperialist upheavals, etc. The study of its transnational character is also a trendy topic[5]; as much as the role of different colonial agents, like travellers and war correspondents[6]. So, let us pay attention to the second subject and the press. From 1860 until around 1910 is considered a 'golden age' of newspaper publication, with technical advances in printing and more advertisements combined with a professionalization of journalism (Briggs and Burke, 2002). Newspapers became more partisan and there was the rise of new or yellow journalism. The socialist press was also increasing its readership (Lee, 1976; Summers, 1994). Since the Napoleonic Wars, *The Times* had established itself as the European masthead with the greatest expense and deployment in recounting wars, first through reports and, coinciding with the Crimean War, by mixing combative articles with photojournalism[7]. In 1859 it sent a correspondent to the area: Frederick Hardman, who was soon to emerge as what the English call an *embedded journalist*. In other words, a reporter committed to one side, in this case, to the strategists at the top of British politics.

It is worth giving a brief introduction to the character. Frederick Hardman (1814-1874) was a connoisseur of Spain. After all, he had lived in Spain, with interruptions, for some twenty years, working as a soldier and reporter. Coinciding with the First Carlist War, he served in the British Legion as a lieutenant of lancers. Later, sent by *The Times*, he covered the revolution of July 1854; and it was five years later that he travelled to Morocco as a correspondent. Hardman had good friends in Madrid and is an authoritative, if little explored, source for the study of nineteenth-century history (Roth Mitchel, 2015: 96). Moreover, at all times, Hardman wanted to be faithful to events and to this end he combined the information he received from the soldiers with that of his contacts in Madrid and Gibraltar. He never concealed the difficulty and haste of his work −"where the army goes everyone must go" (1960: 169)−, and he referred insistently to the circulation of hoaxes that defined the journalistic atmosphere in Gibraltar:

That account differing from the truth, and less unfavourable to the Moors than the glowing Spanish narratives of recent skirmishes, prevail here, will doubtless be taken by the Spaniards as fresh proof of English sympathy with Morocco [...] As to the tales one also hears in Gibraltar of the slaughter of thousands of Moors, and which I suppose are intended as a set-off to the fables unfavourable to the Spaniards, they are scarcely worth alluding to (1860, pp. 39-40).

Hardman denied this slaughter and claimed that only a few skirmishes had taken place. His desire was to denounce both this hostile Gibraltarian atmosphere and the tendency of the Spanish to exaggerate and turn simple skirmishes into epic battles. However, this apparent equidistance disappeared when British diplomacy entered the scene. Hardman then cast his suspicions:

Spanish papers, even those which are generally favourable to England, have lately been unanimous in assailing our government and that portion of our press which has opposed the expedition to Morocco. The publication of the communications between Lord John Russell, Mr. Buchanan and the Spanish Minister for Foreign Affairs, may in part have been the cause of this, but the most recent cause of irritation, at least in the South, has been our Consul's remaining in or off Tangier (1860, pp. 25-26).

In effect, Drummond-Hay became the great enemy of the Spanish press, although Hardman did not perceive these attacks as anything more than a sign of Hispanic paranoia. On the other hand, it is true that the leak of these diplomatic dispatches was more serious because it was intended to compromise the troops by questioning the justice of the declaration of war. Hardman did not delve into the matter, preferring to attack the attitude of the Spanish chroniclers:

In vain may it quote the Audi alteram partem. Few southern journalists admit the maxim, or willingly recognize the virtue of impartiality. I you would stand well with them, you must go through thick and thin, believe only what favours their cause, and set down their enemies as undeserving of credit (1960, p.154).

In a country characterized, moreover, by a growing worker's mobilization and royal overspend, the journalist confessed his sympathy for Espartero, dared to denounce the self-interested patriotism of politicians, their impunity and the excesses of smuggling, and went so far as to recommend the sale of Cuba to the United States. Sharp, didactic and ironic, he disliked getting the laconic comment "things of Spain" when enquiring into the character and customs of the Spaniards: "They have a notion that strangers who write about them prefer exposing their worst traits and institutions to putting their good ones in relief" (Hardman, 1854: 683). Of course, Hardman did not hesitate to point out some virtues of the Spanish army. Usually, to show how historical shortcomings were remedied. This was the case with the cavalry, whose "style of riding is not exactly what would find favour in English eyes, but is better than it used to be" (1860: 168). He also acknowledged the infantryman's temperance and discipline: "He does not irritate his system and his temper by the abuse of strong drinks, as English and French soldiers are but too apt to do" (1860: 248); as well as the fact that he was properly fed thanks, he claimed, to the supply of British bacon and that he received his pay regularly (1860: 189).

However, it must be admitted that, already in his first chronicles, the journalist insisted more on Spanish industrial backwardness and banditry (1860: 7). Analysed as a whole, criticism of the development of the war and, even more so, of those who supported this first explosion of Africanism predominated.

Explaining that *Big War*...

Although the United Kingdom wished to prevent the outbreak of war, O'Donnell eventually imposed its will. Since the 18th century, piracy and the situation of the Spanish presidios on the Moroccan coast had strained bilateral relations. In particular, the security of Ceuta, defined by the Treaty of Meknes (1799) and the Larache Convention of 1845, was repeatedly threatened by the kabyle of Anyera[8]. But hostilities were precipitated by the Spanish attempt to erect a new fortification, the Santa Clara redoubt, in the vicinity of the enclave. On the night of 10-11 August, the Berbers smashed what had been built and trampled the Spanish coat of arms. The incident reached the ears of the Spanish consul in Tangier, Blanco del Valle, because the governor of Ceuta, Ramón Gómez Pulido, wanted to reprimand the kabyle in blood, which firstly alarmed the Minister of War[9].

The Sultan's chief of Foreign Affairs, Mohamed El-Jetib, showed a conciliatory attitude, instigated by Drummond-Hay, who always encouraged him to give in. Nonetheless, the Moroccan representative had limits: he avoided punishing the criminals and argued that he could not accept Spain's desire to build defensive structures without prior consultation. In the end, the Sultan's weakness, death and replacement forced a delay in negotiations, accompanied by an intense exchange of letters marked by escalating Spanish territorial claims (and accompanied, equally, by some military preparations), until the rupture occurred. While British historiography stresses that El-Jetib's refusal to punish the aggressors triggered the war, the question of Ceuta's boundaries features much more prominently in diplomatic documentation. Spain initially claimed the fortification of El Otero, but later claimed absolute rights in the so-called *Moorish camp* and Sierra Bullones (if artillery was used, it meant a strategic military imbalance in the region), extending its borders by almost seven kilometres (Garrido Guijarro, 2014, pp.159-246).

Hardman paid little attention to the background of the conflict, but he did judge the Spanish action as too premature. To begin with, he ironized the near coincidence between the Queen's birthday and the break in hostilities: "It was really hardly worthwhile, in order to flash off a little powder and drive away a few Moors on the Queen's Saint's-day, to begin before all was prepared" (1860, p.36). To continue, he insisted on the poor choice of the moment (1860, pp. 11, 38) and the inexperience of the troops confronted by hundreds of fanatical warriors (1860, p.2). In addition, he made some tactical recommendations. *The*

Times journalist called for greater agility in the management of transport and artillery (1860, p.3) and, above all, urged that this incipient Africanist army should not distance itself from the coast:

If carried away by early triumphs, they attempt too much, and press on into the interior, they will risk reverses [...] A reverse would be much to be deplored, both on account of the fact, and because Spain, in order to retrieve it, might be compelled to an expenditure or men and money far beyond anything that has been contemplated (1860, p.4).

In other words, Hardman wanted a moderate and swift victory to avoid excesses —"the Moors would then be to the Spaniards what the Spanish guerrillas were to the French" (1860, p.21)— that would threaten the United Kingdom's privileged position in the Strait. Thus, during the last months of 1859, he constantly denounced the strategic indecision of the Spaniards —"some think that the first point of attack will be Tetouan, which is easier to reach than Tangier by land from Ceuta" (1860, p.11)—, while revealing British fear of the foreseeable occupation of Tangier. Surprisingly, once this enclave was conquered, his anxiety increased as he wondered: "Is the campaign at an end, or not?" (1860, p.250). Hardman heard a rumour that a squadron, sent from Havana, was preparing to bombard Tangier and took the opportunity to call urgently for an end to the war:

She has already won what she desired and demanded, the tract around Ceuta up to the slopes of the Sierra Bullones. She has gratified her amour propre [...] She has shown that she is not, as she has sometimes been considered utterly effete; and she is gratified by the idea that she has raised herself in the opinion of the nations of Europe (1860, p.202).

O'Donnell, however, preferred to continue the march, a decision that again fits poorly with the supposed lack of sovereignty attributable to an informal colony. In any case, the opacity of his objectives adversely affected the conduct of the campaign and fuelled excessive hopes of unfulfilled conquest. Internationally, on the other hand, the war served to sell a less fratricidal image of Spain. At the same time, however, it was incongruous: neither was a colossal deployment of technical and human resources required to take a city temporarily, nor could these British demands be reconciled with the pressure of Spanish public opinion.

In short, the Liberal Union was not content with punishing some excesses, although it had to comply with the main British demand, renouncing its expansionist plans (Albi, 2018, pp. 344-345). O'Donnell turned something trivial into a *casus belli* because he was conditioned by the experience of a long history of uneasy relations. He sought an excuse to chasten the Anyerinos (Serrallonga, 1998: 140). All the episode coincided, moreover, with a situation of diplomatic success (Inarejos, 2009, p.4) —Spain had just received compensation from the Sultanate for acts of pillage committed in 1856; it had also managed to pay off an old debt contracted with the United Kingdom in the First Carlist War–[10] and the reactivation of the confiscation of lands' process.

... And its *Small Peace* with an Abrupt Halt?

Frederick Hardman was more interested in the development and, above all, the conclusion of the conflict than in its beginnings. He could see, with disgust, how the fighting turned into a ruthless war, with hardly any hostages or ransoms (1860: 61), and he made public his views on O'Donnell by stating that "[the Marshall] is reported to have told his friends that he should eat his Christmas dinner in the Spanish capital. He has eaten it in a much less pleasant place" (1860: 91). Or later: "O'Donnell is certainly in his element [...] enjoys a fight even as much as might be expected from his Irish descent" (1860: 235). Naturally, he was very concerned about the deterioration of Spanish-British relations parallel to the war, although he justified the United Kingdom's actions. Only twice did he allude to the geostrategic importance of Gibraltar. This was the first one:

Is the thorn in the Spaniard's side [...] One hears frequent conversations about Gibraltar, about its capacity of resistance under the altered conditions of modern warfare, and concerning the possibility or its rescue from British hands, either by friendly or by forcible means. Lately, I am told, in one of the large towns of Southern Spain a toast was given to the effect that Gibraltar might, within a year, be crowned with the Spanish standard. Of course, it would be easy to multiply and improve upon such sentiments, and to drink to the recovery of Mexico [...] There is little use in reasoning with Spaniards on the subject; it is one that touches their national pride, and that they will not long regard from any other point of view (1860, p.31).

Hardman, unwittingly revealing what was English's obsession, ridiculed Spanish irredentism. In fact, he saw this war as a quixotic struggle rather than a movement driven by French rapacity. In his chronicles, he also denied that the British were providing military aid to the Sultanate (1860, pp. 62, 103, 138, 146, 151); and he denounced the constant reservations of the Spanish about the conduct of the English consul in Tangiers: "The British Government is reputed, in Spain at least, to be on the most friendly terms with the Sovereign of Morocco, whose chief adviser and dearest friend is, by numbers of Spaniard, believed to be Mr. Drummond Hay" (1860, p.62). He also acknowledged the British eagerness to hasten the end of the conflict and to mediate as soon as Tetouan was occupied: "The moment is favourable for diplomacy" (1860: 235). This thesis, incidentally, coincides with that defended by current British historiography, which insists that it was an unwanted and abrupt halt in hostilities that explained the poor Spanish reaction to the Treaty of Wad Ras (Sharman, 2021, pp. 65-66). However, both sides underestimate the fact that peace was imposed because Muley Abbas, head of the Moroccan army, requested a truce when he realized that the Spanish were not satisfied with the occupation of Tetouan (Hardman, 1860, p.251). Although Drummond-Hay had been persuading the Sultan of the desirability of peace for weeks, the famous treaty came after several conversations between the Spanish and Moroccans, with the question of war indemnity gaining prominence. And generating concern among the British:

A large demand for speedy supplies naturally entailed high prices and heavy charges. Rations and forage of the best quality had to be sought in foreign countries [...] But when the question of indemnity, to be paid by the humbled foe, is brought forward, it may be questioned whether that enemy can fairly be made to bear expenses which were enormously increased by the uncalled-for hurry in which the struggle was commenced [...] My conviction is that the Spaniards, had the to bear the whole cost of the war, would think it a cheap price to pay for the amount of self-satisfaction they have obtained [...], to say nothing of any little pleasant fancies some of the more sanguine may have indulged in respecting possible European complications, with a vision in the distance of a combined French and Spanish fleet bombarding Gibraltar (1860, pp. 253-254).

This fear –Hardman's second allusion to the geostrategic importance of the Strait of Gibraltar– fortunately did not materialise. He did end up regretting the Spaniards' excessive rapacity because, in addition to compensation, he disapproved of the possible creation of a new General Captaincy that would include Ceuta, Tetouan, Melilla and the Chafarinas:

This might be gratifying to Spanish vanity, although it would assuredly be burdensome to Spanish revenue [...] Close to the new Hispano-African province are our old friends the Riffians. How long a time would elapse before forays and outrages on their part would form grounds for fresh disputes between the Madrid and Fez Governments? The Emperor would declare his inability to coerce or chastise those warlike and predatory tribes [...] and request the Spaniards to revenge their own injuries (1860, p.271).

Hardman's predictions are certainly surprising because the reporter justified that, beyond the promotion of officialdom, Spain would not gain any advantages from territorial enlargement in Africa. Moreover, he finished by describing O'Donnell's victory as a parody of the French victory in Algeria (1860: 320) and defending the need to invest at home what was being squandered abroad (1860: 321). However, it must be acknowledged that the Treaty served not only to keep the Liberal Union in power, but also to ensure that Spain was taken into account, albeit as a minor partner, in the subsequent division of the African continent. The benefits, therefore, were not so small.

SOLUTIONS AND RECOMMENDATIONS

After carrying out an analysis of the existing literature and exposing the main arguments developed by Hardman, we can conclude by stating that this journalist amplified many of the postulates also defended by the British government during the development of the War of Africa: the uncertainty about O'Donnell's objectives, the concerns about the security of Tangier, the eternal doubt about the existence of a Spanish-French pact, the dissatisfaction with the excessive achievements of the Treaty of Wad Ras, etc.

The objectives of the chapter have been fully met, since during the work we have learned how the great powers of the Old World, and in particular Great Britain, followed this first major Spanish-Moroccan conflict with great interest and influenced the decision-making process, although it cannot be said that Spain acted as an informal colony under the directives of the London government. Hardman's opinions sometimes reveal discomfort at the Spaniards' unexpected determination, which is why he takes refuge in arguments such as the inopportune wastefulness of the Treasury, a classic of fin-de-siècle socialist thought; the excess of quixotism, which carried enormous weight in historiography until a few years ago; or, finally, the cliché about a suspicious and self-malicious character –those *things of Spain*–, an instinctive defence mechanism against one of the great *living nations* (Lord Salisbury *dixit*) and its supporters.

FUTURE RESEARCH DIRECTIONS

Hardman considered the Spanish reaction to the Treaty of Wad Ras cold and blamed it on Spanish journalists (1860, p.316). However, having analysed his reasoning and fears, it is pertinent to rethink the extent to which the Small Peace really was. The chronicles he published in *The Times* are a good example of what war counter-propaganda was, and it is worth studying this practice in greater depth, both outside and inside Spain, in order to broaden our knowledge of the War of Africa. A comparative reading with Victoriano de Ameller's texts (1861), unknown but very judicious, could be a good way forward.

From a broader perspective, it seems obvious to assert that we need to continue exploring imperialism as a trans-national phenomenon, with enormous importance in shaping Europeanness.

CONCLUSION

It is often argued that the glorification of the War of Africa silenced the account of the suffering it caused and the analysis of the mistakes made. Press censorship, the absence of a strong labour movement and the concealment of logistical and planning problems contributed to this. Hardman's chronicles, however, do not conform to this assertion.

As well as questioning the nationalist bias of contemporary Spanish journalists and writers, Hardman's testimony exemplifies British feelings to the Moroccan question. His testimony helps us better understand why the United Kingdom ended up assuming the largest part of the Moroccan war debt —and the role of informal metropolis—. It had hoped to stop a growing Hispanic influence in the area. However, as quirk of fate, its growing ascendancy over the Maghzen would make it the arbiter of the clashing interests of the Spanish and French in Morocco. In the case of the Sultanate, the Treaty accelerated economic bankruptcy and increased the population's unrest over continued tax increases (Serna, 2001, pp.185-187).

REFERENCES

Albi de la Cuesta, J. (2018). *Españoles a Marruecos! La Guerra de África, 1859-1860 [Spaniards in Morocco! The African War, 1859-1860].* Desperta Ferro.

Ameller, V. (1861). *Juicio crítico de la Guerra de África o apuntes para la historia contemporánea [Critical judgment of the African War or notes for contemporary history.].* Francisco Abienzo Press.

Bachoud, A. (1988). *Los españoles ante las campañas de Marruecos [The Spanish before the Moroccan campaigns].* Espasa-Calpe.

Barbe, A. (2016). *Public debt and European expansionism in Morocco from 1860 to 1956.* [Unpublished doctoral dissertation, Paris School of Economics, France].

Ben-Srhir, K. (2004). *Britain and Morocco during the Embassy of John Dummond Hay.* Routledge. doi:10.4324/9780203494974

Billig, M. (2014). *Nacionalismo banal [Banal Nationalism].* Capitán Swing.

Blanco, A. (2012). *Cultura y conciencia imperial en la España del siglo XIX [Culture and imperial consciousness in 19th century Spain].* University of Valencia.

Briggs, A., & Burke, P. (2002). *Social History of the Media.*

Cain, P. J., & Hopkins, G. (2016). *British imperialism, 1888-2015* (3rd ed.). Routledge.

Claeys, G. (2020). *Imperial esceptics. British critics of empire, 1850-1920.* Cambridge University Press.

Collado Fernández, E. (2019). En el nombre de la reina: La imagen de Isabel II durante la Guerra de África (1859-1860)

Fichter, J. R. (2019). *British and French Colonialism in Africa, Asia and the Middle East Connected Empires across the Eighteenth to the Twentieth Centuries*. Palgrave Macmillan. doi:10.1007/978-3-319-97964-9

Fisher, J. (2013). The Bible dream: official travel in Morocco, 1845-1935. In M. Farr and X. Guéran. (Eds). The British abroad since the eighteenth century. Vol 2: Experiencing imperialism (pp. 176-193). Macmillan. doi:10.1057/9781137304186_10

Fisher, J. (2019). *Outskirts of empire. Studies in British power projection*. Routledge.

Gajate Bajo, M. (2012). *Las campañas de Marruecos y la opinión pública. El ejemplo de Salamanca y su prensa, 1906-1927 [Moroccan campaigns and public opinion. The example of Salamanca and its press, 1906-1927]*. UNED-IUGM.

Gajate Bajo, M. (2021). ¿Guerra de religión o religión de la guerra? Pedro Antonio de Alarcón en la Guerra de África (1859-1860) [War of religion or religion of war? Pedro Antonio de Alarcón in the African War (1859-1860).]. *Siglo XIX. Literatura Hispánica*, 27, 223–256.

García Balañá, A. (2002). Patria, plebe y política en la España isabelina: la Guerra de África en Cataluña (1859-1860) [Homeland, common people and politics in Elizabethan Spain: the African War in Catalonia (1859-1860).]. In E. Martín Corrales (Ed.), *Marruecos y el colonialismo español* (pp. 13–77).

García Balañá, A. (2012). The empire is no longer a social unit. Expectations and Transatlatic crisis in metropolitan Spain, 1859-1860. In A. W. McCoy, J. M. Fradera, & S. Jacobson (Eds.), *Endless Empire. Spais's retreat, Europe's eclipse and America's decline* (pp. 92–103). The University of Wisconsin Press.

Garrido Guijarro, O. (2014). *Aproximación a los antecedentes, las causas y las consecuencias de la Guerra de África (1859-1860) desde las comunicaciones entre la diplomacia española y el Ministerio de Estado [Approach to the background, causes and consequences of the African War (1859-1860) from the communications between Spanish diplomacy and the Ministry of State]* [Unpublished doctoral dissertation, UNED, Spain].

Hardman, F. (1854). A letter from Madrid. *Blackwood's Magazine*, 75(June), 671–686.

Hardman, F. (1860). *The Spanish campaign in Morocco*. Blackwood and Sons.

Iglesias Amorín, A. (2020). The Hispano-Moroccan Wars (1859-1927) and the (De)nationalization of the Spanish People. *European History Quarterly*, *50*(2), 290–310. doi:10.1177/0265691420910946

In the name of the queen: The image of Elizabeth II during the African War (1859-1860).]. Revista de Historia Constitucional, 20(20), 607–621. doi:10.17811/hc.v0i20.576

Inarejos Muñoz, J. A. (2009). La campaña de África de la Unión Liberal. ¿Una Crimea española? [The Liberal Union's Africa campaign. A Spanish Crimea?] *L'Atelier du Centre de Recherches Historique*. doi:10.4000/acrh.1805

Kühne, I. (2017). Pátria, ja tornas á tenir historia! La influencia de la Guerra de África sobre el desarrollo de la identidad catalana [Homeland, you will have history again! The influence of the African War on the development of Catalan identity]. In C. von Tschilschke & J. Witthaus (Eds.), *El colonialismo. España y África, entre imaginación e historia* (pp. 77–103). Iberoamericana-Vervuert. doi:10.31819/9783954876365-005

La Porte, P. (2022). El laberinto marroquí. Piedra de tropiezo de liberales y autoritarios (1912-1926) [The Moroccan labyrinth. A stumbling block for liberals and authoritarians (1912-1926).]. *Hispania Nova. Revista de Historia Contemporánea, 20,* 692–736.

Lécuyer, M. C., & Serrano, C. (1976). *La guerre d'Afrique et ses répercussions sur l'Espagne (1859-1909) [The African War and its repercussions on Spain (1859-1909)].* Presses Universitaires de France.

Lee, A. J. (1976). *The Origins of the Popular Press 1855–1914.* Croom Helm.

Mackenzie, J. (2016). Passion or indifference: popular imperialism in Britain, continuities and discontinuities over two centuries. In J. Mackenzie (Ed.), European empires and the peopel. Popular responses to imperialism in France, Britain, the Netherlands, Belgium, Germany, and Italy (pp. 57-89). Manchester University Press.

Mackenzie, J. M. (1986). *Propaganda and Empire. The Manipulation of British Public Opinion, 1880-1960.* Manchester University Press.

Madariaga, M.ª R. (2009). *Abdelkrim el Jatabi: la lucha por la independencia [Abdelkrim el Khatabi: the struggle for independence.].* Alianza.

Martín Corrales, E. (2004). El patriotismo liberal español contra Marruecos (1814-1848). Antecedentes de la Guerra de África de 1859-1860 [Spanish liberal patriotism against Morocco (1814-1848). Background to the African War of 1859-1860]. *Illes y Imperis, 7,* 11–43.

Martin-Márquez, S. (2011). Desorientaciones. El colonialismo español en África y la performance de la identidad [disorientations. Spanish colonialism in Africa and the performance of identity.]. Bellaterra.

Pedraz Marcos, A. (2000). *Quimeras de África: la Sociedad Española de Africanistas y Colonialistas: el colonialismo español a finales del siglo XIX [Chimeras of Africa: the Spanish Society of Africanists and Colonialists: Spanish colonialism at the end of the 19th century.].* Polifemo.

Pérez Galdós, B. (2004). *Aita Tettauen.* Akal.

Porter, B. (2004). *The Absent-Minded Imperialists. Empire, Society, and Culture in Britain.* Oxford University Press.

Pratt, M. L. (2003). *Imperial eyes. Travel writing and transculturation* (2nd ed.). Routledge. doi:10.4324/9780203106358

Romero Morales, Y. (2014). Prensa y literatura en la Guerra de África (1859-1860). Opinión publicada, patriotismo y xenophobia [Press and literature in the African War (1859-1860). Published opinion, patriotism and xenophobia]. *Historia Contemporánea, 49,* 619–644.

Roth Mitchel, P. (2015). *The Encyclopedia of War Jounalism (1807-2010).* Grey House Publishing.

Sánchez Mejía, M. L. (2013). Barbarie y civilización en el discurso nacionalista de la Guerra de África (1859-1860) [Barbarism and civilization in the nationalist discourse of the African War (1859-1860).]. *Revista de Estudios Políticos*, *162*, 39–67.

Santiáñez, N. (2007). De la tropa al tropo: Colonialismo, escritura de guerra y enunciación metafórica en *Diario de un testigo de la guerra de África* [From the troop to the trope: Colonialism, writing of war and metaphorical enunciation *in Diary of a witness to the war in Africa.*]. *Hispanic Review*, *76*(1), 71–93. doi:10.1353/hir.2008.0002

Sèbe, B. (2013). *Heroic imperialists in Africa. The promotion of British and French colonial heroes, 1870-1936*. Manchester University Press.

Serna, A. (2001). *Al sur de Tarifa. Marruecos-España: un malentendido histórico [South of Tarifa. Morocco-Spain: a historical misunderstanding]*. Marcial Pons.

Serrallonga Urquidi, J. (1998). La Guerra de África (1850-1860). Una revision [The African War (1850-1860). A review]. *Ayer*, *29*, 139–159.

Sharman, N. (2021). *Britain's informal empire in Spain, 1830-1950*. Palgrave Macmillan. doi:10.1007/978-3-030-77950-4

Summers, M. W. (1994). *The Press Gang: Newspapers and Politics 1865–1878*. University of North Carolina Press.

Thompson, A. (2014). *Imperial Britain: The Empire in British Politics, 1880-1932*. Routledge. doi:10.4324/9781315840321

Velasco de Castro, R. (2013). Objetivos y limitaciones de la política exterior española en Marruecos: La batalla de Tetuán (1859-1860) [Objectives and limitations of Spanish foreign policy in Morocco: The battle of Tetouan (1859-1860).]. *Revista Historia Autónoma*, *2*, 93–106.

Villalobos, F. (2004). El sueño colonial. Las guerras de España en Marruecos [The colonial dream. The wars of Spain in Morocco]. *Ariel*.

Zarouk, M. (2007). Revisionismo y colonialismo en Marruecos [Revisionism and colonialism in Morocco]. In B. López García and M. Hernando de Larramendi, Historia y memoria de las relaciones hispano-marroquíes [History and memory of Spanish-Moroccan relations] (pp. 45-76). Ediciones de Oriente y del Mediterráneo.

ENDNOTES

[1]   It has been estimated that Morocco had approximately 50.000 men, fighting between 10.000 and 12.000 individuals in each clash (Albi, 2018: 102).

[2]   Neither could he avoid his prejudices, which led him to act with a certain excess of paternalism. Proof of this assertion can be found in a work by John Fisher on colonial imaginaries, which includes a description of the Sultanate by Drummond-Hay, the man who in 1945 was Consul General in Tangiers: "*The Bible* and the *Arabian Nights* are your best handbooks and would best prepare

you for the scene" (Fisher, 2013: 76). The author argues that British travellers portrayed Morocco as a timeless, fairy-tale land for a long time, resisting to admit that the country's modernisation and openness threatened, day by day, their informal empire. Furthermore, related to this image of Morocco as an example of corrupt oriental state, it is very exceptional the work of Fisher (2019: 141-168) on Foreign Office involvement in British graves located in British, European and international cemeteries in Morocco. He instrumentalizes the construction of churches, cemeteries and, to a lesser extent, missionary work, as a reflection of power projection in Morocco.

3   A panoramic overview of British imperialism can be found in Cain and Hopkins (2016, 3rd edition), both determined to show how the shape of the nation and its economy depended on international and imperial ties. Another very interesting general approach to the phenomenon of British imperialism is the one used by Fichter (2019), employing the comparation with French imperialism as a result of the conviction that they were constantly forming and re-forming in relation to each other: "They shaped each other as opponents, as allies, and, perhaps most commonly, as *frères ennemis,* frenemies who, with one act of competitive collaboration, managed to simultaneously support and undermine each other" (Fichter, 2019: 1).

4   In Britain, imperialist propaganda (newspapers, expositions, foods…) was everywhere. Despite this fact, its permeation is discussed and, while researchers like John Mackenzie have appealed to an internalized and popular imperialism (1986), the theories of Bernard Porter points (2004) to a more reduce effect on the working classes. About the emergence of opposition to the British Empire between 1850 and 1920, it is very useful the contribution by Gregory Claeys (2010: 124-234), who has studied a wide spectrum of socialist writings. For his part, Thompson (2014) prefers to highlight how manifestations of dissent towards imperialism have been exaggerated by academics.

5   John M. Mackenzie (2016) is also the editor of a study about popular responses to imperialism in France, Britain, The Netherlands, Belgium, Germany and Italy. The attractiveness of the book lies in two insights: the permeation was facilitated by popular acceptance rather than resistance and imperialism was always a trans-national process, plenty of parallels. However, while some of the European states had a track record, others were new to the game. The Spanish case, unfortunately, has not been included among the countries examined. However, popular responses to imperialism in Africa have been well analysed both from more classical social history (Bachoud, 1988), and from the mixed field of Political Communication and local, but not localist, history —the example of Salamanca, with a public opinion always attentive to the discourse of Miguel de Unamuno— (Gajate, 2012).

6   It is highly recommended, even when it is not focused on the Moroccan case, the study of Mary Louise Pratt (2003, 2nd edition). This author addresses the theme of how travel writing shaped relations between the European powers and the non-European periphery. For this ambitious purpose, Pratt uses the term "transculturation" and describes the selective borrowings by one culture for another. In her own words: "Borders and all, the entity called Europe was constructed from the outside in as much as from the inside out. Can this be said of its modes of representation?" (Pratt, 2003: 6).

7   Berny Sébe is the author of a very suggestive contribution to the field of popular imperialism with research very focused on the role of press (and audio-visual world) in the promotion of British and French colonial heroes. He shows that an imperial reputation is not made by monumental actions alone. On the contrary, it is rather the result of complex political and cultural mechanics, and networks of *hero-makers* with vested interests in their subject. Sèbe examines the construction of

heroes in popular culture to illustrate that imperial fervour cut across class as well as political lines. From the conviction that the newspaper is closely linked to the market by relationship of reciprocity, he argues that "With war correspondents, the emphasis naturally shifted away from a theoretical and literary approach to what was happening on the battlefield. [They] served not only what they believed was a moral duty of patriotism but also their financial and personal interest when they promoted new heroic reputations, while newspapers were pleased to find in war correspondents good aides in their continual competition for readership" (Sèbe, 2013: 60).

[8]   From 1799 it was stipulated that the Spaniards could settle on the borders of the frontier camp. However, the use of this agricultural space was a nuisance for the inhabitants of Anyera, who disputed the area in 1803 and 1828. They also attacked the defensive line in 1837 (Martín Corrales, 2004: 19; Madariaga, 2009: 16). At no time would the natives tolerate the construction of buildings, while for Spain it was vital to fortify El Otero in the heart of the *Moorish camp* to eliminate the possibility of Ceuta being bombarded with modern artillery. Precisely for the purpose of guarding the convicts who would work on these works, the Santa Clara guard corps began to be built.

[9]   Gómez Pulido has been accused of bad faith because of his aggressiveness and because he relied on a heterodox interpretation of Article 15 of the Treaty of Meknes, overstretching Spanish rights in a pastoral territory; on the other hand, Blanco del Valle is said to have combined a certain anger, because he considered the signing of an agreement on Melilla's borders to be in danger (before the August attack he had already expressed his dissatisfaction with the works carried out in the vicinity of Ceuta), with excessive condescension towards El-Jetib. Despite this, and also the constant Moroccan "yes", which made recourse to war difficult, O'Donnell's wishes prevailed.

[10] The British claim for 42 million of *reales* has been seen by Spanish historiography as a mechanism of extortion coinciding with the mobilization of troops. However, the request was submitted in November 1858 −before the aggression− and the London government allowed it to be paid in four instalments (Albi, 2018: 26).

Chapter 4
Colonial Conflicts in the Horn of Africa:
From European Presence to Ethiopian Imperialism (1880–1930)

César García Andrés
Valladolid University, Spain

Pablo Arconada Ledesma
Valladolid University, Spain

ABSTRACT

This research delves into the colonial conflicts in one of the most confrontational regions of the continent: The Horn of Africa. The geostrategic importance of this area meant that during the first decades of colonisation, several European countries set their sights on these territories, which are currently occupied by Eritrea, Somalia, Djibouti, and Ethiopia. However, the arrival of Europeans in the Horn of Africa was opposed by the local population living in these territories. This resistance to the European invasion is one of the main studies in this analysis, along with the mark it left on the Ethiopian Empire to initiate its expansionism. The object of study is interdisciplinary in nature, but history is undoubtedly the basis of all our argumentation. However, history must be connected to other fields of study, mainly international relations and African studies. The resources that have been used to carry out this research are a list of a wide bibliography on the subject, together with official documents, newspaper, and resources from geographical societies.

INTRODUCTION

Before the beginning of the great period of colonisation in Africa from the 1880s onwards, some European countries such as Portugal, the British Empire, France and Spain had certain enclaves scattered across the continent, mainly port and coastal positions to control trade. The important changes that took place throughout the 19th century led to the expansion of ambitions to control more territories on the

DOI: 10.4018/978-1-6684-7040-4.ch004

African continent given its great wealth in raw materials and cheap labour, together with the development of capitalism, the expansion of the industrial revolution, the explorations of Europeans in Africa since the beginning of the century... In addition to all this, the creation of the last nation states gave rise to a new constellation of power characterised by strong international rivalry and continuous political manoeuvring (Weeseling, 1999, p.452), thus creating a new situation in Europe from the 1870s onwards. Moreover, in the particular case of this chapter's study, the Horn of Africa, since the opening of the Suez Canal in 1869, which facilitated maritime trade between the Mediterranean Sea and the Red Sea to reach the Indian Ocean, has maintained a strategic importance for Europe (Nyaoro, 2019, p.23), both geopolitically and militarily, driving the colonisation of these territories in order to maintain control of the waters and goods that passed through the Suez Canal. This territory is located in the East African region, bordered by the Indian Ocean and the Red Sea, and bounded by the present-day countries of Ethiopia, Somalia, Djibouti and Eritrea.

The explorers began to sign treaties and protectorate or sovereignty agreements with the African chiefs they encountered on their voyages (García Moral, 2016, p.160) promoted by various geographical societies[1], although what this really meant was the subjugation of these populations to the incoming foreign population. A rapid race for control of these places began in several European countries, provoking certain disputes between them. In order to reach an agreement on the division, German Chancellor Otto von Bismarck summoned several powers to the Berlin Conference, which took place between 15 November 1884 and 26 February 1885, but no African representatives were present, and the fate of Africa was decided unilaterally, so that the African continent was invaded by seven European states: France, Italy, Belgium, Germany, the United Kingdom, Portugal and Spain. The European powers each undertook not to proceed with savage acquisitions without notifying the others, in order to allow them to make claims; moreover, the African peoples or kings were not even consulted or informed of all these discussions (Ferro, 2000, p.107). In April 1900 only Liberia[2] and Ethiopia[3] remained independent states south of the Sahara.

The Effects of European Colonization in the Horn of Africa

With the path towards the division of the continent already underway, it is necessary to understand and deepen the effects that the colonisation of the great European metropolises had on the territories of the Horn of Africa, i.e. how it affected the native population and the changes that took place in the relations between the local ethnic groups themselves and between them and the European colonisers. The context of change that took place in the region with the European invasion and the conflicts generated cannot be understood without an analysis of the political, social and economic consequences that took place from the end of the 19th century onwards. This section will provide us with some keys to understanding not only how the clashes took shape, but also their causes and their development.

In the division of this area of East Africa on the shores of the Red Sea at the end of the 19th century, the Europeans had taken over the most important ports: the Italians in Massawa and Mogadishu, the British in Zeila and the French in Obock and then Djibouti (Ki-Zerbo, 1972, p.593). Thus, in Somalia, the Italians had signed various agreements with the sultans and leased several ports, along with the region of Eritrea; within Somali territory, although most of it was occupied by the Italians, the French and British also settled on the shores of the Gulf of Aden, the former in Djibouti and the latter in Somaliland (Ceamanos, 2016, p.87). The other territory that forms part of the Horn of Africa, Ethiopia, had a very different development. At this time, it was known as Abyssinia and after the death of Emperor Yohannes

IV in 1889 it was ruled by his successor Menelik II. He turned the country into a modern, centralised regional power in the face of growing European expansion, as we shall see below.

The first thing the Europeans changed was the political sphere, both its institutions and its pre-existing structures. Given the colonial context, direct rule was necessarily unstable. Their claim to a single legal order and equal rights in a multi-racial context was based on a massive exclusion of 'natives' from the regime of civil power and civil rights (Mamdani, 1999, p.868). Most lines of thought thus converged on what might be called conjunctive administration (usually referred to as 'indirect rule') carried out by the British; that which linked African authorities, in traditional or European-imposed political roles, with the colonial government, but in an obviously subordinate capacity (Betts, 2000, p.315). Despite the above, the French did opt for direct control of their African colonies as in so-called French Somalia (Djibouti), emphasising policies of assimilation, although after World War I they changed their form of government to the British style.

In the social sphere, colonialism had much to do with the idea of the superiority of the white race, the European powers took upon themselves the mission of bringing civilisation to the African continent, which was populated by supposedly inferior races (Ceamanos, 2016, p.39).

This was done in different ways, in the British colonies through missions, while in the French colonies it was done through public schools. It was necessary to form an acculturated social group, introducing them to Western logic and behaviour, familiar with the colonisers' languages and prepared for administrative or economic management tasks (Iniesta, 2000, p.190). Nonetheless, from the very beginning, groups that contested these policies emerged and, by promoting their traditional African customs and habits, ended up claiming their autonomy from European influence, that is to say, originating the first nationalist steps within the African continent. This led to uprisings by the indigenous peoples against the invading powers. One of the main ones was the Dervish movement, led by Maxamed Cabdille Xassan, a religious and politically inspired movement that was active in Somali territory. It mobilised large numbers of Somalis to fight against the colonisers (British, Italian and Ethiopian), so that between 1899 and 1920 the insurgency wreaked havoc in many areas, especially in British Somaliland (Höhne, 2017, p.73).

All these changes also had an effect on the economic field. Their structures were also affected by the arrival of the Europeans, with whom the colonial model that was implemented eliminated local control of the traditional resources that existed on the African continent. In addition, the foreign powers from Europe exercised control over the Red Sea and Gulf of Aden coasts, maintaining a monopoly that closed off local peoples from participating in world trade.

Before beginning this study, we must undertake a historiographical review of how the processes of colonisation and colonial wars in the Horn of Africa have been analysed. Of course, this issue has been central to colonisation studies, with the African continent being an elementary area of research. As early as the 1980s, UNESCO's General History of Africa volumes focused on the role of European powers in the partition of Africa, especially with regard to the instruments of colonisation (Betts, 2000; Uzoigwe, 1985). In the specific case of the Horn of Africa, the main actor studied has been Italy, due to its presence in Eritrea, Somalia and Ethiopia and the conflicts arising from its colonial expansion. Research on Italian colonisation remains central in recent years (Calchi Novati, 1994; Finaldi, 2016; Rivers, 2017; Mayropoulos, 2020). Secondly, some research has also focused on the British Empire, whose presence in the region was more limited, occupying the Somaliland protectorate (Keefer, 1973; Mamdani, 1999; Faulkner, 2021). Finally, there are no specific studies on the processes of French colonisation in the Horn of Africa, a fact that coincides with the scarcity of research on the history of Djibouti. In this case, some information can be found in extensive works on French colonisation.

Regarding local actors, most studies have focused on Ethiopia, as it is one of the few uncolonized territories in Africa. Historical research has varied over the years with studies on Ethiopia's relations with European powers (Keefer, 1973), the construction of the modern Ethiopian state, which allowed it to become a colonising actor (Teshale, 1995), interest in Ethiopia's historical particularities (Tibebu, 1996) and, of course, interest in the Battle of Adwa, which marked the beginning of Ethiopian expansionism (McLachlan, 2011). The role of this actor in colonising the Horn of Africa has also been extensively studied since the 1970s, being a central focus of interest in the processes of colonisation and colonial wars in the region (Harbeson, 1979; Birru 1981; Haggai, 2010). We particularly highlight the effects of colonisation on Oromo peoples (Jalata, 2020).

In relation to colonised spaces, Eritrea and Somalia have been the most analysed case studies. In the case of Eritrea, in addition to colonisation processes, studies have focused on the creation of specific national identities, a fact that has to do with the country's struggles for independence (Okbazghi, 1987; Yemane, 1989; Uoldelul, 2007). A novel case in relation to Somalia has been the growth of studies on Italian cultural influence, which has emerged in recent decades (Calchi Novati, 2005; Mumin Ahad and Gerrand, 2004). Similarly, since 2000, research on Somaliland has been constant, which is due to the fact that this small country became unilaterally independent in 1991 from the rest of Somalia, provoking an interest in its particular history (Millman, 2013; Prunier, 2021). Finally, there have not been many publications on Djibouti in recent decades (Shehim and Searing, 1980).

Finally, there has been a special interest since the 1980s in the role played by African actors against colonisation, highlighting that they had not been passive actors, but that the inhabitants of the Horn of Africa themselves also resisted the European, but also Ethiopian, presence (Geshekter, 1985; Ibrahim, 1985; Kakwenzire, 1986; Iyob, 1993). This area of knowledge needs to be revisited, as we will see throughout this chapter, as studies in the 1980s-1990s had a clear nationalist perspective, sometimes exaggerating its role.

Colonial Resistance and Struggles in the Face of European Invasion

The Berlin Conference represented the turning point in the colonisation process, but it did not lead to a direct territorial division of the continent; rather, the powers progressively settled in different enclaves in order to begin an effective conquest of the territory at a later date. Colonisation, therefore, developed depending on the particular contexts of each region and the colonial model promoted by the main powers, which in the case of the Horn of Africa were France, Great Britain and Italy. However, European expansion was not free of obstacles and confrontations. Historiography has traditionally viewed the populations of the Horn of Africa as passive actors, but as we shall see in the following lines, this was not the case.

It is not appropriate to speak of 'African resistance' because there was no general alliance of the African peoples against the white coloniser, which was easier for the Europeans to fight (García Moral, 2016: 166). Sooner or later, all the regions of the continent that had been divided up at the Berlin Conference ended in the hands of the European invader, with the exception of Liberia and Ethiopia, as we have already mentioned. The myth of easy conquest is belied by twenty years of wars between armies of the line, with frequent colonial defeats despite unequal armaments (Iniesta, 2000: 181), which subsequently resulted in strong resistance from the colonised population. For this reason, the colonial period is called by the black population the 'time of force', because it is by this means, by coercion and physical violence, that the European regime was established (Ki-Zerbo, 1972: 623).

From Eritrea to Somalia, Conflicts in the Italian- occupied Territories

Italy maintained two centres of colonisation in Africa: Cyrenaica and Tripolitania in the north, which later formed Libya, and the Horn of Africa in the east, where it effectively occupied the territories of Eritrea and Italian Somalia but was unable to penetrate Ethiopia. The Wuchale (or Uccialli in the Italian version) agreement signed in 1889 delimited the border between Ethiopia and the Italian colony of Eritrea and was used by Italy as a sign that Ethiopia was its protectorate. However, the defeat of the Italian army by Menelik II at the Battle of Adwa in 1896 certified Ethiopia's right to be an independent state. Meanwhile, the Italians gradually settled and occupied the coasts of Eritrea and central and southern Somalia (Uzoigwe, 1985). The two territories had a different historical process, as most authors have noted the low resistance shown by the local Eritrean population, especially compared to the Somali clans in southern Somalia. However, we consider that when delving deeper into the history of Eritrean resistance, it is also possible to find groups and actors that opposed the Italian presence, as highlighted by Nicola Labanca, whose research reflects colonialist repression against opposition groups (Labanca, 2005).

But why did Italy expand into this area? There seem to be no pre-existing interests, especially since the Italian state was one of the colonial powers that later embarked on colonial conquest, as Germany had done, and its resources for this enterprise were limited. Possibly, the arrival of Italian missionaries and traders may have led Italy to set its sights on the Horn of Africa and remain on its shores (Finaldi, 2016: 23). Moreover, the rapid expansion of France and Britain in the Mediterranean prevented Rome from having a colony nearby, as Libya was not occupied until 1911 (Mayropoulos, 2020, p.94). Against all odds, Italy became the colonial power in the Horn of Africa due to France's inability to penetrate the territory, limiting itself to the colony of Djibouti, and a meagre British presence in the protectorate of Somaliland (Calchi Novati, 2008, p.41).

In the case of Eritrea, the Italian colonial presence can be traced back to 1882, when the Italian state became the owner of the settlement of Assab after signing an agreement with the Rubattino company. Shortly afterwards, it began to occupy other major settlements in the region, such as the city of Massawa, ignoring the historical claims of the Ottoman Empire and Egypt to the territory (Calchi Novati, 1994, p.70) and establishing an intensive and centralist colonial regime (Calchi Novati, 2005, p.54) that, moreover, had no interest in promoting the idea of 'civilisation' among the local population, limiting itself to the exploitation of the resources of the subjugated territory (Yemane, 1989, p.67).

How do we explain the lack of resistance and opposition from the Eritrean population to the Italian presence? Firstly, and as we have already pointed out, we believe that as more research is conducted on this issue, new perspectives on Eritrean resistance will emerge. In addition, Chelati Dirar has already pointed to explanations such as the critical situation in the region prior to Italy's arrival due to ecological and social devastation resulting from the food crisis and a high level of social and political crisis. Thus, it seems that famine and political division prevented the creation of a cohesive opposition capable of standing up to colonisation. In this context, the Italians did not hesitate to make use of the divide et impera motto, allying and confronting various local groups. To maintain this advantage, the Italians used ethnicity, religion and social stratification to further divide the population (Uoldelul, 2007, p. 258).

The situation was quite different in Somalia. From the late 19th century onwards, Italy controlled some of the most important Somali ports, especially in the south and centre of the country. While control of the coast was relatively easy, this was not the case once Italian troops tried to penetrate inland, where the fertile lands around the Jubba and Shabelle rivers were located. In addition to the resistance in that region, there was resistance from the sultanates of Obbia and Midyurtina, two states that became Italian protectorates, and the fierce resistance and struggle of Maxamed Cabdille Xassan and his Dervishes. Prior to the arrival of the Italians on the Somali coast, the most important ports in southern Somalia had been dominated by Oman, which extended its influence as far as the island of Zanzibar, but its power began to wane in the second half of the 19th century, facilitating European expansion (Mumin Ahad, 2004, p.15).

As in Eritrea, the first Italian colonial landmarks were carried out by trading companies that acquired the rights to exploit the Somali ports in the Benadir region. Both the Filonardi Company and the Benadir Company quickly earned high revenues during the 1890s, but lack of investment meant that they had to cede their rights to the Italian state, which took over colonisation at a crucial moment after the defeat of Ethiopia at Adwa in 1896. From then on, the Italian colonisers saw agricultural exploitation as a means of obtaining state benefits, although this implied the occupation of a fairly large territory and the resistance of the local population (Guadagni, 1978, p.5). This southern region, which stretched from Mogadishu almost to the city of Kismaayo, was one of the areas that posed the greatest opposition to Italian rule.

The starting point of the Italian colonial wars in this region was in 1896, at the Battle of Lafole, when an Italian expedition led by Antonio Cecchi was assaulted by a group of local farmers, killing the main promoter of colonisation in Somalia (Guadagni, 1978, p.12). This affront was not overlooked, and the Italians soon retaliated by attacking the town of Lafole shortly afterwards (Bollettino della Società Africana d'Italia, 1897). Unlike the Dervish Movement, which was mostly composed of nomadic peoples, most of the resistance in the south was organised by sedentary people, whose struggle against the Europeans was based on the defence of the land and the rural economy of the area. In some cases, these resistances were also based on religious motives. The Italian colonisation process, contrary to popular belief, was not an easy one. Thus, between 1896 and 1920, the Benadiri, Bimaal, Geledi, Hin-tire or Wa'dan and the religious communities or Jama'a, defended the riverside regions and resisted colonisation. Those who put up the most resistance were undoubtedly the Bimaal who, throughout the period 1907-1908, stood up to Italian expansionism (Bollettino della Società Africana d'Italia, 1908). However, all these forces did not unite in a common front, and this division facilitated Italian expansionism, leading to the first defeats from 1908 onwards. The Benadir coast fell in the same year, as did the Bimaal who lost in the battle of Sabti iyo Ahad. The fall of Mereerey in August 1908 opened up the interior of the coastal regions to the Italians for good (Sorrentino, 2011). The advent of World War I only delayed Italy's expansionist plans, which eventually consolidated control of the entire south in 1923 with the arrival of Cesare Maria Vecchi as Mussolini's appointed governor (Bollettino della Società Africana d'Italia, 1923).

The case of the coastal Somali sultanates was quite different. In 1889 Italy signed an agreement with the Sultanate of Obbia and did the similar for Midyurtina, making both territories Italian protectorates (Alcamo, 2019). However, the good relations between the two sides encountered obstacles at times, especially as Italy's direct control over the territory was limited. This would explain why there were no major anti-colonialist movements in the sultanates, at least not until Vecchi, once in control of the south, moved to effectively control both territories. Thus, the Sultan of Obbia tried to convince the Sultan of Midyurtina to unite against the invaders. However, local differences and the traditional enmity between the two sides made it impossible to forge a pact. Despite the differences, Obbia rose up in 1923, following the uprising in Midyurtina. The revolt did not last long and in 1925 the Italians managed to impose some control over the sultanates, but this did not prevent other resistance movements from rising up against the colonisers, such as El Bur (Ibrahim, 1985: 82). The colonial wars in the region ended in 1927 after the last forces of the Midyurtina sultanate were defeated (Il Popolo d'Italia, 1927).

Finally, the third threat that Italy had to face was that of the Somali religious and political leader Maxamed Cabdille Xassan, who for several years threatened Italy's colonial regions. The Dervish leader posed a real threat not only to Italy, but also to Britain and Ethiopia. Italy went so far as to sign, together with Britain, the Treaty of Illig in 1905, recognising the Dervishes as a pseudo-state in the Walnut, between the sultanates of Obbi and Midyurtina, which served as a buffer zone (Hess, 1964: 422). The role of Cabdille Xassan will not be further discussed in this section as it will be dealt with again in the sections on British Somaliland.

The Small Enclave of Djibouti and the French Invasion

France's interest in this territory was due to the geostrategic position of the enclave on the Red Sea, which became more decisive after the construction of the Suez Canal, as from 1862 the French government established treaties with the leaders of the two main peoples of the area: the Afar and the Issa. Through these treaties, the French began to settle in the north, in the Obock region (Arconada Ledesma, 2020, p. 88), and later extended the pacts to other areas such as Tadjoura. Djibouti's importance lay in the fact that it was a vital supply station for ships and troops travelling from France and Algeria to Indochina and Madagascar, two of the most important outposts of the French colonies (Crouzet, 2019, p.143). But there was another underlying reason: the French wanted to prevent Britain, which controlled the Arabian coast around Bab el-Mandad and the Gulf of Aden, from closing off access to the Mediterranean through the canal (Shelley, 2013, p. 290).

As early as 1885, this European metropolis established its own protectorate in Djibouti, which had its antecedents in a treaty signed in 1883 and a subsequent one in 1887 with the Somali sultans who ruled that region. The colony was established in 1896 with the merger of the territories of Tadjoura, Obock and Djibouti, forming what is known as Coté Français des Somalis, or French Somalia (Shehim & Searing, 1980, p.211), and in that year the capital of Obock was transferred to the city of Djibouti. However, Djibouti's interest was not only for the European powers, but also for the independent African territory in East Africa, Abyssinia. The importance of Djibouti to Menelik II's Empire was due to the fact that Ethiopia, after the Italian occupation of Eritrea, had become a landlocked state, so that almost all international trade had to pass through the French colony (Yusuf Abdi, 1977, p. 62). The prosperity of the port city of Djibouti and the region as a whole was largely due to the rail link with Ethiopia that had been built since 1894. This line cemented a 'special relationship' by making Djibouti, by treaty, the official maritime outlet, which at the time accounted for 60% of Ethiopian trade (Stanley, 2007, p.133), consolidating the development of this French-colonised region.

In this way, the size of this small enclave in the Horn of Africa, together with the treaties that the French made with the region's leaders during the 1880s and the advances in communications and trade that this territory developed, meant that the colonisation of Djibouti did not meet with strong resistance, as was the case in British Somaliland with Maxamed Cabdille Xasan at the forefront of opposition to dependence on the European metropolis.

Colonial Wars in British Somaliland: The Threat of the Dervish Movement

If Italy had encountered serious problems in effectively controlling its portion of the land inhabited by the Somali population, Britain had no less difficulty in the colonised territory in the north, where it had to face the threat of Maxamed Cabdille Xassan and the political-religious movement of the Dervishes between 1899 and 1920. Britain had occupied the northern strip of present-day Somalia since the end of the 19th century for two exogenous reasons: to try to control the entrance to the Red Sea and to supply its colony in Aden with livestock (Prunier, 2021, p.5). However, it had limited itself to effective control of the port city of Berbera and a few coastal points, with no intention of penetrating inland. Moreover, since its arrival, the Empire had to deal with the Somali clans in the area, confronting the Issa, the Habar Gerhajis and the Habar Awal between 1886 and 1895. Although treaties were signed with the clan leaders, they consistently defended their independence (Ibrahim, 1985, p.83). Some British contemporaries went so far as to point out that the British presence was supported by the Somali clans, who avoided any confrontation (Kittermaster, 1928, p.334), but, as we shall see, the colonisers were on several occasions constrained by the colonial wars. Events surrounding the British colonisation of the Somaliland protectorate are sometimes rendered invisible by the lack of sources in the British archives since, as Millman points out, much of the administration's documentation was destroyed after independence (2013, p. 4).

It was around 1899 when the British called him 'Mad Mullah' and launched his anti-colonial campaign with the aim of uniting all Somalis against the foreign invaders, who were also Christians: Italy, the United Kingdom and Ethiopia (Faulkner, 2021, p.338). In that year, the first uprisings against the British began and he gained the support of thousands of warriors, mostly from nomadic Somali clans. There are some chronicles, written by Hamilton, that reflect the ability of this leader to convince the Somali masses: 'He preached continuously in Berbera and gradually gained the reputation and influence of a holy man [...] The fact that he enjoyed immunity increased his influence, including the interior tribes under his command'. The anti-colonial struggle soon threatened the British presence in Berbera and a long colonial war began between 1900 and 1904 in which the British launched four wars to try to undermine Cabdille Xassan's forces (Kakwenzire, 1986, p.662). The balance was disastrous for the British, with numerous human and military losses that led to the Somali leader becoming a figurehead of Somali resistance, allowing him to 'dominate the south of the protectorate, as well as a considerable part of the Italian and Abyssinian spheres' (Hamilton, 1911: 46-53). Moreover, the development of other colonial wars, such as the Anglo-Boer conflict in Southern Africa, allowed the Dervishes some leverage against a Britain that had to divide its forces (Faulkner, 2021, p.338).

The situation was dire for the British in 1904, who foresaw imminent defeat. However, Ethiopia's intervention split the Dervish forces and forced them to sign the Treaty of Illig in 1905 with Italy and Britain, under which they were granted control over the Nogal region and the small port of Eyl in exchange for peace and the avoidance of further fighting (Illig Treaty, 1905). However, the peace was short-lived and allowed Cabdille Xassan and his followers to reorganise, so that in 1908 anti-colonial activities resumed, both in the British and Italian spheres of influence where the Dervishes 'penetrated the sultanate of Obbia and killed 41 men, 28 women, 31 children and stole 3500 head of cattle. They were a force of 1050 men, 500 of whom were armed with rifles (The Times, 1908). The pressure was such that between 1909-1910 the governor of the Somaliland protectorate ordered the evacuation of the colony's internal territories, with only the main urban centres along the coast under his control (Records of the British Parliament, 1910). Nor did the war improve for Britain, which between 1915 and 1918 was involved in the Great War, limiting the number of troops, parties and war material dedicated to the war in Somaliland (The Times, 1914). Moreover, in this same period the Dervishes had a new ally in Ethiopia, where the new emperor, Yasu V, was inclined towards the Central Powers and sought a regional ally among the Dervishes (Zewde, 2007, pp.253-256).

However, the winds in Maxamed Cabdille Xassan's favour came to an end when the Great War ended and Britain was able to redirect its efforts to controlling the situation in the protectorate. Thus, in early 1920, an offensive was launched against the main Dervish positions, which were bombed, defeating the

Mullah, who escaped into the Horn of Africa and died a year later, no longer a threat to European and Ethiopian interests in the region (Records of the British Parliament, 1920).

Ethiopian Expansionism as A Response to The European Presence in The Horn of Africa

When we approach the phenomenon of colonisation and its conflicts, most historiography is linked to Europeans, and it is often forgotten that in Africa there were also local actors who promoted their own particular colonial and imperialist project. In the Horn of Africa, this role belonged to Ethiopia, one of the main historical actors in the region, which set out to control part of the territories inhabited by other peoples on the peripheries of the empire and in neighbouring territories, such as the occupation of Somali territories, especially in the Haud and the Ogaden. The Ethiopian Empire of Menelik II played a key role here, signing several treaties with Britain, France and Italy between 1897 and 1908, which shaped a new map and new realities that affected the peoples of the Horn of Africa.

Thus, after the arrival of the Europeans, the Ethiopian territory set about a series of local conquests and diplomatic manoeuvres with European powers in order not to be left behind in the partition of the Horn of Africa region. In essence, Abyssinia survived the imperialist partition of Africa by becoming one of its participants for, as Menelik II warned in an 1891 letter to the European powers: 'Ethiopia has been for fourteen centuries a Christian island in a sea of heathens. If the powers at a distance go ahead to divide Africa among themselves, I do not intend to remain an indifferent spectator' (Geshekter, 1985: 7).

To explore these issues further, we will look at how Ethiopia reacted to the arrival of Europeans on the shores of the region and try to elaborate on the term African imperialism used in relation to the role played by the Ethiopian Empire and its role as a 'black coloniser'.

Ethiopia's Reaction to European Colonization – African Imperialism?

After the death of Yohannes IV in 1889, Menelik II, the King of Shewa[4], came to power, transforming the Ethiopian Empire into a new territory through his modernisation. Menelik's reign witnessed numerous innovations unprecedented in Ethiopian history. The first, even before his appointment as emperor, was the founding in the mid-1880s of the capital, Addis Ababa, literally 'New Flower', which by 1910 had a population of about 100,000 (Akpan, 1985, p.277). But it also set out to control part of the territories inhabited by neighbouring populations in response to European advance in the region (Ibrahim, 1985, p.82). Indeed, Emperor Menelik II turned the country into a centralised, powerful and modern power, pursuing a policy of expansion in such a way that he brought several surrounding territories under his subjugation (Caranci, 1988), greatly expanding Abyssinia's borders and laying the foundations of the 'Ethiopian' state.

With the Italian occupation of Massawa, the Italian government under Pietro Antonelli and the new Emperor of Ethiopia, Menelik II, signed the Treaty of Wuchale in 1889, which recognised Italian possessions along the Red Sea (Friis, 2001, p.115). Moreover, although contested in the famous Article 17 of the Italian 'protectorate' in Ethiopia, the text fixed the new territorial borders with Italy. From this point onwards Menelik, having reached an agreement with this ambitious European country, turned to the others, declaring firmly: 'I have no intention of waiting with folded arms for European powers from overseas to divide up Africa'. The official creation of the colony of Eritrea in January 1890 was the result of long negotiations (Taddia, 1994, p.494). The text was signed in Italian and Amharic, which introduced a series of contradictions that pitted the parties against each other, with Italy claiming a protectorate over Ethiopia, triggering the Italian-Ethiopian war in 1895.

Previously, Menelik had managed to become a part of the Brussels General Act of 1890 regulating the arms trade in Africa, Articles 8-14, signed by the United States and some European powers. The Act called for the suppression of the slave trade in Africa and the restriction of the importation and sale, within a defined area of the African continent, of firearms, ammunition and spirituous liquors (Metaferia, 2009, p.32). Italy sponsored Ethiopia's participation in the General Act of Brussels, which allowed Addis Ababa to import ammunition legally, thus legitimising the active arms trade it had been conducting for some years with French traders (Abdi, 1981, p.154). Thus, after the outbreak of the conflict with the Italians, the Ethiopians found themselves with a significant amount of modern weapons that could be used to fight under similar conditions as the Europeans. Thus, on 1 March 1896, despite the Italian attempt to surprise the Ethiopians at the Battle of Adwa, the first European defeat in the process of colonisation took place due to Menelik II's potential in terms of weapons and combatants. This military might be (or was) the basis of the Ethiopian leader's success, but even more important was his diplomatic talent (Weeseling, 1999, p.295), and after the Battle of Adwa he became a negotiating partner with the surrounding regions. This event marked the end of Italian expansion in the area, and the beginning of Menelik's conquest of other regions bordering his own borders.

The diplomatic path of the undefeated Ethiopian Empire began after the Battle of Adwa, with the signing of the Treaty of Addis Ababa with the Italians on 26 October 1896. By this agreement, Italy recognised Ethiopian sovereignty and abrogated the controversial Article 17 of the Treaty of Wuchale. In return, Menelik recognised Eritrea as an Italian colony (McLachlan, 2011, p.24). A few months later, on 20 March 1897, the Franco-Ethiopian Friendship Treaty was initialled, ratifying Ethiopia's independence and French preponderance in the country, and establishing the western border of the territory, which reduced the area under French control. Moreover, it was at this time that the two countries agreed on the construction of the 784-kilometre Addis Ababa-Djibouti railway that established the French port as Ethiopia's main outlet to the sea (Lapidoth, 1982, p.82). With the other European power present in the Horn of Africa region, the United Kingdom, Menelik signed a Treaty on 14 May 1897. With this act and taking into account that Ethiopian expansion was heading towards the Red Sea, Ethiopia was granted the possibility of subduing a part of Somalia, which was now occupied not only by France, England and Italy, but also by a foreign, albeit African, power (Weeseling, 1999, p.313). Ethiopia thus received a third of the British-controlled areas in northern Somalia in exchange for Menelik's neutrality in the UK's competition with France for strategic positions in the Horn of Africa, along with some economic concessions. This area was renamed Ogaden, Haud and reserved areas, between Jijjiga in the northwest and the Gumburu Hills in the southeast (Höhne, 2017: 73), a long-standing Ethiopian claim that did not have Somali consent and represented the most fertile parts of the territory. Nevertheless, as Margery Perham wrote: 'Ethiopian sovereignty over the Somalis was expressed mainly through intermittent expeditions, not far removed from raids' (Geshekter, 1985: 10). All these treaties were expanded as Ethiopia entered the 20th century between Ethiopia and the three European colonies with a presence in the Horn of Africa.

Following these agreements, Menelik's power was strengthened in East Africa and the Ethiopian Empire continued to develop and modernise. However, in 1906, the emperor suffered a serious illness, which prompted the three European powers in the Horn of Africa to try to consolidate Ethiopia's power in the region. In December 1906, the Tripartite Agreement was signed between Britain, France and Italy. This instrument analysed the possible internal situation in the territory, even treating an eventual disintegration of Ethiopia as a foregone conclusion, the three signatories began the preamble: 'reaffirming their recognition of the Ethiopian Empire as a full subject of international law, and declaring that it was in their common interest to maintain the integrity of Ethiopia intact, pledging themselves to observe a neutral attitude in the event of internal rivalries or changes in Ethiopia' (Parfitt, 2019, p.260). Nevertheless, by this agreement each of the three signatory countries was given spheres of influence in the territory of Ethiopia.

In 1909 Menelik designated his grandson Lij-Iyasu as his successor, and it was after his grandfather's death in 1913 that he ascended the throne as Iyasu V. However, a period of intrigue ensued as his new policies of rapprochement with Islam provoked a series of protests in Ethiopia that led to his removal from the throne (Arconada Ledesma, 2020, p.264). In 1916 he was deposed in favour of Zauditu, one of Menelik's daughters, who served as empress until 1930. With the relations with the colonisers in the surrounding regions signed by the previous treaties, we should know what were the reactions of the neighbouring populations who were being targeted by Menelik's imperialist ideas.

Clashes Between the Ethiopian Empire and Neighboring Peoples

It is clear that the presence of European countries in the Horn of Africa generated enormous concern among Ethiopian leaders, who saw France, Italy and Britain beginning to settle on the shores of a region where Ethiopia had been a major historical power. This presence led Emperor Menelik II to expand his borders into areas with which he had maintained relations, but not effective rule, especially since the Christian kingdom of Ethiopia had control of the north but not of the lands to the south. Of course, territorial control expanded the kingdom's population (which was also made up of different peoples), land (some of which was highly exploitable and some of which was of little value, such as the desert areas of the Ogaden) and turned Ethiopia into an empire, developing its own colonisation policies. Of course, this move by Ethiopia generated no small amount of conflict with the peoples to be conquered, as well as with its neighbours.

We consider Ethiopia to have been a colonising force in the Horn of Africa, but it was not a unique case of expansionist and centralising states that eventually brought neighbouring peoples under their rule, such as the Sokoto Caliphate, the Zulu state led by Shaka, the Empire of Samori Ture or Buganda. There is still much debate today about using the term 'black coloniser' because it equates European policies with those of these African actors (Tibebu, 1996, p.422). It is clear that it is not comparable due to the extension of the territories, the measures carried out by the Europeans and the effects of their African domination, but neither can it be doubted that some African states, such as Ethiopia, did promote colonial policies on neighbouring populations (Okbazghi, 1987), such as conquest, violence, enslavement, colonisation of land with the transfer of inhabitants from the north to the south or the clear acculturation of the elites, who used Amharic as the main official language (Markakis, 1989, p.119).

But how can we explain that Ethiopia managed not only to expand but also to maintain control of the new territories? First, Ethiopia had established itself as a centralised kingdom, with a remarkable administrative and logistical capacity that allowed it to overcome horizontal societies such as the Somalis of the Ogaden or the Oromo of the central territories (Calchi Novati, 2008: 42). Secondly, the purchase of arms from European powers such as France and Russia undoubtedly gave Ethiopia an advantage over neighbouring peoples who did not have access to modern weapons or the formation of large armies capable of standing up to the regional power (Akpan, 1985: 170). Thirdly, Italy's defeats at Dogali (1887) and Adwa (1896) against Ethiopian armies highlighted the African kingdom's ability to repel European influence and gave the new empire a moral high ground. Finally, and although we have already mentioned it, the European presence generated some pressure on Ethiopia and prompted it to conquer territories that would otherwise and most likely have been dominated by Europeans.

In this context, Ethiopia began a timid expansion with Tewodros II (1855-1868) over the nearest villages, following this policy Yohannes IV (1872 - 1889) began importing arms to prevent internal uprisings and continue expanding the kingdom. This expansion was consolidated under Emperor Menelik II (1889 - 1913), extending the empire to the south, east and west of the country, taking advantage of the Wuchale agreement and the arrival of modern weaponry (Akpan, 1985).

Ethiopia's first target was the rich southern lands in the lower half of the northern plateau, an area not particularly populated, with the longest wet period in the highlands, forests and hunting. Subsequent conquest continued across the Rift Valley, controlling the southern plateau entirely, where fertile, well-watered land was found, with sorghum as the main crop. These territories not only increased agricultural and livestock production capacity, but also prevented internal tensions in the densely populated north of the country, allowing the Amhara-Tigre elites to appropriate land and exploit local labour (Markakis, 2011: 28). Of course, this policy was not carried out without opposition from the peoples who inhabited these regions, especially the Oromo (also known as Galla), which forced the emperors to launch campaigns for the pacification of the territory through the *neftenya-gabbar* model in which Ethiopian soldiers and their families settled in strategically built fortified villages (*katamas*), controlling revolts and supporting the new local officials (Keefer, 1973). Even the alliance between traditional enemies such as the Oromo and the Habaasas could not stop Ethiopia's rapid military expansion (Jalata, 1990: 8). However, the Oromo, along with the Somalis, were the most prominent resisters, resisting the regime of subordination and colonisation and continued to fight after the Ethiopian conquest (Jalata, 2020: 3). Thus, the defeats of the Oromo and other peoples such as the Walyata, Kaffa and Gurage in the south allowed the construction of modern Ethiopia (Teshale, 1995: 48).

The other key piece of empire-building was the lowlands in the east of the country. This region, characterised as a desert territory, was traditionally inhabited by nomadic Somali peoples and did not attract the colonisation of the northern populations, as had been the case in the south (Markakis, 2011: 28). This meant that, although the territory was conquered, intensive colonisation of the local population did not take place. However, the lack of organisation of the Somali clans and the absence of a united state in the interior facilitated Ethiopian expansion into the region where the inhabitants lived by nomadism and pastoralism (Calchi Novati, 2008). The first region targeted by the Ethiopians was the Haud territory, with important economic and commercial centres such as Jijiga and Harar subjugated in 1887 (Keefer, 1973: 472). Although there was rapid expansion into the Ogaden, maintaining effective control of this territory was not so easy because of continued Somali uprisings throughout the 1890s, which were limited to fortified towns. This inability to fully control the territory allowed for the influence of Maxamed Cabdille Xassan and his Dervishes from 1900 onwards, who came to threaten the power of the empire in the region. While the Ethiopians succeeded in curbing their inland expansion, they prevented the Dervish movement from occupying the western part of the Ogaden and kept it away from the highlands (Hess, 1964).

There is no doubt that there is a fundamental difference in the expansion and colonisation of the south and east of the new empire. If in the south the conquest can be justified by the control of land, the increase of agricultural exploitation and the transfer of northern population, in the east the only explanation is the defensive reaction to the European colonial presence (Ibrahim, 1985: 82), establishing the Ogaden as a buffer zone, since the control of the desert responded more to strategic motives than purely economic and commercial ones.

CONCLUSION

The colonial processes in the Horn of Africa were particularly turbulent, although it depended very much on each territory. The most particular fact about this region is that the European powers had to reckon with an independent African actor (a unique case with the exception of Liberia) that also played a role in the division of the Horn of Africa.

Throughout this chapter we have seen how Europeans had to face opposition and resistance that ended up generating large-scale colonial wars, especially in the Somali region and in the case of Ethiopia. Firstly, Italy had no major obstacles in controlling Eritrea, but not Ethiopia, against which it lost two battles, a small one, Dogali in 1887, and the major Italian defeat at the Battle of Adwa in 1896. In addition, it took the Italians several decades to effectively dominate Somali territory, with uprisings in the south and centre of the country, as well as the role played by the Dervish movement. Despite the small size of its Somaliland protectorate, the United Kingdom did not find it easy: for more than two decades it had to contend with Maxamed Cabdille Xassan and his followers, who were able to negotiate with European powers and Ethiopia. It was certainly the French who encountered the fewest complications in their small enclave in Djibouti, with little resistance from the local population, which facilitated their presence until 1977. The differences between the regions seem to respond not so much to the colonial model imposed by the Europeans, but rather to the local context in which the local population found itself when colonisation arrived. The territory of Djibouti is certainly not the same as that of Ethiopia, a centralised and modern power capable of confronting (and defeating) the Europeans. It can therefore be seen how the populations of the Horn of Africa in general stood up to the colonising processes, leaving behind this idealised image of African peoples as passive subjects of their historical processes.

In addition to France, Italy and the United Kingdom, this chapter has also analysed the role played by Ethiopia in the colonial wars. On the one hand, Ethiopia was a victim of European attempts at colonisation, encircled in its traditional sphere of influence by the European advance. But on the other hand, Ethiopia undoubtedly also generated its own colonisation project, expanding its territory beyond the historical borders of Abyssinia and transforming itself into an empire. Although there is still debate as to whether Ethiopia acted as a 'black coloniser', we believe that the Ethiopian case is not comparable in terms of the dimensions and impact of European colonisation on the African continent. However, it cannot be denied that Ethiopia implemented colonising policies at the political, military, economic and socio-cultural levels, profoundly altering the traditional systems of the newly occupied spaces, as we have seen in the case of the Oromo and Somalis. Regarding the Ethiopian reaction to the arrival of the Europeans, we see Ethiopian expansion to the south, east and west of the territory as a direct consequence of colonial pressure. However, there are differences that need to be taken into account: in the case of the southern highlands, Ethiopia had an economic interest, which could have justified its expansion even without European influence. In the case of the eastern lowlands and desert, it seems that the only reason for its domination was to create a buffer-zone between its territory and the spaces colonised by Europeans on the coasts.

Nor can we overlook the fact that there was resistance to Ethiopian expansion among neighbouring populations, especially in the south and east, which forced Ethiopia to devote resources and efforts to effective control of the territory, which in some cases, as in the Ogaden desert, was not effective, allowing local actors such as Maxamed Cabdille Xassan to extend their influence among the different Somali clans. Opposition to Ethiopian colonisation lasted for decades and has led to many conflicts throughout the 20th century.

As a final conclusion, it is clear that the colonising processes in the Horn of Africa were marked by long-lasting colonial wars in the cases of Italy and the United Kingdom in the Somali territories. The second characteristic is the presence of Ethiopia, a Christian and imperialist actor that, after consolidating its position on the regional chessboard, joined in the division of territory, also generating its own wars in the occupied territories. All these confrontations and the distribution of the different areas of influence since the end of the 19th century have marked the most recent history of the Horn of Africa.

REFERENCES

Abdi, S. Y. (1981). Decolonization in the Horn and the outcome of Somali aspirations for self-determination, *Northeast African Studies*, *2/3*(3/1), 153-162. https://www.jstor.org/stable/43660063

Akpan, M. B. (1985). Liberia and Ethiopia, 1880-1914: the survival of two African states. In A. Adu Bohaen (Ed.), General History of Africa VII: Africa under colonial domination 1880-1935, (pp. 249-282). UNESCO.

Alcamo, I. (2019). *Somalia between colonialism and trusteeship: the Italian experience and its legacy*, [Master's thesis, Luiss]. http://tesi.luiss.it/26626/1/082152_ALCAMO_IGNAZIO.pdf

Arconada Ledesma, P. (2020). Brief review of the processes of resistance against colonization in the Horn of Africa. Struggles in Italian Somalia and the Dervish Movement (1890-1930). *Studia Historica. Historia Contemporánea*, (38), 245–266. https://dialnet.unirioja.es/servlet/articulo?codigo=7676254

Arconada Ledesma, P. (2020). El proceso de descolonización en Yibuti: entre la influencia de Francia y la disputa etíope-somalí (1958-1977) [The descolonization process in Yibuti: between the influence of France and the Ethiopian-Somali dispute (1958-1977).]. In C. García Andrés, J. Cuadrado Bolaños, & P. Arconada Ledesma (Eds.), *África, un continente en transformación. Enfoques interdisciplinares [Africa, a continent in transformation. Enfoques interdisciplinares]* (pp. 87–103). Ediciones Universidad de Valladolid.

Benadir, N. (1908). Preludi dell'occupazione militare – Due scontri a Sud di Merca. La zona delle future operazioni [Preludes of Military Occupation – Two clashes South of Merca. The area of future operations,]. *Bollettino della Società Africana d'Italia, [Bulletin of the African Society of Italy]*. http://digitale.bnc.roma.sbn.it/tecadigitale/giornale/TO00017 9105/1908

Betts, R. F. (2000). Methods and institutions of European domination. In A. Adu Boahen (Ed.), *General History of Africa VII. Africa under colonial domination 1880-1935* (pp. 312–331). UNESCO.

Birru, Lubie (1981): Abyssinian Colonialism as the Genesis of the Crisis in the Horn: Oromo Resistance (1855-1913), *Northeast African Studies*, *2/3* (3/1), 93-98.

Caemanos, R. (2016). *El reparto de África. De la Conferencia de Berlín a los conflictos actuales [The department of Africa. From the Conference of Berlin to the actual conflicts.]*. Catarata.

Calchi Novati, G. (1994). Italy in the Triangle of the Horn: Too Many Corners for a Half Power. *The Journal of Modern African Studies*, *32*(3), 369–385.

Calchi Novati, G. (2005). National Identities as a By-Product of Italian Colonialism: A Comparison of Eritrea and Somalia. In J. Andall & D. Duncan (Eds.), *Italian Colonialism: Legacy and Memory* (pp. 47–74).

Calchi Novati, G. (2008). Italy and Africa: How to forget colonialism. *Journal of Modern Italian Studies, 13*(1), 41–57.

Caranci, C. (1988). El pansomalismo: claves históricas del conflicto del Cuerno de África [Pansomalism: historical keys to the conflict in the Horn of Africa]. *África Internacional*, 5-6, 193-212.

Crouzet, G. (2019). A second fashoda? Britain, India, and a French 'Threat' in Oman at the end of the nineteenth century. In, J. R. Fichter (Ed.), British and French colonialism in Africa, Asia and the Middle East. Connected empires across the Eighteenth to the Twentieth Centuries, (pp. 131-150). Palgrave Macmillan.

Digitale. (1897). Gli autori della spedizione Cecchi castigati [The authors of the expedition Cecchi chastised]. *Bollettino della Società Africana d'Italia [Bulletin of the African Society of Italy]*, 88-89. http://digitale.bnc.roma.sbn.it/tecadigitale/giornale/ TO001 79105/1897/

Digitale. (1923). Il Governatore della Somalia [Somalian Government]. *Bollettino della Società Africana d'Italia [Bulletin of the African Society of Italy]*. http://digitale.bnc.roma.sbn.it/tecadigitale/emeroteca/classic/TO00085511/1923

Digiteca. (1927). Brillanti operazoni in Somalia contro ribelli migiurtini [Brilliant operations in Somalia against Migiurtini rebels]. *Il Popolo d'Italia*. http://digiteca.bsmc.it/?l=periodici&t=Popolo%20d%60Italia%2 8Il%29#

Faulkner, N. (2021). *Empire and Jihad: The Anglo-Arab Wars of 1870-1920*. Yale University Press.

Ferro, M. (2000). *La colonización. Una historia global [The colonization. A Global History,]*. Siglo veintiuno editores.

Finaldi, G. (2016). *A History of Italian Colonialism, 1860–1907*. Routledge.

Friis, I., & Edwards, S. (2001). By whom and when was the flora of Ethiopia and Eritrea named. In I. Friis & O. Ryding (Eds.), *Biodiversity research in the Horn of Africa* (pp. 103–136). Biologiske Skrifter.

García Moral, E. (2016). *Breve historia del África subsahariana [Brief history of sub-Saharan Africa]*. Nowtilus.

Geshekter, C. L. (1985). Anti-colonialism and class formation: The Eastern Horn of Africa before 1950. *The International Journal of African Historical Studies, 18*(1), 1–37. https://www.jstor.org/stable/217972

Guadagni, M. M. G. (1978). Colonial Origins of the Public Domain in Southern Somalia (1892-1912). *Journal of African Law, 22*(1), 1–29.

Haggai, E. (2010). *Islam & Christianity in the Horn of Africa: Somalia, Ethiopia, Sudan*. Lynne Rienner.

Hamilton, A. (1911). *Somaliland*. Hutchinson and Co.

Harbeson, J. W. (1979). Ethiopia and the Horn of Africa. *Northeast African Studies*, *1*(1), 27–44.

Hess, R. L. (1964). The 'Mad Mullah' and Northern Somalia. *Journal of African History*, *5*(3), 415–433.

Höhne, M. (2017). Somalí. In S. Uhlig, Siegbert et al (Eds.), Etiopía. History, culture, and challenges, (pp. 73-74). LIT-Michigan State University Press.

Ibrahim, H. A. (1985). African initiatives and resistance in North-East Africa. In A. Adu Bohaen (Ed.), *General History of Africa VIII. Africa under colonial domination (1880-1935)* (pp. 63–86). UNESCO.

Iniesta, F. (2000). *Kuma. Historia de África*. Edicions Bellaterra.

Iyob, R. (1993). Regional Hegemony: Domination and Resistance in the Horn of Africa. *The Journal of Modern African Studies*, *31*(2), 257–276. doi:10.1017/S0022278X00011927

Jalata, A. (1990). *The question of Oromia: Euro-Ethiopian colonialism, global hegemonism and nationalism, 1870s-1980s*, [PhD Doctoral dissertation, State University of New York].

Jalata, A. (2020). *The Oromo Movement and Imperial Politics: Culture and Ideology in Oromia and Ethiopia*. Lexington Books.

Kakwenzire, P. (1986). Resistance, Revenue and Development in Northern Somalia, 1905-1939. *The International Journal of African Historical Studies*, *19*, 659–677.

Keefer, E. (1973). Great Britain and Ethiopia, 1897-1910: Competition for Empire. *The International Journal of African Historical Studies*, *6*(3), 468–474.

Ki-Zerbo, J. (1972). *Historia del África Negra 2. Del siglo XIX a la época actual [History of Black Africa 2. From the 19th century to the present time.]*. Alianza Editorial.

Kittermaster, H. B. (1928). British Somaliland. *Journal of the Royal African Society*, *27*(108), 329–337.

Labanca, N. (2005). Italian Colonial Internment. In R. Ben-Ghiat & M. Fuller (Eds.), *Italian colonialism* (pp. 27–36). Palgrave Mcmillan.

Lapidoth-Eschelbacher, R. (1982). *International straits of the world. The Red Sea and the Gulf of Aden*. Martinus Nijhoff Publishers.

Mamdani, M. (1999). Historicizing power and responses to power: Indirect rule and its reform. *Social Research*, *66*(3), 859–886. https://www.jstor.org/stable/40971353

Markakis, J. (1989). Nationalities and the State in Ethiopia. *Third World Quarterly*, *11*(4), 118–130.

Markakis, J. (2011). Ethiopia: The Last Two Frontiers. James Currey.

Mavropoulos, N. (2020). Why the Italians Set their Sights on East Africa: Developments and Unfulfilled Aspirations in the Mediterranean during the 19th Century, *Historical contributions - Historische Beiträge*, *39*(58), 93-108.

McLachlan, S. (2011). *Armies of the Adowa campaign 1896*. Osprey Publishing.

Metaferia, G. (2009). *Ethiopia and the United States. History, Diplomacy and analysis*. Agora Publishing.

Millman, B. (2013). *British Somaliland. An Administrative History, 1920-1960*. Routledge.

Mumin Ahad, A., & Gerrand, V. (2004). Italian cultural influences in Somalia. A reciprocity? *Quaderni del, 900*(IV), 13–24.

Nyaoro, D. (2019). Refugee hosting and conflict resolution: opportunities for diplomatic interventions and buffeting regional hegemons. In D. Schmidt, L. Kimathi, & M. O. Owiso (Eds.), *Refugees and forced migration in the Horn and Eastern Africa* (pp. 17–32). Springer.

Okbazghi, Y. (1987). The Eritrean question: A colonial case? *The Journal of Modern African Studies, 25*(4), 643–668.

Oxford Historical Treaties. (1905). Agreement of Peace and Protection between Italy and the Mullah of the Somalis (Africa). *Illig, 5*. Oxford Historical Treaties. https://opil.ouplaw.com/view/10.1093/law:oht/law-oht-198-CTS-137.regGroup.1/law-oht-198-CTS-137

Parfitt, R. (2019). *The process of international legal reproduction. Inequality, historiography, resistance*. Cambridge University Press.

Prunier, G. (2021). *The Country That Does Not Exist. A History of Somaliland*. Hurst & Co.

Rivers, C. (2017). *The Italian Invasion of Africa: The History of Italian Colonization in Africa and the Rise and Fall of the Italian Empire*. Create Space Independent Publishing Platform.

Shehim, K., & Searing, J. (1980). Djibouti and the Question of Afar Nationalism. *African Affairs, 79*(315), 209–226.

Shelley, F. M. (2013). *Nation Shapes. The story behind the world's borders*. ABC-CLIO.

Sorrentino, G. (1911). Atraverso il Benadir [Across Benadir]. *Bollettino della Società Africana d'Italia, [Bulletin of the African Society of Italy]*, 225-239. http://digitale.bnc.roma.sbn.it/tecadigitale/giornale/TO00179105/1911

Stanley, B. (2007). Djibouti City. In M. R. T. Dumper & B. E. Stanley (Eds.), *Cities of the middle East and North Africa. A historical encyclopaedia* (pp. 132–135). ABC-CLIO.

Taddia, I. (1994). Ethiopian source material and colonial rule in the Nineteenth Century: The letter to Menilek (1899) by Blatta Gäbrä Egzi'abeher. *Journal of African History, 35*(3), 493–516. https://www.jstor.org/stable/pdf/182645.pdf

Teshale, T. (1995). *The Making of Modern Ethiopia: 1896-1974*. The Red Sea Press Inc.

The Times. (1914) The Dervish Danger in Somaliland: Increase of protective forces, *The Times*. https://www.thetimes.co.uk/archive/article/1914-03-17/7/5.html?region=global#start%3D1785-%2001-01%26end%3D1985-12-31%26 terms%3DMullah%26back%3Dtto/archive/find/Mullah/w:1785-01-0 1%7E1985-12-31/7%26prev%3Dtto/archive/frame/goto/Mullah/w:1 785-01-01%7E1985-12-31/66%26next%3Dtto/archive/%20frame/got o/Mullah/w:1785-01-01%7E1985-12-31/68

The Times. (1908). The Fighting in Italian Somaliland. *The Times.* https://www.thetimes.co.uk/archive/article/1908-04-11/5/23.h tml?region=global#start%3D1785-0101%26end%3D1985-%2012-31%26 terms%3DMullah%26back%3D/tto/archive/find/Mullah/w:1785-0101 %7E1985-12-31/8%26prev%3D/%20tto/archive/frame/goto/Mullah/w :1785-01-01%7E1985-1231/79%26next%3D/tto/archive/frame/goto/ Mullah/w:1785-01-01%7E1985-12-31/81

Tibebu, T. (1996). Ethiopia. The Anomaly and Paradox of Africa. *Journal of Black Studies, 26*(4), 414–430.

UK Parliament(1910). Somaliland. *Actas del Parlamento Británi-co, Cámara de los Comunes [Acts of the British Parliament, Cámara de los Comunes], 16.* https://hansard.parliament.uk/Commons/1910-04-05?showNoDebat eMessage=True

UK Parliament. (1920). Successful operations against Mullah, *Actas del Parlamento Británico [Acts of the British Parliment], 125.* https://hansard.parliament.uk/Commons/1920-02-17/debates/0cc 406be-0086-41c8-8022-a9c16845e9a5/SuccessfulOperationsAgains tMullah?highlight=mullah#contribution-c81a5a2f-4a19-44e2-91e 9-90437b0f2de7

Uoldelul, C. D. (2007). Colonialism and the Construction of National Identities: The Case of Eritrea. *Journal of Eastern African Studies: the Journal of the British Institute in Eastern Africa, 1*(2), 256–276.

Uzoigwe, G. N. (1985). European partition and conquest of Africa: an overview. In A. Adu Bohaen, A. (Ed.), General History of Africa VIII. Africa under colonial domination (1880-1935), (pp. 19-44). UNESCO.

Weeseling, H. L. (1999). *Divide y vencerás. El reparto de África (1880-1914) [Divide and conquer. The division of Africa (1880-1914).].* Ediciones Península.

Yemane, M. (1989). Italian colonialism in Eritrea 1882–1941. *The Scandinavian Economic History Review, 37*(3), 65–72.

Yusuf Abdi, S. (1977). Independence for the Afars and Issas: Complex Background; Uncertain Future. *Africa Today, 24*(1), 61–67.

Zewde, B. (2007). Iyasu. In S. Uhlig (Ed.), *Encyclopaedia Aethiopica* (Vol. III, pp. 253–256). Harrasowitz.

ENDNOTES

[1] These include the Gesellschaft für Erdkunde zun Berlin, the Société de Géographie (Paris) and the Royal Geographical Society (London).

[2] Territory under United States commercial control.

[3] The Ethiopian Empire, also known as Abyssinia, defeated the Italian invasion during the Italian-Ethiopian War (1895-1896) at the Battle of Adwa in March 1896.

[4] Ethiopian region in the centre of the country where the city of Addis Ababa was founded.

Chapter 5

Organistation and Functioning of the Spanish Army in Cuba During the Captaincy Generalship of Valeriano Weyler (1896–1897)

Alberto Guerrero Martín
University of Granada, Spain

ABSTRACT

The aim of this work is to study how the Spanish army developed the counter-insurgency struggle against the Cuban insurgents, what measures were taken, and whether or not they worked, focusing above all on one of the most successful counter-guerrilla units of this war: the Cazadores de Valmaseda (Valmaseda Hunters). The main sources used for this purpose are the operational reports of the Valmaseda Hunters and the memoirs of some of the protagonists of the campaign, as well as the historiography on this conflict and the available bibliography on irregular warfare during the 19th century.

INTRODUCTION

In 1898, what was left of the Spanish Empire was liquidated with the loss of Cuba, Puerto Rico, and the Philippines. This article will look at the land operations that led to the loss of Cuba, focusing above all on the organization of the Spanish Army on the arrival of General Valeriano Weyler in 1896, the reorganization he carried out and the measures adopted to put an end to the insurrection. Thus, the objective will be the study of General Weyler's campaign plan and, through it, the analysis of the organization and functioning of the Spanish Army during Weyler's period as Captain General of the island of Cuba. During the last third of the 19th century, Spain had to face three wars for Cuban independence, the epilogue of which was the confrontation with the United States and the consequent emancipation of the island, in addition to the loss of the remains of the Spanish overseas empire, in what was the annus horribilis of

DOI: 10.4018/978-1-6684-7040-4.ch005

1898. As Puell de la Villa has pointed out, the loss of Cuba, Puerto Rico and the Philippines should not only be attributed to the naval defeats at Cavite and Santiago de Cuba, but also to the political instability Spain was going through, together with the lack of aid from the European powers (Puell, 2013, p. 35).

BACKGROUND

1898 marked the liquidation of the remnants of Spain's overseas empire. Excluding the Philippines and Puerto Rico, the conflict for the emancipation of the island of Cuba resulted in the deaths of more than 50,000 Spanish soldiers, most of them from diseases contracted on the island. Moreover, these conflicts for the independence of Cuba or the Philippines were the origin of the conflicts that European powers had to face in Asia or Africa during the Cold War (Puell, 2013, p. 35).

The study of the campaigns carried out by General Weyler in Cuba and the tactical procedures employed in them are to this day an important source of knowledge and lessons, as he was one of the few military men interested in irregular warfare during the 19th century, developing a series of successful counter-insurgency devices to defeat the Cuban rebels (Fontela, Gómez y Rodríguez, 2007, p. 40). Many of these measures he had already employed during the Cuban War of 1868-1878, where he designed a device for the safe advance of columns and used volunteers from the island, accustomed to its climate and knowledgeable about the terrain, to confront the rebels

MAIN FOCUS OF THE CHAPTER

The article deals with the confrontation between the Cuban rebels and the Spanish army, focusing mainly on the time of General Valeriano Weyler's supreme command in Cuba. It highlights the measures adopted by Weyler to deal with the situation and the state of the army on his arrival. The aim is to make it clear that the Spanish troops and their officers were not prepared for the irregular warfare that took place in Cuba and that thanks to Weyler and his counter-insurgency measures, the situation was subverted. These measures had already been successfully employed during the Ten Years' War (1868-1878), also in Cuba.

However, other of his measures, such as the reconcentration of the Cuban population, had disastrous results and eventually led to his dismissal after the death of Antonio Cánovas del Castillo, his main supporter. However, what is narrated in this work has tended to be overshadowed by the war against the United States and Spain in 1898, which resulted in the defeat of Spain and the liquidation of the remnants of its empire. Authors such as John Lawrence Tone have worked extensively on these three years of war in his *Guerra y genocidio en Cuba 1895-1898*. On the other hand, the controversial measure of reconcentration caused a debate at the time that still persists in the historiography of the Cuban War. In this regard, there is the important work by Andreas Stucki entitled *Las guerras de Cuba. Violencia y campos de concentración 1868-1898*.

Our point of view is that the Spanish army was able to overcome the Cuban War thanks in large part to the measures adopted by Weyler to deal with the guerrillas, which later served as an example to other powers in similar conflicts.

A Brief Portrait of General Valeriano Weyler

General Valeriano Weyler y Nicolau (17 September 1838-20 October 1930) was born in Palma de Mallorca into a family of German origin. The Weyler family had an important military tradition and extensive academic training. His father, Fernando Weyler Laviña, was a doctor of medicine, eventually becoming president of the Academy of Science and Surgery of Palma de Mallorca, member of the Royal Academy of Medicine of Madrid, member of the Academy of Medicine and Surgery of Barcelona, and of the Academy of Science and Arts. He was also a corresponding member of the Royal Academy of History. Weyler notes in his memoirs that his father was a man of extensive knowledge and was fluent in several languages, including French, English, German and Arabic, as well as being able to translate Italian and German (Weyler, 2004, pp.21-25; Guerrero, 2021).

Weyler began his military studies in 1853, being admitted and enrolled in the Infantry College of Toledo on 30 November of that year. He finished his studies in 1856, being promoted to second lieutenant. In 1857 he entered the General Staff College, where Arsenio Martínez Campos taught the Geodesy, Topography and Military History class, a figure who would become particularly important in the history of Spain some time later. This training at the General Staff College was completed with practical training in infantry, cavalry and artillery units. As he recounts in his memoirs, during this period he had the honour of escorting Queen Isabella II to the royal siege of El Pardo. Having been unable to take part in the war in Africa, he decided to ask General Juan Prim for permission to take part in the expedition to Mexico, although he was refused on the grounds that Prim had to finish his training beforehand (Weyler, 2004, pp. 29-36).

After completing his training, he was promoted in September 1862 to captain of the General Staff Corps. At that time, yellow fever was causing many casualties among the soldiers stationed in Cuba, so two vacancies were advertised for overseas staff commanders, which Weyler soon applied for. He arrived on the island on 21 May 1863 and became close friends with Commanders Blanco, Azcárraga, Ortiz and De Miguel. Of these, Blanco, Azcárraga and Weyler attained the rank of captain general. However, he did not spend much time in Cuba, as after the events of Santo Domingo he asked to leave with the expeditionary forces that were to be sent (Weyler, 2004, pp.37-41). It was in this war that he began to establish his reputation as a tough and effective soldier. He pointed out that this campaign had been unjustly forgotten and that no lessons were learned from it that could have been useful in the future (Weyler, 2004, p.54). These skills of military efficiency were later cemented during the Ten Years' War in Cuba (1868-78), where he effectively commanded a unit of volunteers called the Cazadores de Valmaseda and created a marching system for the columns and for confronting the Cuban rebels (Guerrero, 2020). Later, on his return to Spain, he took part in the Third Carlist War (1873-1875). In 1878 he was promoted to lieutenant general (Weyler, 1946, p. 57). He was appointed captain general of the following territories: the Canary Islands (1878-1883), the Balearic Islands (1883-1886), the Philippines (1888-1891), Burgos, Navarre and the Basque Country (1893) and Catalonia (1893-1895). He was also Minister of War in 1901, 1902 and 1906, as well as spending several years in command of the Army General Staff (Alonso, 1971, p. 315).

But Weyler is undoubtedly best remembered for his time as general-in-chief of the army of operations in Cuba between 1896 and 1897, his most important command and one in which he had his ups and downs, especially because he was accused of having acted too harshly against the Cuban insurrectionists. Antonio Cánovas del Castillo had placed all his trust in him, and for the Spaniards he was the man who could put an end to the Cuban rebellion. But his actions in Cuba made him the focus of criticism and insults from some of his compatriots and the foreign press, especially the American press (Alonso, 1971, p. 226). In the prologue that Carlos Seco Serrano wrote for the book that compiles Weyler's memoirs, it is pointed out how his figure is intimately linked to the Cuban problem (2004, p. 9). One of the measures he took to put an end to the insurrection had much to do with this, namely the concentration of the peasants to prevent them from helping the insurgents. Thus, he proceeded to concentrate them in villages controlled by soldiers. It can be said that the measure was not at all unreasonable and that it has been used throughout the 20th century by those countries that had to face a similar problem to Spain's in Cuba. However, it was a measure that was taken hastily and with a lack of means, so that the 100,000 concentrated peasants suffered a lack of means to subsist that caused many of them to die (Puell, 2013, p. 42). The cause is to be found in the health and administration and in the fact that Weyler "undertook a task beyond his means and was able to care for and supply the concentrated population while the war was ruining the island" (Cardona, 2005, p. 115).

The War in Cuba until Weyler's Arrival

The Cuban War had, as Puell de la Villa rightly pointed out, three phases and an epilogue. The first phase was known as the Ten Years' War (1868-1878), which ended with the Peace of Zanjón. The following year, however, the so-called "Little War" broke out, an uprising led by Calixto García that was put down in just two weeks. The third phase is the so-called "war of independence", which ended with the confrontation against the United States (US) and the independence of the island (Puell, 2013, p. 36).

In 1868, Cuba had an estimated population of 1,359,112 inhabitants (Guerra, 1950, p.1). The revolution in Spain that ousted Isabella II from the throne was the trigger for the Ten Years' War. On the night of 9 to 10 October 1868, Carlos Manuel de Céspedes launched his "cry of Yara", which marked the beginning of a long and hard war that lasted for ten years. It cost Spain, which was mired in the revolutionary Sexenio, between 50,000 and 65,000 casualties, most of them because Spanish soldiers were not acclimatised to the island's climate. The historian Antonio Pirala put the figure at 60,000, of whom only 4,720 had fallen in combat (Redondo, 1995, p. 59). In 1876, Arsenio Martínez Campos was appointed general-in-chief of the army of operations, who combined "energy with a left hand", managing to improve the situation for Spain and reaching the agreement of 28 May 1878, known as the Peace of Zanjón. This peace was in reality "more a postponement of the conflict than a definitive peace", as the following year saw some uprisings, such as the aforementioned Calixto García uprising, which gave rise to the "Little War" between 1879 and 1880 (Bastarreche, 1978, pp. 69-71).

It should be noted that the Ten Years' War, the "Little War", the "War of Independence" and the struggle against the US all took place in the eastern part of the island, a place also chosen by Fidel Castro in 1958 to establish his base of operations to confront Fulgencio Batista. This region was chosen because it was an ideal area for irregular warfare, as it was crossed by "two large mountain massifs surrounded by deep valleys". Moreover, the island's climate was hot and humid, "insufferable during the summer" (Puell, 2013, pp. 36-37). It was a war very similar to the one Weyler had experienced in Santo Domingo, based on surprise attacks, small combats and destruction of haciendas and villages. In both campaigns, the Spanish soldiers were unfamiliar with the terrain and unaccustomed to the island's climatic conditions, which led to a high number of casualties from yellow fever (Cardona and Losada, 1998, p. 27).

It is striking how the colonial campaigns that Spain had to face, in which irregular warfare was a predominant factor, received little attention in the military historiography of the period (Guerrero, 2020, p.440). It was the most frequent type of warfare in Spain, as it had the particularity that all the wars it fought until the confrontation with the USA could be considered irregular "in part or in whole" (Barrios, 1893, pp. 9-11). This was also the case in other countries, as the French and British war experiences between Waterloo and the Marne took place outside Europe (Porch, 1992, p.335). The Spanish military 'did not want or did not know how to accept the primacy of irregular warfare in their work'. Instead, they preferred to orient their academic training and doctrine towards irregular warfare, which is why the army never wrote a detailed chronicle of the Cuban wars (Jensen, 2014, pp. 44-47). Hence, Commander Barrios lamented that some campaigns had had an enormous echo among Spanish military writers, such as the Franco-Prussian war, and others, such as the Cuban campaigns, very little (Barrios, 1893, p. 24). The works that do exist on the wars in Cuba were written by military or civilians in a "personal capacity". For the war of 1895-1898, there is the work of Antonio Pirala (1895-1898), a scholar of history, and that of the journalist José Menéndez Caravia (1896). There are also Weyler's works on his command in Cuba (1910) (Guerrero, 2023, p. 38). This scant attention to irregular warfare explains why most officers were slow to grasp the secrets of irregular warfare, "initially seeking to apply academic tactical schemes in the face of an enemy that was blurring into the jungle" (Puell, 1996, p. 252).

Without going into more detail about the Ten Years' War, as this is not the subject of this work, it is necessary to refer to the form of the fighting, as it will be similar to that of the later "war of independence" (Guerrero, 2020, p.446). The insurgents were outnumbered by the Spanish troops and were usually assembled in parties of a hundred men, although they sometimes numbered over a thousand. Most of their men were on horseback, unlike the Spanish, whose main force was on foot. However, the Spanish troops were decimated by disease, as well as being scattered in a multitude of detachments to protect the population. The Mambises also had an advantage over the Spanish soldier, as they were natives of the island and were not affected by the diseases that were depleting the Spanish troops. Knowing their inferiority in regular combat, they resorted to ambushes in favourable terrain (Togores, 2006, p. 542). Since they were specialists in attacking the Spanish columns and then disappearing into the thicket, being experts in the terrain, the Spanish command had no choice but to "use counter-guerrilla tactics that would allow them to fight on equal terms". Weyler was in charge of designing them, as well as calling on locals, acclimatised to the island's conditions, to confront the insurgents (Guerrero, 2020, p.447).

Guerrillas and "trochas" such as the one from Júcaro to Morón, were created to prevent the insurrection from spreading to other parts of the island (Guerrero, 2020, p.448). The "trochas" were fortified lines that divided the island into two parts and were equipped with forts, guard towers and army units (Guerrero, 2023, p. 37). In 1869, Blas Diego de Villate, II Count of Valmaseda, who at the time was acting Captain General of the island, asked Weyler to write a report on the marching device he had devised for the Spanish columns, so that it "could be adopted by all the operational forces" (Weyler, 2008, p. 64). This device appears in the memoirs of an ensign who served in the column under Valmaseda (Guerrero, 2020, p. 448). Ensign Feyjóo noted that the Mambises always attacked "ambushed in the thickets of the mountains, in the ravines and rivers of bad passes, in the cuts and gorges", but never showed their faces. As they were perfectly familiar with the terrain, they were always sure of a place to retreat to. However, the Spanish troops had managed to penetrate the thicket "and deployed on both flanks in guerrilla warfare, so that at the slightest sign of the enemy they can immediately reinforce the guerrillas, opening up a machete in hand". In addition, they had two artillery pieces in the vanguard, with two companies "and at the front of the road ten or twelve flanking pairs". Feyjóo pointed out that this flanking system was due to Weyler, who was "always in the vanguard, foreseeing and arranging the most appropriate thing to do" (Feyjóo, 1869, pp. 11-12).

Weyler had observed and understood the insurgents' way of fighting, who always fought in ambush in the woods, and he wanted them to be confronted under the same conditions. Thus, by going into the thicket they did not offer a good target, but this required a good flanking system for the columns and the vanguard. If the Mambises went into the woods, the Spanish soldiers could also do so as long as they were equipped with machetes. In addition, rows of guerrilla soldiers should march on either side of the column (Pirala, 1895, pp. 335-336; Guerrero, 2020, pp. 448-449).

The war in Cuba from 1895 to 1898 cost the Spanish army 44,500 dead (De Miguel 2010, p. 255), but very few of these were combat casualties, as the vast majority died of disease. The army had still not taken measures to acclimatize the operational forces to the conditions on the island, and a tactical doctrine to deal with the irregular warfare carried out by the Cuban insurgents had still not been developed. The 1882 Field Service Regulations were heavily influenced by the Prussian victory over Germany in 1870. It was based on "hypothetical" wars "in the European style", that is, in conventional conflicts "with mass movements of maneuver, and of a clearly offensive character", something that was of no use in Cuba (Fontela, Gómez and Rodríguez, 2007, pp.37-38). In short, Spanish commanders were strongly influenced by the Prussian way of waging war, which had achieved so many important successes. In the Tactical Regulations of 1881, "guerrilla warfare became the main line of combat" (González-Pola, 2003, p. 275). However, there were very few military works that expressly dealt with irregular warfare, as we can only mention the great work by General Staff Commander José Ignacio Chacón (1883), entitled *Guerras irregulares*; Captain Juan Calero's (1896), entitled *Guerras irregulares y de montaña*; and Colonel Virgilio Cabanellas' short opuscule (1896): *La táctica en Cuba, África y Filipinas y en todo país cubierto y accidentado*. To these could be added the lecture given by Major Leopoldo Barrios in 1893 and published by the Army and Navy Centre under the title *Importancia de las campañas irregulares* (Guerrero, 2023).

The garrison on the island before the insurrection began was small, between 13,000 and 20,000 soldiers, according to the authors and sources consulted. These figures must therefore be treated with caution, as they differ greatly from one author to another. Enrique de Miguel is the one who studied them best. He provides the data of Delgado (1980), who counted 17,776 soldiers, including the Guardia Civil, but not the twelve guerrilla companies, the Camajuani volunteer squadron and other volunteers, which would give a total of 20,238. However, for De Miguel, the most accurate figures are those of Delgado (De Miguel, 2010, p. 249). Moreover, according to his calculations, during the years of the war, 212,336 soldiers were sent to Cuba and 6,175 to Puerto Rico (De Miguel, 2010, p. 253). These enormous numbers were a disproportionate effort for a country like Spain.

The Cuban revolutionary leaders were the same ones who had fought in the Ten Years' War, such as Maceo, Calixto García, Guillermo Moncada, José Martí and Máximo Gómez, among the main ones. It was Moncada who, on 24 February 1895, gave the Grito de Baire, in Bayamo, Santiago province, starting the insurrection. They had foreign aid from the US, while Spain was "isolated in Europe, at odds with Germany since an incident in the Carolinas in 1893, and suspicious of England and France over the Moroccan question". Martínez Campos was sent to the island and asked for reinforcements because most of the soldiers were ill. However, 'his mediating skills and sympathetic character clashed with Cuban determination to see the war through to the end' (Cardona, 2005, pp. 113-115).

Martínez Campos tried in the summer of 1895, in the middle of the rainy season, to enter the Sierra Maestra with 1500 men, but was ambushed by Antonio Maceo, killing General Santocildes and 26 Spanish soldiers, without managing to take Sierra Maestra during the whole war. As if this were not enough, once the rainy season was over, Gómez and Maceo set out on an expedition led by 1,500 mounted men that managed to cross the island from east to west, "ravaging everything in its path" and without being stopped by a garrison that numbered nearly 100,000 soldiers (Puell, 2013, pp. 40-41). The insurgents were armed through expeditions from the US, but they were generally poorly armed and their numerous cavalry used machetes. Moreover, they were outnumbered by Spanish soldiers and their 'best weapons were mobility and terror' (Cardona and Losada, 1998, pp. 162-163).

General Martínez Campos was unable to reverse the negative trend of the campaign and wrote a letter to Cánovas del Castillo to recommend the appointment as captain general of Cuba of General Valeriano Weyler, the only one, in his words, who had the conditions to solve the enormous problem Spain was facing in Cuba. Thus, at the beginning of 1896, he was appointed captain general of Cuba, taking charge of the situation from 10 February 1896, when he arrived in Havana, until he was dismissed in October 1897 (Weyler, 2004, pp.197-204). Weyler indicates in his My Command in Cuba that the army stationed in Cuba at the outbreak of the insurrection consisted, as mentioned above, of 15,900 men (Weyler, 1910, pp. 21-22). Regardless of whether the figures are accurate or not, what is important to note is that it consisted of seven infantry regiments, a battalion of hunters, two cavalry regiments, an artillery battalion, a mixed battalion of engineers and three thirds of the Civil Guard. Given the gravity of the situation, seven provisional infantry battalions and four marine battalions had to be hastily formed, as well as other units to reinforce the forces deployed in Cuba. In addition, he noted that he had to "proceed to contract such armament as was possible to substitute the Remington rifle for the Mauser" (Weyler, 1910, pp.21-22). With Weyler on the island, insurrection leader Gómez wrote in his diary that "the spirit of cruelty and devastation on the part of Spain had become more accentuated" (Gómez, 1940, p. 354). What is certain is that Weyler's arrival aroused enthusiasm, "as if Weyler guaranteed victory". The same thing happened in Cuba, while for the insurgents it was bad news (Cardona and Losada, 1998, p. 175).

Weyler in Cuba

Between April and January 1895, Martínez Campos received 80,000 soldiers and the troops with high-powered Mauser rifles. However, the soldiers were poorly equipped, although better equipped than the Mambises, and their poor diet was conducive to disease, so that a good number of soldiers never saw combat, suffering from yellow fever or black vomit. Deaths from disease far outnumbered those caused by combat (Cardona and Losada, 1998, p. 186). Weyler wrote of Martínez Campos that "more than making war, he strove to make peace, when the insurrectionists were imposing themselves by rigour, and were bringing fire, devastation and misery wherever they went". This was to change, for when he was appointed to go to Cuba, both the press and public opinion demanded "that the necessary energy and rigour be deployed there, and this was the principle on which I have based my military conduct all my life, and I have followed it, but without the fierceness of which the legendary amateurs are wont to speak" (Weyler, 1910, pp. 2-3).

When Weyler arrived in Cuba on 10 February 1896, there were more than 100,000 soldiers, but many were hospitalised, so some 90,000 more were sent over the course of that year (Puell, 2013, p. 39). The Spanish population accepted with 'resignation' those young soldiers who could not afford the costs of paying for a replacement. Moreover, in the Peninsula, the army corps had to call up "reservists, the price of substitution tripled and hundreds of young men crossed the French and Portuguese borders to escape what they considered certain death overseas" (Puell de la Villa, 1996, p. 261). But it was not only the recruits who were reluctant to leave, but also the lieutenants, as so few volunteered that sergeants had to be sent in their place, "who were thus promoted to officers of the reserve scale" (Puell de la Villa, 1996,

p. 261). Shortly afterwards, General Marcelo Azcárraga, Minister of War, ended the practice of sending provisional battalions and sent full units (Cardona and Losada, 1998, pp. 159-160).

The start of the insurrection caught the Spanish troops off guard, whose commanders had forgotten the experiences of previous campaigns, as Weyler had lamented when he left the island of Santo Domingo. Nor had they improved the roads or got good maps of the different regions (Puell, 2013, p. 40). As he indicates in his memoirs, immediately after his arrival on the island, and given that the gravity of the situation required it, he set about putting into practice a plan of operations that he had already been forging during his trip, since he knew Cuba perfectly well for having fought there during the Ten Years' War. Basically, his objective was to imprison Maceo in Pinar del Río, thus preventing him from making contact with the rest of the island. To this end, troops supported by fortifications were set up, also taking advantage of the rugged terrain. His next step was to do the same in the east. He also envisaged the improvement of the Júcaro to Morón road, which had been started during the previous war. On the other hand, he proposed to abolish a good part of the detachments that were stationed on private estates and replace them with volunteers, so as not to "distract forces". He also intended to reorganise the battalions so that the columns would consist of "complete units of each weapon". The cavalry underwent a reduction in its equipment to give it more mobility, as well as replacing machetes with cavalry sabres. Plainclothes guerrillas", known as "volantes", were organised to accompany the columns. More controversial, because of its tragic consequences, was his plan to reconcentrate the inhabitants in villages (Weyler, 2004, pp. 204-205).

Nine days after launching this ambitious plan of operations, he sent a letter to Azcárraga in which he commented on the seriousness of the situation on his arrival and that during those days he had been unable to imprison Maceo in the province of Pinar del Río, but he also reported that he had managed to harass the enemy in all directions, thereby undermining their morale. His memoirs also recounted the harsh campaign the insurgents waged, often setting fire to villages, cane fields and sugar mills "if they were not paid the contribution demanded", as well as "macheteing the cane cutters and those who were working to rebuild the railway; imprisoning many others and raping women and girls, especially Maceo's followers". However, he also acknowledged that other insurgents, such as the forces of Máximo Gómez, behaved more humanely (Weyler, 2004, pp. 206-208).

The move to release troops from the detachments made it possible to organise self-sufficient and co-ordinated columns consisting of a battalion and a twenty-five-man mounted guerrilla force. The convalescing soldiers were responsible for guarding warehouses, offices and toilets. He procured Krupp rapid-fire 75 mm steel guns and provided Mauser rifles for the soldiers in the columns, leaving the Remingtons for the rear troops. In addition, he created a telegraph battalion and a railway battalion, and the coastal artillery was considerably improved, providing the capital with twenty-four coastal batteries and seven auxiliary batteries (Cardona and Losada, 1998, pp. 188-190).

Cuba was divided into three army corps: Cuba, Villar and Pinar del Río. In addition, he considerably reinforced the forces on the north-south line, managing to encircle Maceo in Pinar del Río. As for the cavalry, he formed seven regiments with the expeditionary forces to confront the insurgents, who had a very large cavalry. The results were a success and the rebels were constantly harassed in all directions. However, despite the success in limiting enemy operations, it had not been possible to prevent them from continuing to receive arms and ammunition from the US (Weyler, 2004, pp. 209-212).

Having controlled the province of Havana, Weyler decided to direct the main action against Pinar del Río, where Maceo was stationed, and who died after the heavy encounter known as the "Combate de Punta Brava". In this fight, the son of Máximo Gómez committed suicide to avoid being taken prisoner by the

Spanish troops. Weyler's progress was so significant that by the end of February 1897 the insurrection in the west was practically subdued. However, there was no end to the criticism of his actions from the USA and the opposition on the Peninsula, which called for his immediate dismissal. Weyler deplored these attitudes, especially those of the Spaniards "who had demanded so much rigour" and who had changed their minds. He noted how they denied their triumphs and censured "the reconcentration, which was applied by the English in the Transvaal (called Weylerism without Weyler) and by the Americans in the Philippines, and lately by the Russians in their campaign against Japan". It was the assassination of Cánovas del Castillo and his replacement by Sagasta that precipitated the situation, as he was dismissed and informed of his dismissal on 9 October (Weyler, 2004, pp. 221-236). He was replaced by General Ramón Blanco, who in 1992 had been relieved of his duties in the Philippines for being "appeasing and indecisive" (Cardona and Losada, 1998, p. 237).

In short, Weyler took two important measures to put a stop to the uprising. First, he set out to end peasant support for the rebels by concentrating the population in villages that were protected by soldiers. This re-concentration and the harsh campaign against its creator for the suffering of the population were the cause of its cessation. On the other hand, the reinforcement of the trail from Júcaro to Marón and the construction of another one in Muriel to achieve the objective of encircling Maceo in Pinar del Río. Maceo's death in the autumn of 1896 put an end to the uprising in Pinar del Río. In the winter of 1897, he succeeded in eliminating the parties operating between the two trails. During the spring Calixto García continued to operate with his men, but Gómez "was ready to give up and return to Santo Domingo". The assassination of Cánovas del Castillo and his replacement by Sagasta led to the dismissal of Weyler, who, had he remained in command, would probably have put an end to the insurrection (Puell, 2013, p. 43). A soldier who always marched at the head of his men, ate the same food like them, "rode for hours and slept on a bad mattress or on a cloak thrown on the ground" (Cardona and Losada, 1998, p. 219). He was relieved without the two years he said he needed to subdue the rebellion having passed; "the insurrection in the provinces of Pinar del Río, Havana, Matanzas and Las Villas having already been subdued, and when he intended to achieve the same in the rest of the island" (Weyler, 1910, p. 13).

SOLUTIONS AND RECOMMENDATIONS

As solutions and recommendations for the problems raised in the paper, more precise studies of deaths during the Cuban war are proposed. If accurate data is needed, it is to avoid falling into "conclusions that are far removed from reality" (De Miguel, 2010, p. 243). The same is true of the victims of the reconcentration.

On the other hand, in order to deal with the way Spanish troops fought until counter-insurgency tactics were used, it is necessary to study the military literature of the period, in order to note the lack of works on irregular warfare and the need for them for a country that had to face this type of war almost every time during the nineteenth century.

FUTURE RESEARCH DIRECTIONS

This chapter opens up new lines of research, as has already been made clear in the previous section. On the one hand, that of more precise studies on the deaths in the Cuban War, since historiography has focused mainly on the repatriation of Spanish troops (De Miguel, 2010, p. 243-244). In addition, it is necessary to follow the line of research pursued by Stucki and Tone to see exactly the death toll caused by reconcentration and clearly explain what causes led to this disaster. On the other hand, the present work is part of a field of study that requires a renewal within Spanish historiography. This is more than evident in relation to irregular warfare during the 19th century, since although the conflicts waged by Spain throughout that century were sufficiently studied, the characteristics of these conflicts were not. Hence, future studies are also necessary to see the reason for the rejection of the officialdom to the study of this type of war.

CONCLUSION

Weyler, although a perfect connoisseur of guerrilla warfare, was unaware that its purpose was not military but political, "so that you can win militarily and be defeated". Thus, being more concerned with what was happening on the battlefield, he never "thought that he could be defeated in the rear". On the other hand, the Cuban insurgents were aware that they could not prevail by force, due to their inferior numbers and weapons, but they could exhaust the Spaniards and "destroy their will to resist". Máximo Gómez "invented contemporary guerrilla warfare, while Weyler laid the military foundations of counter-guerrilla tactics" (Cardona and Losada, 1998, p. 192-193).

If one goes to the memoirs left by Weyler, one can see that he always claimed great efficiency in the performance of his duties, but not only in this war, but in all the wars in which he took part. His supporters always praised his qualities, which he undoubtedly had, and his detractors, especially among Cuban historians, accused him of "absolute mediocrity". However, there is no doubt that since his arrival in Cuba the Mambises suffered a heavy blow. We cannot know whether he would have achieved his goal of putting down the rebellion had he remained in office, but some authors argue that it would have been impossible to put down the insurgents completely (Sáiz, 1974, pp. 88-89).

González-Pola points out how Puell de la Villa argues that the Spanish defeat in 1898 was partly due to the fact that the commanders were prepared for conventional warfare, despite the fact that most of the wars fought by Spain in that century had been irregular (González-Pola, 2003, p. 274). The casualties suffered by the insurgents are difficult to quantify. As for the Spanish, from 4 May 1895 to 30 June 1895, "one general, 81 officers and 704 soldiers died in combat; 463 officers and 8164 soldiers died of wounds; and some 70,000 men died of disease. The figures, of course, also vary according to source and author, but they are an example of the magnitude of this war and the economic effort it represented for Spain. "The challenge could only be sustained by cutting supplies and keeping the troops poorly fed, equipped and manned" (Cardona and Losada, 1998, pp. 196-197). As Cardona noted, Spain sent thousands of soldiers "without the support of efficient services". Thus, when disease struck, more recruits were sent back, and when they arrived they too fell ill, "creating a tangle of useless services". Moreover, if the rebels did not achieve victory militarily, "fever, vomiting and dysentery" (Cardona, 2005, p. 117).

REFERENCES

Alonso, M. (1971). El ejército en la sociedad Española [The Army in Spanish Society]. *Ediciones del movimiento [Movement Issues]*.

Barrios, L. (1893). Importancia de la historia de las campañas irregulares y en especial de la Guerra de Cuba: conferencia dada el 13 de febrero de 1893 por D [Importance of the history of irregular campaigns and especially of the Cuban War: lecture given on February 13, 1893 by D]. Comandante de Estado Mayor. Centro del Ejército y de la Armada [Commander of Staff. Army and Navy Center].

Bastarreche, F. (1978). *El ejército español en el siglo XIX [The Spanish army in the 19th century]*. Siglo Veintiuno.

Cabanellas, V. (1896). *La táctica en Cuba, África y Filipinas: prontuario del Oficial en operaciones en todo país cubierto y accidentado (sorpresas, emboscadas e impedimentas) [Tactics in Cuba, Africa and the Philippines: the officer's record in operations in all covered and rugged countries (surprises, ambushes and impediments)]*. Depósito de la Guerra.

Calero, J. (1895). *Guerras irregulares y de montaña [Irregular and mountain warfare]*. Imp. de la Vda. e Hijos de J. Peláez.

Cardona, G. (2005). *El problema militar en España [The Military Problem in Spain]*. Albor.

Cardona, G., & Losada, J. C. (1998). *Weyler. Nuestro hombre en la Habana [Weyler. Our man in Havana]*. Planeta.

Chacón, J. I. (1883). *Guerras irregulars [Irregular wars]*. Depósito de la guerra.

De Miguel, E. (2010). Las tropas españolas en la guerra de Cuba: de las especulaciones cuantitativas a la cuantificación [Spanish troops in the war in Cuba: from quantitative speculation to quantification]. *Anales de la Real Academia de Cultura Valenciana [Annals of the Royal Academy of Valencian Culture], 85*.

Delgado, O. (1980). *The Spanish Army in Cuba 1895-1898: And Institutional Study*. [Thesis doctoral. Columbia University].

Feyjóo, T. (1869). *Diario de un testigo de las operaciones sobre los insurrectos de la isla de Cuba [Diary of a witness of the operations against the insurgents of the island of Cuba]*. Imprenta militar de la V. e Hs. de Soler [Military printing press of the V. and Hs. de Soler].

Fontela, S., Gómez, J., & Rodríguez, P. (2007). *Resumen histórico de la táctica de infantería S [Historical summary of infantry tactics S.]*. Fajardo el Bravo.

Gómez, M. (1940). *Diario de campaña del mayor general Máximo Gómez [Campaign diary of Major General Máximo Gómez]*. Talleres de Centro Superior Tecnológico Ceiba del Agua [Workshops of the Ceiba del Agua Higher Technological Center].

González-Pola, P. (2003). *La configuración de la mentalidad militar contemporánea (1868-1909) [The configuration of the contemporary military mentality (1868-1909).]*. Ministerio de Defensa.

Guerra, R. (1950). *Guerra de los Diez Años (1868-1878) [Ten Years' War (1868-1878)*. Cultural.

Guerrero, A. (2020). Contrainsurgencia en la Guerra de los Diez Años en Cuba (1868-1878): Weyler y los Cazadores de Valmaseda [Counterinsurgency in the Ten Years' War in Cuba (1868-1878): Weyler and the Cazadores de Valmaseda]. In A. Guerrero (Ed.), *Imperialismo y ejércitos [Imperialism and armies]* (pp. 432–457). Editorial Universidad de Granada.

Guerrero, A. (2021). La administración de Filipinas durante la capitanía general de Valeriano Weyler (1888-1891) [The administration of the Philippines during the captaincy general of Valeriano Weyler (1888-1891)]. Studia Humanitatis Journal, *1*(1), 58–80.

Guerrero, A. (2023). La guerra irregular en el pensamiento militar decimonónico español (1863-1898) [Irregular warfare in nineteenth-century Spanish military thought (1863-1898).]. *Revista Universitaria Militar, 11*(23), 16–39.

Jensen, G. (2014). *Cultura militar española: modernistas, tradicionalistas y liberals [Spanish military culture: modernists, traditionalists and liberals].* Biblioteca Nueva.

Menéndez Caravia, J. (1896). La guerra en Cuba: su origen y desarrollo. Reformas necesarias para terminar e impedir la propaganda filibustera [Necessary reforms to end and prevent filibuster propaganda], s. l, s. n

Pirala, A. (1895). *Anales de la guerra de Cuba [Annals of the Cuban War].* Felipe González Rojas.

Porch, D. (1992). Bugeaud, Gallieni, Lyautey: el desarrollo de las guerras coloniales francesas [Bugeaud, Gallieni, Lyautey: the development of the French colonial wars]. En Paret P. (coord.), Creadores de la estrategia moderna: desde Maquiavelo a la era nuclear [Creators of modern strategy: from Machiavelli to the nuclear age] (pp. 395-423).

Puell, F. (1996). *El soldado desconocido. De la leva a la "mili" [The unknown soldier. From the cam to the "milli"].* Biblioteca Nueva.

Puell, F. (2003). *Historia del Ejército [Army History].* Alianza Editorial.

Puell, F. (2013). Guerra en Cuba y Filipinas: Combates terrestres [War in Cuba and the Philippines: Land combat]. *Revista Universitaria de Historia Militar, 2,* 34–17.

Redondo, F. (1995). *La Guerra de los Diez Años [The Ten Years' War].* Monografías del CESEDEN, Núm. 14.

Sáiz, C. (1974). *Guerrillas en Cuba y en otros países de iberoamerica [Guerrillas in Cuba and other Latin American countries].* Editora Nacional.

Stucki, A. (2017). *Las guerras de Cuba. Violencia y campos de concentración (1868-1898) [The Cuban wars. Violence and concentration camps (1868-1898).].* La Esfera de los Libros.

Togores, L. E. (2006). Guerra cubana de los diez años [Cuban Ten Years' War]. In *Aproximación a la historia ilitary de España [Approach to the military history of Spain]* (pp. 537–556). Ministerio de Defensa.

Tone, J. L. (2008). *Guerra y genocidio en Cuba [War and genocide in Cuba].* Turner.

Weyler, V. (2004). *Memorias de un general [Memories of a general].* Destino.

Weyler, V. (1910-1911). *Mi mando en Cuba [My command in Cuba.].* Imp. De Felipe González.

Weyler y López de Puga, V. (1946). *En el archivo de mi abuelo: biografía del capitán general Weyler [In my grandfather's file: biography of Captain General Weyler].* Verdad.

Chapter 6
Expeditionary Light Infantry Battalions During the Philippine Insurgency (1896–1898):
A Historical Approach

Miguel Ángel López de la Asunción
Universidad Complutense, Spain

ABSTRACT

During the second half of 1896, taking advantage of the cruelty of the insurrection of the Revolutionary forces in the district of Cuba, the Philippine Revolutionary society called Katipunan, which had been founded in July 1892 to promote the insurgency against Spanish sovereignty, took up arms in a truly disturbing way on the island of Luzon. After several violent incidents, the situation became extremely worrying and the Spanish government finally listened to the request made by the Governor General of the district to send troops from the Peninsula. Thus, in record time, fifteen expeditionary light infantry battalions were created by the Spanish Army in addition to other small artillery and cavalry expeditionary units for their military deployment in the Philippine archipelago to put down this new and violent insurrection up.

INTRODUCTION

On August 1st, 1896, a masonic inspiration society founded by Andres Bonifacio under the name *Kataastaasang, Kagalang-galangang Katipunan ñg mǧá Anak ñg Bayan* —whose translation into English is Supreme and Venerable Association of the Children of the People and more popularly known as *Katipunan*— began in Manila and in the provinces surrounding this capital an armed insurrection. This initially secret society had been founded on July 7th, 1892, and had as its main goals the achievement of independence of the Philippines from Spain and the expulsion of the religious orders from the archipelago, which the revolutionaries considered guilty of abuses against the local population.

DOI: 10.4018/978-1-6684-7040-4.ch006

Although it had been months since some religious had alerted the Governor-General Ramón Blanco y Erenas —marquis of Peña Plata— about the formation of insurgent groups in the rural areas where they exercised their ministry and, in the same way, a report sent by the Civil Guard lieutenant Manuel Sityar Bernal gave news about the existence of a large group of *katipuneros* in San Juan del Monte and Mandaluyong areas, it was not until August 1896 when the authorities in Manila took the first measures against the revolutionaries who carried out the first violent acts against the Spanish interests on the island of Luzon.

Thus, although Governor-General Blanco declared the state of war on August 24th, it was too late: the revolt quickly spread throughout the province of Manila and in just a few days to the Batangas, Bulacan, Cavite, La Laguna, Nueva Ecija, Pampanga and Tarlac provinces and, worst of all, taking place many massive desertions of native soldiers serving in the Spanish Army Line Infantry regiments in the archipelago.

Faced to the pressing problem and being evident that it was impossible to quell the insurrection with the meager existing regiments, the Governor-General was forced by the situation to request urgently military reinforcements from the Peninsula to the Spanish Government, which, despite being waging a strong war on the island of Cuba and suffer lack of human and financial resources, did not had no choice but to order the creation, from where there was nothing available, of some Light Infantry battalions and a small Cavalry and Artillery contingent.

BACKGROUND

If by itself the subject of the Philippine Revolution against the Spanish hegemony is a topic rarely broadly covered by historians outside the Philippines, a specific chapter on the Expeditionary Light Infantry units sent urgently from the Peninsula to put an end to the armed Insurrection, has few or no precedent studies in this regard. Much of the primary sources and documents which are necessary to face the investigation were simply lost during the campaign, the military repatriation to the Peninsula or in the subsequent decades, therefore, to elaborate this historical approach to such an interesting subject, we have collected documents both from the Spanish military archives, the few existing in the Philippines Archives, from other civilian and ecclesiastical sources and, even, from the diaries and personal memories of the soldiers who took part in the war framed in these units.

MAIN FOCUS OF THE CHAPTER

The main focus in the elaboration of this chapter is the historical approach that would serve as a contribution to the greater knowledge of the Philippine campaign through the knowledge of the units that participated in it and the way in which the Spanish Government faced the problem of the outbreak of the armed revolt in the Philippines and how the quick response they gave despite the lack of financial and human resources prevented the loss of the province already in 1897. How did the peninsular authorities manage to create these Expeditionary Light Infantry battalions despite also having to answer of a serious armed conflict in the island of Cuba? Were its components militarily well trained, well-armed, well-fed and equipped? Knowing the problems mentioned above, how was it possible for reinforcement forces to arrive just weeks after the outbreak of the revolt? Was the participation of private commercial entities and companies essential in the rapid deployment? Would the deployment have been possible without these collaborations? We face the answers of all these and other questions in the following pages. Likewise, we will take a brief tour of the main acts of arms and cases of heroism among the components of the Expeditionary Light Infantry battalions, some of them awarded the San Fernando Laureate Cross, the highest military decoration of the Spanish Army, and already significant part of the Spanish Military and which are still set as an example to the current troops in the Military academies all around the world.

Creation of the Expeditionary Battalions to the Philippine District

At the time of the outbreak of the revolution in the Philippine archipelago, the Military Spanish forces are estimated at approximately 18,000 soldiers, distributed among the seven existing Line Infantry regiments —68th Regiment Legazpi, 69th Regiment Iberia, 70th Regiment Magallanes, 71st Regiment Mindanao, 72nd Regiment Visayas, 73rd Regiment Jolo and 74th Regiment Manila— whose command was held by peninsular commanders and officers and the troops were essentially natives—, a Disciplinary Battalion, a Cavalry Regiment —of little importance in those islands due to its orography—, an Artillery Regiment and two batteries placed in the towns of Manila and Cavite —the artillerymen were always from the Peninsula—, an Engineer Battalion, the 4th Military Sanitary Brigade and some Military Administration staff. In addition, there were three battalions or *tercios* of the *Guardia Civil* (20th, 21st and 22nd), the *Guardia Civil Veterana* of Manila and three companies of *Carabineros*. For its part, the Spanish Navy in the Philippines had a unique company of Marine Infantry. These forces were the ones available to fight on land the more than 25,000 *katipuneros* who are estimated to have started the armed revolt, to which were added the constant desertions from these Spanish units.

Given the first successes of the insurgents on the battlefield, the response from Madrid did not wait. By Royal Order signed on August 29th, 1896, it was given way to the creation of the 1st Expeditionary Light Infantry Battalion —*Batallón de Cazadores Expedicionario núm. 1*—, a light Infantry force initially made up of only six companies and later being made up of a staff and eight companies. Each staff was in turn made up of lieutenant colonel, two majors, assistant captain, cashier captain, subordinate flag-bearer, two first-class or second-class doctors, chaplain, corporal of cornets and gunsmith. Each company was made up of a captain, four subordinates, five sergeants, ten corporals, four buglers or trainees, four first-class soldiers and 152 second-class soldiers.

The commanders, officers and assimilation would be appointed by the Ministry of War, at the same as the bugle corporal, the gunsmith and the classes that were missing for completing the battalion. The classes and troop for the companies will be constituted by the contingents of the personnel destined for Cuba, divided between 25 peninsular regiments and the 14th Battalion Cazadores de Estella —total 1,040 men, corresponding to each unit 40 men—, all of them belonging to the 1st, 3rd, 4th and 6th Military regions. The soldiers assigned to the Expeditionary Light Infantry Battalion would be chosen by lot from the troop classes of each regiment, accepting volunteers not destined for Cuba in a number that did not exceed fifteen men per unit. Just some days later, September 7th, was signed the order for the creation of the 2nd and 3rd Expeditionary Light Infantry Battalions per the same specifications of the first one.

In the same way, by Royal Order on September 22, 1896, it was also decided to send Cavalry and Artillery forces to increase the number of Cavalry squadrons that garrisoned the district to four and provide it with a mounted battery. Thus, the order was given to create the 1st Expeditionary Lancers Squad —*Escuadrón de Lanceros Expedicionario núm. 1*— made up of a major, two captains, three first lieutenants —one of them an assistant—, three second lieutenants, a second-class doctor, a third-class veterinarian, five sergeants, sixteen corporals, four trumpets, four farriers, one blacksmith, four first-class soldiers and 126 second-class soldiers. The 11 horses for officers and the 120 ones assigned to the troop would be delivered to the expedition members at their arrival in the Philippines. As for the Artillery, it was decided to send 170 men to create a mounted battery, made up of a captain, two first lieutenants, two second lieutenants, a second-class doctor, a third-class veterinarian, five sergeants, 20 corporals, three trumpets, two carpenter workers, two blacksmith fitter workers, ten first-class gunners and 128 second-class gunners. Upon arrival in the Philippines, this force would receive seven horses for officers, 18 for troops, and 150 draft horses.

Continuing with the Expeditionary Light Infantry battalions, the Royal Order on September 29th authorizes the creation of the 4th, 5th and 6th battalions and a few days later, on November 2nd, the 7th and 8th ones also receive approval. Finally, it would not be until December 4th, and in view of the events that were taking place in the archipelago, that the Spanish Government had the need to authorize through a new Royal Order the creation of seven new Expeditionary Light Infantry battalions –from 9th to 15th battalions—, thus completing the sending of units to the Philippine islands. However, small contingents of officers and soldiers would continue to be sent to replace those soldiers repatriated to the Peninsula due to illnesses or those who, with worse luck, died on the islands due to illness or on the battlefield.

In times of need for soldiers, civilian volunteers were recruited for the Philippine campaign, receiving an economic compensation at the time of their enlistment. The Army even resorted to private recruiters who, for an economic reward, were looking for candidates to join the Expeditionary forces, whether it was destined for the island of Cuba or the Philippines. Enlisted men had to remain in the ranks until the end of the campaign and six more months. Although it was not the most common, we have could observe in the documentation and military service sheets that some of the volunteers sent to the Overseas provinces to quell the insurrections, although many of them had previous military training, were over 35 years of age.

Given the shortage of officers, many sergeants with more than six years of experience in their rank were offered the chance to go off to the Overseas wars as second lieutenants, but on the condition that they return to their previous rank upon repatriation to the Peninsula. For many, it was a great opportunity for advancement in the Army, since they would earn their promotion to the rank of officer for Merits of War during the campaign.

Equipment, Weapons and Benefits

Even though it has been said that the Expeditionary Light Infantry battalions sent overseas were poorly equipped and armed, the truth is that this statement is far from true. The Royal Orders that organized the battalions established the equipment and individual uniform of each soldier: three shirts, three underpants, a pair of boots, a pair of shoes, a *rayadillo* cloth hat, two *rayadillo* uniforms, a vest, a backpack with gutta-percha sheath, a bow bag, two towels, a kettle, a spoon, a blanket and pair of espadrilles.

The *rayadillo* from which these uniforms were made was a white cotton fabric with parallel lines of blue patron. This fabric was used in the overseas districts of Cuba, Porto Rico and the Philippines by the Spanish army during the last years of the 19th century and later, with some modifications, by the Spanish Army troops to Equatorial Guinea, Morocco and the Spanish Sahara.

The rifle of choice for the Expeditionary Light Infantry battalions was the modern Spanish Mauser model 1893, a bolt-action rifle whose magazine contained five smokeless caliber 7x57 cartridges, which could be quickly reloaded by pressing a piece from the top of the open bolt. The Mauser weapons to armed the troops with and the corresponding ammunition would be provided in the port of boarding. The gun belting and cartridge belts were provided by the battalion that they were part of, which would be provided by the Spanish 4th Military region —the General Captaincy of Catalonia— from the surplus that it had. The garments and effects that the units of the Peninsula provided to the battalions, were previously appraised before being packaged, in order that they could be refunded to them from the budget of the Philippines islands. The battalions were also provided with sanitary material at the time of their embarkation.

The flag, weapons, ammunition, straps and battalion buglers had to be packed aboard the same ship that carried the force consigned to name of the chief of the indicated units, except for the rifles and the corresponding provision of ammunition for the escort on board. For its part, the Military Administration provided in the port of boarding a blanket for navigation, the same as the one they supplied the Deposits for Overseas. The marches by rail and sea, the organization and the transport of material, were on behalf of the Spanish Government. In addition, the battalion was paid 5,000 *pesetas* (25.91 GBP) as an extraordinary payment to face the first expenses of organization and the attentions of the new unit.

The families of the commanders and officials could go to the embarkation points or where they wished to establish their residence, either in the Peninsula, the Balearic Islands, the Canary Islands and Spanish cities in North Africa, on behalf of the Spanish Government. The same benefit would be enjoyed by the families of the classes and married troop individuals.

The Embarkation and Transport of Troops

At the end of the 19th century, and after the opening of the Suez Canal in 1869, the journey between any port placed on the east coast of Spain and the Philippine Islands took, in the best of cases, approximately a month. So, we can classify as a great success of the Spanish authorities having managed to bring the first military reinforcements to the archipelago just one month and six days after the signing of the Royal Order for the creation of the 1st Expeditionary Light Infantry Battalion. To achieve this success was essential the help and willingness of the *Transatlantica Española Co.*, whose ships were used as auxiliary cruisers by the Spanish Army to transport troops to the islands of Cuba, Puerto Rico and the Philippines.

In the archives of the shipping company in Barcelona are kept the telegrams in which the representatives of the firm put on notice their employees of the need to have the ships ready for an eventual massive shipment of troops to the Philippine archipelago, as well as the documents relating to cargo sheets, number of forces planned for embarkation, coal, watery and food needed, accommodation plans for the soldiers and even health recommendations in order to face such a long journey in the conditions in which they were carried out. Preserved from each of the ships that were used in the different troop expeditions, all this unpublished material is, undoubtedly, an interesting source for future studies on the subject.

Paradoxically and faced with the urgent need for troops in the archipelago, while the first infantry battalions were being formed, it was decided from Madrid to send the 1st Marine Infantry Battalion with 3 chiefs, 19 officers and 895 soldiers, which departed from the port of Cadiz on board the ship *Cataluña* on September 3rd, 1896, arriving in Manila on October 1st.

Although both the military authorities and the shipping company took all kinds of care to transport the force, unfortunately, the first deaths among the soldiers belonging the Expeditionary Light battalions took place on the open waters before reaching the archipelago. Thus, on October 7th, the first of the deaths took place, that of the soldier of the 2nd Expeditionary Light Infantry Battalion named Segundo Sanchez Rodriguez, having to mourn, on the 9th, the death of the soldier of the same battalion José Marti

Noguera and the following day that of his mate Pedro Sureda Bibiloni. These three soldiers, therefore, would be the first deaths among the Expeditionary Lught Infantry forces and would be as well the first, but by no means the last, to receive burial at sea.

On September 8th, the first six companies that formed the 1st Expeditionary Light Infantry Battalion with 3 commanders, 28 officers and 1033 soldiers left the port of Barcelona. After disembarking in Manila on October 6th, their newcomers immediately joined the fight against the insurgency. The first death recorded of this battalion in Philippine lands is the soldier Roque Alcubierra Aro, who drowned in a river on January 5th, 1897.

Gradually the rest of the Expeditionary forces arrived in the theatre of operations, to complete a figure of 9 generals,116 chiefs, 881 officers and 27,768 soldiers transported until the month of May 1897. To these figures must be added the arrival of the new Governor-General of the islands, General Camilo Garcia de Polavieja —I marquis of Polavieja— who arrived in the archipelago aboard the *Alfonso XIII* on December 3rd, 1896, after the dismissal of General Blanco.

In appendix 1 can be found a summary of the details of the different expeditions from the first shipment of reinforcements to the Philippines to the month of April 1897.

Regarding the discipline of the units, no revolts took place among the Expeditionary forces against their commanders during the time they served in the Philippines. On the other hand, although it is no less true that since the resurgence of the insurgency in early May 1898, the arrival of the Americans and, mainly, after the Spanish defeat in the military operations, in August 1898, some desertions took place, although the truth is that the numbers of desertions among the peninsular soldiers were not significant.

The Philippine Insurgency: The Fearsome Enemy

To get an idea of the type of enemy that the newcomers in the archipelago had to face with, it could be enough to read some of the instructions that gave one of the main leaders of the Revolution and of the Great Council of the Katipunan to his followers on June 28th, 1896, in order to start the armed insurrection, as it is quoted by the researcher Luis Togores (2019) in his article La defensa de la soberanía española en Filipinas [The defense of Spanish sovereignty in the Philippines]:

- Article 2nd "...each brother will fulfill the duty that this Grand Lodge has imposed on him, assassinating to all Spaniards, their wives and children...".
- Article 4th "Given the coup against the captain-general and other Spanish authorities, the locals will attack the convents and slit the throats of their infamous inhabitants, respecting the riches in those buildings contained, of the which the commissions appointed for this purpose will be seized...".

According these articles, we could get an idea of the aspect that insurrection was taking in these first moments and could stay with the idea the Katipunan as an extremely violent group that did not respect even the lives of non-combatants, including women and children. Even though many of the leaders of the Insurrection the leader of the insurrection had a university education and came from wealthy class families, definitely, many of their followers did not. At this point we could assure that in the first stage of the Philippine Insurgency, in some cases, the lives of the Spaniards in the hands of their captors were not respected, depending the fate of the prisoners on the personal character and benevolence of the Revolutionary commander in the area.

Most the katipuneros were peasants without prior military training, badly uniformed —in the clear majority of cases, not uniformed—, badly armed and worse commanded by their leaders. Although at first the insurgency lacked a significant number of firearms, after the first moments of the revolt, they were getting those from the Spanish army native deserters who crossed over to the Filipino side and those other that were requisitioned from the Spanish prisoners and dead. The smuggling of arms now was scarce, given the tight control that were held on the coasts by the Manila authorities and the position against the Revolution that nations like Great Britain showed in these initial moments of the revolt. Anyway, despite the lack of weapons and the little preparation of the katipuneros, they took some Spanish garrisons and a significant number of towns in the first weeks of fighting.

Thus, these moments also witnessed the existence of Revolutionary units armed only with bows and arrows —called *flecheros*—, and even stones. *Lantacas* —rudimentary cannons made of iron and wood— were built which, as we will see later, ended the life of at least a high-ranking officer of the Spanish Army. Any means was good to combat Spanish hegemony.

All these data can be corroborated by checking the death certificates of the Expeditionary soldiers who were killed on the battlefield or passed way in military hospitals after their evacuation, being the cause of death of many of them injuries caused by arrows, machetes and bladed weapons. At this point we must give due importance to the Spanish Military Sanity establishments scattered across the island of Luzon, the main theater of operations of the Philippine revolt.

The Military Sanity in the Philippines

The Spanish Army 4th Military Sanity Brigade, settled in the Philippines, helped to keep the number of deaths from being higher. Although with few medical professionals in relation to the number of forces deployed in the archipelago at the time of the insurrection, the arrival of doctors who arrived in the ranks of the Expeditionary Light Infantry battalions, helped to increase the number of surgeons in the archipelago. In the same way, the recruitment of civilian doctors was allowed for their enlistment in the Spanish army as temporary military doctors, entering service with the rank of lieutenant. Their permanence in the service lasted as far as the war lasted, leaving the Army and returning to civilian life after the end of the war. The arrival of these volunteers served as a bit of a breather for the already existing Military doctors on the islands.

As is well known, most of the deaths among the expeditionary forces were due to illness —main cause— or accidents. After checking the existing death certificates of hundreds of soldiers, the most common causes of decease were dysentery, pulmonary tuberculosis, acute gastroenteritis, acute bronchitis, and pernicious and typhoid fever. The drowning of soldiers in rivers were not uncommon, since many of them could not swim and were forced by combats to cross rivers loaded with their heavy equipment and weapons during the military operations.

Among the wounds in combat that Spanish military doctors had to deal with, in addition to those produced by bullet impact, were those produced by bladed weapons, mainly those used for field work, such as machetes, which produced terrifying wounds between the soldiers.

As for the existing medical establishments belonging to the Army, apart from the fixed Military hospitals of Manila and Malate placed in the capital, we must add the provisional ones of Cavite, Naig and Indang in the province of Cavite, that of Calamba in La Laguna, Baliuag in Bulacan and Batangas in the province of the same name. Attempts were made to implement infirmaries —not in all cases it was possible— in San Miguel de Mayumo in the province of Bulacan, in San Isidro and Cabanatuan in the province of Nueva Ecija and in Baler in the district of El Principe, not being possible the establishment this one due to the arrival of the insurrection. Precisely in this coastal town, and thanks to the existence of a doctor, the small Spanish garrison, belonging mostly to the 2ⁿᵈ Expeditionary Light Infantry Battalion, maintained a siege for 337 days surrounded by much larger forces of the Philippine Revolutionary Army.

Finally, we found smaller Military Sanity Brigade establishments in Imus, Silang and Alfonso in the province of Cavite, in Santa Cruz in the province of La Laguna and in Taal and Lipa in Batangas. In most of these points there were also military detachments with the presence of Expeditionary forces.

Heroics Among the Expeditionary Light Infantry Battalions Soldiers

During the Philippine campaign, no more and no less than fourteen members of the Expeditionary Light Infantry battalions were awarded the San Fernando Laureate Cross —the highest reward of the Spanish Army, whose purpose is to honour the recognized heroic value and the very distinguished, as virtues that, with self-sacrifice, induce to undertake exceptional or extraordinary actions, individual or collective, always in the service and benefit of Spain—. Let us know briefly all those cases of heroism.

1. The first war action that resulted in the award of the Laureate Cross among the Expeditionary Light Infantry forces —although it was not chronologically the first one to be awarded—, took place on January 1ˢᵗ, 1897, in the fighting at Cacarong de Sile, in the Bulacan province. The second lieutenant Luis Sans Hueling, belonging to the 6ᵗʰ Expeditionary Light Infantry Battalion, was leading his men in extreme vanguard in the taking of insurgent positions when he was wounded by a bullet impact. Nonetheless, he continued advancing leaning on one and encouraging his soldiers to follow him in the melee attack, receiving a second impact and, moments later, a third one that produced the fatal injuries that ended his life. The young second lieutenant was rewarded the Laureate Cross by Royal Order on September 18ᵗʰ, 1900, with an annual pension of 1,000 Spanish pesetas (4.96 GBP) to be collected by his parents.

2. The 5ᵗʰ Expeditionary Light Infantry Battalion first lieutenant Miguel Ruiz Soto was awarded the San Fernando Laureate Cross by Royal Order on March 23ʳᵈ, 1903, for the merits made during the capture of the enemy positions placed at the town of Pamplona (Bayán), province of Manila, on February 15ᵗʰ, 1897. He was the first officer who managed to break through the strongly protected enemy defences, taking their positions and the first commander to manage to form his men inside them, being wounded just after getting his feat. First lieutenant Ruiz Soto did not survive the injuries received, been granted to his widow an annual pension of 1,000 pesetas attached the award of the Laureate Cross.

3. Just one day later Ruiz Soto´s death, the 15ᵗʰ Expeditionary Light Infantry Battalion major Hipolito Vidal Abarca, passed away during the attack to the insurgent Malaguig-Ilang trenches. Leading the vanguard of the Spanish column, he entered the trenches with reckless courage and upon reaching them, unable to climb the parapet that protected the enemy fortification due to its great height, he tried to overcome it by putting his feet in the mouths of the embrasures from where the enemy *lantacas* opened fire, receiving the impact of a shot from one of these rudimentary cannons in his chest, that caused him instant death. His heroism was recognized by Royal Order on February 20ᵗʰ, 1900, receiving his widow an annual 2,000 pesetas (9.92 GBP) pension.

4. On February 19ᵗʰ, 1897, the captain of the 1ˢᵗ Expeditionary Light Infantry Battalion, Andres Jaen Nuñez also deserved to be awarded the highest reward of the Spanish Army for his heroism in

combat. Fulfilling orders received from their superiors after taking part in the combat against the insurgent positions in the town of Silang, Cavite province, led a company under his command to the right flank of the central trench that the Filipinos were still tenaciously defending, taking up positions after advance under heavy fire at a short distance from this entrenchment. Having immediately begun the attack with the bayonet, the Spanish Expeditionary captain, demonstrating dignified behaviour of bravery, was the first who crowned the enemy fortification, receiving two fatal gunshot wounds plus a stab wound, passing away two hours later aboard the ambulance that was carrying out his evacuation. The San Fernando Laureate Cross was awarded to him by Royal Order on December 9th, 1901, granting his widow a 1,500 pesetas (7.44 GBP) annual pension.

5. On December 19th, 1901, by means of Royal Order, the heroism of the 8th Expeditionary Light Infantry Battalion captain Santiago Izquierdo Osorio was rewarded the San Fernando Laureate Cross and a 2,000 pesetas per year pension to be collected by his relatives. Captain Izquierdo Osorio was on the command of a Spanish guerrilla taking part in the action of Bahay Paré (Meycauayan), in the Bulacan province, when he was seriously wounded in one of his leg by a firearm impact after taking an insurrectionary trench. While attacking a second katipunero fortification, despite the wounds received, he continued at the forefront of his troops, encouraging them with his example. Few moments later, he received a new penetrating shot wound, despite which, he continued leading the attack to the enemy positions with a serene spirit and without ceasing for a moment in the target of his mission. Finally, the Spanish captain received a third bullet impact, this time being wounded on his forehead, passing away heroically on the battlefield.

6. The 2nd Expeditionary Light Infantry Battalion second lieutenant Dario Casado Lopez-Novoa was awarded the San Fernando Laureate Cross and 1,000 pesetas annual pension for his heroic behaviour in the action of Lalab, Bataan province, by Royal Order on May 30th, 1903. The date on which the events occurred made him the first Expeditionary survivor among the awarded the Laureate Cross in the Philippine campaign. After being ordered to move back for reinforcements to the end of the column in which he was marching in extreme vanguard after receiving the Spanish forces a Filipino attack, upon his return he found his captain and a soldier of the column engaged in a melee combat against three insurgent soldiers, whom he personally killed with a bladed weapon at despite receiving two serious wounds, thus managing to save heroically his own life and both, his superior´s and his subordinate´s lives.

7. The 4th Expeditionary Light Infantry Battalion captain José Rodríguez Casademunt distinguished himself for his heroic behavior in the defense of the town of Arayat, in the province of Pampanga. Upon receiving the attack of a force of 500 insurgents heavily armed with firearms and *lantacas*, the Spanish officer left his refuge on command of a force of just over 40 soldiers to combat the attackers in the San Jose neighborhood. Having managed to put the enemies to flight, he pursued them, dividing the Spanish forces into two groups and beginning reconnaissance that lasted until the following day, receiving himself fifteen wounds —serious four of them— and losing consciousness due to loss of blood. Thus, the position was saved, with many casualties from the enemy, from whom two lantacas and numerous bladed and firearms were requisitioned. He was awarded the Laureate Cross and annual 1,500 pesetas pension by Royal Order on June 25th, 1900. During the Spanish Civil War, he was vilely assassinated by exalted militiamen of the Republican side.

8. Corporal Manuel Arrojo Lopez, belonging the 8th Expeditionary Light Infantry Battalion, was the soldier with the lowest military rank among the Expeditionary members awarded the San Fernando Laureate Cross, being rewarded for his deed by the Spanish Government by Royal Order

on November 9th, 1900. He was the man in charge of the Pilar garrison, made up of nine other Expeditionary soldiers, in the province of Baatan, when on March 29th, 1898, the detachment was surprised by an insurgent attack. In the first moments of the defense, corporal Arrojo was wounded on his side and a bullet blew off his left hand, nevertheless, the Spaniards managed to take refuge in the village church, being the corporal wounded again —this time on his right hand— and two of his soldiers killed during the assault. Inside the church, an insurgent soldier wounded again Arrojo with a machete on the forehead. Running out of food and ammunition and being all the Spanish defenders wounded, they climbed the bell tower and destroyed the access staircase. Next day, 30th, without ammunition, they put as a condition for their surrender that their lives should be respected and, consequently, they would be sent to a hospital, conditions that were accepted by the besiegers. After hanging from the bell tower using the ropes of the bells, they remained prisoners in Pilar for eight days without receiving medical assistance, until they were transferred to the town of Cavite to be cured by American Navy doctors. After being deprived of liberty for twenty days, they were part of a prisoner exchange and, recovered his freedom, met the Spanish troops in Manila. For his heroic behavior during the defense, he also was awarded an annual pension amounted 400 pesetas (1.98 GBP).

9. Felipe Dugiols Balanzategui was a lieutenant colonel belonging the 9th Expeditionary Light Infantry Battalion when he deserved the San Fernando Laureate Cross and an annual 2,000 pesetas pension due to his heroic behavior during the combats which took place on June 14th, 1898. His merits were awarded by the Royal Order on February 23rd, 1899. On command of the vanguard of the general's Monet column, which was leaving San Fernando de la Pampanga on the way to Manila, the Spanish forces met many enemies heavily armed and entrenched in good positions at the city of Santo Tomas trying to cut off the path of the column. The Spanish vanguard composed of 100 men, tried to take the insurgent positions, but were rejected and messed up. Positioned in front of his soldiers, lieutenant colonel Dujiols harangued them and led his men with his example to attack again, taking the Filipino trenches, suffering during the combat the loss of an officer and eleven troopers, eight officers and 36 soldiers were wounded and eight officers and 29 soldiers were missing.

10. Angel Sequera López, a 12th Expeditionary Light Infantry Battalion captain, got the merits to enter the Royal and Military Order of San Fernando when he stood out in the action of Guaquit on June 2nd and 3rd, 1898. The insurgents, in number of 400 well-armed men and supported by numerous groups armed with bladed weapons, attacked the column commanded by captain Sequera which was made up of two officers and 46 soldiers, maintaining fire for 45 minutes, suffering the small Spanish column 21 casualties that they did not abandon but picked up before undertaking a difficult retreat facing an enemy that, after the combat, were reported to be twenty times greater in number. Without abandoning a man or a rifle, the Spanish column held on the night of June 2nd in the ditch of the road, harassed all the time by the revolutionary forces. On the morning of day 3rd, the strongly reinforced enemy attacked again the Spaniards, offering them the chance to surrender, which was strongly rejected. Despite having only six or seven men unharmed, once the ammunition was over and without any hope of relief, Sequera arranged a desperate attack using bayonets and blade weapons, in which he was wounded in the leg, as well as the officer and the four soldiers who followed him, being all of them eventually taken as prisoners. On February 14th, 1902, by Royal Order he was awarded the San Fernando Laureate Cross in addition to his 1,500 pesetas annual pension.

11. The 9th Expeditionary Light Infantry Battalion major Joaquin Pacheco Yanguas was one of the survivors of the siege of Tayabas, a town in the province of the same name, which was besieged by Filipino revolutionary forces between June 24th and August 16th, 1898. Being commander of the military forces of the town, prepared the defense with all the works of fortification that could be done, being forced to destroy gradually many buildings by controlled fires as they were demanding the needs to prevent the besiegers from taking them. Due to the lack of defenders, the defense ended up being circumscribed only to five buildings, consisting of the Spanish forces available only by one commander, 22 officers and 148 soldiers. Since there were no factories or spare parts, not even gunpowder, the cannons that were in the defense could not be fired, being nailed to disable them. It was necessary for the food lasted, as long as possible, to limit the meat ration supplied to one ounce per person, and this was just possible thanks to the meat obtained from slaughtering the officers' horses. Eventually, the Spaniards had to feed themselves on rice and water which caused the besieged many casualties, among whom there were many civilians, including women. The besiegers never were below 7,800 men armed with rifles and 7,000 with bladed weapons, plus 15 cannons placed in the first line and several others in the second one, having fired, according to own enemy reports, 500,000 cartridges, 300 cannon bullets and 22 dynamite bombs, keeping during the siege continuous fire and being the most significant acts of arms those that took place on July 17th and August 10th, achieving heroic defense and a capitulation that left very high the honor of Spanish arms. After finishing the siege, major Pacheco (1910) was taken prisoner by the Filipino revolutionaries. For his heroic behavior, he was awarded the San Fernando Laureate Cross and an annual 2,000 pesetas pension as ruled by Royal Order on March 18th, 1901. Once in the Peninsula, he wrote an interesting book describing his captivity, whose reading we recommend.

12. Lieutenant colonel of the 12th Expeditionary Light Infantry Battalion Mariano Alberti Leones stood out in the defense of Santa Cruz, in the province of La Laguna. When the town was besieged, the Spanish defense had 700 men. Since June 8th, 1898 was constantly harassed by the adversary forces with artillery and rifle fire until the capitulation of the sieged garrison with all the honors of war, which occurred on August 20th. Despite the inferiority of force, the Expeditionary soldiers carried out various raids to control the besiegers and destroy the enemy trenches that surrounded them. Forced to survive with a third of the usual food ration supply and hardly any medicines, at the end of their defense the Spaniards suffered 133 casualties both dead and wounded. For his exemplary behavior on command his men, lieutenant colonel Alberti was awarded the San Fernando Laureate Cross and 2,000 pesetas annual pension by Royal Order on October 30th, 1902.

13. By Royal Order on July 1st, 1901, the second lieutenant of the 2nd Expeditionary Light Infantry Battalion Saturnino Martín Cerezo (1904) was acknowledged the right to the San Fernando Laureate Cross and 1,000 pesetas annual pension for his merits during the defense of the Baler garrison, a small town placed in the east coast of the island of Luzon in El Principe district. The dramatic defense took place between June 30th, 1898 and June 2nd, 1899. The defense of Baler constitutes a unique military feat in Military History, since this small detachment resisted against Revolutionary forces ten times greater in number, without any help for 337 days, having to fight against the enemy as well against an epidemic of beriberi —a disease caused by poor nutrition and lack of vitamin B1—, which, if prolonged, causes death. Second lieutenant Martin Cerezo was the last man in charge of the defense and years later he wrote his memories in a book that has been recommended reading in the main military academies all around the world, including West Point Academy in the United States and, as it could not be less, we also recommend. After the capitulation of the Spanish

detachment, the first president of the Philippine Republic and former head of the Insurgent forces, general Emilio Aguinaldo, issued an act recognizing the courage of the defenders and ordering the survivors to be treated as friends of the new Philippine Republic and never as prisoners. Currently, every June 30th, the Philippine Army commemorates the feat by presenting honors in front of the church where the Spanish soldiers carried out their defense.

14. We include in this list another of the participants in the siege of Baler, who, although at that time belonged to Passive Classes section and not longer to the Expeditionary Light Infantry battalions, had arrived in the Philippine islands as a captain of the 9th Battalion. Captain Enrique de las Morenas y Fossi was that time the political-military commander of El Príncipe district, headquartered in Baler, the capital city, and he took command of the defense of the garrison from June 30th, 1898, until his death cause by the beriberi epidemic on November 22nd, 1898. A Royal Order on March 5th, 1901, awarded him the San Fernando Laureate Cross and granted his widow the right to receive 2,000 pesetas annual pension. He was the last of the ones awarded the San Fernando Laureate Cross who found his death in the archipelago.

At this point we also should mention the curious case of the provisional medical lieutenant Rogelio Vigil de Quiñones y Alfaro, another of the defenders of Baler's position, who was awarded the San Fernando Laureate Cross by contradictory trial but to which it was later denied. Despite fulfilling all the necessary requirements for a Military doctor to be awarded the Laureate Cross, he was denied the award in second instance for having received a serious injury while praying the Rosary instead of having received it while in combat or caring for a wounded soldier in the battlefield. Given that the praying of the Rosary was a mandatory activity among the soldiers during the siege, it could be considered that the entire garrison was permanently on duty. We can hardly understand this senseless discrimination against this surgeon of the 4th Military Sanitary Brigade.

Although there were fourteen soldiers awarded the San Fernando Laureate Cross, many medals were awarded to many the Expeditionary Light Infantry battalions soldiers, and they are well know the cases of many soldiers who returned the Peninsula with up to five and six Military Merit crosses with a red badge —in the Spanish Army, distinctive of those awards achieved in combat— on their chest, many of them even pensioners for life. It would be interesting to carry out a study on the total amount of rewards that the members of the Expeditionary Light Infantry battalions could have gotten in the Philippine campaign.

The Siege of Baler: An Example of Line of Duty

The Spanish garrison of the town of Baler, El Príncipe district, was the object of an important attack, such as the one suffered by surprise by the detachment of lieutenant Jose Motta Hidalgo and his 50 soldiers, belonging all of them the 2nd Expeditionary Light Infantry Battalion, while they were sleeping on the October 5th, 1897, resulting in the death of the officer himself and several of his soldiers due to machete wounds. Those survivors who were not taken prisoner, were besieged inside the church of the town by the enemy until they were rescued some days later.

The Spanish force that replaced the first besieged detachment suffered a second siege in the same coastal town, taking it place even when the Treaty of peace of Biak-na-Bato —which put an end to the Insurgency in the Philippines— had been signed by the leaders of the Revolution.

On June 30th, 1898, another small detachment belonging to the same unit —in which some of the survivors of the first attack and one soldier of the second one were enlisted— was forced again to take refuge inside the same church after being attacked by a force enemy at least ten times larger than the Spanish garrison, thus beginning a siege, this time of 337 days of duration, something that we could describe as unique and singular. The besieged force was initially made up of two officers and 48 soldiers of the 2nd Expeditionary Light Infantry Battalion, an officer and a sanitary soldier belonging to the 4th Military Sanity Brigade, the political-military commander of El Principe district and a Franciscan friar —although later two more Franciscan friars joined the defenders—. Ignoring the multiple recommendations to surrender from the enemy when the war had ended for weeks and, as well, from two Spanish commissioners who ordered them to abandon their futile resistance, the besieged managed to kept their position without the possibility of receiving any food, fighting the enemy, hunger, disease and despair, facing courageously the siege in truly subhuman conditions until their capitulation on June 2nd, 1899.

According the interrogations that the survivors underwent after their evacuation to Manila, the instinct of self-preservation, camaraderie, patriotism, but mainly the fulfillment of duty and respect for their officers weighed heavily in their heroic behavior. This episode constitutes one of the most brilliant pages in the Spanish Military History and these heroes of the Siege of Baler —several of them, survivors in fact to two sieges of Baler— are an example of the courageous character and the suffering endurance of the Spanish Infantry soldiers.

For those interested in deepening the study of this epic episode, we recommend the historical essay entitled *El sitio de Baler: La heroica gesta de los Últimos de Filipinas* [*The Siege of Baler: The Heroic Deed of the Last of the Philippines*], (López de la Asunción and Leiva Ramírez, 2022) a work that is the result of a 25 years' research *in situ* in three continents.

FUTURE RESEARCH DIRECTIONS

It would be an interesting research topic to study separately and in more detail the different vicissitudes that occurred to the different Expeditionary Light Infantry battalions sent to the Philippines to fight against the supporters of the insurrection. Topics such as figures of casualties, mortality, awards and merits incurred by its components, participation in the different military operations, figures of prisoners —many of them who were in the hands of the Revolutionary army for years— and a long etcetera that, unfortunately, we lack any important paper to this day. Although it would not be an easy task, we encourage the preparation of papers that analyse these issues as relevant as they are unknown, and in general, any research that addresses the Philippine Revolution, which would be undoubtedly welcome.

Despite not being abundant, the opportunity to work today with sources written in the Tagalog language has been greatly facilitated thanks to new technologies, so the approach to these primary sources can provide a lot of information for future studies. Collaboration with Philippine researchers to carry out joint studies could provide us with a more approximate vision for all how the insurrection was experienced in the archipelago.

CONCLUSION

The successful sending of fifteen Expeditionary Light Infantry battalions from the Peninsula to the Philippines in such a short space of time —despite having the Spanish Government to face another bloody battlefront on the island of Cuba— was undoubtedly an achievement of the Spanish Army and particularly of its quartermaster. The rapid arrival of these well-equipped, well-armed and —in most cases— with military training reinforcements in the Philippine archipelago, decanted the victory on the side of the Spanish arms in a few months and put an end to the Insurrection despite the difficult orography of the islands and the lack of knowledge of the terrain. The Military Sanity Brigade establishments in Luzon island were essential to get this victory in the battlefields, as was having control of the sea through warships and transports, which helped the movement of troops and allow the supply of the different military detachments, many of them isolated and without communication with the rest of the deployed forces for weeks even in times of peace.

In the same way, the outbreak of the Spanish-American War of 1898 resulted in the Spanish losing of control of the sea at the hands of the United States Navy and the control of the terrain at the hands of the Revolutionary forces, which made it impossible to supply food and ammunition to the devoid of medical assistance small detachments scattered throughout the island of Luzon, causing the rapid loss of hegemony in the Philippine islands after 335 years of Spanish presence in the archipelago.

However, as we have learnt in these pages, these dramatic last moments of the Spanish presence in the Philippines were plenty of heroism and generosity on the part of those Spanish soldiers who went to defend their flag on the other side of the world but, nevertheless, within the borders of their own country.

The most dramatic part was the 9,000 Spanish prisoners who remained in some cases for years in the hands of the Filipino Revolutionary army. Little has also been written on this subject, which would, undoubtedly, add a strong human factor to the new approaches to the Campaign of Philippines.

REFERENCES

López de la Asunción, M. A., & Leiva Ramírez, M. (2022). *El sitio de Baler. La heroica gesta de los Últimos de Filipinas [Baler's site. The heroic deed of the Last of the Philippines]*. Ed. Actas.

Martín Cerezo, S. (1904). *El sitio de Baler: Notas y recuerdos [The site of Baler: Notes and memories]*. Taller tipográfico del Colegio de Huérfanos [Typographic workshop of the College of Orphans].

Pacheco Yanguas, J. (ca. 1910). *Filipinas: impresiones, notas y memorias de un prisionero [The Philippines: Impressions, Notes, and Memoirs of a Prisoner.]*. Biblioteca Digital._https://bibliotecadigital.aecid.es/bibliodig/es/consulta/registro.do?id=6636

Togores Sánchez, L. (2019) La defensa de la soberanía española en Filipinas [The defense of Spanish sovereignty in the Philippines]. *Revista de Historia Militar, II Extraordinario [Military History Magazine, Extraordinary II.]*. https://publicaciones.defensa.gob.es/media/downloadable/files/links/r/h/rhm_extra_ii_2019_.pdf

ADDITIONAL READING

Blanco, R. (1897). *Memoria que al senado dirige el General Blanco acerca de los últimos sucesos ocurridos en la Isla de Luzón [Memory that General Blanco addresses to the Senate about the latest events that occurred on the Island of Luzón.]*. El Liberal.

Mas Chao, A. (1998). *La guerra olvidada de Filipinas [The Forgotten Philippine War]*. Editorial San Martín.

Puell de la Villa, F. (2002). El Ejército en Filipinas [The Army in the Philippines]. En Elizalde Pérez-Grueso. M.D (2002). *Las relaciones entre España y Filipinas, siglos XVI-XX [Relations between Spain and the Philippines, 16th-20th centuries]*. CSIC. https://asehismi.es/catalogo/capitulos/detalle.php?id=65

Sastrón, M. (1901). *La insurrección en Filipinas y la Guerra Hispano-americana en el archipiélago [The insurrection in the Philippines and the Spanish-American War in the archipelago]*. Imprenta de la sucesora de M. Minuesa de los Ríos.

Togores Sánchez, L. (1996). La revuelta tagala de 1896/97: Primo de Rivera y los acuerdos de Biac-na-Bató [The Tagalog revolt of 1896/97: Primo de Rivera and the Biac-na-Bató agreements]. *Revista española del Pacífico [Spanish-Pacific Magazine], 6.* https://repositorioinstitucional.ceu.es/bitstream/10637/1376/1/Revuelta_Togores_Rev_Esp_Pac_1996.pdf

KEY TERMS AND DEFINITIONS

Carabineros: Spanish armed body whose main mission was the surveillance of coasts and borders, and the repression of tax fraud and smuggling.

Cazadores: In the Spanish Army, soldiers destined to serve as light troops either in companies attached to line regiments or separate, forming independent units.

Guardia Civil: Spanish armed body whose main mission is the preservation of public order, the protection of people and property and the assistance that demands the execution of the laws. Created on the Peninsula in 1844, it was settled in the Philippines in 1868, being the 20th *Tercio* (battalion) was deployed on the island of Luzon, the 21st on the island of Mindanao in 1872 and the 21st in Nueva Ecija province in 1895.

Katipunero: Member or follower of the Katipunan, the secret society that started the independence riots against Spanish hegemony in the Philippine islands.

Lantaca: Small caliber culverin, handcrafted and used by Filipino revolutionaries against Spanish troops during the insurrection.

APPENDIX 1

Table 1. Troops sent to the Philippine district from the creation of the Expeditionary Light Infantry battalions until May 1897

Military unit	Ship	Port	Boarding	Arrival	Generals	Commanders	Officers	Soldiers
1st Marine Infantry Batt.	*Cataluña*	Cadiz	Sep. 4th 1896	Oct. 1st 1896	—	3	19	895
1th - 6th Co. 1st Caz. Exp. Batt.	*Montserrat*	Barcelona	Sep. 8th 1896	Oct. 6th 1896	—	3	28	1.033
Expeditionary Artillery 1st Marine Infantry Batt.	*Antonio Lopez*	Barcelona Cartagena	Sep. 13th 1896 Sep. 14th 1896	Oct. 13th 1896	— —	— *3*	— *24*	*401* *785*
1th - 6th Co. 2nd Caz. Exp. Batt. 1th - 6th Co. 3rd Caz. Exp. Batt. Various	*Isla de Luzon*	Barcelona	Sep. 18th 1896	Oct. 17th 1896	— — —	3 3 1	30 30 1	993 1.002 48
1th - 6th Co. 4th Caz. Exp. Batt. 1st Exp. Lancers Squad Artillery Battery Various	*Colon*	Barcelona	Oct. 6th 1896	Nov. 3rd 1896	— — —	3 1 — 1	34 9 8 14	984 150 160 18
1th - 6th Co. 5th Caz. Exp. Batt. 1th - 6th Co. 6th Caz. Exp. Batt. Various	*Covadonga*	Barcelona	Oct. 16th 1896	Nov. 14th 1896	— — —	3 3 —	35 28 10	996 934 15
7th - 8th Co. 1st & 2nd Caz. Exp. Batt. 2 Co. Marine Infantry Various	*Alfonso XIII*	Barcelona	Nov. 7th 1896	Dec. 2nd 1896	— — 6	— — 24	10 9 45	651 255 152
7th Caz. Exp. Batt. 2 Co. 8th Caz. Exp. Batt. Various	*Leon XII*	Barcelona	Nov. 2nd 1896	Dec. 10th 1896	— — —	3 1 —	26 6 —	1.393 340 41
3rd Marine Infantry Batt. 6 Co. 8th Caz. Exp. Batt. Various	*San Fernando*	Cartagena Barcelona	Nov. 24th 1896 Nov. 27th 1896	Dec. 31st 1896	— — —	3 2 —	26 22 —	1.063 928 40
7th - 8th Co. 3rd, 4th, 5th & 6th Caz. Exp. Batt. Various	*Mindanao*	Barcelona	Dec. 9th 1896	Jan. 7th 1897	— —	— 2	23 12	1.257 141
11th Caz. Exp. Batt. 2 Co. 12th Caz. Exp. Batt.	*Isla de Luzon*	Barcelona	Dec. 17th 1896	Jan. 17th 1897	— —	3 —	23 4	1.389 346
Staff & 6 Co. 12th Caz. Exp. Batt. Various	*Antonio Lopez*	Barcelona	Dec. 17th 1896	Jan. 16th 1897	— —	3 —	17 3	1.042 59
13th Caz. Exp. Batt. 4 Co. 15th Caz. Exp. Batt. Various	*Montevideo*	Valencia	Dec. 18th 1896	Jan. 16th 1897	— — —	3 1 1	24 7 —	1.388 678 28
9th Caz. Exp. Batt. 10th Caz. Exp. Batt. Conscript	*Magallanes*	Cadiz	Dec. 19th 1896	Jan. 25th 1897	— — —	3 3 —	16 21 —	1.323 1.371 89
14th Caz. Exp. Batt. Staff & 4 Co. 15th Caz. Exp. Batt. Various	*Colon*	Barcelona	Dec. 20th 1896	Jan. 25th 1897	— — —	3 2 —	21 12 4	1.394 687 60
Various	*Isla de Panay*	Barcelona	Jan, 2nd 1897	—	—	—	40	275
Various	*Covadonga*	Barcelona	Jan. 30th 1897	—	—	—	46	234
Various	*Leon XIII*	Barcelona	Feb. 27th 1897	—	—	12	52	735
Various Marine infantry	*Montevideo*	Barcelona	Mar. 27th 1897	—	2 —	11 2	65 2	361 856
Various Conscript	*Isla de Luzon*	Barcelona	Apr. 24th 1897	—	1 —	5 —	48 —	78 503
Various Conscript	*Alicante*	Barcelona	Apr. 29th 1897	—	— —	2 —	30 —	25 161
Total					**9**	**116**	**881**	**27.768**

Data Source: López de la Asunción. M.A. & Leiva Ramírez, M. (2022): El Sitio de Baler: La heroica gesta de los Últimos de Filipinas. Ed. Actas.

Chapter 7
Spain, Imperialism, and Genealogy of International Studies in the First Third of the 20th Century

José Luis Neila Hernández

https://orcid.org/0000-0001-7598-9878

Autonomous University of Madrid, Spain

ABSTRACT

In recent decades, international studies have been the subject of exciting debates encouraged from critical perspectives, especially from constructivist approaches. Among these debates, the present text intends to pay attention to the revisionism of the narrative around the genealogy of the scientific study of international relations in the first third of the 20th century and the vindication of imperialism in the genesis of international studies. In Spain, the permeability to such historiographical views has not penetrated too much in the review of the genealogy of international studies and even less in the role of imperialism. A question certainly present in the studies on the foreign policy of the period but absent in the analysis of the academic and institutional habitat of international studies in Spain.

INTRODUCTION

The African reorientation of Spanish imperialism after the crisis of 1898 would not only be transferred to the cartographic projection of the new empire south of the Strait of Gibraltar, but would also be intellectually reflected in Spanish orientalism, specifically Africanism, and in institutional initiatives of a regenerationist nature such as the creation of the Instituto Libre de Enseñanza de las Carreras Diplomática y Consular y Centro de Estudios Marroquíes (the Free Institute of Education of the Diplomatic and Consular Careers and the Centre for Moroccan Studies).

Spain's active reinsertion into the international system of Armed Peace and Imperialism prior to the Great War would be consummated from the overseas window as a means of access to the centre of the

DOI: 10.4018/978-1-6684-7040-4.ch007

system through its connection with the Franco-British Entente Cordiale of 1904 and the whole plethora of diplomatic milestones such as the Algeciras Conference and the Cartagena Agreements on the basis of which Spain built its colonial presence in Africa, and specifically in the Maghreb.

In terms of the development of international studies in Spain at the turn of the century, the most ambitious initiative was the creation of the Instituto Libre de Enseñanza de las Carreras Diplomática y Consular y Centro de Estudios Marroquíes in 1911. Proposed by Rafael María de Labra, its creation was intended to promote and modernise the training of future diplomats and consuls, as well as to meet the needs of the incipient colonial administration, particularly in the Spanish Protectorate in Morocco. The dual dimension of the new institution is in itself illustrative of the centrality of imperialism in Spain's international relations. This institutional and intellectual adaptation would have many similarities with other empires of the time, such as the US imperial practice, which would allocate significant resources from the academic and university world, and which would make the British model its main source of inspiration.

In recent years, historiography has not only recovered attention to imperialism, but has also introduced new approaches to the scale of empires in order to analyse the history and international relations of the period. However, from the perspective of this paper, the genealogy of international studies and the revision of the mythical narrative that located the birth of international relations theory in the post-Great War period has given rise to an exciting historiographical debate. A debate aimed not only at questioning the canonical narrative of the genesis of the theory, but also at recovering the lines of continuity with the pre-Great War academic world and reworking the disciplinary narrative, making the centrality of imperialism visible. In this intellectual framework, it seems pertinent to ask to what extent the academic and institutional world of Spain in the first third of the 20th century participated in or was sensitive to the centrality of imperialism in the studies and practice of international relations?

The approach that encourages this text would be based, first of all, on the historiography of international relations according to the recent revisionist debate on its genealogy from a constructivist perspective. And secondly, it would rest on the cultural history of international relations, in a broad sense, as has been well specified in his reflections by Antonio Niño on the history of intercultural relations. A perspective in whose perimeter of action the study of communication converged, in all its variants, between culturally differentiated societies, and the exchanges that take place of everything that is charged with meaning -cultural products and practices- across borders, political or not, that separate them (Niño, 2009: 26-30). And more explicitly in one of its uses, considering intercultural relations as part of the study of international relations.

On the basis of these argumentative premises, the explicit objectives of the present work are based on the following questions:

Firstly, the enquiry into the historiographical debate that in recent decades has given rise to the revision of the canonical narrative of the origin of the Theory of International Relations after the Great War from a constructivist point of view. This approach has reinterpreted the centrality of imperialism as the Gordian knot at the origin of the scientific study of international relations.

Secondly, the exploration and reinterpretation from these historiographical keys of a terrain that has not been broken in Spanish academic literature. A look not only aimed at contextualising the academic panorama and the genealogy of international studies in Spain in the first third of the century, but also at assessing the role of imperialism in the institutional and academic framework of international studies in Spain, and in particular the performance of the Instituto Libre de Estudios de las Carreras Diplomática y Consular y Centro de Estudios Marroquíes.

And finally, the analysis of the disciplines and areas of knowledge present in the Spanish institutions created at the beginning of the 20th century to undertake the study and praxis of Spain's international and imperialist work in the light of its new African responsibilities. On this level, the impact of Africanism within the intellectual climate of Regenerationism in Spain after the fin-de-siècle crisis is indisputable.

BACKGROUND

One of the most exciting debates in the field of international relations since the beginning of the 21st century has revolved around the genealogy of international studies as a science. The dominant socio-constructivist view in the discipline has promoted a critical revision of the canonical narrative of the origin of international relations theory after the Great War, which sanctioned the Western ethnocentrism of the discipline and the centrality of political science in the construction of international relations theory. Foundational milestones such as the first great debate –idealist *vs.* realist- were thus questioned, and gateways were established to insert the changes in international studies within the framework of the structuralist turn in the intellectual, academic, and political environment preceding the Great War.

In this scenario, as will be specified later in the historiographical debate, imperialism and the political culture in which the theory and practice of imperialism were grounded emerged as a central node in the disciplines that concurred in international studies, such as international law, diplomatic history, geopolitics and anthropology. It is not surprising, therefore, that initiatives such as that of colonial affairs expert Alpheus Henry Snow at George Washington University proposed the creation of a "science of imperial relations" at the beginning of the 20th century. This was a significant symptom of the dynamism of "international studies". A concept that would become standardised in the period between the two world wars, at least within the International Committee for Intellectual Cooperation and the International Institute for Intellectual Cooperation with the creation of the International Studies Conferences, but whose semantic polymorphism would be glimpsed in other institutions such as the Council on Foreign Relations in the United States or the Royal Institute of International Affairs in Great Britain.

The Spanish academic world was in no way alien to this intellectual environment, in keeping with the very nature of the international system since the beginning of the 20th century. It should not be forgotten that the previous century closed with a colonial crisis, the Spanish-American War of 1898. In accordance with the revisionist assumptions surrounding the debate on the genealogy of international studies, the purpose of this paper is to analyse from this perspective the permeability of Spanish intellectuals and academics and the institutional initiatives undertaken at the beginning of the century with the gravity of imperialism both in the practice of foreign policy and in international studies. An unprecedented perspective in Spanish historiography on the genealogy of international studies in Spain.

MAIN FOCUS OF THE CHAPTER

The sensitivity towards the construction of academic discourses on international studies from the centrality of imperialism at the beginning of the 20th century, as one of the great contributions to the debate on the genealogy of international studies, serves as a basis for the other two objectives of this research. Firstly, the incardination of international studies in Spain in the first third of the century and its permeability to the debates and strategies of knowledge about the international in the European and Western spheres.

And secondly, the incidence and presence of Spanish Africanism, as a cultural and political vehicle in an Orientalist key in the institutional strategies to promote theoretical and applied knowledge for the redefinition of Spain's international position and the demands of the new imperialist enterprise in Africa.

The fundamental hypothesis on which this research rests is that although the Spanish academic world did not participate in the standard debate on imperialism, it is no less certain that it did participate in the political and intellectual environment due to the interest, at least among the elites, in international affairs and in particular in imperialism in a context of reconstitution of Spain's coordinates in the international system of imperialism prior to the Great War after the colonial crisis of 1898. In this sense, and in the cultural environment of Regenerationism, Africanists played an obvious cultural and political role. The debate in Spain on imperialism and in particular on the colonial enterprise in Morocco, in any case, was not channelled in the academic arena but in the political arena in conjunction with other structural problems of Alfonso XIII's Spain.

Imperialism as a Foundational Debate in the Scientific Study of International Relations: The Constructivist Approach

The orthodox and canonical narrative of the origins of international relations theory links it to the Great War. In the traditional narrative, according to José Ricardo Villanueva, the first generation of intellectuals specializing in international affairs belonged to a theoretical school known as idealism or utopianism -liberal-. In one of the reference works of this literature, Edward H. Carr stated in *Twentieth Years' Crisis, 1919-1939. An Introduction to the Study of International Relations* (1939) that in the utopian stage of the discipline, researchers "have paid little attention to the facts of reality or to analyses of cause and effect; rather, they have devoted themselves with enthusiasm to the elaboration of visionary projects". Similarly, Edward H. Carr associated those early internationalists with support tout court for the League of Nations (Villanueva, 2019: 196).

The discourse around a new era in international relations and the birth of international relations theory masked, in Barry Buzan and George Lawson's view, the presence and legacies of international thought from the late 19th century and the links to colonialism and racism (Buzan & Lawson, 2015: 52). This mythical narrative constructed from the consolidation of international relations theory in the United States after the Second World War would lead John M. Hobson to question certain dogmas of international relations theory: firstly, the revision of the supposed rupture generated by the birth of the theory of international relations and to vindicate its continuity and insertion with international studies prior to the Great War; to make visible, behind this silence on the racist, imperialist and ethnocentric components of the theory, the atmosphere of resistance in the peripheries with respect to the metropolises in a context of awareness of the decadence of the West; the enunciation of the imperialist dimension underlying the mandatary policy and the explicit imperialism of some of the liberal internationalists, such as Alfred Zimmern, John Hobson, Leonard Woolf, Henry N. Brailsford or Murray Butler; the questioning of the supposed predominance of liberal internationalism in international thought in the period between the two world wars; or the questioning of the very essence of the idealism-realism debate as the discipline's first great debate (Hobson, 2012: 133-135; and Sánchez Román, 2021).

In contrast to the traditional narrative that polarized all its interest in the birth of international relations theory based on political science, authors such as Torbjorn L. Knutsen (1997), Brian Schmidt (1998) and Lucian M. Asworth (2014) have highlighted in their work the more complex panorama surrounding international studies in the first third of the 20th century. In this sense, the gestation of international relations as a scientific discipline took place in a context shaped by the concurrence of different domains of social knowledge that had traditionally dealt with international issues - not only international law and diplomatic history, but also geography and geopolitics, diplomacy, anthropology and orientalism. Disciplines that concurred with all the baggage of Western social and international thought characteristic since the late 19th century - Eurocentrism, social Darwinism, organicism, racism, biopolitics embedded in eugenic policies or the patriarchal dimension of the map of social knowledge (Hobson, 2012: 133-181).

But what really lies behind the first great debate in the discipline? Is it a myth or a reality? And finally, where does imperialism fit into the genealogy of international studies?

One of the arguments put forward by revisionist historiography is the limited interactions between the so-called classical idealists and realists. Authors such as Peter Wilson (1998) and Cameron Thies (2012) deny the very existence of the debate. However, as José Ricardo Villanueva qualifies, the truth is that there were some interactions between these intellectuals and academics in the criticisms of Norman Angell, Alfred Zimmern, Arnold J. Toynbee, or Gilbert Murray to the work of E.H. Carr (Villanueva, 2019: 198-199).

Another problem, continues José Ricardo Villanueva, that derives from the traditional narrative stems from the ambiguity in the use of the term "idealist", since it is often used as a synonym for internationalism or liberal utopianism. Edward H. Carr judged that idealists paid scant attention to the facts of reality, that they dogmatically committed themselves to "visionary projects" such as the League of Nations, and that they ignored the importance of power in the study of international relations. In the light of contributions such as that made by Lucian Asworth (2006) it is "difficult to think that internationalists, who considered imperialism in their writings, could have ignored power and the facts of international reality" (Villanueva, 2019: 200-201). The construction of the liberal international order –the *pax anglosaxonica*- and the League of Nations itself can hardly be understood without the empires and the governance model of the British Empire and the theoretical contributions of experts such as Alfred Zimmern or Leonard Woolf, not to mention the projects of the League of Nations encouraged by Lord Philimore or Jan Smuts (Sánchez Román, 2021: 42-50).

In questioning the very nature and entity of the idealism *vs.* realism debate, John M. Hobson explores the gateways between the two formal poles. In this universe of intersection, consensus would crystallize around the hegemony of the West, the conviction of the superiority of the white man, the myth of progress and the identification of the superiority of the norm -positivism in international law- with the notion of civilization (Hobson, 2012: 135-136).

In José Ricardo Villanueva's assessment of the first great debate in the discipline, he concludes that the discussions were 'very limited' and that there was certainly another, more substantial debate, with a greater flow of exchanges and polarized around imperialism, which began in the early 20th century and lasted until 1935 (Villanueva, 2019: 203-208; and Sánchez Román, 2021: 14).

Analyzing the debate on imperialism from the perspective of international studies allows to enter a broader chronological perspective and to project a map in which the inertias and novelties in the international studies agenda can be better appreciated, taking the Great War as the equator. Brian Schmidt argues that 'although the antecedents of IR are typically identified with international law, diplomatic history, peace movements, moral philosophy, geography, and anthropology, revisionist historians have included colonial administration and the analysis of empire and imperialism' (Schmidt, 2019: 258). Authors such as William C. Olson and A.J.R. Groom (1991) argue that the discipline of international relations had its true beginnings with studies of imperialism rather than world order. Robert Vitalis (2015) would go so far as to argue that empire was indeed the framework in which international relations studies emerged in the United States and in accordance with the context imbued with concerns about empire, imperialism and racism. Symptomatic in this light is the fact that *The Journal of Race Development*, the first academic journal in the field, was renamed *Foreign Affairs* when it was sold to the Council on Foreign Relations in 1922. Brian Schmidt himself, together with David Long, in a paper published in 2005 emphasized the fact that imperialism and internationalism were 'paramount when the field - international relations - began to take recognizable shape in the early 20th century' (Schmidt, 2019: 258-259; and Long & Schmidt, 2005).

In 1904, the American Political Science Association, the discipline of choice from which international relations theory emerged in the United States, was created, appointing Paul S. Reinsch as chairman of the Section of Politics, who was an authority on colonialism and colonial administration. In the context of American tropical empire-building Paul S. Reinsch argued that the 'scientific study of colonial administration should have the practical effect of providing policymakers with the knowledge to design better colonial policies' (Schmidt, 2019: 259-260). In that paradigm of modernity, expressed in terms of the standard of Civilization of the white man and of the racist and patriarchal epistemological model on which imperialism was culturally based, there was no place for pan-Africanist critical approaches to the international order such as those emanating from the Howard School in the United States in the theories of W.E.B Du Bois and Alain Locke (Henderson, 2017: 492-510)

Counting on the precedent of the work of J.A. Hobson, the debate on imperialism, José Ricardo Villanueva points out, began in 1909 with the publication of Norman Angell's *The European Optical Illusion*, which would be republished the following year under the title *The Grand Illusion*. The controversy began with Henri N. Brailsford's review of the 1909 work, in which, along with his praise, he took issue with the assumption that wars did not bring gains to the victors. The socialist Karl Kautsky joined the controversy by rejecting the idea that imperialist wars did not bring economic gains. In 1919 Norman Angell argued that the cause of imperialism was not the capitalists, but nationalist ideas. The Great War introduced new elements into the debate in view of the very outcome of the war and its impact on the peripheries and the revolutionary cycle in Russia. The debate would involve Vladimir Lenin, Leon Trotsky and Harold Laski against the theses of Norman Angell and in the same vein would be staged the writings of Henri N. Brailsford in 1935 criticising the latter for ignoring the gains of the bourgeois class as a result of imperialism. The debate that would close in 1935 would be joined by Leonard Woolf, who would adopt a tempered position in the controversy (Villanueva, 2019: 204-208 y Burón & Redondo, 2022: 85-89).

The Permeability of Spanish Academia to the Gravity of Imperialism in International Studies

The classical study of international relations in Spain throughout the 19th century and the first half of the 20th century, as in other European and American academic and professional spheres, was based on the historicist tradition of diplomatic history and the dominance of international law. In the general framework of the revisionist debate on the birth of the discipline of international relations, the classic narrative in Spain is also shaped by the genetic pattern of the foundational launch of international relations theory, which in Spain's case would last until well after the Second World War.

From the end of the 19th century, says Celestino del Arenal, international studies would experience a great boom in Spain, definitively consolidating the acceptance of the expression "international relations" to designate inter-State relations, at the same time as diplomatic history would reach its full maturity.

However, the production of international law, despite its increase, "would add little, from the perspective of the scientific and autonomous development of International Relations" (Arenal, 1979: 26-27).

The greater preoccupation with international issues in the course of the inter-century was determined by a variety of reasons: the course of Spanish foreign policy itself, after the fin-de-siècle crisis and the redirection of Spain's international policy and position; the rediscovery of the doctrines of the classical theologians and jurists of the 16th century; a greater theoretical concern about the problem of war, in the light of international conflict -at the height of imperialism-, the reception of the classical doctrines of the just war and the very context of the International Conferences of The Hague of 1899 and 1907; and all this in the political-intellectual effervescence that characterized Regenerationism (Arenal, 197: 38-39).

Alongside international law, the other mainstay of international studies in Spain, as historiography has analyzed, is diplomatic history. In Juan Carlos Pereira's opinion, the international historical studies undertaken from the first third of the 19th century onwards were characterized: firstly, the contribution of historians not only to the development of the study of international relations, but also to that of international law; secondly, the pre-eminence given by historians to the study of bilateral relations, especially with Great Britain and France; thirdly, the close collaboration, "intentional or not, between jurists and historians in the elaboration of a documentary corpus of our diplomatic relations"; and finally, the elaboration of the first reflections on the conditioning factors in the elaboration and execution of Spanish foreign policy in the past and the need to incorporate new approaches in accordance with international reality (Pereira, 1987: 271; and other authors such as Antonio Moreno, Francisco Quintana, Susana Sueiro and José Luis Neila, among others, have expressed similar views).

The limited permeability of the historiography on international relations in Spain to the revisionist debate on the genealogy of international relations is due to a large extent to the delay with which the theory of international relations was implanted in Spain. Somehow the canonical account of the gestation of the discipline after the two world wars would contribute to the normalization of a foundational account that tended to accentuate Spanish exceptionalism. It would be essential, therefore, to review the narrative to insert it into its European and Western academic and intellectual references, especially its continental references and the effect that the growing inertia of the Americanization of knowledge would have after the Great War. A perspective already noticed in the recent works of Antonio Niño (Niño, 2022: 9-21). This revisionist approach must consequently lead to assess the gravity of imperialism in the Spanish foreign political culture since the end of the 19th century and its decisive presence in international studies in the academic field. An academic presence due more to the pragmatic needs of Spanish foreign policy and the African imperial project than to motivations derived from academic debate. The reasons are multiple, among them: the condition of Spain as a small power in the international arena, the fasting of a foreign policy defined by the governments and supported by public opinion, the primacy of the domestic conflict as a consequence of the convulsive internal life of the country or the unpopularity of the colonial wars.

The weight of international law and diplomatic history is also an essential part of the canonical narrative in Spain with respect to the panorama prior to the genealogy of the theory of international relations. The analysis of the genesis of international studies in the era of imperialism in Spain has not yet been approached from the perspectives raised in the revisionist debate on the origins of international studies. In this sense, it is essential, firstly, to provide an overview of the disciplines involved in international studies since the beginning of the 20th century, especially on the basis of the role and academic and institutional impact of the Instituto Libre de Enseñanza de las Carreras Diplomática y Consular y Centro de Estudios Marroquíes as an interdisciplinary forum. And secondly, an assessment of the presence of imperialism in political and academic concerns in the work of the aforementioned Institute.

Diplomacy as a theoretical and practical professional field in the development of foreign policy is indispensable for any approach to ways of looking at and analyzing international relations. The training of diplomats for the performance of their profession 'provides a privileged observatory for understanding changes in international relations and their perception by states insofar as such training is regulated by formal methods of selection and education with a state matrix' (Sanz Díaz, 2019: 285).

The creation in Spain of the Instituto Libre de Enseñanza de las Carreras Diplomática y Consular y Centro de Estudios Marroquíes in 1911 is a faithful reflection of the Regenerationism that permeated the modernisation initiatives undertaken by the Monarchy of Alfonso XIII and an echo of the institutionism that enveloped the educational atmosphere of Spain in the first third of the century. It was also a symptom of the situation itself and of the foreign policy challenges facing a small state that was trying to break out of its self-absorption and find its place in the international system. The prominence of imperialism in the debates and international thinking at the beginning of the century and in the Spanish foreign policy agenda would permeate the very conception of the new institution, devoting part of it to the training of specialists for colonial administration.

The creation of the Institute followed the outcome of the second Moroccan crisis, which was settled with the Franco-German agreement of November 1911 and in the wake of which France established the Protectorate in its area of Morocco in 1912. Madrid's reaction was actively aimed at claiming the rights acquired from the Franco-British exchange of notes of 1904 to establish a protectorate in its area, which would crystallize after the Franco-Spanish agreement of 27 November 1912 (Togores & Neila, 1993: 77).

In the 1880s, the Spanish government was inspired by the French model of the grand concours to determine access to diplomatic and consular careers. The only academic requirement to take the competitive examination around 1900 was a university degree in Civil or Administrative Law, but at the beginning of the century it seemed clear that 'law studies, as the only educational credential for young candidates for the career, did not offer the necessary level to achieve the indispensable degree for future civil servants in the international arena' (Sanz Díaz, 2019: 287). In 1910, in his work *Orientación internacional de España*, the politician and legal scholar Rafael María de Labra mentioned the favourable reception that the Minister of State, Manuel Allendesalazar, gave to his recommendation to create a special school for diplomats and consuls, in which studies on Latin America, Portugal and North Africa would be privileged. In 1901 it was published his work *La crisis colonial de España (1869-1898). Estudios de política palpitante y discursos parlamentarios*. His political and intellectual activity was aimed at promoting public awareness of Spain's international and colonial problems and at "laying the foundations of what Spain's policy should be if it was to emerge from the critical situation in which it had found itself since the crisis at the end of the century". The path towards these objectives inevitably required the creation of centres for international studies, in which, alongside international law, other sciences related to international society would be addressed, "as the only way to be able to understand it and develop an international policy".

The Royal Decree of 21 December 1911 created the Instituto Libre de Enseñanza de las Carreras Diplomática y Consular y Centro de Estudios Marroquíes, by virtue of which a "vacuum" in official education was filled, in whose establishments "the scientific subjects indispensable to the performance of the aforementioned careers, to the correct appreciation of international questions and to the knowledge of the geography, history and political and legal institutions of the Muslim peoples" would be studied" [1].

The Institute's activities were located at the Real Academia de Jurisprudencia y Legislación. From its foundation, the Institute was conceived as a centre for the training of the monarchy's civil service elites, who were to work in three areas: diplomatic, consular and colonial administration, but it would also become a scientific institution dedicated to the dissemination and study of international relations (Sanz Díaz, 2019: 288; and Togores & Neila, 1993: 77).

The real impact of the teachings imparted at the Institute was limited, insofar as passing through its classrooms was never a compulsory requirement for access to diplomatic and consular careers or to carry out functions in the colonial administration (Togores & Neila, 1993: 90-102). Despite all this and the discreet numbers of students in the course of the 1920s, it consolidated its prestige as a specialized training body for future members of the diplomatic and consular careers. The modernization and adaptation initiatives undertaken by the Dictatorship of Primo de Rivera in the foreign administration also reached the Institute, whose regulations were reformed in 1926 and later in 1929 on the occasion of the merger of the diplomatic and consular careers undertaken in 1928. These changes made it necessary to modify the curricula in an attempt to maintain:

(...) as a whole and in its general lines, the curriculum that had been in force until now, since it should not be forgotten that the Institute was not created for the limited and exclusive purpose of preparing candidates for Diplomacy and Consulship, but for the establishment of courses related to the development of Spain's international interests and which are not studied, or are studied for a different purpose, in other educational centers[2].

The end of the war in Morocco opened up new expectations for the colonial administration in Morocco, which is why the Governing Board of the Real Academia de Jurisprudencia y Legislación sent a proposal to the president of the Civil Directory to ensure that the studies being pursued at the Institute would be recognized for access to the colonial administration[3].

The decline of the center, renamed after the last reform as the Instituto Diplomático y Centro de Estudios Marroquíes, was largely due to the opposition to the dictatorship of some of the members of the Real Academia de Jurisprudencia y Legislación. In 1929 the dictatorship acted against the Royal Academy, "the seat of rebelliousness and political passion", dissolving the Governing Board and imposing an internal executive committee. The Institute's activities were temporarily suspended. The fact is that activity was never to return to normal in the wake of the final crisis of the Monarchy and the institutional and training initiatives undertaken by the Republic from 1931 onwards.

The teaching map that took shape in the successive curricula from the foundation of the Institute focused on three areas: the broad field of the study of international issues, professional qualification for the development of the "different applications or requirements" in the performance of diplomatic and consular functions and, finally, training geared to the exercise of colonial administration in Morocco.

From the academic year 1913-1914, the academic year in which the centre began to function fully, the syllabuses were divided into three sections - Diplomatic, Consular and Moroccan Studies. The subjects taught were: Political history of Europe since the fall of Napoleon and of America since independence; Social and political evolution of Asian states in the 19th and 20th centuries; Universal economic and mercantile geography; Progress of contemporary international, public and private law; Geography and history of Morocco; Spanish and foreign colonisation; and Comparative customs and transport legislation. These subjects were studied at greater length and in greater depth depending on their place in the curriculum. The Centre for Moroccan Studies offered the following subjects in its own right: Geography and history of Morocco, Legal institutions of Muslim peoples and especially of the Moroccan Empire; Systems of colonization in Africa; and Arabic language, both vulgar and literary (Togores & Neila, 1993: 87).

The Regulations of May 1917 modified the curriculum in order to adapt it to the syllabus of the competitive examinations for diplomatic and consular careers, and to adapt it to the transformations and the impact that the Great War was having on international relations. In the new teaching design, two of the issues of priority attention at the Centre - America and Morocco - would increase their presence with independent subjects in Contemporary American History and two common subjects in the three sections, apart from the courses in the Moroccan Studies section, on the Geography and History of Morocco and on the organization of the Spanish protectorate, in comparison with the systems of colonization in Africa. In the new plan, the presence of economic studies would be maintained with the course on Universal Economic and Mercantile Geography for the first two sections, but in the second year of the consular section it was replaced by a new subject, Special Studies in the Economic Geography of Spain, aimed specifically at the new consuls. In the field of diplomatic history, a History of Spain's international treaties from 1815 replaced the old subject on the Progress of International Law. The respective sections included courses on diplomatic law and consular law. Novel subjects, such as the impact of the domestic politics of states on international politics and vice versa, trade or the financial penetration of the American republics by European powers, already appeared in the curricula of a historical nature (Togores & Neila, 1993: 98-100).

The pillars of international studies were primarily international law and diplomatic history and the history of treaties. Interest in international law was already reflected in the 1913 curriculum in the subject History of International Law, with a special focus on Spain's treaties and diplomatic relations from 1815 onwards. It is worth remembering that from 1883 - as María Victoria López Cordón states - the study of international law, both public and private, began to spread to all Spanish universities and "new ideas penetrated from its hand", including the ideas and humanitarian sentiment of the law of nations towards the search for peace through arbitration. The Spanish presence at the 1907 Hague Conference was more active both within the conference and in public opinion (López Cordón, 1982: 709). This presence was mainly mediated by Spain's Mediterranean policy interests.

After the Great War and during the dictatorship of Primo de Rivera, the expectations raised by the League of Nations as a useful platform for the pursuit of Spanish foreign policy objectives stimulated the strengthening of an internationalist legal education adapted to the needs of multilateral diplomacy and the new framework of international relations. The 1929 reform would ultimately complete the emphasis on international law and the organization of international society through subjects such as International Law and History of Treaties, and World Political and Diplomatic Organization (Togores & Neila, 1993: 107-109).

The other pillar was historical studies and, in particular, diplomatic history. The history taught at the Institute had a practical purpose, insofar as it had to provide knowledge of the background to international issues in order to guide a coherent and effective national foreign policy, as the historian of diplomacy Jerónimo Becker formulated in his 1925 lecture - "Causes of the sterility of Spain's foreign action"- at the Real Academia de Jurisprudencia y Legislación. He was undoubtedly the person who best illustrated the scholarly and positive component of diplomatic history in Spain and the intellectual and political commitment, shared by other intellectuals of his generation and by the legal and historiographical tradition itself, of concern and denunciation of the shortcomings of Spanish foreign policy. Between the 1890s and the date of his death in 1925, he undertook a rigorous and extensive study of the diplomatic history of Spain. In this respect, his work has three strands. Firstly, his interest in America. Secondly, his concern, as a member of the Liga Africanista Española and secretary of the Junta Superior de Historia y Geografía de Marruecos, with the question of Morocco and Spanish penetration, which would basically bear fruit in two books: *España en Marruecos. Sus relaciones diplomáticas durante el siglo XIX* (1903) and *Historia de Marruecos. Apuntes para la historia de la penetración europea y principalmente de la española en el Norte de África [Spain in Morocco. Its diplomatic relations during the nineteenth century* (1903) and *History of Morocco. Notes for the history of European penetration and mainly Spanish penetration in North Africa]* (1915). And lastly, the work dedicated to the study of the history of Spanish foreign policy.

Other speakers at the same forum, such as Rafael Altamira in 1916, R. Spottorno in 1921 and C.A. Goicoechea in 1922, coincided in calling for a precise definition of foreign policy objectives. After the World War, Rafael Altamira, who taught Contemporary Political History of America at the Institute, advocated in his writings that the "international spirit" should be included in history texts and in the teaching of history, making room for contemporary knowledge of the League of Nations and pacifism.

To these pillars in the study of international relations, geographical and economic studies would be added as a complement to the training of students at the Institute. The teaching of geography, argues Carlos Sanz, was "directly linked to the regenerationist impulse that was encouraged at the Institute". This 'drive made the protectorate over Morocco a vital necessity for Spain'. The Centro de Estudios Marroquíes was to 'alleviate the lack of expert knowledge on African issues in government, administration and public opinion' (Sanz Díaz, 2019: 294). The permeability of Orientalist discourse in an Africanist key was thus channelled into the generic framework of international studies based on the needs arising from the colonial enterprise in Morocco. In this sense, the Instituto Libre de Enseñanza de las Carreras Diplomática y Consular y Centro de Estudios Marroquíes included subjects *ad hoc* to colonial action, in particular geography, which at this time was strongly influenced by Ratzellian political and determinist geography and by the conception of the state as a "territorial organism" - from which the notion of "vital space" coined by G. von Treitsche would derive. The influence of Ratzellian thought in Spain would crystallize in the development of an embryonic geopolitical thinking which, from the last decades of the 19th century, would provide a legitimizing discourse for colonial practice, strengthened by the regenerationist environment (Reguera, 1990: 79-104).

Ratzellian geopolitics was incorporated into the teaching of the Institute through the teaching of Eloy Bullón y Fernández, who began to teach at the Centre in 1916. Eloy Bullón had held the chair of Political and Descriptive Geography at the University of Madrid since 1907 and was the forerunner of a whole generation of geographers such as Gonzalo de Reparaz, E. Huguet del Villar and L. Martín Echevarría, whose works "justified with geographical and political arguments with Ratzellian roots the Spanish colonial penetration in Africa" (Sanz Díaz, 2019: 294).

Finally, the presence of economic studies responded to the very adaptation of diplomacy to the evolution of international relations. The growing presence of economic and commercial subjects in the curricula reflected the increasing weight of these subjects in the daily work of diplomatic and consular representatives. The growing interpenetration between economic and diplomatic interests, as well as between the domestic and international spheres, had influenced the 1928 reform of the diplomatic and consular careers (Sanz Díaz, 2019: 295-296).

The Instituto Libre de Enseñanza de las Carreras Diplomática y Consular y Centro de Estudios Marroquíes was, likewise, a centre oriented to accommodate scientific studies and promote the dissemination of international studies among public opinion. For its founding fathers, especially Rafael María de

Labra, the regeneration of the country required the encouragement and dissemination of international knowledge and the awakening of public interest and awareness. In 1901, Rafael María de Labra had "vehemently defended the free and public discussion of foreign policy issues, and even diplomatic affairs, thus anticipating one of the elements of the 'new diplomacy' formed after the War of 14" (Sanz Díaz, 2019: 294). Within the Institute, both aims would be channeled through the library of the Real Academia de Jurisprudencia y Legislación, whose facilities were expanded to increase the capacity of reading places with the intention of attracting politicians and diplomats in need of a specialized library. The confluence of publications of a historical, geographical, literary, economic, legal or travel nature would favour an "environment conducive to the circulation of ideas and intercommunication between different branches of knowledge". The Real Academia de Jurisprudencia y Legislación was to become one of, if not the most active center for the promotion of international studies in Spain until the 1920s. The impact of the World War, as in other European and American states, would lead to an unusual interest in the causes of war and the peaceful conduct of international relations, especially from a legal and moral point of view. In 1918, shortly after the signing of the armistice with Germany, a special war library was established at the Real Academia de Jurisprudencia y Legislación.

At the same time, the Real Academia de Jurisprudencia y Legislación organised a series of lectures with the aim of disseminating knowledge and interest in international affairs. From 1918 onwards, the Institute itself published the texts of these lectures, inaugural lectures and other texts in order to multiply their impact and their dissemination in public opinion.

The syllabuses, the teaching staff and the programming of the lectures, as well as the library of the Real Academia de Jurisprudencia y Legislación, show the close connection between foreign policy and colonial policy, whose convergence planes would be staged in Mediterranean policy or, to be more rigorous, in Moroccan policy. The incidence of Spanish Orientalism, specifically Africanism, is a fundamental cultural construction for understanding international studies from the perspective of the Institute and Spanish foreign policy in the first half of the 20th century.

Spanish Africanism and the New Imperial Adventure of the Spain of Alfonso XIII

The dimension of imperialism in foreign policy and international thought, sanctioned in the very nature and reasons that led to the creation of the Instituto Libre de Enseñanza de las Carreras Diplomática y Consular y Centro de Estudios Marroquíes, cannot be dissociated from the textual force of Spanish Africanism.

Spanish Orientalism has certain specificities, as underlined by Edward W. Said himself, as a consequence of the extremely complex and dense relations between Spain and Islam in historical and geographical terms. Spanish Orientalism, unlike that of other European powers - Britain, France or Germany - does not manifest itself exclusively as an imperial relationship. The Orient, in these states, is created by "conquerors, administrators, scholars, travellers, artists, novelists and poets" - it is "something that is 'outside'". In Spain, by contrast, the imperial dimension - of the outsider - that undoubtedly exists and nourishes much of the culture emanating from Orientalism is interwoven by the historical fact that "Islam and Spanish culture inhabit each other rather than confronting each other belligerently" (Saïd, 2002: 9-10).

This double dimension of Orientalism in the Spanish case would shift the very sphere of cultural production and even political culture towards the East - in particular towards the Arab world and the Mediterranean. The 'Spanish colonial experience in northwest Africa had a limited impact on the development of Arab studies, which remained focused on the study of its 'domestic Orient''. Unlike in France and Britain, 'Spanish university Arabists did not become actively involved in the colonial adventure'. It would be the Africanists who, linked to the projection towards the near Mediterranean-African overseas, would become the architects of the production of most of the studies on North Africa - basically Morocco and Western Sahara - (Hernando de Larramendi & Azaola, 2006: 87). The official attitude of the Spanish administration influenced, in the opinion of Vicente Moga Romero, the split between 'academic Arabism and the more militant Africanism with an ideological wedge centred on ethnic and religious determinism'. A legacy that would remain unchanged for decades (Moga Romero, 2008: 141).

Africanism, as the term began to be used in the mid-19th century, would refer to those who, either personally or within the framework of institutions or opinion groups, claimed "the existence of vital interests for Spain south of the Strait of Gibraltar - strategic, economic, historical and even moral - and advocated decisive action, both on the part of the state and private initiative, in defence and promotion of these interests" (Villalobos, 2004: 55).

Spanish Africanism would be the sociological nucleus around which a political discourse would be articulated, as an expression of the geoculture of domination characteristic of Orientalism. Africanism, the "star of Spanish Orientalism" - in the expression of Víctor Morales Lezcano - developed in the second half of the 19th century, spurred on by the colonialism and European imperialism of the time.

The French presence in Northwest Africa constituted the 'triggering factor of Spanish Africanism, that is, of the Hispanic attempt to safeguard its historical rights and the security of its southern border with the neighbouring continent' (Morales Lezcano, 1993: 20). In the context of the defeat of the Sultan of Morocco by France at the Battle of Isly in 1844, Spain took advantage of the situation to occupy the Chafarinas Islands in 1848 and colonise the cities of Ceuta and Melilla - the 'Gateway to Africa' - which had been conquered three centuries earlier. That incipient Africanism around 1850 was of the opinion that a 'timely intervention in North Africa could guarantee the security and image of Spain, which had become a small state within the European system inherited from the Congress of Vienna and the readjustments it underwent until 1870'. With France in Algeria, Morocco became the focus of Spanish Africanism's expectations, spurred on by the African War of 1859-1860. Throughout the second half of the 19th century:

(...) Spanish colonial circles tried to alert governments, material interests and public opinion in the country to the ineluctable consummation of the partition of North Africa in the short or medium term. Legal titles, historical allegations, the imperatives of security and defence of the peninsular territory and the waters of the Strait of Gibraltar from the presidios (Ceuta, in particular), the need to re-establish a foreign trade weakened since the loss of the Empire in America, and a diffuse conviction of a civilising power in Africa, fed the pages of the current of opinion known as Spanish Africanism at the end of the century (Affayi & Gerraoui, 2005: 52).

The Spanish 'neo-colonial' lobby, in Sebastian Balfour's view, was not a clique or an organized pressure group like the French colonial party, but a range of interests promoting the penetration of Spanish capitalism in Africa, and especially in Morocco. An Africanism sponsored by prominent members of the regenerations intellectual elites such as Joaquín Costa and Ángel Ganivet, journalists such as Gonzalo de Reparaz, and liberal politicians such as the Count of Romanones and José Canalejas, as well as from associationist platforms – the Sociedad Geográfica de Madrid (1876), the Asociación Española para la Exploración de Áfricaca (1877) and others created later such as the Sociedad Española de Africanistas y Colonialistas (1883) - (Morales Lezcano, 1990: 17-34; Rodríguez Esteban, 1996; and Pedraz Marcos, 2000). After a certain languishing of Africanism, the redirection of Spanish foreign policy at the beginning of the century and the privileged role of the Mediterranean would shake up the ecosystem of Spanish Africanism, in the light of the publication of works such as Gonzalo de Reparaz *España en África*, the creation in 1904 of a Centro de Arabistas with a view to the action that Spain was to take in North Africa, and the appearance in 1912 of the Liga Africanista. To these should be added the activity of financial, industrial and commercial interest groups, such as Catalan industrialists, shipping companies, insurance companies attracted by the potential business of the Rif mines and the construction of infrastructures. These groups would act close to the aforementioned associations and would promote the holding of Africanist congresses - four between 1907 and 1910 - to unite the different pressure groups. They defended a typically positivist program of peaceful penetration, somewhere between enlightened liberalism and social Darwinism (Balfour, 2007: 9; and Neila, 2011: 88-112).

Spanish Orientalism -Africanism- would codify a discourse through which Spain would project an imperialism, consented to by the great powers -Britain and France- and through which its new incardination in the international system was staged. Based on the superiority of European/Western civilization, Spain projected, as another axis of its regeneration, its convinced civilizational superiority over the nearby African overseas territories (Martín Corrales, 2002: 24).

The dramatic start of Spanish penetration into Morocco from 1909 onwards and the successive military disasters of that year and of 1921 in Annual exacerbated social unrest and highlighted the unpopularity of the war in Africa. A literature would emerge, often based on the authors' own Moroccan experience, critical of the Spanish presence and activity in Morocco, such as the writings of Giménez Caballero *Las notas marruecas* (1922), Giménez Fernández, author of *El blocao*, or the best-known texts of Ramón J. Sender *Imán* (1931) and Arturo Barea *La forja de un rebelde* (1946) (Morales Lezcano, 1993: 67-69).

In the first decades of the 20th century, the "unfolding of the textual forces of Spanish Africanism" would take place. In the course of these years, works would be published that would allow on the one hand, an approach to the unknown Morocco, such as those of Jerónimo Becker and R. Fernández de Castro, and on the other, a typology of works that "stage the codification of the colonial imaginary. During the first third of the century, as illustrated in the excellent study by Eloy Martínez Corrales, the official press and the spokesmen of colonization in Spain and the Spanish part of Morocco gradually took on board the imaginary generated by Africanism, in which a primitive and savage image, impregnated with paternalism, would converge. The image of "sympathy for the 'Moritos'" would derive in the heat of military penetration into a negative, cruel, savage and treacherous image, accentuated by the military disasters of 1909 and 1921 (Martín Corrales, 2002: 99-144).

The Africanist sector of the army tended to occupy a more prominent role in Africanism, as the military solution expanded the army's sphere of action in the colonial enterprise. Within the framework of the tragic military, political, economic and human conditions of the occupation of the Protectorate, the creation in Ceuta in 1924 of the *Revista de Tropas Coloniales. Propagadora de estudios hispanoafricanos*, founded under the direction of Gonzalo Queipo de Llano, would channel the consolidation of the guidelines for action and the ideology of the Africanist military. Its main supporters were, in addition to Queipo himself, Millán Astray and Francisco Franco, who would direct the magazine in its second stage from 1925, since then *called África. Revista de Tropas Coloniales.*

SOLUTIONS AND RECOMMENDATIONS

The revisionist approach projected in these pages from a constructivist perspective, inspired by recent debates on the genealogy of international studies, has made it possible to paint a broader horizon in the cartography of international studies in early twentieth-century Spain. In this way, the gravity of international law and diplomatic history pre-eminent in the canonical narrative is inserted into a more complex panorama in which, without questioning their centrality, they share a more complex academic space in which other disciplines such as economics or geography and geopolitics converge, in addition to administration studies.

This research has made the centrality of imperialism in international studies visible at the academic level. Studies on Spain's foreign policy at the beginning of the 20th century and institutional initiatives in a regenerationist vein, such as the creation of the Instituto Libre de Estudios de las Carreras Diplomática y Consular y Centro de Estudios Marroquíes created in 1911, always valued the colonial component and the new imperial enterprise as a fundamental factor in Spain's international position. However, the relevance of imperialism from an interdisciplinary perspective in international studies and its connections with such essential cultural and political platforms as Africanism had not been appreciated. This new perspective is relevant for the reconstruction of the academic and institutional ecosystem in the genealogy of international studies in Spain.

FUTURE RESEARCH DIRECTIONS

The approaches developed in this text are part of a broader research project whose aim is to analyze the genealogy of international studies in Spain and its participation in intellectual cooperation in the international system of Versailles after the Great War. This research is part of the Research Group "Conflicts and international relations in today's world. Historical analysis", approved by the Research Commission of the Universidad Autónoma de Madrid on 11 December 2018 and under the direction of Dr. Álvaro Soto Carmona (Universidad Autónoma de Madrid).

CONCLUSION

In the light of the research presented in these pages, the validity of the fundamental hypothesis on which this work is based has been fully demonstrated.

The analysis of the genealogy of international studies in Spain since the beginning of the 20th century required a look in a very similar sense to that projected from the debates on the origins of the theory of international relations by revising the canonical account of its birth. This debate not only questioned the first great debate in theory - idealism v. realism - but also reclaimed pre-Great War inertias in order to reconstruct the academic cartography of international studies. It is within this framework that imperialism emerged as the first major interdisciplinary debate in international studies. A founding debate that illustrated the multidisciplinary nature of international studies – international law, diplomatic history, geopolitics, anthropology and economics, among the preeminent areas. An academic framework that promoted an epistemology of domination based on Western ethnocentrism, racism and patriarchy on which imperialism and the modern discourse around the civilizing mission would be based.

Spanish historiography, although it is true that in the works of authors such as Celestino del Arenal and Antonio Niño some prisms of this debate such as the Americanisation of international studies are raised, lacks an approach that reconstructs the cartography of international studies from the beginning of the century. This text, based on an analysis of the nature and activity of the Instituto Libre de Enseñanza de las Carreras Diplomática y Consular y Centro de Estudios Marroquíes, has contributed to showing the interdisciplinary nature of international studies, going beyond the gravity of international law and diplomatic history to highlight other disciplines of knowledge such as economics, geography and geopolitics, and colonial administration studies.

The importance of imperialism in international relations at the end of the 19th century and the first half of the 20th century can be seen in the leading role played by the Mediterranean and Morocco in Spain's integration into the international system after the fin-de-siècle crisis. This research makes the protagonist of imperialism visible in the interdisciplinary cartography of international studies through the activity of the aforementioned Institute. There is no doubt that Spanish intellectuals and academics did not participate in the formalized debate on imperialism, nor was the possibility of a science of imperial relations contemplated in any way, but it is indisputable that imperialism was a central foreign policy concern in political and academic circles. The academic work carried out by these academics was basically oriented towards the needs of Spain's foreign policy after the end of the century crisis and to promote international awareness in the Spanish political class.

And lastly, the impact of Spanish Africanism in the context of imperialism and the search for a new place in the international system after the crisis of 1898 would be profound and constant in an institution in which one of its fundamental tasks was precisely the intellectual and professional preparation of the managers of the new North African imperial adventure.

REFERENCES

Affaya, N., & Gerraoui, D. (2005). *La imagen de España en Marruecos [The image of Spain in Morocco].* CIDOB.

Altamira, R. (1916). *Cuestiones internacionales: España, América y los Estados Unidos [International issues: Spain, America and the United States.].* Jaime Ratés.

Altamira, R. (1932). Observaciones sobre la realidad internacional presente (writting in 1925) [Observations on the present international reality (writing in 1925).]. In R. Altamira (Ed.), *Cuestiones internacionales y de pacifism [International issues and pacifism.].* C. Bermejo.

Angell, N. (1913). *The Great Illusion.* G.P. Putnam & Sons.

Arenal, C. del (1979). *La teoría de las relaciones internacionales en España [The theory of international relations in Spain.].* International Law Association (Sección Española).

Asworth, L. M. (2006). Where are the idealists in interwar international relations? *Review of International Studies, 32*(2), 291–308. doi:10.1017/S0260210506007030

Asworth, L. M. (2014). *A History of international thought. From the origins of the modern state to academic international relations.* Routledge. doi:10.4324/9781315772394

Balfour, S. (2007) España, Marruecos y las grandes potencias, 1898-1914 [Spain, Morocco and the great powers, 1898-1914]. In Gómez-Ferrer, G. & Sánchez, R. (eds.) Modernizar España. Proyectos de reforma y apertura internacional (1898-1914) [Modernize Spain. Reform projects and international opening (1898-1914)] (pp. 143-151). Biblioteca Nueva.

Becker, J. (1903) *España en Marruecos. Sus relaciones diplomáticas durante el siglo XIX [Spain in Morocco. Their diplomatic relations during the 19th century]*.

Becker, J. (1905). *Historia de Marruecos. Apuntes para la historia de la penetración europea y principalmente de la española en el Norte de África [History of Morocco. Notes for the history of European penetration and mainly of the Spanish in North Africa]*. Jaime Ratés.

Becker, J. (1925). *Causas de la esterilidad de la acción exterior de España [Causes of the sterility of Spain's foreign action]*. J. Cosano.

Brailsford, H. N. (1914). *The war of steel and gold. A study of the armed peace*. G. Bell & Sons Ltd.

Brailsford, H. N. (1917). *A League of Nations*. MacMillan.

Brailsford, H.N. (1935) War and Capitalism. *The New Statesman and Nation*.

Burón Díaz, M., & Redondo Carrero, E. (2022). *Imperios e imperialismo. Orden internacional, historia global y pensamiento politico [Empires and imperialism. International order, global history and political thought.]*. Síntesis.

Buzzan, B., & Lawson, G. (2015). *The Global Transformation. History, Modernity and the Making of International Relations*. Cambridge University Press. doi:10.1017/CBO9781139565073

Carr, E.H. (1939) *Twentieth Years' Crisis, 1919-1939. An Introduction to the Study of International Relations*, (consulted edition: *La crisis de los veinte años, 1919-1939 [The twenty year crisis 1919-1939)*. Madrid, Los Libros de la Catarata, 2004).

de Reparaz, R. G. (1924). *Política de España en África [Politics of Spain and Africa]*. Espasa-Calpe.

Goicoechea, C. A. (1922). *La política internacional de España en noventa años (1814-1904) [Spain's international policy in ninety years (1814-1904).]*. Ed. Reus.

Henderson, E. A. (2017). The Revolution will not be theorized: Du Bois, Locke and the Howard School's challenge to White Supremacist IR Theory. Millenium *Journal of International Relations*, *45*(3), 452–510.

Hernando de Larramendi, M., & Azaola, B. (2006) Los estudios sobre el Mundo Árabe y Mediterráneo contemporáneo en España [Studies on the contemporary Arab and Mediterranean world in Spain] (pp. 87-147). In Investigando el Mediterráneo, monografías [Studies on the contemporary Arab and Mediterranean world in Spain]. CIDOB.

Hobson, J. A. (1902). *Imperialism. A study*. Nisbet.

Hobson, J. M. (2012). *The Eurocentric conception of world politics. Western international theory 1760-2010*. Cambridge University Press. doi:10.1017/CBO9781139096829

Huguet, E. (1969). El factor geográfico y el gran problema de España [The geographical factor and the great problem of Spain]. In *Velarde Fuentes, J. Lecturas de economía Española [Spanish economy readings]* (pp. 82–98). Gredos.

Knutsen, T. J. (1997). *A History of International Relations Theory*. Manchester University Press.

Labra, R.M. (1901). La crisis colonial de España (1869-1898) [The colonial crisis of Spain (1869-1898)]. *Estudios de política palpitante y discursos parlamentarios [Studies of throbbing politics and parliamentary speeches]*.

Labra, R.M. de (1910) *La orientación internacional de España [The international orientation of Spain]*. Tip. de Alfredo Alonso.

Laski, H.J. (1935) Capitalism and War. *The New Statesman and Nation*.

Lenin, V. (1917). *Imperialism, the Highest Stage of Capitalism*. Foreign Languages Press.

Long, G., & Schmidt, B. (dirs.) (2005) Imperialism and Internationalism in the Discipline of International Relations. State University of New York Press.

López Cordón, Mª.V. (1982). España en las Conferencias de La Haya de 1899 y 1907 [Spain at the Hague Conferences of 1899 and 1907]. *Revista de Estudios Internacionales, 3*(3), 703–756.

Martín Corrales, E. (2002) La imagen del magrebí en España. Una perspectiva histórica. Siglos XIX-XX [The image of the North African in Spain. A historical perspective. 19th-20th centuries]. Bellaterra.

Martín Echevarría, L. (1937). *Geografía de España [Geography of Spain]* (Vols. 1–3). Labor.

Moga Romero, V. (2008) La cuestión marroquí en la escritura africanista. Una aproximación bibliográfica y editorial española al conocimiento del norte de Marruecos (1859-2006) [The Moroccan question in Africanist writing. A Spanish bibliographical and editorial approach to the knowledge of northern Morocco (1859-2006)].Bellaterra.

Morales Lezcano, V. (1990). El Norte de África, estrella del Orientalismo español [North Africa, star of Spanish Orientalism.]. *AWRAQ*, anejo al v. XI, 17-34

Morales Lezcano, V. (1993). *España y el mundo árabe: imágenes cruzadas [Spain and the Arab world: crossed images]*. AECI.

Moreno, A. (2001) La historia de las relaciones internacionales y de la política exterior Española [The history of international relations and Spanish foreign policy.]. In Pereira, J.C. (ed.) La historia de las relaciones internacionales [The history of International Relations], Ayer, 42, 71-96.

Neila, J. L. (2007). La historia de las relaciones internacionales en España: Un marco interpretative [The history of international relations in Spain: An interpretive framework.]. *Estudios de Historia de España, IX*, 177–212.

Neila, J. L. (2011). *España y el Mediterráneo en el siglo XX. De los acuerdos de Cartagena al proceso de Barcelona [Spain and the Mediterranean in the 20th century. From the Cartagena agreements to the Barcelona process]*. Sílex.

Niño, A. (2009) Uso y abuso de las relaciones culturales en la política internacional [Use and abuse of cultural relations in international politics]. In NIÑO, A. (ed.) La ofensiva cultural norteamericana durante la Guerra Fría [The American cultural offensive during the Cold War] Ayer, n. 75(3), 25-61.

Niño, A. (2022). Historiografía de las relaciones internacionales españolas en democracia [Historiography of Spanish international relations in democracy]. In *Ortíz Heras, M. & González, D.A. (coords.) La transición exterior. La asignatura pendiente de la democratización [The outer transition. The unfinished business of democratization]* (pp. 3–34). Comares Historia.

Olson, W. C., & Groom, A. J. R. (1991). International relations then and now: origins and trends in interpretation. HarperCollins.

Pedraz Marcos, A. (2000). *Quimeras de África. La Sociedad Española de Africanistas y Colonialistas. El colonialismo español de finales del siglo XIX [Chimeras of Africa. The Spanish Society of Africanists and Colonialists. Spanish colonialism at the end of the 19th century].* Ediciones Polifemo.

Pereira, J. C. (1987). Reflexiones sobre la historia de las relaciones internacionales y la política exterior Española [Reflections on the history of international relations and Spanish foreign policy.]. *Cuadernos de Historia Moderna y Contemporánea*, (8), 269–290.

Quintana, F. (1996). La historia de las relaciones internacionales en España: apuntes para un balance historiográfico [The history of international relations in Spain: notes for a historiographical balance]. In *Comisión Española de Historia de las Relaciones Internacionales La Historia de las Relaciones Internacionales: una visión desde España [Spanish Commission for the History of International Relations The History of International Relations: a vision from Spain]* (pp. 9–65). CEHRI-Ministerio de Asuntos Exteriores-Ministerio de Educación y Ciencia.

Reguera, A. T. (1990). Orígenes del pensamiento geopolítico en España. Una primera aproximación [Origins of geopolitical thought in Spain. A first approximation.]. *Documents d'Analisi Geografica*, (17), 79–104.

Rodríguez Esteban, J. A. (1996). *Geografía y colonialismo. La Sociedad Geográfica de Madrid (1876-1936) [Geography and colonialism. The Geographical Society of Madrid (1876-1936).].* Universidad Autónoma de Madrid Ediciones.

Saïd, E. W. (2002). *Orientalismo.* Debolsillo.

Sánchez Román, J. A. (2021). *La Sociedad de Naciones y la reinvención del imperialismo liberal [The League of Nations and the reinvention of liberal imperialism.].* Marcial Pons Historia.

Sanz Díaz, C. (2019). Relaciones internacionales y formación para la diplomacia en torno a la Primera Guerra Mundial: un estudio de caso [International relations and training for diplomacy around the First World War: a case study.]. In Lozano Vázquez, A., Sarquís Ramírez, D.J., Villanueva Lira, Jorge, D. ¿Cien años de relaciones internacionales? Disciplinariedad y revisionism [One hundred years of international relations? Disciplinarity and revisionism] (pp. 285–299). Siglo XXI.

Schmidt, B. (1998). *The Political discourse of anarchy. A disciplinary history of international relations.* SUNY Press.

Schmidt, B. (2019). Revisando la historia temprana de las relaciones internacionales: imperialismo, colonialismo y raza [Revisiting the early history of international relations: imperialism, colonialism, and race]. In Lozano Vázquez, A., Sarquís Ramírez, D.J., Villanueva Lira, Jorge, D. ¿Cien años de relaciones internacionales? Disciplinariedad y revisionism [One hundred years of international relations? Disciplinarity and revisionism] (pp. 250–264). Siglo XXI.

Spottorno, R. (1921). *Consideraciones generales y de carácter histórico acerca de la Diplomacia [General and historical considerations about Diplomacy.].* Ed. Reus.

Sueiro, S. (2004) La historia de las relaciones internacionales en España [The history of international relations in Spain]. Un balance. Tendencia actuales y perspectivas de future [A balance. Current trends and future prospects.]. In Rémond, R.-Tusell J.-Pellistrandi, B.-Sueiro, S. Hacer la historia del siglo XX [Making 20th century history] (pp. 95-118). Biblioteca Nueva (UNED).

Thies, C. (2021). Myth, half-truth, reality or strategy? In C. Thies (Ed.), *International relations and the first great debate* (pp. 118–132). Routledge.

Togores, L. E., & Neila, J. L. (1993). *La Escuela Diplomática: cincuenta años de servicio al Estado (1942-1992) [The Diplomatic School: fifty years of service to the State (1942-1992).].* Escuela Diplomática.

Villalobos, F. (2004). El sueño colonial: Las guerras de España en Marruecos [The colonial dream: Spain's wars in Morocco]. *Ariel.*

Villanueva, J. R. (2019). El primer gran debate en relaciones internacionales: ¿mito disciplinario? [The first great debate in international relations: disciplinary myth?] In *Lozano Vázquez, A., Sarquís Ramírez, D.J., Villanueva Lira, Jorge, D. ¿Cien años de relaciones internacionales? Disciplinariedad y revisionism [One hundred years of international relations? Disciplinarity and revisionism]* (pp. 195–211). Siglo XXI.

Vitalis, R. (2015). *White world order, black power politics: the birth of American international relations.* Cornell University Press.

Wilson, P. (1998). The myth of the first great debate. *Review of International Studies, 24*(5), 1–13. doi:10.1017/S0260210598000011

Woolf, L. (1928/1933). *Imperialism and Civilization.* Hogarth Press.

Woolf, L. (1935) War and Capitalism. *The New Statesman and Nation*, February 16th.

ENDNOTES

[1] *Boletín Oficial del Ministerio de Estado*, Madrid, 31 de diciembre de 1911, p. 148.

[2] Archivo del Ministerio de Asuntos Exteriores R-246 exp. 2. Proyecto de reforma elaborado por el Claustro de profesores del Instituto Libre de Enseñanza de las Carreras Diplomática y Consular y Centro de Estudios Marroquíes. Madrid, 17 de noviembre de 1928.

[3] Archivo del Ministerio de Asuntos Exteriores R-246 exp. 2. Informe de R. Spottorno, Sección de Personal del Ministerio de Estado, Madrid, sin fecha.

Chapter 8
A Multi-Faceted Military Campaign:
German Operations Against the Hereros and Nama (1904–1908)

Roberto Muñoz Bolaños

https://orcid.org/0000-0001-6444-2797

Camilo José Cela University, Spain

ABSTRACT

The German army's campaigns against the Herero and Nama peoples between 1904 and 1907 were the result of the sum of several dynamics that defined their development: Western military culture, the emergence of Total War, German military doctrine, and biological racism linked to the cultural revolution that took place in Europe in the last decades of the 19th century. However, the defining factor in its development was the international position of the German Empire at the beginning of the 20th century. The result was not only the defeat of two indigenous peoples, but also the first genocide of the 20th century. However, this genocide was not a planned action but the result of the German military's inability to defeat the indigenous warriors. After the victory of the Kaiser's soldiers, the imperial general staff was unable to draw any lessons from this colonial war, despite the limitations of the concept of the decisive battle, the cornerstone of its military doctrine.

INTRODUCTION

The German military campaigns against the Herero and Nama peoples between 1904 and 1907 constituted not only the first genocide of the twentieth century, but also a manifestation of a set of dynamics –Western military culture, Total War, German military doctrine and racism– that had developed over the previous decades. The key element, however, was the system of international relations that had developed between the late nineteenth and early twentieth centuries (Muñoz Bolaños, 2021: 77). Based on this idea, we set out the following objectives to be developed:

DOI: 10.4018/978-1-6684-7040-4.ch008

Explain the characteristics of the dynamics that defined these campaigns: Western military culture, Total War, German military doctrine and biological racism

Put this campaign in its international context

Analyse the evolution of operations against the Hereros and Nama not only in terms of the military actions that defined them, but also in terms of contemporary international events, especially the Russo-Japanese War (1904-1905)

Describe its limited influence on German military doctrine

BACKGROUND

The 1960s saw two very important processes in the field of German historiography. The Marxist historian of the German Democratic Republic (GDR), Horst Drechsler (1966), published a study on the campaign against the Herero and Nama in which he developed the theory of genocide and tried to link this "criminal" process to the Federal Republic of Germany (1966: 158). At the same time, two historians of the same GFR school, Fritz Fischer (1967) and Hans-Ulrich Wehler (1985), proposed the theory of the Deutsche Sonderweg (German special road), according to which the modernisation process in Germany was partial, as economic transformations were not accompanied by social changes, which resulted in an undemocratic aristocratic elite provoking two world wars with the sole aim of maintaining its dominant position. Thus, for both historians, there was continuity between Imperial Germany (1871-1918) and Nazi Germany (1933-1945). The military campaign against the Hereros and the Nama in German South West Africa (1904-1907) would be an example of this relationship and, consequently, a forerunner of the holocaust unleashed during the Second World War (1939-1945). The result of this approach was the thesis that a direct path from Windhoek (capital of German South West Africa) to Auschwitz can be established (Madley, 2005; Steinmetz, 2005; Erichsen and Olusoga, 2010). This thesis was also defended by the American historian Isabel Hull (2005), albeit on the basis of the existence of an extremely violent German military culture, developed during the imperial period, which would be the link between the genocidal dynamics that took place before 1914, during the First World War (Belgium) and after 1918. However, Helmuth Bley (1968), who studied this campaign in detail and considered the Herero and Nama to have been victims of genocide, questioned this approach, arguing that the events that took place in South West Africa and the genocidal dynamics that were triggered during the Second World War belonged to different historical moments. His position was defended by a broad group of historians: Birthe Kundruss (2003), Wolfgang Benz (2007), Robert Gerwath and Stephan Malonowski (2007), Jürgen Zimmerer (2011), Richard Evans (2015) and Susanne Kuss (2017). Finally, Matthias Häussler (2021: 14-19), who also rejected the idea of continuity, developed the theory of colonialism as an open system to explain what happened in German South West Africa.

But beyond this divergence of positions, one aspect that should be emphasised is that this group of authors considered the internal factors of the German Empire –*Primat der Innenpolitik* (Primacy of Domestic Policy)– as opposed to the international situation at the time –*Primat der Aussenpolitik* (Primacy of Foreign Policy)– to be dominant in their explanations of the events that unfolded in the military campaign against Hereros and Nama.

MAIN FOCUS OF THE CHAPTER

The question we posed before writing these pages and to which we will try to give an answer is: was the campaign against the Herero and Nama peoples a military operation of annihilation determined by the internal factors defining the German Empire or was its development influenced by the international situation in Berlin and the events linked to the Russo-Japanese War? Our hypothesis is that these operations were an episode of Total War, defined by a set of factors internal to the German Empire –military culture or tactical doctrine– but not an orchestrated operation of genocide. Its development and radicalisation was related, on the one hand, to the progressive degradation and isolation of the German Empire on the international stage, culminating in the signing of the *Entente Cordiale* between France and the United Kingdom on 8 April 1904, and, on the other, to the inability of the Kaiser's army to defeat the Indians. This combination of dynamics, which further weakened Berlin's position vis-à-vis its enemies, forced Wilhelm II and the German military elite to try to achieve victory at any cost. They therefore accepted the extreme measures taken by the military command in South West Africa (Major General Lothar von Trotha) in the face of the position of the civilian arm of the government, which was more concerned with the external image of the *Reich*. This position was to be modified by another external event: the Russo-Japanese War (1904-1905). When, at the end of 1904, the defeat of Tsar Nicholas II's forces by Tokyo became irreversible, German pressure on the indigenous peoples eased, Trotha's ceasefire was lifted and a negotiated way to end the conflict was accepted. Thus ended an unsuccessful war for German troops and one from which no military lessons were learned.

In order to develop this hypothesis, we have used official German documents on this campaign, the memoirs of some of its protagonists and the extensive bibliography on the subject as fundamental sources.

Triggering Dynamics

If there is one key factor for all authors who defend the *Primat der Innenpolitik* thesis in the development of these campaigns, it is undoubtedly the military culture of the German Empire. According to Hull, this was characterised by the use of extreme violence as the best solution for dealing with politico-military problems (Feld, 1977: 71-84). This approach entailed the search for a "final solution" that would provide "permanent results" (Hull, 2005: 1). "This kind of thinking led to the desire to exterminate" (Hull, 2005: 100). The annihilation campaign against the Hereros and Nama was thus a manifestation of this imperial military culture. However, this extreme position was not unique to the *Reich*'s military. On the contrary, parallel to the outbreak of the German Unification Wars, the Russian Empire launched a campaign to exterminate the Circassians, a Muslim people inhabiting the Caucasus with whom the Russians had been in conflict since the 18th century. As a result, between 1864 and 1867, 400,000 Circassians were killed by the Tsar's soldiers and 490,000 driven from their lands. Only 80,000 Circassians continued to live in their region of origin after this campaign (Richmond, 2013).

In fact, this extreme approach to military operations is linked to the second dynamic that defined the campaign against the Hereros and Nama: the emergence of Total War. This form of combat originated as a consequence of the sum of elements that emerged from the three great revolutions that defined the First Modernity (1789-1870): liberal, national and industrial. Its fundamental characteristic is that it considers as a military target not only the enemy army, but also any civilian who can support the soldiers: peasants, workers, railway conductors, etc. (Ludendorff, 1964: 15). The first manifestations of this form of combat occurred during the Civil War (1861-1865): campaigns of destruction by federal troops under Major Generals William Sherman and Philip Sheridan and massacres of civilians accused of being guerrillas (10,000 men were killed by federal troops in the state of Missouri) (Förster and Nagler, 2002: 295-310 and 501-549). Thus, the campaigns against the Hereros and Nama were yet another example of this form of conflict, but not the first.

The third dynamic that we are going to analyse defined these campaigns from a tactical point of view: German military doctrine, articulated by four theorists. The first, Frederick II (1740-1788) –mobile warfare and *oblique order* to overwhelm the enemy from the flank, thus achieving a quick victory (Frederick II, 1793: 17-18, 123, 126)– whose principles were embodied in a famous phrase: "Unsere Kriege kurtz und vives seyn musen" (Prussia's wars must be short and intense). The second, Brigadier General Carl von Clausewitz (1780-1831), established the importance of the decisive battle as opposed to the small victories that Frederick II was banking on, and defined the different types of war –in accordance with Hegelian dialectics– according to the political objectives pursued: limited –partial defeat– or absolute –complete destruction– in relation to the enemy. The latter form of war, he called "absolute war" or *Vernichtungsschlacht* (War of Annihilation), as it involved an extreme unleashing of violence (Clausewitz, 1999: 682-685), and was considered the basis on which Total War was later articulated. Thus, Basil Liddell Hart (1946: 205-208) held the Prussian military theorist responsible for the great slaughters of the First World War. Finally, *Generalfeldmarshall* Helmuth von Moltke *the Elder* (1800-1891) and Alfred von Schlieffen (1834-1914). The former was in favour of always taking the offensive initiative in order to encircle the enemy in whole or in part, and then destroy him in a decisive battle or *Kesselschlacht*, while the latter advocated continuous and combined movement with the aim of achieving a complete envelopment of the entire theatre of operations to bring about the complete defeat of a nation or group of nations by annihilating their armies in a *Gesamtschlacht* (Total Battle), as he put forward in his famous "Schlieffen Plan" (1905) (Muñoz Bolaños, 2015: II, 1467). If this initial objective was not achieved, the enemy had to be pursued in order to force him into a new combat that would allow his complete annihilation (Hull, 2005: 45-47). The campaign against the Hereros and Nama developed along these tactical lines, although the initial results were not what the Germans had hoped for. This failure led to a radicalisation of the campaign, which resulted in a high death toll among the indigenous people.

The fourth dynamic was linked to a characteristic that was common to all imperialist nations: racism. This ideology took "scientific" form from the German zoologist Ernst Haeckel's re-reading of social Darwinism. According to the "father of Ecology", there were "primitive" races that were in their infancy and needed the supervision and protection of more mature societies, from which he extrapolated a new philosophy, which he called "monism". His works served as a reference and scientific justification for imperialism, and were at the basis of Nazi theories in this field (Larson and Brauer 2009: 59-123). This dynamic was of great importance in the campaigns against the Hereros and Nama because the Germans could not accept that an "inferior race" would defeat them on the battlefield, thus discrediting them internationally (Haussler, 2021: 19-22). It was precisely this unprecedented fact that explains the extermination orders issued by General Trotha after the unsuccessful battle of Waterberg (11 August 1905).

However, while these four dynamics had a major influence on this conflict, the defining element was the international situation of the German Empire. During the nineteen years (1871-1890) that Bismarck was at the helm of the German government, he pursued a policy –*Realpolitik*– aimed at preventing a new war in Europe –by isolating his great enemy, France– that would endanger his great work. Hence his refusal to interfere in the imperialist dynamics in which other states on the continent were involved: "Here is Russia, here is France and here we are, in the centre. This is my map of Africa" (Craig, 1978: 117). Nevertheless, from 1880 onwards, he allowed German expeditions in South West Africa (Namibia)

–which caused great irritation in London (Clark, 2014: 177)–, East Africa (Tanganyika), Togo, Papua New Guinea, the Bismarck Archipelago and the Marschall, Solomon and Nauru islands in the Pacific (Gründer, 2018: 55-65). At the same time, however, he withdrew from Zululand in South Africa so as not to annoy the British, and the two countries jointly defeated the Sultan of Zanzibar and divided East Africa in 1885. The chancellor even considered several times abandoning German colonial possessions so as not to create sources of conflict with the UK and France (Wehler, 1976, 423). The result of Bismarck's policy was a set of agreements that allowed him to isolate France completely, while maintaining a solid agreement with the Austro-Hungarian Empire and Italy (Triple Alliance, 1882), and a cordial relationship with the Russian Empire (Treaty of Reinsurance, 1888) and the United Kingdom.

However, Bismarck's diplomacy failed with an emerging state, whose position would ultimately lead to his downfall: the United States. The rise of American power after 1870 was overshadowed by the economic, political and diplomatic development of the German Empire. However, Washington had embarked on a policy of commercial expansion beyond continental America, supported by its industrial power and its emerging war fleet (Palmer, 1999, 12-22). These mercantile interests led to a clash with Berlin in the 1980s in Samoa. As a result of a series of incidents, linked to the internal politics of this territory, and the potential threat of conflict, Bismarck convened a conference in the Empire's capital to discuss the fate of this territory with the United Kingdom and the United States. The final agreement, known as the Treaty of Berlin, established a tripartite condominium over Samoa, as the American representatives had demanded. For German public opinion, this agreement was a real international humiliation, which was used by Wilhelm II (1888-1918) to dismiss Bismarck on 20 March 1890 (Herwig, 1976, 14-18). This cessation did not mean the end of Berlin's divergences with Washington, which would reach their peak in 1917 when the United States entered the First World War.

The fall of the chancellor meant the end of *Realpolitik* and opened the way for a new dynamic in German diplomacy: the kaiser thought in global terms –*Weltpolitik*– as opposed to the realist terms –*Realpolitik*– on which Bismarck had developed his foreign policy. The aim of this new policy was to create a great German colonial empire. To achieve this it was necessary to make the British Empire Berlin's main ally, while at the same time maintaining good relations with Russia, since the strong tension between the two countries in India made it impossible to be an ally of both nations at the same time.

However, over the next fourteen years, the *Reich* failed to establish an alliance with London, with whom it would end up at odds as a result of Germany's attitude in the Second Boer War (1899-1902) and the Kaiser's decision to build a powerful navy from 1897 onwards. Berlin also lost its privileged relationship with Russia after the non-renewal of the Reinsurance Treaty in 1890. By contrast, Paris succeeded in establishing an alliance with St. Petersburg (1892) and signed a secret treaty of friendship with Italy (1902). The culmination of this dynamic would come in 1904 with the signing of the *Entente Cordiale (*Clark, 2014: 176-188).

This sum of events was reflected in the progressive reduction of the German Empire's influence on the international stage, which felt increasingly encircled by its enemies. However, Berlin still retained great prestige thanks to its economic power and, above all, its military capability, which was recognised worldwide. It was at this juncture that the revolt of the Hereros and the Nama took place.

Germans in South West Africa (1883-1904)

On 1 May 1883, Heinrich Vogelsang bought the bay of Angra Pequena (Lüderitz Bay) and five miles of inland land on behalf of the Bremen tobacco merchant Adolf Lüderitz. This contract marked the beginning of the German presence in South West Africa (Großer Generalstabes, 1906: I, 2-3). A year later, this territory was acquired as a protectorate rather than a colony by Berlin. However, its subtropical climate, arid terrain, sparse vegetation, lack of water and difficult communications made it unattractive for colonisation. This is how the German military themselves explained it (Großer Generalstabes, 1906: I, 6):

The geographical location makes it a difficult area to access. Only one really good harbour, Lüderitz Bay, and a few less useful harbours, such as Swakopmund, Ogdenhafen, Sandwichhafen, allow the seafarer to land on the coast, which is dangerous due to fog and swell. All landing sites, with the exception of Lüderitz Bay, are exposed to the danger of being gradually dragged northwards by the cold Benguela current. This coast is almost inaccessible from the interior by an 80 to 100 km wide belt of completely desolate, totally barren sand and rock deserts with very low rainfall. Only in the far north and south do water-bearing rivers, the Kunene and Orcmje, allow a way inland. However, the deep riverbeds of the Hoanib, Ugab, Omaruru, Swakop and Kuiseb, enclosed by high mountain walls, are poor in water and only slightly favourable to advance from the coast (...).

Only after overcoming the barren coastal strip does one reach the more fertile highlands (...).

The characteristics of the indigenous population (200,000 people) did not favour the presence of Europeans either (Großer Generalstabes, 1906: I, 9-10). The northern part of the territory was inhabited by the Herero (Bantu), hardy pastoralists who moved their herds across the sparse grasslands between the Namib and Kalahari deserts. Their principal chief, from the late 19th century, was Samuel Maharero. In the south were the Nama, immigrants from the Cape Colony, where they had mixed with the Boers, adopting their language and Christian religion. They were expert horsemen and marksmen (Fergusson, 2012: 246). Their "captain" was Hendrik Witbooi. Other ethnic groups inhabiting the territory were the Sans (Bushmen) and the Damara. From 1894, Maharero and Witbooi maintained good relations with the Germans after the end of the first revolt against the colonisers (Großer Generalstabes, 1906: I, 4-5; Schwabe, 1899). The key figure in this change of attitude was the then commander and later Colonel Theodor Leutwein, governor of the territory, whose aim was to attract white settlers while trying to integrate the Herero herders into the German colonial system, taking advantage of the great tension that still existed between the Herero herders and the Namas. This policy was known as the "Leutwein System" (Gründer, 2018: 121-124).

To maintain control over this territory, the governor also had a military force at his disposal: the *Kaiserliche Schutztruppe für Deutsch-Südwestafrika* (Imperial Protective Forces *for* German South West Africa) created on 9 June 1895 under the initial control of the *Kaiserliche Marine* (Imperial *Navy*). A year later, these troops came under the direct command of the Kaiser through the Colonial Department of the Foreign Office. This change was significant because it placed the colonial forces under the command of a civilian authority (Kuss, 2017: 91).

The hierarchical structure of the *Schutztruppe* was similar to that of modern armies: commanders, officers, non-commissioned officers, classes and soldiers. Applications for a commission in the Schutztruppe were open to all active army or *Landwehr* (reserve) commanders and officers. The criteria used for selection were primarily professional qualifications (service record) and a strong character. However, no in-depth knowledge of the geography, customs and languages of the colonies was required, although applicants were offered voluntary training in these fields. Service in the colonies was very lucrative. Officers and NCOs who served in the *Schutztruppe* for an uninterrupted period of more than three years received a minimum 16% and a maximum 100% increase in their pension, as six months of uninterrupted colonial service was equivalent to 12 months in the metropolis. Chiefs and officers who had been stationed for a minimum of one year in a colony were entitled to receive their pension without having to prove their unfitness for service (Gann and Duignan, 1977: 112-113; Kuss, 2017: 89-94). Soldiers could either volunteer from the army or the Kaiserliche Marine or be recruited from among the natives. The *Kaiserliche Schutztruppe für Deutsch-Südwestafrika* consisted exclusively of German and also Austrian volunteers, with no natives in their ranks (Schulte-Varendorff, 2007: 386-390). This aspect would be decisive in explaining their behaviour vis-à-vis the enemy.

The Campaign Against Herero and Nama (1904-1907)

The revolt of the Hereros and Nama against the Germans was the result of two parallel causes. The first was the economic crisis that affected the first of these indigenous peoples from 1897 onwards as a result of rinderpest, which wiped out 95 per cent of their livestock, and malaria, which killed 8/10 per cent of their population. This catastrophe forced the Hereros to sell their land to Germans, while at the same time incurring large debts to German traders and being forced to work as day labourers for white landowners. This led to a process of progressive proletarianisation of these people, which could mean the end of their existence as a cultural entity. The governor, perceiving the latent danger posed by this situation, tried to alleviate the situation by establishing a period of limitation for debts. This decision provoked the creditors to demand immediate payment of the debts. The result was an escalation of the confrontation between the indigenous population and the German settlers (Gründer, 2018: 126-128).

The second cause was inequality before the law, the result of colonial racism. Indians were forbidden to ride horses, own bicycles, go to the library or walk on the pavement, and were obliged to salute whites. Moreover, in the judicial sphere, the word of a German was equivalent to the word of seven Africans, and crimes committed by whites, including the most serious ones –rape and murder– were punishable by simple fines, while those committed by blacks were punishable by hanging. It was the murder, after an attempted rape, of the daughter-in-law of a Herero chief in 1903 that precipitated the events, following a meeting later that year of Herero chiefs. The revolt began on 12 January 1904 when Herero warriors killed 125 settlers on farms near Windhoek. However, they spared the lives of women and children, who were placed under the protection of German missionaries (Gründer, 2018: 128-131; Großer Generalstabes, 1906: I, 1).

From then on, a military campaign began in three phases. The first phase lasted from January to June 1904. During this period, the strategy of Samuel Majarero and the rest of the indigenous leaders focused on disrupting communications, destroying the railway and telegraph lines between Swakopmund and Windhoek, and laying siege to fortified settlements in the north of the protectorate. At all times, however, they respected the lives of women and children. In the first two weeks of the conflict, the Indigenous killed 158 men, 5 women and no children, as an eyewitness acknowledged (Rust, 1905: 140). However, the German press and eyewitness accounts portrayed the Herero warriors as "savages" who murdered women and children and mutilated the men (Hull, 2006: 10-11). For his part, Leutwein tried his best to restore order and protect the 4,640 German settlers, even though he was confronted with three serious problems from the beginning of the conflict. The first was the revolt of the Bondzelwarts, a Nama group living in a 45,000-square-kilometre territory in the southwest with 300-400 warriors. To fight them, the governor sent the 2nd Field Company, commanded by Captain Victor Franke (Großer Generalstabes, 1906: I, 17 and 19). Second, the area over which the fighting was to take place: "between the coastal strip and the Kalahari steppe, the terrain in the far north is flat" (Großer Generalstabes, 1906: I, 7). The third, linked to the previous one, was the few troops at the governor's disposal: 27 officers, nine doctors, three veterans, one paymaster, 729 men and about 800 horses, which he divided into a police force and a field force of about 500 men. They were equipped with 88 and 71/84 infantry rifles and five 60 mm rapid-fire mountain guns; five 90 mm L/73 field guns from earlier times, intended for station defence, and five machine guns (Großer Generalstabes, 1906: I, 12-13). Following the outbreak of the revolt, 1,141 reservists were mobilised, to which were added 82 sailors from the *Habicht*, a German gunboat sent to the region after the outbreak of the uprising (Großer Generalstabes, 1906: I, 16), and on 17 January, the Kaiser –who from the outset considered the revolt to have been encouraged by the British (Bülow, 1931: 19)– ordered the head of the Colonial Office, Oscar Stübel, to form the Marine Expeditionary Corps. This unit was to be dispatched on 21 January and its functions were (Admiralstab der Marine, 1905: 1):

1.   Restoration of order in the protectorate by all available means. available means.
2.   Occupation of the country's capital
3.   Ensure communication with the coast
4.   If the railway is interrupted, re-establish it

On 3 February, 231 men arrived under the command of Captain Alfred von Winkler (1912: 5-11) and the Marine Corps and Major Hermann Ritter's unit (741 men) on the 9th. Among the officers sent was Major Ludwig von Estorff, one of Germany's leading experts in colonial warfare (Admiralstab der Marine, 1905: 97). Leutwein was then able to field about 2,000 front-line men against some 8,000 Herero warriors equipped with little more than 4,000 rifles. This numerical inferiority forced the governor to focus his operations on the built-up areas. In the ensuing actions, Germans and Hereros suffered similar casualties: 210 and 250 respectively. However, the battles of Ovikokorero (13 March), Onganjira (9 April) and Oviumbo (13 April) demonstrated the Germans' inability to defeat their enemies, although the Indians suffered heavy casualties (Hull, 2006: 22). Against this background, Berlin sent further reinforcements and operations were suspended until their arrival (Großer Generalstabes, 1906: I, 127). In May, the German military presence amounted to 4,654 frontline soldiers (Kuss, 2017: 51-52). At the same time, the Hereros, encircled by the Germans, began to retreat with their families and livestock to the Waterberg massif –on the edge of the Omaheke Desert– from where they hoped to begin negotiations. This retreat to an area far from the railway lines forced the Germans to transport their supplies by ox cart, which posed a major logistical problem.

Leutwein then drew up plans to provoke a decisive battle at Waterberg, which would inflict a final defeat on his enemies. Only after this triumph would peace talks begin (Hull, 2006: 27). However, William II, surprised by a revolt that had turned into open warfare, decided on a change in military leadership. On 3 May 1904 he relieved Leutwein by General Trotha, a veteran of the colonial campaigns in Tanganyika (1894-1897) and China (1900-1901), where he had demonstrated a harsh treatment of the indigenous people and strong racism (Hull, 2006: 25-27; Kuss, 2017: 38). This decision of the Kaiser was made against the Chief of the Great General Staff Schlieffen and the Prussian Minister of War (Major General Karl von Einem). Stübel and Chancellor Bernhard von Bülow also expressed their opposition to Wilhelm II's decision, believing Trotha to be "a man only capable of thinking in purely military terms" (Bley, 1998: 155, 159).

The general arrived in June 1905, and the second phase of the campaign began. Trotha followed the strategy of his predecessor, whose aim was to defeat the Hereros in a decisive battle. His aim was not the physical extermination of the enemy, but to put down the revolt in a conventional battle. To achieve this, he had 4,000 men, 30 artillery pieces and 12 machine guns. For his part, Maharero had 6,000 armed men and 54,000 non-combatants under his command. The German general arranged his men in six divisions to outflank, encircle and defeat the Hereros in accordance with the principles of German military doctrine. The battle took place on 11 August and the Kaiser's troops advanced according to plan. However, one of the divisions was diverted to seize a mission building in the area. This action forced the Hereros to retreat south, where they encountered the weaker German unit –Hayde Division– at the Hamakari watering hole. The Germans were overwhelmed –three officers and 22 soldiers killed– preventing the Herero force from being surrounded. The indigenous warriors then moved into the desert, accompanied by their wives and children and some of their livestock. In their flight they left behind all their valuables, including most of their weapons and ammunition (Großer Generalstabes, 1906: I, 152-184). This flight prevented Trotha from achieving a great victory that would have increased his prestige and that of the German Empire. The decisions he took from this moment on cannot be understood without considering the frustration that this failure caused him. At the same time, Schlieffen's and Wilhelm II's attitude to the general's actions was related to their surprise at the inability of the German troops to defeat the Hereros.

After the failure at Waterberg, Trotha set out to pursue his enemies in order to force a new battle and prevent them from taking refuge in Bechuanaland –under UK control– and using this territory as a base from which to launch new operations. On 13 August, the general ordered Colonel Berthold von Deimling and Majors Franke and Estorff to launch a pursuit operation along the area between the end of the prairie and the beginning of the desert. These forces were decisive in the end of the campaign by progressively pushing the Indigenous into the desert (Großer Generalstabes, 1906: I, 185-187). Shortly afterwards, he issued a set of regulations stipulating that all "plundered cattle" should be driven to German posts whenever possible, prioritising the "destruction of the enemy" and expressly forbidding negotiation with the Hereros. However, Trotha also ordered that women and children should not be shot, although some German soldiers did not obey this order. Cruelty and acts of brutality by German soldiers towards the Indigenous occurred on a daily basis (Haussler, 2021: 13). Leutwein would state that it was "natural after all that has happened that our soldiers showed no leniency" (Kuss, 2017: 59). However, this new campaign failed again, as Trotha did not have the necessary forces to cover such a wide terrain and face a mobile enemy. This was demonstrated by his attempt to force a new decisive battle at the end of August (Großer Generalstabes, 1906: I, 198). This new setback further radicalised his position, and he opted for a policy of extermination of his enemies. On 13 September 1904, when he learned that scattered groups of Hereros were attempting to gather at the Eiseb River, he intensified his pursuit to push them back into the desert, achieving his goal on the 28th, although German troops were unable to pursue them for lack of water (Großer Generalstabes, 1906: I, 199-202). It was then that he ordered the border with the Omaheke to be sealed so that the Hereros would die of dehydration. This decision –a pure manifestation of Total War where no distinction was made between combatants and non-combatants– was justified by Trotha in a report sent to Berlin (Großer Generalstabes, 1906: I, 207):

No effort or hardship was spared to strip the enemy of the last vestige of his power of resistance; like a half-dead deer he was driven from watering-hole to watering-hole, until at last he was left without will, a victim of the nature of his own country. The waterless Omaheke was to complete what the German guns had begun: the destruction of the Herero people.

But was this the common position of the entire German military? Apparently not. Estorff and Lieutenant Colonel Karl Ludwig von Mühlenfels were highly critical of the general's decision (Zimmerer, 2011: 183; Häussler, 2021: 167). These divergences show that the annihilation campaign against the Herero people was not the result of a particular military culture –as Hull claimed– but the product of circumstances and Trotha's decisions (Benz, 2007: 37). The culmination of this dynamic came on 2 October, when the general issued his famous "Words to the Herero people". In this proclamation, after warning the Indigenous to hand over their leaders –offering a reward in return– he threatened them with extermination, not excluding women and children. The Indians became outlaws in their own country (Hull, 2006: 55-59).

The general's proclamations were immediately known in Berlin. Wilhelm II and Schlieffen, frustrated by Germany's inability to defeat its enemies, accepted its full content. In a letter to the chancellor dated 23 November 1904, the chief of the Great General Staff stated that peace with the insurgents could only take place in the form of unconditional surrender (Häussler, 2011: 64). In contrast, the political elite, led by Bülow, quickly understood the damage this proclamation did to the international image of the German Empire and convinced the Kaiser on 8 December to order their withdrawal (Hull, 2006: 63-66). Significantly, the chancellor's success came only two days after the Japanese seizure of Port Arthur, which significantly improved Berlin's international standing. Not only was the Russian Army weakened, but relations between St. Petersburg and Paris were going through a difficult time in the face of the French refusal to help the Russians in order not to break their recent friendship with the United Kingdom, an ally of Japan. Bülow did not hesitate to link the two conflicts –the Herero rebellion and the Russo-Japanese War– although he gave much more importance to the latter (Bülow, 1931: II, 19). Moreover, and this was no minor detail, the tsar's troops also clashed with non-Whites (Häussler, 2021: 33-34).

The repeal of Trotha's proclamation marked the beginning of the third phase of the campaign, characterised by Hereros being interned in concentration camps or used as forced labour on German property and in German enterprises. The protagonist of this period was no longer Trotha, who was dismissed on 19 November 1905, but a civilian, Friedrich von Lindequist, who was appointed governor of the colony (Hull, 2006: 63-66). This event, together with the withdrawal of the "Words to the Herero People", demonstrated that civilians were once again in control of the territory after the end of the military campaign.

Parallel to the Herero rebellion, in October 1904 the Nama revolted under the leadership of their captains Hendrik Witbooi and Jakob Morenga. The causes of this outbreak were, on the one hand, the treatment inflicted by the Germans on the Hereros and, on the other, the perception that the Nama might suffer the same fate, for without Leutwein's protection, they would succumb to the demands of the white settlers. The uprising took place on the same terms as that of the Hereros: the Indigenous attacked the German farms, killing 60 men but sparing the lives of women and children. From the outset, however, their movement was limited by its small size, as it was centred on Rietmond and Gibeon, mobilising less than 2,000 warriors (Kuss, 2017: 53-54).

The German campaign against this rebellion was also conducted in three phases, with as little success as in the north and using the same means. In the first, the Kaiser's soldiers, led by Colonel Deimling, sought a decisive battle that would enable him to encircle and destroy his enemies. They almost succeeded in doing so in the homeland of the Witbooi Nama –the most important group of the Witbooi Nama people– who were forced into battle at Rietmond and Auob in December. However, as at Waterberg, the indigenous escaped, although they abandoned 15,000 head of cattle, supplies, arms and ammunition. The second phase began in December 1904 and was marked by two events. First, Witbbooi and his commanders came to the conclusion that a pitched battle with the Germans would be a disaster. From that point on, they opted for a mobile guerrilla war that would allow them to defy their enemies and force a negotiation. The Nama attacked railway stations, transport columns, posts and military detachments, inflicting losses on the Germans that, while not decisive, did weaken the morale of the troops and forced them to remain inactive, as supplies and water had to be transported by ox carts from the coast. The second development was Trotha's refusal, in despair at the limited success of his soldiers, to engage in any further negotiations. On 23 April 1905, unable to defeat the enemy, the general issued a proclamation threatening the Nama with the same punishment as the Hereros had received if they did not surrender (Erichsen and Olusoga, 2018: 178-187). This second phase ended on 29 October with the death of Hendrik Witbooi in an attack on a car belonging to a German battery. The third phase was marked by the collapse of the Nama's power - after the loss of their leader - and the cessation of Trotha on 19 November. At this point, German commanders considered their enemies' tactics so effective and the terrain so inhospitable that they could not win the war (Erichsen and Olusoga, 2018: 193). Therefore, they abandoned the idea of the decisive battle and opted instead to organise mobile detachments to pursue and destroy the Nama contingents. This new tactic, combined with the lack of indigenous cohesion after Witbooi's death and a German position more open to negotiation, caused most Nama groups to abandon the fight. The recently promoted Brigadier General Deimling ended the campaign on 31 March 1907 (Hull, 2006: 67-69).

After the end of the conflict, the Nama prisoners were sent to concentration camps where they lived with the Hereros. These facilities had been established shortly after the start of the Maharero rebellion. They were located on *Shark Island* –a peninsula– and in the main towns of the colony: Okahandja, Omaruru, Karibib, Keetmanshoop, Lüderitz Bay, Swakopmund and Windhoek. They were initially under military control, but after Trotha's dismissal their administration passed to civilians, except for the first one, until they were closed on 27 January 1908 (Häussler, 2021: 10). The harsh living conditions resulted in the deaths of 7,682 of the 17,000 internees –15,000 Hereros and 2,000 Nama– between October 1904 and March 1907 (Hull, 2006: 89). Thus, 45 per cent of all inmates. However, although the death toll was very high, it did not exceed the number of deaths in the concentration camps set up during the Second Boer War (1899-1902). The British took 28,000 Boers prisoner, sending 25,630 to camps in Bermuda, Ceylon, India and St. Helena. Another 27,927 non-combatant Boers –elders, women and children–died in camps set up in South Africa, and 20,000 blacks of the 120,000 imprisoned. In total, 50,000 non-combatants lost their lives in these establishments (Clive, 1957: 31; Mongalo and Du Pisani, 1999: 170).

The operations against the Hereros and Nama were a sad experience for the German Army, which lost 2,000 men out of the 14,000 sent, at a cost of 585 million. In fact, the budget debate was so arduous that it led to the dissolution of the Reichstag and the calling of the *Hottentot Elections* in 1907 (Häussler, 2021: 12). For the Hereros and Nama, the consequences were more catastrophic. It is estimated that 75-80 per cent of the Herero population –some 100,000 before the conflict, 16,000 after it– and 50 per cent of the Nama population –20,000 before the conflict, 9,000-13,000 after it– died (Kuss, 2017: 55).

SOLUTIONS AND RECOMMENDATIONS

The German operations against the Hereros and Nama were one more colonial campaign in a historical process known as Imperialism. In this sense they were similar to those unleashed by the British Empire against the Boers or the Russian Empire against the Circassians. What is more. Like the former, the international situation played a role in their brutal development and in the enormous mortality among non-combatants. However, it cannot be said that its aim was the complete annihilation of the enemy, like the Russian campaign against the Circassians. Similarly, the British and Germans saw these campaigns as specific to the colonial space.

FUTURE RESEARCH DIRECTIONS

The campaigns against the Hereros and Nama have been the subject of in-depth study since the 1960s by German, British and American historiography. However, international factors have been neglected in favour of those internal to the *Reich*. This research demonstrates the importance of the German position in the international context in explaining the development of the war. For this reason, we believe that this thesis should be explored further in future research.

CONCLUSION

The revolt of the Herero and Nama peoples in South West Africa –a consequence of the harsh economic and political conditions under which these peoples lived– occurred at a time when the international situation was particularly unfavourable to the German Empire, leading to a punitive campaign by the German Government and Army that resulted in the near-total destruction of both peoples. At no time, however, was this an orchestrated genocidal operation, but a Total War aimed at defeating the enemy in a battle of annihilation in order to enhance the prestige of the German Army. The impossibility of achieving this victory, coupled with racism and contempt for non-whites in Europe, led to a radicalisation of the position of the German command –General Trotha– who sought the physical annihilation of the enemy, without distinguishing between combatants and non-combatants. This decision was initially approved by Wilhelm II and Schlieffen, who were astonished and frustrated that a group of black rebels could challenge the strongest army in the world and call into question their war doctrine. It was only when the international situation changed as a result of the defeat of the Russian Empire by the Japanese that the Kaiser, encouraged by the civilian arm of the government, decided to change his position, influenced by the negative consequences of these extermination actions for the image of the *Reich*. This conflict between civilians and the military, which would manifest itself again during the First World War, and the conflict within the military elite itself –Estorff and Mühlenfels *versus* Trotha– demonstrates the non-existence of an imperial military culture of genocide and a continuity between the events in South West Africa and the actions unleashed during the Second World War. Nor, for the same reasons, can such continuity be established in the Russian case between the Circassian genocide and Stalinism.

Finally, these operations did not influence German military doctrine, despite their obvious failure. The Great General Staff did not evaluate this campaign –as it had not evaluated the American Civil War– and therefore could not determine why the strategy on which German military doctrine was based –the decisive battle by means of a double flank to destroy the enemy and achieve victory in a short war– had failed (Häussler, 2021: 13):

The esteemed Prussian/German war machine did not live up to expectations, although its organisation and performance had been considered exemplary throughout the world. With the utmost effort and sacrifice, it achieved results that hardly anyone was satisfied with, indeed, that hardly anyone foresaw.

A little more than 10 years after the revolt of the Hereros and Nama began, the Battle of the Marne (6/12 September 1914) would take place, where German troops again failed to encircle and destroy the French and British forces.

REFERENCES

Admiralstab der Marine. (1905). *Das Marine-Expeditionskorps in Südwest-Afrika während des Herero-Aufstandes* [*The Marine Expeditionary Corps in South-West Africa during the Herero Uprising*]. Mittler.

Benz, W. (2007). Kolonialpolitik als Genozid. Der 'Herero-Aufstand' in Deutsch-Südwestafrika [Colonial Policy as Genocide. The 'Herero Uprising' in German South-West Africa]. In Wolfgang Benz (ed.), Ausgrenzung, Vertreibung, Völkermord. Genozid im 20. Jahrhundert [Expulsion, expulsion, genocide. Genocide in the 20th Century] (27-53). München, Dtv.

Bley, H. (1968). *Kolonialherrschaft und Sozialstruktur in Deutsch-Südwestafrika 1894-1914 [Colonial rule and social structure in German South West Africa 1894-1914.]*. Leibniz-Verl.

Bülow, B. v. (1931). *Memoirs, 1903-1909*. Putnam.

Clark, Ch. (2014). *Sonámbulos: Como Europa fue a la guerra en 1914 [Sleepwalkers: How Europe went to war in 1914]*. Galaxia Gutenberg.

Clausewitz, K. v. (1999). *De la guerra [On war]*. Ediciones Ejército.

Craig, G. A. (1978). *Germany, 1866-1945*. Oxford University Press.

Drechsler, H. (1966). *Südwestafrika unter deutscher Kolonialherrschaft: Der Kampf der Herero und Nama gegen den deutsche Imperialismos (1884-1915) [South West Africa under German Colonial Rule: The Struggle of the Herero and Nama against German Imperialism (1884-1915)]*. Akademie-Verlag.

Erichsen, C., & Olusoga, D. (2010). *The Kaiser's Holocaust: Germany's Forgotten Genocide and the Colonial Roots of Nazism*. Faber and faber.

Evans, R. (2015). *The Third Reich in History and Memory*. Oxford University Press.

Feld, M. D. (Ed.). (1977). *The structure of violence: Armed forces as social systems*. Sage Publications.

Fischer, F. (1967). *Germany's Aims in the First World War*. W.W. Norton.

Förster, S., & Nagler, J. (Eds.). (2002). *On the Road to Total War: The American Civil War and the German Wars of Unification, 1861-1871*. Cambridge University Press.

Frederick, I. I. (1793). *El Arte de la Guerra* [The Art of War]. Imprenta Real.

Gann, L., & Duignan, P. (1977). The Rulers of German Africa, 1884-1914. Stanford University Press.

Gerwath, R., & Malonowski, S. (2009). Hanna Arendt's Ghost: Reflections on the Disputable Path from Windhoek to Auschwitz. *Central European History*, *42*(2), 279–300. doi:10.1017/S0008938909000314

Großer Generalstabes. (1906). *Die Kämpfe der deutschen Truppen in Südwestafrika I* [*The battles of the German troops in South West Africa*]. Mittler.

Gründer, H. (2018). *Geschichte der deutschen Kolonian* [*History of the German colonian*]. Panderborn, Brill Deutschland GmbH. doi:10.36198/9783838549729

Häussler, M. (2011). From destruction to extermination: Genocidal escalation in Germany's war against the Herero 1904. *Journal of Namibian Studies*, *10*, 55–81.

Häussler, M. (2021). *The Herero Genocide: War, Emotion and Extreme Violence in Colonial Namibia*. Berghahn. doi:10.2307/j.ctv2tsx91h

Herwig, H. (1976). *Politics of Frustration: The United States in German Naval Planning, 1889-1941*. Little, Brown and Company.

Hull, I. V. (2006). *Absolute Destruction: Military culture and The practices of war in Imperial German*. Cornell University Press.

Kundruss, B. (2003). Von Windhoek nach Nürnberg? Koloniale 'Mischehenverbote' und die national-sozialistische Rassengesetzgebung. [From Windhoek to Nuremberg? Colonial 'intermarriage bans' and National Socialist racial legislation] In B. Kundrus (Ed.), *"Phantasiereiche". Der deutsche Kolonialismus aus kulturgeschichtlicher Perspektive [*"Imaginative". German colonialism from a cultural-historical perspective] (110-131)*. Campus.

Kuss, S. (2017). *German Colonial Wars and the Context of Military Violence*. Harvard University Press. doi:10.4159/9780674977358

Larson, B. & Brauer, F. (2009). *The Art of Evolution. Darwin, Darwinism and Visual Culture*. Lebano, University Press of New England.

Lidell Hart, B. (1946). *Estrategia. La aproximación indirecta* [*The strategy of indirect approach*]. Iberia.

Ludendorff, E. (1964). *La Guerra Total* [*The Total War*]. Ediciones Pleamar.

Madley, B. (2005). From Africa to Auschwitz: How German South West Africa Incubated Ideas and Methods Adopted and Developed by the Nazis in Eastern Europe. *European History Quarterly*, *35*(3), 429–464. doi:10.1177/0265691405054218

Martin, A. C. (1957). *The Concentration Camps, 1900-1902: Facts, Figures and Fables*. Howard Timmins.

Mongalo, B. E., & Du Pisani, K. (1999). Victims of a White Manís War: Blacks in concentration camps during the South African War (1899-1902). *History (London)*, *44*(1), 148–182.

Muñoz Bolaños, R. (2015). *Griff nach der Weltmacht*: Hacia el poder mundial. El desarrollo de la doctrina militar alemana (1808-1945). [*Griff nach der Weltmacht*: Towards world power. The development of German military doctrine (1808-1945)] In E. Martínez Ruiz & J. Cantera Montenegro (Eds.), *Perspectivas y Novedades de la Historia Militar: una aproximación global [Perspectives and News of Military History: a global approach]* (Vol. II, pp. 1.469–1.488). Ministerio de Defensa.

Muñoz Bolaños, R. (2021). Wo ist heute das Volk der Herero, wo sind heute seine Häuptlinge? [The German Military Campaign in South West Africa (1904-1907)]. *Guerra Colonial*, *9*, 75–96.

Palmer, M. (1999). *Guardians of the Gulf: A History of America's Expanding Role in the Persion Gulf, 1883-1992*. Simon and Schuster.

Richmond, W. (2013). *The Circassian Genocide*. Rutgers University Press.

Rust, C. (1905). *Krieg und Frieden im Hererolande. Aufzeichnungen aus dem Kriegsjahre 1904* [*War and Peace in Hereroland. Notes from the War Year 1904*]. Kittler.

Schulte-Varendorff, U. (2007). Schutztruppe. [Protection Force] In U. Van der Heyden & J. Zeller (Eds.), *Kolonialismus hierzulande: Eine Spurensuche in Deutschland [Colonialism in this country: A search for traces in Germany]* (pp. 386–390). Sutton Verlag.

Schwabe, K. (1899). *Mit Schwert und Pflug in Deutsch-Südwestafrika. Vier Kriegs und Wanderjahre. Mit zahlreichen Karten und Skizzen sowie Abbildungen und Tabellen [With Sword and Plough in German South-West Africa. Four Years of War and Travel. With numerous maps and sketches as well as illustrations and tables]*. Berlin, Ernst Siegfried Mittler u. Sohn.

Steinmetz, G. (2005). Von der 'Eingeborenenpolitik' zur Vernichtungsstrategie: Deutsch-Südwestafrika, 1904 [From 'Native Policy' to Extermination Strategy: German South-West Africa, 1904]. *Peripherie, 97/98*, 195–227.

Wehler, H.-U. (1976). *Bismarck und der Imperialismus* [*Bismarck and Imperialism*]. Deutscher Taschenbuch Verlag.

Wehler, H.-U. (1985). *The German Empire, 1871-1918*. Berg.

Wincler, A. v. (1912). *Im afrikanischen Sonnenbrand* [*In the African sunburn*]. Verlag Abel & Müller.

Zimmerer, J. (2011). *Von Windhuk nach Auschwitz: Beiträge zum Verhältnis von Kolonialismus und Holocaust [From Windhoek to Auschwitz: Contributions to the Relationship between Colonialism and the Holocaust]*. LIT Verlag.

Chapter 9
Spain in China:
A "Dove" in the Midst of Imperial "Hawks" at the End of the Qing Dynasty

Raúl Ramírez Ruiz
Rey Juan Carlos University, Spain

Guanjie Niu
Renmin University, China

ABSTRACT

This article explores the links between China and Spain since the establishment of formal diplomatic relations in 1864 until the fall of the Qing Dynasty in 1912. To this aim, the authors investigate documents kept by the Ministry of Qing Foreign Affairs at The First Historical Archives of China, in Beijing. Specifically, the authors examine 809 documents of diplomatic communications between the Qing central government and the Spanish institutions in Chinese, French, Spanish, and English. Based on these documents, a database was designed that allowed a full quantitative, diachronic, and thematic analysis of their content. Once the four main topics were defined (diplomatic agreements, protocol, economic and minority issues), each one was independently presented and analyzed. The chapter finds that Spain's relations with late Qing China were characterized by the search for mutual diplomatic support, but lacked an economic or strategic background to cement them. As the authors argue, the documents of the Waiwubu demonstrate how Spain was a friendly but irrelevant nation for the Chinese Qing administration.

INTRODUCTION

China lived for millennia in isolation from the world. The Tianxia, "All Under Heaven" was confused with its own identity. "All Under Heaven" was ruled by the "Son of Heaven", who had received the "Mandate of Heaven". There was no difference between foreigners and Chinese, but only between civilized and barbarians. China was equivalent to Civilization and, on its margins, barbarian peoples could aspire to join civilization.

DOI: 10.4018/978-1-6684-7040-4.ch009

China was an ordered world: Sinocentric. The arrival of Iberian naval powers, Spain and Portugal, and later the Dutch changed little between the 16th and 18th centuries. However, at the end of the last century the British appeared. They, the English, managed to attract the attention of mandarins and merchants from southern China to a new product: Opium.

The Sinocentric world collapsed as drugs corrupted its official elite and poisoned its youth. The Qing state tried to halt the decline through the honest civil servant Lin Zexu sent as anti-drug commissioner to Canton. His intervention provoked the First Opium War (1840-1842), the defeat, the Taiping Rebellion (1851-1864) and in between, the Second Opium War (1856-1860). A process of loss of sovereignty that began the period of the "Unequal Treaties" and "Open Door Policy".

"Open Door Policy" is the fruit of what is known as the "Treaty System" or the "Unequal Treaties", by which we mean the West's control of China. From the 1840s onwards, through the signing of international treaties under military threats, large areas of China's territory were ceded to other countries; foreign settlements were created in numerous cities; China's foreign trade and exchanges were directly controlled by foreign powers; and extraterritoriality was guaranteed for foreigners (Ramírez-Ruiz. 2018: 54-55).

The great powers came in for the plunder: the United Kingdom, France, Russia, then Japan, and later the United States with its growing power. Finally, Spain, Portugal, Austria-Hungary, Italy, the Netherlands, less powerful countries, but eager to position themselves in the "sharing out of China".

The ultimate expression of this "century of humiliation" was the entry of the "Eight-Nation Alliance" expeditionary force into Peking on 14 August 1900. The Boxer Rebellion and Chinese sovereignty came to an end. The imperial family fled and the Qing capital was sacked. Spain took advantage of this occasion to appear to the world as one of the great powers that "ruled" China. But it was a fiction. The "Boxer Protocol" negotiations were to be hosted by the Spanish ambassador to China, Bernardo Cólogan y Cólogan. Spain had suffered from the siege but had no troops or strong interests in China. The Spanish representative might appear to be the most even-handed of the foreigners. Moreover, he was the doyen of the diplomatic representatives in Beijing and had a close relationship with the Dowager Empress Cixi. His prominence in this historic event came despite opposition from the United States. The American power, having just finished the war with Spain, did not understand that such a 'diminished' power with so little political-military weight could capitalise on the victory over China (Cologan Soriano, 2015, 181). Spain was, in the eyes of the Chinese, a dove among hawks.

BACKGROUND

Relations between Spain-China at the end of the 19th century and throughout the 20th century have been largely forgotten in Spanish historiography. Undoubtedly, the causes of them are multiple, but we can summarize them in the following: decline of Spain as an imperial power, scarcity of documentary sources in Spain, the excessive weight of the Philippine sphere and the end of the Spanish presence in the Far East after 1898.

After the reestablishment of diplomatic relations between Spain and the People's Republic of China in 1973, there was a timid revival of historiographic interest in that period. In those years, we had the works of Ojeda (1978) and Folchs (1985), continued by José E. Borao (1994), Rodao (1997) and Togores, (1997). At the beginning of the 21st century, Spanish sinology has grown spectacularly, diversifying into the most varied fields of science. Among which we must include the historical studies of Sino-Spanish relations. They are far-reaching investigations that confirm the existence of relations between the two countries. The publications of García Ruiz-Castillo (2009); García-Tapia (2009); Martínez-Robles (2007); Borao (2017); Brasó Broggi (2018); Brasó Broggi and Martínez-Robles, (2018); Cologan (2015); Ramírez-Ruiz, (2016 and 2017); Toro (2016). While on the Chinese side, we must highlight the profound and comprehensive academic work of Professor Zhang Kai (2003).

Despite this, there are still important gaps in the research of the historical relations between China and Spain. This is mainly due to two causes: On the one hand, the non-preservation of an important part of the Spanish diplomatic documentary collections, especially of internal consular correspondence. And on the other, the non-incorporation in Spanish research of Chinese archives.

MAIN FOCUS OF THE CHAPTER

This chapter has been written to make up for this last lack. In the present paper, original Chinese sources unknown in the Spanish historiographic world and barely in Chinese are presented. We are working with documents from the Archive of the Ministry of Foreign Affairs in the central government of Qing, known in Chinese as the *Waiwubu*, which are kept in the "*First Historical Archive of China*", located next to the Forbidden City. In that place we had access to the facsimile edition published by *Zhong Hua Book Company* in 2004, the article explores a collection of 809 documents, including 302 attachments (The First Historical Archives of China, Peking University & Macao Polytechnic Institute, 2004).

This collection includes all the diplomatic communications between Spain and China preserved by the Imperial government since the signing of the *Spanish-Chinese Friendship Treaty*, in October 1864, until the abdication of the last Emperor of China, in January 1912.

These documents are little known in Spain and sparsely worked elsewhere, including China. On the Spanish side, only the aforementioned J.E. Borao (2017) worked on sources located in the Academia Sinica de Tapei and collaterally cites some of these documents, referring to them as AICPP: Imperial Palace Archives (Beijing). On the Chinese side, Xu Kai, Mu Yinchen refers to these documents in the "The Symposium of Conference on China and Spain during the Ming and Qing Dynasties, Macao Polytechnic Institute (2009)". In both cases they are partial visions that lack the totalizing vision of this article. Because, our objective is to analyze the documentation as a whole. In order to describe Sino-Spanish relations what they were like, of what type and with what characteristics and shortcomings.

For research purposes, we used an already tested methodology, consisting of the design of an Access Database in which to dump the information. This allowed us to analyze all the documents and identify comprehensive findings, after cataloguing them first by date, author, origin or destination and, in a second analysis, by subject.

Diachronic Analysis

A chronological analysis of the documentation reveals the first significant piece of information. And this is that 91% of the documents of *The First Historical Archives of China* were issued between 1902 and 1912. There are several reasons that explain this highly unbalanced distribution. The first refers to the special circumstances of Qing state institutions. This collection includes all the communications between the Chinese and Spanish governments of the two central institutions dedicated to international relations that took place in the last decades of the Dynasty: The Zongli Yamen and the Waiwubu.

Before the establishment of these two institutions, China lacked a centralized agency dedicated to diplomatic relations, which were entrusted to the Provincial Governors or, in exceptional cases, to a delegate of the emperor appointed *ad hoc*. Following the disastrous diplomatic experience of the two opium wars, senior government bureaucrats urged the emperor to centralize contacts with foreigners in a single entity. Thus, on January 20, 1861, Emperor Xianfeng established *Zongli Yamen* or *Department of Foreign Relations*, but as an office within the Council of State, on a temporary basis, since he thought that when foreign affairs were not "so complicated" he could avoid using it (Li, 2017, pp. 40-42). This meant that all the officials assigned to the *Zongli Yamen* worked part-time and that their services there did not count towards promotion in the official career. This situation not only influenced the diligence of these officials, but also facilitated the *de facto* maintenance of broad diplomatic powers by the provincial governors. Furthermore, following tradition, these governors did not feel the obligation to forward their agreements with foreigners to this office in Beijing (Martínez Robles, 2010, p. 497).

In 1901, when the Boxer Protocol was signed, at the request of the victorious powers, the Department of Foreign Affairs (*Zongli Yamen*) was transformed into the Ministry of Foreign Affairs (*Waiwubu*). This Ministry was raised to the same level as the traditional *Six Ministries*, making their officials' status equal to that of other ministerial posts. Its professionalization and standardization with international uses was completed with reforms in 1906 and 1907 (Li, 2017, pp. 64-65).

Thus, the exponential increase in diplomatic communications with Spain, starting in 1902, is due, in part, to the greater efficiency of the *Waiwubu*. However, as this study will later illustrate, such increase also followed the reactivation of China's foreign relations after the return of Empress Cixi from her exile in Xi'an coinciding with the beginning of the reign of Alfonso XIII. This unbalanced temporal distribution of the documents by date illustrates the attempts by two outward "regenerationist" monarchies to establish mutual legitimizing ties in the international arena.

Thematic Analysis

Further analysis of the documentation, the next step was the definition and standardization of the topics covered at the collection. Such, we identify sixteen issues of relevance. These topics can be grouped into four blocks, with the following percentage distribution of documents.

Table 1. Thematic blocks

Thematic blocks	Percentage of documents
International Treaties and agreements of the Diplomatic Corps	10%
Protocol diplomatic communications	68%
Economy	11%
Minority issues	11%

Source: FHACh. Compiled by the authors.

As we can see (table 1) seven out of ten documents are devoted to purely protocol matters. This is the most significant information in the table above. However, in order to give coherence to our wording we must start with the documents that we have framed as "International Treaties and agreements of the Diplomatic Corps".

INTERNATIONAL TREATIES AND DIPLOMATIC CORPS AGREEMENTS

Documents that refer to "International Treaties and agreements of the Diplomatic Corps" account for 10% of the total. The "International Treaties" refer to the establishment of Sino-Spanish relations and "agreements of the Diplomatic Corps" give Spain a more important role in the international arena than it had, thanks mainly to the weight of the Spanish ambassadors in Beijing. The low political and economic weight of Spain meant that when Spain played a significant role before the Qing Court, it was due to the Spanish ambassador occupying the position of "Dean" of the Diplomatic Corps. We will indicate this situation in each of the corresponding points.

The most important of all the treaties signed by Spain with China was the Tientsin Treaty of 1864, as it is known in China, established the foundations of modern diplomatic relations between China and Spain. This was no easy achievement. In 1843 when the Spanish and the Portuguese saw Great Britain, France and Russia sign commercial treaties with China, they established as their aspiration to receive the same treatment as these powers. To this aim, they claimed that they had been trading with China for more than 200 years. However, they were ignored. Martínez-Robles has described the hardships that the Spanish Special Envoy, Sinibaldo de Mas, endured on his various missions in 1845, 1847 y 1864 (Martínez Robles, 2018, pp. 460-465). After the accession to the throne of Emperor Tongzhi (1861), and the establishment of the *Zhongli Yamen*, Spain again sent Sinibaldo de Mas (1809-1868) to achieve the signing of a treaty. Manchu China refused to receive the Spanish envoy in Beijing, forcing him to negotiate in Tianjin. There, de Mas, met with Imperial Commissioners Xue Huan and Chonghou. Finally, on October 10, 1864, the *Treaty of Tientsin* was signed between China and Spain. This agreement, also known as the *China-Spain Friendship Treaty* (Chen Xulu et al., 1982, p. 759).

Spain achieved a less advantageous agreement than other countries (Martínez Robles, 2010, p. 497-503). The Spain-China treaty is more egalitarian than unequal, as it includes terms of parity with China that are not found in those achieved by the great powers (Martínez-Robles, 2007, p. 246). The greatest example of this was the reciprocity of 'most favoured nation' treatment, which Spain granted to China, a concession unimaginable in any of the other 'unequal treaties' (Martínez-Robles, 2018, pp. 187-189).

More than half of the articles of the Friendship Treaty between Spain and China focus on trade issues: tariffs, tariffs, embarkation and disembarkation procedures, jurisdictional attributions of Spanish consuls, etc. In all of them, the possibilities for the Chinese authorities to act in the event of the involvement of Chinese citizens in various matters are clearly spelled out (Martínez-Robles, 2007, p. 251). The treaty guaranteed the personal and property security of Spanish merchants, however, if the Spanish deliberately cheated and extorted Chinese citizens, the Qing government had more prerogatives to prosecute and punish them than against merchants from other powers (Xu and Mu, 1997, pp. 330-337).

Protocolary Diplomatic Communications

The diplomatic communication with merely protocol matters account for 68% of all Sino-Spanish documents (1864-1912). There can be no greater example of this peripheral or "disinherited" role in the Far East of Spain (Rodao, 1997).

This thematic block, which we have called protocol, is made up of: Coronations, births, marriages, deaths and birthdays of royal families; Imperial hearings/Audiences and Consular visits; awards; notices about changes in the Spanish Diplomatic Corps and Diplomats' personal affairs.

We will not provide an exhaustive account of all the issues dealt with in this section, but rather, within each of them, we will point out those issues that portray the essence of the Spain-China relationship at that time.

In this section we have gathered those documents that refer to the coronations, marriages, births, deaths and birthdays of the royalty of both countries. It is the most numerous issues among the documentation of the Chinese Foreign Archive, practically a quarter of the total, 24%.

Alfonso XIII's ascent to the throne was scheduled for May 17, 1902. On March 6, the Spanish ambassador Manuel de Cárcer (Li, 1989, p. 798) requested Prince Ching (Yikuang, 1836-1918), Minister of Foreign Affairs of China, that a representative of suitable rank be appointed to attend the ceremony. In a matter of days, Vice-General Zhang Deyi (1847-1918), ambassador to London (Cao, 2014, pp. 652-653), was appointed through an edict signed by both emperors. The Archive shows all his communications with Beijing in preparation for the trip. His stay in Madrid would last between May 13 and 16 (Xiong, 2013, p. 216).

Alfonso XIII married Princess Victoria Eugenia of Battenberg on May 31, 1906, however, references to this matter appear in First Historical Achives two years earlier, on April 3, 1904, when Wang Daxie (1859-1929) (Shi Yuanhua, 1996, p. 841), ambassador to the United Kingdom, wrote to the Waiwubu in appreciation for being appointed "Special Ambassador" for the wedding of the Spanish monarch. This decision was communicated to the Spanish embassy three days later, which will immediately lead one of the most important figures in China at the time, Robert Hart (1835-1911), British officer who from 1863 to 1911 was the Inspector General of Customs of China (Chen Xulu et al., 1982, p. 730), to recommend Juan Mencarini (Zhaickuan, 1997, p. 397), the only Spaniard in the service of the Great Qing, as Wang Daxie's translator during his time in Spain (First Historical Archive of China, hereinafter, FHACh, Doc. 138, Vol. 1, p. 688; Doc. 241, Vol. 1, pp. 700-702).

After this last communication, the matter is not found again until two years later, on March 14, 1906, when Liu Shixun (Tang Jiaxuan, 2000, p. 184), ambassador to Spain and France, wrote to the Waiwubu, informing that the Spanish King had become engaged to the British princess Victoria Eugenie. Fifteen days later the communication will arrive from the Spanish ambassador, informing that the wedding will be held in May or June and requesting that a "special ambassador" be sent. The Spanish government wanted to know as soon as possible who would form the entourage and, again, asked that Juan Mencarini be included; because he was "close" to the Duke of Almodóvar, and "Hart agrees". On June 1 a direct letter from Alfonso XIII to Guangxu will be dated, announcing that "yesterday May 31" he married Victoria Eugenie.

The death and burial of Emperors Cixi and Guangxu demonstrated the real weight of Spain in China and the world. Spain played a leading role in both events, as its ambassador, Manuel de Cárcer, was "the Dean of the Diplomatic Corps" in Beijing. But things would turn out very differently.

According to the documents of the *First Historical Archives of China*, on the day of the death of the emperors, November 14, 1908, the Spanish ambassador receives a note in which he is told that "Prince Ching, Yi Kuang, has something important to communicate to you. Please wait at the Ministry of Foreign Affairs at 3 p.m.". Two days later, Cárcer writes to Prince Ching sending the King of Spain's condolences for the death of the two emperors. Already, as dean, on November 17, he will write that

He wishes to convey his respectful sympathy to the entire Chinese imperial family for the double loss suffered [foreign legations will observe] 27 days of mourning and flags at half-mast... for another side, on behalf of the entire Diplomatic Corps, wishes to offer the Regent its condolences and congratulations on his elevation to the highest institution of the State (FHACh, Doc. 371, Vol. 3, pp. 1.059-1.601).

A day later, the Waiwubu informs him that the condolences of each country will be received on November 28, 1908. However, and in a very significant way, on November 26, 1908, "the Spanish ambassador, Jia Sili [Cárcer], had to leave Beijing for something important and the main issues were transferred to the American ambassador William W. Rockhill". Cárcer, as Rockhill will report, will not return until December 24, 1908, when Puyi had already been crowned (FHACh, Doc. 367, Vol. 3, p. 1.051; FHACh, Doc. 368, Vol. 3, p. 1.052; FHACh, Doc. 372, Vol. 3, p. 1.062; FHACh, Doc. 376, Vol. 3, p. 1.075; FHACh, Doc. 377, Vol. 3, p. 1.076).

Following the official ritual, the funeral will be delayed until May 1909. In his role as "Dean", Cárcer is informed by Prince Ching of everything related to the transfer of the emperor's coffin, but, at all times, he will show a subordinate position to Rockhill (FHACh, Doc. 427, Vol. 3, pp. 1208-1209; FHACh, Doc. 414, Vol. 3, p. 1.192; FHACh, Doc. 434, Vol. 3, p. 1.223).

On the other hand, Puyi's accession to the throne appears in the archive on 23 November 1908 with a letter from Spanish Ambassador, Manuel de Cárcer, to Prince Ching, in which he conveys the congratulations of the King of Spain to Emperor Puyi on his "accession to the throne". The Spanish leadership in this matter, again, is due to the role of the Spanish ambassador as "Dean of the Diplomatic Corps". However, the enthronement took place on 2 December 1908, when Ambassador Carcer was away from Peking. His role was reduced to matters of protocol thereafter, where he ceded the limelight to US Ambassador Rockhill. Thus, on February 3, 1909, the *Waiwubu* sent him the credentials of the entire Diplomatic Corps so that they could write to the Great Emperor of the Great Qing. But his real role was limited to being Spain's ambassador, not acting as "Dean". So that, on June 9, 1909, an original letter from Alfonso XIII to Emperor Puyi was dated on June 9, 1909, congratulating him and "wishing Your Imperial Majesty a prosperous and happy reign and whatever may be to His satisfaction and pleasure" (FHACh, Doc. 374, Vol. 3, p. 1.070; FHACh, Doc. 384, Vol. 3, p. 1.091; FHACh, Doc. 435, Vol. 3, p. 1.224).

Spain's role as a secondary power and friend of China is clearly reflected in the treatment received by diplomats in China. It is a friendly treatment, aimed more at specific individuals than at the state they represent. So, the Diplomats' role of Spain in China is limited, in essence, to the individual role of its diplomats (Cologan, 2015, pp. 107-116; 120; 180-191). Cólogan, Cárcer and Pastor (Ramírez Ruiz, 2017, pp. 40-42), in this order, will be "Spain" in the eyes of the Qing government.

Imperial Audiences and Consular Visits

Communications regarding the audiences granted to Spanish diplomats and their families account for 13% of the documents. The period 1864-1902 is a time of hesitation, few contacts and disconnected news. Afterwards, the average exchanges are reduced to a single fixed annual audience with the occasion of the New Year. There were also some occasional Chinese official receptions at the Spanish embassy and palace audiences. In almost all these meetings there are delays "with allegations of unforeseen events" by the Spanish diplomat, such as when Cárcer missed "the audience with the emperor and the widow empress of the Great Qing due to his terrible health" (FHACh, Doc. 7, Vol. 1, pp. 30-31; FHACh, Doc.

184, Vol. 2, p. 547). These are excuses that we interpret as "acts of Western authority," within what has come to be called "colonial pedagogy" (Martínez Robles, 2010, p. 493).

This monotony is broken by one issue of historical significance: the audiences of diplomats' wives and the succession to the imperial throne. In 1902, with the return of Cixi from his exile in Xi'an, the diplomatic activity started to follow Western standards. According to Jung Chang, Empress Dowager Cixi, on January 27, 20 days after her return to Beijing, received the Diplomatic Corps without a screen. A few days later, as she was unable to socialize with men, she welcomed her wives and children (Jung Chang, 2016, pp. 413-416). The first news of this came on January 13, 1902, when Qu Hongji (1850 -1918) (Cao Zixi, 2014, pp. 653-655), from Waiwubu, requested a meeting with the Spanish ambassador, in his role as "dean of the Diplomatic Corps". After which, on February 2, 1902, Manuel de Cárcer wrote to Prince Ching thanking "the treatment that has been given to his wife and children". In his eagerness to please the Empress Cixi he went beyond what courtesy could allow and, Cárcer, as dean of the Diplomatic Corps, had to write to Ching again rejecting the gift of silver coins that Cixi made to the children: "are they are contrary to western customs".

Awards

The Great Qing rewarded officials, both Spanish and Chinese, when leaving their posts for a special service. Before 1902 the awards were occasional, but from the beginning of the century, with the coronation of Alfonso XIII, a new dynamic started that tended to the trivialization or generalization of these honorary recognitions. As we will see, later, 1908 represented an important Spanish consular renewal, as reflected in the delivery of Chinese awards to those who left. But, it will be with the end of the Empire when this tradition of rewarding for the most trivial causes will reach its maximum quota.

Changes in the Spanish Diplomatic Corps

There are many second-level diplomats that we see reflected in the FHACh Documents: Tiburcio Faraldo, Luis de Aryon, Tiburcio Rodríguez, Eduardo Aparicio y Mota, Hilarión González de Castillo y Velarde, Federigo Rodrigo Alemela, Conde Jezierski, J. F. Velasco, Rafael Seco Fabres, M. de Ynclan, Justo Garrido. But, as we have already said, Spain only had three diplomats in China in those years: Bernardo de Cólogan y Cólogán (1894-1902), Manuel de Cárcer (1903-1909) and Luis Pastor y de Mora (1910-1919) (Li Shengping, 1989, p. 768). Their long stay in Beijing, normally with few personnel at their service, meant that they established strong ties with the Qing government's top officials. This "guanxi" is best reflected in two events. On the one hand, in Empress Cixi's attempt to prevent Cárcer from leaving his post. The documents talk to us about private audiences that, in the case of Cárcer, show a certain degree of confidence, as demonstrated by the fact that due to his dismissal, the Chinese government ordered its ambassador in Madrid to initiate various procedures before the Foreign Ministry to prevent his departure (FHACh, Doc. 132, Vol. 1, pp. 435-436; FHACh, Doc. 351, Vol. 3, pp. 997-998; FHACh, Doc. 438, Vol. 3, pp. 1230-1231; FHACh, Doc. 472, Vol. 3, p. 1332; FHACh, Doc. 448, Vol. 3, p. 1252).

We have a lot of information about tourism. Diplomats ask for passports and protection to visit the Great Wall, the inland provinces, the Summer Palace or the Western Qing Tombs (nine documents of 1902, 1908 y 1909). Others issue affects their servants and reflects the power and influence of foreign representatives. In 1903, Cárcer's wife asks Empress Cixi for help, directly, so that her European servant is well cared for in the hospital "due to a small outbreak of smallpox." In July 1908 the embassy *rickshaw* driver will be arrested and mistreated by the police. This will lead to Cárcer taking initiatives that will resulting achieving immunity for diplomatic transport in Beijing. Finally, in April 1910 the embassy requests that its cook will be released after being detained for "fighting with others".

Economic Relations

Economic relations between Spain and China appear as extremely weak (Brasó Broggi, 2017, pp. 109-117). The documents that make mention of economic matters are only 11% of the total. Trade rarely appears in news isolated, disconnected and unfinished business. Those relevant involve the role of the ambassador as "Dean of the Diplomatic Corps." These are cases such as the following: on January 1894, China addresses the Spanish ambassador to establish an agreement on "the importation of machinery." It is a communication in which the mandarins are trying to avoid direct negotiation with the United States. The Spanish representative refuses to interfere, since the American "acts as representative of the diplomatic corps". Or when Cólogan will protest "the modification of customs fees, especially in the port of Tiensin" o will lead the negotiation to establish a regulation on the "trafficking of hides and game feathers". In those years, raw hides became one of the most exported products to Spain (Brasó Broggi, 2017, p. 117).

The final crisis of the empire had the new ambassador of Spain, Carcer, the opportunity of played the similar role of the previous one about the crash of the financial system. In 1907, Cárcer, as dean, must face the double taxation suffered by the products sent from Qinhuangdao to Niuzhuang compared to those sent from Qinhuangdao to Tientsin. And, on March 31, 1909, he will write two letters to Prince Ching. In the first, he complains about the devaluation of the *Hua-pao sycee* silver bullion in Tientsin and transmits the complaint of foreign merchants for paying a 2% tax surcharge and their demand for compensation. In the second, he recommends creating a centralized national minting system to solve similar issues. Almost a year later, the Waiwubu again insisted to *the Beiyang Minister*, recalling that, at the request of the Spanish ambassador, he should proceed to "return the additional tax paid by foreign businessmen" (FHACh, Doc. 292, Vol. 2, pp. 830-831; FHACh, Doc. 405, Vol. 3, pp. 1.156-1.157; FHACh, Doc. 406, Vol. 3, pp. 1.163-1.164; FHACh, Doc. 454, Vol. 3, p. 1.263).

The second important topic was the Boxer Protocol signed on 7 September 1901. Arduous negotiations immediately began to make its payment to the victorious powers effective. Spain signed two consecutive agreements (1903 and 1905) (Borao, 2017, p. 114) on compensation. The first mention of the compensation appears with a meeting that took place on December 31, 1902, after which Cárcer protested to Prince Ching about the obstructionism of the Shanghai Customs Official (*taotai*). Negotiations will continue, and in 1905, the "Friendship Agreement" between Spain and China will be modified because article 11 of the Final Protocol, obliged China to negotiate the amendments that Spain considers useful to the Treaty of Commerce and Navigation between Spain and China.

The final agreement on compensation was closed on July 2, 1905, but in the final months of that year, again, the Shanghai *taotai*, in charge of the payment, hindered the operation. According to the Spanish point of view, the payment had to be made following the Portuguese model, but Spain was not a partner of the Hong Kong Bank. What made the operation difficult, since the collection had to be made in London, in silver taels, at the cost of Shanghai. The Spanish government was not willing to assume the freight charges between London and Shanghai. Finally, China agreed to change the form of payment of the compensation but not Cárcer's suggestion to pay a bonus of 50 cents per 100 taels for the costs of moving the silver.

Finally, we have the Spanish businessmen in China. In reviewing the FHACH's "Spanish collection", the picture of the Spanish business presence that emerges is one of a scarce presence, punctual and related to the Philippines. All the deals undertaken by Spaniards, and reported in the FHACh, are problematic or unfinished. And they always show Spain's weakness as an imperialist power in China.

The first of these is the recruitment of coolies. The issue of Chinese workers, known as coolies, taken abroad to work as a substitute for slave labour, marked relations between China and Spain from the moment of their establishment, although it was not initially a major problem for the signing of the treaty (Borao, 2017, p.41). It appears as a minority issue in the documents of the FHACh, although it does so with the case that represented its historical turning point.

In 1866, after the signing of the Trade Treaty between Spain and China, several Spanish businessmen, tried to find a "House of Contracting of Chinese settlers for the island of Cuba". This request was rejected in 1871 by the "tax bureau of Chinese Customs in Canton". The reason was the complaints received from the consuls of the United States, Denmark, Great Britain and France, who warned the Chinese authorities that "their intention to recruit was based entirely on earnings, regardless of whether the workers' lives were hard or not. The US consul also emphasized the terrible situation of Chinese workers in Spanish colonies such as Peru" (FHACh, Doc. 5, Vol. 1, pp. 85-115). This case will be the end of the Spanish recruitment of coolies and will force China and Spain to sign the "Spanish-Chinese Emigration Agreement" of 1877 (Zhang Kai, 2003, 196-210).

The most important, or at least the most controversial, Spanish businessman in China was known to Chinese sources as Ma Ganbao. Joaquín Malcampo will be the main protagonist of the communications related to the activities of the Spanish businessmen in China, monopolizing 44% of the documents between 1902-1909. He is a Chinese citizen who, after a period of residence in the Philippines, acquired Spanish nationality, resides in Amoy (Xiamen) and is the owner of "Malcampo & Co. Merchants and Commission Agents". His business will always end in legal controversies, in which he will use the privileges granted by the European passport (Xiamen Archives, 1997, pp. 531-532).

In 1896 he founded the *Ruixiang Bank*, for which he hired Ouyang Ruiquan, who, after a time, became his partner. The bank was poorly managed and Malcampo, in 1899, denounced Ouyang to the ambassador alleging a debt of 55,000 yuan. For the Waiwubu the matter begins in December 1902 when the Spanish ambassador asks for *"the justice that should be expected"*. Meanwhile, Malcampo extended his claim to Huang Zide, Ouyang's nephew and guarantor. In January 1905 Wei Guangtao, envoy of the Viceroy of Minzhe (Xu Kai, Mu Yinchen, 2009, p. 332), communicated stated that not only he did not recognize the debt alleged by Malcampo, but also ordered him to pay 3,280 taels for the costs (FHACh, Doc. 113, Vol. 1, p. 398; FHACh, Doc. 201, Vol. 2, pp. 583-586).

The second case is a national scandal, Malcampo ran a theater in Xiamen, and, in November 1908, he dared to open it, circumventing the legal prohibition of holding shows during the hundred days of mourning for the death of the emperors. Malcampo, already known and hated by the local authorities, was, together with his son, beaten and detained. Again, he did not hesitate to use the privileges granted him by his nationality. In the absence of a Spanish diplomatic representative in Xiamen, the French consul should take charge of the case. The news came to appear in the international press and thanks to this we found out that, in the end, as was usual on these occasions, the *taotai* was ceased.

Following the chronological order (September 1903) the third businessman to appear is Francis Gogar Leyles, who intends to establish a mining company, extraction of coal in Anhui, called Yutong. At the same time, he requests permission to build a narrow-gauge railway to serve the mining operation (FHACh, Doc. 157, Vol. 2, pp. 485-491). The Spanish businessman had a Chinese partner named Ning

Qingbo. The initial start-up capital was 50,000 taels of silver. This is a case that perfectly explains the characteristics of the source and of Spanish entrepreneurship in China. Firstly, we have unfinished news of a business venture whose final solution cannot be verified. Secondly, we have a large project that is difficult to encompass and possibly unfinished.

Next, we meet a smuggler called Perez. In 1904, a businessman named "Pérez" appeared for the first time and saw that his request to establish a wooden walkway, as a boat landing stage, in the Port of Shanghai was rejected because it did not comply with international treaties. In response, the Spanish ambassador, Cárcer, wrote directly to Prince Ching protesting the rejection and claiming that the Spanish businessman was being treated in a discriminatory manner, causing him economic losses with the paralysis of his file. Ching's response came in the form of a communiqué from the Ministry, which, after reviewing the arguments of the customs official, ratified its decision and denied discriminatory treatment, as similar requests from Japanese and American businessmen had also been rejected.

However, this Pérez, who we identify as Ramigio Pérez Aura, appears again in 1906. He complains before Cárcer that the Shanghai *taotai* denied him the establishment of a wood depot or lumber yard. Cárcer protests to Prince Ching claiming that he is entitled by Article 5 of the treaty. But the matter of Pérez is much more important than it claims, since the claim that the facility is indeed a "wood warehouse" is suspicious considering that "... the Customs of that port [has seized Pérez] 11 boxes containing 3 shotguns and 14,000 cartridges ... ".

Faced with the presence of these weapons, Cárcer argued that "being for his use, I see no reason why Mr. Pérez cannot import these goods. Cárcer claimed that "arms and bullets for hunting are not explicitly prohibited in the treaty". For the "treaty does not permit the smuggling of arms and the like [art. 49]. Although there is no explicit stipulation that arms and bullets used for hunting are forbidden to be imported".

Prince Ching replies to Cárcer that, although certainly no treaty expressly prohibited the importation of arms and bullets for personal use, the large quantity of ammunition he intended to import "made one suspect that it must belong to persons other than one" (cita).

In his next communication, Cárcer is forced to acknowledge that the weapons are "more for selling than for hunting", but that both Belgian and British businessmen had imported weapons into the port of Tientsin "under unilateral most-favoured-nation treatment", a privilege to which the Spanish businessman is also entitled.

Finally, on 18 May 1906, in a long report, the Waiwubu tells Cárcer the correct procedure for importing arms. But, Perez transported thousands of bullets to sell them for profit, using the shotguns to try to hide his intention, lying that they were for his own use and hunting, and consciously did not inform the customs to avoid paying taxes, so Perez's case could not be compared to that of the English and Belgian Tientsin businessmen (Xu Kai, Mu Yinchen, 2009, pp. 334-335). Therefore, on May 28, 1906, Pérez's commercial establishment will be prohibited, on suspicion of smuggling (FHACh, Doc. 248, Vol. 2, pp. 717-718; FHACh, Doc. 245, Vol. 2, pp. 709-710; FHACh, Doc. 247, Vol. 2, p. 715; FHACh, Doc. 252, Vol. 2, pp. 729-730).

Finally, as is usual among Spanish entrepreneurs abroad, we find large projects: *Beijing Water Company*. According to the documents issued between July-August 1907, a group of Spaniards, called by the Chinese source "Celia et al.", want to take advantage of the Cixi Palace fire in 1907 to promote a running water project to the capital, a Running-water Company in Pekin.

On July 19, 1907, the Waiwubu communicated to the Ministry of Civil Affaires the inconvenience of this project because it had already been tried by the American diplomat Charles Denby in 1902-1903, while he was the main adviser to the Viceroy of Zhili Yuan Shikai. It failed because of the "cultural atavism of the people", which had not changed (FHACh, Doc. 314, Vol. 2, pp. 902-905).

On 30 July the Ministry of Civil Affairs replied to the Foreign Office that it had agreed to reject the Spanish request, not only because of the Denby precedent, but also because it considered that "such an important civil work should be carried out by its own country".

On 1 August 1907, the Ministry of Foreign Affairs sent the same reply to the Spanish ambassador. But Cárcer was not prepared to accept this refusal, and on 10 August 1907, he wrote to the Waiwubu trying to refute the reasons given for the refusal and pointing out alternative ways and the advantages that China could obtain.

Manuel de Cárcer intended to go ahead with the project despite this first official rejection. But, once again, the documentation ends up not giving us a solution to the matter. Although we know, from historical reality, that the Spanish businessmen did not complete the project. The person in charge was the powerful Yuan Shikai, Viceroy of Zhili (Peking region) at the time, who, under the direct order of the Dowager Empress Cixi, entrusted this mission to Zhou Xuexi, an efficient official who, within the framework of the Westernisation Movement, had already played a leading role in the establishment of various industries throughout China. In April 1908, the Jingshi Tap Water Co. was founded (Su Xiuying, 2009, 63).

Minor Topics

In the First Historical Archives of China we have found a miscellany of news items. We have classified it in four issues as minor: Epidemics, military issues, culture, and justice. All can be considered secondary and subordinate to others.

The only one with historical interest is those that show what kind of relations existed between the two countries. We are talking about historical facts, for example: On 1882 Tiburcio Rodríguez communicating that the Chinese community in the Philippines has suffered little from the cholera outbreak that hit the islands at the time thanks to their intra-ethnic solidarity (FHACh, Doc. 14, Vol. 1, pp. 135-137). Or in October 1894, Cárcer announced the arrival of E. Herrera de la Rosa as military attaché to the embassies of Beijing and Tokyo (Rodao, 2002, pp. 144-145). Or reported the gift of books to the Chinese authorities, whose themes refer to Spanish art and culture. And finally, a 3% of the documents speak of legal cases. The vast majority are related to businessmen or servants of diplomats.

SOLUTIONS AND RECOMMENDATIONS

In this article we have carried out an exhaustive analysis of the 809 documents related to Spain kept in the First Historical Archive of China from the "Qing Foreign Ministry" from its creation as Zongli Yamen (1861) until the fall of the empire, already renamed as Waiwubu. This collection includes all communications between the Spanish government through its embassy, and the Chinese imperial government, as well as the internal documentation generated between Chinese institutions regarding their contacts with Spain since the signing of the treaty of Spanish Chinese friendship in 1864 until January 1912.

There are several findings to emphasize from this study. In the first place, China-Spain relations between 1864 and 1912 were characterized by high levels of formality and protocol. Specifically, 68% of the documents deal with coronations, births, marriages, birthdays, and deaths of both royal families;

imperial hearings and consular visits; appointments of officials; delivery of awards or personal affairs of Spanish diplomats.

This predominance of protocol shows us two monarchies that wish to establish and maintain mutual legitimizing ties, seeking a nominal foreign prestige that they were unable to achieve by more effective means. This second finding emerges from the fact that 91% of the documents are concentrated between 1902 and 1912, coinciding with the appearance of two "regenerationist moments" in both monarchies. On the one hand, in 1902 Alfonso XIII, who dreamed of being the "regenerationist" king, ascended to the throne of Spain. On the other, the Empress Dowager Cixi, returning from exile to Xi'an after the taking of Beijing by the allied armies following the Boxer Rebellion, initiated the Constitutional Reform of the old dynasty, the New Plant Decrees, as a last chance to save the Qing dinasty. Both states looked at each other from afar and sought gratuitous and non-binding sympathies.

The third conclusion leads us to economic matters, to which only 11% of the documents are devoted. This appears to be the main reason for the timid Spanish presence and impact in the Far East. Economic relations revolve around two themes. On the one hand, issues related to banking and currencies, in which Spain claims the payment of the Boxer compensation as part of broader international agreements. On the other, the performance of Spanish businessmen in China. Spanish businesses are characterized by a personal, punctual presence frequently related with the Philippines. In addition, the Waiwubu usually preserves information about fragmentary and unfinished projects, such as the attempt to create a "Beijing Water Company" or the Yutong mining company. There are also reports of smugglers, such as the case of Perez's "Lumber Warehouse" in Shanghai, and a small but significant presence of documents related to the hiring of coolies. At the end, there is only one Spanish company that maintained a controversial presence over time, and that is "Malcampo y Cía.".

Spanish economic activity is characterized more by its absence than its presence. This is also the case of other minor issues, which illustrate the abundant deficiencies in these relations between China and Spain. As such we have found mention of epidemics, military, cultural and judicial affairs. The first two are again protocol matters informing on an epidemic in the Philippines in 1882, practically the only mention of the Philippines in the Archives of the Chinese Foreign Ministry. Military affairs are limited to protocol matters. Meanwhile, cultural and judicial issues replicate the business model: they are punctual, personal and unfinished.

A conclusion refers to the role of Spain as a secondary power and friend of China. A 10% of the agreements refer to international treaties and agreements of the diplomatic corps. At this point, the role of the various Spanish ambassadors as "Deans" of the diplomatic corps is especially important. Cólogan, Cárcer and Pastor will occupy that position for years. The lack of a specific agenda in China will make Spain a "neutral" country and a friend of China. And it also will confer a strong personal role on these diplomats. But their low weight will mean that, at critical moments such as the death of the emperors in 1908, they are relegated to secondary positions, despite the official position they occupy.

In short, the vision that the Qing State probably had of Spain was that of a secondary nation in the international context, without economic or strategic interest (since 1898) in the field of the Far East. A friendly and weak nation, useful in seeking international recognition for the Qing Dynasty, but irrelevant.

FUTURE RESEARCH DIRECTIONS

This line of research continues with the comparison of these sources from the People's Republic of China with those located in Taiwan and Spain. The former come from the evacuation of official documents carried out by the Chiang Kaisek regime in the last days of the Republic of China. They are in the custody of the Academia Sinica in Taipei. The second, the Spanish documents, are distributed between the National Historical Archive and the General Administration Archive. From this joint analysis, we will be able to confirm whether the type of relations between the late Qing and Spain really followed the path that made Spain a "dove" among the European "imperialist hawks" in China.

CONCLUSION

In essence, this research portrays the existence of a relationship between Spain and China that can be characterized as "formal but insubstantial". Analyzing the current situation, we can see that the type of relations that the Kingdom of Spain has established with the People's Republic of China continue to run along very similar lines. A century later, cultural remoteness and the lack of a strong, constant economic relationship based on symbiotic complementarity mean that Spain continues to be a friend of China. But this friendship is based on a lack of interests, both convergent and divergent. China's Eurasia One Road One Belt (OBOR) project may bring about a change.

REFERENCES

Bai, S. (Ed.). (2008). *An outline history of China*. Foreign Languages Press.

Borao Mateo, J. E. (2017). *Las miradas entre España y China. Un siglo de relaciones entre los dos países (1864-1973) [The looks between Spain and China. A century of relations between the two countries (1864-1973).]*. Miraguano Ediciones.

Brasó Broggi, C. (2017). Las Aduanas Marítimas de China y el comercio sino-español, 1900-1930 [Chinese Maritime Customs and Sino-Spanish trade, 1900-1930.]. *Revista de Historia Industrial, 70*(XXVI), 109–143.

Cao, Z. (Ed.). (2014). *Beijing Lishi Renwu Zhuan [The Biography of Historical Persons in Beijing]*. (Vol. 2). Beijing Yanshan Press.

Chang, J. (2016). *Cixí, La emperatriz. La concubina que creó la China moderna [Cixi, The Empress. The concubine who created modern China]*. Taurus.

Chen, X. (Ed.). (1982). *Zhongguo Jindaishi Cidian [The Dictionary of Chinese Modern History]*. Shanghai Lexicographical Publishing House.

Cologán Soriano, C. (2015). *Bernardo Cologán y los 55 días en Pekín [Bernardo Cologán and the 55 days in Beijing]*. Gobierno de Canarias.

García Ruiz-Castillo, C. (2009). Los fondos de las representaciones diplomáticas y consulares de España en China conservados en el Archivo General de la Administración: Su context [The funds of the diplomatic and consular representations of Spain in China conserved in the General Archive of the Administration: Its context.]. *Cuadernos de Historia Contemporánea, 31*, 223–241.

García-Tapia Bello, J. L. (2009). Relaciones bilaterales con China [Bilateral relations with China]. *Boletín Económico ICE [Economic Bulletin ICE], 2.972* (1), 69-93.

Li, S. (Ed.). (1989). *Zhongguo Jinxiandai Renming Dacidian [The Dictionary of Modern and Contemporary Chinese Celebrities]*. China's International Broadcasting Publishing House.

Li, W. (2017). *The Emergence of the Modern Chinese Diplomats: Officials in the Zongli Yamen, Waiwu Bu and legations, 1861-1911 [Zhōngguó jìndài wàijiāo guān qúntǐ de xíngchéng(1861-1911)]*. SDX Joint Publishing Company.

Martínez-Robles, D. (2010). Más allá de los tratados desiguales: reciprocidad en el tratado sino-español de 1864 [Beyond unequal treaties: reciprocity in the Sino-Spanish treaty of 1864]. In P. San Ginés (Ed.), *Cruce de miradas, relaciones e intercambios [Crossing glances, relationships and exchanges]* (pp. 487–505). Editorial Universidad de Granada.

Martínez-Robles, D. (2018). Los desheredados de la empresa imperial: Implantación diplomática de España como potencia colonial periférica en China [The disinherited of the imperial company: Diplomatic implantation of Spain as a peripheral colonial power in China]. *Historia Contemporánea, 57*(57), 460–465. doi:10.1387/hc.17724

Martínez-Robles, D. (2018). *Entre dos Imperios. Sinibaldo de Mas y la empresa colonial en China (1844-1868) [Crossing glances, relationships and exchanges]*. Macial Pons.

Palacios, L. & Ramírez-Ruiz, R. (2011). *China. Historia, pensamiento, arte y cultura [China. History, thought, art and culture.]*. Almuzara.

Ramírez Ruiz, R. (2017). Neto and Giadán: The Last Two Spanish in the Qing Dynasty. *Sinologia Hispanica, 4*(1), 1–46. doi:10.18002in.v4i1.5266

Ramírez Ruiz, R. (2018). *Historia de China Contemporánea. De las guerras del opio a nuestros días [History of Contemporary China. From the opium wars to the present day]*. Síntesis.

Rodao, F. (1997). *Españoles en Siam, 1540-1939: una aportación al estudio de la presencia hispana en Asia [Spaniards in Siam, 1540-1939: a contribution to the study of the Hispanic presence in Asia]*. CSIC.

Rodao, F. (2002). *Franco y el imperio japonés. Imágenes y propaganda en tiempos de Guerra [Franco and the Japanese Empire. Images and propaganda in times of war.]*. Plaza & Janés.

Rodríguez Caparrini, B. (2014). Alumnos españoles en el internado jesuita de Beaumont (Old Windsor, Inglaterra), 1880-1886 [Spanish students at the Jesuit boarding school at Beaumont (Old Windsor, England), 1880-1886.]. *Hispania Sacra, LXVI* (Extra I), 403-452.

Shi, Y. (Ed.). (1996). *Zhonghua Minguo Waijiaoshi Cidian [The Dictionary of Diplomatic History of the Republic of China]*. Shanghai Ancient Books Press.

Tang, J. (Ed.). (2000). *Zhongguo Waijiao Cidian* [*Dictionary on China's Diplomacy*]. World Affairs Press.

The First Historical Archives of China, Peking University, & Macao Polytechnic Institute (Edit.). (2004). The Collection of Sino-foreign Relation Archives of the Ministry of Foreign Affairs in Qing Dynasty, China and Spain. Zhong Hua Book Company.

VVAA. (1909). Taotai Liu's dimissal causes demostration. *San Francisco Call*, https://cdnc.ucr.edu/cgi-bin/cdnc?a=d&d=SFC19090329.2.21

Xiong, Y. (2013). *Zhongguo Jinxiandai Shi Juan* [*The Chinese Modern History*]. Shanghai Lexicographical Publishing House.

Xu, K., & Mu, Y. (2009). An overview on the Late Ching Government's Commercial Policy towards Spain. In X. Li, & Ch. Li (Ed.), *The Symposium of Conference on "China and Spain during the Ming and Ching Dynasties* (pp. 329-339). Macao Polytechnic Institute.

Zhaickuan, (Ed.). (1997). *Zhongguo Jiyou Cidian* [*Diccionario de Filatelia de China*], vol.2. Beijing Press.

Zhang, K. (2003). *Historia de las Relaciones Sino-Españolas [History of Sino-Spanish relations]*. Elephant Press.

Chapter 10
Japanese Colonialism:
The Rise of a New Colonial Empire

Pedro Panera Martinez
General Gutierrez Mellado University Institute, Spain

ABSTRACT

This chapter attempts to explain the historical process by which Japan succeeded in becoming a leading colonial power in the Far East. It will analyze the dramatic changes that took place in Japanese foreign policy and international relations from the mid-nineteenth century onwards. Changes that enabled a country with a feudal-type structure to build a national and centralist state and to achieve an unprecedented expansion in the Pacific Ocean and continental Asia. In short, it will describe the process by which Tokyo created in a few decades one of the largest and most ephemeral colonial empires in the history of mankind, supported by rampant nationalism and militarism.

INTRODUCTION

Writing the history of Japan or any other Asian country from a Western perspective can lead to certain cultural nuances being partially misunderstood or maybe overlooked altogether. However, during recent decades, there has been growing popular demand for works on the history of the Far East, especially from the specific perspective of International Relations or Military History. Japan's significance in the contemporary evolution of humanity is unquestionable. Today it is more necessary than ever to understand the current problems of diplomacy in the Asia-Pacific region, insofar as a review of the past can contribute to a better understanding of the contemporary panorama of international relations.

This chapter aims to identify the principles that guided the territorial and colonial expansion of a country that, in a few decades, was transformed from a small island nation with a feudal-type structure into the heart of one of the largest and most ephemeral colonial empires in history. To this end, an attempt has been made to provide a new critical point of view of when this process started, supported by the study and reinterpretation of a wide range of relevant secondary sources. As a consequence of the historical profile of the analysis, the description of events and their chronological order has played an essential role. Thus, the structure of the text is divided into two main sections, corresponding –broadly

DOI: 10.4018/978-1-6684-7040-4.ch010

speaking– to the nineteenth and twentieth centuries. The first section reviews the distant historical background of Japanese expansionism, as well as the end of the country's international isolation and its entry into the international arena and the beginning of territorial expansion in the nineteenth century. The second section corresponds to twentieth-century territorial gains until the end of World War II, and it is divided into four parts which correspond to the main events of the period: the Russo-Japanese War and the annexation of Korea; the Great War and the Siberian Intervention; the interwar period and the ephemeral expansions which took place until the end of World War II; and the collapse of the colonial empire in 1945.

The primary objective of this contribution is to explain the process by which Japan succeeded in becoming a leading colonial power in the Far East at the beginning of the twentieth century and how the roots of this rise lay in the nineteenth century.

BACKGROUND

Colonial processes have traditionally been regarded as historical phenomena exclusively developed by some countries of Western civilization and, more specifically, by European countries. In recent years, some very relevant works have highlighted the need to reconsider whether or not the relations of territorial domination developed in the seventeenth and eighteenth centuries by the Quing Empire can be described as colonialist (Schneider, 2020). Despite the fact that the process of Japanese colonialism is generally believed to have been the "only successful attempt by a non-Western power", albeit based on political and ideological assumptions far removed from those of the West (Souyri, 2005, p. 479).

Because of its socio-political and geographical constraints, "Japan seemed destined to remain politically immature, economically backward and militarily impotent in terms of world power" (Kennedy, 2006, p. 333). However, against all the odds, it embarked on a strategy of Westernization that enabled it to join in the game of territorial rivalries with the great empires of the time, on an equal or even a superior footing. Of course, the country's Westernization did not occur as a consequence of a fondness for or affinity with European culture, but after drawing "the painful conclusion that Japan must adapt Western civil and military institutions in order to fend off the West", having observed "with horror China's vivisection by Russia and its subjugation" (Paine, 2016, pp. 425-426).

In response, many ideologists of the time advocated the country should join "the colonialist banquet", as Fukuzawa Yukichi did in 1885 in his publishing house *Datsu-A Ron* (Martínez Taberner, 2015, p. 136). In line with this idea, Japanese leaders soon became convinced that successful European national models –i.e. those with greater economic and political power– maintained powerful navies and strong military structures that had allowed them to expand into vast overseas territories. It was not long before the obvious conclusion was drawn: Japan had to "conquer or be conquered", to adopt the knowledge and modes of action of the European powers and the United States or resign itself to suffering a fate identical to that of India and China (Torre del Río, 1985, pp. 7-8, 13-14).

The subsequent process of imperial construction is often divided into two phases. A domestic one, in which the reforms necessary to modernize the whole country were undertaken between 1869 and 1894, followed by another focused on securing territories, from 1895 onwards (Paine, 2016, pp. 426-427). In reality, it is perhaps more appropriate to argue that the two phases overlapped and that Japanese empire-building began much earlier. However, Nipponese historiography has vehemently differentiated between pre- and post-1895 expansion. This is a clear attempt to legitimize the territorial aggrandizement of a nation-state in the making by illegitimately and violently phagocytizing other neighboring states, and does not seem to admit the slightest debate, given the alleged difference in scale, aims and means of the two processes. Thus, the Japanese academy confines the colonial phenomenon exclusively to the first half of the twentieth century, neglecting the fact that it acquired shape and took form from the mid-nineteenth century onwards, although its origins can be traced back much further.

From the point of view of European historiography, it would be more correct to distinguish three phases: an initial one, which would include the formation of the state itself, the development of its expansive mentality and the annexation and demographic occupation of certain groups of adjacent islands to the north and south of the archipelago until the decade of the 1890s. Another, from the occupation of Taiwan in 1895 until the outbreak of World War II, whereby the adjoining territories gradually came under Tokyo's domination and were subjected to the process of forced cultural assimilation. And the third, which would correspond to the occupation of the Western colonies in the area –Burma, Indochina, Indonesia, Malaysia and the Philippines– and their integration into the Greater East Asia Co-Prosperity Sphere from 1941 until the end of the Asia-Pacific War. However, it is not clear that one should speak of colonization in the strict sense in these cases, just as occupied France did not become Germany's colony during those years (Souyri, 2005, pp. 483-484).

Discussions aside, it seems clear that the costs of territorial expansion always offset any potential benefits, initiating a dangerous vicious circle whereby colonial expansion could never stop: the progression towards Korea meant setting sights on Manchuria; once the latter was subjugated, Tokyo made greater demands on China, and these entailed further aspirations in relation to Indochina and Southeast Asia (Morgan, 2016, p. 493). If Japan had been successful in these scenarios, Australia, India, Siberia or even the Latin American coast would definitely have constituted the next steps in the expansionist spiral.

The history of the country seems to have shaped it into an ever-expanding state, seeking to assimilate and encompass annexed territories (Souyri, 2005, p. 481). Since time immemorial, Japan's political evolution has been defined by the continuous and constant struggles between local clans to impose themselves on their neighbors, with the ultimate aspiration of dominating the entire archipelago. Once this primordial unity had been achieved, far from confining themselves to their island borders, the rulers immediately set their sights on the surrounding territories, until the debacles of their first expeditions against Korea, European military superiority and the growing penetration of Christianity finally convinced the ruling class of the need to remain within their own natural borders to guarantee their perpetuation in power.

EARLY TERRITORIAL DOMINANCE

Precedents and Historical Background

Leaving aside the mythical explanations present in the *Kojiki* and the *Nihon Shoki* about the *Kuniumi* or "formation of the country", historians do not appear to have reached a consensus on the origin of the Japanese people, who were most likely an amalgam of Tungus tribes from the north, people from southern China and Mongols from Korea. In the absence of written records prior to the introduction of *kanji* or Chinese characters in the fifth and sixth centuries –and bearing in mind that early chronicles are nothing but the self-interested production of a court seeking to justify its power– it is not easy to determine with any accuracy the evolution of political processes during the *Jomon* (to 250 BC) the *Yayoi* (to 250 AD) and the *Kofun* period (250-538 AD) of the *Yamato* era (250-710 AD).

Nevertheless, Japanese historians are in agreement with regard to the existence of archaeological and written testimonies that would support the deployment of expeditions against Korea, some of which would have succeeded into imposing themselves upon the neighboring peninsular kingdoms at the end of the fourth century and initiating a period of Nipponese influence in the region. Scholars on the other side of the strait, meanwhile, triumphantly affirm the existence of Korean groups that initiated the first organized societies in the archipelago (Rodríguez Jiménez, 2020, pp. 15-16). Despite this apparent difference in criteria, what seems quite clear is that Nipon cultural origins were initially concentrated on the island of Kyushu, before expanding into southern Honshu. The territory witnessed continuous struggles between different warlords for control of the land, with the victor eventually settling in the Yamato area and establishing an imperial dynasty that has survived to the present day (Hane, 2013, pp. 22-25).

However, the result of this political process was not the imposition of a centralized state, but rather the articulation of an amalgam of territories under independent political rule, but culturally related and ceremonially subject to the Imperial Court. Despite the aspiration of several rulers to establish a robust government like that of the Tang dynasty in China, the impossibility of raising standing armies eventually led to the emergence of a social group that made warfare its way of life. These were the *bushi* or samurai, thanks to whose loyalty some *shugos* or provincial administrators ended up becoming true *daimyos* –a sort of feudal lord (Rodríguez Jiménez, 2020, pp. 22-23). The power struggles between these daimyos would culminate in the ascension in 1192 of Minamoto no Yoritomo (1147-1199), who was proclaimed *Seii Taishogun* –abbreviated as *shogun*– or "Great general appeaser of the barbarians", establishing a system of politics known as *Bakufu* or "Government from the curtain"[1].

The shogunate failed to put an end to internal conflicts, which were constant until the sixteenth century, perhaps because the archipelago was not seriously threatened from the mainland. The only major exceptions were the two campaigns of conquest launched by the Mongol Kublai Khan (1215-1294) in the late thirteenth century, after his conquest of China and Korea. These campaigns, however, were thwarted by providential typhoons that destroyed the invading fleets and were known as *kamikaze* or "divine wind". By contrast, in the late sixteenth century, from the relative safety of the archipelago, the unifier Toyotomi Hideyoshi (1537-1598) sent two consecutive expeditions against the continent, while the *daimyo* Shimazu Tadatsune (1576-c.1640) did the same against the Ryukyu Islands. The Korean raids of 1592-1593 and 1597-1598, known as the Imjin Wars, failed miserably, but the Satsuma fiefdom fared better in its action against the Nansei archipelagic kingdom in 1609, and Okinawa became doubly subservient to the Celestial Empire monarchy and the Satsuma princes (Souyri, 2005, p. 488).

Further evidence of Japan's outward-looking vocation can be found in the operation of the *shuinsen* or "red seal ship" system. In essence, these were a few hundred-armed merchantmen who were granted patents to trade throughout Southeast Asia, thus encouraging the emergence of *Nihonmachis* in the major ports in their routes. One of the most important of these "Japanese towns" was Dilao, near Spanish Manila, which welcomed the famous Catholic Justo Takayama (c.1550-1615) after his departure from Honsu due to the upsurge of religious persecution. Despite the welcome the Spaniards extended to the *Kirishitan* in the Philippines, the arrival of Japanese in Manila was usually viewed with much suspicion. In 1589, there was something of an alarm when it became known that a large fleet was being prepared against Korea. The Spanish Governor of the time stated that, thanks to their numerous spies, the Japanese were aware of the few Castilian troops who garrisoned the Philippines and might be falsely announcing their intention to attack the mainland in order to converge by surprise on Luzon (Reyes Manzano, 2014, p. 318).

In any case, the first contacts with Portuguese and Spanish were even initially encouraged by Japan, but the fear of a possible Spanish military intervention due to the growing community of Catholic

Christians led to Hideyoshi's partial proscription of the faith in 1587. The total ban on Catholicism was introduced in 1614 by Tokugawa Ieyasu (1543-1616), only one year after the departure of the embassy of Hasekura Tsunenaga, who visited Spain and the Holy See.

It should not be forgotten, however, that it was not only religious motives that prompted the Tokugawa shogunate to break contact with the outside world. This also responded to the intention of preventing the *daimyos* from accessing imported firearms that could threaten centralized power, to the fact that foreign trade was about to drain the country of precious metals, and to the fear that Western penetration would end up representing serious competition for Japanese international trade (Reyes Manzano, 2005, p. 53; Laborde Carranco, 2011, p. 116; Rodríguez Jiménez, 2020, pp. 27-28). Likewise, it should not be forgotten that *rangaku* or "Schools of Foreign Studies" continued to exist in Japan, where information about the West was gathered and ambitious plans for reforming the country were drawn up, such as that of Sato Nobuhiro (1769-1850), who even advocated territorial expansion through the occupation of Luzon, among other places (Martínez Taberner, 2015, p. 130).

From Isolation to the Entry into the International Arena

In the last decades of the Takugawa shogunate (1600-1868) –and thus of the Edo period (1603-1867) – an intense process took place that historiography has come to know as *Bakumatsu*. In essence, this was an unprecedented social, cultural, and industrial modernization, whereby the country abandoned its feudal structure to build a heavily industrialized national and centralist state, headed by the emperor instead of the shogun. The influence of Western armed forces in this process was decisive, as it was initially the "gunboat diplomacy" expeditions of US Commodore Matthew C. Perry (1853) and the subsequent interventions by France, the United Kingdom and Russia –between 1863 and 1865– that put the final seal on the traditional *Sakoku* or "closing of the country"[2].

As a result of the shogunate government's weakness in dealing with such foreign intrusions, the confidence in its power professed by some *daimyo* diminished drastically. They were perfectly aware that Westerners were imposing their will on China by force. So, in an attempt to prevent the nation from suffering a fate similar to that of other Asian states and to achieve the traditional aspiration of the *fukoku kyohei* or "rich nation, strong army" motto, the imperial court seized power from the shogun during the enthronement of the young prince Meiji Tenno (Souyri, 2005, p. 480; Hane, 2013, p. 124). The result was a bloody civil war known as the Boshin War or Japanese Revolution (1868-1869).

This conflict was the catalyst for the search for Western military instructors and equipment, both by allies of imperial power and those of the Tokugawa clan. After the consolidation of the Meiji period (1868-1912), the government of the newly founded Great Empire concentrated a large part of its resources on obtaining all sorts of information from foreign peoples, paradoxically considered "barbarians". This was in harmony with the fifth premise of the *Charter of the Oath*, promulgated during the Meiji enthronement, according to which "knowledge was to be sought anywhere in the world to strengthen the power of the emperor" (Hane, 2013, p. 126). The idea was to combine the "Eastern spirit with Western science" or *wakon yosai*, a slogan coined in the pre-Meiji era (Rodríguez Jiménez, 2020, p. 51).

Without going into further detail about this period, once the Boshin War ended in 1869 –and after a decade-long period of internal instability– the territory's centralized power was consolidated, despite the brief threat posed by the Satsuma Rebellion of 1877, which was crushed in the famous Battle of Shiroyama. Thereafter, Tokyo began to review its international position, more in line with the aforementioned motto of "rich nation, strong army". The intention was to recover from the humiliation of the signing of the

Treaty of Kanagawa with Washington in 1854, which began the signing of the *Ansei Treaties* with the United Kingdom, Russia, the Netherlands and France. Even Spain adhered to these unequal agreements with the belated signing of the *Treaty of Friendship, Commerce and Navigation* in 1868 (Martínez Taberner, 2017, pp. 106-112). However, that treaty already incorporated several modifications with respect to previous ones, including a sort of reformulation of extraterritoriality rights (Martínez Taberner, 2015, p. 134). Not surprisingly, it was the first treaty signed by the new Meiji government, and the imperial court was already seriously rethinking its own relevance and weight in the international sphere: in the face of European expansion into Asian territories, it was "more logical, in the opinion of the Tokyo government, for Japan to do so" (Rodríguez Jiménez, 2020, p. 61).

The entire Meiji renewal had succeeded in reproducing institutional structures in domestic politics, but it also involved importing from the West patterns of action in foreign policy (Laborde Carranco, 2011, p. 120). Thus, the Chrysanthemum Throne had understood that in order to be accepted among the great powers, it would not be enough to achieve full modernization or the revision of the vexatious conditions imposed by the Europeans, but that it had to expand territorially and obtain new territories that would guarantee access to raw materials, new markets and provide strategic enclaves (Togores Sánchez, 2000, p. 9). In other words, the colonialist mentality permeated the upper echelons of society, which understood that the country had to act as one of the main imperialist powers and participate in the game of territorial rivalries with other colonial empires at a moment when other non-Western power was really capable of doing so (Souyri, 2005, p. 481).

Initial Expansion and Birth of a New Colonial Power

Japanese penetration of Ezo Island dates back as far as the *Muromachi* period (1336-1573), with the early occupation of the Oshima Peninsula. However, it was during the last years of the *Tokugawa* shogunate that regular expeditions began to be launched to the northern islands of the archipelago, in the face of growing competition with the Russian Empire in the area and the fear that St. Petersburg would completely take over Ezo, Sakhalin and the Kurils. Tokyo's expansion in the area began to be particularly encouraged in the wake of the Boshin conflict, mainly through the establishment in 1869 of the Hokkaido Colonial Development Commission, as the island of Ezo was known henceforth.

Moreover, in 1874, Tokyo launched the expedition against Taiwan, in its first overseas deployment in contemporary times, in response to the murder of several sailors by Paiwan Indians, a campaign that opened the door to the subsequent incorporation of the Ryukyu Empire in 1879, following its transformation into a simple manor in 1872 and the abolition of the monarchy (Souyri, 2005, p. 488)[3].

Furthermore, the Ganghwa Island Incident of 1875 enabled Tokyo to force the signing of the *Korean-Japanese Friendship Treaty or Treaty of Ganghwa* in 1876, which opened up the trade circuit of the Joseon kingdom after unsuccessful attempts by France and the US in 1866 and 1871[4]. This treaty, similar in content to the unequal treaties that the Japanese had been enduring, not only established the opening of Korean ports to trade with Japan, but also implied the definition of Korea as an independent and non-tributary state to Peking (Rodríguez Jiménez, 2020, pp. 64-65). As a result of this agreement, the Hanseong political elite was deeply divided between those in favor of modernizing the country along the Tokyo model and those opposed to the opening of the hermit kingdom to the world. In 1882, a series of riots within the army eventually spread to some popular strata due to food shortages, resulting in the storming of some official government buildings and an attack on the Japanese consulate.

The revolt only ended after the intervention of a Chinese contingent, which provided the perfect excuse for Tokyo to justify increasing its military and naval strength (Hane, 2013, p. 186). The *Chemulpo Convention* of 1882, under which Tokyo negotiated a series of reparations and indemnities, also served to give Japan permission to deploy a military contingent to protect its diplomatic mission and interests. Tensions, far from easing, escalated until the Gapsin Coup in December 1884, in which the pro-Japanese forces were quickly defeated by Chinese military intervention. Tokyo was not prepared for confrontation with Peking –as was corroborated in 1886, when the Nagasaki incident was ended without a satisfactory response– and so in 1885 the *Tianjin Convention* was signed: both nations withdrew their troops from Korea and agreed to inform each other before any future military deployment in the zone (Hane, 2013, p. 186).

The reality is that Japan was postponing the conflict until better options of victory arose, given the far superior naval power of the Chinese Northern Seas Fleet, which had modern vessels such as the *Dingyuan*, the *Zhenyuan* or the *Jiyuan*. Something not dissimilar had happened a few years earlier. Through the *Treaty of St. Petersburg* (1875), by which Japan poured oil on troubled waters with its other major competitor in the region: Russia. Although Tokyo momentarily renounced its claims Sakhalin Island in exchange for control of the Kurils, the agreement was revised after the Russo-Japanese War (1905), when Japan was granted administration of some territories on the northern side of the Strait of La Pérouse.

The importance of the events of the 1870s and 1880s, though relative, should not be minimized. Japan was no longer a timid Asian country incapable of resisting Western penetration and was clearly embarking on its own forms of pressure and domination over other states in the area. On balance, it could be argued that it had failed to oppose its two great strategic rivals head-on. But the truth is that it was beginning to behave in much the same way as great colonial powers, achieving some successes that lent impetus to new aspirations.

Colonial Aspirations and Territorial Expansion in the *fin-de-siècle era*

It was in this context of expansion that Japanese interests in the *Nanshin-ron* or "southward advance theories" emerged. According to these, the Philippine Islands and other uninhabited Spanish possessions in the Pacific were a priority target for a country eager for land to settle its growing population and for natural resources to support its industry. The naval program for the defense of the Philippines, presented in 1880 by Spanish Admiral and Navy Minister Santiago Durán, pointed to the islands' inexhaustible wealth of raw materials and agricultural production that could "flood Asia" with goods of all kinds if properly administered. This undoubtedly made them the object of Tokyo's desire, which the admiral considered the most direct threat to the preservation of Spanish sovereignty over the Philippines if Madrid did not carry out an ambitious defense plan (Rodríguez González, 1989, pp. 203-205). Such a plan was never formalized, and the reality is that Spain could not even protest after the occupation of the Arzobispo and Volcano islands shortly afterwards[5]. The value of such groups of islands was small, except from a strategic point of view. Of far greater economic importance were other archipelagos in Spanish Micronesia, as evidenced by the successive proposals to purchase the Marinas between 1876 and 1892 and the constant attempts to establish trading companies or agricultural colonies on some of the islands. These were quite logical aspirations for a country with only fourteen percent of its territory under cultivation, but with such a demographic expansion that its population grew from 35 to 46 million between 1873 and 1900 (Togores Sánchez, 2000, p. 9). In this context, intellectuals such as Suganuma Sadakaze began openly to advocate the displacement of large masses of settlers to Luzon, where, in addition to developing local agriculture, they should work alongside the locals to put an end to Spanish colonial rule (Martínez Taberner, 2015, p. 139).

In similar vein, the press, which was largely state-controlled, highlighted the weakness of the "once sovereign nation of the seas" and recurrently expounded that "the Philippines will not remain under Spanish domination for long", with the *Kukomin Shinbun* wondering whether the time had not already come for the enterprising spirit of the Japanese people to extend beyond south of the Bashi Channel (Rodríguez González, 2016, pp. 119-10; Martínez Taberner, 2017, p. 292). The sad lament of the Spanish plenipotentiary in Yokohama is very revealing: after bitterly declaring in 1891 "our Philippines will eventually be to this Empire what Cuba is to the United States" (Martínez Taberner, 2015, p. 143).

The truth was that Tokyo's interest was primarily focused on expanding its economic and military influence on the mainland, where it hoped significantly to increase its living space at China's expense. In the summer of 1894, a new series of protests in Korea prompted the entry of Chinese and Japanese troops into the peninsula. If ten years earlier Tokyo had decided to sheathe its sword because of Peking's superiority, the rapid modernization of Japanese forces now led to a succession of victories, thanks to their logistical and tactical superiority. Within weeks, Japan occupied most of Korea and dominated the Yellow Sea. The advance through southern Manchuria, the seizure of the Liaodong Peninsula and the real possibility of a major offensive on Peking forced the Manchu Court to sign peace under very unfavorable conditions (Rodríguez Jiménez, 2017, p. 69). Thus, by the *Treaty of Shimonoseki* on 17 April 1895, which put an end to the war, the Chinese renounced retaining Korea –which in practice meant handing it over to Japan–, directly ceding Taiwan, the Pescadores Islands and the Liaodong Peninsula; in addition to allowing Japanese trade in seven mainland ports and agreeing to the occupation of the port of Wei-Hai-Wei until completing the payment of a war compensation of two undress million taels (Togores Sánchez, 2000, p. 12).

However, just six days after the signing of the Treaty, Berlin, Paris, and St. Petersburg, fearful of the effects of Japanese expansionism, acted in concert –in what historiography has come to know as the *Triple Intervention*– to force Tokyo to return Liaodong to China, quickly transforming the sweet flavor of a great military victory into a bitter and embarrassing political defeat. Even a weakened Spain took the opportunity, with the support of France and Germany, to force the signing of the 1895 *Declaration of Limits*, which Japan could not reject without raising serious doubts about its further intentions.

As a result of all these humiliations, many, like Baron Hayashi, believed that the time had come for the nation to remain calm and quiet. The point was not to arouse suspicion while it consolidated its power and awaited the opportunity to decide its own destiny: to exact revenge and settle its grievances with the West (Kennedy, 2006, pp. 336-337). This attitude was pointed out by the Spanish military attaché on his arrival in Tokyo in August 1895, when he noted that "Japan aspires to become the England of the Far East" through a colonial expansion that was only impeded by the recently signed treaties and the impossibility of attending to more simultaneous campaigns, due to the difficulties imposed by the military occupation of the latest territorial acquisitions[6]. The Spanish attaché was not far off the mark. In 1897, during US negotiations with the Hawaiian monarchy to develop a large naval base at Pearl Harbor –which would grant Washington considerable capacity for strategic projection in the North Pacific while denying the latter to Tokyo–, the Japanese ambassador in US urged a swift attack and recommended to Tokyo that "strong naval armament should be at once disposed of for the purpose of occupying the islands by force" (Morgan, 2016, p. 479).

Be that as it may, the humiliated Tokyo government was convinced that the main brake on its Pacific expansion was Russian policy. In particular, St. Petersburg's interest in obtaining an ice-free port in the Far East clashed with the Japanese intention completely to dominate Korea and to expand into Manchuria, just as respective aspirations also collided in Hokkaido and Sakhalin. The next conflict was brewing, just as it had with China in 1880, and Tokyo only had to wait for the right moment, which would come a decade later.

JAPANESE EXPANSIONISM IN THE TWENTIETH CENTURY

Japan's entry into the twentieth century could be said to have taken place in 1899, with the entry into force of the *Anglo-Japanese Treaty of Commerce and Navigation*, which was actually signed in 1894. According to this agreement, unequal treaties between the two nations came to a definitive end, as did the unfair system of extraterritoriality for British citizens in Japan.

The growing influence of Western powers in China finally provoked a xenophobic rebellion in the north of the country which, supported by Empress Cixi (1835-1908), became known as the Boxer Uprising (1898-1901). With Japanese society convinced that the resolution of the conflict would imply the division of the Celestial Empire, Tokyo decided to send the largest contingent of the coalition, surpassing the contributions of Austro-Hungary, France, Germany, Italy, Netherlands, Russia, the United Kingdom, or the United States. Although the international expeditionary force took control of the situation within weeks, this victory did not bring the longed-for colonial distribution. The latest rebuff to Tokyo's expectations was however accompanied by a consolation prize in the form of a much closer rapprochement with London, which crystallized in the 1902 alliance between the two nations and Japan's rise to the status of major regional power in the Far East[7]. This was evidenced by its inclusion in the negotiations that led to the signing of the *Boxer Protocol* and the right it obtained to station troops in the Peking-Tianjin area (Togores Sánchez, 2000, p. 12; Rodríguez Jiménez, 2020, p. 71).

The Russo-Japanese War and the Annexation of Korea

By virtue of the *Nishi-Rosen Agreement* of 1898, Russia had agreed not to interfere in Japanese commercial activities in Korea. Similarly, as it had done earlier with Peking, Tokyo agreed with St. Petersburg that it would not interfere by sending military or financial advisors without prior agreement between the parties. Japan's aspirations to extract natural resources in the Yalu River area soon clashed with those of Russia, which expected to open an ice-free port in East Asia. To this end, St. Petersburg obtained from China a twenty-year cession of the Liaodung Peninsula. In addition, in order to connect Port Arthur to the Trans-Siberian network in the direction of Vladivostok, Russia initiated construction of the East China Railway Network in southern Manchuria; something that directly clashed with Japan's interest in expanding its dominions through the area (Hane, 2013, pp. 189-190).

Despite two years of negotiations over the future of the region, the Japanese and Russian governments not only failed to reach an understanding, but tension gradually increased, until the preemptive initiation of hostilities by Japan as a result of the sudden entry into Korea of some Russian troops garrisoned in Manchuria (Rodríguez Jiménez, 2020, p. 73). Diplomatic relations were broken off at the beginning of February 1904. Immediately after that, but without having declared a state of war, the Japanese fleet launched a surprise attack on the First Russian Pacific Squadron stationed in the roadstead of Port Arthur, which would remain under siege until January 1905. Simultaneously, the Army landed at Chemulpo and quickly crossed the Yalu River, obtaining a series of triumphs in Manchuria and a decisive victory in the Battle of Mudken (1905). In the maritime theatre, following the defeats in the battles of the Yellow Sea and Ulsan (1904), a large Russian reinforcement fleet –after a hazardous seven-month voyage from the Baltic Sea– was destroyed in the Battle of Tsushima (1905).

After half a century of continued humiliation at the hands of Western powers, Japan finally seemed "destined to expand and rule other nations" (Chang, 2016, p. 39). It was no coincidence that, with the 1905 *Treaty of Portsmouth*, the Russians recognized Japanese interests in Korea and Japan obtained the Trans-Manchurian Railway and its associated mining deposits, the southern half of Sakhalin Island, and fishing rights in the Okhotsk and Bering Seas (Torre del Rio, 1985, p. 16). Once again, the public's reaction was one of disappointment; much larger territorial gains had been expected and the treaty was received with indignation and violent demonstrations in the capital. In truth, it was a very advantageous peace treaty that reflected Japan's conversion into an imperialist power. Not only in military terms, but also commercially and financially, thanks to the foundation of the Bank of Taiwan (1899), the Oriental Development Company (1908) and the Bank of Korea (1909) (Togores Sanchez, 2000, pp. 21-22).

Meanwhile, the assassination in 1909 of the Japanese Resident General in Seoul –a sort of colonial governor– by a Korean nationalist was the perfect pretext to proceed with the foundation of a Ministry of Colonies and the final annexation of the country in 1910. Japan had already been in control of Korean international relations since 1905, thanks to the forced signing of the *Treaty of Eulsa*. Only two years later, in 1907, Tokyo had also assumed control of the country's internal affairs. Consequently, following the outbreak of the Chinese Revolution of 1911, Japan became undisputedly the most important nation in the Far East, constrained only by the Asian possessions of the great Western powers (Langa Laorga, 1985, p. 22).

The Great War and Siberian Intervention

Despite its military successes against Russia, the truth is that Japan was not in a position to compete economically with Europe or the United States, neither in terms of volume nor quality of products. Only the outbreak of the Great War (1914-1918) reversed this situation, with the country meeting the demands of the Allied markets and supplying the Asian world with all kinds of manufactured goods, including ships and armaments in general. This involved a seventy percent increase in the number of manufacturing factories and the doubling of the size of Japan's merchant navy (Langa Laorga, 1985, p. 22; Rodríguez Jiménez, 2020, p. 81).

Tokyo's entry into the global conflict was directed exclusively against Germany's Asian interests. Although the French press took for granted the arrival in Europe of a large expeditionary contingent, Japan's real objective in entering the war was to expand its territory at the expense of German possessions in the Pacific –the Carolines, Marianas, Marshall and Palau Islands– which it occupied without much resistance and managed to retain by mandate of the League of Nations. As far as China was concerned, Japan succeeded in occupying the German concession of Kiau Chau, seizing the naval base of Tsing-tao and quickly taking over the railroad route built by Berlin to exploit the mining areas of the interior (Togores Sanchez, 2000, p. 27). As early as the beginning of 1915, Tokyo even submitted to the Peking Government the *Twenty-One Demands*, a series of requirements, divided into five groups, each more draconian than its predecessor. The many demands included more control over the Chinese territory, reinforcement of rights over the railroads and the Manchurian mineral deposits, and the appointment of Japanese officials to control administrative and financial affairs throughout the country (Langa Laorga, 1985, p. 22; Rodríguez Jiménez, 2020, pp. 85-86). However, the concentrated pressure exerted by the

United States and the United Kingdom finally forced the withdrawal of the Fifth Group of Demands, those relative to placing Japanese officials in the Chinese administration. Nevertheless, Washington finally acknowledged that "territorial contiguity creates special relations", referring to Japan and the regions of Shandong, Manchuria and North China, but without specifying much more (Morgan, 2016, pp. 488-489)[8].

If Japan's participation in the Great War was very limited, its interest in intervening in the Russian Civil War (1917-1923) between the Red and White Armies was far greater. Tokyo participated in the Siberian Intervention by sending a contingent of seventy thousand men –surpassing by twenty thousand men the force of the Czech Legion and almost ten times the Anglo-Canadian and American contingents. However, despite its size, the Japanese force remained mainly in the rearguard, acting as if they were mere observers, despite the seriousness of the combat in which the allied forces found themselves involved (Togores Sanchez, 2000, 34). This was because one of Tokyo's main interests with regard to this expedition was the acquisition of rights in the area, to build a buffer against Moscow –designated capital of the USSR in 1917– and to lay the foundations of control of Siberian resources in the event of an eventual collapse of the Russian state (Morgan, 2016, p. 489).

The Interwar Period

It was only after the *Washington Conference* (1921-1922) that the Nipponese Siberian Expeditionary Army, which progressed along the Trans-Siberian lines as far as the distant Lake Baikal, was withdrawn. At the same Conference, Japan was forced to accept the *Four-Power Treaty*, the *Five-Power Treaty*, and the *Nine-Power Treaty*. According to the first accord, Tokyo agreed, along with the US, France, and Great Britain, to maintain the status quo in the Pacific. The second, also known as the *Washington Naval Treaty* (1922), enforced reduction of the Japanese fleet to sixty per cent of the size of its Anglo-American counterpart. The third treaty sought agreement to respect the territorial integrity and political-administrative independence of the Republic of China and the reinforcement of the *Open Door* principle (Rodríguez Jiménez, 2020, p. 92)[9].

After Meiji Tenno's death in 1913, the *Taisho* period (1913-1926) was characterized by democratization, the proliferation of political parties, the emergence of leagues for the protection of the constitution when military interventions were sensed and, finally, the approval of universal suffrage in 1925 (Langa Laorga, 1958, p. 20). However, the situation changed drastically following the ascension to the throne of Showa Tenno –better known as Hirohito– in 1926, with a gradual imposition of the most exacerbated militarism, aggressive imperialism and totalitarianism. The increase of voters from three to fourteen million coincided with a reduction of enlisted men in the Army –which decreased from twenty-one to seventeen divisions. The reasons for such a reduction were various, but some political sectors were quick to establish a link between democratization and military weakness (Togores Sánchez, 2000, p. 39). By the end of the 1920s, Japan's glories began to be overshadowed by Western limitations upon its territorial ambitions and the growing hostility of the outside world to Japanese expansionism (Langa Laorga, 1985, p. 20). The Army soon expressed growing animosity towards the unstable civilian governments –there were eleven prime ministers between 1918 and 1932, six of whom were assassinated in office–, which they blamed for the severe economic crisis that engulfed the country, especially after 1929. The increase in nationalist propaganda against the "liberal traitors" implied the extension of the idea that, sooner rather than later, Japan would have to fight for its own survival. It was only a matter of time before politics would soon be subordinated to the designs of the Army General Staff (Togores Sanchez, 2000, p. 52).

By 1930, the rise of the Chinese *Kuomintang* and its progression into Manchuria after the *Northern Expedition* of Chiang Kai-shek (1926) was the cause of some concern in Tokyo. The more conservative groups soon began to demand greater intervention in China and better conditions for military development than those obtained at the *London Conference* of 1930 (Morgan, 2016, pp. 492-494). Peking tried to resist Japanese predation by means of a four hundred percent increase in export taxes on Fushun coal and oil shales. The response was not long in coming. Using the explosion of a "Chinese" bomb on the Mukden Railway as a pretext, Tokyo reacted by occupying Manchuria and establishing the puppet state of Manchukuo. This ensured Japanese industry direct access to one of the largest energy production areas on the continent (Goralski & Freeburg, 1989, p. 105). However, the occupation of China's richest province not only provided an extensive market for raw materials, but it also placed Japan in an unparalleled position for future territorial expansion (Togores Sanchez, 2000, p. 59)[10].

From Expansion During World War II to the End of the Empire

At the beginning of July 1937, after a small incident in Huan-Ping in which shots were exchanged between Chinese and Japanese troops, Tokyo sent an ultimatum that was followed on July 26 by a crushing attack on Peking –which was conquered in 48 hours– and on numerous coastal cities and ports, such as Shanghai, with the city of Nanking falling at the end of the year. By the end of 1938, Japan dominated the entire southern coast and controlled forty percent of the Chinese population and one fifth of the territory (Togores Sanchez, 2000, p. 61).

Expansion into mainland China gave Japan control of territories rich in raw materials, especially coal and iron, but not in hydrocarbons. In 1937, eighty percent of Japan's oil was obtained from wells in California, since of the nearly one hundred thousand barrels a day consumed in the country, only eight thousand were produced domestically, including Taiwanese extractions. China was not the imagined source of energy supplies, and in the quest for self-sufficiency to guarantee "national defense", Tokyo began to look more and more towards the poorly protected oilfields in Southeast Asia. Oilfields that by 1930 equaled the production of all the countries of Europe, excluding the Soviet Union: "it was manna for a fuel-poor nation like Japan" (Goralski & Freeburg, 1989, pp. 102, 106-107).

By means of the attempted coup d'état in 1936 known as the Incident of February 26, a group of young officers in command of barely fifteen hundred men tried to establish an ultranationalist government with an anti-Western bias (Rodríguez Jiménez, 2020, p. 108). Although it was quickly crushed, the coup revealed the growing anti-liberal sentiment among society and the Armed Forces, as was revealed by the immediate adherence to the *Anti-Komintern Pact* and the signing of the *Tripartite Pact* four years later. By virtue of the latter, Berlin and Rome recognized Japan's interest in establishing its great zone of Co-Prosperity in Asia, emboldening Tokyo to start the occupation of Indochina (Laborde Carranco, 2011, p. 125).

Maintaining an independent –and certainly very opportunistic– foreign policy, Tokyo signed a non-aggression pact with Moscow in April 1941 and refrained from acting in concert with Berlin after the beginning of *Operation Barbarossa*, hoping for a Soviet defeat that would allow its army to invade Siberia at a minimum cost (Togores Sanchez, 2000, p. 64). Meanwhile, the development of the war in Europe –with France and Holland occupied and the United Kingdom fighting to avoid invasion– left China, Hong Kong, Indochina, Malaysia, Singapore, and the Philippines practically defenseless. The subsequent freezing of Japanese bank deposits and Washington's oil embargo pushed Japan into war with the United States, with the surprise naval air attack on Pearl Harbor on December 7, 1941.

Although the attack was less successful than had been expected –a number of sunken ships were refloated and none of the American aircraft carriers were at the base during the strike–, it allowed Tokyo to control the Western Pacific: the conquest of the Philippines was almost immediate, as well as Guam, Wake, Hong Kong, Singapore, Burma and Indonesia. In less than four months, Japan achieved its objectives, acquiring an empire of over four hundred million people, one that had a virtual monopoly on the world's rubber, quinine and tin production, harvested seventy percent of the global rice crop, and held huge reserves of strategic resources. Boosted by its initial successes, Tokyo created the Ministry of Asian Affairs, encouraged the development of the Co-Prosperity Area and began to elaborate the construction of a common market free from Western control (Togores Sanchez, 2000, pp. 64-67).

The reality is that rather than the liberation of the Asian peoples, what Japan brought was a harsh, new colonization, stricter and more oppressive than the one it came to replace. Nevertheless, Tokyo tolerated and even encouraged indigenous nationalist movements, especially with the beginning of the US counter-offensives that cut back Japanese territories at a very high cost in material and human lives until 1945 (Rodríguez Jiménez, 2020, pp. 143-144). In any case, at the end of the II World War, Japan was stripped of all its territorial gains since 1868 and Tokyo's sovereignty was limited to the islands of Hokkaido, Honshu, Shikoku, and Kyushu, plus some adjacent minor archipelagos (Togores Sánchez, 2000, p. 73; Rodríguez Jiménez, 2020, p. 168).

CONCLUSION

The preceding pages have attempted to explain the process by which Japan succeeded in becoming a leading expansionist power in the Far East from the nineteenth century onwards. The most interesting aspect of this topic is the fact that Japan is generally believed to have been the only non-Western power to success in doing so, despite lacking, a priori, the most conducive socioeconomic and political conditions. It is also interesting because of the fact that Japanese historians have confined the study of the colonial process of their country to the territorial expansion that took place after 1895. This is due to a genuine interest in legitimizing an enlargement of the State's territory during its period of national construction, rather than the cruel posterior invasion of other neighboring states' territories. On the contrary, it has been sought to argue that the country's own past seems to have destined it from time immemorial to become a state in permanent expansion, with echoes of this aspiration evident very early on in Japan's history. However, it was in the mid-nineteenth century that the foundations of Japanese colonial expansion were laid, and to ignore the study of this period would, undoubtedly, preclude correct understanding and contextualization of the events that took place later, in the twentieth century.

REFERENCES

Chang, I. (2016). *La violación de Naking* [*The Rape of Nanking: the Forgotten Holocaust of World War II*]. Capitán Swing.

Goralski, R., & Freeburg, R. W. (1989). *El Petróleo y la Guerra* [*Oil & War*]. Servicio de Publicaciones del EME.

Hane, M. (2013). *Breve historia de Japón* [*Brief history of Japan*]. Alianza Editorial.

Kennedy, P. (2006). *Auge y caída de las grandes potencias* [*The Rise and Fall of the Great Powers*]. Debolsillo.

Kuromiya, H. (2023). *Stalin, Japan, and the Struggle for Supremacy over China, 1894–1945*. Routledge Open History.

Laborde Carranco, A.A. (2011). Japón: Una revisión histórica de su origen para comprender sus retos actuales en el contexto internacional [Japan: A historical review of its origin to understand its current challenges in the international context]. *EN-CLAVES del pensamiento, 9*, 111-130.

Langa Laorga, A. (1985). El Japón en el siglo xx [Japan in the 20th Century]. *Cuadernos de Historia (Santiago, Chile), 16*(255), 18–31.

Martínez Taberner, G. (2015). Comercio intra-asiático y dinámicas inter-imperiales en Asia Oriental: el Japón Meiji y las colonias asiáticas del imperio español [Intra-Asian Trade And Inter-Imperial Dynamics in East Asia: Japan During the Meiji Peiod and the Asian Colonies of the Spanish Empire]. *Millars. Espai i Història, 39*, 125–157.

Martínez Taberner, G. (2017). *El Japón Meiji y las colonias asiáticas del imperio español* [*Meiji Japan and the asitaci colonies of the Spanish Empire*]. Edicions Bellaterra.

Morgan, W. M. (2016). Pacific Dominance. The United States versus Japan. In J. Lacey (Ed.), *Great Strategic Rivals from the Classical World to the Cold War* (pp. 479–509). Oxford University Press.

Paine, S. C. M. (2016). China, Russia, and Japan Compete to Create a New World Order. In J. Lacey (Ed.), Great Strategic Rivals from the Classical World to the Cold War (pp. 417-446). Oxford University Press.

Reyes Manzano, A. (2005). Mitos y realidades sobre las relaciones hispano-japonesas durante los siglos XVI-XVII [Myths and Realities of the Spanish-Japanese Relations in the 16th-17th Centuries]. *BROCAR, 29*(29), 53–75. doi:10.18172/brocar.1680

Reyes Manzano, A. (2014). *La Cruz y la Catana: relaciones entre España y Japón (siglos XVI-XVII)* [*The Cross and the Catana: Relations between Spain and Japan (16th-17th centuries)*]. Universidad de La Rioja.

Rodríguez González, A. R. (1989). El peligro Amarillo en el pacífico español 1880-1898. [The yellow peril in the Spanish Pacific 1880-1898] In F. Rodao (Ed.), *España y el Pacífico* [*Spain and the Pacific*]. AECI.

Rodríguez González, A. R. (2016). *Tramas ocultas de la guerra del 98* [*Hidden plots of the war of '98*]. Actas.

Rodríguez Jiménez, J. L. (2020). *Historia contemporánea de Japón* [*Contemporary Japanese history*]. Síntesis.

Schneider, J. C. (2020). A Non-Western Colonial Power? The Qing Empire in Postcolonial Discourse. *Journal of Asian History, 54*(2), 311–341. doi:10.13173/jasiahist.54.2.0311

Souyri, P. F. (2005). La colonización japonesa: un colonialismo moderno pero no occidental. [Japanese colonisation: a modern but non-Western colonialism] In M. Ferro (Ed.), *El libro negro del colonialismo. Siglos XVI al XXI: del exterminio al arrepentimiento* [*The Black Book of Colonialism. Sixteenth to twenty-first centuries: from extermination to repentance*]. La Esfera de los Libros.

Togores Sánchez, L. E. (2000). *Japón en el siglo XX. De imperio a potencia económica* [*Japan in the 20th Century. From Empire to Economic Power*]. Arco Libros S.L.

Torre del Río, R. de la. (1985). El Japón Meiji [Meiji Japan]. *Cuadernos de Historia (Santiago, Chile)*, *16*(255), 4–16.

ADDITIONAL READING

Allen, L. (1971). *Japan: The Years of Triumph.* TBS.

Beasley, W. G. (1972). *The Meiji Restoration.* Stanford University Press. doi:10.1515/9780804779906

Iriye, A. (1995). Japan's Drive to Great-Power Status. In M. B. Jansen (Ed.), *The Emergence of Meiji Japan* (pp. 268–329). Cambridge University Press. doi:10.1017/CBO9781139174428.006

Miñano Medrano, S. (2018). *Tratado de 1868: los cimientos de la amistad Japón-España* [*Treaty of 1868: the foundations of Japan-Spain friendship*]. Ministerio de Asuntos Exteriores, Unión Europea y Cooperación.

Moreno, J. (1993). La descolonización de Asia [The Decolonization of Asia]. *Historia (Wiesbaden, Germany)*, 16.

Mutel, J. (1972). *El fin del Shogunato y el Japón Meiji, 1853-1912* [*The End of the Shogunate and Meiji Japan, 1853-1912*]. Vicens Vivens.

Perkins, D. (1997). *Japan Goes to War. A Chronology of Japanese Military Expansion from the Meiji Era to the Attack on Pearl Harbor (1868-1941).* Diane Pub Co.

Rodao, F. (2002). *Franco y e l imperio japones* [*Franco and the Japanese Empire*]. Plaza & Janes.

Rodríguez González, A. R. (1994). España y Japón ante la crisis de 1898. Antecedentes e hipótesis [Spain and Japan before the crisis of 1898. Background and hypothesis]. *Mar océana: Revista del humanismo español e iberoamericano*, 1, 181-193.

Togores Sánchez, L. E. (1997). *Extremo Oriente en la política exterior de España (1830-1885)* [*The Far East in Spanish Foreign Policy (1830-1885)*]. Prensa y Ediciones Iberoamericanas.

ENDNOTES

[1] In reference to the *maku,* a sort of bamboo and cloth screen decorated with the commander's *mon* or family crest, from which the great samurai leaders led their troops on the battlefield.

[2]   In mid-1853, Commodore Perry's squadron arrived in Tokyo Bay with the task of forcing the Japanese to accept a letter from President Fillmore formally proposing the establishment of diplomatic ties between the two nations. In practice, however, it ordered the opening of Japanese trade with the US, requiring a formal response within a year. On his return on 13 February 1854, Perry showed up with an intimidating squadron and more than fifteen hundred men to force the signing of the *Convention of Kanagawa*, which opened the ports of Shimoda and Hakodate to American merchantmen, while establishing a consulate in Shimoda as a permanent representation. The *Kanagawa* treaty was followed four years later by the *Treaty of Amity and Commerce between Japan and the United States,* better known as the *Harris Treaty.* This involved opening the ports of Kanagawa, Nagasaki, Niigata and Hyogo, obtaining a number of rights for US citizens in those ports and implementing the system of judicial extraterritoriality for foreign residents, as well as establishing low taxes on imports and exports of goods on the island.

[3]   Despite this "formal integration" into the national territory, there were no deputies from the Nansei archipelago in the Lower House until 1920, schools marginalized the local language, and during the Battle of Okinawa (1945), the Imperial Army acknowledged that it would be the last major battle before the war was fought "on the soil of the motherland" (Souyri, 2005, p. 489).

[4]   Under the pretext of a punitive expedition following the murder of several Catholic missionaries in 1866, Paris launched a brief campaign against Ganghwa Island, which it briefly occupied but had to withdraw from after unsuccessful attempts to land on the Peninsula. Washington, for its part, sent an expedition in 1871 following the incident involving the merchant ship *General Sherman.* The ship was destroyed and its crew killed after sailing up the Taedong River towards Pyongyang, against the warnings of the Korean authorities and with unclear intentions. In retaliation, the US seized Ganghwa Island, massacring the two hundred or so defenders, but failed to enforce the opening of Korean trade.

[5]   After its annexation to Tokyo's Prefecture in 1891, the most important of these, Sulphur Island, was renamed Iwo Jima or *Io To*, a direct translation of the original Spanish name given by Bernardo de la Torre circa 1543.

[6]   Spain. Ministry of Defence. General Military Archive of Madrid, 6198. Letter from the military attaché in Tokyo to the Minister of War, 28 August 1895.

[7]   The confluence of British and Japanese interests in the face of Russian expansion in Asia led to the signing of the *Anglo-Japanese Alliance* on January 30, 1902. Both countries committed themselves in "the first alliance on equal terms between a Western and a non-Western state" to maintaining their respective areas of influence over China and Korea, as well as the status quo in the region. It was also agreed that they would remain neutral in any armed conflict, unless one or the other was simultaneously attacked by more than one power. Renewed in 1905 and 1911, it was in force until 1921 (Hane, 2013, p. 190; Rodríguez Jiménez, 2020, p. 73; Kuromiya, 2023, p. 30).

[8]   Similarly, in 1917, when the United States and Japan committed themselves by the *Lansing-Ishii Agreement* to maintaining China's independence and territorial integrity and to following the principles of the *Open Door* to Chinese trade and industry. As had happened two years earlier, Washington recognized Japanese "special interests" over China, "but did not spell out either the geographic range of 'China' or exactly what 'special interests' meant" (Morgan, 206, p. 489).

[9]   The *Open Door* concept was interpreted very differently in the US and Japan. While for the former only economic and commercial factors were considered, for Tokyo the main motivation was to

ensure its autonomy and that of its security sphere in the construction of Greater Japan (Morgan, 2016, p. 498).

10 With the Japan's exit from the League of Nations in 1933, the pan-Asian program, projected since the end of the nineteenth century, was revived. The Japanese Empire was called upon to be the organizer of Greater Asia, in accordance with the idea of Asia for the Asians: however, this idea really meant "Asia for the Japanese". If the American manifest destiny had been the nineteenth-century expansion to the Pacific, Japan's manifest destiny seemed to be expansion through China (Chang, 2016: 42).

Chapter 11
The Decolonization of the Spanish–French Protectorate of Morocco (1953–1956):
Between Terrorism and International Negotiation

José Manuel Azcona Pastor
Rey Juan Carlos University, Spain

José Carlos Aránguez Aránguez
iD https://orcid.org/0000-0002-1175-5471
European University of Madrid, Spain

ABSTRACT

The decolonization of the Spanish-French Protectorate of Morocco initiated after the dethronement of Sultan Mohammed V on August 20, 1953 was a process that was accelerated as a result of the action of terrorism. The way in which the French protectorate administration managed this event unilaterally, without the favor of either Spain or the international community, ended up precipitating that over the next three years the Protectorate of Morocco was plunged into a climate of strong socio-political instability capitalized by the action of terrorism sponsored by the nationalist elements as an instrument to achieve the emancipation of the Alaouite country. The colonial conflict in the Protectorate could only be quelled when France finally agreed to hold diplomatic negotiations with the Moroccan nationalist movements and the legitimate sultan, culminating in the recognition of Morocco's independence in March 1956.

DOI: 10.4018/978-1-6684-7040-4.ch011

INTRODUCTION

The Afro-Asian decolonization processes of the mid-20th century are a field of study that require a precise technique of analysis in which multiple conditioning factors such as autochthonous nationalism, the evolution of the international system or the political-social conflict are what determine the development of these emancipation processes. In the case of Morocco, being a Protectorate and not a colony or a mandate, moreover, administratively divided by zones of influence between France and Spain since 1912, it requires a special treatment in the way of proceeding in the study of its decolonization process.

In view of the scarce historiographic production on the colonial conflict in this context, the decolonization process of Morocco by France and Spain, between the dethronement of Sultan Mohammed V (1953) and the accession of the Alawi country to independence (1956), still harbors a multitude of enigmas that need to be investigated, and this work is an opportunity to do so. In this sense, the consultation of the diplomatic documentation generated by both protective administrations in the course of the events preserved in the *Archivo General de la Administración* (AGA) in Madrid and in *Les Archives Diplomatiques du Ministère des Affaires Étrangères* in Paris are fundamental. In this sense, the main objectives of this work revolve around two questions:

1. To analyze the genesis of terrorism in the Protectorate of Morocco and to determine its activity as an instrument of colonial conflict to accelerate the emancipation process of the Alaouite country after the dethronement of Sultan Mohammed V on August 20, 1953.
2. To try to determine what was the role of the Moroccan nationalist movement during the diplomatic negotiation process carried out with the colonial powers so that Morocco finally acceded to independence in 1956.

BACKGROUND

The approach from which this work is approached has allowed us to corroborate that the historiographical production generated up to now has hardly taken into consideration the factors described above, such as the action of terrorism or the influence of the nationalist element to understand the colonial conflict in the Spanish-French Protectorate of Morocco during the decolonization process. A situation that has necessarily led us to have to supplement this scarce historiographical production with period documentation -primary sources- preserved in the main archives of the protectorate administrations, since they are the ones that are currently most easily accessible to researchers. Consequently, this work is pioneering in its use of primary documentation to approach this object of study so scarcely worked by historiography. A field of analysis such as that of colonial conflict which, on the other hand, we consider necessary to strengthen and lay the foundations for future research to take as a reference the methodology of approach used in this work in order to open new lines of research, either from the discipline of the history of international relations or from any other academic discipline.

MAIN FOCUS OF THE CHAPTER

Some of the questions we asked ourselves before beginning to write these pages, and which we will try to answer in the course of this paper, are the following: to what extent was the colonial conflict a determining factor in Morocco's accession to independence in 1956? why is it in this context of the mid-1950s that the protecting powers finally decided to recognize the independence of the Alawi country? what role did Moroccan nationalist leaders and parties play as informal diplomats in achieving Morocco's emancipation? What role did Moroccan nationalist leaders and parties play as agents of informal diplomacy in the achievement of Morocco's emancipation, and what led to the unleashing of terrorist action in the hitherto non-existent Spanish-French Protectorate of Morocco during this period?

These questions are in tune with many of the works that have approached this object of study from different approaches. In our case, the text turns out to be pioneering because, from the perspective of the history of international relations, and taking into consideration the bibliographical and diplomatic documentation (primary sources) generated on the subject of study, we delve into an unknown historical process by jointly analyzing how the events are triggered and what repercussions they have, both in both areas of the Moroccan protectorate and on the international scene, and in the respective metropolises.

In this sense, our starting hypotheses are a clear attempt to answer the questions posed:

1. In line with the majority of Afro-Asian decolonization processes of the mid-20th century, the action of terrorism was decisive in accelerating the process of emancipation of Morocco from its respective protective powers.
2. International negotiation eventually proved to be the only real alternative to reach an agreement by which both the protecting powers and the Alawi country could undertake a peaceful decolonization process that would establish the basis for future relations between the new Moroccan state, France and Spain.
3. The actions of the African country's nationalist leaders and parties, together with the support of Sultan Mohammed V, made it possible for Morocco to finally gain independence through diplomatic action in 1956.

As mentioned above, in order to carry out this research we have relied on a vast historiographical production of academic texts written by prestigious Spanish, Moroccan, French and Anglo-Saxon authors. Likewise, this work is based mainly on diplomatic documentation -period sources- preserved in the *Archivo General de la Administración* (AGA) in Alcalá de Henares (Madrid, Spain) and in *Le Centre des Archives Diplomatiques du Ministère des Affaires Étrangères* in La Courneuve (Paris, France).

The Protectorate of Morocco and the Fall of Sultan Mohammed V

The manner in which Sultan Mohammed V was dethroned by the French on August 20, 1953, evacuated from the palace with his two sons and transferred by military plane from the Rabat airfield to Corsica, quickly aroused the protests of the Arab countries and Moroccan nationalism (Bernard, 1968). At the UN, the complaint presented by the Arab-Asian bloc had little effect, since it was not finally admitted by the Security Council, which did not have the necessary votes to include it on the agenda of the next session, and considered that this incident did not disturb the world order (AGA, Box 2968). As María Concepción Ybarra (1993) indicates with regard to Spain, the determination adopted unilaterally by the Gallic power to depose Mohammed V and replace him with Ben Arafa was the pretext awaited by Francoism to publicly denounce France for having violated the Treaty of Fez of 1912.

The fact that the Spanish High Commissariat had not been officially notified by the French General Residence contributed to encourage the animosity of Franco and the High Commissioner Rafael García-Valiño to try to reach -from now on- any understanding with the French concerning Morocco (Dulphy, 2002). A position that was quickly reinforced due to the fact that the Arab countries and the nationalists exonerated Spain of any responsibility for this maneuver attributed exclusively to the French, given that Francoism showed from the beginning its opposition to recognize Ben Arafa as the new sultan of Morocco (Velasco de Castro, 2012). Among the gestures that Francoism put into practice to gain sympathy, one of the most applauded was not opposing the fact that Friday prayers in the mosques continued to be held in the name of Sultan Mohammed V. In this way, Spain guaranteed its confidence and collaboration, becoming the Northern Zone of Morocco, together with Tangier, a sort of base of operations of nationalism against France and against the new Sultan Ben Arafa.

On the other hand, Francoism, in its determination to continue to maintain its recognition of the deposed Mohammed V, saw a propitious opportunity to promote abroad and among the Moroccan public opinion the image of the Khalifa Mehdi Ben Ismael, of the Alaouite dynasty, as the highest authority in Morocco. The triumph of this strategy would allow Spain to manage the Khalifa Zone as an autonomous entity with respect to the Sultan Zone, since the Khalifa would not be obliged to obey the new Sultan by not recognizing either his political or spiritual authority (Ibn Azzuz Hakim, 1990) (Madariaga, 2013). In addition, the signing of the Concordat with the Holy See on August 27, 1953 and the signing of the pacts with the United States the same year for the establishment of military bases in Spain -which would finally take effect on September 23-, would allow Francoism to strengthen its presence in the international sphere since, it should be recalled, that on January 30 Spain had already joined the United Nations Educational, Scientific and Cultural Organization (UNESCO). Thus, by the end of the summer, Spain was in a very favorable international position to achieve its goal of joining the UN in the short term.

Meanwhile, the situation of socio-political instability in the French Zone, which General Augustin Guillaume had tried to resolve with the deposition of Mohammed V, was aggravated by the refusal of the majority of Moroccans, nationalism, Arab countries and Madrid to recognize Ben Arafa as the legitimate Sultan of Morocco. To this contributed that, since his arrival on the throne, the new Sultan adopted an attitude of total collaborationism with the French power. In a declaration made on September 4 from Meknes, Ben Arafa announced that, except for the canonical festivities of *Aid el-Sghir*, *Aid el-Kebir* and *Mulud*, the celebration of the other festivities, in particular that of the Throne -which, it should be recalled, had been officially established on November 18, 1934 at the request of the nationalists- were henceforth suppressed (ADMAE, Dossier AP3-30).

As for the reform projects presented by the French General Residence, which Mohammed V had refused to endorse until his deposition, Ben Arafa declared that "*nous sommes persuadés que par la réalisation des diverses mesures que nous venons d'exposer la paix règnera dans ce pays et que l'évolution vers un avenir de justice et de bien-être se poursuivra en plein accord avec le Gouvernement français, l'ami des bons et des mauvais jours*" (ADMAE, Dossier AP3-30).

Proof of Ben Arafa's willingness to sanction any reform project presented to him by the French Residence General was the promulgation of a *dahir*, dated September 9, in which his prerogatives to sanction laws were transferred to a Council of Viziers and Directors composed in equal numbers of Moroccans and French. Moreover, if after a first veto by the Sultan the draft submitted to the sovereign was again approved by this Council in a second round, it would automatically be sanctioned with the royal seal (BOECPRFM, no. 2133).

With regard to the activity of nationalism in the Sultanian Zone, the repression to which the Gallic protective administration had subjected the main nationalist party -the *Istiqlal* (Independence Party), founded on December 10, 1943 by Ahmed Balafrej- after the serious incidents of Casablanca the previous December had led to its practical disarticulation. However, since the dethronement of Mohammed V the French General Residence had to deal with a new threat in its Zone, the appearance of terrorism (AGA, Box M-2976; Bernard, 1968; Julien, 1978; Spillmann, 1967).

The Genesis of Terrorism in the French Zone of the Protectorate

In this order of things, on September 11, 1953, Sultan Ben Arafa was the object of an attack in Rabat perpetrated by Allal Ben Abdallah -who first tried to run him over and then to stab him- when he was on his way from the Imperial Palace to the mosque (AGA, Box 2236). Although the Sultan escaped unharmed from this attempt of assassination -which was filmed-, on March 5, 1954 he was again the object of another attack perpetrated in Marrakesh with a grenade, when he was about to perform the Friday prayer in the Berrima mosque in the company of Thami el-Glaoui. On this occasion, Ben Arafa was slightly wounded by the shrapnel in the head (AGA, Box 2236), (ADMAE, Dossier AP3-30). Between these two violent events, and in order to appease the multiple terrorist actions carried out in the French Zone, on December 23, Ben Arafa signed a *dahir* introducing the death penalty to punish these destabilizing acts (BOECPRFM, No. 2148).

As for the Khalifa Zone in relation to the attitude of nationalism after the fall of Sultan Mohammed V, at first Tomás García Figueras -at the head of the Delegation of Indigenous Affairs as a body under the High Commissariat of Spain in Morocco with headquarters in Tetouan- considered it appropriate to adopt measures of containment in order to avoid that an eventual exacerbation of the mood of the National Reformist Party (PRN) could affect the interests of Spain in the Protectorate. As preventive measures always inscribed in the traditional suspicion and control of the activities of this movement, at the end of August the Delegate of Indigenous Affairs sent telegrams to the territorial Interventions with clear guidelines on how to act in relation to the situation of instability generated in the Protectorate. According to his indications (AGA, Box 2965), it was necessary to continue exactly as before August 20, not allowing nationalism to use this pretext to implement its actions in the Zone.

However, as soon as the High Commission realized that the activity of nationalism in the Zone was directed against France and the new Sultan, exonerating Spain of all responsibility, General García-Valiño immediately understood the advantages of gaining their confidence in order, on the one hand, to consolidate his permanence in Morocco and, on the other hand, to consolidate his position in the international concert with a view to his early integration into the UN. In the same way, the PRN, under the guidelines of Abdeljalak Torres, warned of the need to maintain good relations with Spain, which would make it possible to turn the Khalifa Zone into a sort of bastion of nationalist resistance from which to direct its attacks against France and Ben Arafa. In this context, on October 8, 1953, the newspaper *Al-Umma*, suspended a year earlier, was put back into operation in Tetouan as the only nationalist press in existence in the Protectorate (AGA, Box 2953).

In this context of early autumn 1953, under the auspices of the PRN, the birth of the Moroccan Liberation Army (ELM) was witnessed. In order to make its development possible, during an interview held in Madrid between García-Valiño and Allal al-Fassi, the High Commissioner undertook to facilitate the freedom of action of the Moroccan resistance in the Khalifa Zone, including the right to carry arms, as long as they did not attack Spanish positions. In addition, García-Valiño showed his commitment not to hand over to the French authorities those who sought refuge in the Northern Zone (Velasco de Castro, 2012), (Wolf, 1994).

The good harmony between the High Commissariat and Moroccan nationalism in the Northern Zone was publicly confirmed from November 1953 onwards on the occasion of the celebration on the 8th of the feast of the Throne of the Khalifa Mehdi Ben Ismael, but above all after the celebration on the 18th of the Feast of the Throne in honor of Mohammed V. During the events, Torres thanked both Spain and the Khalifa for their adherence to Mohammed V for having refused to recognize Ben Arafa as the legitimate Sultan of Morocco (AGA, Box 2953). However, it was necessary to bear in mind the opposition of nationalism to elevate the Khalifa Mehdi Ben Ismael to the rank of Sultan, as the Franco regime intended to do in order to advance towards the autonomy of the Northern Zone. This situation, which deeply irritated France, was answered on the occasion of the celebration of the *Mulud* holiday on the 21st with the imposition by Resident General Guillaume on Sultan Ben Arafa -recognized in some circles as Mohammed VI- of the *Grand-Croix de la Légion d'Honneur* (AGA, Box 2236).

While at the beginning of 1954 the possibility of replacing General Guillaume at the head of the French General Residence began to gain weight due to the situation of serious socio-political instability in which the Sultanian Zone had been plunged since the dethronement of Sultan Mohammed V, whom the Government of the Republic was now considering transferring to Tahiti -more than 12,000 kilometers away from Morocco, in the Pacific Ocean-, in the Khalifa Zone, a great act of adhesion on the part of the Moroccan notables towards Spain took place, while the Arab League reiterated its recognition of Mohammed V as the legitimate Sultan of Morocco. With regard to the event of January 21, 1954, organized in Tetouan as a large gathering of notables of the Zone to participate in a public tribute to Spain, represented by High Commissioner García-Valiño, it again showed the gratitude towards Madrid for its determination to continue opposing the recognition of Ben Arafa as Sultan of Morocco for having been arbitrarily imposed by France. In this order of things, and following the thesis of Francoism, in a document signed by 430 personalities of the Zone, they were in favor of separating the Khalifa Zone from the Sultan Zone, recognizing the Khalifa as the highest authority. It goes without saying that this act aroused all kinds of misgivings on the part of France, especially in the press (Benjelloun, 1983; Dulphy, 2002). Among other measures taken by the French Government, on January 25, 1954, Mohammed V was transferred from Corsica to Madagascar.

Although Torres had shown his reservations to the Spanish strategy of continuing to promote the image of the Khalifa as sovereign of the Northern Zone, nevertheless, the position of Francoism with respect to Ben Arafa and the actions undertaken by France in its Protectorate Zone favored that, during the following months, the expressions of affection of nationalism towards Spain were a constant, especially through manifestos published in its press organ *Al-Umma* (AGA, Box 2965). Likewise, from the Arab League, its Secretary General, Abdeljalak Hassuna, spared no praise for Franco for his determination to continue to maintain his recognition of Mohammed V as the legitimate Sultan of Morocco, in addition to praising the civilizing work carried out by Spain in its Protectorate Zone.

Moroccan Nationalism and the Commitment to the Diplomatic Route

In spite of Franco's diplomatic efforts to win over the sympathies of the nationalist element since the dethronement of Sultan Mohammed V by the French, these were unexpectedly altered in the second half of 1954 as a consequence of two events of special importance for the future of France. On the one hand, the serious situation of socio-political instability in the Sultanian Zone, where the activity of terrorism intensified considerably since the attack against Ben Arafa on March 5 in Marrakesh, which precipitated the replacement on May 20, 1954 of General Guillaume by the diplomat Francis Lacoste at the head of the French General Residence (ADMAE, Dossier AP3-30). On the other hand, the resounding defeat of France in the battle of Dien Bien Phu on May 7 in the course of the Indochina War against *Viet Minh* nationalism, led by Ho Chi Minh, which precipitated the French country to definitively abandon the Indochina peninsula, triggering the beginning of a complex Afro-Asian decolonization process (Aránguez, 2017).

As soon as the new French government led by Pierre Mendès-France -which was formed on June 18 after the fall of the Cabinet chaired by Joseph Laniel- resolved the Indochina issue -through the Geneva Agreements of July 20, 1954- it determined to undertake negotiations in its protectorates of Morocco and Tunisia that would make it possible to move towards a decolonization formula that would not be too burdensome for France's interests in the region. The reason for this change of attitude was that the new government in Paris -it should be noted that Mendès-France also held the *Quai d'Orsay*- was beginning to focus its attention on Algeria, its main French-populated colony in Africa (Bernard, 1968).

Thus, in August 1954, the secretary general of *Istiqlal*, Ahmed Balafrej, went to Geneva to start negotiations with representatives of the French government in order to outline a consensual solution to the "*problème marocain*". At the same time, General Georges Catroux and Léon Marchal traveled to Madagascar to hold talks with the deposed Sultan Mohammed V in order to prepare his eventual return to the Alawite throne. However, the French Government agreed that it was necessary to avoid the misgivings of the French colonists in Morocco, as well as those of the local notables who had supported the deposition of Mohammed V exactly one year earlier, for as indicated in the diplomatic documentation (AGA, Box 2236) "trataban de buscar una solución con los únicos verdaderos representantes del Marruecos francés: el Sultán depuesto y el *Istiqlal*" ["they were trying to find a solution with the only true representatives of French Morocco: the deposed Sultan and the *Istiqlal*."]

Although the arrival of the diplomat Lacoste at the head of the French General Residence on June 14 had been welcomed with hope by nationalism -not being, among other things, a military man- it did not, however, prevent terrorist action and acts of sabotage in the Sultanian Zone from continuing (Bernard, 1968). At the end of July 1954, the Delegation of Indigenous Affairs (DAI) echoed a news item in which the nationalists claimed to have prepared up to 20,000 armed men to act in the French Zone in order to obtain the return of Mohammed V to the Alaouite throne and the accession of Morocco to independence (AGA, Box 81/12648). One year later, the terrorist action in the French Zone, attributed by the Joint Information Office of Tangier to the nationalist activity of the *Istiqlal*, continued unabated. In January 1955, on the occasion of a trip made by Lacoste to Paris to discuss this question with Fouchet, the Resident General had conveyed to him his concern about the escalation of the terrorist action in Morocco, since between December 20, 1954 and January 11, 1955, 35 assassinations and more than 100 wounded had been recorded. According to information published by *La Dépêche Marocaine*, the nationalist leaders were determined to carry this action to the extreme until France agreed to satisfy their aspirations (AGA, Box 81/12648).

Similarly, the international activity of Moroccan nationalism against France, promoted by al-Fassi from Cairo and by the *Istiqlal* Information Office from Washington, was also a constant (ADMAE, Dossier AP3-30), (AGA, Box 81/10918). As on previous occasions, its main objective was to try to promote again -through the Arab bloc- the debate on the "*Morocco question*" in the UN, since it had been blocked since December 1952 after France had managed to convince its partners that it was an internal question that only it was up to it to resolve (ADMAE, Dossier AP3-30) (AGA, Box M-2669).

Change of Course in the French Administration

The outbreak of the Algerian War on November 1, 1954 and the unstable situation the French Protectorate of Morocco was going through due to the upsurge of terrorist action, among other factors, precipitated the fall of the government headed by Mendès-France and his replacement by Edgar Faure in February 1955 (Bernard, 1968). Just a few months later, on July 6, the new Cabinet decided to replace Lacoste at the head of the French General Residence in Rabat with Ambassador Gilbert Grandval, until then head of the French diplomatic mission in Saarland (ADMAE, Dossier AP3-30).

During the year in which Lacoste remained at the head of the French General Residence, his mandate was characterized by an attempt to implement a conciliatory policy in the Zone -despite the ravages caused by terrorist and counter-terrorist activity- that would make it possible to open cordial negotiations with nationalism in order to move towards a solution that would diplomatically resolve the "*problème marocain*". Although since the summer of 1954 the *Istiqlal* leaders had managed to acquire the status of recognized political negotiators, nevertheless, Lacoste considered it appropriate that other Moroccan nationalist parties that had traditionally operated in the French Zone, as was the case with the *Parti Démocrate de l'Indépendance* (PDI), should also participate in the negotiations, which would prevent *Istiqlal* from capitalizing on them (Bernard, 1968).

The other issue with which Lacoste also had to be particularly concerned was that of trying to set up a Regency Council in charge of assuming the Sultan's own powers between the abdication of Ben Arafa and the return of Mohammed V to the Alawite throne. During the spring of 1955 Resident General Lacoste worked hard to finalize the details of this undertaking (Spillmann, 1967). At the beginning of July, some of the names that were being considered to constitute the Council of the Throne were: Mbarek Bekkaï, Fatmi ben Sliman, Abbas Tazi, Bahnini and Ben Laarbi El Alaoui (AGA, Box 81/12648).

Since one of the objectives of the new Cabinet headed by Faure was to normalize the situation in Morocco before August 20 in order to avoid that the second anniversary of the dethronement of Sultan Mohammed V might cloud the negotiations, at the beginning of July 1955 the new Minister responsible for Moroccan and Tunisian affairs, Pierre July, sent Grandval a long report with precise instructions to be implemented in Morocco (ADMAE, Dossier AP3-30). In his instructions, July began by informing the newly appointed Resident General of the serious political crisis that Morocco was going through as a consequence -in his opinion- of two trends that had also been driven in the world after World War II: on the one hand, the emancipation movement of Afro-Asian peoples subjected to any foreign domination; and, on the other hand, the nationalist actors consolidated by geographical, economic and political sentiments. In the case of Muslims, July estimated that in the last decade, 400 million Muslims had managed to throw off the colonial yoke, which had inevitably had repercussions in North Africa. In this context, it is worth bearing in mind the Bandung Conference held in April 1955, which brought together as many as thirty Afro-Asian countries, most of which had just gained independence (Mesa, 1993).

To achieve this purpose in the remainder of July and during the first three weeks of August, July structured his instructions around four lines of action that had to be addressed immediately. In the first place, it was necessary to neutralize terrorist activity in the Zone, so recovering the police's capacity for action was an unavoidable necessity, but limiting their procedures, since on occasions the forces of law and order had also gone too far in their interventions. As a special measure, it was advised that the

General Residence should examine its amnesty or pardon measures from which nationalists could benefit when they had been condemned for actions not linked to terrorism, such as because of their opinions. It was also necessary to introduce changes among the personnel in administrative posts, equalizing the number of positions between French and Moroccans, facilitating the entry of young people from the Alawi country for their abilities and not for their political ideals. Consequently, it was necessary for the protective administration to facilitate freedom of expression in the Zone (ADMAE, Dossier AP3-30).

Regarding the question of the throne, it was warned from Paris that the existence of a Council of Viziers and Directors in Morocco could not be considered as a representative government. It was therefore necessary to make further progress on the project outlined by Lacoste on the constitution of a Council of Regency. In this sense, it was necessary for Morocco to move towards a system of constitutional monarchy. With regard to the throne, the most extreme nationalists -those of the *Istiqlal*- demanded as an indispensable condition the return of Mohammed V, while the most moderate -those of the PDI- were in favor of exploring the possibility of enthroning a third member of the Alaouite dynasty. In any case, the French General Residence should manage to convince Ben Arafa, who was practically confined to his Palace as a consequence of the attacks he had suffered, to agree to abdicate the throne (ADMAE, Dossier AP3-30).

Regarding the political system to be implemented in Morocco, the Sultan would continue to maintain his prerogatives -spiritual and temporal- such as that of sanctioning the decrees with his seal, but a mechanism of transfer of powers should be installed whereby the sovereign would entrust a person, who could hold the position of Grand Vizier or Grand Chancellor, with the affairs of the Empire as his delegate. The first step of this political leader should be to appoint a Prime Minister, whose initial step should be to form a representative government in which the various trends of opinion would have a place. With regard to the structure of this new Government, it was specified that it should be composed of eight Moroccan ministers -holding the portfolios: of Prime Minister; of State; of Justice; of the *Habús*; of Agriculture; of Public Health; of Labor and Social Affairs; and of Housing- and six French representatives -who would assist as delegates to the Ministries in the following areas: In the General Secretariat of the Government; in that of Finance; in that of Public Instruction; in that of Public Labor; in that of Commerce and Merchant Marine; and in that of Industrial Production and Mines- (ADMAE, Dossier AP3-30).

As for the ambitious program of *reforms*, although July warned Grandval of the deterioration of this concept in the Protectorate, it was necessary to undertake those that were necessary to modernize the representative institutions. For example, in the case of the municipal organization, it was essential that the Moroccans ceased to be underrepresented in relation to the French. In addition, the participation of Moroccans in municipal management should be encouraged. However, the most complex issue for the French General Residence would be how to articulate administratively the Sultanian Zone in provinces -overcoming regional problems of a cultural, ethnic, geographical and/or religious nature- by placing a Moroccan Governor at the head of each one of them. In order to counteract the centralizing influence of the central government -of the *makhzen*-, Provincial Assemblies could be constituted to elect their own Governors. In the provinces where the French presence was important, parity among the members of the Assembly should be maintained, while in those where it was less, it would not matter if their representation was in a minority. Regarding the method of appointing the members of these Assemblies, it was proposed that the French should be elected by direct universal suffrage and the Moroccans by the *deux degrés* system (ADMAE, Dossier AP3-30).

Among the reforms to be undertaken in Morocco, it was necessary to grant Moroccans freedom of association, since it was considered essential for the industrialization of the country by allowing the Moroccan proletariat to organize itself in a trade union manner. It was also necessary to introduce reforms in the judicial system in relation to the courts of first instance and the regional courts; the creation of an Administrative Court; the promulgation of a Civil Code, a Penal Code and a Code of Penal Procedure adapting to Moroccan jurisdiction the codes hitherto applied by the French jurisdiction. With regard to public education, it was emphasized that the progression of schooling after the age of ten for Moroccan, French and Israeli boys and girls was showing a very favorable trend, and that it was therefore necessary to increase the number of schools, especially in rural areas (ADMAE, Dossier AP3-30). Similarly, it was necessary to undertake reforms in secondary and higher education, encouraging technological studies as opposed to those of a theoretical nature, which would reduce the lack of opportunities for young people. Reforms were also needed in the area of social action, especially in rural areas, where 80% of the population was concentrated and whose main occupation was agriculture, the basis of Morocco's economy. Meanwhile, in the cities it was necessary to introduce reforms that would make possible the evolution of industrialization (ADMAE, Dossier AP3-30).

With regard to Morocco's fiscal policy, the current fiscal year of the Zone was expected to end the year -for the first time- with a deficit. Given this novel situation, July proposed to increase the proportion of indirect taxes for the 1956 fiscal year. In any case, it was emphasized that State control over the collection of all taxes should be generalized and that regular remuneration should be provided to those in charge of administration, which would help to remedy one of the main problems of corruption. Finally, it was essential to safeguard the investments made by the French State since the establishment of the Protectorate in services and infrastructures financed with its own funds, such as airfields, military installations, schools and lyceums, telephone cables or buildings intended for administrative service, among others (ADMAE, Dossier AP3-30).

With respect to Spain's position, France's commitment to move towards a conciliatory policy in its Protectorate zone since the summer of 1954, promoted from Paris by the successive governments of Mendès-France and Faure and from the French General Residence in Rabat by Lacoste and Grandval, began to be perceived by Francoism as a serious threat to its interests in Morocco. If France finally agreed to abrogate the Treaty of Fez of 1912, its permanence in the Alawi country could be seriously compromised despite the support given to nationalism and to Sultan Mohammed V since the crisis of August 1953. Consequently, Spain had to succeed in taking part in the negotiations that were about to take place that summer between the French and Moroccan representatives of the Sultanian Zone, otherwise its situation in Morocco would be totally conditioned by the agreements reached by the former.

Negotiations in Aix-les-Bains

While Grandval was trying to put into practice the instructions transmitted from Paris -*le plan Grandval*- the head of the French Government constituted, under his presidency, a committee of experts composed of Antoine Pinay -Minister of Foreign Affairs-, Robert Schumann - Minister of Justice-, General Pierre Koenig -Minister of National Defense- and Pierre July -Minister of Moroccan and Tunisian Affairs- to study with the representatives of the various trends of opinion of the Moroccan society the possible solutions to the "*problème marocain*". Since the holder of the *Quai d'Orsay* was on retreat in the spa resort of Aix-les-Bains -a French town near the Alps, 100 km from Lyon-, Faure agreed that the interviews would take place in this thermal village (Spillmann, 1967).

Between August 22 and 27, 1955, each of the different tendencies of opinion, which had been formed during the previous weeks to represent the different interests of the inhabitants of the French zone of the Protectorate of Morocco, were received in Aix-les-Bains in an atmosphere of excellent cordiality. During these days, up to eight delegations with different proposals passed through this site: the one in favor of maintaining Ben Arafa as Sultan of Morocco; the one in favor of Ben Arafa, because of his fatigue, leaving the throne and setting up a Council of the Throne; the one in favor of Ben Arafa leaving the throne but appointing a third person other than Mohammed V. in his place; the one in favor of Ben Arafa leaving the throne but appointing a third person in his place; the one advocated by the nationalists of the *Istiqlal*; the one advocated by the nationalists of the PDI; the one advocated by the moderate nationalist movements of the Zone; and the one advocated by the Israelis and the French inhabitants of the Zone (ADMAE, Dossier AP3-30).

As for the talks with the *Istiqlal* nationalists, these took place on August 25 through Mohammed Lyazidi, Mehdi Ben Barka, Abderrahim Bouabid and Omar Abdeljalil (ADMAE, Dossier AP3-30). Among its proposals to resolve the crisis of the throne, the *Istiqlal* demanded the abdication of Ben Arafa and the constitution of a Regency Council, on a transitional basis, to safeguard national sovereignty until Mohammed V returned to the throne. However, this action would entail the fulfillment of a series of essential guarantees, pointing out as essential that Mohammed V should approve the constitution of this body, so that the French Government should allow his transfer to France to be able to express himself freely on the matter. Moreover, no one who had been implicated in the plot which had led to the dethronement of Mohammed V in August 1953 could be a member of the Council of Regency.

However, what the *Istiqlal* really focused on was the problem of Franco-Moroccan relations, whose solution, they warned, would depend on the determination of the French Government. In this regard, the nationalist representatives pointed out that the problem would not be solved by the implementation of new reforms, but that France should move towards the suppression of the 1912 Treaty of Fez and the establishment of a mutual cooperation agreement as a safeguard of Franco-Moroccan friendship: "*c'est donc un système de coopération franco-marocain, librement accepté par les deux partenaires, et impliquant la permanence des liens économiques, culturels et stratégiques, qui serait le plus sûr garant de l'existence d'un Maroc indépendant*" (ADMAE, Dossier AP3-30). In the meantime, the *Istiqlal* would accept the establishment of a Franco-Moroccan interdependence relationship, limited in time, while France advanced -evidently- in the preparations to lead Morocco to its definitive emancipation.

With regard to the proposal put forward by France to set up a local government, the *Istiqlal* agreed, provided that the Council of Regency would determine the form of its constitution. Among the first functions of the Moroccan government, it would have to promote the introduction of structural political reforms leading to the establishment of a regime of constitutional monarchy. With regard to the democratization of the institutions and the fundamental principles by which Morocco should be governed, it was necessary to guarantee: the equality of all Moroccan citizens, without distinction of race or confession, to the exercise and enjoyment of political rights and the security of property; the possibility for all Moroccan citizens to access any post in the State administration under equal conditions; and the division of powers, on the one hand, administrative and judicial and, on the other hand, legislative and executive (ADMAE, Dossier AP3-30).

The conciliatory mood demonstrated by *Istiqlal* in its meeting with the French representatives -"*nous formulons le vœu, que la Conférence d'Aix-les-Bains, à laquelle le Gouvernement française a bien voulu nous faire l'honneur de prendre part, aura été une rencontre préparatoire d'un avenir meilleur*"- was symptomatic of nationalism's readiness to explore a consensual solution that would definitively resolve the *"problème marocain"* (ADMAE, Dossier AP3-30). Among the first news received in the nationalist branch of the *Istiqlal* in Tangier -echoed by the Tangier Joint Information Office- it was assured that in the talks held in Aix-les-Bains an agreement had been adopted whereby the abdication of Ben Arafa and the immediate transfer of Mohammed V to France would take place. With regard to the Council of Regency, although its composition was still being studied, the possibility that the grand vizier Mohammed el-Mokri would be the one to preside over it was being considered at this time. However, it would be necessary to wait for the French Council of Ministers to officially publish in the next few days the agreements to which it had committed itself to resolve the *"problème marocain"* (AGA, Box 2236).

However, what the Faure Cabinet did not count on was that both Resident General Grandval and Sultan Ben Arafa, deeply irritated at feeling displaced from the negotiations, would be the main stumbling block to the resolution of the *"problème marocain"*. In the case of Grandval, he resigned, so that on August 29 the Council of Ministers had to proceed immediately to appoint a new Resident General, this task falling to General Pierre Boyer de Latour, who had just held the post of Resident General in Tunisia (ADMAE, Dossier AP3-30). As for Ben Arafa, who during the last months had been in favor of abdicating for fear of being again the victim of another attack, now refused to renounce voluntarily to the throne, putting at serious risk the negotiations held in Aix-les-Bains to solve the crisis of the Crown.

Moreover, it should be borne in mind that the action of terrorism and counter-terrorism in the French Zone had intensified, especially during the last week of August (Morales, 1998). Of 108 violent attacks recorded during this month, the official balance sheet showed 28 dead -3 Europeans and 25 Moroccans- and 78 wounded -11 Europeans and 67 Moroccans-. As for attacks against the public domain, 33 attacks were recorded, while those against private property amounted to 378. As a result of the fight against terrorism, 144 suspects were arrested, five of whom were sentenced to death in Casablanca, one of the most active centers of destabilizing action (ADMAE, Dossier AP3-30).

New Direction in the Protectorate

In this context, the fragile understanding reached in Aix-les-Bains between the French Government and the *Istiqlal* nationalists to reach a consensual solution to the *"problème marocain"* was seriously compromised by the publication on September 1 in *Le Monde* of the letter that Grandval -on the occasion of his resignation- had sent to the President of the French Republic, René Coty. The seriousness of this fact lay in the fact that in the letter Grandval used extracts from secret documents and instructions that the French Government had sent him during the summer for their implementation in Morocco. Immediately Boyer de Latour addressed the Government warning that *"vous reconnaîtrez sans doute avec moi qu'il me serait peu aisé d'assurer le développement des négociations aussi délicates que celles qui m'ont été confiées si nous devions continuer à révéler ainsi au grand jour tous les éléments qui conditionnent notre attitude"* (ADMAE, Dossier AP3-30).

Since the French Government was fully aware that the return of Mohammed V to the Moroccan throne was for nationalism a sine qua non condition for making progress in the resolution of the *"problème marocain"*, from September 1955 onwards, events accelerated very rapidly. In compliance with the *Istiqlal*'s demands, the French Government ordered General Catroux, stationed with other representatives in the Malagasy town of Antsirabe, to communicate to Mohammed V -on the basis of a convention presented at the beginning of September, the main points of which provided for the dethronement of Ben Arafa and the constitution of a Throne Council and a Moroccan Government- its wishes that he should go to France to make further progress in the talks (Bernard, 1968; Spillmann, 1967). As for the French General

Residence, the main stumbling block that General Boyer de Latour had to face was to try to convince Ben Arafa to agree to renounce, voluntarily, the Alaouite throne (AGA, Box 2236). In a telegram sent to the French Government on September 10, among the conditions imposed by the old Sultan to agree to abdicate the throne and retire to his mansion in Tangier, was that France would undertake to prohibit the return of Mohammed V or any of his offspring to the Moroccan throne (ADMAE, Dossier AP3-30).

In addition to the serious situation of socio-political instability in the Sultanian Zone, where the action of terrorism was still very active, the international pressure to which France was subjected also contributed to accelerate events. At this point, the position of France in Morocco could hardly be sustained, especially when the Afro-Asian nations represented at the UN maneuvered so that the "Morocco question" would be debated again during the autumn at its 10th General Assembly (ADMAE, Dossier AP3-30). Only with the support of the United States, which feared that the Moroccan territory might leave the Allied orbit, and hiding behind the progress of the negotiations between the parties after the talks opened in Aix-les-Bains, the French representatives managed to impose, once again, their criterion that the "Morocco question" was a matter for France alone to resolve as an internal matter (ADMAE, Dossier AP3-30).

Finally, on October 1, 1955, the French Government made a public statement expressing its wish that the talks held at Aix-les-Bains with the different trends of opinion in Moroccan society should lead -among other ends- to the establishment between France and Morocco of a freely agreed relationship of interdependence:

"Ainsi la France, fidèle à son idéal de liberté et de solidarité, entende conduire le Maroc au statut d'Etat souverain et démocratique et maintenir avec lui liens permanents d'une interdépendance librement consentie" [Thus, the France, faithful to its ideal of freedom and solidarity, intends to lead Morocco to the status of a sovereign and democratic State and maintain with it permanent links of freely consented interdependence."] (ADMAE, Dossier AP3-30).

However, this purpose was seriously compromised when Ben Arafa went into exile that same day in Tangier without having formally abdicated the throne (AGA, Box 2236).

However, this circumstance allowed the constitution in Rabat on October 15 of a Council of Regency composed of four members: Bekkaï and Sbihim -representing the nationalist current- and el-Mokri and Tahar Uassu -as representatives of the Francophile current- (AGA, Box 2236). Two days later, the Council of the Throne entrusted Sliman with the formation of a Moroccan government according to the guidelines agreed upon in Aix-les-Bains (Spillmann, 1967). Faced with the transformations that were taking place in the French protectorate of Morocco, on October 25 el-Glaoui made a public declaration requesting the return of Mohammed V to the Moroccan throne (ADMAE, Dossier AP3-30). In the same vein, on the 28th Abdlhai el-Kittani also made a public statement in favor of the return of the prayer in the mosques to be pronounced in the name of Sultan Mohammed V (Spillmann, 1967). Finally, on October 31, from Tangier, Ben Arafa addressed a letter to the President of the French Republic officially renouncing the Alawite throne in favor of Mohammed V (AGA, Box 2236).

The Return of Mohammed V to the Moroccan Throne and Spain's Difficult Position

The official renunciation of the Alaouite throne by Ben Arafa at the time Mohammed V landed in Nice for the opening of talks with the French Government on the procedure for the definitive settlement of the *"problème marocain"* considerably smoothed the course of the negotiations (La Vanguardia). In declarations to the press provided by Sliman, in charge of the formation of the Moroccan Government, the latter reaffirmed this circumstance on the grounds that *"le retour de Ben Youssef sur le trône «constituait la clé de la solution du problème marocain"* [*"Ben Youssef's return to the throne 'was the key to the solution of the Moroccan problem'*] (AGA, Box 2236). Unlike in Aix-les-Bains, which had been attended by representatives of all the tendencies of opinion of the Moroccan society, on this occasion Mohammed V participated directly in the negotiations with the French foreign minister, Minister Pinay, between November 5 and 6 at the castle of La Celle-Saint-Cloud, near Versailles.

As soon as the negotiations were concluded, the French Government recognized Mohammed V as Sultan of Morocco. In this context, on November 6, Pinay and Mohammed V delivered to the press a joint declaration on the principles reached during the meeting. According to this declaration, Mohammed V confirmed his will to set up a Moroccan Government of management and negotiation in which the different tendencies of opinion in Moroccan society would be represented. Among its functions, the new government was to have the task of elaborating the institutional reforms necessary to make Morocco a democratic state in the form of a constitutional monarchy. Pending his return to Morocco, scheduled for the 16th, the Sultan agreed with the French Government that the Council of the Throne should continue to administer the internal affairs of the Alawi country. In order to make further progress in the negotiations, both Pinay and Mohammed V had agreed that France and Morocco should jointly settle, without the intervention of third parties, the status of future relations between the two sovereign states. The formula put forward in this joint declaration -obviously introduced by France- was that the negotiations should lead to

"faire accéder le Maroc au statut d'Etat indépendant uni à la France par les liens permanents d'une interdépendance librement consentie et définie" [*"to establish Morocco as an independent State united to the France by the permanent links of freely consented and defined interdependence"*] *(ADMAE, Dossier AP3-30).*

Before Mohammed V returned to Morocco, on November 11, General Boyer de Latour resigned and was replaced at the head of the French General Residence by André-Louis Dubois, prefect of police in Paris and elevated to the rank of ambassador for the occasion, who would be in charge of managing this new stage that was opening in the Franco-Moroccan relations (ADMAE, Dossier AP3-30). In this order of things, on November 15, on the eve of the arrival of Sultan Mohammed V in Rabat and in compliance with his instructions, the president of the executive Sliman proceeded to decree the dissolution of the Moroccan government in functions (ADMAE, Dossier AP3-30).

On November 16, Mohammed V returned to Morocco and on the 18th, on the occasion of the celebration of the 28th anniversary of his ascension to the Throne, he pronounced a speech in which he solemnly announced -without having agreed with France- the end of the tutelage and the Protectorate regime over Morocco (ADMAE, Dossier AP3-30). In this context, on the 26th, he entrusted Bekkaï with the formation of the new Moroccan government. Barely a week later, on December 7, 1955, it was formally constituted (BOECPRFM, No. 2252). Presided over by Bekkaï, the new executive was composed of nineteen ministries and two secretaries of state, with the nationalists of the *Istiqlal* and the PDI occupying most of the ministerial portfolios (Julien, 1978), (Wolf, 1994).

With the nationalists in the government and Mohammed V restored to the Alawite throne, before the beginning of the new year, the French government was convinced that it had lost control of the situation with regard to the process by which Morocco would gain its independence. In a speech delivered by Faure on November 27, the Head of the French Government had declared that:

Parmi les Marocains et les Tunisiens, beaucoup reconnaissent qu'ils ne peuvent se passer de notre concours. Les bienfaits que nous leur apportons n'empêchent pas leur conscience de s'éveiller et de devenir plus exigeante et ils nous rappellent nos propres leçons et nos propres exemples pour réclamer plus d'indépendance. Nous aurions été obligés de partir et de renoncer à toute notre œuvre si nous nous étions accrochés au système colonial.

[...] En ce qui concerne le Maroc où nous avons rendu de très grands services, nous avons commis, il faut le reconnaître, quelques erreurs et notamment celle d'oublier la leçon du Maréchal Lyautey. Lyautey était opposé au système de l'administration directe. Il voulait maintenir l'unité marocaine et il cherchait une formule d'association. Depuis la guerre nous n'avons pu faire aboutir aucune réforme importante et aujourd'hui il faut réparer la conséquence de cette lacune. Il fallait nous prémunir contre une nouvelle guerre d'Indochine. C'est pourquoi j'ai pris l'initiative d'une politique d'évolution, d'apaisement et de réconciliation au Maroc, au prix des plus grandes difficultés.

À Aix-les-Bains, même les partis nationalistes nous ont assuré qu'ils ne voulaient pas la guerre sainte, mais coopérer avec la France. Si la France connaît aujourd'hui des déceptions, c'est dans la mesure où l'on avait nourri des illusions.

Il faut aujourd'hui prendre conscience d'un fait: c'est qu'il est possible de faire la synthèse des deux France, la France de 1789 qui enseigne le liberté et qui guide les peuples dans la voie de la maturité, et la France qui a compté dans son sein de grands bâtisseurs d'Empire

Translation: Among Moroccans and Tunisians, many recognize that they cannot do without our support. The benefits we bring them do not prevent their consciousness from awakening and becoming more demanding, and they remind us of our own lessons and examples to demand more independence. We would have had to leave and give up all our work if we had clung to the colonial system.

[...] As far as Morocco is concerned, where we have rendered very great service, we have committed, it must be admitted, some mistakes, in particular that of forgetting the lesson of Marshal Lyautey. Lyautey was opposed to the system of direct administration. He wanted to maintain Moroccan unity and he was looking for a formula of association. Since the war we have not been able to bring about any major reforms and today we must repair the consequence of this shortcoming. We had to guard against a new war in Indochina. That is why I have taken the initiative of a policy of evolution, appeasement and reconciliation in Morocco, at the cost of the greatest difficulties.

In Aix-les-Bains, even the nationalist parties assured us that they did not want holy war, but to cooperate with the France. If the France is experiencing disappointments today, it is to the extent that we had nurtured illusions.

Today we must become aware of a fact: it is possible to synthesize the two France, the France of 1789 which teaches freedom and guides peoples on the path of maturity, and the France which counted in its midst great builders of Empire (ADMAE, Dossier AP3-30).

As for Spain, which hoped not to be dragged down by the events that were precipitating in the Sultanian Zone, the policy practiced during the last years by Francoism and by High Commissioner García-Valiño, encouraging nationalism in its Protectorate Zone against France, was now turning against it. At this point, the consequences of explicit support for the ELM could not have been more counterproductive in guaranteeing Spain's permanence in Morocco (Velasco de Castro, 2012). In an October report, it was certain that the ELM had created terrorist cells in almost all the important cities of the Spanish Protectorate, although at the time their objective was to act against the French in the Sultanian Zone (AGA, Box 2759). Now, the risk of the Spanish Zone becoming a field of sabotage and attacks perpetrated by the ELM was extremely high. Even more so when, recently, this organization had made it clear that, among its objectives, was the achievement of independence and the reunification of all Morocco (Velasco de Castro, 2012).

Although on the occasion of the celebration of the Feast of the Throne on November 18 the nationalists had praised Franco and High Commissioner García-Valiño for having maintained their recognition of Sultan Mohammed V against Ben Arafa since his fall on August 20, 1953, nevertheless, from this moment on they began to demand that Spain follow in the footsteps of France to lead Morocco towards independence (AGA, Box 2965). On the occasion of a meeting held in Madrid on November 21, the Executive Committee of the *Istiqlal* -chaired by al-Fassi and with Ahmed Balafrej occupying the general secretariat- issued an official communiqué urging the Spanish government to recognize the independence and territorial unity of the Maghrebi country (ADMAE, Dossier AP3-30). According to the testimony of Guy de la Tournelle, French ambassador in Madrid, the reason for this communiqué was that Spain had distorted the speech delivered by the Sultan by replacing the formula used by the sovereign in which he appealed to the "independence and unity of Morocco" by that of "independence and later the unity of Morocco" (ADMAE, Dossier AP3-30).

With respect to the PRN, also on November 21 its leader made a speech in Tetouan encouraging the population to fight for an early independence from Morocco and for the unity of the territory. In this sense, Torres reproached the Spanish Government for the delay in fulfilling its promise to grant autonomy to the Jalifian Zone in the following terms: "el Estado español ha perdido la batalla del Protectorado ante Francia, pero debe ser lógico y ayudar a que Marruecos obtenga pronto su independencia" ["the Spanish State has lost the battle of the Protectorate against France, but it must be logical and help Morocco soon obtain its independence"] (Ybarra, 1998). In addition, the nationalist weekly *Al-Umma* began to insistently demand the independence and territorial unity of Morocco, and the nationalists urged the High Commissioner García-Valiño for Spain to adopt a resolution in this sense (Velasco de Castro, 2012).

However, Franco was adamant about exploring this possibility, since it would mean putting an end to his North African colonial dream. Since the deposition of Sultan Mohammed V in August 1953, both Franco and García-Valiño had put all their efforts into making the Northern Zone of Morocco -with the connivance of nationalism, the Khalifa and the countries of the Arab League- an autonomous territory with respect to the Southern Zone. However, the opening of negotiations by France with the representatives of all the tendencies of opinion of the Moroccan society -including the nationalists- in Aix-les-Bains in August 1955 -in order to find a consensual solution to the "*problème marocain*"- seriously compromised the future permanence of Spain in Morocco. Although Spanish diplomacy, with Alberto Martín-Artajo at its head, had tried to maneuver since then so that France and the Moroccan representatives would recognize Spain as an interested party in the negotiations -which should therefore take place on a tripartite basis- this strategy had failed. In this order of things, and on the occasion of the interview held in La Celle-Saint-Cloud between Pinay and Mohammed V, on November 11, Francoism, through its ambassador in France, Count de Casa-Rojas, tried to persuade -without success- the Sultan to recognize Spain -given its presence in the Alaouite country- as an active party in the negotiations held with France on the independence process and the new status of Morocco (ADMAE, Dossier AP3-30).

In reality, what Franco's regime was after by trying to take part in the negotiations was to delay *sine die* Morocco's accession to independence. In a statement made by Franco to the American press on November 30, the Generalissimo had said -according to the testimony of his cousin, Lieutenant General Francisco Franco Salgado-Araujo (2005)- that Morocco:

[...] no está aún preparado para su independencia, por falta de personal competente para atender a los muchos servicios que lleva consigo un Estado moderno. Creo que si Francia rectificase su política, podría imponer allí el orden, lo que es muy necesario. [...] En Marruecos estamos para cumplir un mandato internacional y para prepararlo para su completa independencia.

[...] it is not yet ready for independence, for lack of competent personnel to attend to the many services that a modern State entails. I believe that if France were to rectify its policy, it could impose order there, which is very necessary. [...] We are in Morocco to fulfil an international mandate and to prepare it for complete independence.

According to Franco himself in an interview granted to the Director of the *EFE Agency* Pedro Gómez Aparicio, and published in *ABC* on December 16, Morocco would not be ready to achieve its independence for another 25 years (ABC). A position that was beginning to oppose that defended by High Commissioner García-Valiño, who considered that Spain should go ahead of France and facilitate Morocco's emancipation if it wanted to keep its influence in the region. Even more so when on December 14, 1955 Spain had joined the UN, so the pressure from the rest of the member states -particularly the Afro-Asian bloc- for Franco to facilitate the resolution of the "Moroccan question" would henceforth be constant (Ybarra, 1998).

On the occasion of the statements made by Franco and other personalities of the regime to the press -such as those of the Minister of Foreign Affairs Martín-Artajo to the newspaper *Ya* on January 3, 1956-, the nationalists began to distrust both the attitude maintained by Spain during the last few years in support of Sultan Mohammed V and its connivance with his actions and aspirations. A mistrust which grew when they perceived the resistance of the Regime to publicly recognize the principle of independence and unity of Morocco, using as a pretext that the formula of interdependence proposed by France was inconceivable, since it would have as its purpose to whitewash Morocco's entry into the French Union, in addition to clinging to the demand that negotiations on the future of the Alawite country should be carried out in a tripartite manner (ADMAE, Dossier AP3-31).

Morocco in the Home Stretch to Independence

At the beginning of 1956, the nationalists of the Northern Zone began to promote -with the support of their press organ *Al-Umma*- the story that France was the only power with which the Alaouite country had signed the Treaty of Fez of March 30, 1912, establishing the Protectorate regime over Morocco, and what Spain exercised in the Jalifian Zone was a sort of sublease agreed with the French power by means of the Spanish-French Treaty of November 27, 1912 (Ibn Azzuz Hakim, 1990). Consequently, if France agreed to abrogate the Treaty of Fez and to recognize the independence of Morocco, Spain would have no alternative but to abandon the Khalifa Zone.

Based on this strategy of action, the efforts of nationalism were concentrated on pressuring the French Government to advance in the negotiating process that would make possible the definitive independence of Morocco, rejecting outright the formula of interdependence. The four Moroccan personalities in charge of preparing the talks with France to negotiate independence were Mehdi Ben Barka and Abderrahim Bouabid, on behalf of the *Istiqlal* -who had participated in the Aix-les-Bains negotiations-; Mohammed Charkaui, for the PDI; and Ahmed Reda Guedira, for the independents (Madariaga, 2013). Taking advantage of the serious situation of socio-political instability in which France was plunged -it should be noted that on February 1 the government presided over by Faure was replaced by another one headed by Guy Mollet, of the *Section Française de l'International Ouvrière* (SFIO)-, finally, on February 15, 1956, the nationalists succeeded in getting the President of the Republic René Coty, meeting in Paris with the Sultan Mohammed V, to announce the opening of Franco-Moroccan negotiations which were to lead Morocco definitively to achieve its full independence (ADMAE, Dossier AP3-31).

After weeks of intense negotiations, a joint declaration and an additional protocol were finally promulgated on March 2, 1956, an act that was accompanied by an exchange of letters between Foreign Minister Pineau and the head of the Moroccan Government Bekkaï (ADMAE, Dossier AP3-31). With regard to the joint declaration signed by the two signatories, France announced the abolition of the Treaty of Fez of March 30, 1912 on the grounds that it *"ne correspond plus désormais aux nécessités de la vie moderne et ne peut plus régir les rapports franco-marocains"*, so that *"en conséquence, le Gouvernement de la République Française confirme solennellement la reconnaissance de l'indépendance du Maroc"* [*"no longer corresponds to the necessities of modern life and can no longer govern Franco-Moroccan relations"*, so that *"consequently, the Government of the French Republic solemnly confirms the recognition of the independence of Morocco"*] (ADMAE, Dossier AP3-31). In Spain, the ABC newspaper - in its Seville edition - published on the 3rd the full text of the joint declaration and the additional protocol subscribed by Pineau and Bekkaï the day before, of which the Count of Casa-Rojas, in his capacity as Spanish Ambassador to France, had received a copy from the Secretary General of the *Quai d'Orsay*.

In this context, on March 7, Mohammed V delivered a speech in Rabat proclaiming the independence of Morocco (ADMAE, Dossier AP3-31). However, in the Khalifa Zone, the Franco regime, which was reluctant to accept the fait accompli, decided to censor part of the radio speech delivered by the Sultan. In particular, those parts in which the sovereign had made reference to the recent violent events that had taken place in the Northern Zone, since on the 4th and 5th there had been in cities like Tetouan, Alcazarquivir and Larache multiple clashes between demonstrators and the forces of order that had resulted in several deaths and dozens of wounded (Benjelloun, 1983), (Ibn Azzuz Hakim, 1990), (Julien, 1978). Since Torres was not willing to compromise with the measures adopted by Franco to try to preserve the Khalifa Zone at all costs, the PRN proceeded to print and distribute the full speech delivered by Mohammed V on March 7 in Rabat and the words addressed by the sovereign to the Moroccans denouncing the bloody incidents in the Northern Zone.

The speed with which France had recognized Morocco's independence, since Madrid expected the process to take a long time, finally led Franco to extend an official invitation to the Sultan to visit Spain on March 13 (Ibn Azzuz Hakim, 1990). With no other alternative, the aim of this meeting was to inaugurate a negotiating process in which, beyond recognizing the fait accompli of Morocco's independence, a consensual agreement could be reached in which, on the one hand, Spain's interests in the North African region would be guaranteed and, on the other hand, the status by which Spanish-Moroccan relations would henceforth be governed would be established.

While the situation in the Northern Zone was becoming more violent and the action of nationalism, promoted through its press organ *Al-Umma*, was exerting more and more pressure on the Spanish authorities to speed up the process of recognition of Morocco's independence, on March 18 Torres and al-Fassi, representing the PRN and *Istiqlal*, announced from Tangiers the merger of both nationalist parties into *Istiqlal* (Wolf, 1994). In this order of things, on March 21 the Sultan accepted the invitation extended by Franco to visit Spain in the first days of April.

Finally, on April 4, Mohammed V went to Madrid. As part of the ceremonial, Franco entertained the Sultan with a visit to the Infantry Academy of Toledo and the Royal Monastery of El Escorial. On April 6, in the Council Chamber of the Palace of El Pardo, the opening of the Spanish-Moroccan negotiations that would result in the recognition by Spain of Morocco's independence and full sovereignty was preceded. In the early morning of April 7, 1956, the Minister of Foreign Affairs Martín-Artajo and the President of the Moroccan Government Bekkaï signed in the Palace of Santa Cruz the joint Spanish-Moroccan declaration and the additional protocol (BOE, 1956, n° 63).

Following the structure of the Franco-Moroccan joint declaration of March 2nd, in the Spanish-Moroccan document the parties recognized that "the regime established in Morocco in 1912 does not correspond to the present reality, they declare that the Agreement signed in Madrid on November 27th, 1912 cannot henceforth govern Spanish-Moroccan relations" (ABC). Consequently, *"el Gobierno español reconoce la independencia de Marruecos proclamada por S.M.I. el Sultán Mohammed V y su plena soberanía [...]"* ["the *Spanish Government recognizes the independence of Morocco proclaimed by HMI Sultan Mohammed V and its full sovereignty [...]* "] (ABC). Thus, and after more than 44 years of Protectorate regime over Morocco, the Alaouite country regained its independence and full sovereignty. As a gesture of this feat, on April 9, Sultan Mohammed V traveled for the first time in his life to Tetouan, symbol of the unification of both zones.

Only a few months later, on October 29, 1956, the city of Tangier and its hinterland became part of the Moroccan territory when its international status was abolished, and on November 12, Morocco was admitted as a member state of the UN. However, Spain would still continue to exercise its presence over the territory of Ifni and the southern zone of the Spanish Protectorate in Morocco, known as the strip of Tarfaya or Cape Juby, which the Francoist regime had managed -skillfully- to detach from the Spanish-Moroccan declaration initialed on April 7 (Montoro, 1991), (Salas, 1992). Finally, with the signing of the Angra de Cintra Agreements on April 1, 1958, Spain returned the Tarfaya strip to Morocco. With respect to Ifni, which became a Spanish province in 1958, it was not until June 30, 1969 when -in compliance with *Resolution 2072 (XX)* approved by the UN General Assembly- Franco's regime agreed to its retrocession to Morocco (Azcona et al., 1994).

SOLUTIONS AND RECOMMENDATIONS

After analyzing the scientific literature and the existing diplomatic documentation on the object of study, we can make an assessment of the main hypotheses and objectives set out, responding in a generic way to the questions we formulated at the beginning of this work. In general terms, our hypotheses have been corroborated, since our research has shown that both the action of terrorism inciting colonial conflict and that of the nationalist movement as an agent of informal diplomacy pressuring the protectorate administration to seek a negotiated solution to Morocco's independence was decisive.

In the same way, it has been noted that the recognition by Spain and Moroccan nationalism of the legitimate Sultan Mohammed V against the French candidate, the old Sultan Ben Arafa, allowed that from September 1955 the diplomatic route overcame the action of terrorism. A circumstance which allowed Mohammed V to be taken into account again as a valid interlocutor between all the actors to lead the final straight of the access to the independence of the Alawite country by placating the action of terrorism, especially after the talks with the French protective power in La Celle-Saint-Cloud and his return to Morocco in November 1955.

FUTURE RESEARCH DIRECTIONS

Undoubtedly, both the approach to the history of international relations from which the present work has been approached and the use of diplomatic documentation of the period give rise to multiple lines of research from which it is hoped that in the future researchers will be able to approach works in which colonial conflict as part of the decolonization processes will be the cornerstone of study.

As far as the Afro-Asian decolonization processes of the mid-20th century are concerned, as has been corroborated in the present work, both the action of terrorism and that of indigenous nationalist movements prove to be decisive. Analyzing the colonial conflict in all these scenarios, taking into consideration the aforementioned determining elements, will undoubtedly contribute to the further development of this field of study. A field which, to a certain extent, to date continues to be approached mainly from the perspective of the discipline of international relations through the postcolonial paradigm, but which requires other methodologies and determining factors to be taken into account in order to understand the "*forces profondes*" -as Pierre Renouvin would say- involved in the Afro-Asian decolonization processes of this period.

CONCLUSION

Between the end of the Rif War (1927) in the Spanish zone and the pacification of the Atlas region (1934) in the French zone up to the time of the dethronement of Sultan Mohammed V on August 20, 1953, colonial conflict in the Moroccan Protectorate had hardly been testimonial. However, the international context of the mid-twentieth century encouraging the Afro-Asian decolonization process and the appearance in the French zone of the Protectorate of Morocco of the action of terrorism will end up proving to be decisive in bringing the Alawite country to independence in just three years. A process that, on the other hand, could not be fully understood if we did not take into consideration, on the one hand, the determination of Moroccan nationalism as an agent of informal diplomacy during the negotiation process with the colonial powers and, on the other hand, the involvement of Sultan Mohammed V as a unifying element of Moroccan society against the French candidate Ben Arafa, who will end up capitalizing on the independence and unification of the Moroccan territory in 1956 under his authority.

REFERENCES

ABC (periódico español) ADMAE--> *Archives Diplomatiques du Ministère des Affaires Étrangères* AGA--> Archivo General de la Administración BOE--> Boletín Oficial del Estado (España) BOECPRFM--> *Bulletin Officiel de l'Empire Chérifien. Protectorat de la République Française au Maroc*

Aránguez, J. C. (2017). El factor nacionalista en el proceso descolonizador afroasiático de mediados del siglo XX [The nationalist factor in the Afro-Asian decolonization process of the mid-twentieth century.]. En Ferrer, C. (coords.). Fronteras contemporáneas: identidades, pueblos, mujeres y poder. Actas del V Encuentro de Jóvenes Investigadores en Historia Contemporánea [Contemporary borders: identities, peoples, women and power. Proceedings of the V Meeting of Young Researchers in Contemporary History], Vol. 2, 19-31. Bellaterra.

Azcona, J. M., Rodríguez, A., & Azaola, G. (1994). La Guerra de Sidi Ifni-Sahara (1957-1958) [The Sidi Ifni-Sahara War (1957-1958).]. *Estudios de Ciencias Sociales [Social Science Studies]*, 7, 68–91.

Benjelloun, A. (1983). *Contribution à l'étude du mouvement nationaliste marocain dans l'ancienne zone nord du Maroc (1930-1956) [Contribution to the study of the Moroccan nationalist movement in the former northern zone of Morocco (1930-1956).]*. Université Hassan II. Faculté des sciences juridiques, économiques et sociales de Casablanca [Hassan II University. Faculty of Legal, Economic and Social Sciences of Casablanca].

Bernard, S. (1968). *The Franco-Moroccan Conflict 1943-1956*. Yale University Press.

Dulphy, A. (2002). *La politique de la France à l'égard de l'Espagne de 1945 à 1955: entre idéologie et réalisme [France's policy towards Spain from 1945 to 1955: between ideology and realism.]*. Ministère des Affaires Étrangères.

Franco Salgado-Araujo, F. (2005). *Mis conversaciones privadas con Franco [My private conversations with Franco]*. Planeta.

Ibn Azzuz Hakim, M., & Ibn Azzuz Hakim, F. (1990). *Mohammad V frente al Protectorado [Mohammad V against the Protectorate]*. Arabian Al Hilal.

Julien, C. A. (1978). *Le Maroc face aux impérialismes: 1415-1956 [Morocco facing imperialism: 1415-1956]*. Éditions J.A.

La Vanguardia (periódico español)

Madariaga, M. R. (2013). *Marruecos, ese gran desconocido. Breve historia del protectorado español [Morocco, that great unknown. Brief history of the Spanish protectorate]*. Alianza Editorial.

Mesa, R. (1993). La Conferencia de Bandung [The Bandung Conference]. *Historia (Wiesbaden, Germany)*, 16.

Montoro, G. (1991). La retrocesión de Tarfaya e Ifni [The retrocession of Tarfaya and Ifni]. *Espacio, Tiempo y Forma. Serie V, Historia Comtemporánea, 4*, 181–189.

Morales, V. (1998). *El final del protectorado hispano-francés en Marruecos: el desafío del nacionalismo magrebí (1945-1962) [The end of the Spanish-French protectorate in Morocco: the challenge of Maghreb nationalism (1945-1962).].* Instituto Egipcio de Estudios Islámicos.

Salas, R. (1992). *El Protectorado de España en Marruecos [The Protectorate of Spain in Morocco.].* Mapfre, 1992.

Spillmann, G. (1967). *Du protectorat à l'indépendance: Maroc [From protectorate to independence: Morocco] (1912-1955).* Plon.

Velasco de Castro, R. (2012). España ante la «crisis del Trono» alauí: ¿una política de oportunidades perdidas? [Spain in the face of the Alaouite "throne crisis": a policy of missed opportunities?] In *Martínez, L. (coords.): La presencia española en África: del "fecho de Allende" a la crisis de Perejil [The Spanish presence in Africa: from the "Allende date" to the Perejil crisis]* (pp. 131–162). Asociación Veritas.

Wolf, J. (1994). *Maroc, la vérité sur le protectorat franco-espagnol: l'épopée d'Abd el Khaleq Torres [Morocco, the truth about the Franco-Spanish protectorate: the epic of Abd el Khaleq Torres.].* Ballànd.

Ybarra, M. C. (1993). Acción política española en la independencia de Marruecos (1951-1956) [Spanish political action in the independence of Marruecos (1951-1956).]. In J. Tusell (Eds.), *El Régimen de Franco (1936-1975): política y relaciones exteriores, Tomo II [Franco's Regime (1936-1975): politics and external relations, Tomo II]* (pp. 401–4013). UNED.

Ybarra, M. C. (1998). *España y la descolonización del Magreb. Rivalidad hispano-francesa en Marruecos (1951-1961) [].* UNED.

ADDITIONAL READING

Ageron, C. R. (1973). *Politiques coloniales au Maghreb [Colonial policies in the Maghreb].* Presses Universitaires de France.

Aragón, M. (dir.) (2013). El Protectorado español en Marruecos: la historia trascendida [The Spanish Protectorate in Morocco: the transcended history,], vols. I, II, III. Iberdrola.

Aránguez, J. C. (2019). *España y Francia frente al desafío del nacionalismo en el Protectorado de Marruecos (1930-1956): tensiones internacionales y conflictos internos [Spain and France facing the challenge of nationalism in the Protectorate of Morocco (1930-1956): international tensions and internal conflicts.].* [Thesis Doctoral, La Universidad Complutense de Madrid].

Bekkaï, N. E. (2007). Une indépendance bâclée: Maroc 1950-1961 [A botched independence: Morocco 1950-1961.]. Top Press.

Benbaruk, L. (1979). *The Moroccan monarchy and the nationalist movement, 1930-1965.* McGill University.

García, T. (1957). *España y su Protectorado en Marruecos (1912-1956) [Spain and its Protectorate in Morocco (1912-1956).]*. CSIC.

Hernando de Larramendi, M. (Eds.). (2015). *El Instituto Hispano-Árabe de Cultura. Orígenes y evolución de la diplomacia pública española hacia el mundo árabe [The Hispanic-Arab Institute of Culture. Origins and evolution of Spanish public diplomacy towards the Arab world]*. AECID.

Julien, C. A. (1972). *L'Afrique du Nord en marche. Nationalismes musulmans et souveraineté française [North Africa on the move. Muslim nationalisms and French sovereignty]*. Julliard.

Mateo, J. L. (2003). La «hermandad» hispano-marroquí. Política y religión bajo el Protectorado español en Marruecos (1912-1956) [The Spanish-Moroccan "hermandad". Política y religión bajo el Protectorado español en Marruecos (1912-1956).]. Bellaterra.

Pennell, C. R. (2000). *Morocco since 1830. A History*. Hurst & Company.

Chapter 12

Idealism vs. Pragmatism:
The Role of Yugoslavia During the Algerian War of Independence

Luis Illanas García

https://orcid.org/0000-0002-7229-1180

University of Granada, Spain

ABSTRACT

The case of Yugoslavia is paradigmatic in the light of its traumatic decomposition, through a war resulting from religious tensions, nationalism, and revanchism. However, in the decades following the end of the Second World War, Yugoslavia was one of the major protagonists of the historical period known as the Cold War. From a position of theoretical independence from the two opposing blocs, Yugoslavia led the Non-Aligned Movement, and from this organisation it was, as a state, an active defender of the processes of decolonisation and on numerous occasions the main supporter of the new states that were gaining independence from their metropolises. The case of Algeria was significant in the relationship between Yugoslavia and anti-colonialism, for never before had Yugoslav involvement been so intense as in this French colony in North Africa.

"... the colonial problem can no longer be solved in the same way as at the beginning of the twentieth century or in the same way as during and immediately after the Second World War, nor as an issue occasionally referred to by the great powers. The fate of peoples who have freed themselves from colonialism, or are on the way to freedom, can no longer be decided without their participation".

Josip Broz, speech to the Ghanaian parliament, 1961.

DOI: 10.4018/978-1-6684-7040-4.ch012

INTRODUCTION

The case of Yugoslavia is paradigmatic in the light of its traumatic decomposition, through a war resulting from religious tensions, nationalism and revanchism. However, in the decades following the end of the Second World War, Yugoslavia was one of the major protagonists of the historical period known as the Cold War. From a position of theoretical independence from the two opposing blocs, Yugoslavia led the Non-Aligned Movement, and from this organisation it was, as a state, an active defender of the processes of decolonisation and on numerous occasions the main supporter of the new states that were gaining independence from their metropolises. The case of Algeria was significant in the relationship between Yugoslavia and anti-colonialism, for never before had Yugoslav involvement been so intense as in this French colony in North Africa.

RESEARCH METHODOLOGY

The national archives, both in Algiers and Belgrade, are for the most part not digitised, which is a huge handicap for the researcher. The French national archives, on the other hand, have a large amount of accessible material.

This is a complex research project structured around relations between France and Yugoslavia with respect to the Algerian question, based on a number of primary sources and pre-existing works.

The theory underpinning this theoretical chapter is that Algeria marked the turning point in Yugoslavian internationalist praxis, involving Belgrade for the first time in a conflict resulting from a process of decolonisation, with support that went beyond diplomatic finance.

The questions to be answered are what motivated the escalation of Yugoslav aid to Algeria. What were the repercussions for both Algeria and France. What role did the US and the USSR play.

The type of research is empirical and descriptive, answering the questions: What was Yugoslavia like in the early 1950s? What were its relations with France and with the leaders of the opposing blocs? What were France's relations with the US and the USSR? How did Yugoslav aid materialise? What was the role of the Non-Aligned countries? On the basis of the answers to these questions, we have sufficient data to draw conclusions regarding the main issues raised about Yugoslavia's aid to Algeria, relations with France, the US, the USSR and the Non-Aligned countries.

The research is approached from an objective position, to know the role that Yugoslavia played during the process of Algerian independence through pre-existing archives and research works, it is a qualitative type of research, analysis of sources, establishing a theoretical framework around a pre-existing analysis, conclusions are exposed and demonstrated according to the information gathered from different sources, fragments of press conferences, statements and speeches, typical of a qualitative research.

The Balkan Pact and Cooperation with the Western Bloc

In Europe, at the beginning of the 1950s, Yugoslavia was moving between two waters, its political positioning and state model, and the confrontation with the USSR, which theoretically brought it closer to the Western bloc. This estrangement from its theoretical allies had two important repercussions for Belgrade, the first was the establishment in 1951 of the tripartite aid program for Yugoslavia, made up of France, the US, and the UK. The second was the signing of the Balkan Pact with Greece and Turkey, which was preceded by a political pact signed in Ankara in 1953, after which the defensive pact between the three states was signed. Two unnatural moves, which de facto integrated the theoretically independent Yugoslavia into the orbit of the Western bloc in the Balkans, taking advantage of the estrangement of Belgrade and Moscow. A further event that consolidated this first stage of relations between Yugoslavia and the Western bloc was the 1954 agreement on Trieste with Italy.

Internally, the Balkan Pact created a series of inconveniences for Tito with the League of Yugoslav Communists, who beyond the political divergences with the USSR, did not understand the rapprochement to the Western bloc, in spite of being a strictly defensive alliance with two neighbouring states. The Balkan Pact was based on the principles of the United Nations Charter and was structured around the political pact of 1953, indicating in its article XI:

The Treaty of Friendship and Cooperation concluded between the Contracting Parties at Ankara on February 28, 1953, shall remain in force insofar as it is not modified by the provisions of the present Treaty.

The Contracting Parties agree to apply the provisions of Article XIII of this Treaty with respect to the duration of the Treaty of Ankara.

Among other things, the signatories to the pact undertook not to participate in any alliance opposed to the other signatories to the treaty or to participate in or take any action incompatible with the articles of the treaty, i.e., contrary to the interests of the treaty. The treaty would not affect the obligations of Greece and Turkey within NATO and placed Yugoslavia de facto under NATO protection without being a member of the alliance itself.

At the end of the decade, with Europe immersed in the midst of the Cold War, and the peripheral conflicts motivated by the anti-colonial movements and, secondarily, by the indirect conflict between blocs in ferment, the Algerian question demanded a peremptory resolution in the face of France's immobilism and the possibility of destabilizing the whole of North Africa in a traumatic way, with Nasser in full political effervescence. Some states, such as Turkey, pragmatically understood that the alliance with France was more important than the anti-colonial, pan-Arabist or religious idealism represented by support for the FLN.

Yugoslavian-Style Internationalism

The Yugoslav foreign doctrine was based on two principles, independence from the USSR and, in practice, socialist internationalism. This political doctrine, theoretically based on the cooperation of the proletarian states, was structured around a series of principles such as non-interference, respect and defence of national sovereignty, equal rights between nations and peaceful coexistence, organizing these points on the basis of the United Nations Charter (Socialist Democracy in Yugoslavia, 1963). In relation to the Algerian question in particular and to the processes of decolonization, he understood that it was the proletariat of the colonized territories that should unite and channel the effort for emancipation. In this sense, it was extremely paradoxical, something that had already been a contradiction since the beginning of the century, nationalism, from which in part came many anti-colonial movements, was a movement opposed to both socialism and internationalism (Hobswbawn, 1998).

However, as Hobswbawn himself determines, most national movements during the second half of the twentieth century theoretically went beyond issues such as ethnicity, race, or history, so crucial for nationalist movements, they were popular movements, which fit perfectly within the Yugoslav conception of internationalism. Ethnic, cultural, and racial tensions would be subsequent to the processes of emancipation, as would happen in Algeria itself after independence (Hobswbawn, 1998). It was precisely during the conflict in Algeria that Yugoslavia put its model of foreign relations into practice.

Yugoslavia embraced issues inherent to socialist internationalism, such as anti-colonialism, disarmament, a certain anti-militarism or the rejection of war as a means to solve conflicts (Socialist Democracy in Yugoslavia, 1963). This question would become one of the main lines of action of Yugoslav foreign policy during these years, based on the Organization of Non-Aligned Countries since 1961 and always acting under the principles defined by the United Nations. From this organization, diplomatic support was provided to countries immersed in processes of decolonization and self-determination, turning anti-colonialism into one of the hallmarks of Yugoslavia's foreign action with respect to the Third World. At the political level, relations were fostered with communist and socialist parties and organizations, both Western, Great Britain, France, Belgium, Denmark, Netherlands, Norway, and belonging to the Eastern bloc, Poland, USSR, Slovakia, Germany and Albania. These relations were continuous and fluid in most cases, although the divergences with the USSR, which became more acute throughout 1958, cooled Belgrade's relations with the parties of the countries closest to the USSR, while at the same time there was a rapprochement with the Western Social Democratic parties.

Yugoslavia and France

On a few occasions, Algeria being one of them, Yugoslavia acted unilaterally, at the cost of endangering relations with the Western powers, in this case with France and with some allies of Paris, such as Turkey. The main Yugoslav praxis will be that already mentioned, of supporting developing countries immersed in processes of self-determination and independence and guaranteeing the support and aid of third states. France's relations with Serbia first, and with the Kingdom of Serbs, Croats, and Slovenes later, were traditionally good. After the war, Yugoslavia inherited these relations with France, which were maintained despite the great ideological differences between the two countries, to the point that in 1946 the France-Yugoslavia trade association was created, the predecessor, as we have seen, of the Tripartite Agreement on aid to Yugoslavia. Aid to Yugoslavia ended in 1954, although still a communist country, a year later, 1955, the USA, maintained minimal economic cooperation with Belgrade, while the France-Yugoslavia trade partnership continued to function, improving especially after the Tito-Stalin conflict.

Other factors such as Yugoslavia's cooperation with the Western bloc on security issues, the Balkan Pact, good relations with Italy, the Trieste agreement, led Yugoslavia in the early 1950s, hand in hand with France, to move closer to NATO. Thus, relations were good and smooth between the two governments during the early stages of the Algerian war. Yugoslavia and France did not clash overnight over the Algerian question, both countries maintained close positions after Indochina war, determined both by the French withdrawal from this territory and the French government's desire to decolonize Morocco and Tunisia. Even at times of open Yugoslav criticism of France, Paris sought Yugoslav mediation with the Arab countries. In 1956 Tito made a state visit to France, where various issues were discussed, always with the Algerian crisis in the background and Yugoslavia's position of support for the FLN. France pressured Belgrade to mediate with the Arabs and Egypt, to lead negotiations with the Algerians without the participation of the FLN, which the French government considered a terrorist organisation. The Algerians refused to meet with the French, with independence out at the negotiating table.

As we shall see, the meeting of the future leaders of the Non-Aligned Movement at Brijuni in 1956 will have a definitive influence on the future of Franco-Yugoslav relations with regard to Algeria. Belgrade, with its position in Algeria, jeopardised its relations with Paris until they were formally broken off in 1959 with the recognition of the Algerian provisional government, given Algeria's political, economic, and strategic weight. The way in which the two states dealt with the rupture of relations brought bilateral relations to a virtual standstill. Paradoxically, cultural, and scientific cooperation between the two countries was not compromised by the Algerian issue. This was because many of Yugoslavia's political elite had been educated at French universities, including one of Tito's most trusted men, Koča Popovic, the hero of Sujetska and Yugoslav foreign minister from 1953 to 1965. Two years earlier Yugoslavia and Federal Germany had broken off relations following the recognition of the Yugoslav government of the German Democratic Republic. Diplomatic relations between France and Yugoslavia would not be restored until January 31, 1968.

The Non-Aligned

The foundations of the so-called third way, States, most of which emerged from post-colonial processes, opposed to the policy of blocs in the sense of political alignment, and its embodiment in the Organization of Non-Aligned Countries has its germ in the Conference of Afro-Asian countries in Bandung in 1955, the meeting in Brijuni in 1956 between Nasser, Nehru and Tito to finally formally constitute the organization at the Belgrade Conference in 1961. This meeting was also of decisive importance for the Algerian war as the Algerian question was included in the joint statement of the representatives of India, Egypt and Yugoslavia and their support for the FLN.

The precedent of Bandung, the Colombo Conference of 1954, which brought together the neutral countries, had already had far-reaching consequences on the emerging Algerian question. In the final considerations of the conference, it refused to mention Algeria, considering that this was an internal problem to be dealt with among the members of the newly created Arab League (Conelly, 2001). A year later, at the Bandung conference, the incipient but very strong and belligerent pan-Arabist movement took up the Algerian question as its own, perhaps in the hope of integrating the future state within the belligerent pan-Arabist movement led by the president of Egypt, Gamal Abd El Nasser. The public proclamation of The Algerian revolution was broadcast on November 1, 1954, from the Voice of the Arabs Radio in Cairo (Mihić, 2018).

With the Non-Aligned Movement, relations are fluid during Algerian crisis, Yugoslavia participates in all the initiatives proposed by this organization and maintains deep relations with some of the key players in the Algerian question, such as Egypt, participating in the conferences on Algeria and in the Asian-African youth conference, both held in Cairo. Nasser had positioned himself as the Algerians' closest ally because of the rejection of France, the French government being one of Israel's main arms suppliers. However, the Egyptian leader had a surprise meeting in March 1956 with the French foreign minister, Pineau. At this meeting, the Egyptian leader pledged to mediate a meeting between the warring parties and a decrease in Egyptian arms supplies to the FLN in exchange for France limiting the number of French Jews emigrating to Palestine and a decrease in military aid to Israel (Conelly, 2001).The French intervention in the Suez Canal in July of the same year led to the breakdown of the agreements, the French believed that military intervention in Egypt would bring Nasser's remove and eliminate one of the most important factors in the Algerian affair.

At the end of the 1960s, the GPRA, *Gouvernement Provisoire de la République Algérienne*, the provisional government - parallel to the French colonial government - organized by the Algerian independence fighters and constituted a year earlier, deployed an intense foreign policy effort, trying to obtain as much support as possible for its cause within the international community. The Arab countries, with the exception of Lebanon, were the first states to recognize the GPRA.

The USSR and the US

Since 1955, the USSR, very skilfully, seeing the development of the decolonization processes, had developed what Matthew Conelly calls the New Strategy for the Third World (Conelly, 2001). Khrushchev visited India, Burma, and Afghanistan, promising close cooperation between the USSR and these states (Conelly, 2001) while supplying arms to Nasser's Egypt. Meanwhile, in the United Nations the USSR positioned itself as the main diplomatically of the FLN, *Front de Libération Nationale,* the main organisation around which the fight against France in Algeria was structured until the formation of the GPRA.

Moscow's main interest was to totally eliminate French influence in the region, without deteriorating bilateral relations too much, while at the same time it saw a window of opportunity to weaken relations between France and the US. They also feared the growing influence of Arab states and states such as Yugoslavia that were not under USSR control, in addition to losing influence in the Middle East, on the one hand it would complicate access to hydrocarbons, which were beginning to become a major factor in determining Washington's relations with the various regional players, and on the other, it would push the Arabs definitively into the arms of pan-Arabism and Nasser, or worse still, bring them definitively closer to the Soviet orbit.

For the US, the option was to follow an ambiguous policy, without offering firm support to France, at the risk of provoking the breakup of NATO or, at the very least, the defection of France. So, the solution that the US considered the least harmful from the beginning of the conflict was to give France limited support, conditioned by the adoption of structural reforms with respect to Algeria, including the autonomy of the territory while maintaining French sovereignty, while NATO's main allies and the US itself declared their unconditional support for Paris. By the summer of 1956, France had increased the length of military service to 30 months and had about half a million soldiers deployed in Algeria, compared to about 50,000 FLN fighters.

The situation was further complicated when in 1958 the GPRA requested, in addition to economic military aid, Chinese volunteers to China, North Korea and Vietnam and it was considered quite plausible that France, a NATO member, would invoke Article V of the Washington Treaty (Conelly, 2001). Up to that point, the major concern regarding France as a NATO member was that Paris would decide to send to Algeria units deployed on European soil under NATO command (Conelly, 2001). In the eyes of the international community and the United States itself, it seemed that the Algerian conflict was inexorably heading towards internationalization, with the participation of foreign volunteers and even an undeclared co-belligerency of Arab countries.

France, on the contrary, after the defeat of the French army in Indochina led to a growing distrust of partnership with the Americans, but expected unconditional support from the US, both at the diplomatic level and in terms of material resources that would help to sustain the war in Algeria with guarantees. France did not have it all its own way after the entry in 1955 of 17 new States, most of them belonging to the Eastern bloc or new countries, which had emerged as part of the decolonization processes in Asia and Africa. For France it was obvious that these new members of the UN would take the Algerian side in the face of the immobilism of the metropolis. This perception was confirmed in October 1956 when fifteen states denounced in a letter to the General Assembly the situation of repression in Algeria, describing it as genocide in the terms of Articles 11 and 14 of the United Nations Charter and denouncing France's failure to apply the United Nations Convention on Genocide, to which France was a signatory.

The ambivalent position was compromised in 1957 when France entered into conflict with Tunisia over the French militarization of the border. Tunisia, which had been granted independence by France in 1956, welcomed a large number of Algerian refugees, including a considerable number of FLN members. From their bases in Tunisia, the FLN operated inside Algeria, bringing in supplies and material and bringing in foreign volunteers who joined the FLN, including Yugoslavs, some of whom managed to enter through the Tunisian border as late as 1959 (Nikolić, 2016). The porosity of the border and the French impossibility to stop the incursions of the FLN, led to the establishment in June 57 of a defensive line, called Maurice line, which along 300 km, covered the border with Tunisia with barbed wire, minefields, and observation posts (Mihić, 2018).

After the French bombardment of Sakiet Sidi Youssef in the spring of 1958, the Tunisian government threatened to request armaments from the USSR or the Arab states - Nasser - to defend itself against France, its main arms supplier, in the event of a hypothetical action against the Algerian refugees inside Tunisia. The United States and the United Kingdom finally opted to supply a minimal amount of military equipment to Tunisia, which provoked indignation in France. From this point on, the UK's position of support was maintained for what it was worth, although in private meetings, the Foreign Office was very skeptical about the situation in Algeria. The US continued to play a double game with regard to France, as did Germany and Italy (Conelly, 2001).

Finally, after de Gaulle came to power on 1 June 1958 and the formal constitution of the Algerian provisional government in Cairo in June 1958, relations with Tunisia became even more strained, which, coupled with the US refusal to support France at the UN in December, caused de Gaulle to withdraw the French Mediterranean fleet from NATO command. France ran out of support in the region, and even States isolated by the international community such as Spain refused to support its neighbour unless Paris agreed to cooperate in handing over political dissidents to Madrid (Conelly, 2001).

Breakdown of Relations

Very soon Yugoslavia began to show interest in the Algerian independence movements, initiating the first contacts with the FLN in Cairo between 1953 and 1954 (Davidović, 2017). The uprising came as a surprise not only to the French in Algeria, but also to the metropole and the international community, including Yugoslavia. With the beginning of the popular uprising in Algeria, under the leadership of this organization on November 1, 1954, Belgrade manifested Yugoslavia's support for the FLN and its cause, initiating before the United Nations a campaign in support of the Algerian independence process and the organizations involved. This first diplomatic initiative was intended to dismantle the French government's official account of the situation in Algeria, which claimed that these were isolated actions by extremists (Davidović, 2017) groups, since the targets selected by the FLN during the first months of the war, such as police stations, were of relative strategic importance.

Cases such as the French response to the FLN action in Philippeville in August 1955, (Mihić, 2018). where, following an FLN attack that killed 123 people, including 52 Algerian supporters of the French, the subsequent crackdown by the French authorities resulted in a death toll around 1,250 Algerians according to the French government to 20,000 according to Mathew Connelly, greatly facilitated Yugoslavia's work at the UN, condemning the French solution for Algeria as a military solution, requesting the General Assembly to recognize and legitimize the Algerian cause and recognize its right to self-determination. France's representatives, and at first the few states that timidly supported Paris, tried to argue that Algeria was part of France's metropolitan territory, and the matter was essentially within France's internal jurisdiction.

In 1954, Algeria was an integral part of French territory, it is estimated that before the uprising there were around 1.1 million Europeans in Algeria, the majority of whom were French or naturalised French, representing around 12-13% of Algeria's population. The rest of the population consisted of Muslim Arabs and Berbers, estimated at just over 7 million at the start of the conflict. Despite their numerical inferiority, the European minority concentrated all political and economic power in Algeria (Mihić, 2018).

Between 1956 and 1957, FLN attacks became primarily terrorist actions in urban areas, targeting the French population. In the so-called Battle of Algiers, General Jacques Massu was given extraordinary powers, increasing the repression against the Algerian population. In this context, some of the tensest moments in the relations between France and Yugoslavia occurred between August 1957 and January 1958 when the French Navy intercepted the Yugoslav freighters *Srbija* with a cargo of 70 tons of arms and ammunition and *Slovenija*, with a cargo of 150 tons of arms destined for the Algerian rebels (Davidović, 2017). Since these two events, the interception of Yugoslav ships in international waters by the French navy became frequent, leading to a strong diplomatic confrontation between the two countries. France considered it was within its rights to stop and search ships likely to carry supplies to the Algerians. Yugoslavia considered it illegal to stop ships in international waters and demanded compensation from France.

In September 1958, the Provisional Government of the Republic of Algeria, the GPRA was formally constituted in Cairo. Ferhat Abbas was the first president to head it, within 10 days, it was recognised by 13 countries, including the People's Republic of China. No member of the socialist bloc, nor the USSR made a formal recognition of the GPRA, but through different meetings at the highest level, a de facto recognition was given, and the Algerians sent representatives to most of the European socialist states, in October 1958 had representatives in 20 countries, outside the USSR-led bloc, North Korea, and North Vietnam recognized the GPRA.

It was Ferhat Abbas himself, during a meeting with Tito in June 1959, who pleaded with the Yugoslav president to accept De Gaulle's offer of a peaceful solution to the conflict in Algeria (Davidović, 2017). Up to this point, Yugoslavia, like the USSR, had not taken a public position of formal recognition of the GRU, but, like the Soviets, the Yugoslavs recognized de facto the parallel Algerian government and its highest representative.

De Gaulle's declaration of September 16, 1959, in which he admitted the right of self-determination of peoples as a principle for the resolution of conflicts, with the consequences that this declaration has for Algeria, slightly relaxed the relations between Yugoslavia and France. In Belgrade they hoped for an agreement between the warring parties that would lead to the process of independence, under the terms of resolution 1184, 12 December 1957, and a return to official relations between France and Yugoslavia. Instead, despite the fact that the United Nations had already stated in Resolution 1573, 15 December 1960, that France recognised Algeria's right to self-determination as a basis for the resolution of the conflict, Paris increased military pressure on Algeria, further straining relations between France and Yugoslavia (Davidović, 2017). At the same time, initiated a policy aimed at improving the living conditions of Algerian citizens, thus trying to soften the effect of the indiscriminate repression against the civilian population. In the army, while increasing the number of troops in Algeria, he carried out a purge of officers, eliminating those who were most belligerent towards Algeria affair.

Throughout the 1960s relations between France and Yugoslavia became even more strained, practically reaching a breaking point with Tito's intervention at the United Nations in September 1960 in which he had harshly attacked de Gaulle's declaration on the right to self-determination, the hardening of the military solution and the brutality of French troops towards the civilian population, openly calling for the convocation of a referendum on self-determination in Algeria under the United Nations. In response, Paris prepared a very harsh reply to Tito's speech, which further complicated relations between France and Yugoslavia.

On June 12, 1961, Yugoslavia was the first European country to recognize the Algerian provisional government. France and Belgrade broke off diplomatic relations, Paris expelled the Yugoslav ambassador in February 1962, a little more than a month before France recognized Algeria's independence. From this moment on, relations gradually relaxed, reaching a point of normalization in 1964 (Davidović, 2017).

The French Communist Party

The Communist Party of France was sympathetic to Yugoslavia until the severance of relations with the USSR in 1948, after which there was a change in the stance towards Yugoslavia of the French communists. Belgrade's relations with the French Communist Party were ambivalent throughout the war, given the official position adopted by the party on Algeria and the request made to the Yugoslav government by a section of the party leadership which opposed the official line. Meanwhile, the leadership of the French Communist Party had requested the support of the League of Yugoslav Communists in order to advocate a de-escalation in the tone of the Yugoslav government's statements in support of the Algerian provisional government and against the policy of the French government. This triggered a debate within the League of Yugoslav Communists and within the Yugoslav government, with two opposing views, those who preferred a less belligerent policy against France and the hardliners led by Tito.

The dissidents of the French Communist Party also tried to obtain support in Belgrade, in the face of the position of the FLN, which in opposition to the position adopted by the French Communist Party, had denied any kind of protagonism to the Communist Party of Algeria, condemning at the same time the position of the French Communists (Conelly, 2001). Another issue that complicated relations between Yugoslavia and the French communist party was the intervention in Suez by the French army. Tito urged the French communists to condemn the intervention in a sovereign country in what he considered a new act of colonialism by France and the UK.

In May 1958 the Yugoslav government and the party leadership met to discuss the future of relations with the Western communist and socialist parties, among these, the French Communist Party, weighing in the debate on the future relations between the two parties, the Algerian question, and the internal dissidence within the French Communist Party. Also of concern in Belgrade was the constitutional referendum called in September 1958 by the French government to legitimise the constitution of the Fifth Republic, and the November elections to legitimise de Gaulle's leadership, because of the position the French Communist Party would take. De Gaulle's party won the elections with about three-quarters of the total votes. The second most voted party was the French Communist Party.

Within the party leadership there were serious divergences on the attitude towards the FLN, some members of the Central Committee of the League of Yugoslav Communists accepted the arguments of the French Communist Party, supporting reforms and a statute of autonomy for Algeria, instead of nurturing a revolutionary process and a traumatic rupture with the Metropolis, through which to achieve independence. They were equally sceptical about the capacities of the FLN to defeat the French army.

The hardliners led by Tito pushed to maintain support for the FLN, which had also stated that the partisan movement in Yugoslavia had been one of his models in structuring the armed struggle in Algeria.

The Yugoslav Friend

At the same time that Belgrade initiated the diplomatic offensive in the United Nations, the Yugoslav government considered the possibility of delivering military material to the FLN via Cairo, where the FLN had established its headquarters. Once the military aid was approved in 1958, the first shipments consisted mainly of light weapons (Conelly, 2001). In May of the same year, the Yugoslav government and the party leadership met to discuss the future of relations with the Western communist and socialist parties, within this meeting the relations with the Arab countries were also discussed, with the Algerian question weighing again, more than likely.

In 1959 the Commission for International Relations of the Central Committee of the League of Yugoslav Communists, SJK for its acronym in Serbo-Croatian, had sent a mission of observers to Algeria which presented its conclusions to the SJK in mid-September. At the end of the month the reports of the SJK members sent to the Middle East and to the Anti-Colonial Rome and Oslo Peace Conferences were received, and at the beginning of October the report of the envoy of the International Relations Committee of the League of Serbian Communists to the conference on Algeria held in Cairo.

Consequently, after Tito's intervention in the United Nations in 1960, the Yugoslav government approved an increase in the sending of material aid to the FLN, increasing in proportion its influence over this organization. Belgrade's position on the internationalization of the conflict did not change even when the Algerian representatives in Yugoslavia were exultant at the fear of France, seeing itself internationally isolated, that the holding of a referendum of self-determination in Algeria promoted by the UN, as Tito had requested before the General Assembly, would lead to a hypothetical intervention of the United Nations in Algeria, similar to that which had taken place in the Congo (Conellyl, 2001).

Yugoslavia, both at the level of the collegiate structure of government and at the level of its individual republics - the presence of members of the League of Serbian Communists at the Cairo conference in 1958 - was involved in the Algerian question both by intervening in the various forums organized at the international level and by sending representatives to the Arab countries and observers to Algeria itself and receiving at the same time Algerian representatives in Belgrade. Yugoslavia's official position concerning Algeria had centred on aid to refugees channelled through the JCK (Yugoslav Red Cross), especially those settled in Tunisia, to whom they provided trucks on at least one occasion, and to a lesser extent in Morocco, to whom they constantly provided clothing and food. According to the testimony of Stevan Labudović, numerous Yugoslav doctors were mobilized during the war to care for wounded Algerian fighters, Yugoslav hospitals regularly took in combatants and seriously ill (Nikolić, 2001) and Algerian doctors were trained (Davidović, 2017). This testimony contrasts with the intense campaign developed by the JCK in Algeria and Tunisia and the presence at the border of Yugoslav doctors belonging to this organization.

In this context, requests for Algerian aid to the countries of the socialist bloc and Arab countries had multiplied, so that in June 1959 members of the League of Yugoslav Communists met with the President of the Provisional Government of Algeria, Ferhat Abbas (Davidović, 2017). The FLN asked the Israeli committee for Free Algeria for instructors and technicians to give training courses for FLN militants in training camps in Yugoslavia (Nedjar, 2008). Yugoslav military aid was constant, contributing decisively to the success of the FLN. Other initiatives were also carried out, such as initiatives in the field of education, granting university scholarships to Algerian students in Yugoslavia, or cultural exchanges, promoting the performance of Algerian folklore and drama groups in Yugoslavia.

At the political level, figures such as Ramdane Abbane led the FLN from nationalist positions to internationalism as a political stance, introducing organisational measures such as the collective leadership of the FLN. Observers from this organization were invited to the Seventh Congress of the SKJ in Ljubljana, April 1958 and to the Congress of the Union of Yugoslav Trade Unions (Davidović, 2017). After independence, Yugoslav political influence, made the FLN became interested in the Yugoslav model of autonomous socialism.

CONCLUSION

After the defeat in Indochina, France needed time to stabilise, reorganise as a state and set priorities for a future determined by bloc-to-bloc conflict. The uprising in Algeria, unexpected by France, ended up completely destabilising the country. The development of the conflict and its consequences damaged the structure of the French state, tearing apart its social fabric, its cohesion as a nation and its international prestige. Internally, due to the intransigent attitude and without an effective solution to the Algerian uprising, the governments of the French Fourth Republic fell, giving way to the French Fifth Republic, led by De Gaulle, a consensus solution around the father of the nation, which in the end fell victim to a process, Algeria's independence, that was unstoppable.

The French Fifth Republic itself was on the verge of collapse after an attempted coup d'état by the army at the beginning of 1960, which refused to give up on Algeria, even at the cost of the complete destabilisation of France, Algeria was an integral part of French territory, so the number of European settlers, mostly French, was very high. The internationalisation of the Algerian conflict was a very painful issue for the French, who for a long time remained in a kind of international isolation. The battles and the confrontation, both military and in counter-terrorist actions, were won by France, using means and methods that provoked the defeat at the international level, which France did not know how to identify well, and where Yugoslavia played the trump card of the military solution in front of the world public opinion in all those forums where the GPRA did not have a voice, such as the UN.

Apparently, the very deteriorated relations between Yugoslavia and France as a result of the war in Algeria were restored relatively quickly, according to the speech delivered by De Gaulle in January 1969 on the occasion of the visit, one year after the re-establishment of diplomatic relations, of Mika Spiljak, President of the Federal Executive Council of Yugoslavia, to Paris. It is clear from de Gaulle's speech that during that visit, the two governments discussed, among other issues, the right to self-determination and the processes of decolonization. This speech came 10 years after de Gaulle himself had declared Algeria's right to self-determination and received a harsh attack from Tito at the United Nations.

With respect to the US and their allies, French disaffection with Washington will lead Paris to conclude that the best way to enhance its security and interests is to develop its own nuclear capabilities in the next years, achieving the first successful test of a nuclear weapon in 1960, adding yet another player in the complex Cold War nuclear equation.

REFERENCES

Democracia socialista en Yugoslavia. [Socialist democracy in Yugoslavia.] (1963). Revista Política Internacional; Revista mensual yugoslava; Belgrado, 1963.

Connelly, M. (2001). Rethinking the Cold War and decolonization: The grand strategy of the Algerian war for independence. *International Journal of Middle East Studies, 33*(2), 221–245. doi:10.1017/S0020743801002033

Davidović, N. (2017). *Kako je Jugoslavija pomagala oružanu borbu protiv Zapada! [How Yugoslavia helped the armed struggle against the West!]* Princip Info. https://princip.info/2017/01/03/kako-je-jugoslavija-pomagala-borbu-protiv-zapada/

Hobswbawn, E. (1998). *Naciones y nacionalismo desde 1780 [Nations and nationalism since 1780.].* Grijalbo Mondadori.

Nedjar, M. (2008). *Argelia y la cuestión palestina durante el periodo de gobierno de FLN (1962-1988). [Algeria and the Palestinian question during the period of FLN rule (1962-1988).]* [Tesis doctoral; Universidad Autónoma de Madrid].

Nikolić, M. (2016) Jugosloven na prvim linijama fronta u Ažiru. [Yugoslav on the front lines in Ažir.] Princip Info.

Mihić. I. (2018). Diplomatski odnosi Francuske i Jugoslavije 1954. - 1962. i Alžirski rat za neovisnost. [Diplomatic relations between France and Yugoslavia 19541962 and the Algerian War of Independence.] Zagreb University

Yale Law School. (1954). *Lillian Goldman Law Library; The Avalon project; Treaty of Alliance, Political Cooperation, and Mutual Assistance Between the Turkish Republic, the Kingdom of Greece, and the Federal People's Republic of Yugoslavia (Balkan Pact).* Yale Law School.

United Nations General Assembly. (1957). *United Nations General Assembly Resolutions.* UN.

UN. (1957). *Resolution 1012.* UN. http://www.worldlii.org/int/other/UNGA/1957/15.pdf

UN. (1957). *Resolution 1184.* UN. http://www.worldlii.org/int/other/UNGA/1957/127.pdf

UN. (1960). *Resolution 1573.* UN. https://www.noticieroficial.com/Internacional/DIH/ONUAG/ONUAGR1576-1960.pdf

United Nations Office of Legal Affairs. (1959). *Article 2 (para. 7); Case N°- 27; The Algerian Question.* UN. https://legal.un.org/repertory/art2/spanish/rep_supp2_vol1_art2_7.pdf

Archives Nationales. (1960). *Allocutions et discours de Charles de Gaulle (1944-1969; Communiqué non diffusé, faisant suite à la déclaration du maréchal Tito, président de la République de Yougoslavie, à l'ONU [National Archives; Allocutions and speeches by Charles de Gaulle (1944-1969; Unpublished communiqué, following the declaration of Marshal Tito, President of the Republic of Yugoslavia, at the UN].* Archives Nationales.

Archives Nationales. (1969). *Allocutions et discours de Charles de Gaulle (1944-1969); Toast adressé à Mika Spiljak, président du Conseil exécutif fédéral de Yougoslavie, déjeuner, palais de l'Élysée, [peeches and speeches by Charles de Gaulle (1944-1969); Toast addressed to Mika Spiljak, President of the Federal Executive Council of Yugoslavia, lunch, Élysée Palace].* Archives Nationales.

Arhiv Jugoslavije [Archives of Yugoslavia]. (1958). Fond number 142; Materijali komisije za društvene organizacije (društvene organizacije, savezi i udruženja); Materijali o radu jugoslovenskog crvenog krsta [Fund number 142; Materials of the commission for social organizations (social organizations, alliances and associations); Materials on the work of the Yugoslav Red Cross]. Archives of Yugoslavia.

Arhiv Jugoslavije [Archives of Yugoslavia]. (1959). Fond number 142; Materijali komisije za međunarodne veze saveznog odbora SSRNJ; Materijali sa sastanaka komisije za međunarodne veze so SSRNJ [Fund number 142; Materials of the commission for international relations of the federal board of SSRNJ; Materials from the meetings of the commission for international relations with SSRNJ]. Arhiv Jugoslavije [Archives of Yugoslavia].

Chapter 13
Interventionism and the Third World:
The Crisis of the Dominican Republic in the Global Cold War (1965–1966)

Pedro Martinez Lillo
Autonomous University of Madrid, Spain

Javier Castro Arcos
Gabriela Mistral University, Chile

ABSTRACT

The present paper analyzes the occupation of Santo Domingo in 1965 which was the largest US military operation directed against a Latin American country, not only during the Cold War, but in the entire century. In a global Cold War framework, on the one hand, by the détente between the superpowers after the Cuban missile crisis and, on the other, by the force of the Third World and Third World internationalism, the authors explain the impact of the events that occurred on this Caribbean Island had on post-colonial construction, as well as defining a global anti-imperialist struggle. Finally, and according to the review of historical archives from North America, France, and Latin America, among others, which are the primary and secondary sources that accompany the analysis of the proposed research, these conclusions will be delivered in accordance with this historical research.

INTRODUCTION

The 1965 occupation of Santo Domingo, one of the largest U.S. military operations against a Latin American country in the contemporary era, has remained relatively marginalized in regional historiography, as well as in studies on the Cold War. Despite its hemispheric and international impact and transcendence, the Dominican crisis (*April Revolution*, civil war, US intervention) was obscured by a double process of collective amnesia and diplomatic expediency, blurring those dramatic events that nevertheless must be placed among the most outstanding in the recent evolution of Latin America (Halliday, 2010:2-3, 9). In

DOI: 10.4018/978-1-6684-7040-4.ch013

recent years, valuable North American and Dominican research contributions have been correcting this anomaly (Chester, 2001; Grimaldi, 2016; Gleijeses, 2014; Gleijeses, 1984; de la Rosa, 2015; Hermann, 2009), even though the popular mobilization and the constitutionalist movement of the Dominican Republic still does not appear on the *Tree of Revolutions* (Rojas, 2021).

The paradigmatic case around which this chapter is structured is based on the approach of the global Cold War, projecting the history of American intervention and its repercussions during the 1960s in the Third World under a Cold War hegemonic context. For this reason, the main objectives of this work revolve around two questions:

- An analysis of the historical context that led the United States to implement military intervention as a model of containment of possible revolutionary scenarios in the Dominican Republic in 1965.
- An exploration of the intervention model and its political repercussions in the Inter-American system, in the Third World, and in intermediate powers such as France.

BACKGROUND

At the end of April 1965, Ernesto Che Guevara accompanied by fourteen Cuban guerrillas crossed Lake Tanganyka from Dar es Salaam, entering a liberated zone of the Congo to intervene in favour of the emancipation struggle of this African country (Gott, 1996, 6-7). Far away from there, but almost simultaneously, American troops landed in Santo Domingo neutralizing the *Dominican Revolution,* in a similar scenario to their occupations of the Caribbean country in the early twentieth century (Smith, 2010, 93). Although chance made the dates and the events coincide in such distant geographical spaces, sub-Saharan Africa and The West Indies, what happened illustrated a transnational historical process that defined by a global Cold War and the emergence of the Third World and popular movements, would mark the decade of the sixties.

MAIN FOCUS OF THE CHAPTER

The present chapter is an attempt to contribute to the recovery of that forgotten memory by studying the impact that the events on this Caribbean Island had on post-colonial construction, as well as on the definition of a global anti-imperialist struggle. It situates the events that took place in the Dominican Republic during the spring and summer of 1965, in a regional and, above all, a global framework, defined on the one hand by the détente between the superpowers after the Cuban missile crisis and on the other, by the strength of the Third World and Third World internationalism. The decolonization after World War II and the Afro-Asian Bandung Conference in 1955 transformed international society. Our hypothesis suggests the need to interpret the brief existence of the *Dominican Revolution* by integrating it into the global social reality and therefore, as a complement to the analyses which are more focused on the causes of the *post-Trujillo* political crisis. We have also studied the reactions within the Western bloc, to highlight how the discrepancies between some of its allies, e.g. the Johnson administration versus de Gaulle's France, were illustrative of their different visions of the Third World or, of the defence of their interests in a different way in the face of the thrust of the liberation movements.

The work presented here is organized under different headings describing the nature of the subject, its relevance and main characteristics, and the proposal from upon which it is based, as well as ways of transferring the contributions obtained.

The Latin American Global Cold War

In addition to the consultation of documentary collections in France, Spain and the United States, our research is based both conceptually and methodologically, on two historiographical proposals. On the one hand, within the *new Cold War history, it* takes advantage of the concept of the *Global Cold War* formulated by Arne Odd Westad, as well as other studies that focus on a decentralizing vision of the bipolar conflict, taking advantage of *transnational history* and *global history* approaches. The Cold War goes beyond the Soviet-American rivalry and the spheres of geopolitics, security or military balances. By opening up the *periphery*, it allows a play of scale between the global, the regional, the national and the local, enriching its understanding. Where we have numerous actors, other states, leaders, and have even incorporated and considered non-state actors such as transnational groups, organizations and individuals (Faure and Del Pero, 2020: 9-11).

Westad has included for the first time, the Third World as the central object of a conflict between the superpowers of a global scope (Westad, 2018), where the peripheries are not only seen as a static scenario of the struggle between Soviets and Americans, but above all, as active subjects (Pettiná, 2018: 21-22; Westad, 2018: 15-17). All of which is relevant to the Latin American case as shown by the recent works of Thomas C. Field Jr., Stella Krepp, Vanni Pettiná, Tanya Harmer or Germán Alburqueque (Field, 2020; Alburquerque, 2020; Field, Krepp and Pettiná, 2020; Garrard-Burnet, Lawrance and Moreno, 2013). Harmer lucidly indicates that:

(...) More than a mere spectator of the rivalry between the two superpowers, the Third World also played an important role in shaping the international politics of the second half of the twentieth century. In Latin America, Africa and Asia, the ideological divisions that were at the heart of the Cold War led to revolutionary reaction (with and without superpower intervention), and it was where the hot wars of the Cold War were fought, with foreign arms, funds and assistance (Harmer, 2009).

In this way, and in accordance with Pettiná, it is possible to point out that, as in other regions of the Third World, in Latin America the conflict between the two superpowers overlapped with complex local processes of social, economic, and political transformation (Pettiná, 2018). There were local dynamics, which dynamized processes of a global nature with respect to power schemes in a bipolar era. After the Cuban revolution of 1959, Latin America was inserted into the radars of the powers, however, after the tensions generated by a nuclear threat, the Missile Crisis of 1962, the region gained greater geopolitical and media relevance at a global level (Pettiná, 2018:59).

Aldo Marchesi emphasizes that the sixties were more global than their historical narrative, and his criticism makes sense regarding the role of the bibliography of global history that has underestimated the role of the processes and active roles of the peripheries, and of the events that occurred there, which when analyzed, will grant a more complete understanding of the globality of that period (Marchesi, 2017). The recent discussion between Gilbert Joseph and Marcelo Casals in *Cold War history* shows how the predominance of the North continues to be hegemonic when it comes to accommodating works that focus not only on the issues that occurred in the global Latin American Cold War, but also limit the contributions of studies in this field of research (Joseph, 2019; Casals, 2020). Casals indicates that in the balance made by Joseph, for a synthesis of Latin American Cold War studies, of the 264 works cited by the author, 92% were published in English while only 8% are in Spanish.

The paradigm of the 'global south' opens up a research vein that calls for a thorough study to locate or highlight the junctures, contact zones or processes of the socio-cultural, political and economic transfer in significant moments of the global and Latin American Cold War. Since many of the Latin American actors, influenced by the global conflict, were surely guided by the ideological principles of the Cold War and set goals and objectives in its direction. Part of the challenge is to think and work the global conflict on the Latin American scale, in order to unravel multiple memories and webs of global interaction. In this sense, the hermeneutics of the historian of the global cold war in Latin America should go beyond Eurocentric epistemologies (Palomino, 2019).

Third Worldism as a Theoretical Reference

If we speak of a *Global Cold War*, we also subscribe, as a second reference, to the analytical proposals of Vijay Prashad when he states that the *Third World was not a place, it was a project* (Prashad, 2012:15; Prashad, 2013). The ideas of this project sustained the solidary capacity of the decolonized states after World War II to create a power bloc, to integrate other peoples in their emancipatory struggles, and the conviction that non-Europeans assumed a key responsibility in the world system. With the help of important leaders, the Third World included diverse aspirations from anti-colonialism, anti-imperialism, the preservation of peace, non-alignment, or development, as well as the institutions to put them into practice, such as the Afro-Asian meetings in Bandung or Cairo, the Non-Aligned Movement, the Tricontinental Conference in Havana, or the UN. Little by little these ideas would manage to become an ideology, *Third Worldism,* not too elaborated, but with a sufficient nucleus of statements capable of representing very diverse realities (Alburquerque, 2020: 16). Faced with this scenario, the superpowers and the heirs of the colonial empires were defining their strategies.

According to Cristoph Kalter, the Third World was a very influential organizational category in the 20th century. The concept was created by the French demographer Alfred Sauvy in *L'Observateur*, in 1952, cataloguing in an exercise of political geography the so-called underdeveloped spaces in the Third World. Kalter specifies that the concept established nothing less than a new model of the world, whose rapid and incomplete devaluation still needed explanation as much as the fact that for thirty years before that, the idea of the Third World had dominated, almost overwhelmingly, the way in which political-economic spheres and social disparities could be conceived on a global scale (Kalter, 2016:10). It is important to emphasize that such a conceptual framework was constructed in the midst of post-war decolonization, the first phase of the Cold War, and the dispute over modernization models between the 'developed' economies and the rest (Palomino, 2019:23). It is in this sense, to indicate as Bergel, the Third Worldist reference proliferated in a spectrum of initiatives that sought to make visible and discuss global social fractures (Bergel, 2019: 130-131). For many of the decision-makers in the geopolitical agencies of the powers, it made strategic calculations in order to determine centres of influence in a process in which Third Worldism was synonymous with vulnerability, reconfiguration and spaces of opportunity to influence the chessboard of the global Cold War.

The strategic need for hemispheric security, and to foresee the future focal points of revolutions such as that in Cuba, led the United States, via the Department of State, to work on methods to investigate the problem of Third World poverty and, secondly, to link it to traditional (non-capitalist) values and practices on the one hand, and to the lack of capital and technology on the other. According to Aram Ziai, the solution was then to propose to Third World countries that they abandon traditional social structures and import Western values on the one hand, and import Western capital and technology through investments and integration into the world market on the other (Ziai, 2016: 32). Ultimately, the goal of the modernizing discourse was to produce African, Asian, and Latin American subjects who of their own free will would support an international order in line with the interests of the First World metropolises. 'The burden' of the colonial period shifted from civilizing the uncivilized, to global governance and the production of a world in which the American way of life could flourish (Ziai, 2016). If the phenomena of adaptation to planned modernization did not occur, the solutions to be explored would be to move away from a *softpower* approach and to transit directly to *hardpower*.

Michael Latham observed that the superpowers assumed that their national security depended on spreading their visions of modernization or socialist transformation, depending on the case. This projection led them to deploy strategies of persuasion in their propagation. Ultimately, many 'Third World' elites, eager for rapid economic and social progress, also embraced those approaches, with some even employing repression in the name of transformation, and others adapting packages of resolute reforms in order to achieve the standards derived from the theory of modernization itself (Latham, 2011:280).

In order to safeguard the self-determination of the peoples, the idea of the Third World was increasingly deployed to generate unity and support among a growing number of non-aligned nation-states whose leaders sought to displace the 'East-West' (Cold War) conflict and bring the 'North-South' conflict to the forefront (Berger, 2004). In this way, in the 1960s the anti-colonialist movements worked to create an internationalist fraternity or solidarity, which derived in spaces and/or forums of mutual support against the superpowers, a matter that led them to perceive themselves as a 'Third Force', driving, not without the direct or indirect participation of the bipolar powers, in national liberation movements in Latin America, Africa and Asia, i.e. from the Global South (Hatzky, 2015: 12).

According to Berger, Third Worldism as a historical movement was shaped by political currents that grew out of the ideas of anti-colonial nationalists and their efforts to combine often highly romantic interpretations of pre-colonial traditions and cultures with the utopianism embodied specifically by Marxism and socialism, as well as their reticence to 'Western' visions of modernization and development in general (Berger, 2044:11). Now, for authors such as Marchesi, Third Worldism clearly contributed to shape an anti-imperialist discourse that implied imagining a community that transcended the nation, and in opposition to the empire. As Marchesi explains, many times 'anti-imperialists' denounced 'imperialist' practices or actors within their own national communities, so that the boundaries between Third Worldism, anti-imperialism, and imperialism were political rather than territorial (Marchesi, 2006: 136).

Anticolonialist Links and Transnational Resistance Networks

The Third World in Latin America would find its apogee during the 1960s and 1970s (Field, Krepp and Pettiná, 2020: 394; Alburquerque, 2020: 17). The European sociocultural heritage of its elites, their racial biases or disinterest in linking the region's development to the newly independent states of Africa and Asia, limited the immediate impact of global anticolonial resistance in the Latin American imaginary (Field, Krepp and Pettiná, 2020: 394). On the contrary, the cultures of resistance forged during the nineteenth and early twentieth centuries, in defence of their sovereignty against the growing control of the United States, together with the impact of the Komintern in the countries of the region, generated a background of anticolonialist ties among peripheral actors.

The Cold War, whether as an international system or as a global conflict between two models of social modernization, accentuated this regional scheme of hegemony-resistance and established a key constant. Pan-Americanism, the backbone of Latin American foreign policy, was strengthened after World War II under the leadership of the United States, through the commitment of the Pact of Bogota (OAS) and the Inter-American Treaty of Reciprocal Assistance (TIAR). Its instrumentalization in terms of U.S. interests led to the resurgence, after the intervention in Guatemala in 1954, of an ever latent Latin American autonomist tendency, which was strengthened by the Cuban Revolution and the aggression in Santo Domingo, to finally be enhanced by the emergence of *Third Worldism* (Alburquerque, 2020:20-21).

No less important would be the Caribbean contribution to global anti colonialism. It is true that Bandung (1955) focused on the new states, but Third Worldism grew out of *transnational resistance networks,* whose antecedents included intellectuals such as Martinique's *Frantz Fanon,* Trinidad's *George Padmore* and *Cyril Lionel Robert James, Guyana's Leon Damas and black poet Aimé Césaire of Martinique*; *Leon Damas*, from Guyana, or the black poet *Aimé Césaire* from La Martinique, who in one way or another, through negritude, Pan-Africanism or neocolonial denunciation conceptualized the Third World, and connected their positions with other anti-imperialist movements (Westad, 2018: 288-289, 294). On the other hand, the Caribbean was experiencing a geopolitical reconfiguration in a Third Worldist tune. Along with the triumph of the Cuban Revolution, the independence of most of the former British colonies: Jamaica and Trinidad and Tobago since 1962, Guyana and Barbados in 1966, was witnessed, while secessionist traces took hold in the French territories of Guadeloupe and Martinique. National liberation parties, organizations, and movements, including those in Puerto Rica, flowed and circulated throughout the Antilles, projecting themselves onto other continents (Dumont, 2010: 258-259).

In the long run, the determining element was linked to the triumph of the Cuban Revolution and the development of a foreign policy based on solidarity internationalism and the conviction of contributing to a fairer world through a revolutionary strategy (Domínguez, 2009: 65-67). Likewise, pressure from the United States made the Havana leadership understand the need to be part of an anti-imperialist front at a world level (Lentin, 1966: 30). Cuba's involvement with the postcolonial states within the Third World, as well as its support for African liberation movements, generated a new space for the interrelation of Latin America with the rest of the world. Before them, Havana assumed the role of spokesman for the poor and uprooted people of the continent, far from being a North American puppet. Despite its close ties with the USSR, in 1961 Castro's Cuba became a founding member of the Non-Aligned Movement (NAM), and through it was able to interact with numerous countries that had recently acceded to independence and reaffirm its role as the vanguard for social-political change throughout Latin America. The fact that Cuba continued to support anti-colonial projects with concrete actions, sending material aid and soldiers to fight alongside those liberation movements, increased its prestige in Asia and Africa (Field, Krepp and Pettiná, 2020:397).

From then on, *Third Worldism* penetrated among Latin American students and intellectuals and even the nationalist elites. From the left, above all, Latin American dependence on the United States began to be seen in terms similar to African and Asian dependence on their former metropolises. As in Europe and the United States, the discovery of the Third World fuelled the establishment of new leftist movements, often critical of the already established socialist and communist parties, and at times dedicated to guerrilla struggle, for which they found inspiration in Cuba, Vietnam, Algeria, and South Africa (Field, Krepp and Pettiná, 2020:397-398). Progressively, in the 1960s, the Third World option gave way to other forms of organization in the South, such as the Group of 77 and the Non-Aligned Movement, options that were more developed in Latin America, although they included right-wing nationalist regimes and even military dictatorships.

As Palieraki has shown, linkages within the Third World, counted on a growing number of activists who travelled from one country to another, and from one continent to another, to help revolutionary movements, attend military or intelligence training, or to seek refuge from dictatorial regimes. The emancipation of the Third World had a double meaning for its protagonists: the strengthening of their nation-states and at the same time, transnational networks (Palieraki, 2017: 276).

Interventionism: Hemispheric Security Scheme

During the 1950s, American exceptionalism grew together with an anti-communist globalism that profoundly shaped U.S. policy in Latin America and the entire underdeveloped world (Berger, 2002:64-65). The paternalistic attitude towards Latin America included military intervention as a variable promoting democracy and modernization. To be more precise, military intervention is defined as the movement of troops or regular forces, airborne, maritime, bombing, etc. from one country into the territory or territorial waters of another country, or the forcible military action of troops already stationed by one country within another, in the context of some political issue or dispute (Peksen and Olson, 2012). In the words of Hermann and Kegley, this mode of military force is particularly attractive because, unlike other forms of coercion, such as full-scale war or protracted economic sanctions, intervention gives policymakers relative control over both 'in and out' and the costs of military action and can be justified in the name of such lofty ideals as the promotion and restoration of democracy (Hermann and Kegley, 1998:92-93).

In Washington's calculations, the distant socio-political reality of the Latin American actors and the global south meant evaluating a variety of political, ideological, and economic orientations that made the negotiation routes more complex. Interventions functioned as a more direct and practical way to influence the internal politics of the countries monitored in alert of possible revolutions of a socialist nature (Parrot, 2022:5). Pearson and Baumann note that between 1945 and 1992 there were 64 discrete, non-overlapping U.S. events that adhered to the international legal definition of overt and direct uses of U.S. military force in other countries. Each of these actions had as at least one of its primary purposes to protect or promote the democracy of the target; that is, the action involved military force to (1) support a government that leaned toward the liberal democratic community or (2) to oppose an autocratic government (Hermann and Kegley, 1998:94). The 64 interventions involved varying degrees of U.S. troop commitments, from sending military advisors and equipment to assist a combatant in a civil war, to shows of force with naval warships, to moving large numbers of U.S. ground forces into the target country (Peksen and Olson, 2012).

The global Cold War added multiple episodes of US and USSR intervention in the internal affairs of other states, sometimes directly such as that which occurred with the US intervention in the civil war in Vietnam, Dominican Republic, Grenada and Panama, or that of the USSR in Hungary, Czechoslovakia and Afghanistan, and sometimes indirectly by the use of allied or dependent states, such as Cuba in Angola, and Ethiopia or the Franco-Belgian interventions in Shaba in 1977-78 (Adelphi, 2002:38) (Adelphi, 2002:38). Undoubtedly, the interventions were the local reflection of the global bipolar competition. In the American case, the strategic interests for an invasion were probably defined in terms of the degree of possible Soviet intervention, as well as the intervention of a Soviet ally, an internal communist presence in the country of internal war, military assistance and/or the geographical distance of the country from the United States (Yoon, 1997, 580).

In the case of the invasion of the Dominican Republic, its design is one of multilateral intervention. Fundamentally, the United States, through the OAS, sent a multilateral force to replace U.S. units in the Dominican Republic in 1965. As we shall see, the regional debates surrounding the operation suggested a growing disillusionment with US hegemonic policy in the region, and the Dominican experience strongly reinforced regional norms of non-intervention (Adelphi, 2002, 45).

Crisis of the Dominican Republic (1965-1966)

In April 1965, the attention of the international community was focused on Vietnam, who became worried after the US military escalation that began in February with the bombing of the North, and the arrival of the Marines in March at the Dag Nam base. Surprisingly, everything turned to the Dominican Republic where, on the 28th, the President of the United States, Lyndon B. Johnson had ordered the landing of 30,000 marines and airborne forces, in the midst of the crisis that had just broken out in the Caribbean country. Three days earlier, a plot, the so-called *April Revolution*, bringing together liberal military, nationalist, reformist, and leftist elements, had overthrown the ruling Triumvirate and attempted to reestablish the power of the country's former president, Juan Bosch, a reformist democrat, head of the Dominican Revolutionary Party (PRD), who had been overthrown by a coup d'état in 1963. The *constitutionalists*, supported by a popular uprising, managed to corner the conservative and anti-communist sectors of the Dominican army, the armed wing of a still active Trujillo oligarchy, and Colonel Francisco Caamaño emerged as the leader of the rebel side. The euphoria was short-lived: the U.S. deployment managed to sustain the initially defeated, giving rise to a bloody civil conflict between two de facto Dominican governments[1].

Lyndon Johnson instructed Secretary of State Rusk and Undersecretary Ball to seek a means to involve the OAS in the actions in order to resolve the crisis as quickly as possible and to avoid any isolation of the United States from the other members of the Organization. The objective was to gain Latin American support and understanding for the military intervention, and their receptiveness to constructive suggestions about how to proceed. The former coordinator of the Alliance for Progress, Teodoro Moscoso, was quickly summoned to work on a Special Committee for the agreement of an inter-American force. Consideration was given to sending Ambassador Ralph Dungan of Chile to San Jose to brief Costa Rican leaders and seek their advice. The assistance of the former White House advisor Arthur Schlesinger, Jr. was also solicited, and preparations were begun to send Ambassador Averell Harriman to the major Latin American capitals (Lowenthal, 1973, 117).

Shortly afterwards, Washington succeeded in getting the Organization of American States (OAS), which was very divided, to give legal coverage to the operation, creating an Inter-American Pacification Force (Brazil, Nicaragua, Honduras, Paraguay, El Salvador, Costa Rica) to interpose itself between the parties and facilitate a peace agreement. As Harvey points out, the approval of the Inter-American Force meant the transformation of the forces present in Dominican territory into another force that would not belong either to a State or a group of States, but to an inter-State organization, such as the OAS, in charge precisely of interpreting the democratic will of its members (Harvey, 2020, 35).

Figure 1. Palmer, Bruce, Jr., and General Bruce, Jr. Palmer. Intervention in the Caribbean: The Dominican Crisis Of 1965, University Press of Kentucky, 1989, p. 74

Chart 2 - Inter-American Peace Force
(Dominican Republic, 1965-1966)

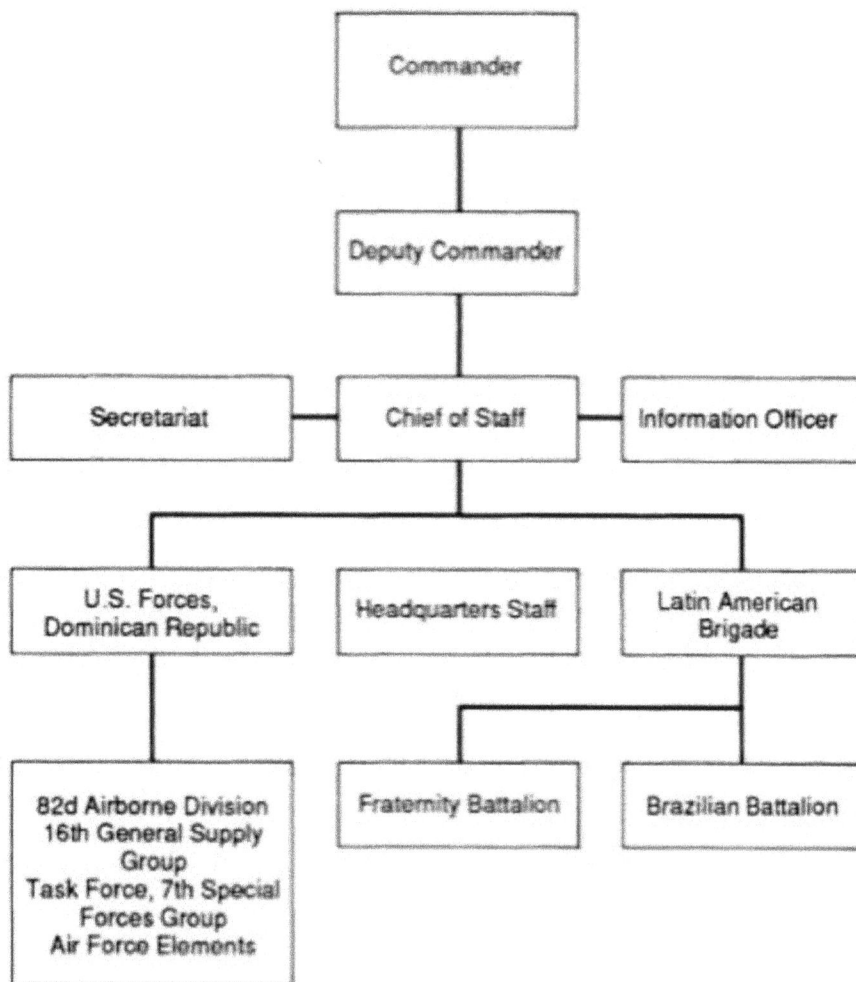

```
                        ┌──────────────┐
                        │  Commander   │
                        └──────────────┘
                               │
                        ┌──────────────┐
                        │Deputy Commander│
                        └──────────────┘
                               │
   ┌─────────────┐     ┌──────────────┐     ┌──────────────────┐
   │ Secretariat │─────│Chief of Staff│─────│Information Officer│
   └─────────────┘     └──────────────┘     └──────────────────┘
                               │
   ┌─────────────┐     ┌──────────────┐     ┌──────────────────┐
   │U.S. Forces, │     │Headquarters  │     │ Latin American   │
   │Dominican    │     │   Staff      │     │    Brigade       │
   │Republic     │     └──────────────┘     └──────────────────┘
   └─────────────┘                                  │
          │                                  ┌──────┴───────┐
   ┌─────────────┐                    ┌──────────────┐ ┌──────────────┐
   │82d Airborne │                    │  Fraternity  │ │  Brazilian   │
   │Division     │                    │  Battalion   │ │  Battalion   │
   │16th General │                    └──────────────┘ └──────────────┘
   │Supply Group │
   │Task Force,  │
   │7th Special  │
   │Forces Group │
   │Air Force    │
   │Elements     │
   └─────────────┘
```

Under the Inter-American umbrella, unilateralism was transformed into multilateralism, despite the violation of the Pact of Bogota and the mandate of non-interference in the internal affairs of a State. After months of conflict and attempts at negotiation through OAS mediation and US supervision, on August 31st an Act of Reconciliation put an end to the civil war, dissolved the two governments, and appointed a provisional president who was to lead the country until elections were held in 1966. The occupation had left more than 3,000 Dominicans dead (Veeser & Bobea, 2020, 40-41). The elections were won by the North American candidate and lost by Juan Bosch[2].

After the Vietnam disaster, Nixon and Kissinger observed that there was an urgent need to reduce direct U.S. intervention in the Third World. Instead of using U.S. military power in crises, regional 'policemen' would have to take responsibility, with U.S. support, for keeping communism contained in their regions. As Westad argues, the Third World police states, i.e., Brazil, Turkey, South Africa, Iran and Indonesia would receive assistance and training from the United States, while Washington would interfere as little as possible in the way they solved their local communist problems (Westad, 2005, 197). The assumptions of 'manifest destiny' and the Monroe Doctrine re-emerged. Not forgetting the application of the Truman Doctrine of the containment of communism, as a backbone of the pro-American bloc alignments, in this case, within the Inter-American system. With the events thus generated, the Johnson administration reinforced and extended the hegemonic pretension, that is, the idea that Latin America was a sphere of influence for the United States in its own right (Lowenthal, 2010, 561-562).

The intervention in the Dominican Republic proved that the Third World was a Cold War battleground during the 1960s. U.S. policies toward underdeveloped regions became increasingly militarized, culminating in the invasion of the Dominican Republic in 1965. Kennedy's characterization of Latin America as "the most dangerous area in the world" apparently alerted the Johnson administration to take expeditious action (Brands, 2010, 37).

The Johnson Doctrine: American Reaction

In addition to the economic interests of sugar at stake, the White House had justified the intervention in avoiding a *second Cuba*, given the control, it argued, that communists and Castroists exercised over the Dominican popular movement. If the choice was between another "Castro revolution" and a right-wing dictator, in Johnson's view, the United States should prefer the latter a thousand times over (Westad, 2018, 370-371). The *Johnson Doctrine* meant the return of the old *big stick policy*, now updated within the strategy of the containment of communism, in an area of national interest, the Caribbean, under tension since the Cuban Revolution. These justifications were unfounded: although communist Dominicans and supporters of the guerrilla struggle had participated in the struggle, they neither controlled the uprising nor were they in the majority. Moreover, the three radical groups in the country, the Castroist M14J, the pro-Chinese Popular Democratic Movement (MPD), and the communist Dominican Socialist Party (PSP), were wary of the plot by the constitutionalist forces and Juan Bosch, and only later joined the popular resistance (Veeser & Bobea, 2020, 40-41). There was also no direct involvement by Cuba, although young Cubans, Puerto Ricans, Venezuelans of the FALN or anti-Duvalier Haitians circulated in the streets of Santo Domingo. Although evidence of communist activity among the pro-Bosch forces was very scarce, Johnson concluded that the risk of subversion was simply intolerable (Latham, 2010, 271).

Jonathan Colman details the implications of the Dominican affair and the impending Cuban threat on the reactions of Johnson and his cabinet,

(...) Undersecretary of State George Ball suggested that upon learning of the news of the rebellion, President Johnson experienced an 'increasing absorption in the Dominican problem, to the point where he took over the day-to-day direction of policy and became, in effect, the Dominican desk.' Johnson felt, according to Ball, that 'his own position was very much at stake in this issue of whether we had another Cuba on our hands or not.' The Johnson White House also had to consider the Dominican Republic not only in terms of U.S. Cold War security interests, but in the context of a powerful anti-Communist constituency in the United States that had coalesced around the Republican candidate in the 1964 presi-

dential election, Barry Goldwater, amounted to a policy of 'double containment': restraining Communism abroad and anti-Communism at home.

Johnson asked, "How can we send troops 10,000 miles away and let Castro take power right under our noses?" Concerns about the spread of communism in both the Caribbean and Southeast Asia meant that by mid-May there were 100,000 U.S. troops engaged in two widely separated 'wars' (Colman, 2010, 176-177).

In line with Hal Brands' proposal, Johnson's fear of a 'Castro operation' in the Dominican Republic was misplaced, since Cuban participation was basically non-existent. Moreover, it ended up demonstrating the State Department's superficial understanding of Latin American affairs, while underestimating the complexity of events on the ground, in view of the fact that such an intervention only brought marginal benefits for Washington (Brands, 2010,66).

The reason for the intervention had been to prevent the return of Juan Bosch, whom Washington distrusted, and to avoid the collapse of the Dominican armed forces. Washington, especially after the Cuban Revolution, tended to identify, almost as natural allies, Latin American radicalism and progressivism with communism, in a precedent forged in Arbenz's Guatemala (Westad, 2018). From that point of view, the formidable popular support for Juan Bosch in a country still subjected to the inertia of the Trujillo dictatorship illustrated the strength of nationalism and social movements in the region (Halliday, 2010).

The geopolitics of the Caribbean is a necessary, but not a sufficient lens through which to insert the Johnson Doctrine. His vision is broader, encompassing globalizing, interrelated, transnational dynamics. *What are we doing in Vietnam if we are not able to intervene in Santo Domingo,* Johnson shouted (Faligot, 2013, 159). Or the other way around. Throughout 1965 and 1966, the president was convinced that showing weakness in Vietnam would translate into further setbacks elsewhere in the Third World, and perhaps in Europe as well. But Johnson, encouraged by his advisors, also had the feeling that events might turn in America's favour in some important regions of Asia, Africa and Latin America. In his view, the important thing was to hold out in Vietnam as other new countries, with the assistance and encouragement of US aid programs had turned away from radicalism and opted for freedom and economic growth (Westad, 2018).

International Impact of the Dominican Crisis

The U.S. intervention in Santo Domingo provoked a broad wave of protest around the world, placing the Dominican crisis at the centre of the international agenda and forcing many countries to speak out. In Latin America, its governments were divided between those who supported Washington's determination to curb Castro-communism, and those who criticized the violation of the Pact of Bogota and the return of the imperialist garrote, a position adopted by Mexico, Chile, Venezuela, Uruguay and Peru. The State Department had to mobilize by sending Ambassador Harriman on a tour of the region to curb, eventually successfully, these criticisms. Even so, the misgivings were not immediately dispelled by Washington's intention to take advantage of the Dominican events to go further and create within the OAS a permanent multilateral intervention mechanism - not a temporary one like the Inter-American Peace Force - capable of acting ex officio in the face of any internal crisis. In any case, the inter-American system was weakened and what happened became a black mark on the OAS in the collective memory of Latin America. A few years ago, its Secretary General apologized to the Dominican people for the role played by the organization at that time.

More forceful were the Afro-Asian reactions. The fact that the Dominican crisis coincided with the American escalation in Vietnam and the preparation in Algiers of the *Second Bandung Conference*, created the right climate to give a definitive impulse to the incorporation of Latin America in the global anti-imperialist struggle, a pending issue since 1961 due to the Sino-Soviet disputes, while strengthening the most radical *Third Worldist* sector[3]. *Vietnam, Santo Domingo, same combat!* ended up becoming one of their favourite expressions (Faligot, 2013, 149).

This was the case at the IVth meeting of the Afro-Asian Solidarity Organization, in Winneba (Ghana), from May 9 to 16, 1965 where it was decided, one: to admit Latin America for the first time to the orga-nization; two: to convene the Tricontinental Conference of African, Asian and Latin American Peoples in Havana in 1966 (Bouamama, 2017, 212-213); and three: to condemn the aggression on Santo Domingo, as a result of a Cuban motion that also denounced the colonial vestiges in American lands[4]. This hap-pened again at the OSPAA meeting in Cairo on 1 to 2 September, 1965, which was preparatory to the Tricontinental Conference in Havana where the Dominican Republic crisis was mentioned in the section on Hot Points of the Anti-imperialist Struggle in the Three Continents, together with the Vietnam War, the Congo, the Portuguese colonies, Palestine and Rhodesia (Brieux, 1966, 21)[5]. The Tricontinental Confer-ence in Havana incorporated these claims, although the civil war had ended months before it took place.

Many leaders took advantage of the U.S. invasion to support their vision of Third World interna-tionalism, with combative speeches. In addition to Castro, it is also worth mentioning Ben Bella and Mao Zedong. For the hero of Algerian independence, it was the whole revolutionary project that was in danger. A defender of a Third World revolution incorporating the Latin American space with Cuba in an essential role, Ben Bella saw the Dominican events as a threat to Castro[6]. Also the pronouncement of the People's Republic of China was relevant as it represented the most radical line of the emancipation struggles, determined that the liberation movements should adopt as a guide its model and to transform the poor and underdeveloped countries of Asia, Africa, and Latin America into a force to overthrow the existing international order (Zhai, 2004: 283-284). Just at that time its diplomacy was mobilizing to succeed in imposing such criteria in the upcoming *Second Bandung Conference* (Gettig, 2015, 129-133). On May 3, the Beijing government described the US action in Santo Domingo as armed aggression, in line with its imperialist dynamics in Vietnam, Latin America, and Africa. The events also highlighted two facts: one: the failure of *peaceful coexistence,* and two: the ineffectiveness of the UN[7]. In criticizing peaceful coexistence, Beijing was lashing out against the USSR; and in denouncing the United Nations it claimed the need to transform that international organization. For Mao, in the face of Santo Domingo, it was necessary to *respond tooth by tooth to the aggression of US imperialism[8]*.

But the protests and debates were not limited to Latin America or the Afro-Asian world. They also reached the United Nations, as well as the Western bloc. In New York, the Security Council met up to 30 times on the subject between May and June 1965, approving two specific resolutions[9]. In this forum Moscow would launch its denunciations of *Yankee* imperialism. The USSR protested, but little. Firstly, because little could be done; and, secondly, because by recognizing the hegemony of the United States over the Caribbean, it hoped, in reciprocity, to legitimize its actions in Eastern Europe, as happened in Hungary in 1956, or later in Czechoslovakia (Halliday, 2010: 3). In any case, according to Getchell, the prominence of the issue in the Soviet Foreign Ministry report suggests that to a large extent the Cuban fears and concerns remained central to the Soviet perceptions of U.S.-Latin American relations (Getchell, 2020: 158).

The Paris-Washington Controversy over the Intervention in Santo Domingo

Within Western Europe, if the British Labour government remained close to its *transatlantic solidarity*, President de Gaulle' France, with a nationalist and prestigious foreign policy, *la grandeur* (Vaïsse, 1998) criticized the action in Santo Domingo, as it did with Vietnam, rejecting interference in the internal affairs of a State and the actions of the OAS. This would be his first spectacular diplomatic stance against an action by Washington (Grosser, 1989: 209). Only the United Nations was competent in the matter. Politically, moreover, Paris was wary of the argument of the communist threat, showing its support for the *constitutionalists*. The Security Council would witness the struggle between the thesis of French diplomacy and that of the United States[10].

The Paris-Washington controversy was interesting because it showed the discrepancies and contradictions that the Third World and the liberation processes had generated between allied countries and NATO partners, certifying, in this case at least, the different conception between Johnson and de Gaulle on the Cold War. The Gaullist conception of the world order did not revolve so much around ideologies as nations, like many Americans he did not believe in a monolithic communist threat, or in national liberation processes under absolute communist control (Friedman, 2015: 249). For de Gaulle, Washington was incapable of understanding the historical dimension of the Third World. As he would admit to his minister Alain Peyrefitte, on May 18, in the midst of the Dominican crisis, the United States had refused to recognize the changes that had taken place in an international system where the peoples had acquired a self-awareness of their national personality; on the contrary, they responded to their demands with an old-fashioned, and already non-existent, policy of gunboats. Something that France had learned in Algeria (Peyrefitte, 1997, 522). In those days, at the NATO spring meeting in London where Vietnam was being discussed, the head of the Quai d'Orsay, Maurice Couve de Murville, would reply to Dean Rusk, the US Secretary of State, that *"it would not be wise for the Atlantic Alliance to criminalize en bloc the wars of national liberation because it would lead to pit NATO against many peoples. If that happens, what would the Third World countries think of the Atlantic Alliance? Nor can the impression be given that we consider these movements to be necessarily communist-inspired. Around this table are delegates representing countries emerging from wars of national liberation. You can conquer a country, but you cannot conquer a people"[11]*.

Therefore, what role did the Third World play in Gaullist foreign action? The answer allows us to contemplate, not without difficulties, a construction ranging from the defence of principles to the safeguarding of national interests. Since his arrival in power and the end of the Algerian question, de Gaulle had sought to put France back at the centre of world affairs, overcoming strict bipolarity, acting as a sort of intermediary between the blocs, through a *third way*, by leaning on the Third World, prioritizing its role in the UN, and enjoying greater autonomy vis-à-vis the United States. Paris lacked the great instruments of power, hard *power,* but it could use a moral force, a *soft power,* to develop a framework of good relations with the newly independent countries and in the long run, also with the Soviet Union and Eastern Europe. The Third World, where nationalism and not the communists prevailed, was the instrument and the opportunity to regain international prestige, taking advantage of Washington's mistakes to reduce its influence and, instead, enjoy greater protagonism. There is no *Third Worldist* position, as an ideology or doctrine. As in a theory of communicating vessels, everything the US lost, France could gain (Wahl, 1984:383). Criticizing its peripheral interventionism earned it praise from Third World countries for its independence and courage (Torikata, 2007:937).

The events that unfolded in 1965 are illustrative in this regard. Let us look at three examples. On the one hand, the American military escalation in Southeast Asia when in February Johnson began bombing North Vietnam, and in March when he landed the first Marines in Dag Nam, caused de Gaulle enormous anger because at that time French diplomacy was trying to find a peaceful solution to the conflict with Hanoi. Vietnam was then the nerve centre of the Third World struggles. It is possible that de Gaulle preached in the desert with these peace initiatives, but they made him the leader of a moral crusade with all the advocates of this third way (Vaïsse, 2004, 162-163). His approach to the Third World would be greater from then on (Torikata, 2007, 912). On the other hand, a month later, in April 1965, in the face of the US invasion of the Dominican Republic, Paris turned the Security Council into the visible arena of the struggle with Washington, becoming the spokesman of the Third World and a measured adversary of US interventionism against the uncomfortable governments of the American continent (Grosser, 1989, 209-210). It is worth remembering that, in 1964, de Gaulle made a tour of almost a whole month, throughout South America where in his speeches he denounced hegemonies, praised national independences, underlined Latinity, offered help in the face of economic-social backwardness, and vindicated the right of peoples to self-determination (Vaïsse, 2014, 7-12). Contributing, in his imaginary, to a renewed international balance through Latin American cooperation. In any case, his position on the Dominican Republic was certainly indebted to other concerns: the stability of his overseas Antillean territories of Martinique and Guadeloupe where the lack of development and inequality generated protests and the emergence of incipient communist, nationalist and pro-independence organizations and, therefore, the need to maintain cordial relations with Castro's Cuba (Couffignal, 2011, 59-72).

The third reference visualized the French rejection of radical Third Worldist drifts. Mao's policy of backing revolution and insurgency in the Third World, and promoting the Chinese revolutionary model, alerted de Gaulle, fearing the loss of his influence in the French-speaking African countries. Paris was pressing these countries to improve their defences and coordinate their economic development policies in order to resist the infiltration of Chinese ideology. De Gaulle insisted that they not attend the so-called *Second Bandung Conference* in Algeria, actively promoted by Beijing (Zhai, 2004, 286).

SOLUTIONS AND RECOMMENDATIONS

In accordance with the line of analysis proposed, this paper demonstrates that the Dominican crisis was not limited to the American space but had a broad international repercussion. The involvement of the Elysée Palace was demonstrative. The American action in the Dominican Republic was not only a dramatic moment in the history of Latin America, but also became a 'watershed' in the Cold War due to the global vision of the United States as an interventionist force, and its attempts to neutralize the processes of popular change in the Third World. Its actions were thus inserted in a counter-revolutionary response to the Third Worldist thrust, reflected in what happened in Panama and Brazil (1964) for example, just as Vietnam and the Congo were happening, just as shortly after it would happen with the anti-communist coup in Sukarno's Indonesia (Westad, 2010, xxi-xxii; Bevins, 2021, 9-17) or at a diplomatic level, with the mobilization of the State Department so that in the Second Bandung Conference the radical approaches of China, or the advocates of world revolution would not triumph, being able to shape the direction of Third World internationalism, and through it, the Global Cold War (Gettig, 2015).

FUTURE RESEARCH DIRECTIONS

Based on the case study developed, we propose to delve deeper into the interweaving of the interactions that arose from the Global Cold War in Latin America in the 1960s. In America, the invasion shaped a singular model of political polarization. Although the right-wing coups d'état in Brazil and Bolivia had taken place in March and November 1964, both regimes only fully implemented their repressive measures after the invasion. As in the case of Barrientos with the attacks on the mining sectors in May 1965, or Castel Branco approving the Institutional Act No. 2 in November, which withdrew constitutional guarantees in a decade. In Argentina the government banned union activities in October, and in Uruguay a state of siege was imposed. The signal from Santo Domingo was so strong that Fidel Castro announced that Che Guevara had decided to resume a guerrilla struggle that would take him to Bolivia in the following years. For Latin American radicalism, it is permissible to speak of the 'long sixties', in a sequence that spans from the triumph of the Cuban Revolution to the fall of Allende in September 1973 (Halliday, 2010).

CONCLUSION

The Kennedy and Lyndon B. Johnson administrations considered that they were losing the pulse of the Third World to communists and radicals, and therefore to the USSR. Johnson's decision to send ground forces to Vietnam stemmed from this idea, as did his support for the military coups that took place between 1964-1966 in Brazil, Indonesia, Algeria, and Ghana. The fierce US response to the attempts to reintroduce a constitutional system in the Dominican Republic must be analyzed and, therefore, understood under that broad framework and context of the Cold War (Westad, 2018).

The objectives, hypotheses, and research questions that we originally proposed were oriented in the direction of answering the motives of the US intervention in the Dominican Republic (1965) and are intended to be one more piece in the puzzle of the implications of the global Cold War in the contemporary history of Latin America.

REFERENCES

Alburquerque, G. (2020). *Tercermundismo y No Alineamiento en América Latina durante la Guerra Fría*. Santiago de Chile, Ediciones Inubicalistas.

Bergel, M. (2019). *Futuro, pasado y ocaso del "Tercer Mundo", Nueva Sociedad N°284*. Ensayo, November-December.

Berger, M. (2002). 'Toward Our Common American Destiny?' Hemispheric history and pan American politics in the twentieth century. *Journal of Iberian and Latin American Research*, 8(1), 57–88. doi:10.1080/13260219.2002.10431761

Berger, M. (2004). After the Third World? History, destiny and the fate of Third Worldism. *Third World Quarterly*, 25(1), 1, 9–39. doi:10.1080/0143659042000185318

Bevins, V. (2021). *The Jakarta Method. La cruzada anticomunista y los asesinatos masivos que moldearon nuestro mundo*. Capitán Swing.

Bouamama, S. (2017). *Figures de la révolution africaine. De Kenyatta à Sankara*. La Découverte. doi:10.3917/dec.bouam.2017.01

Brands, H. (2010). Latin America's Cold War. Harvard University Press.

Brieux, J. (1966), La Tricontinentale. Politique étrangère, n° 1, 31 année. doi:10.3406/polit.1966.2227

Casals, M. (2020). Which borders have not yet been crossed? A supplement to Gilbert Joseph's historiographical balance of the Latin American cold war. *Cold War History, 20*(3), 367–372. doi:10.1080/14682745.2020.1762311

Chester, E. T. (2001). *The US intervention in the Dominican Republic (1965-1966). Rag-Tags, Scum, Riff-Raff and Commies*. Monthly Review Press.

Colman, J. (2010). *The Foreign Policy of Lyndon B. Johnson: The United States and the World, 1963-1969*. Edinburgh University Press.

Couffignal, G. (2011), *La politique étrangère de la France vis-à-vis Latin America*. Observatoire des changements en Amérique Latine, Paris, La Documentation Française-IHEAL.

De la Rosa, J. (2015). *La Revolución de abril de 1965*. LetraGráfica.

Domínguez, J. (2009). *La política exterior de Cuba (1962-2009)*. Editorial Colibrí.

Dumont, J. (2010). *L'amère patrie. Histoire des Antilles françaises au XXe siècle*. Fayard.

Faligot, R. (2013). *Tricontinentale. Quand Che Guevara, Ben Barka, Cabral, Castro et Hô Chi Minh, préparaient la révolution mondiale (1964-1968)*. La Découverte.

Faure, J., & Del Pero, M. (November 2020). La Guerre Froide Globale. In J. Faure & M. Del Pero (Eds.), *La Guerre Froide Globale, Monde(s) no. 18*. doi:10.3917/mond1.202.0009

Field, T. Jr, Krepp, S., & Pettiná, V. (2020). *Latin America and the Global Cold War*. University of North Carolina Press. doi:10.5149/northcarolina/9781469655697.001.0001

Friedman, M. (2015). *Rethinking anti-Americanism: The history of an exceptional concept in American international relations*. Machado Grupo.

Garrard-Burnet, V., Lawrence, M., & Moreno, J. (2013). *Beyond the Eagle's Shadow: New Histories of Latin America's Cold War*. University of New Mexico Press.

Getchell, M. (2020), Cuba, the USSR, and the Non-Aligned Movement: Negotiating Non-Alignment. In Latin America and the Global Cold War, edited by Field, T., Krepp, S., Pettinà, V., 148-73. University of North Carolina Press.

Gettig, E. (2015). Trouble ahead in Afro-Asia: The United States, the Second Bandung Conference, and the Struggle for the Third World, 1964-1965. *Diplomatic History, 39*(1), 126–156. doi:10.1093/dh/dht133

Gleijeses, P. (1984). *La crisis dominicana*. FCE.

Gleijeses, P. (2014), *Hope Denied. The US Defeat of the 1965 Revolt in the Dominican Republic*, Washington, Woodrow Wilson Centre for Scholars, Cold War International History Project no. 72.

Gott, R. (1996) Che Guevara and the Congo, *New Left Review*, pp. 6-7.

Grimaldi, V. (2016). *Golpe y revolución. El derrocamiento de Juan Bosch y la intervención norteamericana*. Editorial Búho.

Grosser, A. (1989). *Affaires extérieures. La politique de la France, 1944-1989*. Champs-Flammarion.

Halliday, F. (Ed.). (2010). *Caamaño in London. The exile of a Latin American revolutionary*. University of London.

Harmer, T. (2008) *The Rules of the Game: Allende's Chile, The United States and Cuba, 1970-1973*, [PhD Thesis, London School of Economics and Political Sciences, England].

Harvey, H. (2020), Revisiting the inter-American turning point in the Cold War: the Dominican crisis of 1965, U.S. intervention, and the Inter-American Peace Force. *Humanidades: revista de la Universidad de Montevideo*, 7, (2020): 25-63.

Hatzky, C. (2015). *Cubans in Angola. South-South Cooperation and Transfer of Knowledge, 1976-1991*. The University of Wisconsin Press.

Hermann, H. (2009). *Eslabón perdido. Gobierno provisional (1965-1966)*. Editorial Búho.

Hermann, M., & Kegley, C. Jr. (1998). The U.S. use of military intervention to promote democracy: Evaluating the record. *International Interactions*, 24(2), 91–114. doi:10.1080/03050629808434922

Joseph, G. (2019). Border crossings and the remaking of Latin American cold war studies. *Cold War History*, 19(1), 141–170. doi:10.1080/14682745.2019.1557824

Joseph, G. (2020). The continuing challenge of border crossing: A response to Marcelo Casals' commentary. *Cold War History*, 20(3), 373–377. doi:10.1080/14682745.2020.1762312

Joseph, G., & Spencer, D. (Eds.). (2008). *In from the Cold: Latin America's New Encounter with the Cold War*. Duke University Press. doi:10.1215/9780822390664

Kalter, C. (2016). *The Discovery of the Third World: Decolonization and the Rise of the New Left in France, c. 1950-1976*. Cambridge University Press. doi:10.1017/CBO9781139696906

Latham, M. (2010). The Cold War in the Third World, 1963-1975. In M. Leffler & O. Westad (Eds.), The Cambridge History of the Cold War. Cambridge: Cambridge University Press.

Latham, M. (2011). *The Right Kind of Revolution: Modernization, Development, and U.S. Foreign Policy from the Cold War to the Present*. Cornell University Press.

Lentin, A. (1966). *La lutte tricontinentale. Imperialisme et revolution après la conference de La Havane*. Maspero.

Lowenthal, A. (1973). *The Dominican intervention*. Harvard University Press.

Lowenthal, A. (2010), The United States in Latin America, 1960-2010: From hegemonic pretension to diverse and complex relations. *International Forum*, (3-4), 552-626.

Marchesi, A. (2006), Imaginación política del antiimperialismo: intelectuales y política en el Cono Sur a fines de los sesenta. *E.I.A.L. Montevideo*, *17*(1).

Marchessi, A. (2017), Writing the Latin American Cold War: between the "local" South and the "global" North. *Estudos Históricos (Rio de Janeiro)*, *30* (60), 187-202.

Palieraki, E. (2017). From Peking to Havana. The Chilean radical left and its revolutions, 1963-1970 [s]. *Monde*, *11*(1), 119–138. doi:10.3917/mond1.171.0119

Palomino, P. (2019). On the Disadvantages of "Global South" for Latin American Studies. *Journal of World Philosophies*, *4*(2), 22–39.

Papers, A. (2002). Intervention during the cold war. *The Adelphi Papers*, *42*(350), 33–45. doi:10.1080/05679320208459466

Parrott, R. (2022). Tricontinentalism and the Anti-Imperial Project. In R. Parrott & M. Lawrence (Eds.), *The Tricontinental Revolution: Third World Radicalism and the Cold War*. Cambridge University Press. doi:10.1017/9781009004824.002

Peksen, D., & Lounsbery, M. (2012). Beyond the Target State: Foreign Military Intervention and Neighboring State Stability. *International Interactions*, *38*(3), 348–374. doi:10.1080/03050629.2012.676516

Pettiná, V. (2018). *Historia mínima de la Guerra Fría en América Latina*. El Colegio de México. doi:10.2307/j.ctv8bt0xr

Peyrefitte, A. (1997). *C'était de Gaulle. La France reprend sa place dans le monde* (Vol. II). Fayard.

Prashad, V. (2012). *Las naciones oscuras. A history of the Third World*. Península.

Prashad, V. (2013). *Las naciones pobres. A possible global history of the South*. Península.

Rojas, R. (2021). *El árbol de las revoluciones. Ideas y poder en América Latina*. Turner.

Smith, P. (2010). *Estados Unidos y América Latina. Hegemony and resistance*. PUV.

Torikata, Y. (2007). Reexamining de Gaulle's Peace Initiative on the Vietnam War [November]. *Diplomatic History*, *31*(5), 5. doi:10.1111/j.1467-7709.2007.00659.x

Vaïsse, M. (1998). *La grandeur. Politique étrangère du général de Gaulle*. CNRS Éditions.

Vaïsse, M. (2004). De Gaulle and the Vietnam War. In L. C. Gardner & T. Gittinger (Eds.), *The search for peace in Vietnam (1964-1968)*. Texas A&M University Press.

Vaïsse, M (dir). (2014), *De Gaulle et l'Amérique Latine*. Rennes, PUR.

Veeser, C., & Bobea, L. (2020). Guerrilla movements in the Dominican Republic. In D. Krujit, E. Rey, & M. Alvarez (Eds.), *Latin American guerrilla movements. Origins, evolution, outcomes*. Routledge.

Wahl, N. (1984), *De Gaulle et le Tiers Monde. Une alliance de raison?* in VV.AA, *De Gaulle et le Tiers Monde.*, Éditions Pedone.

West, O. (2010). Introduction: The United States, the Dominican intervention, and the Cold War. In F. Halliday (Ed.), *Caamaño in London. The exile of a Latin American revolutionary*. University of London.

Westad, O. (2005). *The Global Cold War: Third World Interventions and the Making of Our Times*. Cambridge University Press. doi:10.1017/CBO9780511817991

Westad, O. (2018). *The Cold War. A world history*. Galaxia Gutenberg.

Yoon, M. (1997, August). Explaining U.S. intervention in Third World internal wars, 1945-1989. *The Journal of Conflict Resolution, 41*(4), 580–602. doi:10.1177/0022002797041004005

Zhai, Q. (2004). China's response to French peace initiatives. In L. C. Gadner & T. Gittinger (Eds.), *The search for peace in Vietnam (1964-1968)*. Texas A&M University Press.

Ziai, A. (2016). *Development discourse and global history: from colonialism to the sustainable development goals*. Routledge.

PRIMARY SOURCES

Despacho del Embajador de España en Argelia al Ministro de Asuntos Exteriores. (1965). Reserved. AGA, Foreign Affairs, 82-19053.

Despacho del Embajador de Francia en La Habana al Ministerio de Asuntos Exteriores. (1965). AMFAE, Conférence Tricontinentale de La Havane, Dossier Général.

Fond des Archive Orales, Ministère des Affaire Étrangères. (1984). AO10 Entretien Roger Seydoux, Ambassadeur de France.

Mao Tse-Tung's Statement Supporting The Dominican People's Resistance to U.S. Armed Aggression. (1965). In Support The Dominican People's Resistance to U.S. Armed Aggression.

Note de la Direction Politique. (1965). *Intervention sur le Vietnam prononcée par Mr. Couve de Murville devant le Conseil Atlantique à Londres, le 12 de mai de 1965*. AMFAE, Services des Pactes (1961-1970), 1667INVA/271 BIS.

Security Council. (1966). Situation in the Dominican Republic. University of Wisconsin Press, Wisconsin.

foreign Languages Press. (1965). Statement of The Government of The People's Republic of China Opposing U.S. Armed Aggression against The Dominican Republic. In Support The Dominican People's Resistance to U.S. Armed Aggression (pp. 5–7). Foreign Languages Press.

ENDNOTES

[1]   Both sides would end up forming two power structures. The constitutionalists, a provisional government presided over by Colonel Caamaño and the anti-communist bloc, a National Reconstruction Board, organized by Washington.

2   Héctor García Godoy. In 1966, they gave victory to the Reformist Party (PR) of Joaquín Balaguer, a former Trujillo collaborator, against Bosch's Dominican Revolutionary Party (PRD), who having been harassed, went into exile again.

3   . These demands - so radical - were surprising due to the fact that the main Dominican, Soviet communist, Castro-influenced or pro-Chinese left-wing forces had shown from the beginning a certain detachment from the movement in favour of Bosch. These three elements, that is, the American incorporation into the Afro-Asian bloc and solidarity with the Dominican people, associating their struggle with the rest of the liberation resistance, were linked in the Third World project of those months.

4   Dispatch from the French Ambassador in Havana to the Ministry of Foreign Affairs nº 198 (Havana, May 20, 1965). AMFAE, Conférence Tricontinentale de La Habana, Dossier Général (May 1965/ August 1968), 92 QONT.

5   - In the same line were the declarations of Mehdi Ben Barka -president of the Tricontinental Preparatory Committee- who pointed out that the problems of Vietnam, Congo and Santo Domingo shared the same aggressor: imperialism. Mehdi Ben Barka in La Havana. https://www.ina.fr/video/ VDD13020553. [Accessed May 19, 2021].

6   Dispatch from the Ambassador of Spain in Algeria to the Minister of Foreign Affairs nº 360 (Algiers, May 5, 1965). Reserved. AGA, Foreign Affairs, 82-19053. For the Algerian politician, the Johnson Doctrine turned Washington into a world gendarme, capable of acting in any part of the globe, from Congo-Brazaville, Vietnam, or Santo Domingo.

7   Statement of The Government of The People's Republic of China Opposing U.S. Armed Aggression against The Dominican Republic (May, 3, 1965), in Support The Dominican People's Resistance to U.S. Armed Aggression, Peking, Foreign Languages Press, 1965, pp. 5-7.

8   Mao Tse-Tung's Statement Supporting The Dominican People's Resistance to U. S. Armed Aggression (May 12, 1965), in Support The Dominican People's Resistance to U.S. Armed Aggression, Op. cit, pp. 1-4.

9   <<Security Council, Situation in the Dominican Republic>>, International Organization, Vol. 20, nº 1, winter 1966, University of Wisconsin Press, Wisconsin, page. 111.

10   -Fond des Archive Orales, Ministère des Affaire Étrangères, AO10 Entretien Roger Seydoux, Ambassadeur de France, nº 3 (mardi, 5 juin 1984).

11   Note de la Direction Politique (Paris, 21 mai 1965): "Intervention sur le Vietnam prononcée par Mr. Couve de Murville devant le Conseil Atlantique à Londres, le 12 de mai de 1965". AMFAE, Services des Pactes (1961-1970), 1667INVA/271 BIS. Pacte Atlantique Nord. Organismes de l'OTAN. Sessions ministerielles. 38 session (Londres, 11-13 mai 1965).

Chapter 14
The Practical Geopolitics of the Portuguese Estado Novo in the Context of the Colonial War (1955–1974)

Mariano García de las Heras
https://orcid.org/0000-0001-5978-2156
Complutense University of Madrid, Spain

Jerónimo Ríos
Complutense University of Madrid, Spain

ABSTRACT

Based on critical geopolitics, and more specifically on the possibilities offered by practical geopolitics, the following chapter aims to analyse the essence of the discourse of the Portuguese state authorities in relation to Portugal's status as a colonial power, especially after the beginning of the decolonization process, from the early 1960s onwards. Specifically, the period covered by this paper runs from 1955, the year of Portugal's accession to the United Nations, until the end of the dictatorship in 1974. For this purpose, the primary sources used are the parliamentary sessions held in the Portuguese National Assembly and the public speeches delivered by the head of state, António de Oliveira Salazar. The paper thus shows how the foundations of the country's foreign policy were evolving at a particularly convulsive moment in its history, when the legitimization/threat binomial held a central position in terms of discourse.

DOI: 10.4018/978-1-6684-7040-4.ch014

INTRODUCTION AND METHODOLOGICAL CRITERIA

The end of World War II marked the beginning of a new geopolitical order, the shaping of which was debated during the armed conflict itself. Portugal's neutral position in the war responded to its long-standing alliance with London and this circumstance allowed the Estado Novo to be integrated into the construction of the post-war world. However, the immediate post-1945 scenario was also witness to a phenomenon of liberation from European colonial powers taking place in the Afro-Asian territories.

Lisbon maintained a dispute in international forums, especially following its admission to the United Nations in 1955, with the firm intention of preserving its overseas territories. Against this background, the Salazar regime introduced a series of reforms guided by the "new winds" of decolonization and offering an image in line with the demands for independence coming from the colonies.

The aim of this paper is to shed light on the reasoning used by the political elites of the Portuguese Estado Novo during the period 1955-1974. The year 1961 marks the beginning of the colonial war and serves to divide the chronological arc under consideration from an earlier stage, reflecting the diplomatic wrangling between Lisbon and the demands formulated by the United Nations Assembly. Moreover, in the second half of the 1950s, Portugal experienced the first stirrings of the independence movements in its colonies in Goa. In a second phase, coinciding fully with the armed conflict between the mainland forces and the liberation guerrilla fighters operating in African territories, this analysis is based on a two-fold narrative thread: the affirmation of legitimating arguments and the identification of a set of threats.

In methodological terms, the paper draws on primary sources provided by the political elites of the Estado Novo. The parliamentary sessions held in the Portuguese National Assembly and the public speeches delivered by António de Oliveira Salazar form the subject of study. These criteria have guided the research into the foundations of Portugal's foreign policy during the selected historical period and coincide, from a critical perspective, with the practical dimension of geopolitical discourse.

THE CRITICAL PERSPECTIVE OF GEOPOLITICAL STUDIES

Geopolitics is a cultural issue fraught with complexities due to the representation or omission of identities formulated in contemporary political discourses (Dalby, 2002, p. 295). The fundamental purpose of critical approaches is to uncover the schemas and operative plots of power embedded in the lines of reasoning articulated from different angles of social reality through the narrative construction of ideas ordered by heterogeneous actors (Dalby, 1991; Ó'Tuathail & Agnew, 1992; Sharp, 1993; Ó'Tuathail, 2002).

Recognising multiple agencies in producing and disseminating geopolitical reasoning implies, on the one hand, a saturation of everyday life through numerous channels (the media, national security reports, specialised think tanks, the film industry, literature, etc.). Yet, also the gradual emergence of new lines of research that provide fertile ground for the analysis of the interrelations between space and power.

The notion of discourse is at the epicentre of the critical currents of geopolitics that emerged in the latter part of the last century. Intersections between geographical references and political patterns have dominated studies grounded in such epistemological perspectives because "strategies of power always require the use of space (...) to create particular spatial images, primarily of territory and boundaries in statecraft" (Sharp, 1993, p. 492).

According to Ó'Tuathail and Agnew (1992), the term "geopolitical discourse" refers to the instrumentalization of a set of socio-cultural resources to endow global dynamics with meaning. In this sense, the images and representations that spatially shape the scenario of the world-economy system are multiple, artificial and subject to constant reformulation.

Geopolitical analysis focuses on the definition of threats, both real and figurative, and the construction of identities through the prescription of political behaviour in specific contexts. Building geopolitical models based on certain geographic-political assumptions seeks to provide certainty by upholding precise ideals or values, previously selected by civilian or military elites. This exercise is indicative of an intellectual process and aspires to transform theoretical approaches into practical codes, which guide the foreign policy of states. For this reason, the ability to construct a popular understanding of context is an essential task of the discipline of geopolitics (Dalby, 2002, p. 295).

Contributions by Carol Cohn (1987) and Joanne Sharp (2000) have highlighted the relevance of the so-called "scientific" culture produced by strategic studies during the bipolar conflict between Washington and Moscow in establishing a particular identity through a specific language. The collapse of the scripts established by Cold War "ideological geopolitics" (Agnew, 2005) inaugurated a stage defined by an ongoing political discussion regarding the shaping of a new order, even though its foci of production were restricted to the Western space.

References to security agendas, the role of diplomacy and the patterns set by politico-military elites convey a series of issues that are visibly intertwined with concerns about popular culture and the representation of identities in geopolitical reasoning (Dijkink, 1996). The specialised critical literature shows that war practices and the design of policies aimed at providing a certain style of governance respond to the crystallization of historical-cultural archetypes (Walker, 1993; Shapiro, 1997; Dalby, 2003; Cairo, 2006, 2020).

Myths and historical traditions are cultural ingredients, which operate in defining boundaries capable of differentiating between "Us" and "Them". At the same time, as Dijkink (1996) pointed out, the existence of cultures labelled as "national" implies the recognition of national "geopolitical visions". Critical studies emphasise geographical references to argue for and legitimise the various lines that make up the foreign policy of state entities.

The contributions of critical geopolitical studies negotiate the contradictions caused by the notion of culture. Their analyses focus on questions of identity and, in particular, on the narrative construction of otherness as central to security and defence policy agendas. Literary production specialising in this subject line emphasises the importance of images and spatial representations affirmed, symbolically or overtly, in the three strands of geopolitical discourse: practical, formal and popular (Ó'Tuathail & Dalby, 2002, p. 5).

That said, practical geopolitics is related to the geopolitics emanating from state bureaucracies, and thus relates to narratives, discourses and practices coming from military and diplomatic academies in fields such as security, defence, cooperation or diplomacy. Formal geopolitics, on the other hand, originates from theoretical proposals, models and doctrines that are constructed by the state intelligentsia, think tanks and universities, and serve as a guide to develop practical geopolitics and the geopolitical action of the state. Finally, popular geopolitics is developed through cultural manifestations, *lato sensu*, such as cinema, radio, press or literature. The discourse generated by and from popular geopolitics is related to the construction of identities, narratives or imaginaries embedded in the geopolitical sense of a given society or social group. Thus, these three aspects of geopolitics are not watertight compartments, but on the contrary, are in continuous interaction.

In the case at hand, the focus is on the practical geopolitical vision of the Portuguese Estado Novo during the period of the Colonial War, between 1961 and the transformative process of the Carnation Revolution in April 1974. The connections established between imperial centres and colonial peripheries show the relevance of spatial metaphors in the construction of geopolitical imaginaries (Agnew, 2005).

THE PERSISTENCE OF IMPERIAL NARRATIVES IN THE ESTADO NOVO

Portugal's colonies were a source of national ostentation, as illustrated by the so-called 'Cor-de-rosa' map (the Rose-Coloured Map), dated 1886, which shows Lisbon's territorial claims on the African continent at the time of the British ultimatum (Image 1). The plan was to control the strip of land between the Portuguese possessions of Angola and Mozambique. However, Portugal's ambitions clashed with the interests of London and its intention to build a north-south link between Cairo and Cape Town.

Figure 1. The Cor-de-Rosa map
Source: Sociedade de Geografía de Lisboa (1886)

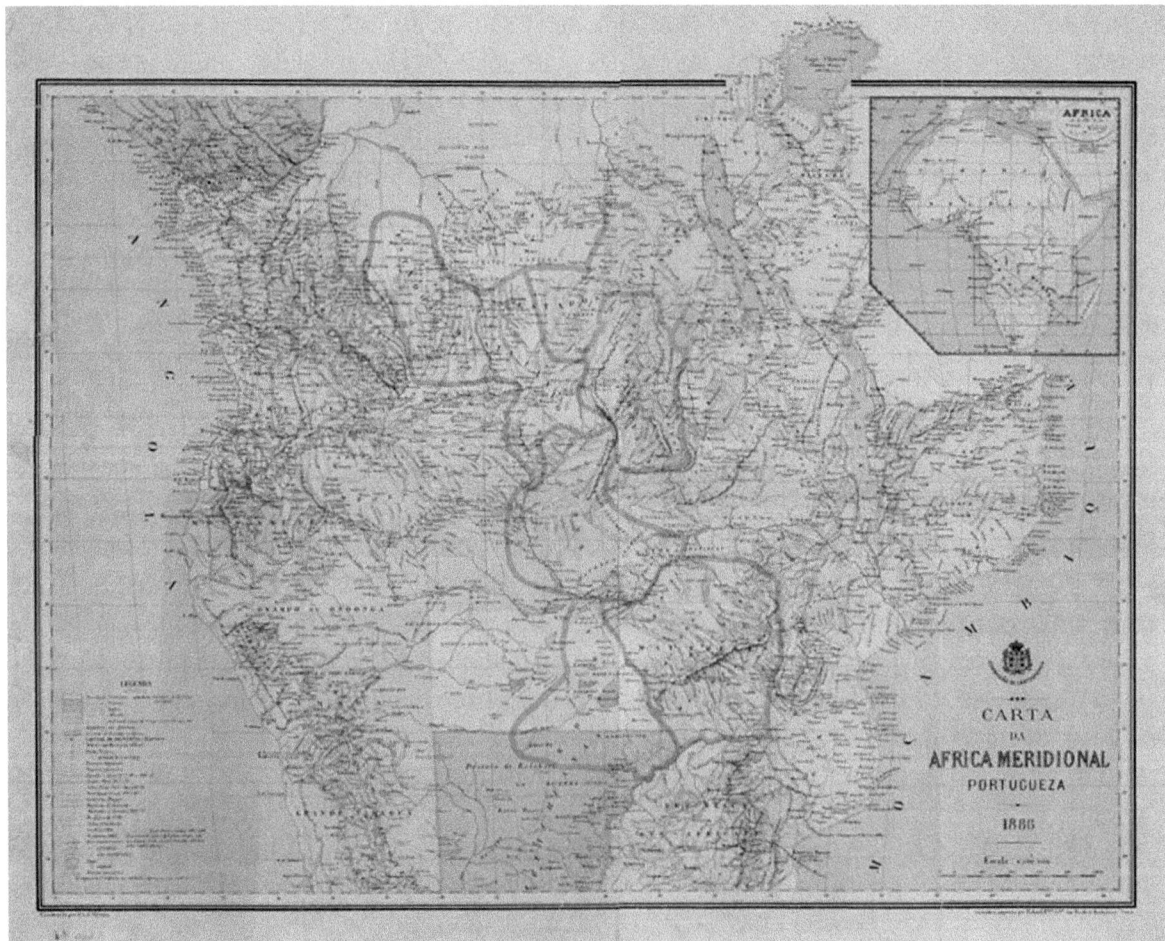

Cartographic representations were a potential tool for political propaganda by circulating ideas that served to promote certain inclinations, generally described as "national interests" (Cairo, 2006; Corkill & Pina, 2009). An example of this is the Colonial Exhibition organised by the Estado Novo in the city of Porto and held under the slogan 'Portugal não é um país pequeno' ('Portugal is not a small country') (Image 2) in 1934. This event gave the Salazar regime the opportunity to convey the territorial magnitude of the Portuguese Empire through the illustration entitled 'No rumo do Imperio' that accompanied the event, directed by the army officer Henrique Galvão.

Figure 2. Portugal is not a small country
Source: Galvão (1934)

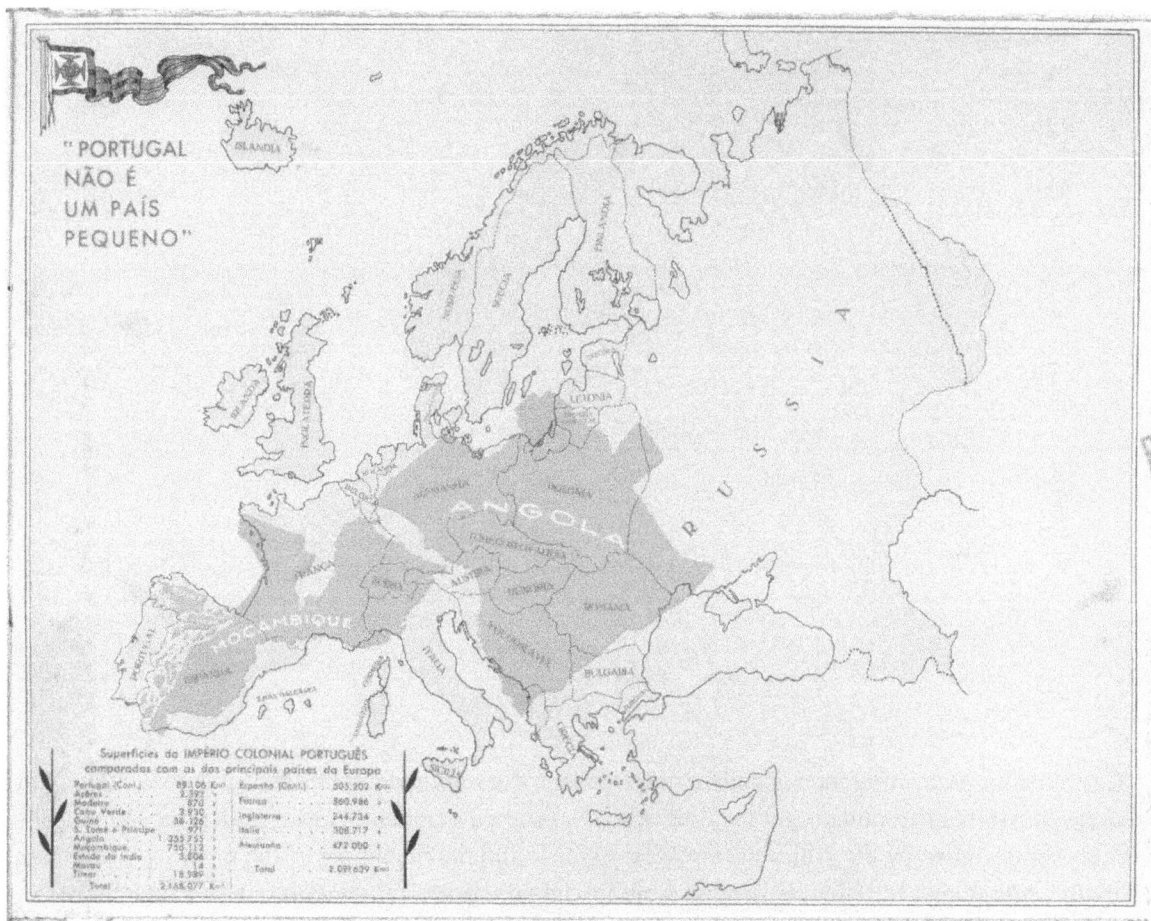

Like the previous example, we can highlight Roberto Araujo's creation (1947), reflecting the routes travelled by Portuguese explorers[1] during the historical period between 1482-1606. The expeditions led by Diego Cão (1482-1485), Bartolomé Díaz (1487-1488), Vasco da Gama (1497-1498) and Pedro Alvares Cabral (1500) were responsible for circumnavigating the land contours of the African continent. The cartographic representation bears the following caption: "Portugal, the country that has contributed most to geographic knowledge of the globe. Over one century, she discovered and explored nearly two-thirds of the inhabited globe" (Araujo, 1947). This document (Image 3) sought to vindicate the role of the so-called país pequeno in a global enterprise and to assert its imperial legitimacy based on a bygone era.

Figure 3. Portugal: the country that has contributed most to geographic knowledge of the globe
Source: Araujo (1947)

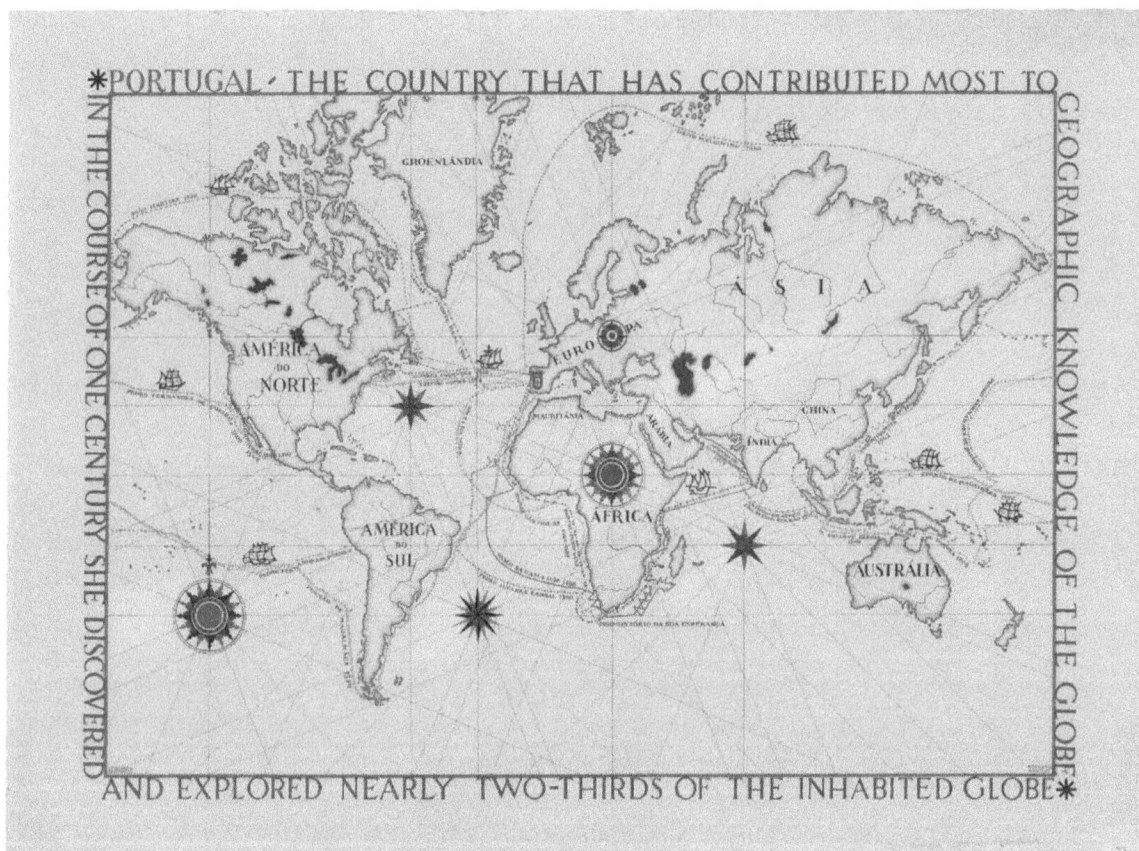

Cartographic production encouraged the development of certain geographical imaginaries and strengthened the geopolitical arguments put forward by the Salazar government. However, the shaping of a new world order designed by the Allies during World War II and the beginning of the process of liberation led by the Afro-Asian colonies challenged the imperial pretensions of the Portuguese Estado Novo.

Lisbon's first response was to introduce a series of changes to its legal-administrative system, which failed to prevent armed struggle in its colonial territories on the African continent. However, the constitutional reforms implemented in 1945 and 1951 sought to mask the central position of the Portuguese mainland government in the hierarchical connections with its various "overseas provinces".

The 1950s was a period of imperial exaltation. Thousands of Portuguese settlers left for the dominions in search of opportunities they did not have at home (Evans, 2012, p. 499). Yet, the spread of African nationalism was unstoppable and, as a result, Portugal became embroiled in a series of colonial wars that began in Angola in 1961, followed by Guinea in 1963 and Mozambique in 1964. Goa was annexed by India in 1961.

COLD WAR, UNITED NATIONS, AND THE DECOLONIZATION PHENOMENON

A particular feature of the geopolitical codes produced from Lisbon was Portugal's admission into the defence system structured around NATO. Portugal was one of the founding members of NATO and Salazar unsuccessfully sought to expand the perimeter of NATO's treaty provisions to include the overseas territories. Discussions on the mechanisms of integration in the new order designed by Washington involved the military establishment, but the centrality of the Empire maintained its privileged position in the geopolitical imagination of the Estado Novo (Sidaway, 2003, p. 126).

The invitation extended to Lisbon to participate in the North Atlantic Treaty, signed in 1949, responded to the strategic value the United States attached to the Azores archipelago in the event of a possible US intervention in a Europe dominated by a bipolar order during the Cold War. Portugal's NATO membership was precisely the main diplomatic trump card played by the Salazar regime to stop pressure from Washington and London, which were seeking a moderate and negotiated solution to the aspirations for independence expressed by the Portuguese colonies. In a speech broadcast on radio and television on 12 August 1963, Salazar stated that "the fight against the presence of Portugal in international technical organisms, in which we have full rights, is something that does no favours to Africans and no credit to Westerners" (Salazar, 2016 [1963], p. 1047).

At no point did the Salazar authorities ever put forward decolonization as an option for their "overseas problem". Maintaining imperial support was a fundamental principle for the Estado Novo, strengthened by the broad backing of Portuguese society (Cueto, 2011). The only exceptions that showed sympathy for the recognition of the right to self-determination were the youth section of the Movimento de Unidade Democrática in 1953 and the Portuguese Communist Party from 1957 onwards.

Lisbon retained a colonial mindset until the mid-1950s. Portugal's entry into the United Nations in 1955 was a milestone in the process of restoring Salazar's Estado Novo within the political order established after the Second World War. At the same time, this episode neutralised its arguments aimed at making its imperial architecture invisible in response to Resolution 1514 (XV) issued by the international forum founded in the Californian city of San Francisco in October 1945, which "solemnly proclaims the necessity of bringing to a speedy and unconditional end colonialism in all its forms and manifestations" (United Nations, 1960, p. 71).

A number of features were prevalent in Portuguese geopolitical discourse after World War II. One of its main focuses lay in safeguarding colonial territories in a scenario marked by a new geopolitical order built on the terror introduced by nuclear armament and on the ongoing dynamism of formal decolonization on the periphery of the world system.

One peculiarity of Portuguese decolonization was Lisbon's intransigence in ceding sovereignty over its African territories. According to the developmentalist theory, this attitude prevented "the necessary journey "into the modern world" of Africans" (Davidson, 1973, p. 5). The interpretation of the pro-Salazar political elites led to developing a discourse with a markedly paternalistic tone regarding the colonial situation. However, the mainland authorities did not ignore the changes in the geopolitical scene after World War II and proceeded to introduce a series of minimal modifications to the existing web of colonial relations.

Salazar and the Portuguese leaders rejected the proposals put forward on the other side of the Atlantic because they considered that agreeing to access to independence would mean opening the floodgates to demands for democratization in Lisbon. Against this background, the notion of "empire" was replaced by the idea of "overseas", while "colonies" were transformed into "provinces" and access to citizenship was restricted to natives who admitted to a "European" way of life. The Estado Novo considered this semantic game to be sufficient to avoid UN scrutiny of its imperial practices.

The structure of Salazarism's geopolitical reasoning regarding the decolonization phenomenon and admission to the UN brought about a substantive change: the reinforcement of a constitutional reform in 1951, replacing the term "colonies" with "provinces". This revision of the juridical-administrative order of the Portuguese colonies represented a throwback to the conception that predated the Republic and whose ideals underpinned the notion of a unitary imperial entity, albeit with a contemporary purpose (Sidaway, 2003, p. 127).

Increasing pressure on Lisbon to dismantle its colonial territories forced it to tighten its surveillance mechanisms. The request made by the UN Secretary-General, Swedish diplomat Dag Hammarskjöld, called on the Estado Novo to submit detailed information on the political and socio-economic conditions of its colonial territories (Oliveira, 2017). However, this request met with an evasive response from Lisbon, which claimed that legal equality existed between the inhabitants of its "provinces" and the citizens of mainland Portugal. This narrative thread is reflected in the following words spoken by Américo Tomás:

Surprise at the resentment of the Portuguese people and the reaction seen everywhere against the attitudes and resolutions of the UN force me to believe that the United States, whose policy has always been one of total understanding and friendship towards us, found itself faced with a new reality different from the one it had assumed. Clearly a grave error was made in considering the Portuguese overseas territories as a purely colonial expression; an error in thinking that our Political Constitution could integrate dispersed territories without there being a community of sentiments that sufficiently expressed the unity of the Nation. (Diário das Sessões, 1961a, p. 924)

Within this context, the UN activated the Special Committee for the Territories Administered by Portugal, which aimed to gather information on the socio-political situation of the populations under Lisbon's control. Investigations carried out by the Organization concluded that the aspirations enshrined in the principle of self-determination remained unfulfilled despite the reformist rhetoric of the Estado Novo. Salazar used the tension produced by the global dispute between Washington and Moscow to justify Lisbon's position from a strategic point of view:

Leaving aside what is important for the defence of Europe, strongly shaken by the African policy of the United States, one fact stands out clearly: the African continent is today the great area of competition between the two most powerful nations, the United States and Russia, or three, since communist China has already made its appearance [...]. This competition for the African space may lead to an understanding that used to be known as defining spheres of influence and may now have another name. (Salazar, 2016 [1963], p. 1056-1057)

The political atmosphere in Lisbon was permeated by the final annexation of Goa to the Union of India in December 1961 and the previous outbreak of independence movements in the African colonies, which had opted for armed struggle in February of the same year. Moreover, Lisbon was facing pressure from the United Nations in an environment defined by the political turmoil caused by a failed coup attempt in April and a major student mobilization against the Estado Novo. Portugal's reaction was to set up PIDE agencies in all its overseas possessions from 1957 onwards to quash any subversive initiatives. Portugal thus launched a consular battle against the UN-led anti-colonial coalition.

Portugal decided to leave Goa to concentrate its forces on the African continent following the peasant uprising in the Angolan district of Malanje in the first weeks of 1961. Lisbon reacted violently to suppress the subversion detected in Baixa de Cassanje, resulting in a very high death toll, albeit with considerable discrepancies depending on the available sources (Oliveira, 2017). This episode marked the definitive turning point in the independence process of the Portuguese colonies in Africa through the offensive against the colonists' properties initiated by the União das Populações de Angola (UPA), which forced Salazar to mobilise a disproportionate number of military resources to curb the situation. In short, the Estado Novo opted for a militarised solution to "pacify" the demands for independence coming from its "provinces" and proof of this is the following statement by Silva Mendes:

At this moment in the life of the Nation, a grave responsibility rests on the shoulders of the men of the Government [...] Errors of unpredictability and lack of preparation have already been made, but nothing is gained by alluding to them. Action is needed now, but quickly, considering that we are truly at war and the region where the acts of terrorism are being carried out needs to be secured with sufficient troops and police forces. (Diário das Sessões, 1961b, p. 534)

Oliveira (2017) points to two explanatory factors for Lisbon's refusal to accept the "winds of change"[2] detected on the African continent in the late 1950s. Firstly, the ideological doctrine underpinning the Salazar dictatorship expressed through the corporatism of the Estado Novo. Secondly, the perception of the Portuguese authorities on the decolonization process compared to the rest of the old European imperial powers, as they believed that Portugal lacked an advantageous political strategy in the face of a hypothetical rupture of the ties of dependence towards her colonies. Salazar stressed that "the disintegration of the [colonial] system would in itself reduce its [Western Europe's] economic and political potential" (Salazar, 2016 [1963], p. 1055).

BUILDING LEGITIMACY AND THREATS

The Portuguese Empire from Minho to Timor

Portugal repeated the image of the "colonial paradigm" in tune with the modernising stimuli coming from other European powers. Lisbon opted for maintaining an "integralist" approach, which consisted of rescuing the ancestral ideas linked to assimilationism in order to present its colonial rule as equivalent to a socio-cultural experience free of prejudices and based on the notion, formulated by Gilberto Freyre, of "Luso-tropicalism". The speech made by Artur Águedo de Oliveira in the Estado Novo's parliamentary seat summarises these ideas as follows:

We have been in Angola, without any significant reaction, since 1482 and in Mozambique since 1505; we have already been invaded several times by enemies and plunderers; we will remain there! [...] Integration also means decolonising because it ensures national independence, development and a life that can be called their own. To integrate means to decolonise and yet they do not want it to be so [...]. Integration means raising the level of morality and civilization to the European level [...] It means moral and political unity. This is the contrary, the opposite of decolonization. (Diário das Sessões, 1961c, p. 511-513)

The Estado Novo adopted a set of measures aimed at reforming the colonial elements of its legal system because of the cycle of protests that originated in Angola. The most salient feature of this move was to eliminate the Statute of the Indigenous Peoples, which involved recognising Portuguese citizenship for the native inhabitants of African territories.

Portugal's role in the defence of the Christian values of the West represented a second strand in the practical geopolitical discourse of the Portuguese elites "in the face of an enemy with modern weapons, entrusted to them by countries that are enemies of civilization and envious of the situation we occupy in Africa as a civilising people", as Moreira Longo pointed out (Diário das Sessões, 1966, p. 808). A few years earlier, Member of Parliament, Alexandre Lobato, made a similar argument:

We were the first in the world to declare valid and legitimate the indigenous populations' own institutions, which were respected in everyday life and in law, leaving to State action the dialogue of cultural values and to freedom of conscience the problem of the choice of institutions [...] All this at a time when the conclusion that universal values exist in all types of civilization had not yet been reached [...]. Let there be no doubt that if Portugal exists overseas, it is due to the secular Portuguese respect, in law and in practice, for native institutions. (Diário das Sessões, 1963a, p. 1905)

In the case of Portugal, a NATO country and recipient of Marshall Plan aid, the empire was the price of Portuguese adherence to international anti-communism. For Salazar, imperial possessions provided prestige, as well as raw materials and markets that acted as a buffer against economic uncertainty (Evans, 2012, p. 499). The ideological underpinnings of this geopolitical narrative thread were subordinated to the imperial myth, sustained by the integral territorial dimension from "Minho to Timor" (Coelho, 2003, p. 179).

The Communist Threat

Liberation movements organised in the Afro-Asian colonies intensified their challenge to Portuguese colonialism as a result of Portugal becoming a member of the UN General Assembly. Redefining the colonies as "provinces" took on greater relevance and Lisbon sought to reassign, in defence of its territories, the representation of geopolitical codes based on ideological criteria of a bipolar nature. The aim was to replace the North-South divide with a binary split between two extremes represented by a communism-anti-communism duality. Proof of this was the intervention by Artur Águedo de Oliveira, as representative of Angola in the National Assembly of the Estado Novo, defining the notion of decolonization in the following terms:

[...] It means submission to the communist party, atheism and economic servitude [...] Confusion and criticism result, therefore, from what some writers call the solidarity of pre-Marxists, the "impact of colour" and the export of revolutions as shortcuts to social cataclysm (Diário das Sessões, 1961b, p. 513)

During the Colonial War, the African territories under Portuguese mainland administration underwent a process of militarization. The use of armed struggle initiated by the liberation movements in the colonies found legitimacy, therefore, in the mainland's refusal to support access to political independence. This dynamic responded to a logic based on a categorical interpretation, which foreseen the potential transformation of native peoples into "terrorists". In a speech delivered by Salazar on the situation on the African continent in 1967, the Portuguese leader noted that in "Africa there are ideologies that lead to subversion, and there are also interests that thrive on chaos and hope to obtain facilities and privileges". (Salazar, 2016 [1967], p. 1106)

Strategic reasoning consisted of activating codes aimed at involving local societies in the defence of the colonial order by reinforcing psychological actions (Coelho, 2003). Lisbon's counter-subversive strategies highlighted the importance of the psychological factor. The narratives of the Estado Novo resorted to constructing an enemy, driving militarised reaction to protect Lisbon's interests in Africa. A central line of this reasoning was to attribute the responsibilities of the anti-colonial movements to communist ideology (Power, 2001, p. 474). In April 1963, MP João Ubach Chaves concluded that political emancipation served the interests of communism, since "poor states that became independent more through the selfishness of the mother nations than through the deadly ideals of decolonization, depend today on a policy of Russian or Chinese penetration and expansion". (Diário das Sessões, 1963b, p. 2370)

Communism symbolised a threat in the geopolitical imaginary of the Portuguese dictatorship and the Estado Novo made use of this narrative to legitimise its rejection of the demands to surrender its colonies in Africa. Salazar considered that "African countries would not have the strength to impose expulsion on us, if they were not supported by the vote of communist governments that want to destroy the West, and the attitude of some Western countries should be considered a desertion". (Salazar, 2016 [1963], p. 1047).

Problems in the Mainland: Protests, Conscription, and Desertions

In the mainland, the cycle of anti-war protest was confined to certain circles of anti-colonial activism. In this area, the politically motivated student sector was particularly prominent, and the reasons for this were twofold: the influence exerted by the Casa dos Estudantes do Império, and their potential enlistment in the Armed Forces deployed in African territories (Cardina, 2020, p. 189).

The decolonization phenomenon in Afro-Asian countries was framed by global tensions arising from the dispute between Washington and Moscow, which is in line with so-called "ideological geopolitics" (Agnew, 2005). In the specific case of the dismantling of the Portuguese territories on the African continent, Lisbon relied on local recruitment to swell the ranks of its fighters (Power, 2001, p. 470).

The number of African combatants underwent substantial changes in the course of the Portuguese Colonial War fought simultaneously in Angola, Guinea and Mozambique. Their distribution also reflected differences depending on the territories and the different strategies devised by Lisbon to hold on to its territories in Africa.

The increase in local enlistment during the course of the war was politically and economically motivated. The insufficient level of recruitment in the Armed Forces was mainly due to the high number of desertions and emigration figures recorded in Portugal in the decade prior to the war. The high cost of the military garrisons installed in African territory and the progressive demoralization of the armed contingents further hampered the interests of the powers in the mainland. This process of Africanization was also linked to Lisbon's financial problems in sustaining its military presence over such a large geographical area (Coelho, 2002; Afonso & Gomes, 2005).

In quantitative terms, the military forces deployed in Angola amounted to 6,500 soldiers mobilised in the year before the start of the war, approximately 5,000 of whom were locally recruited (Rodrigues, 2013). These figures underwent a remarkable transformation in the last part of 1961 with the African colonies witnessing an increase in the number of expeditionary troops rising from 1,500 combatants to 28,000 individuals deployed in the war zone (Antunes, 1995, p. 710; Teixeira, 2006, p. 86).

The Portuguese Colonial Wars in Africa involved an estimated one million people (Power, 2001, p. 462). Overall recruitment figures amounted to 1.4 million soldiers, according to the official sources of the Estado Maior do Exército, with approximately 400,000 of them coming from local enlistment (Rodrigues, 2013). Military forces of African origin in the mainland army steadily increased in Angola and Mozambique, while the trend was reversed in Guinea.

Lisbon protected its imperial territories in Africa with mainland military troops that, at the beginning of the Portuguese colonial conflict, numbered only a few thousand soldiers. However, by 1968, this figure had reached between 120,000 and 150,000 soldiers, absorbing 40% of the Estado Novo's budget (Guerra, 1994). Data from official sources put the number of wounded soldiers at 30,000, with an added 9,000 fatalities (quoted in Power, 2001, p. 462).

Research by Cardina and Martins (2019) found that there were approximately 9,000 deserters, apart from occasional gaps in certain years and military sectors, in addition to the number of young people who refused to join, which ranged from 10,000-20,000 to 200,000 insubordinate youth. These numbers were equivalent to 20% of the young people called up for recruitment in the mainland, according to data issued by the army itself (Cardina & Martins, 2019). The category of "desertion" was subject to semantic changes through narrative appropriations based on legal or political criteria to establish, while the war, a difference between those who refused to join and those who deserted (Cardina, 2020. p. 183).

The administration led by Marcelo Caetano, after succeeding Salazar, sought to soften the climate of protests in Lisbon by presenting an open-minded political line. However, resistance to ceding sovereignty over colonial territories persisted right up to the time of the Carnation Revolution. An example of this can be found in the words of Mota Amaral:

As we are already far from the political and ideological content of the "Portuguese colonial empire" of the first period of the Salazar era [...] errors must be corrected! Because the government's handling of foreign policy has been hesitant and backtracking, at least in appearance. Suffice it to recall the revision of the Organic Law of the Overseas Provinces and, subsequently, of the political and administrative statutes of each territory, which did not come about without protests from certain sectors of opinion, both on the mainland and overseas [...]. Moreover, those with special responsibilities prefer to speak of administrative and financial decentralization of the overseas territories instead of political-administrative autonomy, which is different and is enshrined in the Constitution, and they continue to refer to Angola and Mozambique as provinces, when their status is that of States, in accordance with the law and the Constitution itself (Diário das Sessões, 1974, p. 748)

The defence of the African colonies represented a heavy financial burden for Lisbon, and its protracted duration led to a gradual wearing down of the ranks of the Armed Forces. The denouement coincided with the episodes framed by the Revolução dos Cravos of 25 April 1974 and the leading role played by the organization of the Movimento das Forças Armadas, which reflected the exhaustion of a very specific sector within the military ranks: the low-ranking officers. The restoration of democracy in Portugal led to the recognition of the independence of the former Portuguese colonies in African territory: Guinea-Bissau in September 1974, Mozambique in June 1975, and Angola in November of the same year.

CONCLUSION

The Estado Novo managed to resist the attempts at national emancipation by its overseas colonies in Africa, which resorted to armed struggle with the political goal of gaining independence. However, the delays in this process, due to the entrenchment of the mainland authorities, led to discontent among the Portuguese Armed Forces. In April 1974, a cycle of revolution led by various democratising currents and backed by broad sectors of the military succeeded in overthrowing a dictatorship that had been in place for half a century.

The rupture of the Salazar regime rescued democracy in mainland Portugal and prompted the establishment of power transfer agreements in the colonial enclaves. The result was a disorderly transition caused by the excessive speed of events, the political inexperience of the new ruling elites in Lisbon, the intransigent attitude of the white settlers, the divisions between African nationalist factions and the interference of foreign powers.

Nevertheless, the evolution of the discursive foundations of the Portuguese governmental authorities provides great potential for analysis to understand how the former adapted to a changing geopolitical scenario, which demanded transformations and confrontations that, sooner rather than later, were to overturn the foundations of the country's foreign policy.

Thus, although in this paper aspects such as the dominant colonial legitimacy or the sense of threat are central to the events occurring since 1961, they may be enriched in the future by the inclusion of other voices, such as, for example, from within the military. Similarly, the incorporation of "other geopolitics", such as formal geopolitics or popular geopolitics, can also lead to the discovery of new polysemies, contradictions and discursive tensions, which, even today, make the study of the processes of rupture of the former Portuguese colonies an object of study with countless possibilities for analysis and debate.

REFERENCES

Afonso, A., & Gomes, C. M. (2005). *Guerra Colonial*. Editorial Notícias.

Agnew, J. (2005). *Geopolítica. Una re-visión de la política mundial*. Trama.

Antunes, J. F. (1995). *A Guerra de África (1961-1974)*. Círculo de Leitores.

Araujo, R. (1947). Portugal: the country that has contributed most the geographic knowledge of the globe. Litografia Nacional Assambleia Nacional.

Cairo, H. (2006). "Portugal Is not a Small Country": Maps and Propaganda in the Salazar Regime. *Geopolitics*, *11*(3), 367–395. doi:10.1080/14650040600767867

Cairo, H. (2020). Geopolítica popular del coronavírus: el poder de las viñetas editoriales en la prensa diaria. Geopolítica(s). Revista de estudios sobre espacio y poder, 11(Special), 303-317. doi:10.5209/geop.69373

Cardina, M. (2020). A deserção à Guerra colonial: História, memoria e política. Revista de História das Ideias, 38, 181-204. https://impactum-journals.uc.pt/rhi/article/view/2183-8925_38_8/6400

Cardina, M., & Martins, S. (2019). Evading the war: deserters and draft evaders from the Portuguese army during the colonial war. e-Journal of Portuguese History, 17(2). https://repository.library.brown.edu/studio/item/bdr:1104360/

Coelho, J. P. (2003). Da violencia colonial ordenada à orden pós-colonial violenta. Sobre um legado das guerras coloniais nas ex-colonias portuguesas. Lusotopie, 10, 175-193. https://www.persee.fr/doc/luso_1257-0273_2003_num_10_1_1554

Coelho, J. P. B. (2002). African troops in the portuguese colonial army, 1961-1974: Angola, Guinea-Bissau and Mozambique. *Portuguese Studies Review*, *10*(1), 129–150.

Cohn, C. (1987). Sex and Death in the Rational World of Defense Intellectuals. *Signs (Chicago, Ill.)*, *12*(4), 687–718. doi:10.1086/494362

Corkill, D., & Pina, J. C. (2009). Conmemoration and Propaganda in Salazar's Portugal: The 'Mundo Portugués' Exposition of 1940. *Journal of Contemporary History*, *44*(3), 381–399. doi:10.1177/0022009409104115

Cueto, A. (2011). Portugal y su imperio frente a la descolonización, 1945-1962. *Espacio, Tiempo y Forma. Serie V, Historia Comtemporánea*, *23*(23), 161–200. doi:10.5944/etfv.23.2011.1579

Dalby, S. (1991). Critical geopolitics: Discourse, difference and dissent. *Environment and Planning. D, Society & Space*, *9*(3), 261–283. doi:10.1068/d090261

Dalby, S. (2002). Geopolitics and global security: culture, identity and the 'pogo syndrome. In G. Ó'Tuathail & S. Dalby (Eds.), *Rethinking Geopolitics* (pp. 295–313). Routledge. doi:10.4324/9780203058053-18

Dalby, S. (2003). Calling 911: Geopolitics, security and America's new war. *Geopolitics*, *8*(3), 61–86. doi:10.1080/14650040412331307712

Davidson, B. (1973). La lucha por la independencia en el África 'portuguesa'. El Correo: África "portuguesa". La lucha por la independencia. UNESCO, 4-8

Dijkink, G. (1996). *National Identity and Geopolitical Visions*. Routledge.

Evans, M. (2012). Colonial Fantasies Shattered. In D. Stone (Ed.), *The Oxford Handbook of Postwar European History* (pp. 480–501). Oxford University Press.

Galvão, H. (1934). *No rumo do império*. Litografia Nacional.

Guerra, J. P. (1994). *Memorias das Guerras Coloniais*. Edições Afrontamento.

Ó'Tuathail, G. (2002). Theorizing practical geopolitical reasoning: The case of the United States' response to the war in Bosnia. *Political Geography*, *21*(5), 601–628. doi:10.1016/S0962-6298(02)00009-4

Ó'Tuathail, G., & Agnew, J. (1992). Geopolitics and discourse: Practical geopolitical reasoning in American foreign policy. *Political Geography, 11*(2), 190–204. doi:10.1016/0962-6298(92)90048-X

Ó'Tuathail, G., & Dalby, S. (2002). Introduction: Rethinking Geopolitics. Towards a critical geopolitics. In G. Ó'Tuathail & S. Dalby (Eds.), *Rethinking Geopolitics* (pp. 1–15). Routledge.

Oliveira, P. A. (2017). Decolonization in Portuguese Africa. In *T. T. Spear (Dir.), Oxford Research Encyclopedia of African History*. Oxford University Press. doi:10.1093/acrefore/9780190277734.013.41

Power, M. (2001). Geo-politics and the representation of Portugal's African colonial wars: Examining the limits of 'Vietnam syndrome'. *Political Geography, 20*(4), 461–491. https://www.sciencedirect.com/science/arti-cle/pii/S0962629801000038. doi:10.1016/S0962-6298(01)00003-8

Rodrigues, F. C. (2013). A desmobilização dos combatentes africanos das Forças Armadas Portuguesas da Guerra Colonial. *Ler História, 65*(65), 113–128. doi:10.4000/lerhistoria.484

Salazar, A. O. (2016). A política de África e os seus erros. In *Discursos e Notas Políticas, 1928 a 1966 (1101-1107)*. Coimbra Editora.

Salazar, A. O. (2016]). Política Ultramarina. In Discursos e Notas Políticas, 1928 a 1966 (1041-1060). Coimbra Editora.

Shapiro, M. (1997). Violent Cartographies. Mapping Cultures of War: University of Minnesota Press.

Sharp, J. P. (1993). Publishing American identity: Popular geopolitics, myth and the Reader's Digest. *Political Geography, 12*(6), 491–503. doi:10.1016/0962-6298(93)90001-N

Sharp, J. P. (2000). *Condensing the Cold War. Reader's Digest and American Identity*. University Minnesota Press.

Sidaway, J. D. (2003). Iberian geopolitics. In K. Dodds & D. Atkinson (Eds.), *Geopolitical Traditions. A century of geopolitical thought* (pp. 118–149). Routledge.

Sociedade de Geografía de Lisboa. (1886). Mapa de cor-de-rosa. Lisboa. https://purl.pt/93/1/iconografia/imagens/cc976a/cc976a_3.jpg

Teixeira, R. A. (2006). Guerra de África: Angola, 1961-1974. QuidNovi

Walker, R. B. J. (1993). *Inside/Outside: International Relations as Political Theory*. Cambridge University Press.

ENDNOTES

[1] The document includes Ferdinand Magellan, although the expenses for his voyage were borne by the coffers of the Crown of Charles I.

[2] An expression used by British Premier Harold Macmillan to define the process of decolonization during his address to the Parliament of the Union of South Africa in February 1960.

Chapter 15
The Rhodesian War (1965–1980):
Counter-Guerrilla and Black-Market Armaments as an Example of Counter-Insurgency Warfare

Miguel Madueño Álvarez
Rey Juan Carlos University, Spain

Julio Alfonso Gonzalez
National University of Distance Education, Spain

ABSTRACT

The Rhodesian War (1965-1980), known to Anglo-Saxons as The Bush War and to Zimbabweans as the Second Chimurenga conflict or War of Liberation, was the conflict that pitted Ian Smith's unilateral white minority government against pro-independence Zimbabwean guerrillas supported by various communist countries. The nature of the conflict, which was characterized for the small number of combatants, the isolation of the Rhodesian regime, the presence of guerrillas, and the difficulties in obtaining materials, led to the mechanisms of counter-insurgency warfare being set in motion. In this text, the different characteristic elements of this type of warfare have been analysed in terms of combat tactics and military operations, the kind of troops, and the weaponry used as an example of a counterinsurgency conflict.

INTRODUCTION

The Rhodesian War (1965-1980) became a long conflict that lasted for 15 years and had special characteristics that could well be classified as a war between guerrilla elements and a government, that is, a priori an irregular war (Gianluigi, 1974). However, Ian Smith's executive, due to problems inherent to the characteristics of its population and the difficulties in supplying its army with military resources, was quickly inclined to turn the conflict into a counterinsurgency war (Fox, 1915; Bratton, 1979; Pulido,

DOI: 10.4018/978-1-6684-7040-4.ch015

2017). This was demonstrated by the operations carried out by Rhodesian forces, the systematic and punitive execution of guerrillas (De Boer, 2012) and the strategic defence plan against the Zimbabwean guerrillas, which eliminated the likely sympathies they might have aroused in the eyes of the international community and reduced collateral damage to the civilian population. Therefore, the objectives of this paper are:

- To analyse the nature of counterinsurgency warfare through the case study of the Rhodesian war.
- To examine the conduct of warfare through military operations, strategic plans and the adaptation of regular troops to a counterinsurgency environment, with the intention of eliminating the guerrillas.
- To analyse the weaponry available to the Rhodesian army in this war and its varied origins or forms of procurement.

BACKGROUND

The Rhodesian War has attracted a great deal of interest in academic circles, especially in the Anglo-Saxon sphere, because of the national proximity - the main force involved was heir to the British Empire and Rhodesians were regarded as such. As a result, an important bibliography has been built up around this context, especially by authors linked to the UK or English-speaking authors. Researchers such as Rossi, Bratton, Gott and Cilliers analysed the Rhodesian War in terms of guerrilla warfare and the international context of the Cold War.

A second batch of works was produced during the first decade of the 21st century, in which colonial wars began to be treated as conflicts with a certain degree of differentiation and counterinsurgency began to be discussed in greater detail, with the works of De Boer, Evans and Wood standing out, without forgetting the elements of the Cold War concerning the special operations that were becoming known at that time.

Interest continues today with recent works such as those by Preller, Davidow and Cross, even crossing language barriers and attracting the attention of researchers such as Pulido and Mañes Postigo.

MAIN FOCUS OF THE CHAPTER

We approached the Rhodesian War through the use of bibliographical sources. The method used is the hypothetico-deductive method subject to the traditional historical method in which we have differentiated four phases: collection of sources; reading; internal and external criticism; and interpretation of these sources. Throughout the work we have followed a study focused especially on the Rhodesian forces, as a means of approaching the counter-insurgency model that Smith's government put in place. Before undertaking this detailed analysis, we set out to develop a series of hypotheses in order to give the text a scientific character that could be debated in the concluding chapter.

In our understanding, the Rhodesian War was a counter-insurgency conflict in which Ian Smith's government based its military operations on eliminating members of the native guerrillas who threatened the newly created and internationally unrecognised state of Rhodesia. The worldview of the whites who had been settled in the region for generations due to the colonialist episodes that had spread since the late 19th century was that they possessed the right to own property and furthermore, they considered that the native population lived in sufficient comfort to pretend to rebel (Godwin & Hancock, 1993). The Rhodesian government showed some signs of opposition to the British Empire and remained ideologically aloof from the Cold War power struggle between the Soviet Union and the United States (Evans, 2007), which did not prevent the latter from assisting Rhodesia in the face of the threat of Marxist guerrillas. This attitude ran counter to the new scenarios that were emerging around decolonisation. This isolation and the particular perspective on the conflict were enough for Ian Smith's executive to believe that the threat lay solely in the rise of the guerrillas and therefore set their destruction as the main objective (De Boer, 2012). Thus, the scenario of irregular warfare became one of counter-insurgency warfare.

On the other hand, this type of conflict is characterised by a number of unique elements. Firstly, the existence of a guerrilla group to fight, of an evidently insurgent nature that appeared in dual form and the imitation of its combat tactics; and secondly, the type of actions carried out by both sides, such as terrorist attacks, kidnappings, executions and disappearances. In addition to all this, there was one element specific to the Rhodesian war that prevented Ian Smith's government from proving superior to the guerrillas it was fighting: technical resources. Under normal conditions, a well-supplied government fighting a guerrilla army would have enormous logistical superiority and on that basis could extend the conflict or even win it. But in the case of Rhodesia, the limitations imposed by the British embargo and the international isolation of both the communist orbit and many of the Western bloc countries meant that supplies were scarce and came from illicit operations, which is why Smith's government was sustained for so long by the imposition of this type of counter-insurgency strategy (Melson, 2005).

Rhodesia, the name given to the vast region now occupied by Zambia and Zimbabwe, was named after the entrepreneur Cecil Rhodes, who, in the course of building the railway linking Cairo and Cape Town, discovered its mineral wealth and conquered the area on behalf of the British South Africa Company. The British colony was quickly divided into two territories: one in the north and one in the south, plus Nyasaland (present-day Malawi). The three areas were soon differentiated according to the mining capabilities they offered, and Northern Rhodesia, given its mining characteristics, developed an important industry that drew skilled workers from England and Europe (Rotberg, 1988).

When in 1964 Nyasaland and later in 1965, Northern Rhodesia, in line with the decolonisation process affecting the whole of Africa, gained their independence and Southern Rhodesia, on the other hand, prolonged its policies of white domination with a unilateral proclamation of independence not recognised by Britain, a large white population was soon concentrated in Southern Rhodesia, estimated at 240,000 people and accounting for almost five percent of the population (Godwin & Hancock, 1993). This led to a worsening of the country's civil war situation, with an internationally unrecognised white minority government and Soviet and Chinese communist-backed African guerrillas seeking control of the country, as had happened in Zambia and Malawi.

Even before the unilateral declaration of independence in 1957, the guerrillas had carried out important civil disobedience actions in Southern Rhodesia against British domination, and although they were controlled by the metropolis, the seed of those insurgencies had germinated and remained uncontrolled in many parts of the territory, especially on the borders with Mozambique and Zambia. These guerrillas, which had been active since the early 1960s, were ZANLA (Zimbabwe African National Liberation Army) under ZANU (Zimbabwe African National Union), supported by China, and ZIPRA (Zimbabwe People's Revolutionary Army), the armed wing of ZAPU (Zimbabwe African People's Union), supported by the Soviet Union (Preller, 2018). Both were at odds with each other, but held London as a common enemy and united in a patriotic front. The real support for the guerrillas, however, was not the indirect presence of the Soviet Union or China in the conflict, but the backing these guerrillas received from the country's two major ethnic groups. ZIPRA was backed by a large majority of the Ndebele ethnic group, which made up twenty percent of the population, and ZANLA by a large number of the Shona ethnic group, which made up almost eighty percent (De Boer, 2012).

This conglomerate of acronyms was joined by FRELIMO (Front for the Liberation of Mozambique), whose main activity was the armed struggle against the Portuguese colonial government and which developed important support for the Zimbabwean guerrillas along its hundreds of kilometres of borders. The MK (Spear of the Nation), the armed wing of the African National Congress, also operated from Zambia, although its impact was less significant given that the white Apartheid government still maintained a tight grip on the black population of South Africa and operated directly in support of Smith's executive. The presence of these guerrillas was indicative of black discontent with white minority rule, and this was exacerbated when Zambia and Malawi gained independence and the white population of all three territories was concentrated in Southern Rhodesia.

To better understand the war situation in the region, it is interesting to know the military capabilities of its hostile neighbouring states, from which the liberation forces and guerrillas operated. In 1979, the Mozambican armed forces numbered 24,000. In 1979, Mozambique's armed forces numbered 24,000 troops and included 350 medium tanks of the *T-34/T-54* and *T-55* models; 50 *PT-76* light tanks; 150 *BRDM-2* armoured reconnaissance vehicles; 250 armoured personnel carriers of the BTR-40 and BTR-152 models; artillery pieces of 76, 85, 105, 122, 130 and 152mm calibres; 122mm *BM-21* multiple rocket launchers; *AT-3* Sagger anti-tank missiles; *SA-3* anti-aircraft missiles; and *SA-7* man-portable missiles. Its main combat aircraft were 36 *MIGs* of the -17/-19 and -21 models (Military Balance, 1980: 75). This warfare capability is all the more interesting because Mozambique, after the Carnation Revolution (1974) that ended the Salazar dictatorship in Portugal, became a new battlefront for Rhodesia (Meneses & McNamara, 2012).

Zambia, which had been the main base of operations for the guerrillas against Ian Smith's government, had at the end of the war some 16,000 troops and its most important war material was 30 T-54 battle tanks; 28 Ferret armoured reconnaissance vehicles and 50 BRDM-1 and -2; they had 18 105mm multiple rocket launchers and 30 BM-21 122mm; possesed some SA-7 portable anti-aircraft missile systems; and 12 Rapier and 3 Tigercat anti-aircraft missile systems. In addition, they were buying more equipment such as T-55 medium tanks and more modern armoured reconnaissance and armoured personnel carriers. Their main combat aircraft were 12 Chinese F-6s, 6 Galeb and 6 Yugoslav-made Jastreb, and 16 MIG-21s were due to arrive (Balance Militar, 1980: 79).

Finally, Botswana had an insignificant military consisting in little more than 3,000 men and an air branch of only five armed BN-2 Defender aircraft used for counter-insurgency tasks, but it was a sovereign country in the region opposed to the Smith regime, which meant support for the guerrillas and the existence of another border to worry about (Balace Militar, 1980: 80)). As a result, by the late 1970s, Rhodesia was internationally isolated and only the South African government, under its own international pressures, and the Mozambique National Resistance (RENAMO) could offer their support.

All in all, the stage was set for a long war in which both sides were convinced of their ideological integrity. The state led by Ian Smith represented a white minority threatened by guerrilla elements, and it was precisely on this aspect that it focused its war discourse, creating its own strongly rooted identity among this small demographic sector (Melson, 2005). For their part, the Zimbabwean guerrillas pursued an emancipatory process and were based on the remembrance of the Chimurenga or struggle against

British occupation in the 19th century, rebranding it with a national liberation component (Martin & Johnson, 1982).

Development of the War

The Rhodesian civil war can be divided into several phases according to the political conditions surrounding the conflict and the development of military operations. Thus, a pre-war phase can be distinguished, from 1957 to 1965, when revolts and episodes of civil disobedience by the black majority took place and the ZIPRA and ZANLA guerrillas were formed.

In 1964 the situation began to worsen more clearly and the guerrillas, with greater material support and more resources, began to demand independence for the region, as practically all the surrounding territories had already done. At this time ZANU and ZAPU were already in control of the guerrillas, the former led by Robert Mugabe, Herbert Chitepo and Ndabaningi Sithole and the latter by Joshua Nkomo. During this period, ZANLA guerrillas, trained in Tanzania, began to concentrate in the north-east of the border with Mozambique, supported by FRELIMO, triggering one of the first combined defence operations of the Rhodesian command known as Hurricane in December 1972. It had also led to heavy fighting in the Zambian border area against both guerrillas between 1965 and 1974 (Mtisi, Nyakudya & Barnes, 2009).

After this pre-war period full of tension and isolated clashes between the Rhodesian - still British - forces of order and the guerrillas, the civil war began when Ian Smith's government proclaimed independence from the British Empire in contempt of London's authority. The new executive was unwilling to hand the country over to the African political movements as had apparently been agreed, or at least discussed between them and the British representatives, and installed, based on the 4.5 percent of the population represented by whites, a South African apartheid-style government (Pulido, 2017), convinced that the black population agreed with its leadership and considering the guerrillas already operating in the region as the only problem (De Boer, 2012).

This worsened the situation and ushered in a period of war in which the Rhodesians, with greater military superiority, controlled the territory. It must be said that this supposed superiority was conditioned by the difficulties of Ian Smith's executive in receiving material, since Britain had not recognised his government and maintained on the region. The international community, with the exception of some Arab countries, Israel, South Africa and Portugal, had refused to do any business with Smith's cabinet. Southern Rhodesia had to source supplies across the border from its ally South Africa, from Mozambique - still Portuguese - and from intricate smuggling networks that bypassed the countries that belonged to the trade veto, which may explain the number and variety of types of weaponry and war materiel that were mixed throughout the conflict (Moorcraft and McLaughlin, 1982: 92).

From 1974 onwards another phase began, conditioned by Mozambique's independence from the Portuguese Empire, which meant that FRELIMO, hitherto a communist guerrilla force that circumstantially supported Zimbabwean guerrillas, became the main force in government, harassed by the anti-communist RENAMO guerrillas financed and organised by the Rhodesian and South African governments (Melson, 2005). Firstly this meant that Rhodesia saw its hostile borders increased by almost a thousand kilometres in addition to those of Zambia and Botswana, and secondly, that the clandestine support that FRELIMO had given until then was converted into full backing for the ZIPRA and ZANLA guerrillas.

Rhodesia also stopped receiving so much support from South Africa from 1976 onwards due to strong international pressures, conditioned by the geostrategic context of the time. It could be said that from that point onwards Ian Smith's government found itself surrounded by hostile states and beginning to show signs of exhaustion. With the sharp increase in ZANLA military actions from Mozambique (Flower, 1988), the eastern border was compromised, which led to a large proportion of Rhodesian forces being mobilised in the Thrasher operations in the Untali and Repulse area in the south-eastern territory in February and May 1976 (Lohman and MacPherson, 1983: 28). At the same time ZIPRA was consolidating its positions in Botswana, forcing the emergence of the combined operation Tangent in August of the same year. The increase in guerrilla infiltration into Rhodesian territory led to the activation of Operation Grapple in the summer of 1977 (Abbott and Botham, 1986: 13).

By that year, negotiations began, with international mediation, for a dignified exit that would guarantee a white presence in the important sectors of the country, while actions against the guerrillas increased with the intention of ensuring that, when the time came for peace, their enemies would be weakened and in a better position to negotiate. In early 1978, due to increased armed action in the capital, a combined operation was formed for the defence of Salisbury. Meanwhile in the north, along the Zambian border, the main area of fighting with both guerrillas since the beginning of the war, features such as Lake Kariba and the Zambezi River had served as a natural barrier, with Rhodesian defences concentrated in the area between Kariba and the Mozambican border with a series of minefields, barbed wire and guard posts every 18 kilometres (Abbott and Botham, 1986: 23). Operation Splinter was activated in July 1978 in anticipation of the conventional attack by ZIPRA, which had already amassed Soviet artillery, tanks and armour (Moorcraft & McLaughlin, 2010).

One indication of the intensity of the conflict in recent years was the increase in mine detonations inside Rhodesian territory, from around 900 mine incidents in 1978 to over two thousand in 1979, indicating an increased guerrilla presence of around 12,500 in the interior and almost 38,000 on the hostile borders (Beckett, 2007).

In 1979 Smith's government disappeared and the country was handed over to a provisional government made up of all political forces, except ZANU and ZAPU, under British supervision in a new country called Zimbabwe-Rhodesia headed by black leader Abel Muzorewa. Mugabe and Nkomo denounced this new government as a continuation of white supremacy and the fighting continued until the Lancaster House Accords (Davidow, 2019). The fines imposed on the country were lifted, a ceasefire was agreed and the continuation of Zimbabwe was decided in democratic elections. Months later the country achieved full independence and was renamed Zimbabwe and ruled by Robert Mugabe, who did not have much competition in the democratic elections that were held due to the demographic superiority of the Shona ethnic group.

Combat Tactics

The war in Rhodesia was largely infantry-based with some unique characteristics. Firstly, the number of casualties amounted to 40,000, of wich 15,000 were seriously wounded and to which should be added around 1.5 million displaced persons, of whom almost 200,000 were white. These figures do not seem too high, especially considering the length of the conflict. In fifteen years, seven people died every day, a figure far lower than those recorded in other conflicts of the time (Vietnam 184, Korea 1348). Even so, these are figures that stand out within Rhodesia itself, considering that the population was no more than five million. This was for one fundamental reason: it was a war based on small-scale, rapid and targeted operations, focused on hunting guerrillas in very specific areas and in scenarios far from population centres. Nevertheless, there were episodes related to terrorist actions that did harmed the civilian population in accordance with the collateral effects of this type of conflict. To give an-idea of the precision of the targeting, between 1972 and 1979, more than 10,000 guerrillas were killed in internal and cross-border operations, compared to some 1,300 black civilians, only 130 whites and a total of 1,361 Rhodesian troopers, suggesting that the proportion of civilian casualties was quite low (Cilliers, 1985).

While the ZIPRA and ZANLA groups fought as guerrillas because their capabilities, especially at the beginning of the conflict, were very limited and they lacked heavy equipment and aircraft, the Rhodesian army adopted a counter-insurgency approach to fighting the guerrillas. It based its tactics on simulating the fighting style of African guerrillas and made its army so flexible that it was able, despite the small size of its troops, to fight the guerrillas effectively. The army was nourished by a limited number of foreigners, who may have numbered around 1,400 combatants of various nationalities such as French, South Africans, Americans, Portuguese and British, who served in the Rhodesian Light Infantry (Mañes Postigo, 2016).

It should not be forgotten that Rhodesia, despite the trade embargo it was subjected to after the unilateral declaration of independence, possessed technology that the ZIPRA and ZANLA guerrillas lacked, despite Soviet and Chinese support. Aviation, combined with ground forces, implemented the army's operability and provided cover for all units deployed in the territory, both through the support of Hawker Hunter FGA.9 fighter-bombers and transport aircraft that gave the Rhodesian troops the quasi-general status of airborne troops (Moorcraft and McLaughlin, 1982: 96). On many occasions there were raids across the Mozambican border or into Zambia by small groups ferried in Alouette III helicopters or dropped as paratroopers behind the enemy lines from C-47 Dakotas.

The Rhodesian army was a flexible army, not driven by its supposed technological and material superiority in what could have led to asymmetric warfare with many more casualties and little effectiveness, but adapting to the circumstances and fighting its enemy with the same tactics. It confronted the guerrillas with a well-trained counter-guerrilla that knew the terrain, imitated their movements and was able to mimic them. A counter-guerrilla that helped to minimise the conflict to just the insurgents, taking large numbers of casualties among the insurgents and affecting the civilian population to a lesser extent than in other conflicts.

Much of the operations carried out in the Rhodesian war were counter-insurgency in nature. At other times, raids were conducted along the borders of both Zambia and Mozambique in pursuit or hunting of guerrilla groups. These were organised operations which aimed to elimine as many guerrillas as possible, and were usually carried out by Rhodesian light infantry, considered elite troops, in line with the army's usual strategy. One type of operation that worked well for the Rhodesian army was the so-called Fire Force, which combined light infantry attack and air support from Alouette helicopters and Lynx aircraft (Wood, 2009). The Fire Force was based on the location of the guerrillas by the Selous Scouts, infiltrated among them. A rapid and accurate attack on the guerrilla groups was then deployed with the help of helicopters and the dropping of paratroopers from C-47 Dakotas, encircling the enemy and causing them to be eliminated or captured, the latter option being rarely considered. Finally, a continuous intelligence and observation operation that relied almost exclusively on Selous Scouts, infiltrated into guerrilla-held territory, played a crucial role in determining the strategy of the Rhodesian command.

As for ZIPRA and ZANLA, the strategies they adopted were that of guerrilla warfare, with the exception that ZANLA, supported by China, maintained this form of combat as an objective in itself, that is, as a way of systematically wearing down the enemy by forcing him to carry out punitive operations that brought the people closer to the guerrillas and in which he did not have the usual success due to the adoption of counter-insurgency as a primordial means of combat. ZIPRA, on the other hand, operating from the borders of Zambia and Botswana, and with Soviet material support, maintained a guerrilla war based on attrition while equipping itself with heavy equipment in search of a conventional confrontation that would allow it to win (Mtisi, Nyakudya & Barnes, 2009).

Troops

The only way for the Rhodesian army to cope with the continuing influx of guerrillas across the border from Zambia and especially Mozambique from 1974 onwards was counter-insurgency and the army therefore specialised in such operations. The Rhodesian armed forces consisted of a core of professionals reinforced by compulsory military service for the white population and black volunteers (constituting up to 70% in the army and police, only 25% in the air force and non-existent among all reservists) (Military Balance, 1980: 73). There were a small number of European and American mercenaries and veterans of recent conflicts such as Kenya, where they had already made significant gains against the Mau-Mau insurgency (Evans, 2007). It also had a large number of reservists who could be mobilised at any time by Ian Smith's government, and arguably virtually all white males of fighting age were soldiers in the Rhodesian armed forces. This permanent state of militarisation meant that farm productivity declined and many whites began to emigrate from 1977 onwards. There are photographs and accounts of the state of alarm in which white farmers found themselves at the end of the conflict, with many of the ranchs being barbed-wire fortresses and the land owners themselves armed soldiers (Cilliers, 1985).

The Rhodesian army relied on a very effective system and to this end subjected its soldiers to periods of training consisting of six weeks of basic training, six weeks in conventional warfare drill and finally, and this is what made them special, five weeks of preparation for irregular combat in guerrilla warfare or counter-insurgency, this period being longer in the case of the Selous Scouts. Survival was emphasised and the method was based on a single objective: to eliminate the enemy (Cocks, 2006).

Soldiers who received this training were inducted into a select group of trained counter-guerrillas who complemented the actions of the Rhodesian African Rifles (RAR) and the Rhodesian Regiment (RR) of Whites, essentially the regular army, which was extremely important as a base for the infantry. By the end of 1979 the army had some 10,800 regulars and over 40,000 reservists (15,000 active) (Lohman and MacPherson, 1983: 2).

The police (BSAP) carried out security tasks in the interior of the country, including direct confrontation with guerrillas. Its elite unit was the PATU (Anti-Terrorist Police Unit). In 1980 the number of BSAP amounted to 7500 in service and more than 35000 reservists, indicating a strong guerrilla presence in the interior (Balance Militar, 1980: 76).

The Ministry of Internal Affairs, responsible for the tribal areas, had an armed corps (Guard Force), very important for the control and infiltration of the guerrillas with more than 8000 men in 1979 and one of the most punished units in the confrontation with the guerrillas. The Rhodesian army (Beckett, 1985) was organised as follows:

- Prime Minister
- Combined Operations Commands
- Army (10,800 Regulars and 15,000 Active Reserves)
- RAR (Rhodesian African Rifles)
- RR (Rhodesian Regiment)
- RA (Rhodesian Artillery)

- RACR (Rhodesian Armour Car Regiment)
- REC (Rhodesian Enginer Corps)
- Special Forces
- SAS (Special Air Forces)
- Selous Scouts
- Grey`s Scouts
- RLI (Rhodesian Light Infantry)
- RHAF (Rhodesian Air Force) (2300)
- BSAP (British South African Police) (11000 Regulars and 19 Active Reservists)
- Internal Affairs
- Guard Force (8000)
- CIO (Central Intelligent Office) (1300)

Four units of the Rhodesian army should be singled out for their uniqueness and significance in counter-insurgency warfare:

The Selous Scouts were the best Rhodesian troops in terms of spotting, infiltration and guerrilla hunting. They could move as a group commanded by one or more white officers, combining white and black soldiers, of about 30 individuals who moved into hostile terrain as guerrillas. The whites went unnoticed by wearing black make-up or moving as prisoners of their coloured comrades. They were expert hunters and survivors in the jungle environment, living on the ground hunting their own food and dressing in the clothes of the guerrillas they eliminated. They were able to live in very adverse conditions, handle Russian or Chinese weapons and blend in with the peasant population by posing as communist guerrillas. Their mission usually consisted of observation, infiltration and informing the Rhodesian army of the location of enemy targets. It was the unit that caused the most casualties among the guerrillas (French, 2012; Cole, 1984 & Parker, 2006).

-The Rhodesian Light Infantry (RLI) was, prior to the Civil War, a regiment of the regular army, distinguished by the fact that it was composed of white soldiers. Throughout the war it combined soldiers from a variety of backgrounds, with most of the foreign volunteers being placed in this unit, and was the enforcement arm of the operations known as the Fire Force. This unit specialised in airborne operations and direct combat against guerrillas.

-Grey`s Scouts was the name given to a mounted infantry unit that played an important role in the war from its formation in 1975 until the unit was disbanded in 1979 as part of the Rhodesian Army and in 1986 as a special unit of the Zimbabwean forces. They were engaged in wide-area scouting and patrolling and developed a successful frontal attack. One of the great advantages of the Grey`s Scouts was their ability to carry ammunition and materiel compared to an infantryman on foot, and also their speed, being able to cover large distances in a single day that could be three times that of an infantryman. They were also important for their ability to move through minefields or terrain inaccessible to vehicles.

-The final unit of note was the Special Air Services (SAS). It was Rhodesia's premier elite special operations unit. Its main missions were the most dangerous commando operations in enemy territory against particularly strategic targets (Wessels, 2015).

Counter Insurgency Operations

The Rhodesian war has often been labelled an example of counter-insurgency warfare, given the struggle between conventional government armed forces and outlawed armed guerrillas, but could an executive such as Ian Smith's be considered legitimate? The government had proclaimed independence unilaterally and with little international support. The fact that the white minority ruled without having won power through the ballot box, that the distribution of land was unfair, and that the black population was subjugated and its freedoms curtailed, explain the right of the natives to demand their liberties.

The ZANLA and ZIPRA guerrillas were insurgents and committed terrorist actions at the cost of civilian lives, all within the context of open warfare and as part of an asymmetrical fighting strategy due to the great disproportion of forces. ZIPRA guerrillas shot down a Vickers Viscount airliner in September 1978, killing 48 people. Ten of them had survived the crash but were executed on the spot by the guerrillas. Months later, in February 1979, a similar passenger plane was shot down again and all 59 people on board were killed.

In June 1978 eight missionaries and four children from the Elim Pentecostal mission were tortured and executed by bayonet in cold blood; and almost a year earlier, on 6 August 1977, 11 people were killed and 70 injured when a device exploded in the Woolworth shop in Salisbury. The guerrillas' terrorist actions were combined with other military actions and raids from the borders of Zambia, Botswana and Mozambique. However, as mentioned above, Ian Smith's government carried out a counter-insurgency struggle that involved some army units, especially the Selous Scouts, the RLI and the SAS in actions very similar to those of the guerrillas.

In an interesting article entitled "Rhodesia's Approach to Counterinsurgency Operations: A Tendency to Kill", Marno de Boer reviewed the violence carried out by Rhodesian troops in their operations. According to the author, prisoners were rarely taken and violence was carried out on the enemy that even the Rhodesian government itself began to feel uncomfortable (De Boer, 2012). The Geneva Convention obliged Rhodesian troops to take prisoners after their surrender, but it rarely happened. It should also be added that the Selous Scouts did not conduct classic military operations but rather infiltration operations in foreign countries such as Zambia and Mozambique, so that their actions violated international law.

It has already been mentioned that Rhodesia's tactics were close to guerrilla tactics and therefore on many occasions were on a par with them. The difference between terrorism and surgical military actions, both based on the elimination of human beings in a context not of peace, the preferred scenario for terrorism, but in an environment of war, was evident and once again demonstrates the singularity of counter-insurgency actions that surpass international legality as well as those established in the Universal Charter of Human Rights.

Punitive operations were also part of the regular actions of the Rhodesian army. Two of the most notable were Operation Dingo or the Chimoio massacre and the attack on Nyadzonya. The former was carried out in retaliation for the ZANLA bombing of the Woolworth's shop in Salisbury. The operation allegedly annihilated two guerrilla camps located in Chimoio and Tembue, causing more than three thousand casualties and thousands more wounded, probably a high percentage of civilians linked to the guerrillas. The proof of the ambiguity referred to above about the morality of such action lies in the use of language. For some it was Operation Dingo, for others the Chimoio massacre.

Another operation that caused a large number of casualties was the attack on Nyadzonya. A group of 72 Selous Scouts entered Mozambican territory completely infiltrated and camouflaged with the FRELIMO guerrillas, to such an extent that they passed several checkpoints in FRELIMO vehicles and went deep into the guerrilla centre located in Nyadzonya. Once inside at the camp, and without anyone suspecting their true identity, they set up points around the square and announced over a loudspeaker that the Rhodesian government had fallen, which caused the guerrillas to gather in the centre of the square to celebrate. The Selous Scouts opened fire from vehicle-mounted machine guns, triggering a massacre that resulted in the deaths, according to Rhodesian sources, of more than 1,200 people (Baxter, 2014: 159).

Weapons for All

The highly irregular and changing conditions of the Rhodesian civil war profoundly affected the weaponry used during the conflict, including the use of biological and chemical material (Cross, 2017). Ian Smith's government had great difficulties when obtaining modern weaponry due to the international embargo, which was only partly overcome by the support of South Africa, Israel and Portugal until the loss of its colonies (Melson, 2005). Also, the black market of smuggled armament an the local production mitigated as far as possible the ever-increasing need for buy modern and heavy equipment to counter the guerrillas' improved equipment.

The armament of the Rhodesian Security Forces had different origins. Mainly, it came from the arsenal inherited from the British colonial period, mostly from the Second World War, with a few exceptions such as airborne equipment of more modern provenance. It was sent to Africa in the wake of the Mau Mau rebellion in Kenya and the tense situation with the Apartheid South African government independent of the British Empire. Other major source of military aid would come to the Rhodesian government of South Africa from 1965 onwards, albeit conditioned by periods of shortages depending on the international context and the Cold War scenario (Gott, 1967). Much of the South African material was ceded and not handed over to Rhodesia, sometimes being recovered by South Africa in response to strong international pressure. On many occasions this material was camouflaged as part of Rhodesia's existing arsenal, using similar models (Baxter, 2014: 187). To a lesser extent, Ian Smith's government relied on Portuguese assistance until 1974, when the political situation in Portugal changed after the Carnation Revolution, putting an end to the dictatorial regime and forming a democratic government that allowed the independence of its colonies. Until then, Mozambique had been Rhodesia's main trade route in and out of the country.

As the war progressed, the weaponry captured from the guerrillas became another important source of equipement for the Rhodesian army. This material was quite abundant and in some cases better than that of the Rhodesians themselves, but in return it required instruction in its handling. This problem was solved with the help of Portuguese military advisers already accustomed to dealing with it. The regular incorporation of ex-guerrillas into the government side helped in this learning process, as did the assimilation of Chinese and Soviet weaponry and equipment. Eventually Rhodesia itself produced as much material as possible, with particular attention paid to the domestic transformation of commercial vehicles into armoured and mine-proof vehicles. This was achieved by increasing the height and altering the chassis so that the explosion of the mines was deflected as much as possible and the deflagration was not carried by the main cabin of the vehicle, (Moorcraft and McLaughlin, 1982: 95).

The use of weaponry was fairly homogenous between the army and law enforcement forces, although with a prioritisation of the best and most modern parts and models for the shock troops such as the RLI or SAS and the more antiquated relegated to Guard Force units. The main light weapons used by the Rhodesian forces ranged from Browning HI-Power pistols to the 9mm Star, or the Walther PP, favoured by the police forces. Rhodesia even produced its own model, called the Mamba (Locke and Cooke, 1995:

108). Enfield N2 MKI revolvers were also used especially in police duties at the beginning of the war. Many second-line units were equipped with WWII Lee-Enfield rifles, although these were gradually phased out and replaced by more modern weaponry, although the sniper version was used until the end of the war because of its high accuracy and reliability.

At the time of the Unilateral Declaration of Independence by the Smith Cabinet, the regular forces were equipped with the British L1A1 SLR assault rifle, which was the British Army's standard issue weapon and immediately became unavailable due to the UK embargo on Rhodesia (Baxter, 2014: 80). This forced it to be replaced with copies of the original Belgian FN FAL model, from which the British L1A1 was derived. The South African R1 assault rifles, a copy of the FN FAL, of which probably just over 30,000 copies arrived, provided the Rhodesian forces with greater range and more power than their guerrilla counterparts, but they also had a major handicap over the latter, namely that they were weapons that required much more thorough cleaning and maintenance than rival assault rifles, which in a savannah environment was a problematic issue due to be extreme temperatures and dust accumulation, were more problematic. In the mid-1970s, at a time of dwindling South African support, several thousand HK G3s made in Portugal were purchased under licence and were widely used until the end of the war, although they were considered inferior by Rhodesian troops.

For airborne operations, very common on the borders and in the context of counter-insurgency warfare, the FN FAL variant with the folding stock model 50/61 was used, as this feature allowed it to take up less space, very important given the limitations on board the Alouette III or any the time during a parachute jump. Smuggled from the USA, a number of Mini-14 automatic carbines were also available, which were also very useful that kind of actions.

The submachine gun models used, mainly for surveillance tasks and by vehicle crews, were the popular UZI of Israeli origin, the British L2A1 Sterling and Sten MK2. A number of Australian Austen and Owen Gun submachine guns were also available, as well as numerous submachine guns manufactured in small local workshops, commonly known as "Rhuzies", which shows the imperative need to cover the shortages of materials and armament due to the embargo and the contrary international context. Their small size was ideal for the limited space inside the vehicles and their volume of fire was very useful in close-range engagements common in attacks on installations inside Rhodesia. The FN Browning Auto-5, Ithaca-37 and Greener shotguns also played an important role, and were highly appreciated in confrontations that required the elimination of guerrillas in buildings, due to their effectiveness at short and inaccurate distances.

As for machine guns, the 7'62 mm FN MAG multi-purpose machine gun was used as a squad weapon as its weight was acceptable for long foot-march operations in conflict zones, as well as for sustained fire support (Moorcraft and McLaughlin, 1982: 91-92). Tripod-mounted, it was a weapon with a high rate of fire and mechanically very reliable, with little or no stoppage or jamming. The Bren MK2 Cal .303 light machine gun was more common and had already proved its worth in service with the British Empire during World War II, although as the war progressed, it was relegated to the second line by the more modern L4A1 7.62mm NATO-calibre version. Also used as a squad support weapon was the 50/41 heavy-barrelled version of the FN FAL and the Browning M1919. Their Browning MK2 version, originally mounted on the Spitfire fighters that were in service in Rhodesia in the 1940s and 1950s, were adapted to vehicles (Moorcraft and McLaughlin, 1982: 91-92). In their urgent need for armament from every possible source, the Rhodesians were quick to find another use for these weapons, which proved to be excellent. The familiar 12.7mm Browning M2 HB was also present as a heavy machine gun used in fixed positions and mostly mounted aboard vehicles.

Most of the 7'62, 9 and 0'303 ammunition used in all these weapons came from South African factories and although it often performed worse than the original batches, it was one of the only sources of supply for the army under Smith's command. The wick variety of small arms in Rhodesia was overwhelming, and a telling statistic that shows the easy path to militarisation and diversity of models in Rhodesia was the presence of 120,000 registered small arms in civilian hands for a community of less than 300,000 inhabitants (Moorcraft and McLaughlin, 1982: 91-92). Thus, we can state that white society under Ian Smith's leadership was familiar with the use of small arms, and although many items were obtained through illicit operations, many of these weapons were already present at the time of the conflict.

Between Black Market and Home Production

The problem for the Rhodesians was the supply of heavy weapons that would provide superior firepower to the guerrillas, so they had to go to great lengths to obtain them on the black market, as few countries were willing to negotiate with Smith's executive. Among the most common support weapons for the Rhodesian forces were the British-made L16 81mm mortars and the South African M4 60mm commando mortar, which were widely used as fire support against the poorly protected infantry typical of fighting in the Rhodesian savannah against guerrilla parties. Some pieces, such as the M40 106mm recoilless cannon and the M20 Super Bazooka anti-tank rocket launcher, were adapted to counter-insurgency fighting and especially to guerrilla warfare (Baxter, 2014: 248). Although they were originally anti-tank weapons, they were rarely used in anti-armour roles, being used to destroy fortified guerrilla positions or transport vehicles by taking advantage of their direct fire capability. This kind of weaponry also had diverse origins as a small number of American M-72 Law portable anti-tank rocket launchers were available at the end of the war and it is possible that Rhodesian forces had 9 Milan anti-tank missile launchers, including a complement of 75 missiles, which would have entered via South Africa and were reserved to meet the expected conventional ZIPRA attack with tanks and armoured vehicles (Moorcraft & McLaughlin, 2010).

The only anti-aircraft weapon available, not including the weaponry captured from the guerrillas, was the 37mm M1 anti-aircraft gun, also of American origin, from the Second World War. Its insufficient characteristics in the event of a confrontation with the modern aerial material available in Zambia or Mozambique meant that it was destined for a few fixed positions in the most important cities, with the anti-aircraft material captured from the guerrillas, such as the ZPU-1, ZPU-4 or ZU-23-2, being the main support for the Rhodesian troops. The imprecision of enemy targets contributed to the Rhodesians once again adapting the conventional functions of these weapons to counter-insurgency warfare and using them against infantry, given their firepower and rate of fire (Lohman and MacPherson, 1983: 32).

Armoured vehicles were also very heterogeneous, and it was here that the ingenuity of the Rhodesians was most clearly displayed in the form of home-made contributions, as they carried out many modifications, given the near impossibility of obtaining armoured material suitable for combat against the guerrillas. Most notably, eight Polish-made T-55 LD battle tanks were received in 1979 from South Africa, from a shipment of Libyan arms destined for the army of Ugandan dictator Idi Amin when he was fighting his war with Tanzania, whose transport ship, the French merchantman "Astor", was eventually confiscated by the Pretoria authorities. They were then made to look as if they had been captured by the Rhodesians from the Mozambican army (Baxter, 2014: 185).

The most widely used and effective armoured vehicles, until the arrival of the T-55, were the South African Eland-90s, a copy of the French AML-90s, armed with a 90mm gun. Rhodesian forces also had several Eland-60s armed with a 60mm rear-loading mortar, but they were used in defence of vital air bases rather than in the field (Moorcraft and McLaughlin, 1982: 94).

Some twenty World War II veteran Ferrets, inherited from the British Army, were the mainstay of armoured reconnaissance vehicles until the 1970s, although some were upgraded and were used until the very end of the conflict. Initially a few outdated South African Marmon Herringtons were also available, but they were withdrawn in the early 1970s and at least two Shorlands were used by the police for reconnaissance and patrol duties, ending up in the hands of the Selous Scouts to support their raids in Mozambique and with a clear focus on counter-insurgency warfare.

With the unilateral Declaration of Independence, Rhodesia inherited 30 old fashioned Universal Carriers of British origin (Locke and Cooke, 1995: 152). These vehicles were no longer used on the front line, but were used in modified and better armed form to defend vital installations within Rhodesia and for the safe armoured transport of troops in combat zones. The absolute lack of such means led Rhodesia to produce a large number of armoured personnel carriers, adapted to the mine warfare so prevalent on the country's roads and highways. They were built on the chassis of civilian trucks of brands such as Unimog, Nissan and Bedford, all of which were already present in Rhodesia before the outbreak of hostilities.

The only foreign models they were able to acquire were small numbers of the South African-made Buffel and Hippo armoured mine-proof transports. Notable in this regard were another 130 Crocodile; between 200 and 300 MAP75; between 100 and 200 MAP45; 60 Spook, which was an unlicensed copy of the German armoured UR-416 adapted for mine warfare; 2 PIG exact copies, also unlicensed, of the UR-416 manufactured by the Selous Scouts for their cross-border raids; and an unspecified number of Leopards (Moorcraft and McLaughlin, 1982: 95). However, penalties in obtaining modern equipment on international markets due to embargoes and external conditions meant that the Rhodesians produced their own armoured vehicles such as the Pookie, whose function was to detect and clear minefields laid by ZANLA and ZIPRA guerrillas in certain positions and communication routes.

As elsewhere, the lack of artillery and especially its ammunition was a chronic problem for the Rhodesians. Even so, they got a very high return on what was available and also managed to fulfil their tasks of fire support and even in some case of counter-battery, in border duels against neighbouring armies supporting the guerrillas or even against the guerrillas when they began to rely on heavy Chinese and Soviet origin material. The main field artillery pieces of the Rhodesian forces were 36 Ordnance QF 25 Pdr 88mm howitzers and the famous 25-pounders of World War II, the standard weapon of British field artillery that demonstrated enormous quality and remained in service around the world for decades (Baxter, 2014: 185). At the end of the war and on loan from South Africa, they had nine 140mm BL 5'5 howitzers, more powerful and longer-range weapons than the 25 rpdr, which were a vital contribution during the heavy fighting at the end of the war. They also had six 105mm M-101 howitzers, standard issue in 1965 in the only regular battery then available to the Rhodesian artillery, which were rarely used due to the lack of spare parts and ammunition (Lohman and MacPherson, 1983: 32).

One of the fundamental differences and a major tactical advantage of the Rhodesian security forces was aviation, which was practically non-existent on the guerrilla side. Despite the age of their equipment and the difficulties in buying modern models, they were able to take great advantage of their superiority in the sky. Ian Smith's government had 12 Hawker Hunter FGA 9 fighter-bombers, and 16 De Havilland Vampire FB 9s inherited from the British presence, reinforced by another 13 FB.52s on loan from South Africa (Moorcraft and McLaughlin, 1982: 96). The Hunter was the most modern and powerful fighter-bomber in their arsenal, although the British embargo prevented its modernisation with more potent engines. It ensured the superiority and security of Rhodesian airspace, and was widely used in cross-border attacks on rebel bases and in support of gaps opened by Selous Scout counter-guerrilla expeditions. The Vampires were very old and outdated by 1965, but the Rhodesians made much use of them, both for ground attack and for advanced pilot training.

They also had ten English Electric Canberras, already deployed before the Unilateral Declaration of Independence and which in many operations would be supplemented or replaced by the more modern South African Canberras operating directly in the conflict. They were jet bombers, but classically used for saturation bombing missions. Like the Hunter, they could not be re-engined due to the British embargo and by the end of the war were in poor condition, being replaced by more modern and refurbished South African Air Force Canberras, masquerading as their Rhodesian counterparts (Moorcraft and McLaughlin, 1982: 96).

The Rhodesian air force had 21 Reims Cessna FTB.337.G Lynx, 14 SIAI Marchetti SF.260 Warrior and 11 AL-60 Trojan F5s that acted both as light transport and armed in counter-insurgency actions. These light attack aircraft played a major role in close support of the typical guerrilla combat so common in the conflict. They were often armed with external weapons containers with multiple rocket launchers and machine guns or light bombs. They were more vulnerable to guerrilla small arms anti-aircraft fire, but their high manoeuvrability allowed them to provide essential close support to anti-guerrilla operations. Moreover, their use was boosted by the impossibility of obtaining more modern and powerful fighter aircraft on the international arms markets. This equipment was purchased as if it were intended for the civilian market and thus avoided embargoes (Moorcraft and McLaughlin, 1982: 96).

Among the transport aircraft, Rhodesia had twelve Douglas C-47 Dakota, four Canadair C4 Argonaut and two DC-7Cs. The role of the Dakotas was central to the paratroop actions used in Fire Force operations. In addition, such air capability was essential for the rapid movement of materials and personnel from one end of the country to the other. Among the light transport, they had 17 Cessna 185s, six BN-2A Islanders, two Percival Pembrokes, one Cessna 421, one Cessna 402 and one Baron Beechcraft 95 C-55 (Military Balance, 1978: 99). The lack of adequate airstrips in much of the country made the importance of these light transport aircraft enormous, as they could operate from almost any flat surface. The urgent transport of ammunition or personnel in small quantities was one of their main missions, along with the evacuation of seriously wounded to hospitals in Salisbury or Bulawayo.

As had been evident in wars such as Vietnam and other conflicts where guerrilla warfare played a major role, the British confrontation against Indonesia in Borneo or the Portuguese colonial wars, the helicopter and its tactical use proved to be essential in such conflicts. Rhodesia had between 34 and 60 Aerospatiale SA 316 Alouette IIIs, many on loan from South Africa and even flown directly by South African pilots; 11 Augusta Bell 205A Cheetahs, obtained from Israel; and 6 Aerospatiale SA 313 Alouette IIs also supplied by South Africa (Moorcraft and McLaughlin, 1982: 97). The Alouette IIIs played a leading role in Fire Force actions, some used as transport for Rhodesian G-Car soldiers with four men on board and others on fire support missions, usually equipped with a 20mm gun called a K-Car. The Israeli induction of AB-205s, which were licensed copies of the famous Vietnam War UH-1 Huey, with far greater payload capacity and range than the ubiquitous Alouette, was a major contribution. The South African Army's SA-332 Puma and Super Frelon helicopters were heavily involved in major deep incursion operations in neighbouring country territories, especially in Mozambique, again supporting counter-guerrilla raids (Moorcraft and McLaughlin, 1982: 97).

It is important to note the extensive use of material captured from the guerrilla liberation forces, such as RPGs. They came to replace the M20 and became the standard anti-tank weapon of Rhodesian frontline units. The light weapons of infiltration units, such as the Selous Scout, were almost always captured from enemy guerrillas to reinforce the camouflage of these units (Warren & Higginson, 2006). The 12.7mm DShK heavy machine gun, specially mounted on vehicles, was also widely used. The Salisbury government's anti-aircraft defence was reinforced with at least a dozen ZPU-4s and some ZU-23-2s and there were also BM-21 units to reinforce the artillery or captured BTR-152s to reinforce the mechanised capabilities of the Rhodesian infantry.

FUTURE RESEARCH DIRECTIONS

The study of colonial wars, both the wars of independence and the later decolonisation, show a different type of conflict that the different metropolitan governments confronted in different ways, with the same end, the withdrawal and independence of the native forces. Colonial wars must be contextualised in their time and studied in detail as they moved away from the prerogatives of regular warfare, whether with irregular warfare tactics or, as in this case, counter-insurgency. The importance of these colonial wars in the development of contemporary history and the processes of decolonisation in the context of the Cold War is evident better to understand the geopolitical situation, nowadays a question that is also linked to a contemporary phenomenon of neo-colonialism.

CONCLUSION

Throughout the precedent pages we have described and analysed the particular conditions of the Rhodesian war in order to establish, through this case study, an example of counterinsurgency warfare. The objectives of this paper have been to analyse the Rhodesian war on the basis of both tactical and strategic warfare behaviour and the adaptation of Rhodesian troops to an irregular fighting environment that was primarily based on the counterinsurgency model. In order to better understand the war environment, we have considered it important to describe the weaponry used, where it came from and the difficulties in obtaining it as a circumstantial part of this conflict.

However, we see how the Rhodesian army, despite having a clear British heritage and therefore a regular organisational character, was quick to adapt to the conditions of the conflict and adopt an effective tactic to combat the guerrillas. Ian Smith's government was convinced that the guerrillas were the problem and that they lacked sufficient social support to seize power, so they considered it essential to end ZANLA and ZIPRA as a means to end any threat (Cilliers, 1985). The Rhodesian military therefore adapted to guerrilla warfare and responded to its enemies with punitive tactics focused on eliminating insurgents (De Boer, 2012). In this case, the adoption of counter-insurgency methods such as systematic attacks on guerrilla bases, bombings, kidnappings, extortion and ultimately copying their role model, worked well for Rhodesia, at least from a tactical point of view, and allowed Ian Smith's executive to remain at war for 15 years in an unfavourable situation, but also became its own end as it was unable to sustain it and focused its efforts solely on fighting the guerrillas (Preston, 2004). The British embargo, the international measures on arms sales arranged in response to the palpitations of the Cold War, and the existence of guerrillas on its borders - which from 1974 onwards were consolidated into hostile government forces - bear witness to this. We have checked the tactics, troop types and operations and everything points to a very effective form of counter-insurgency fighting, which reduced the number of casualties that would have occurred in the case of an irregular war between a militarised state with regular tactics and a guerrilla. We have also noted the seriousness of the isolation of the Smith regime, which was unable to obtain modern weaponry and was forced to adapt the equipment it possessed to the service of counter-insurgency warfare. In short, the chronic supply difficulties of the Smith regime meant that virtually anything captured from the guerrillas was put into service and used by the Rhodesian military and security forces.

REFERENCES

Abbott, P., & Botham, P. (1986). *Modern African Wars (I): Rhodesia 1965-80*. Osprey Publishing.

Balance Militar. (1978). *Revista Ejército*, 461.

Balance Militar. (1979). *Revista Ejército*, 478.

Balance Militar. (1980). *Revista Ejército*, 490.

Barroso, L. F. M. (2014). The independence of Rhodesia in Salazar's strategy for Southern Africa. *The American Historical Review*, *46*(2), 1–24. doi:10.1080/17532523.2014.943922

Baxter, P. (2014). *Bush War Rhodesia*. Helion & Company.

Beckett, I. F. (1985). *The Rhodesian army: counter-insurgency, 1972-1979. Armed forces and modern counter-insurgency*. St. Martin Press.

Bratton, M. (1979). Settler state, guerrilla war and rural underdevelopment in Rhodesia. *African Issues*, *9*(1-2), 56-62.

Cilliers, J. (1985). *Counter-Insurgency in Rhodesia*. Routledge.

Cocks, C. (2006). *Fireforce: One Man's War in the Rhodesian LightInfantry*. 30° South Publishers.

Cole, B. (1980) *The Elite. The Story of the Rhodesian Special Air Service*. WYD 4.

Cross, G. (2017). *Dirty War: Rhodesia and Chemical Biological Warfare 1975-1980*. Helion and Company.

Davidow, J. (2019). *A Peace in Southern Africa: The Lancaster House Conference on Rhodesia 1979*. Routledge.

De Boer, M. (2012). El enfoque de Rodesia hacia las operaciones de contrainsurgencia: Una tendencia a matar. *Military Review*.

Evans, M. (2007). The wretched of the empire: Politics, ideology and counterinsurgency in Rhodesia, 1965-1980. *Small Wars & Insurgencies*, *18*(2), 175–195. doi:10.1080/09574040701400601

Flower, K. (1988). Serving Secretly—An Intelligence Chief on Record- Rhodesia into Zimbabwe—1964 to 1981. *African Affairs*, *87*(348), 465–466. doi:10.1093/oxfordjournals.afraf.a098063

Fox, H. W. (1915). Rhodesia and the War. *Journal of the Royal African Society*, *14*(56), 345–354.

French, P. (2012). *Shadows of a Forgotten Past: To the Edge with the Rhodesian SAS and Selous Scouts*. Helion and Company.

Godwin, P., & Hancock, I. (1993). *Rhodesians Never Die—The Impact of War and Political Change on White Rhodesia, 1970-1980*. OUP Oxford. doi:10.1093/acprof:oso/9780198203650.001.0001

Gott, R. (1967). El sur de Africa y el fin de la guerra fría. *Estudios Internacionales (Santiago)*, 95–109.

Grant, N. (2015). *Rhodesian Light Infantryman 1961-80*. Osprey Publishing.

Locke, P. G., & Peter, D. F. (1995). *Fighting Vehicles and Weapons of Rhodesia 1965-80*. P & P. Publishing.

Lohman, M. y MacPherson, R. (1983). *Rhodesia: Tactical victory, strategic defeat*. Marine Corps Command and Staff College, Marine Corps Development and Education Command.

Mañes Postigo, J. (2016). *Soldados Sin Bandera*. Editorial Magasé.

Martin, D., & Johnson, P. (1982). *The Struggle for Zimbabwe: The Chimurenga War*. Faber and Faber.

McNamara, R. (2012). The last throw of the dice: Portugal, Rhodesia and South Africa, 1970–74. *Portuguese Studies*, *28*(2), 201–215. doi:10.5699/portstudies.28.2.0201

Melson, C. D. (2005). Top secret war: Rhodesian Special Operations. *Small Wars & Insurgencies*, *16*(1), 57–82. doi:10.1080/0959231042000322567

Moorcraft, P., & McLaughlin, P. (2010). *The Rhodesian War: A Military History*. Stackpole Books.

Moorcraft, P. L., & McLaughlin, P. (1982). *The Rhodesian War a Military History*. Stackpole Books.

Mtisi, J., Nyakudya, M., & Barnes, T. A. (2009). War in Rhodesia, 1965-1980. In Becoming Zimbabwe: a history from the pre-colonial period to 2008, 141-166. Jacana.

Parker, J. (2006). *Assignment Selous Scouts: Inside Story of a Rhodesian Special Branch Officer*. Galago Pub.

Preller, G. (2018). *ZIPRA and ZANLA war stories*. Independently editorial.

Preston, M. (2004). Stalemate and the termination of civil war: Rhodesia reassessed. *Journal of Peace Research*, *41*(1), 65–83. doi:10.1177/0022343304040050

Pulido López-Rodríguez, G. (2017). Rhodesia: Guerra sucia, insurgencia y violencia política. *Análisis GESI*, *24*.

Rossi, G. (1974). *Anatomy of a Rebel. Smith of Rhodesia: a biography*. Graham Publishing.

Rotberg, R. (1988). *The founder: Cecil Rhodes and the pursuit of power*. Oxford University Press.

Warren, C., & Higginson, C. (2006). At the Going Down of the Sun, 77-78. Zanj Press.

Wessels, H. (2015). *A Handful of Hard Men: The SAS and the Battle for Rhodesia*. Casemate.

Wood, J. R. (2009). *Counter-strike from the Sky: The Rhodesian All-Arms Fireforce in the War in the Bush, 1974-1980, 30.°* SouthPublishers.

Chapter 16
The Russian–Ukrainian War With Historical Approximation:
From Colonial Wars to Digital Spaces

Felipe Rodolfo Debasa Navalpotro

 https://orcid.org/0000-0001-6459-1469

Rey Juan Carlos University, Spain

Yuliia Andriichenko

Taras Shevchenko National University of Kyiv, Ukraine

Nataliia Popova

Taras Shevchenko National University of Kyiv, Ukraine

Iryna Sytdykova

Taras Shevchenko National University of Kyiv, Ukraine

ABSTRACT

This chapter raises the problems of colonial wars in the modern world. According to the generally accepted point of view, the elimination of the colonial system had been completed by the end of the twentieth century, as a result of which 90 independent new states arose. But in practice, colonialism has not ceased to exist, but rather continues developing, though in new hybrid forms. Despite numerous international legal norms which were adopted to combat colonialism, more developed countries have repeatedly resorted to armed intervention to restore their interests on the territories they once controlled, including the establishment of a political regime loyal to them, since the end of the last century.

DOI: 10.4018/978-1-6684-7040-4.ch016

INTRODUCTION

This article raises the problems of colonial wars in the modern world. According to the accepted point of view, the elimination of the colonial system had been completed by the end of the twentieth century, as a result of which 90 independent new states arose.

But in practice, colonialism has not ceased to exist, but rather continues developing, though in new hybrid forms. Despite numerous international legal norms which were adopted to combat colonialism, more developed countries have repeatedly resorted to armed intervention to restore their interests on the territories they once controlled, including the establishment of a political regime loyal to them, since the end of the last century.

Finding new forms of colonialism such as technological or data colonialism (Alister Fraser, 2019), or the one that takes place in digital societies (Michael Kwet, 2019).

The chapter exposes that the Russian-Ukrainian war of the 21st century is not an armed conflict on national or language issues but postcolonial war aiming to own independent state's territory and resources. Proving that the modern world is already in the process of another redivision since Russia also decided to become a participant in this process. The first steps in this direction were taken by the country in 1994, almost after the collapse of the USSR. The state launched the First Chechen War, followed by Georgia and by an attack on Ukraine this year.

Having analyzed Putin's regrets on USSR collapse in his speeches, we have managed to determine his sacred mission to unify the "Russian" lands and create a semblance of the USSR. The general perception is that the Russian mass media were given new methodological instructions on the coverage of the war in Ukraine and on Putin's role in the international political arena. So, a clear indication of a parallelism between the current president and the Russian prince Alexander Nevsky was revealed. This historical figure (1220-1263 AD) is known for the fact that he did not lose a single battle in his entire life. Alexander, prince of Nóvgorod, was considered clergy's favorite prince and the patron of the Orthodox Church. Nowadays Putin applies this role to himself. Therefore, a possible loss in the war with Ukraine is tantamount to complete collapse for him.

There is also a possible Russian society reaction on its military defeat. It will not be accepted by Russian society, been subjected to powerful propaganda over the past eight years, which, in turn, may lead to a change in the ruling elites of Russia. This loss may entail not only the resignation of Putin, but also the disintegration of Russia into separate uncontrolled states.

In this chapter, we state that, the portioned allocation of military assistance to Ukraine and their constant attempts to establish a negotiation process with the leader of Russia demonstrate the fear of Western countries to receive those vast uncontrolled territories with a mostly impoverished population and with even more inadequate leaders in command.

According to opposition Russian journalists, there are approximately 3,000 Chechen troops led by Ramzan Kadyrov in Moscow, which will try to take control of the decision-making center in the Kremlin at the first sign of Putin's weakness. Therefore, Putin who has quarreled with almost all highly developed countries except China has only one way. He is going for broke and realizes that he simply has no other choice.

Russia needs this conflict to guarantee its access to the sea via the Mediterranean and through Suez and Gibraltar to be able to access the great maritime routes. Russia could consider as its great area of influence the Mediterranean (Nechaev, Chikharev, Irkhin, & Makovskaya, 2019) that includes the Black and Azov seas.

THE ROOTS OF THE CONFLICT

Russia invades Ukraine on February 24th, 2022, starting a war that is analyzed differently depending on the belligerent side. With a cursory review it could seem that the conflict began in 2014 after the Euromaidan protests, impeachment of President Viktor Yanukovch, Russian annexation of Crimea and conflict in the Donbas region. The Minsk agreements signed among representatives of Russia, Ukraine, and the Donetsk and Lugansk People's Republics on September 5th, 2014, attempted to end the fighting in eastern Ukraine. The Russian President Vladimir Putin states that the Minsk agreements have been for nothing. Also, that he feels threatened by NATO's expansion to the East, saying that the red line not being tolerated by him is Ukraine's possible applying for NATO membership.

Therefore, a broader vision rooted directly from the agreements of the Western allied countries that won World War II and Gorbachev 2+4 Treaty is required.

The Treaty 2+4 quota; was signed in Moscow by the foreign ministers of the FRG, the GDR, and the four victorious powers in World War II: the USSR, the USA, Great Britain, and France. This document put an end to the division of Germany (Debasa, 2022). New borders were established, full sovereignty returned, and security issues clarified, including NATO membership, the reduction of the armed forces to 370.000 in a reunified Germany (up to that point, there were half a million troops only in Western Germany) and the withdrawal of the Soviet military from the former GDR.

The question of the existence of an agreement for the non-expansion of NATO into Eastern Europe, allegedly reached in some form during the negotiations between the USSR and the USA on the unification of Germany in 1990, is one of the conflicting moments in relations between Russia and NATO.

The Russian authorities claim that such an agreement took place orally and the alliance violated it by its expansion (Memorandum, 1990), while the leaders of the alliance claim that such a promise was not given and that such a decision could only be made in writing (Kaiser, 1991). In the scientific community, opinions about the existence or absence of an agreement on non-expansion also differ.

The former allies of the Soviet Union changed sides from friends to adversaries. Shortly after those agreements, the independence of Ukraine took place without Russia being asked. In 1991, a referendum was held to dissolve the Ukrainian Socialist Republic and proclaim its independence. In all Ukrainian provinces and regions, the votes exceeded 50% including Crimea, Kherson, Zaporizhian, Donetsk, Luhansk and Kharkiv.

Russia needs this post-Soviet colonialism for several reasons. The most outstanding is to maintain an image of world superpower facing the outside. Another one is that the President Putin tries to maintain a high rating for country´s population. In terms of globalization, Russia does not want to lose the influence on the seas inherited from the Soviet Union and its nuclear potential in the form of submarines and icebreakers. Control of Ukraine allows Russia an exit to the Mediterranean, a scenario that must be taken with caution by the European Union. Great Britain, being now outside the European Union, happens to maintain military bases on the island of Cyprus off the coast of Turkey. Likewise, Great Britain has the last colony that exists in Europe and that controls the exit from the Mediterranean, the Rock of Gibraltar. Mussolini's words were completely relevant when he said that Italy had to prey to the English in the Mediterranean Sea since they were controlling both accesses, the Gibraltar and the Suez Canal. Nowadays they no longer control the Suez Canal, but they maintain the military bases of Akrotiri and Dekelia in Cyprus, facing the Suez Canal and at the outlet of the Black Sea through the Dardanelles Strait (Debasa & Aznar, 2021).

Before the Russian-Ukrainian war, the Russian army was the second most powerful in the world. However, the excessive duration of the conflict and Russian defeats have revealed an old, no motivated and obsolete military structure. Some analysts maintain that China wants to take advantage of this position in order to show itself as the second world military power.

Vladimir Putin uses complex propaganda systems through television networks in some European countries. Germany has already banned them, but Spain did not, although the propaganda can be seen on Internet channels and on the YouTube platform all over the world. Through these systems he has intended to generate a European opinion favorable to his interests and contradicting Ukrainians' goals.

We could consider that the Russian-Ukrainian conflict conceived many years ago has been latent in these propaganda actions, and it could include the approach to relevant politicians in European countries. Those are the cases of the Austrian Foreign Minister Karin Kneissl, of right-wing ideas; also the German former chancellor Gerhard Schröder, a socialist, who finished his mandate and was hired by a Russian public oil company.

Russia no longer has support in Europe (may be only Hungary with its leader Victor Orban is an exception) and therefore must seek it in the East, especially in Iran, Syria, Eritrea, China and Northern Korea.

Russian neo-colonialism with an expansionist base is even leading to the denial of the existence of the Ukrainian nation and people, as happened with the Poles before the Second World War.

If Russia establishes a strong and solid union with Belarus, the Donets and Lugansk People's Republics, the Republic of Crimea and the area surrounding the Prussian city of Konisberg, renamed Kaliningrad after World War II, it will be only a few kilometers away from important European centers due to this enclave. This situation of confrontation with NATO could build a New Berlin wall that already exists de facto due to sanctions and create a new page of the Cold War which may be even more dangerous due to Putin's unpredictability.

These events pose a new type of the Colonial War due to the setting, the modern time and the media, in which conventional and nuclear warfare is joined by cybernetic and robotic warfare, drones and the data economy. The political regime of the modern world is faced with challenges every day. Colonial wars that were considered a thing of the past a short time ago have emerged with new force today, threatening to become the third world war. Before giving the analysis of the current situation that has been created in Europe we are going to discover what the Colonial War is and what characteristics it has.

Historical Background

The term "colonialism" has a moral, political, and legal weight because it implies that the separation of the peripheral territory of the State, called empire, is legitimate but the separation of the peripheral territory of the country called nation-state no longer exists.

The Colonial warfare is a general term that refers to the various armed conflicts that arose as a result of the settlement of overseas territories by foreign powers that established a colony (Miguel Maldueño, 2017). The term applies exclusively to conflicts in the colonies of Great Britain, France, Spain, Portugal, Denmark, and Holland which were fought in the 19th century by European armies in Africa and Asia.

The obstinacy and brutality with which the aggressor countries acted and continue to act in colonial wars, are due to the determination of each of the rival states to monopolize the spoils of the dependent states and, on the other hand, to the exceptional importance of colonial markets, which has usually managed to block foreign competition. In addition, the trade has always been unequal for the colonies and its profitability for the metropolis has increased with the advance of technological progress.

Moreover, the colonizers have often received the products of the colonial countries for free through direct looting. At the time of manufacturing capitalism development, the colonial states would gain commercial, maritime and colonial hegemony and thus provide the most favorable conditions for the development of their own industries. The conflicts associated with the republics of the former USSR do not officially fall under the definition of "Colonial War", what is a wrong opinion because not all the republics entered or left the USSR exclusively on a "voluntary" basis (Debasa, Andriichenko, & Popova, 2022).

A Civil War was started on purpose and citizens were gathered and colonized by force of the Caucasian regions that overthrew and seized power in Russia and the rest of the soviet territories. At the same time, they could be legally formalized as sovereign and independent countries but in fact they were suppressed by a stronger country using mercenaries from different nationalities to destabilize a weaker one, including collaborators, military equipment, weapons, special services, military overtly or covertly, propaganda based on national or language issues, etc.

All these characteristic features can be observed in the last armed conflict in central Europe. We are talking about the Russian invasion in Ukraine, considering it a Colonial War and not an armed conflict as some European politicians calls it. To justify our opinion, we will take a look at the 20th century. The Soviet Union was one of the last colonial empires in the modern world.

It collapsed in 1991 not because of an economic crisis or disillusionment with the dominant communist ideology, not because of the scarcity of products in supermarkets, not because of the difficulty of leaving the country, but because of the simultaneous attempts of its former Soviet republics to gain sovereignty. Russia became the successor to the USSR not only of goods but of colonial policy. The claim that the USSR was a colonial empire persisted throughout the post-Soviet period. The orientalist and political scientist Prazauskas wrote, a month and a half after the collapse of the USSR: "The Union of Indestructible Free Republics that has sunk into oblivion was undoubtedly an imperial-type formation" (Prazauskas, 1991).

The USSR by force and through total control held together a multi-tribal world, a kind of Eurasian panopticon of peoples who had nothing in common with each other except the generic properties of *Homo sapiens* and artificially created disasters. Like other empires in the Union, powerful imperial structures, an ideology and a quasi-class system of inequality developed.

If we analyze the history of this country, we can see that for centuries Tsarist Russia was an empire that tried to expand its territory at the expense of neighboring lands. Two stages of Russian colonialism can be indicated. The first lasted from the 11th to the 14th centuries, when the Moscow principality became the ancient predecessor of Russia (in years 1000-1150). The young princes of the Kyiv Rus's founded the cities that later became the nodal points of the Moscow principality: Vladimir, Suzdal, Ryazan and Moscow. The second stage began in the 16th century with the beginning of the overseas expeditions of Muscovites who wanted to expand in the north and east where they had captured the lands of the Ugrians in 1502 and they had taken Ryazan in 1520. Moscow conquered the Kazan Khanate in 1552 and the Astrakhan Khanate in 1556. It put an end to the existence of the Great Nogai Horde in 1557 and captured the Siberian Khanate in 1582. In time, these captures roughly coincide with the Spanish conquests in Central and South America: Haiti in 1496, Cuba and Puerto Rico in 1508, New Spain in 1519-1521, Peru and the Río de la Plata in 1535-1536 and Florida in 1565. But the Russians took much larger territories for themselves continuing their colonial policy into the next century. In1610, they captured the Piebald Horde, reaching the Yenisei River and they approached the Chinese border in the mid-17th century. Moscow had conquered all northeastern Eurasia up to the Bering Strait by 1689. After Mongol rule the Russians also adopted their enslavers methods.

Based on an assessment in terms of the total area subject to Moscow, the Russian Empire was the largest and longest lasting of all existing empires leaving behind the British and Roman Empires.

Tsarist Russia turned into the Soviet Union in the 1920s. The old imperial legacy merged again but already with the new communist ideology. Memories of the mighty empire led Soviet leaders to fight for the revival of "Imperial Russia", that resulted in the renewal of control over Central Asian territory and the restoration of central government authority over most imperial territories in 1922. It also led to reconciliation with Germany in 1939, after that western Belarus, western Ukraine and Bessarabia were quickly "liberated".

The three Baltic States were annexed by Soviet Russia in 1940. The incorporation of the semi-independent Republic of Tuva into the USSR in 1944 and East Prussia in 1945 were the last territorial acquisitions by the Soviets after which Moscow began to form puppet states throughout Central Europe.

During the Soviet period the communist government was aware of the incomplete character of the colonization of Siberia and the Far East, which represented about 20% of the country, and directed its policy to conquer these lands. There is a historical fact that took place a little before the beginning of the Second World War: Karl Burkhardt, who was the Commissioner of the League of Nations in Danzig, had a conversation with A. Hitler to find out about his objectives and, he told him directly, that he needed Ukraine. It has been revealed recently that the communist government offered Hitler part of the Ukrainian lands in the first days of the German-Soviet war (1941) to quell the conflict, but Hitler no longer wanted to negotiate.

The concept of colonial war is limited to a series of considerations, many of them historical, and based mainly on the territory. With this work we show that it is necessary to take into account the new scenarios with a high technological level, with a purely digital society, and where physical spaces transcend the metaverse. The new scenarios go through the digital society and this raises new questions. Is digital colonialism an old form of colonialism that has been updated? Can digital colonialism lead us to new colonial wars? (Elisabetha Demeshkova, Ivan Rudov, & Julia Afanasieva 2021).

MAIN FOCUS OF THE CHAPTER

Analyzing the current situation in Ukraine, it is necessary to understand first: how the new war has happened in the globalized world of the 21st century, when the memory of the two bloody world wars is still alive and how an aggression of unprecedented proportions has made possible.

Analogies with Nazi Germany of almost a century ago do not answer the question of its causes, although some associations with the consequences are already visible.

Vladimir Putin's regional reforms have turned Russia into a unified, bureaucratized, and corrupt neo-empire where many regions of the Federation have become internal colonies that are just appendages of the resources of the Russian Federation modern empire. One of the modern Russian ideologues, Dugin, in his book published in accordance with the decision of the Department of Sociology of International Relations of the Faculty of Sociology of Moscow State University, formulates the task of integrating Russia, Ukraine and Belarus into a single strategic space. And the integration of Ukraine is indicated as a necessary condition for the transformation of Russia into a global power (Dugin, 1999).

The Foundations of Geopolitics more openly formulates the principles of Russian neo-colonialism: Ukraine's existence within its current borders and its current status as a sovereign state is inadmissible to Russia. Consequently, after ten years of massive propaganda, the Russian population perceives the invasion of Ukraine and Putin's internal rating is growing.

Twenty years ago, Putin expressed his desire, first covertly and then openly, to revive the Soviet Union. He considers himself a "land collector' and treats other independent states that were part of the Soviet Union as temporarily lost, but as those that must be returned "home". This raises the question: can Ukraine really be considered a part of Russia? Most modern historians in their works prior to Russia's military aggression against Ukraine on February 24th, 2022, had viewed Russia as a colonial power with some caution and paid more attention to the analysis of classical imperial powers such as the British Empire, France, the Netherlands, and the United States.

Russia was still a somewhat mysterious country for them, and they saw it very indirectly. But, for example, the collapse of the USSR fits neatly into the late decolonization of the 1970s and 1980s, when there was a struggle against the apartheid regime and decolonization in the Caribbean. The collapse of the Soviet Union was also decolonization, though a very specific one.

Ukraine was a part of the Russian Empire but according to the established definition of the term it was not a colony. In our opinion, its certain industrial backwardness in comparison with the countries of Western Europe could be explained by its agricultural orientation. From the time of Tsarist Russia, the policy of forced Russification began to be applied to Ukrainians, which was continued by the Soviet leadership until the complete collapse of the USSR. This element can be considered inherent in the colonial policy, but at the same time heavy industry was built on the territory of Ukraine and Ukrainians held high positions in the central government. This fact contradicts the definition of colonial policy.

It is interesting to mention that in 1914 V. Lenin described the logic of separating Ukraine from Russia, as well as the fact that Russia should have had its own nation-state without subjects of other nationalities. In his speech, he pointed out that Russia "was getting everything" out of Ukraine but did not give anything instead. That statement could be interpreted as an acknowledgment of economic colonialism. However, Lenin's speech was never quoted or published in the USSR, as if it did not exist at all. Although he considered Ukraine and other dependent territories of Eastern Europe before the war as oppressed nations rather than colonies, the difference between them was, in his view, only in degree: the colonies had no capital as opposed to the oppressed nations.

The liberal Marxist political currents (Kautsky and Bernstein) marked Ukraine's status as a "European-type colony" at the end of the 20th century. Such colonies at that time were also Ireland, Finland, Slovakia and Poland. In 1895, the social democrat Yulian Bachinsky from Galitzia, published the book "Ukraine Irredenta" (1924) in which he complied with the demands of the Ukrainian conciliar state, based on an analysis of the most important economic events. In Bachinsky´s opinion, only political independence has prevented further successful social, economic and cultural development of the colony of two great empires, under whose influence Ukraine had been (Bachinsky, 1924).

The first step that Iósif Stalin made having come to power in the Soviet Union was power centralization. He ordered to kill everybody who tried to oppose to Bolsheviks. Thus, wide repressions helped to revive Russian imperial colonialism. The history of Ukraine, written in 1986 by a scientist living out of the country, reveals that the country was a colony within the USSR (Subtelny, 2009). Some historians supported this opinion, representing the Soviet Ukraine and the republics which entered the warehouse of the USSR earlier and then gained independence as colonies.

Russia hangs on itself the image of the "older brother" and made everything to be considered the motherland of the unity of 15 sisters, but with the head of the greater Russia. Making all the republics use Russian language, it tried to promote the entire foundation of the Soviet Union through propaganda materials imposed by Moscow.

From the beginning of Soviet Union´s founding a clear centralization of vertical power was pushed in it. To maintain such decision the principal executives of the republics were to go to Moscow. All the numerous local insurrections which rose on the territory of the USSR were severely suppressed and that information never appeared in mass media. All the republics united by Russia were seen by the Kremlin as colonial raw materials appendages, while the official political doctrine and propaganda obviously staggered the common discourses.

Russia's first military intervention began immediately after the collapse of the Soviet Union, when, due to ethnic conflicts, it tried to suppress the shoots of freedom and independence of the republics that left the USSR, by a long-known method, to capture and govern.

The war in Nagorno-Karabakh between Azerbaijan and Armenia can be considered the first serious military conflict on the territory of the Soviet Empire. The roots of the conflict between the Christians of Armenia and the Muslims of Azerbaijan are lost in the depth of centuries and have more than 1500 years of history. But at the start of the war in 1988, the population of Nagorno-Karabakh was overwhelmingly Armenian. They wanted to join Armenia which supported that desire.

Then there was Transnistria, Georgia, two Chechen wars, the annexation of Crimea and Donbas and it is the whole Ukraine now.

In our opinion, December 11st, 1994 can be considered Russia's first serious step towards neo-colonialism. It was the day when the First Chechen War began in the North Caucasus, which Russian propagandists called the "First Chechen Campaign". Russia´s troops and the self-proclaimed republic of Ichkeria began to fight for the territory. Despite the enormous military and technical superiority of Russia, this bloody war lasted for two years. It is unknown how many Russian and Chechen soldiers were killed in the clashes at that time. According to various estimations, as a result of the hostilities the lives of from 3.860 to 14.000 soldiers of the Russian Armed Forces were claimed.

Thousands of people, both military and civilian, simply disappeared. Dzhokhar Dudayev declared the independence of the Republic of Ichkeria on June 8th, 1991. He accused Russia of having a colonialist policy, called for the abolition of state structures and the withdrawal of Ichkeria from Russia. Four months later, when elections were held in the self-proclaimed republic, Dudayev officially became the President of Ichkeria (Ahsan Habib, 2001). Russian deputies declared the elections illegal and imposed a state of emergency on the territory. The corresponding decree was signed by then President Boris Yeltsin. The Supreme Soviet of the Russian Federation decided to withdraw Russian military units and units of the Ministry of Internal Affairs.

On September 30, 1999, in an interview with the Russian daily newspaper "Kommersant" Russian Prime Minister Vladimir Putin said that there would be no new war with Chechnya. The war called officially the anti-terrorist operation lasted more than 10 years and claimed the lives of more than 20.000 soldiers and 125.000 civilians. Despite a significant advantage, as noted above, Russia was still defeated in the First Chechen War on August 31, 1996, and was forced to conclude a peace agreement under which Russian troops withdrew from the Chechen Republic of Ichkeria and the provisions on interstate relations between the Chechen Republic and the Russian Federation were postponed until 2001. Many influential Russian political and military circles of the so-called "war party" considered that state of affairs shameful for such a powerful colonial power. It was also feared that the "bad" example of an independent Chechnya might be followed by other national autonomies within the Russian Federation.

However, the "war party's" quota was not dominant in President Boris Yeltsin's entourage. It was only after the 1998 default when Russia's economy collapsed and the government was headed by Vladimir Putin after numerous reshuffles.

The idea of a quick victorious war was considered to help society´s consolidation and separatism prevention. To solve those problems, Putin resorted to the FSB's favorite trick, creating a terrible pretext "under someone else's flag". It could be a real or staged attack by one side of the conflict, in which it blamed the other. Enemy symbols, paraphernalia, equipment and weapons might be used during such operations, the purpose of which were to discredit the opponent, accuse him of aggression and even create a pretext for war. Such attacks got their name in the 16th century, when pirates "disguised" their ships, raised the official flags of some states and then attacked peaceful ships or cities.

To bring the idea to life, a series of explosions were carried out in an apartment building on the Kashirsky highway in Moscow on September 13rd, 1999 at 5 o´clock in the morning. The explosion took place in the basement of an 8-storey brick residential building n. 6. The capacity of the explosive device was 300 kilograms. Since the house was made of brick, it was completely destroyed as a result of the explosion and, almost everyone, who lived in it was killed. Russia immediately blamed the Chechens. That served as the beginning of a new military invasion of Ichkeria. But the official version of the explosions is highly disputed by experts, and after careful investigation most of them are inclined to believe that it was the Russian authorities that caused that tragedy to blame Chechnya. Having a reason, a press conference was called after the explosions and journalists asked Putin what he was going to do. The President responded immediately: "Wet them in the toilets". That phrase became very popular among Russian society and turned into the slogan of the Invading War against Chechnya.

Russian troops began the massive shelling of Grozny and its surroundings, and on September 30th, 1999 they entered Chechnya. Using artillery and aircraft, the Russians occupied a third of the republic on October 16th and had controlled the entire plain by December. The siege of the capital Grozny began on December 26th and lasted until February 6th, 2000; the assault on the city cost the lives of about 2.5 thousand Russian soldiers. The loss of civilians was terrible, tens of thousands of people, and the city itself was almost completely destroyed. The resistance center of the Russian troops moved to the mountains in the spring of 2000, where active guerrilla action took place.

By the end of 2004, after the destruction of most of the field commanders, guerrilla activity in Chechnya had subsided and on April 16th, 2009, the Second Chechen War was considered to be over. The republic was proclaimed as the inalienable part of Russia. Akhmat Kadyrov was appointed as the president of Chechnya, but he did not rule for a long time. He was killed in a terrorist attack seven month later in 2004. His son Ramzan Kadyrov after a series of intrigues and tricks was proclaimed as the new president of Chechnya in 2007. Most of the armed conflicts that took place at the end of the 20th century, beginning of the 21st, took place exclusively within one state or another and did not spread to neighboring countries. The conflicting parties usually faced negative consequences, in particular, refugees' influx or catastrophic fluctuations in energy prices and basic needs.

If we take the countries that were part of the Soviet empire, the examples of such a conflict are the events in Kazakhstan, on the eve of the beginning of Russia's aggression against Ukraine, or the long military territorial disputes between Azerbaijan and Armenia. The conflicts have local limits and do not go beyond them.

In the first case, the Kazakh authorities cracked down on opposition forces also with the help of Russia. The Russian army entered Kazakhstan under the banner of bringing order to the country, at the request of President Kasim Jormat Tokayev. He addressed Putin directly when the situation in the country got out of hand. After the brutal suppression of the uprising, Putin seemed to expected something different from the "friendly" Kazakh leader because Russian media called for another "liberation" of the predominantly Russian-populated region of northern Kazakhstan. Russian parliamentarians also joined. For example, the chairman of the Committee on Education and Science of the Russian State Duma (by the way, grandson of the head of the Stalinist Foreign Ministry V. Molotov) said that Kazakhstan had not existed before, North Kazakhstan was not inhabited, and the entire territory of modern Kazakhstan was a gift given by generous Russia during the Soviet Union period to Kazakh nomads. The Russian side also reported that the Russian soldiers who participated in the resolution of the conflict would remain in Kazakhstan as peacekeepers and permanent observers.

The same rhetoric, but from President Putin, was heard about Ukraine a month later. But unlike Ukraine, Kazakhstan is more fortunate. The interests of China and Turkey are concentrated in Kazakhstan, and the two countries watched the turbulent events of early 2022 with concern. In our opinion, China is not interested in strengthening Russia's position in Kazakhstan, and that is why, after defusing the situation, the Chinese Foreign Ministry issued a statement containing a veiled demand for Russia to withdraw its troops from the country. Putin did not dare to go against Xi Jinping and the Russian soldiers returned to their barracks.

We can say that Ukraine's war against Russian aggression is exceptional because it takes place during the existence of mobile devices, social networks and the Internet. All enemy movements are immediately recorded by drones, satellite communications and video surveillance. At the very beginning of the Russian aggression, the Ukrainian military appealed to the population through social networks, asking for help in locating the movement of one or another enemy column. Today, soldiers, using new technologies, can show the whole world what is really happening in the zone of military conflict (Zijderveld, den Bol, & Zwick, 2022).

We must not forget that Putin's Russian imperial claims to Ukrainian territory began much earlier and were demonstrated eight years ago. Taking advantage of the situation during the 2014 revolution in Ukraine, Russia seized some territory in the Donetsk and Lugansk regions and carried out an almost bloodless annexation of the Crimean peninsula. On March 16th, 2014, the so-called "referendum" was held in Crimea, after which the Crimean Peninsula was occupied by the Russian Federation. Subsequently, the British Foreign Office posted on Twitter five reasons why Ukraine or the international community did not recognize it. Ukrainian and international publications have taken the word "referendum" in stride since that time, emphasizing that there was an occupation in Crimea, but not as a legitimate expression of the people´s will.

One of the reasons for the illegality of the referendum was that it violated the Ukrainian Constitution. Russia, based on paragraph 10 of Article 138 of the Constitution of Ukraine, legalized the "Crimean referendum", arguing that according to that paragraph, local referendums in Crimea were possible. However, if we read article 73 of the Ukrainian Constitution, it states that the question of changing the territory of Ukraine is decided exclusively in an all-Ukrainian referendum. Therefore, according to the Constitution of Ukraine, the referendum held in 2014 was not legal. This contradicts the State Constitution.

Putin's colonial imperial claims are not limited to Ukraine. At different historical moments, taking advantage of one or another circumstance, Russia annexed many neighboring territories. Almost all the states that border Russia have lost part of their territory. If you look at the modern borders of Russia, you can see that it has several countries, including Ukraine, Belarus, Kazakhstan, USA, Georgia, China, Poland and others. The Kremlin has territorial claims, veiled or open, over almost all of them. But it is understandable that, on the contrary, most of these countries should present their territorial claims to the Kremlin.

As for Georgia, the Russian-Georgian conflict has been going on since the early 1990s when Abkhazia and South Ossetia decided to lose control of Tbilisi (with the support of Moscow). In 2008 the conflict escalated into the Russian- Georgian war, whereby Russia seized part of the territory of a sovereign state and created these pseudo-republics. For example, Georgian-controlled South Ossetia and Abkhazia had come under Russian protectorate until the early 1990s through a direct military operation. Later the conflict turned into the Russian-Georgian war in 2008, coursed by blackmail which Putin liked to use. That war lasted on August 5th and ended with Georgia losing part of its territory. The well-known Russian opposition journalist Arkady Babchenko described it as a victorious little war which significantly raised the rating of puppet president Dmitry Medvedev, a Putin´s protégé who at the time was at the forefront of deja vu.

The Abkhaz enclave was created with the help of Russia and has territorial claims on it. In particular we are talking about the village of Aibga through which the border between Russia and Abkhazia passes. The Abkhazians in their claims refer to Soviet laws, according to which the people were Abkhazians. Now the former deputy speaker of the Abkhaz parliament, Irina Agrba, has even called the issue "a test of trust and friendship" between Moscow and Sukhumi.

Even Lukashenko in October 2014 during a speech in Minsk at a press conference for Russian and regional media, recalled that "part of the lands of Pskov, Smolensk and Bryansk belonged to Belarus" (Kalinovsky, 2014). He expressed claims about the Kaliningrad region which, according to him, the BSSR should have received after the war because it was "not Russia".

Putin planned to recreate such a small victorious war in Ukraine based on the data received by his agents acting on the territory of Ukraine. And this intention has been exactly what led to a big mistake. The Russian leadership has allocated a large amount of agents to create an intelligence base in Ukraine for last 5 years. One of the leaders of the process was Putin's godfather, the Ukrainian politician Viktor Medvedchuk who was also the leader of the pro-Russian opposition party. It was represented in the Ukrainian parliament by a large faction of the Opposition Bloc. The leaders of the intelligence units took Russian money and informed his sponsor about his enormous contribution to building pro-Russian sentiment among the citizens of Ukraine. His agents cheated Putin and stole all the money intended for Russian propaganda. Before the military conflict, this political force had a significant following among the population of eastern Ukraine, including Kharkiv, Zaporizhia, and Mariupol. But after February 24th the number of supporters of the "Russian world" even in those pro-Russian regions dropped to almost zero. After the destruction of 90 percent of Mariupol and Kharkiv, which is bombed every day, even the most ardent supporters of Putin have changed their attitude towards Russia.

One of the reasons for the failure of Putin's blitzkrieg which he was sure would take Kyiv in three days was the misinformation of his intelligence network in Ukraine, which assured him that Russian soldiers would be received with flowers, the army would not be able to resist, and President Zelensky would flee on the first day of the war. There is a confirmed fact that several high-ranking Russian military and civilian officials, on the eve of the February 23rd attack, booked in Kyiv restaurants for February 25th to celebrate the victory. When going through the things of the deceased Russian soldiers during the first weeks of the invasion, Ukrainians found the festive military uniform. That says that those soldiers were preparing to take part in the military parade in occupied Kyiv.

Announcing the decision to recognize the Donetsk and Lugansk republics in February 22sd 2022, Putin delivered a speech that lasted almost an hour in which, among many other accusations and claims, he declared that "Ukraine, in fact, never had a stable tradition of its true state", arose "as a result of Bolshevik policy and therefore today the entire Ukraine could be called in honor of Vladimir Ilyich Lenin". Putin attacked the European Union and the United States with a series of aggressive rebukes, threats and taunts, calling them "the so-called civilized world" and he continued: "the only representatives of which our Western colleagues have declared themselves". He in fact accused Gorbachev of "disintegrating historical Russia under the name of the USSR" and, not without regret, claimed that that was due to "historical and strategic errors of the Bolshevik leaders and the leadership of the communist party." Vladimir Putin made several direct threats against Ukraine (including the comment "Do you want decommunization? Well, we agree. But we don't need to stop halfway. We are ready to show you what real decommunization means for Ukraine", as well as the end of the speech: "Those who seized and hold power in Kyiv, we demand an immediate cessation of hostilities (albeit led by the Russian side). Otherwise, all responsibility for the possible continuation of bloodshed will fall entirely in the conscience of the ruling regime in Ukraine". In this speech the list of claims to Ukraine was surprising (Putin, 2022).

It can be compared with the world of George Orwell described in his famous work "1984". The main one we have already mentioned, and it is that Ukraine was created by Lenin. The second was that Ukraine wanted nothing to do with the common past with Russia and tried to be a member of the European Union and NATO. These factors show that we are right in our hypothesis when we speak of the war between Ukraine and Russia as a colonial war in modern circumstances.

POSSIBLE SCENARIOS AND FUTURE RESEARCH

It is not known where the Russian-Ukrainian military conflict may lead. It could be understood as a conflict between East and West (Gutiérrez, López, & González, 2023) in which the weapons of classical propaganda and manipulation appear; but developed in new scenarios such as the digital of social networks (ElHawary, 2022) and the immediate offered by the Internet. The authors have identified four possible scenarios without going into assessing what the conflict should be.

The first option for ending the military confrontation is a frozen conflict on the model of two North and South Koreas with a line of demarcation at the points of the occupied territories after February 24, which risks resuming with even greater intensity in a few years when Russia restores its reserves. The second option is the expulsion of Russia from the territory of Ukraine and a return to the borders that existed at the time of February 24, 2022. The third option is the complete seizure of the territory of Ukraine by Russia and its proclamation as part of Russian territory. And, finally, the fourth option, is the complete liberation of Ukraine from Russian troops, including Crimea and the entire Donbass.

The research can be continued in deep analysis of possible geopolitical, demographic and economic consequences of the Russian-Ukrainian post-colonial war for European, Eastern and American countries, which are inevitable. Also, another question is the existence of Russia, and not only it, as a big colonial empire in confrontation with other world powers and the relations among them.

We can affirm that there are concerns confronted after the hypothetical resolution of the conflict, such as social wounds, war crimes (Nantawaroprai 2022) and environmental damage (Pereira, Bašić, Bogunovic, & Barcelo, 2022). All this without taking into account a hypothetical nuclear disaster not addressed in this work.

CONCLUSION

Of the scenarios presented, the authors consider that the most plausible scenarios are the first two. A chronic conflict with diffuse borders or a return to the borders of February 24, 2022. Due to the internationalization of the conflict, a total disappearance of the Ukrainian State is not expected, although a situation of fragmentation of the territory could be found in the future.

The evolution of the story in Putin's speech that points to the West as guilty of the war is significant, where he also specifies that it is influenced by modern "woke" ideologies that, according to Putin, have been imposed in Europe and America. In some Eurasian countries Putin is perceived as the guarantor of classical traditions.

In the construction of the story of the dramatic arc, Putin has modified the enemy of the war that has gone from being Ukrainian nationalism to becoming the entire NATO bloc. Including NATO instead of an isolated country is a safeguard for Putin in case he loses the conflict. It will present the defeat as a conflict with the United States and its NATO allies instead of a single country like Ukraine. As a result of the foregoing, there are indications that Russia is preparing a defeat since, in the eyes of the people, losing to NATO is not ashamed as it would be to do so against Ukraine. Putin could show as a victory uniting Kherson and part of Zaporizhzhia to Russia.

Colonial wars are aimed at controlling physical territory for different reasons. The colonial war transcends the old scenarios and this work proposes that digital scenarios and social networks be taken into account as new spaces for propaganda actions. That is why in these conflicts cybersecurity plays a leading responsibility.

The prominent role of control of the seas and their access through channels and straits, necessary for world trade, is significant and little discussed.

The need for Russia to guarantee small fragments of Ukrainian territory allows it to consolidate the exit to the Mediterranean Sea and begin construction of the so-called Greater Mediterranean, which includes the Black and Azov seas.

REFERENCES

Aguirre, Y., & Diego, J. R. (2008). *La última guerra colonial de España*. Editorial Algazara.

Amo B., (2009) *Humo y estrellas. Sidi Ifni, la guerra ignorada*. Editorial Nemira, s.l.

Asenjo España, J. M. (2003). *Sidi Ifni (A.O.E.): años felices, años inquietos 1953-1958*. Asenjo.

Azcona Pastor, J. M. (2019). *Historia del Tiempo Presente*. Ediciones URJC Santander Presdeia.

Bachinsky, Y. (1924). *Ukraine Irredenta*. Rady.

Baker (1988) *US-Soviets; Have Made Substantial Progress. Press conference in Moscow*. Public Diplomacy Query.

Balf Barkawi, T. and Laffey, M. (2018). *Democracy, liberalism, and war: Rethinking the democratic peace debate*. A text in time edition.

Debasa, F. (2022). *Algorithms, Social Rejection, and Public Administrations in the Current World. Handbook of Research on Artificial Intelligence in Government Practices and Processes.* IGI Global.

Debasa, F., Andriichenko, Y., & Popova, N. (2022). Ukrainian Social Realities and Emotivities in the Political Speeches of Yuliia Tymoshenko: A Data-Based Approach. In *Handbook of Research on Artificial Intelligence in Government Practices and Processes* (pp. 264–283). IGI Global. doi:10.4018/978-1-7998-9609-8.ch015

Debasa, F., & Sánchez, T. A. (2021). El discurso político de la presidencia Trump antes del Covid. *Historia Actual Online, 56*, 21–34.

Demeshkova, E., Rudov, I., & Afanasieva, J. (2021). Digital cultural colonialism: Measuring bias in aggregated digitized content held in Google Arts and Culture. *Digital Scholarship in the Humanities, 36*(3), 607–640. doi:10.1093/llc/fqaa055

DuginA. (1999). *Основы геополитики. Геополитическое будущее.* России: АРКТОГЕЯ – центр.

ElHawary, D. M. M. (2022). *TikTok Battlefield: Comparative Analysis of English and Arabic Language Representations of The 2022 Russian Ukrainian Conflict On TikTok.*

Fraser, A. (2019). Curating digital geographies in an era of data colonialism. *Geoforum, 104*, 193–200. doi:10.1016/j.geoforum.2019.04.027

Gutiérrez, F. C., López, F. O., & González, A. L. (2023). Lawfare or the War Behind the Curtains: An Analysis of the Russian-Ukrainian Conflict. In *Handbook of Research on War Policies, Strategies, and Cyber Wars* (pp. 239–255). IGI Global. doi:10.4018/978-1-6684-6741-1.ch013

Habib, A. (2001). *Chechen Refugees: A Forgotten History of Caucasus; Who Remembers and Who Cares?* Green University of Bangladesh.

Hegre, H., Ellingsen, T., Gates, S., & Petter, N. Gleditsch. (. (2001). Towards a democratic civil peace: Democracy, democratization, and civil war 1834-1992. *The American Political Science Review, 95*(1), 33–48. doi:10.1017/S0003055401000119

Henderson, E. A. (2002). *Democracy and war: The end of an illusion.* Lynne Rienner.

Hermann, M. G., & Kegley, C. W. Jr. (1998). The US use of military intervention to promote democracy: Evaluating the record. *International Interactions, 24*(2), 91–114. doi:10.1080/03050629808434922

Kaiser, K. (1991). Deutschlands Vereinigung. Die internationalen Aspekte. Mit den wichtigsten Dokumenten. Bergisch Gladbach.

Kalinovsky, V. (2014). *Lukashenko accuses Russia and says he is Ukrainian.* Euromaidan Press.

Kwet, M. (2019). Digital colonialism: US empire and the new imperialism in the Global South. *Race & Class, 60*(4), 3–26. doi:10.1177/0306396818823172

Madueño, M. (2017). Aproximación al concepto y tipologías de la guerra colonial. *Guerra Colonial, 1*, 7–26.

Magocsi, P. E. (2010). *A History of Ukraine: The Land and Its Peoples.* University of Toronto Press.

Mann, M. (2001). *Democracy and ethnic war. Democracy, liberalism, and war: Rethinking the democratic peace debate.* Lynne Rienner.

Maoz, Z., & Russett, B. (1993). Normative and structural causes of democratic peace, 1946-86. *The American Political Science Review, 87*(3), 623–638. doi:10.2307/2938740

Memorandum of conversation between Mikhail Gorbachev and James Baker in Moscow. (1990). U.S. Department of State, FOIA.

Memorandum of conversation between Robert Gates and Vladimir Kryuchkov in Moscow. (1990). George H.W. Bush Presidential Library.

Nantawaroprai, D. (2022). Role of the International Criminal Court in War Crimes, Crimes against Humanity, and Acts of Aggression by Threats of the Usage of Nuclear Weapons under International Law "Jus Cogens". *Journal of Positive School Psychology*, pp. 5567-5576.

Nechaev, V. D., Chikharev, I. A., Irkhin, A. A., & Makovskaya, D. V. (2019). Framework of the geostrategic atlas of the greater mediterranean. *Vestnik Moskovskogo universiteta. Seriya* 5. *Geografiya, 1,* 67–74.

Pereira, P., Bašić, F., Bogunovic, I., & Barcelo, D. (2022). Russian-Ukrainian war impacts the total environment. *The Science of the Total Environment,* 837–865. PMID:35569661

Prazauskas, A. (1991). Ethnic conflicts in the context if democratizing political systems. *Theory and Society, 20*(5), 581–602. doi:10.1007/BF00232661

Putin, V. (2022) *Address by the President of the Russian Federation.* Kremlin. http://en.kremlin.ru/events/president/news

Rodríguez Esteban, J. A. (1996). *Geografía y colonialismo. La Sociedad Geográfica de Madrid (1876-1936).* Ediciones de la Universidad Autónoma de Madrid.

Segura Valero, G. (2006). *Ifni. La guerra que silenció Franco,* Ediciones Martínez Roca, S.A.

Snider, T. (2022) The war in Ukraine is a colonial war. *The New Yorker. s*https://www.newyorker.com/news/essay

Subtelny Orest. (2009) Ukraine. A History. University of Toronto Press.

Vanhanen, T. (2000). A new dataset for measuring democracy, 1810-1998.

Wylegala, A., & Glowacka-Grajper, M. (2019). *The Burden of the Past: History, Memory, and Identity in Contemporary Ukraine.* Indiana University Press.

Zijderveld, A., den Bol, L., & Zwick, S. (2022). How social media proves to be a vital instrument in times of war in the year 2022. *Shaping Europe. Ideas to bring the European Union forward.* https://shapingeurope.eu/en/

Compilation of References

Abbott, P., & Botham, P. (1986). *Modern African Wars (I): Rhodesia 1965-80*. Osprey Publishing.

ABC (periódico español) ADMAE--> *Archives Diplomatiques du Ministère des Affaires Étrangères* AGA--> Archivo General de la Administración BOE--> Boletín Oficial del Estado (España) BOECPRFM--> *Bulletin Officiel de l'Empire Chérifien. Protectorat de la République Française au Maroc*

Abdi, S. Y. (1981). Decolonization in the Horn and the outcome of Somali aspirations for self-determination, *Northeast African Studies, 2/3*(3/1), 153-162. https://www.jstor.org/stable/43660063

Admiralstab der Marine. (1905). *Das Marine-Expeditionskorps in Südwest-Afrika während des Herero-Aufstandes* [*The Marine Expeditionary Corps in South-West Africa during the Herero Uprising*]. Mittler.

Advisory Opinion, I. C. J. (1971). Legal consequences for states of the continued presence of South Africa in Namibia (South West Africa) notwithstanding. *Security Council Resolution 276* (1970). https://www.icj-cij.org/en/case/53/advisory-opinions

Affaya, N., & Gerraoui, D. (2005). *La imagen de España en Marruecos [The image of Spain in Morocco]*. CIDOB.

Afonso, A., & Gomes, C. M. (2005). *Guerra Colonial*. Editorial Notícias.

Ageron, C. R. (1973). *Politiques coloniales au Maghreb [Colonial policies in the Maghreb]*. Presses Universitaires de France.

Ageron, Ch.-R. (1978). *France coloniale ou parti colonial? [Colonial France or colonial party?]* Presses Universitaires de France.

Agnew, J. (2005). *Geopolítica. Una re-visión de la política mundial*. Trama.

Aguirre, Y., & Diego, J. R. (2008). *La última guerra colonial de España*. Editorial Algazara.

Akpan, M. B. (1985). Liberia and Ethiopia, 1880-1914: the survival of two African states. In A. Adu Bohaen (Ed.), General History of Africa VII: Africa under colonial domination 1880-1935, (pp. 249-282). UNESCO.

Albi de la Cuesta, J. (2018). *Españoles a Marruecos! La Guerra de África, 1859-1860 [Spaniards in Morocco! The African War, 1859-1860]*. Desperta Ferro.

Alburquerque, G. (2020). *Tercermundismo y No Alineamiento en América Latina durante la Guerra Fría*. Santiago de Chile, Ediciones Inubicalistas.

Alcamo, I. (2019). *Somalia between colonialism and trusteeship: the Italian experience and its legacy*, [Master's thesis, Luiss]. http://tesi.luiss.it/26626/1/082152_ALCAMO_IGNAZIO.pdf

Aldrich, R. (1996). *Greater France. A History of French Overseas Expansion*. Palgrave Macmillan.

Alonso, M. (1971). El ejército en la sociedad Española [The Army in Spanish Society]. *Ediciones del movimiento [Movement Issues]*.

Altamira, R. (1916). *Cuestiones internacionales: España, América y los Estados Unidos [International issues: Spain, America and the United States.]*. Jaime Ratés.

Altamira, R. (1932). Observaciones sobre la realidad internacional presente (writting in 1925) [Observations on the present international reality (writing in 1925).]. In R. Altamira (Ed.), *Cuestiones internacionales y de pacifism [International issues and pacifism.]*. C. Bermejo.

Ameller, V. (1861). *Juicio crítico de la Guerra de África o apuntes para la historia contemporánea [Critical judgment of the African War or notes for contemporary history.]*. Francisco Abienzo Press.

Amo B., (2009) *Humo y estrellas. Sidi Ifni, la guerra ignorada*. Editorial Nemira, s.l.

Anaya, J. (1996). *Indigenous peoples in international law*. Oxford University Press.

Anaya, J., & Puig, S. (2017). Mitigating state sovereignty: The duty to consult with indigenous peoples. *University of Toronto Law Journal, 67*(4), 435–464. doi:10.3138/utlj.67.1

Angell, N. (1913). *The Great Illusion*. G.P. Putnam & Sons.

Antunes, J. F. (1995). *A Guerra de África (1961-1974)*. Círculo de Leitores.

Aragón, M. (dir.) (2013). El Protectorado español en Marruecos: la historia trascendida [The Spanish Protectorate in Morocco: the transcended history,], vols. I, II, III. Iberdrola.

Aránguez, J. C. (2017). El factor nacionalista en el proceso descolonizador afroasiático de mediados del siglo XX [The nationalist factor in the Afro-Asian decolonization process of the mid-twentieth century.]. En Ferrer, C. (coords.). Fronteras contemporáneas: identidades, pueblos, mujeres y poder. Actas del V Encuentro de Jóvenes Investigadores en Historia Contemporánea [Contemporary borders: identities, peoples, women and power. Proceedings of the V Meeting of Young Researchers in Contemporary History], Vol. 2, 19-31. Bellaterra.

Aránguez, J. C. (2019). *España y Francia frente al desafío del nacionalismo en el Protectorado de Marruecos (1930-1956): tensiones internacionales y conflictos internos [Spain and France facing the challenge of nationalism in the Protectorate of Morocco (1930-1956): international tensions and internal conflicts.]*. [Thesis Doctoral, La Universidad Complutense de Madrid].

Araujo, R. (1947). Portugal: the country that has contributed most the geographic knowledge of the globe. Litografia Nacional Assambleia Nacional.

Archibugi, D. (2003). A critical analysis of the self – determination of peoples: A cosmopolitan perspective. *Constellations (Oxford, England), 10*(4), 488–505. doi:10.1046/j.1351-0487.2003.00349.x

Archives Nationales. (1960). *Allocutions et discours de Charles de Gaulle (1944-1969; Communiqué non diffusé, faisant suite à la déclaration du maréchal Tito, président de la République de Yougoslavie, à l'ONU [National Archives; Allocutions and speeches by Charles de Gaulle (1944-1969; Unpublished communiqué, following the declaration of Marshal Tito, President of the Republic of Yugoslavia, at the UN]*. Archives Nationales.

Archives Nationales. (1969). *Allocutions et discours de Charles de Gaulle (1944-1969); Toast adressé à Mika Spiljak, président du Conseil exécutif fédéral de Yougoslavie, déjeuner, palais de l'Élysée, [peeches and speeches by Charles de Gaulle (1944-1969); Toast addressed to Mika Spiljak, President of the Federal Executive Council of Yugoslavia, lunch, Élysée Palace]*. Archives Nationales.

Arconada Ledesma, P. (2020). Brief review of the processes of resistance against colonization in the Horn of Africa. Struggles in Italian Somalia and the Dervish Movement (1890-1930). *Studia Historica. Historia Contemporánea*, (38), 245–266. https://dialnet.unirioja.es/servlet/articulo?codigo=7676254

Arconada Ledesma, P. (2020). El proceso de descolonización en Yibuti: entre la influencia de Francia y la disputa etíope-somalí (1958-1977) [The descolonization process in Yibuti: between the influence of France and the Ethiopian-Somali dispute (1958-1977).]. In C. García Andrés, J. Cuadrado Bolaños, & P. Arconada Ledesma (Eds.), *África, un continente en transformación. Enfoques interdisciplinares [Africa, a continent in transformation. Enfoques interdisciplinares]* (pp. 87–103). Ediciones Universidad de Valladolid.

Arenal, C. del (1979). *La teoría de las relaciones internacionales en España [The theory of international relations in Spain.]*. International Law Association (Sección Española).

Arhiv Jugoslavije [Archives of Yugoslavia]. (1958). Fond number 142; Materijali komisije za društvene organizacije (društvene organizacije, savezi i udruženja); Materijali o radu jugoslovenskog crvenog krsta [Fund number 142; Materials of the commission for social organizations (social organizations, alliances and associations); Materials on the work of the Yugoslav Red Cross]. Archives of Yugoslavia.

Arhiv Jugoslavije [Archives of Yugoslavia]. (1959). Fond number 142; Materijali komisije za međunarodne veze saveznog odbora SSRNJ; Materijali sa sastanaka komisije za međunarodne veze so SSRNJ [Fund number 142; Materials of the commission for international relations of the federal board of SSRNJ; Materials from the meetings of the commission for international relations with SSRNJ]. Arhiv Jugoslavije [Archives of Yugoslavia].

Asenjo España, J. M. (2003). *Sidi Ifni (A.O.E.): años felices, años inquietos 1953-1958*. Asenjo.

Asworth, L. M. (2006). Where are the idealists in interwar international relations? *Review of International Studies*, *32*(2), 291–308. doi:10.1017/S0260210506007030

Asworth, L. M. (2014). *A History of international thought. From the origins of the modern state to academic international relations*. Routledge. doi:10.4324/9781315772394

Atkinson, D. (2005). Constructing Italian Africa: Geography and Geopolitics. In R. Ben-Ghiat & M. Fuller (Eds.), *Italian Colonialism* (pp. 15–27). Palgrave Macmillan. doi:10.1007/978-1-4039-8158-5_2

Azcona Pastor, J. M. (2019). *Historia del Tiempo Presente*. Ediciones URJC Santander Presdeia.

Azcona, J. M., Rodríguez, A., & Azaola, G. (1994). La Guerra de Sidi Ifni-Sahara (1957-1958) [The Sidi Ifni-Sahara War (1957-1958).]. *Estudios de Ciencias Sociales [Social Science Studies]*, 7, 68–91.

Bachinsky, Y. (1924). *Ukraine Irredenta*. Rady.

Bachoud, A. (1988). *Los españoles ante las campañas de Marruecos [The Spanish before the Moroccan campaigns]*. Espasa-Calpe.

Bai, S. (Ed.). (2008). *An outline history of China*. Foreign Languages Press.

Baker (1988) *US-Soviets; Have Made Substantial Progress. Press conference in Moscow*. Public Diplomacy Query.

Balance Militar. (1978). *Revista Ejército*, 461.

Balance Militar. (1979). *Revista Ejército*, 478.

Balance Militar. (1980). *Revista Ejército*, 490.

Balf Barkawi, T. and Laffey, M. (2018). *Democracy, liberalism, and war: Rethinking the democratic peace debate.* A text in time edition.

Balfour, S. (2007) España, Marruecos y las grandes potencias, 1898-1914 [Spain, Morocco and the great powers, 1898-1914]. In Gómez-Ferrer, G. & Sánchez, R. (eds.) Modernizar España. Proyectos de reforma y apertura internacional (1898-1914) [Modernize Spain. Reform projects and international opening (1898-1914)] (pp. 143-151). Biblioteca Nueva.

Barbe, A. (2016). *Public debt and European expansionism in Morocco from 1860 to 1956.* [Unpublished doctoral dissertation, Paris School of Economics, France].

Barrios, L. (1893). Importancia de la historia de las campañas irregulares y en especial de la Guerra de Cuba: conferencia dada el 13 de febrero de 1893 por D [Importance of the history of irregular campaigns and especially of the Cuban War: lecture given on February 13, 1893 by D]. Comandante de Estado Mayor. Centro del Ejército y de la Armada [Commander of Staff. Army and Navy Center].

Barroso, L. F. M. (2014). The independence of Rhodesia in Salazar's strategy for Southern Africa. *The American Historical Review, 46*(2), 1–24. doi:10.1080/17532523.2014.943922

Bastarreche, F. (1978). *El ejército español en el siglo XIX [The Spanish army in the 19th century].* Siglo Veintiuno.

Baxter, P. (2014). *Bush War Rhodesia.* Helion & Company.

Becker, J. (1903) *España en Marruecos. Sus relaciones diplomáticas durante el siglo XIX [Spain in Morocco. Their diplomatic relations during the 19th century].*

Becker, J. (1905). *Historia de Marruecos. Apuntes para la historia de la penetración europea y principalmente de la española en el Norte de África [History of Morocco. Notes for the history of European penetration and mainly of the Spanish in North Africa].* Jaime Ratés.

Becker, J. (1925). *Causas de la esterilidad de la acción exterior de España [Causes of the sterility of Spain's foreign action].* J. Cosano.

Beckett, I. F. (1985). *The Rhodesian army: counter-insurgency, 1972-1979. Armed forces and modern counter-insurgency.* St. Martin Press.

Bekkaï, N. E. (2007). Une indépendance bâclée: Maroc 1950-1961 [A botched independence: Morocco 1950-1961.]. Top Press.

Benadir, N. (1908). Preludi dell'occupazione militare – Due scontri a Sud di Merca. La zona delle future operazioni [Preludes of Military Occupation – Two clashes South of Merca. The area of future operations,]. *Bollettino della Società Africana d'Italia, [Bulletin of the African Society of Italy].* http://digitale.bnc.roma.sbn.it/tecadigitale/giornale/TO00179105/1908

Benbaruk, L. (1979). *The Moroccan monarchy and the nationalist movement, 1930-1965.* McGill University.

Ben-Ghiat, R., & Fuller, M. (2005). *Italian Colonialism.* Palgrave Macmillan. doi:10.1007/978-1-4039-8158-5

Benjelloun, A. (1983). *Contribution à l'étude du mouvement nationaliste marocain dans l'ancienne zone nord du Maroc (1930-1956) [Contribution to the study of the Moroccan nationalist movement in the former northern zone of Morocco (1930-1956).].* Université Hassan II. Faculté des sciences juridiques, économiques et sociales de Casablanca [Hassan II University. Faculty of Legal, Economic and Social Sciences of Casablanca].

Ben-Srhir, K. (2004). *Britain and Morocco during the Embassy of John Dummond Hay.* Routledge. doi:10.4324/9780203494974

Benz, W. (2007). Kolonialpolitik als Genozid. Der 'Herero-Aufstand' in Deutsch-Südwestafrika [Colonial Policy as Genocide. The 'Herero Uprising' in German South-West Africa]. In Wolfgang Benz (ed.), Ausgrenzung, Vertreibung, Völkermord. Genozid im 20. Jahrhundert [Expulsion, expulsion, genocide. Genocide in the 20th Century] (27-53). München, Dtv.

Bergel, M. (2019). *Futuro, pasado y ocaso del "Tercer Mundo", Nueva Sociedad N°284*. Ensayo, November-December.

Berger, M. (2002). 'Toward Our Common American Destiny?' Hemispheric history and pan American politics in the twentieth century. *Journal of Iberian and Latin American Research*, 8(1), 57–88. doi:10.1080/13260219.2002.10431761

Berger, M. (2004). After the Third World? History, destiny and the fate of Third Worldism. *Third World Quarterly*, 25(1), 1, 9–39. doi:10.1080/0143659042000185318

Bermúdez, A. (2016). Movilizaciones contra la Guerra Del Rif en Francia (1925). [Mobilizations against the Rif War in France (1925).] In P. Hernández (Ed.), *Las Violencias y la Historia [Violence and History]* (pp. 667–686). Hergar Ediciones Antema.

Bernard, S. (1968). *The Franco-Moroccan Conflict 1943-1956*. Yale University Press.

Bertella, P., & Dau Novelli, C. (2015). *Colonialism and National Identity*. Cambridge Scholars Publishing.

Betts, R. F. (2000). Methods and institutions of European domination. In A. Adu Boahen (Ed.), *General History of Africa VII. Africa under colonial domination 1880-1935* (pp. 312–331). UNESCO.

Bevins, V. (2021). *The Jakarta Method. La cruzada anticomunista y los asesinatos masivos que moldearon nuestro mundo*. Capitán Swing.

Bhalla, R. S. (1991). The right of self-determination in international law. In W. Twining (Ed.), *Issues of self-determination* (pp. 91–101). Aberdeen University Press.

Billig, M. (2014). *Nacionalismo banal [Banal Nationalism]*. Capitán Swing.

Biondi, J. P. (1993). *Les Anticolonialistes (1881-1962) [The Anticolonialists (1881-1962)].* Hachette Littératures.

Birru, Lubie (1981): Abyssinian Colonialism as the Genesis of the Crisis in the Horn: Oromo Resistance (1855-1913), *Northeast African Studies*, 2/3 (3/1), 93-98.

Blackbourn, D., & Eley, G. (1984). *The Peculiarities of German History*. Oxford University Press. doi:10.1093/acprof:oso/9780198730583.001.0001

Blanco, A. (2012). *Cultura y conciencia imperial en la España del siglo XIX [Culture and imperial consciousness in 19th century Spain]*. University of Valencia.

Bley, H. (1968). *Kolonialherrschaft und Sozialstruktur in Deutsch-Südwestafrika 1894-1914 [Colonial rule and social structure in German South West Africa 1894-1914.]*. Leibniz-Verl.

Boddi, M. (2012). *Letteratura dell'Impero e romanzi coloniali (1922-1935) [Empire literature and colonial novels (1922-1935).]*. Caramanica.

Borao Mateo, J. E. (2017). *Las miradas entre España y China. Un siglo de relaciones entre los dos países (1864-1973) [The looks between Spain and China. A century of relations between the two countries (1864-1973).]*. Miraguano Ediciones.

Borkowski, A., & du Plessis, P. (1994). *Textbook on Roman Law*. Oxford University Press.

Bouamama, S. (2017). *Figures de la révolution africaine. De Kenyatta à Sankara*. La Découverte. doi:10.3917/dec.bouam.2017.01

Bowersow, J. (2010). Boy's and Girl's Own Empires. Gender and the Uses of the Colonial World in Kaiserreich Youth Magazines. In M. Perraudin & J. Zimmerer (Eds.), *German Colonialism and National Identity* (pp. 57–69). Routledge.

Brailsford, H.N. (1935) War and Capitalism. *The New Statesman and Nation*.

Brailsford, H. N. (1914). *The war of steel and gold. A study of the armed peace*. G. Bell & Sons Ltd.

Brailsford, H. N. (1917). *A League of Nations*. MacMillan.

Brands, H. (2010). Latin America's Cold War. Harvard University Press.

Brasó Broggi, C. (2017). Las Aduanas Marítimas de China y el comercio sino-español, 1900-1930 [Chinese Maritime Customs and Sino-Spanish trade, 1900-1930.]. *Revista de Historia Industrial*, *70*(XXVI), 109–143.

Bratton, M. (1979). Settler state, guerrilla war and rural underdevelopment in Rhodesia. *African Issues, 9*(1-2), 56-62.

Brieux, J. (1966), La Tricontinentale. Politique étrangère, n° 1, 31 année. doi:10.3406/polit.1966.2227

Briggs, A., & Burke, P. (2002). *Social History of the Media*.

Brilmayer, L. (1991). Secession and self-determination: A territorial interpretation. *Yale J. Int'l L.*, (16), 177–202.

Brioni, S., & Bonsa Gulema, S. (2018). *The Horn of Africa and Italy. Colonial, Postcolonial and Transnational Cultural Encounters*. Peter Lang.

Brownlie, I., & Crawford, J. (2012). *Brownlie's Principles of Public International Law*. Oxford University Press.

Buchanan, A. (2003). The Quebec secession issue: democracy, minority rights and the rule of law. In S. Macedo & A. Buchanan (Eds.), *Secession and self –determination* (pp. 238–272). Nomos XLV.

Buchheit, L. C. (1978). *Secession, the legitimacy of self-determination*. Yale University Press.

Bülow, B. v. (1931). *Memoirs, 1903-1909*. Putnam.

Burón Díaz, M., & Redondo Carrero, E. (2022). *Imperios e imperialismo. Orden internacional, historia global y pensamiento politico [Empires and imperialism. International order, global history and political thought.]*. Síntesis.

Buzzan, B., & Lawson, G. (2015). *The Global Transformation. History, Modernity and the Making of International Relations*. Cambridge University Press. doi:10.1017/CBO9781139565073

Cabanellas, V. (1896). *La táctica en Cuba, África y Filipinas: prontuario del Oficial en operaciones en todo país cubierto y accidentado (sorpresas, emboscadas e impedimentas) [Tactics in Cuba, Africa and the Philippines: the officer's record in operations in all covered and rugged countries (surprises, ambushes and impediments)]*. Depósito de la Guerra.

Caemanos, R. (2016). *El reparto de África. De la Conferencia de Berlín a los conflictos actuales [The department of Africa. From the Conference of Berlin to the actual conflicts.]*. Catarata.

Cain, P. (2002). *Hobson and Imperialism: Radicalism, New Liberalism, and Finance 1887-1938*. Oxford University Press. doi:10.1093/acprof:oso/9780198203902.001.0001

Cain, P. J., & Hopkins, G. (2016). *British imperialism, 1888-2015* (3rd ed.). Routledge.

Cairo, H. (2020). Geopolítica popular del coronavírus: el poder de las viñetas editoriales en la prensa diaria. Geopolítica(s). Revista de estudios sobre espacio y poder, 11(Special), 303-317. doi:10.5209/geop.69373

Cairo, H. (2006). "Portugal Is not a Small Country": Maps and Propaganda in the Salazar Regime. *Geopolitics*, *11*(3), 367–395. doi:10.1080/14650040600767867

Calchi Novati, G. (1994). Italy in the Triangle of the Horn: Too Many Corners for a Half Power. *The Journal of Modern African Studies*, *32*(3), 369–385.

Calchi Novati, G. (2005). National Identities as a By-Product of Italian Colonialism: A Comparison of Eritrea and Somalia. In J. Andall & D. Duncan (Eds.), *Italian Colonialism: Legacy and Memory* (pp. 47–74).

Calchi Novati, G. (2008). Italy and Africa: How to forget colonialism. *Journal of Modern Italian Studies*, *13*(1), 41–57.

Calero, J. (1895). *Guerras irregulares y de montaña [Irregular and mountain warfare]*. Imp. de la Vda. e Hijos de J. Peláez.

Cao, Z. (Ed.). (2014). *Beijing Lishi Renwu Zhuan [The Biography of Historical Persons in Beijing]*. (Vol. 2). Beijing Yanshan Press.

Caranci, C. (1988). El pansomalismo: claves históricas del conflicto del Cuerno de África [Pansomalism: historical keys to the conflict in the Horn of Africa]. *África Internacional*, 5-6, 193-212.

Cardina, M. (2020). A deserção à Guerra colonial: História, memoria e política. Revista de História das Ideias, 38, 181-204. https://impactum-journals.uc.pt/rhi/article/view/2183-8925_38_8/6400

Cardina, M., & Martins, S. (2019). Evading the war: deserters and draft evaders from the Portuguese army during the colonial war. e-Journal of Portuguese History, 17(2). https://repository.library.brown.edu/studio/item/bdr:1104360/

Cardona, G. (2005). *El problema militar en España [The Military Problem in Spain]*. Albor.

Cardona, G., & Losada, J. C. (1998). *Weyler. Nuestro hombre en la Habana [Weyler. Our man in Havana]*. Planeta.

Carr, E.H. (1939) *Twentieth Years' Crisis, 1919-1939. An Introduction to the Study of International Relations*, (consulted edition: *La crisis de los veinte años, 1919-1939 [The twenty year crisis 1919-1939)*. Madrid, Los Libros de la Catarata, 2004).

Casals, M. (2020). Which borders have not yet been crossed? A supplement to Gilbert Joseph's historiographical balance of the Latin American cold war. *Cold War History*, *20*(3), 367–372. doi:10.1080/14682745.2020.1762311

Cassese, A. (1995). *Self- determination of the peoples, a legal reappraisal*. Cambridge University Press.

Castellino, J. (2014). International law and self-determination: peoples, indigenous peoples, and minorities. In Christian, W, von Ungern-Sternberg, A., & Abushov, K. (Eds.), Self-determination and secession in international law (pp. 27-45). Oxford University Press.

Castellino, J. (2000). *International law and self- determination*. Kluwer Law International. doi:10.1163/9789004480896

Castellino, J. (2008). Territorial integrity and the "right" to self- determination: An examination of the conceptual tools. *Brooklyn Journal of International Law*, *33*(2), 499–564.

Chacón, J. I. (1883). *Guerras irregulars [Irregular wars]*. Depósito de la guerra.

Chafer, T., & Sackur, A. (2002). *Promoting the Colonial idea: Propaganda and Visions of Empire in France*. Palgrave Macmillan. doi:10.1057/9781403919427

Chang, I. (2016). *La violación de Naking [The Rape of Nanking: the Forgotten Holocaust of World War II]*. Capitán Swing.

Chang, J. (2016). *Cixí, La emperatriz. La concubina que creó la China moderna [Cixi, The Empress. The concubine who created modern China]*. Taurus.

Chen, X. (Ed.). (1982). *Zhongguo Jindaishi Cidian [The Dictionary of Chinese Modern History]*. Shanghai Lexicographical Publishing House.

Chester, E. T. (2001). *The US intervention in the Dominican Republic (1965-1966). Rag-Tags, Scum, Riff-Raff and Commies*. Monthly Review Press.

Cilliers, J. (1985). *Counter-Insurgency in Rhodesia*. Routledge.

Claeys, G. (2020). *Imperial esceptics. British critics of empire, 1850-1920*. Cambridge University Press.

Clark, Ch. (2014). *Sonámbulos: Como Europa fue a la guerra en 1914 [Sleepwalkers: How Europe went to war in 1914]*. Galaxia Gutenberg.

Clausewitz, K. v. (1999). *De la guerra [On war]*. Ediciones Ejército.

Cobo Martínez, J. (1986). *Study on the problem of discrimination against indigenous populations*. UN Doc E/CN.4/Sub.2/1986/Add.4.

Cocks, C. (2006). *Fireforce: One Man's War in the Rhodesian LightInfantry*. 30° South Publishers.

Coelho, J. P. (2003). Da violencia colonial ordenada à orden pós-colonial violenta. Sobre um legado das guerras coloniais nas ex-colonias portuguesas. Lusotopie, 10, 175-193. https://www.persee.fr/doc/luso_1257-0273_2003_num_10_1_1554

Coelho, J. P. B. (2002). African troops in the portuguese colonial army, 1961-1974: Angola, Guinea-Bissau and Mozambique. *Portuguese Studies Review*, *10*(1), 129–150.

Cohn, C. (1987). Sex and Death in the Rational World of Defense Intellectuals. *Signs (Chicago, Ill.)*, *12*(4), 687–718. doi:10.1086/494362

Cole, B. (1980) *The Elite. The Story of the Rhodesian Special Air Service*. WYD 4.

Collado Fernández, E. (2019). En el nombre de la reina: La imagen de Isabel II durante la Guerra de África (1859-1860)

Colman, J. (2010). *The Foreign Policy of Lyndon B. Johnson: The United States and the World, 1963-1969*. Edinburgh University Press.

Cologán Soriano, C. (2015). *Bernardo Cologán y los 55 días en Pekín [Bernardo Cologán and the 55 days in Beijing]*. Gobierno de Canarias.

Connelly, M. (2001). Rethinking the Cold War and decolonization: The grand strategy of the Algerian war for independence. *International Journal of Middle East Studies*, *33*(2), 221–245. doi:10.1017/S0020743801002033

Conrad, S. (2006). *Globalisierung und Nation im Deutschen Kaiserreich*. C. H. Beck.

Cooper, F., & Stoler, A. L. (1997). *Tensions of Empire. Colonial Cultures in a Bourgeois World*. University of California Press.

Corkill, D., & Pina, J. C. (2009). Conmemoration and Propaganda in Salazar's Portugal: The 'Mundo Portugués' Exposition of 1940. *Journal of Contemporary History*, *44*(3), 381–399. doi:10.1177/0022009409104115

Couffignal, G. (2011), *La politique étrangère de la France vis-à-vis Latin America*. Observatoire des changements en Amérique Latine, Paris, La Documentation Française-IHEAL.

Craig, G. A. (1978). *Germany, 1866-1945*. Oxford University Press.

Cristescu, A. (1981). *The right to self-determination, historical and current development on the basis of United Nations instruments*. United Nations.

Cross, G. (2017). *Dirty War: Rhodesia and Chemical Biological Warfare 1975-1980*. Helion and Company.

Crouzet, G. (2019). A second fashoda? Britain, India, and a French 'Threat' in Oman at the end of the nineteenth century. In, J. R. Fichter (Ed.), British and French colonialism in Africa, Asia and the Middle East. Connected empires across the Eighteenth to the Twentieth Centuries, (pp. 131-150). Palgrave Macmillan.

Cueto, A. (2011). Portugal y su imperio frente a la descolonización, 1945-1962. *Espacio, Tiempo y Forma. Serie V, Historia Comtemporánea, 23*(23), 161–200. doi:10.5944/etfv.23.2011.1579

Dalby, S. (1991). Critical geopolitics: Discourse, difference and dissent. *Environment and Planning. D, Society & Space, 9*(3), 261–283. doi:10.1068/d090261

Dalby, S. (2002). Geopolitics and global security: culture, identity and the 'pogo syndrome. In G. Ó'Tuathail & S. Dalby (Eds.), *Rethinking Geopolitics* (pp. 295–313). Routledge. doi:10.4324/9780203058053-18

Dalby, S. (2003). Calling 911: Geopolitics, security and America's new war. *Geopolitics, 8*(3), 61–86. doi:10.1080/14 650040412331307712

Davidović, N. (2017). *Kako je Jugoslavija pomagala oružanu borbu protiv Zapada! [How Yugoslavia helped the armed struggle against the West!]* Princip Info. https://princip.info/2017/01/03/kako-je-jugoslavija-pomagala -borbu-protiv-zapada/

Davidow, J. (2019). *A Peace in Southern Africa: The Lancaster House Conference on Rhodesia 1979*. Routledge.

Davidson, B. (1973). La lucha por la independencia en el África 'portuguesa'. El Correo: África "portuguesa". La lucha por la independencia. UNESCO, 4-8

De Boer, M. (2012). El enfoque de Rodesia hacia las operaciones de contrainsurgencia: Una tendencia a matar. *Military Review*.

De la Rosa, J. (2015). *La Revolución de abril de 1965*. LetraGráfica.

De Miguel, E. (2010). Las tropas españolas en la guerra de Cuba: de las especulaciones cuantitativas a la cuantificación [Spanish troops in the war in Cuba: from quantitative speculation to quantification]. *Anales de la Real Academia de Cultura Valenciana [Annals of the Royal Academy of Valencian Culture], 85*.

de Reparaz, R. G. (1924). *Política de España en África [Politics of Spain and Africa]*. Espasa-Calpe.

Debasa, F. (2022). *Algorithms, Social Rejection, and Public Administrations in the Current World. Handbook of Research on Artificial Intelligence in Government Practices and Processes*. IGI Global.

Debasa, F., Andriichenko, Y., & Popova, N. (2022). Ukrainian Social Realities and Emotivities in the Political Speeches of Yuliia Tymoshenko: A Data-Based Approach. In *Handbook of Research on Artificial Intelligence in Government Practices and Processes* (pp. 264–283). IGI Global. doi:10.4018/978-1-7998-9609-8.ch015

Debasa, F., & Sánchez, T. A. (2021). El discurso político de la presidencia Trump antes del Covid. *Historia Actual Online, 56*, 21–34.

Degl'innocenti, M. (1976). *Il socialismo italiano e la guerra di Libia [Italian socialism and the war in Libya.]*. Editori Riuniti.

Del Boca, A. (1992). *Gli Italiani in Africa Orientale I, dall' Unita alla Marcia su Rome* [*The Italians in East Africa I, from the United to the March on Rome.*]. Mondadori.

Delgado, O. (1980). *The Spanish Army in Cuba 1895-1898: And Institutional Study.* [Thesis doctoral. Columbia University].

Demeshkova, E., Rudov, I., & Afanasieva, J. (2021). Digital cultural colonialism: Measuring bias in aggregated digitized content held in Google Arts and Culture. *Digital Scholarship in the Humanities, 36*(3), 607–640. doi:10.1093/llc/fqaa055

Demhardt, I. J. (2002). *Deutsche Kolonialgesellschaft 1888-1918. Ein Beitrag zur Organisationsgeschichte der deutschen Kolonialbewegung* [*German Colonial Society 1888-1918. A contribution to the organizational history of the German colonial movement.*]. Selbstverlag.

Democracia socialista en Yugoslavia. [Socialist democracy in Yugoslavia .] (1963). Revista Política Internacional; Revista mensual yugoslava; Belgrado, 1963.

Digitale. (1897). Gli autori della spedizione Cecchi castigati [The authors of the expedition Cecchi chastised]. *Bollettino della Società Africana d'Italia [Bulletin of the African Society of Italy]*, 88-89. http://digitale.bnc.roma.sbn.it/tecadigitale/giornale/TO001 79105/1897/

Digitale. (1923). Il Governatore della Somalia [Somalian Government]. *Bollettino della Società Africana d'Italia [Bulletin of the African Society of Italy].* http://digitale.bnc.roma.sbn.it/tecadigitale/emeroteca/class ic/TO00085511/1923

Digiteca. (1927). Brillanti operazoni in Somalia contro ribelli migiurtini [Brilliant operations in Somalia against Migiurtini rebels]. *Il Popolo d'Italia.* http://digiteca.bsmc.it/?l=periodici&t=Popolo%20d%60Italia%2 8Il%29#

Dijkink, G. (1996). *National Identity and Geopolitical Visions.* Routledge.

Domínguez, J. (2009). *La política exterior de Cuba (1962-2009).* Editorial Colibrí.

Drechsler, H. (1966). *Südwestafrika unter deutscher Kolonialherrschaft: Der Kampf der Herero und Nama gegen den deutsche Imperialismos (1884-1915)* [*South West Africa under German Colonial Rule: The Struggle of the Herero and Nama against German Imperialism (1884-1915)*]. Akademie-Verlag.

Dreesbach, A. (2005). *Gezähmte Wilde: die Zurschaustellung «exotischer» Menschen in Deutschland 1870-1940* [*Tamed savages: the display of "exotic" people in Germany 1870-1940.*]. Campus.

Dugard, J. (2003). A legal basis for secession - relevant principles and rules. In J. Dahliz (Ed.), *Conflict avoidance and - regional appraisals* (pp. 89–97). Asser press. doi:10.1007/978-90-6704-699-2_7

Duggan, C. (2001). *Creare la nazione: vita di Francesco Crispi* [*Creating the nation: life of Francesco Crispi.*]. Laterza.

Dugin A. (1999). *Основы геополитики. Геополитическое будущее.* России: АРКТОГЕЯ – центр.

Dulphy, A. (2002). *La politique de la France à l'égard de l'Espagne de 1945 à 1955: entre idéologie et réalisme [France's policy towards Spain from 1945 to 1955: between ideology and realism.].* Ministère des Affaires Étrangères.

Dumont, J. (2010). *L'amère patrie. Histoire des Antilles françaises au XXe siècle.* Fayard.

Duncan, I., Patton, P., & Sanders, W. (2000). Introduction. In Duncan, I., Patton, P., & Sanders, W. (Eds.), Political theory and the rights of indigenous peoples (pp.1- 25). Cambridge University Press.

Duursma, J. S. (1997). Fragmentation and the international relations of micro-states: Self-determination and statehood. *Leiden Journal of International Law, 10*, 579–586.

Eckart, W. U. (1997). *Medizin und Kolonialimperialismus: Deutschland 1884-1945.* [*Medicine and Colonial Imperialism: Germany 1884-1945.*] Schöningh Verlag.

Eley, G. (1991). *Reshaping the German Right: Radical Nationalism and Political Change after Bismarck.* University of Michigan Press. doi:10.3998/mpub.8157

ElHawary, D. M. M. (2022). *TikTok Battlefield: Comparative Analysis of English and Arabic Language Representations of The 2022 Russian Ukrainian Conflict On TikTok.*

El-Tayeb, F. (2001). *Schwarze Deutsche. Der Diskurs um 'Rasse' und Nationalität 1890–1933* [*Black Germans. Der Diskurs um 'Rasse' und Staatsangehörig 1890–1933.*]. Campus.

Epstein, P. (2009). Behind closed doors:"autonomous colonization" in post United Nations era- the case of Western Sahara. *Annual Survey of International and Comparative Law*, *15*(1), 107–143.

Erichsen, C., & Olusoga, D. (2010). *The Kaiser's Holocaust: Germany's Forgotten Genocide and the Colonial Roots of Nazism.* Faber and faber.

Evans, M. (2004). *Empire and culture: the French experience, 1830-1940.* Palgrave Macmillan. doi:10.1057/9780230000681

Evans, M. (2007). The wretched of the empire: Politics, ideology and counterinsurgency in Rhodesia, 1965-1980. *Small Wars & Insurgencies*, *18*(2), 175–195. doi:10.1080/09574040701400601

Evans, M. (2012). Colonial Fantasies Shattered. In D. Stone (Ed.), *The Oxford Handbook of Postwar European History* (pp. 480–501). Oxford University Press.

Evans, R. (2015). *The Third Reich in History and Memory.* Oxford University Press.

Faligot, R. (2013). *Tricontinentale. Quand Che Guevara, Ben Barka, Cabral, Castro et Hô Chi Minh, préparaient la révolution mondiale (1964-1968).* La Découverte.

Falk, R. (2002). Self-determination under international law: the coherence of doctrine versus the incoherence of experience. In Danspeckgruber, W. (Ed.), *Self – determination of peoples, community, nation and state in an interdependent world* (pp.31- 67). Lynne Rienner Publishers.

Faulkner, N. (2021). *Empire and Jihad: The Anglo-Arab Wars of 1870-1920.* Yale University Press.

Faure, J., & Del Pero, M. (November 2020). La Guerre Froide Globale. In J. Faure & M. Del Pero (Eds.), *La Guerre Froide Globale, Monde(s) no. 18.* doi:10.3917/mond1.202.0009

Feld, M. D. (Ed.). (1977). *The structure of violence: Armed forces as social systems.* Sage Publications.

Ferro, M. (2000). *La colonización. Una historia global [The colonization. A Global History,].* Siglo veintiuno editores.

Feyjóo, T. (1869). *Diario de un testigo de las operaciones sobre los insurrectos de la isla de Cuba [Diary of a witness of the operations against the insurgents of the island of Cuba].* Imprenta militar de la V. e Hs. de Soler [Military printing press of the V. and Hs. de Soler].

Fichter, J. R. (2019). *British and French Colonialism in Africa, Asia and the Middle East Connected Empires across the Eighteenth to the Twentieth Centuries.* Palgrave Macmillan. doi:10.1007/978-3-319-97964-9

Field, T. Jr, Krepp, S., & Pettiná, V. (2020). *Latin America and the Global Cold War.* University of North Carolina Press. doi:10.5149/northcarolina/9781469655697.001.0001

Finaldi, G. (2011). The peasants did not think of Africa: empire and the Italian state's pursuit of legitimacy, 1871-1945. In Mackenzie J. M. (Ed.), European empires and the people: popular responses to imperialism in France, Britain, the Netherlands, Belgium, Germany and Italy (pp. 195-228). Manchester University Press.

Finaldi, G. (2016). *A History of Italian Colonialism, 1860–1907*. Routledge.

Fischer, F. (1967). *Germany's Aims in the First World War*. W.W. Norton.

Fisher, J. (2013). The Bible dream: official travel in Morocco, 1845-1935. In M. Farr and X. Guéran. (Eds). The British abroad since the eighteenth century. Vol 2: Experiencing imperialism (pp. 176-193). Macmillan. doi:10.1057/9781137304186_10

Fisher, J. (2019). *Outskirts of empire. Studies in British power projection*. Routledge.

Fisher, L. (2007). *The Socialist Response to Antisemitism in Imperial Germany*. Cambridge University Press. doi:10.1017/CBO9780511511783

Flower, K. (1988). Serving Secretly—An Intelligence Chief on Record- Rhodesia into Zimbabwe—1964 to 1981. *African Affairs*, *87*(348), 465–466. doi:10.1093/oxfordjournals.afraf.a098063

Fontela, S., Gómez, J., & Rodríguez, P. (2007). *Resumen histórico de la táctica de infantería S [Historical summary of infantry tactics S.]*. Fajardo el Bravo.

Förster, S., & Nagler, J. (Eds.). (2002). *On the Road to Total War: The American Civil War and the German Wars of Unification, 1861-1871*. Cambridge University Press.

Fox, H. W. (1915). Rhodesia and the War. *Journal of the Royal African Society*, *14*(56), 345–354.

Franck, T. M. (1992). The emerging right to democratic governance. *Am. J. Int'l L.*, *86*(1), 46–91. doi:10.2307/2203138

Franck, T. M. (2000). Legitimacy and democratic entitlement. In G. H. Fox & B. R. Roth (Eds.), *Democratic governance and international law* (pp. 25–47). Cambridge University Press. doi:10.1017/CBO9780511522307.002

Franco Salgado-Araujo, F. (2005). *Mis conversaciones privadas con Franco [My private conversations with Franco]*. Planeta.

Fraser, A. (2019). Curating digital geographies in an era of data colonialism. *Geoforum*, *104*, 193–200. doi:10.1016/j.geoforum.2019.04.027

Frederick, I. I. (1793). *El Arte de la Guerra* [The Art of War]. Imprenta Real.

French, P. (2012). *Shadows of a Forgotten Past: To the Edge with the Rhodesian SAS and Selous Scouts*. Helion and Company.

Friedman, M. (2015). *Rethinking anti-Americanism: The history of an exceptional concept in American international relations*. Machado Grupo.

Friis, I., & Edwards, S. (2001). By whom and when was the flora of Ethiopia and Eritrea named. In I. Friis & O. Ryding (Eds.), *Biodiversity research in the Horn of Africa* (pp. 103–136). Biologiske Skrifter.

Gajate Bajo, M. (2012). *Las campañas de Marruecos y la opinión pública. El ejemplo de Salamanca y su prensa, 1906-1927 [Moroccan campaigns and public opinion. The example of Salamanca and its press, 1906-1927]*. UNED-IUGM.

Gajate Bajo, M. (2021). ¿Guerra de religión o religión de la guerra? Pedro Antonio de Alarcón en la Guerra de África (1859-1860) [War of religion or religion of war? Pedro Antonio de Alarcón in the African War (1859-1860).]. *Siglo XIX. Literatura Hispánica*, *27*, 223–256.

Galvão, H. (1934). *No rumo do império*. Litografia Nacional.

Gann, L., & Duignan, P. (1977). The Rulers of German Africa, 1884-1914. Stanford University Press.

García Balañá, A. (2002). Patria, plebe y política en la España isabelina: la Guerra de África en Cataluña (1859-1860) [Homeland, common people and politics in Elizabethan Spain: the African War in Catalonia (1859-1860).]. In E. Martín Corrales (Ed.), *Marruecos y el colonialismo español* (pp. 13–77).

García Balañá, A. (2012). The empire is no longer a social unit. Expectations and Transatlatic crisis in metropolitan Spain, 1859-1860. In A. W. McCoy, J. M. Fradera, & S. Jacobson (Eds.), *Endless Empire. Spais's retreat, Europe's eclipse and America's decline* (pp. 92–103). The University of Wisconsin Press.

García Moral, E. (2016). *Breve historia del África subsahariana [Brief history of sub-Saharan Africa]*. Nowtilus.

García Ruiz-Castillo, C. (2009). Los fondos de las representaciones diplomáticas y consulares de España en China conservados en el Archivo General de la Administración: Su context [The funds of the diplomatic and consular representations of Spain in China conserved in the General Archive of the Administration: Its context.]. *Cuadernos de Historia Contemporánea, 31,* 223–241.

García, T. (1957). *España y su Protectorado en Marruecos (1912-1956) [Spain and its Protectorate in Morocco (1912-1956).]*. CSIC.

García-Tapia Bello, J. L. (2009). Relaciones bilaterales con China [Bilateral relations with China]. *Boletín Económico ICE [Economic Bulletin ICE], 2.972* (1), 69-93.

Garrard-Burnet, V., Lawrence, M., & Moreno, J. (2013). *Beyond the Eagle's Shadow: New Histories of Latin America's Cold War*. University of New Mexico Press.

Garrido Guijarro, O. (2014). *Aproximación a los antecedentes, las causas y las consecuencias de la Guerra de África (1859-1860) desde las comunicaciones entre la diplomacia española y el Ministerio de Estado [Approach to the background, causes and consequences of the African War (1859-1860) from the communications between Spanish diplomacy and the Ministry of State]* [Unpublished doctoral dissertation, UNED, Spain].

Gerwath, R., & Malonowski, S. (2009). Hanna Arendt's Ghost: Reflections on the Disputable Path from Windhoek to Auschwitz. *Central European History, 42*(2), 279–300. doi:10.1017/S0008938909000314

Geshekter, C. L. (1985). Anti-colonialism and class formation: The Eastern Horn of Africa before 1950. *The International Journal of African Historical Studies, 18*(1), 1–37. https://www.jstor.org/stable/217972

Getchell, M. (2020), Cuba, the USSR, and the Non-Aligned Movement: Negotiating Non-Alignment. In Latin America and the Global Cold War, edited by Field, T., Krepp, S., Pettinà, V., 148-73. University of North Carolina Press.

Gettig, E. (2015). Trouble ahead in Afro-Asia: The United States, the Second Bandung Conference, and the Struggle for the Third World, 1964-1965. *Diplomatic History, 39*(1), 126–156. doi:10.1093/dh/dht133

Gissibl, B. (2011). Imaginaton and beyond: cultures and geographies of imperialism in Germany, 1848-1918. In Mackenzie J. M. (Ed.), European empires and the people: popular responses to imperialism in France, Britain, the Netherlands, Belgium, Germany and Italy (pp. 158-194). Manchester University Press.

Gleijeses, P. (2014), *Hope Denied. The US Defeat of the 1965 Revolt in the Dominican Republic*, Washington, Woodrow Wilson Centre for Scholars, Cold War International History Project no. 72.

Gleijeses, P. (1984). *La crisis dominicana*. FCE.

Godwin, P., & Hancock, I. (1993). *Rhodesians Never Die—The Impact of War and Political Change on White Rhodesia, 1970-1980*. OUP Oxford. doi:10.1093/acprof:oso/9780198203650.001.0001

Goicoechea, C. A. (1922). *La política internacional de España en noventa años (1814-1904) [Spain's international policy in ninety years (1814-1904).]*. Ed. Reus.

Gómez, M. (1940). *Diario de campaña del mayor general Máximo Gómez [Campaign diary of Major General Máximo Gómez]*. Talleres de Centro Superior Tecnológico Ceiba del Agua [Workshops of the Ceiba del Agua Higher Technological Center].

González-Pola, P. (2003). *La configuración de la mentalidad militar contemporánea (1868-1909) [The configuration of the contemporary military mentality (1868-1909).]*. Ministerio de Defensa.

Goralski, R., & Freeburg, R. W. (1989). *El Petróleo y la Guerra [Oil & War]*. Servicio de Publicaciones del EME.

Gott, R. (1996) Che Guevara and the Congo, *New Left Review*, pp. 6-7.

Gott, R. (1967). El sur de Africa y el fin de la guerra fría. *Estudios Internacionales (Santiago)*, 95–109.

Grant, N. (2015). *Rhodesian Light Infantryman 1961-80*. Osprey Publishing.

Grimaldi, V. (2016). *Golpe y revolución. El derrocamiento de Juan Bosch y la intervención norteamericana*. Editorial Búho.

Großer Generalstabes. (1906). *Die Kämpfe der deutschen Truppen in Südwestafrika I [The battles of the German troops in South West Africa]*. Mittler.

Grosser, A. (1989). *Affaires extérieures. La politique de la France, 1944-1989*. Champs-Flammarion.

Gründer, H. (2018). *Geschichte der deutschen Kolonian [History of the German colonian]*. Panderborn, Brill Deutschland GmbH. doi:10.36198/9783838549729

Guadagni, M. M. G. (1978). Colonial Origins of the Public Domain in Southern Somalia (1892-1912). *Journal of African Law*, *22*(1), 1–29.

Guerra, J. P. (1994). *Memorias das Guerras Coloniais*. Edições Afrontamento.

Guerra, R. (1950). *Guerra de los Diez Años (1868-1878) [Ten Years' War (1868-1878)*. Cultural.

Guerrero, A. (2020). Contrainsurgencia en la Guerra de los Diez Años en Cuba (1868-1878): Weyler y los Cazadores de Valmaseda [Counterinsurgency in the Ten Years' War in Cuba (1868-1878): Weyler and the Cazadores de Valmaseda]. In A. Guerrero (Ed.), *Imperialismo y ejércitos [Imperialism and armies]* (pp. 432–457). Editorial Universidad de Granada.

Guerrero, A. (2021). La administración de Filipinas durante la capitanía general de Valeriano Weyler (1888-1891) [The administration of the Philippines during the captaincy general of Valeriano Weyler (1888-1891)]. Studia Humanitatis Journal, *1*(1), 58–80.

Guerrero, A. (2023). La guerra irregular en el pensamiento militar decimonónico español (1863-1898) [Irregular warfare in nineteenth-century Spanish military thought (1863-1898).]. *Revista Universitaria Militar, 11*(23), 16–39.

Guettel, J.-U. (2012). The Myth of the Pro-Colonialist SPD: German Social Democracy and Imperialism before World War I. *Central European History*, *45*(3), 452–484. doi:10.1017/S0008938912000350

Gutiérrez, F. C., López, F. O., & González, A. L. (2023). Lawfare or the War Behind the Curtains: An Analysis of the Russian-Ukrainian Conflict. In *Handbook of Research on War Policies, Strategies, and Cyber Wars* (pp. 239–255). IGI Global. doi:10.4018/978-1-6684-6741-1.ch013

Habib, A. (2001). *Chechen Refugees: A Forgotten History of Caucasus; Who Remembers and Who Cares?* Green University of Bangladesh.

Haggai, E. (2010). *Islam & Christianity in the Horn of Africa: Somalia, Ethiopia, Sudan.* Lynne Rienner.

Halliday, F. (Ed.). (2010). *Caamaño in London. The exile of a Latin American revolutionary.* University of London.

Halperin, M. H., Scheffer, D. J., & Small, P. L. (1992). *Self – determination in the new world order.* Carnegie Endowment for International Peace.

Hamilton, A. (1911). *Somaliland.* Hutchinson and Co.

Hanauer, L. (1995). The irrelevance of self – determination law to ethno- national conflicts: A new look at the Western Sahara case. *Emory International Law Review, 9*(1), 133–178.

Hane, M. (2013). *Breve historia de Japón* [*Brief history of Japan*]. Alianza Editorial.

Hannum, H. (1990). *Autonomy, sovereignty, and self-determination, the accommodation of conflict rights.* University of Pennsylvania Press.

Harbeson, J. W. (1979). Ethiopia and the Horn of Africa. *Northeast African Studies, 1*(1), 27–44.

Hardman, F. (1860). *The Spanish campaign in Morocco.* Blackwood and Sons.

Hardman, F. (1854). A letter from Madrid. *Blackwood's Magazine, 75*(June), 671–686.

Harmer, T. (2008) *The Rules of the Game: Allende's Chile, The United States and Cuba, 1970-1973,* [PhD Thesis, London School of Economics and Political Sciences, England].

Harvey, H. (2020), Revisiting the inter-American turning point in the Cold War: the Dominican crisis of 1965, U.S. intervention, and the Inter-American Peace Force. *Humanidades: revista de la Universidad de Montevideo, 7,* (2020): 25-63.

Hatzky, C. (2015). *Cubans in Angola. South-South Cooperation and Transfer of Knowledge, 1976-1991.* The University of Wisconsin Press.

Häussler, M. (2011). From destruction to extermination: Genocidal escalation in Germany's war against the Herero 1904. *Journal of Namibian Studies, 10,* 55–81.

Häussler, M. (2021). *The Herero Genocide: War, Emotion and Extreme Violence in Colonial Namibia.* Berghahn. doi:10.2307/j.ctv2tsx91h

Hegre, H., Ellingsen, T., Gates, S., & Petter, N. Gleditsch. (. (2001). Towards a democratic civil peace: Democracy, democratization, and civil war 1834-1992. *The American Political Science Review, 95*(1), 33–48. doi:10.1017/S0003055401000119

Henderson, E. A. (2002). *Democracy and war: The end of an illusion.* Lynne Rienner.

Henderson, E. A. (2017). The Revolution will not be theorized: Du Bois, Locke and the Howard School's challenge to White Supremacist IR Theory. Millenium *Journal of International Relations, 45*(3), 452–510.

Henrard, K. (2000). *Devising an adequate system of minority protection.* Kluwer Law International. doi:10.1163/9789004482500

Hermann, H. (2009). *Eslabón perdido. Gobierno provisional (1965-1966).* Editorial Búho.

Hermann, M., & Kegley, C. Jr. (1998). The U.S. use of military intervention to promote democracy: Evaluating the record. *International Interactions, 24*(2), 91–114. doi:10.1080/03050629808434922

Hernando de Larramendi, M., & Azaola, B. (2006) Los estudios sobre el Mundo Árabe y Mediterráneo contemporáneo en España [Studies on the contemporary Arab and Mediterranean world in Spain] (pp. 87-147). In Investigando el Mediterráneo, monografías [Studies on the contemporary Arab and Mediterranean world in Spain]. CIDOB.

Hernando de Larramendi, M. (Eds.). (2015). *El Instituto Hispano-Árabe de Cultura. Orígenes y evolución de la diplomacia pública española hacia el mundo árabe [The Hispanic-Arab Institute of Culture. Origins and evolution of Spanish public diplomacy towards the Arab world]*. AECID.

Herwig, H. (1976). *Politics of Frustration: The United States in German Naval Planning, 1889-1941*. Little, Brown and Company.

Hess, R. L. (1964). The 'Mad Mullah' and Northern Somalia. *Journal of African History, 5*(3), 415–433.

Hobson, J. A. (1902). *Imperialism. A study*. Nisbet.

Hobson, J. M. (2012). *The Eurocentric conception of world politics. Western international theory 1760-2010*. Cambridge University Press. doi:10.1017/CBO9781139096829

Hobswbawn, E. (1998). *Naciones y nacionalismo desde 1780 [Nations and nationalism since 1780.]*. Grijalbo Mondadori.

Höhne, M. (2017). Somalí. In S. Uhlig, Siegbert et al (Eds.), Etiopía. History, culture, and challenges, (pp. 73-74). LIT-Michigan State University Press.

Howe, S. (1998). *Anti-Colonialism in British Politics: The Left and the End of Empire, 1918-1964*. Oxford University Press.

Huguet, E. (1969). El factor geográfico y el gran problema de España [The geographical factor and the great problem of Spain]. In *Velarde Fuentes, J. Lecturas de economía Española [Spanish economy readings]* (pp. 82–98). Gredos.

Hull, I. V. (2006). *Absolute Destruction: Military culture and The practices of war in Imperial German*. Cornell University Press.

Hyrkkänen, M. (1986), *Sozialistische Kolonialpolitik. Eduard Bernsteins Stellung zur Kolonialpolitik und zum Imperialismus 1882-1914. [Socialist Colonial Policy. Eduard Bernstein's position on colonial politics and imperialism 1882-1914.]* Ein Beitrag zur Geschichte des Revisionismus. SHS.

Ibn Azzuz Hakim, M., & Ibn Azzuz Hakim, F. (1990). *Mohammad V frente al Protectorado [Mohammad V against the Protectorate]*. Arabian Al Hilal.

Ibrahim, H. A. (1985). African initiatives and resistance in North-East Africa. In A. Adu Bohaen (Ed.), *General History of Africa VIII. Africa under colonial domination (1880-1935)* (pp. 63–86). UNESCO.

ICJ. (1975). *Reports of judgments, advisory opinions and orders. Western Sahara, advisory opinion.* https://www.icj-cij.org/public/files/case-related/61/061-19751016-ADV-01-00-EN.pdf

ICJ. (1986). *Frontier Disputes (Burkina Faso/Republic of Mali)*. ICJ. https://www.icj-cij.org/en/case/69

Iglesias Amorín, A. (2020). The Hispano-Moroccan Wars (1859-1927) and the (De)nationalization of the Spanish People. *European History Quarterly, 50*(2), 290–310. doi:10.1177/0265691420910946

In the name of the queen: The image of Elizabeth II during the African War (1859-1860).]. Revista de Historia Constitucional, 20(20), 607–621. doi:10.17811/hc.v0i20.576

Inarejos Muñoz, J. A. (2009). La campaña de África de la Unión Liberal. ¿Una Crimea española? [The Liberal Union's Africa campaign. A Spanish Crimea?] *L'Atelier du Centre de Recherches Historique*. doi:10.4000/acrh.1805

Iniesta, F. (2000). *Kuma. Historia de África*. Edicions Bellaterra.

Iyob, R. (1993). Regional Hegemony: Domination and Resistance in the Horn of Africa. *The Journal of Modern African Studies*, *31*(2), 257–276. doi:10.1017/S0022278X00011927

Jalata, A. (1990). *The question of Oromia: Euro-Ethiopian colonialism, global hegemonism and nationalism, 1870s-1980s*, [PhD Doctoral dissertation, State University of New York].

Jalata, A. (2020). *The Oromo Movement and Imperial Politics: Culture and Ideology in Oromia and Ethiopia*. Lexington Books.

Jensen, G. (2014). *Cultura militar española: modernistas, tradicionalistas y liberals [Spanish military culture: modernists, traditionalists and liberals]*. Biblioteca Nueva.

Joseph, G. (2019). Border crossings and the remaking of Latin American cold war studies. *Cold War History*, *19*(1), 141–170. doi:10.1080/14682745.2019.1557824

Joseph, G. (2020). The continuing challenge of border crossing: A response to Marcelo Casals' commentary. *Cold War History*, *20*(3), 373–377. doi:10.1080/14682745.2020.1762312

Joseph, G., & Spencer, D. (Eds.). (2008). *In from the Cold: Latin America's New Encounter with the Cold War*. Duke University Press. doi:10.1215/9780822390664

Julien, C. A. (1972). *L'Afrique du Nord en marche. Nationalismes musulmans et souveraineté française [North Africa on the move. Muslim nationalisms and French sovereignty]*. Julliard.

Julien, C. A. (1978). *Le Maroc face aux impérialismes: 1415-1956 [Morocco facing imperialism: 1415-1956]*. Éditions J.A.

Kaiser, K. (1991). Deutschlands Vereinigung. Die internationalen Aspekte. Mit den wichtigsten Dokumenten. Bergisch Gladbach.

Kakwenzire, P. (1986). Resistance, Revenue and Development in Northern Somalia, 1905-1939. *The International Journal of African Historical Studies*, *19*, 659–677.

Kalinovsky, V. (2014). *Lukashenko accuses Russia and says he is Ukrainian*. Euromaidan Press.

Kalter, C. (2016). *The Discovery of the Third World: Decolonization and the Rise of the New Left in France, c. 1950-1976*. Cambridge University Press. doi:10.1017/CBO9781139696906

Keefer, E. (1973). Great Britain and Ethiopia, 1897-1910: Competition for Empire. *The International Journal of African Historical Studies*, *6*(3), 468–474.

Kennedy, P. (2006). *Auge y caída de las grandes potencias* [*The Rise and Fall of the Great Powers*]. Debolsillo.

Kittermaster, H. B. (1928). British Somaliland. *Journal of the Royal African Society*, *27*(108), 329–337.

Ki-Zerbo, J. (1972). *Historia del África Negra 2. Del siglo XIX a la época actual [History of Black Africa 2. From the 19th century to the present time.]*. Alianza Editorial.

Knop, K. (2002). *Diversity and self- determination in the international law*. Cambridge University Press. doi:10.1017/CBO9780511494024

Knutsen, T. J. (1997). *A History of International Relations Theory*. Manchester University Press.

Kolonder, E. (1994). The future of the right to self-determination. *Connecticut Journal of International Law*, *10*, 153–168.

Kühne, I. (2017). Pátria, ja tornas á tenir historia! La influencia de la Guerra de África sobre el desarrollo de la identidad catalana [Homeland, you will have history again! The influence of the African War on the development of Catalan identity]. In C. von Tschilschke & J. Witthaus (Eds.), *El colonialismo. España y África, entre imaginación e historia* (pp. 77–103). Iberoamericana-Vervuert. doi:10.31819/9783954876365-005

Kundrus, B. (2011). From the Periphery to the Center: On the Significance of Colonialism for the German Empire. In S. O. Müller & C. Torp (Eds.), *Imperial Germany Revisited: Continuing Debates and New Perspectives* (pp. 253–266). Berghahn Books.

Kundruss, B. (2003). Von Windhoek nach Nürnberg? Koloniale 'Mischehenverbote' und die nationalsozialistische Rassengesetzgebung. [From Windhoek to Nuremberg? Colonial 'intermarriage bans' and National Socialist racial legislation] In B. Kundrus (Ed.), *"Phantasiereiche". Der deutsche Kolonialismus aus kulturgeschichtlicher Perspektive ["Imaginative". German colonialism from a cultural-historical perspective] (110-131)*. Campus.

Kuokkanen, R. (2019). *Restructuring relations, restructuring relations: indigenous self-determination, governance, and gender*. Oxford University Press. doi:10.1093/oso/9780190913281.001.0001

Kuromiya, H. (2023). *Stalin, Japan, and the Struggle for Supremacy over China, 1894–1945*. Routledge Open History.

Kuss, S. (2017). *German Colonial Wars and the Context of Military Violence*. Harvard University Press. doi:10.4159/9780674977358

Kwet, M. (2019). Digital colonialism: US empire and the new imperialism in the Global South. *Race & Class*, *60*(4), 3–26. doi:10.1177/0306396818823172

La Porte, P. (2022). El laberinto marroquí. Piedra de tropiezo de liberales y autoritarios (1912-1926) [The Moroccan labyrinth. A stumbling block for liberals and authoritarians (1912-1926).]. *Hispania Nova. Revista de Historia Contemporánea*, *20*, 692–736.

La Vanguardia (periódico español)

Labanca, N. (1994). *Storia dell'Italia coloniale*. [*History of colonial Italy*.] Fenice 2000.

Labanca, N. (2005). Italian Colonial Internment. In R. Ben-Ghiat & M. Fuller (Eds.), *Italian colonialism* (pp. 27–36). Palgrave Mcmillan.

Laborde Carranco, A.A. (2011). Japón: Una revisión histórica de su origen para comprender sus retos actuales en el contexto internacional [Japan: A historical review of its origin to understand its current challenges in the international context]. *EN-CLAVES del pensamiento, 9*, 111-130.

Labra, R.M. (1901). La crisis colonial de España (1869-1898) [The colonial crisis of Spain (1869-1898)]. *Estudios de política palpitante y discursos parlamentarios [Studies of throbbing politics and parliamentary speeches].*

Labra, R.M. de (1910) *La orientación internacional de España [The international orientation of Spain].* Tip. de Alfredo Alonso.

Langa Laorga, A. (1985). El Japón en el siglo xx [Japan in the 20th Century]. *Cuadernos de Historia (Santiago, Chile)*, *16*(255), 18–31.

Lapidoth-Eschelbacher, R. (1982). *International straits of the world. The Red Sea and the Gulf of Aden*. Martinus Nijhoff Publishers.

Larson, B. & Brauer, F. (2009). *The Art of Evolution. Darwin, Darwinism and Visual Culture*. Lebano, University Press of New England.

Laski, H.J. (1935) Capitalism and War. *The New Statesman and Nation.*

Latham, M. (2010). The Cold War in the Third World, 1963-1975. In M. Leffler & O. Westad (Eds.), The Cambridge History of the Cold War. Cambridge: Cambridge University Press.

Latham, M. (2011). *The Right Kind of Revolution: Modernization, Development, and U.S. Foreign Policy from the Cold War to the Present.* Cornell University Press.

Lécuyer, M. C., & Serrano, C. (1976). *La guerre d'Afrique et ses répercussions sur l'Espagne (1859-1909) [The African War and its repercussions on Spain (1859-1909)].* Presses Universitaires de France.

Lee, A. J. (1976). *The Origins of the Popular Press 1855–1914.* Croom Helm.

Lenin, V. (1917). *Imperialism, the Highest Stage of Capitalism.* Foreign Languages Press.

Lentin, A. (1966). *La lutte tricontinentale. Imperialisme et revolution après la conference de La Havane.* Maspero.

Levy, J. T. (2003). Indigenous self- government, secession and self- determination. In Macedo, S. and A. Buchanan, Secession and self- determination, (pp. 119-136). Nomos XLV.

Lidell Hart, B. (1946). *Estrategia. La aproximación indirecta [The strategy of indirect approach].* Iberia.

Li, S. (Ed.). (1989). *Zhongguo Jinxiandai Renming Dacidian [The Dictionary of Modern and Contemporary Chinese Celebrities].* China's International Broadcasting Publishing House.

Li, W. (2017). *The Emergence of the Modern Chinese Diplomats: Officials in the Zongli Yamen, Waiwu Bu and legations, 1861-1911 [Zhōngguó jìndài wàijiāo guān qúntǐ de xíngchéng(1861-1911)].* SDX Joint Publishing Company.

Locke, P. G., & Peter, D. F. (1995). *Fighting Vehicles and Weapons of Rhodesia 1965-80.* P & P. Publishing.

Lohman, M. y MacPherson, R. (1983). *Rhodesia: Tactical victory, strategic defeat.* Marine Corps Command and Staff College, Marine Corps Development and Education Command.

Long, G., & Schmidt, B. (dirs.) (2005) Imperialism and Internationalism in the Discipline of International Relations. State University of New York Press.

López Cordón, Mª.V. (1982). España en las Conferencias de La Haya de 1899 y 1907 [Spain at the Hague Conferences of 1899 and 1907]. *Revista de Estudios Internacionales, 3*(3), 703–756.

López de la Asunción, M. A., & Leiva Ramírez, M. (2022). *El sitio de Baler. La heroica gesta de los Últimos de Filipinas [Baler's site. The heroic deed of the Last of the Philippines].* Ed. Actas.

Lowenthal, A. (2010), The United States in Latin America, 1960-2010: From hegemonic pretension to diverse and complex relations. *International Forum,* (3-4), 552-626.

Lowenthal, A. (1973). *The Dominican intervention.* Harvard University Press.

Ludendorff, E. (1964). *La Guerra Total [The Total War].* Ediciones Pleamar.

Lü, Y. (2010). The War That Scarcely Was. The Berliner Morgenpost and the Boxer Uprising. In M. Perraudin & J. Zimmerer (Eds.), *German Colonialism and National Identity* (pp. 45–57). Routledge.

Mackenzie, J. (2016). Passion or indifference: popular imperialism in Britain, continuities and discontinuities over two centuries. In J. Mackenzie (Ed.), European empires and the peopel. Popular responses to imperialism in France, Britain, the Netherlands, Belgium, Germany, and Italy (pp. 57-89). Manchester University Press.

Mackenzie, J. M. (1986). *Propaganda and Empire. The Manipulation of British Public Opinion, 1880-1960*. Manchester University Press.

Mackenzie, J. M. (1992). *Popular imperialism, and the military, 1850-1950*. Manchester University Press.

Madariaga, M.ª R. (2009). *Abdelkrim el Jatabi: la lucha por la independencia [Abdelkrim el Khatabi: the struggle for independence.]*. Alianza.

Madariaga, M. R. (2013). *Marruecos, ese gran desconocido. Breve historia del protectorado español [Morocco, that great unknown. Brief history of the Spanish protectorate]*. Alianza Editorial.

Madley, B. (2005). From Africa to Auschwitz: How German South West Africa Incubated Ideas and Methods Adopted and Developed by the Nazis in Eastern Europe. *European History Quarterly*, *35*(3), 429–464. doi:10.1177/0265691405054218

Madueño, M. (2017). Aproximación al concepto y tipologías de la guerra colonial. *Guerra Colonial*, *1*, 7–26.

Magocsi, P. E. (2010). *A History of Ukraine: The Land and Its Peoples*. University of Toronto Press.

Mamdani, M. (1999). Historicizing power and responses to power: Indirect rule and its reform. *Social Research*, *66*(3), 859–886. https://www.jstor.org/stable/40971353

Mañes Postigo, J. (2016). *Soldados Sin Bandera*. Editorial Magasé.

Mann, M. (2001). *Democracy and ethnic war. Democracy, liberalism, and war: Rethinking the democratic peace debate*. Lynne Rienner.

Maoz, Z., & Russett, B. (1993). Normative and structural causes of democratic peace, 1946-86. *The American Political Science Review*, *87*(3), 623–638. doi:10.2307/2938740

Marchesi, A. (2006), Imaginación política del antiimperialismo: intelectuales y política en el Cono Sur a fines de los sesenta. *E.I.A.L. Montevideo*, *17*(1).

Marchessi, A. (2017), Writing the Latin American Cold War: between the "local" South and the "global" North. *Estudos Históricos (Rio de Janeiro)*, *30* (60), 187-202.

Markakis, J. (2011). Ethiopia: The Last Two Frontiers. James Currey.

Markakis, J. (1989). Nationalities and the State in Ethiopia. *Third World Quarterly*, *11*(4), 118–130.

Marshall, P. (1996). *The Cambridge Illustrated History of the British Empire*. Cambridge University Press.

Martín Cerezo, S. (1904). *El sitio de Baler: Notas y recuerdos [The site of Baler: Notes and memories]*. Taller tipográfico del Colegio de Huérfanos [Typographic workshop of the College of Orphans].

Martín Corrales, E. (2002) La imagen del magrebí en España. Una perspectiva histórica. Siglos XIX-XX [The image of the North African in Spain. A historical perspective. 19th-20th centuries]. Bellaterra.

Martín Corrales, E. (2004). El patriotismo liberal español contra Marruecos (1814-1848). Antecedentes de la Guerra de África de 1859-1860 [Spanish liberal patriotism against Morocco (1814-1848). Background to the African War of 1859-1860]. *Illes y Imperis*, *7*, 11–43.

Martín Echevarría, L. (1937). *Geografía de España [Geography of Spain]* (Vols. 1–3). Labor.

Martin, A. C. (1957). *The Concentration Camps, 1900-1902: Facts, Figures and Fables*. Howard Timmins.

Martin, D., & Johnson, P. (1982). *The Struggle for Zimbabwe: The Chimurenga War*. Faber and Faber.

Martínez Taberner, G. (2015). Comercio intra-asiático y dinámicas inter-imperiales en Asia Oriental: el Japón Meiji y las colonias asiáticas del imperio español [Intra-Asian Trade And Inter-Imperial Dynamics in East Asia: Japan During the Meiji Peiod and the Asian Colonies of the Spanish Empire]. *Millars. Espai i Història, 39*, 125–157.

Martínez Taberner, G. (2017). *El Japón Meiji y las colonias asiáticas del imperio español [Meiji Japan and the asitaci colonies of the Spanish Empire].* Edicions Bellaterra.

Martínez-Robles, D. (2010). Más allá de los tratados desiguales: reciprocidad en el tratado sino-español de 1864 [Beyond unequal treaties: reciprocity in the Sino-Spanish treaty of 1864]. In P. San Ginés (Ed.), *Cruce de miradas, relaciones e intercambios [Crossing glances, relationships and exchanges]* (pp. 487–505). Editorial Universidad de Granada.

Martínez-Robles, D. (2018). *Entre dos Imperios. Sinibaldo de Mas y la empresa colonial en China (1844-1868) [Crossing glances, relationships and exchanges].* Macial Pons.

Martínez-Robles, D. (2018). Los desheredados de la empresa imperial: Implantación diplomática de España como potencia colonial periférica en China [The disinherited of the imperial company: Diplomatic implantation of Spain as a peripheral colonial power in China]. *Historia Contemporánea, 57*(57), 460–465. doi:10.1387/hc.17724

Martin-Márquez, S. (2011). Desorientaciones. El colonialismo español en África y la performance de la identidad [disorientations. Spanish colonialism in Africa and the performance of identity.]. Bellaterra.

Mateo, J. L. (2003). La «hermandad» hispano-marroquí. Política y religión bajo el Protectorado español en Marruecos (1912-1956) [The Spanish-Moroccan "hermandad". Política y religión bajo el Protectorado español en Marruecos (1912-1956).]. Bellaterra.

Mavropoulos, N. (2020). Why the Italians Set their Sights on East Africa: Developments and Unfulfilled Aspirations in the Mediterranean during the 19th Century, *Historical contributions - Historische Beiträge, 39*(58), 93-108.

McLachlan, S. (2011). *Armies of the Adowa campaign 1896.* Osprey Publishing.

McNamara, R. (2012). The last throw of the dice: Portugal, Rhodesia and South Africa, 1970–74. *Portuguese Studies, 28*(2), 201–215. doi:10.5699/portstudies.28.2.0201

Melson, C. D. (2005). Top secret war: Rhodesian Special Operations. *Small Wars & Insurgencies, 16*(1), 57–82. doi:10.1080/0959231042000322567

Memorandum of conversation between Mikhail Gorbachev and James Baker in Moscow . (1990). U.S. Department of State, FOIA.

Memorandum of conversation between Robert Gates and Vladimir Kryuchkov in Moscow . (1990). George H.W. Bush Presidential Library.

Menéndez Caravia, J. (1896). La guerra en Cuba: su origen y desarrollo. Reformas necesarias para terminar e impedir la propaganda filibustera [Necessary reforms to end and prevent filibuster propaganda], s. l, s. n

Mesa, R. (1993). La Conferencia de Bandung [The Bandung Conference]. *Historia (Wiesbaden, Germany), 16.*

Metaferia, G. (2009). *Ethiopia and the United States. History, Diplomacy and analysis.* Agora Publishing.

Migenmi, A. (1984). *Immagine coordinata per un impero. [Coordinated image for an empire.] Etiopía 1935-1936,* Gruppo editoriale Forma.

Mihić. I. (2018). Diplomatski odnosi Francuske i Jugoslavije 1954. - 1962. i Alžirski rat za neovisnost. [Diplomatic relations between France and Yugoslavia 19541962 and the Algerian War of Independence.] Zagreb University

Miillerson, R. (2003). Sovereignty and secession: then and now, here and there. In J. Dahlitz (Ed.), *Secession and international law, conflict avoidance and regional appraisals* (pp. 125–167). Asser press. doi:10.1007/978-90-6704-699-2_10

Millman, B. (2013). *British Somaliland. An Administrative History, 1920-1960*. Routledge.

Moga Romero, V. (2008) La cuestión marroquí en la escritura africanista. Una aproximación bibliográfica y editorial española al conocimiento del norte de Marruecos (1859-2006) [The Moroccan question in Africanist writing. A Spanish bibliographical and editorial approach to the knowledge of northern Morocco (1859-2006)].Bellaterra.

Mongalo, B. E., & Du Pisani, K. (1999). Victims of a White Manís War: Blacks in concentration camps during the South African War (1899-1902). *History (London)*, *44*(1), 148–182.

Montoro, G. (1991). La retrocesión de Tarfaya e Ifni [The retrocession of Tarfaya and Ifni]. *Espacio, Tiempo y Forma. Serie V, Historia Comtemporánea*, *4*, 181–189.

Moorcraft, P. L., & McLaughlin, P. (1982). *The Rhodesian War a Military History*. Stackpole Books.

Moorcraft, P., & McLaughlin, P. (2010). *The Rhodesian War: A Military History*. Stackpole Books.

Moore, M. (2003). An historical argument for indigenous self- determination. In Macedo, S. and A. Buchanan, Secession and self- determination, pp. 89–118. Nomos XLV.

Morales Lezcano, V. (1990). El Norte de África, estrella del Orientalismo español [North Africa, star of Spanish Orientalism.]. *AWRAQ*, anejo al v. XI, 17-34

Morales Lezcano, V. (1993). *España y el mundo árabe: imágenes cruzadas [Spain and the Arab world: crossed images]*. AECI.

Morales, V. (1998). *El final del protectorado hispano-francés en Marruecos: el desafío del nacionalismo magrebí (1945-1962) [The end of the Spanish-French protectorate in Morocco: the challenge of Maghreb nationalism (1945-1962).]*. Instituto Egipcio de Estudios Islámicos.

Moreno, A. (2001) La historia de las relaciones internacionales y de la política exterior Española [The history of international relations and Spanish foreign policy.]. In Pereira, J.C. (ed.) La historia de las relaciones internacionales [The history of International Relations], Ayer, 42, 71-96.

Morgan, W. M. (2016). Pacific Dominance. The United States versus Japan. In J. Lacey (Ed.), *Great Strategic Rivals from the Classical World to the Cold War* (pp. 479–509). Oxford University Press.

Mtisi, J., Nyakudya, M., & Barnes, T. A. (2009). War in Rhodesia, 1965-1980. In Becoming Zimbabwe: a history from the pre-colonial period to 2008, 141-166. Jacana.

Mumin Ahad, A., & Gerrand, V. (2004). Italian cultural influences in Somalia. A reciprocity? *Quaderni del*, *900*(IV), 13–24.

Muñoz Bolaños, R. (2015). *Griff nach der Weltmacht*: Hacia el poder mundial. El desarrollo de la doctrina militar alemana (1808-1945). [*Griff nach der Weltmacht*: Towards world power. The development of German military doctrine (1808-1945)] In E. Martínez Ruiz & J. Cantera Montenegro (Eds.), *Perspectivas y Novedades de la Historia Militar: una aproximación global [Perspectives and News of Military History: a global approach]* ((Vol. II, pp. 1.469–1.488). Ministerio de Defensa.

Muñoz Bolaños, R. (2021). Wo ist heute das Volk der Herero, wo sind heute seine Häuptlinge? [The German Military Campaign in South West Africa (1904-1907)]. *Guerra Colonial*, *9*, 75–96.

Murphy, S. (2000). Democratic legitimacy and the recognition of states and governments. In G. H. Fox & B. R. Roth (Eds.), *Democratic governance and international law* (pp. 123–154). Cambridge University Press. doi:10.1017/CBO9780511522307.005

Nantawaroprai, D. (2022). Role of the International Criminal Court in War Crimes, Crimes against Humanity, and Acts of Aggression by Threats of the Usage of Nuclear Weapons under International Law "Jus Cogens". *Journal of Positive School Psychology*, pp. 5567-5576.

Nechaev, V. D., Chikharev, I. A., Irkhin, A. A., & Makovskaya, D. V. (2019). Framework of the geostrategic atlas of the greater mediterranean. *Vestnik Moskovskogo universiteta. Seriya 5. Geografiya*, *1*, 67–74.

Nedjar, M. (2008). *Argelia y la cuestión palestina durante el periodo de gobierno de FLN (1962-1988). [Algeria and the Palestinian question during the period of FLN rule (1962-1988).]* [Tesis doctoral; Universidad Autónoma de Madrid].

Neila, J. L. (2007). La historia de las relaciones internacionales en España: Un marco interpretative [The history of international relations in Spain: An interpretive framework.]. *Estudios de Historia de España*, *IX*, 177–212.

Neila, J. L. (2011). *España y el Mediterráneo en el siglo XX. De los acuerdos de Cartagena al proceso de Barcelona [Spain and the Mediterranean in the 20th century. From the Cartagena agreements to the Barcelona process]*. Sílex.

Nikolić, M. (2016) Jugosloven na prvim linijama fronta u Ažiru. [Yugoslav on the front lines in Ažir.] Princip Info.

Niño, A. (2009) Uso y abuso de las relaciones culturales en la política internacional [Use and abuse of cultural relations in international politics]. In NIÑO, A. (ed.) La ofensiva cultural norteamericana durante la Guerra Fría [The American cultural offensive during the Cold War] Ayer, n. 75(3), 25-61.

Niño, A. (2022). Historiografía de las relaciones internacionales españolas en democracia [Historiography of Spanish international relations in democracy]. In *Ortíz Heras, M. & González, D.A. (coords.) La transición exterior. La asignatura pendiente de la democratización [The outer transition. The unfinished business of democratization]* (pp. 3–34). Comares Historia.

Nyaoro, D. (2019). Refugee hosting and conflict resolution: opportunities for diplomatic interventions and buffeting regional hegemons. In D. Schmidt, L. Kimathi, & M. O. Owiso (Eds.), *Refugees and forced migration in the Horn and Eastern Africa* (pp. 17–32). Springer.

Ó'Tuathail, G. (2002). Theorizing practical geopolitical reasoning: The case of the United States' response to the war in Bosnia. *Political Geography*, *21*(5), 601–628. doi:10.1016/S0962-6298(02)00009-4

Ó'Tuathail, G., & Agnew, J. (1992). Geopolitics and discourse: Practical geopolitical reasoning in American foreign policy. *Political Geography*, *11*(2), 190–204. doi:10.1016/0962-6298(92)90048-X

Ó'Tuathail, G., & Dalby, S. (2002). Introduction: Rethinking Geopolitics. Towards a critical geopolitics. In G. Ó'Tuathail & S. Dalby (Eds.), *Rethinking Geopolitics* (pp. 1–15). Routledge.

Okbazghi, Y. (1987). The Eritrean question: A colonial case? *The Journal of Modern African Studies*, *25*(4), 643–668.

Oliveira, P. A. (2017). Decolonization in Portuguese Africa. In *T. T. Spear (Dir.), Oxford Research Encyclopedia of African History*. Oxford University Press. doi:10.1093/acrefore/9780190277734.013.41

Olson, W. C., & Groom, A. J. R. (1991). International relations then and now: origins and trends in interpretation. HarperCollins.

Oxford Historical Treaties. (1905). Agreement of Peace and Protection between Italy and the Mullah of the Somalis (Africa). *Illig*, *5*. Oxford Historical Treaties. https://opil.ouplaw.com/view/10.1093/law:oht/law-oht-198-CTS -137.regGroup.1/law-oht-198-CTS-137

Pacheco Yanguas, J. (ca. 1910). *Filipinas: impresiones, notas y memorias de un prisionero [The Philippines: Impressions, Notes, and Memoirs of a Prisoner.]*. Biblioteca Digital. https://bibliotecadigital.aecid.es/bibliodig/es/consulta/reg istro.do?id=6636

Paine, S. C. M. (2016). China, Russia, and Japan Compete to Create a New World Order. In J. Lacey (Ed.), Great Strategic Rivals from the Classical World to the Cold War (pp. 417-446). Oxford University Press.

Palacios, L. & Ramírez-Ruiz, R. (2011). *China. Historia, pensamiento, arte y cultura [China. History, thought, art and culture.]*. Almuzara.

Palieraki, E. (2017). From Peking to Havana. The Chilean radical left and its revolutions, 1963-1970 [s]. *Monde*, *11*(1), 119–138. doi:10.3917/mond1.171.0119

Palmer, M. (1999). *Guardians of the Gulf: A History of America's Expanding Role in the Persion Gulf, 1883-1992*. Simon and Schuster.

Palomino, P. (2019). On the Disadvantages of "Global South" for Latin American Studies. *Journal of World Philosophies*, *4*(2), 22–39.

Papers, A. (2002). Intervention during the cold war. *The Adelphi Papers*, *42*(350), 33–45. doi:10.1080/05679320208459466

Parfitt, R. (2019). *The process of international legal reproduction. Inequality, historiography, resistance*. Cambridge University Press.

Parker, J. (2006). *Assignment Selous Scouts: Inside Story of a Rhodesian Special Branch Officer*. Galago Pub.

Parrott, R. (2022). Tricontinentalism and the Anti-Imperial Project. In R. Parrott & M. Lawrence (Eds.), *The Tricontinental Revolution: Third World Radicalism and the Cold War*. Cambridge University Press. doi:10.1017/9781009004824.002

Pedraz Marcos, A. (2000). *Quimeras de África. La Sociedad Española de Africanistas y Colonialistas. El colonialismo español de finales del siglo XIX [Chimeras of Africa. The Spanish Society of Africanists and Colonialists. Spanish colonialism at the end of the 19th century]*. Ediciones Polifemo.

Pedraz Marcos, A. (2000). *Quimeras de África: la Sociedad Española de Africanistas y Colonialistas: el colonialismo español a finales del siglo XIX [Chimeras of Africa: the Spanish Society of Africanists and Colonialists: Spanish colonialism at the end of the 19th century.]*. Polifemo.

Peksen, D., & Lounsbery, M. (2012). Beyond the Target State: Foreign Military Intervention and Neighboring State Stability. *International Interactions*, *38*(3), 348–374. doi:10.1080/03050629.2012.676516

Pennell, C. R. (2000). *Morocco since 1830. A History*. Hurst & Company.

Pereira, J. C. (1987). Reflexiones sobre la historia de las relaciones internacionales y la política exterior Española [Reflections on the history of international relations and Spanish foreign policy.]. *Cuadernos de Historia Moderna y Contemporánea*, (8), 269–290.

Pereira, P., Bašić, F., Bogunovic, I., & Barcelo, D. (2022). Russian-Ukrainian war impacts the total environment. *The Science of the Total Environment*, 837–865. PMID:35569661

Pérez Galdós, B. (2004). *Aita Tettauen*. Akal.

Perraudin, M., & Zimmerer, J. (2010). *German Colonialism and National Identity*. Routledge. doi:10.4324/9780203852590

Pettiná, V. (2018). *Historia mínima de la Guerra Fría en América Latina*. El Colegio de México. doi:10.2307/j.ctv8bt0xr

Peyrefitte, A. (1997). *C'était de Gaulle. La France reprend sa place dans le monde* (Vol. II). Fayard.

Pirala, A. (1895). *Anales de la guerra de Cuba [Annals of the Cuban War]*. Felipe González Rojas.

Porch, D. (1992). Bugeaud, Gallieni, Lyautey: el desarrollo de las guerras coloniales francesas [Bugeaud, Gallieni, Lyautey: the development of the French colonial wars]. En Paret P. (coord.), Creadores de la estrategia moderna: desde Maquiavelo a la era nuclear [Creators of modern strategy: from Machiavelli to the nuclear age] (pp. 395-423).

Porter, B. (2004). *The Absent-Minded Imperialists. Empire, Society, and Culture in Britain*. Oxford University Press.

Potter, S. J. (2003). *News and the British World: The Emergence of an Imperial Press System 1876-1922*. Oxford University Press. doi:10.1093/acprof:oso/9780199265121.001.0001

Power, M. (2001). Geo-politics and the representation of Portugal's African colonial wars: Examining the limits of 'Vietnam syndrome'. *Political Geography*, *20*(4), 461–491. https://www.sciencedirect.com/science/arti-cle/pii/S0962629801000038. doi:10.1016/S0962-6298(01)00003-8

Prashad, V. (2012). *Las naciones oscuras. A history of the Third World*. Península.

Prashad, V. (2013). *Las naciones pobres. A possible global history of the South*. Península.

Pratt, M. L. (2003). *Imperial eyes. Travel writing and transculturation* (2nd ed.). Routledge. doi:10.4324/9780203106358

Prazauskas, A. (1991). Ethnic conflicts in the context if democratizing political systems. *Theory and Society*, *20*(5), 581–602. doi:10.1007/BF00232661

Preller, G. (2018). *ZIPRA and ZANLA war stories*. Independently editorial.

Preston, M. (2004). Stalemate and the termination of civil war: Rhodesia reassessed. *Journal of Peace Research*, *41*(1), 65–83. doi:10.1177/0022343304040050

Prior, C. (2010). Empire before Labour: The 'Scramble for Africa' and the Media. In Frank, B. Horner, C. & Stewart, D. (eds.). The British Labour Movement and Imperialism (pp. 23-40). Cambridge Scholars Publishing.

Prunier, G. (2021). *The Country That Does Not Exist. A History of Somaliland*. Hurst & Co.

Puell, F. (1996). *El soldado desconocido. De la leva a la "mili" [The unknown soldier. From the cam to the "milli"]*. Biblioteca Nueva.

Puell, F. (2003). *Historia del Ejército [Army History]*. Alianza Editorial.

Puell, F. (2013). Guerra en Cuba y Filipinas: Combates terrestres [War in Cuba and the Philippines: Land combat]. *Revista Universitaria de Historia Militar*, *2*, 34–17.

Pulido López-Rodríguez, G. (2017). Rhodesia: Guerra sucia, insurgencia y violencia política. *Análisis GESI*, *24*.

Putin, V. (2022) *Address by the President of the Russian Federation*. Kremlin. http://en.kremlin.ru/events/president/news

Quintana, F. (1996). La historia de las relaciones internacionales en España: apuntes para un balance historiográfico [The history of international relations in Spain: notes for a historiographical balance]. In *Comisión Española de Historia de las Relaciones Internacionales La Historia de las Relaciones Internacionales: una visión desde España [Spanish Commission for the History of International Relations The History of International Relations: a vision from Spain]* (pp. 9–65). CEHRI-Ministerio de Asuntos Exteriores-Ministerio de Educación y Ciencia.

Ramírez Ruiz, R. (2017). Neto and Giadán: The Last Two Spanish in the Qing Dynasty. *Sinologia Hispanica, 4*(1), 1–46. doi:10.18002in.v4i1.5266

Ramírez Ruiz, R. (2018). *Historia de China Contemporánea. De las guerras del opio a nuestros días [History of Contemporary China. From the opium wars to the present day]*. Síntesis.

Ratner, S. (1996). Drawing a better line: Uti possidetis and the borders of new states. *AJIL, 90*(4), 590–624. doi:10.2307/2203988

Redondo, F. (1995). *La Guerra de los Diez Años [The Ten Years' War]*. Monografías del CESEDEN, Núm. 14.

Reguera, A. T. (1990). Orígenes del pensamiento geopolítico en España. Una primera aproximación [Origins of geopolitical thought in Spain. A first approximation.]. *Documents d'Analisi Geografica*, (17), 79–104.

Reyes Manzano, A. (2005). Mitos y realidades sobre las relaciones hispano-japonesas durante los siglos XVI-XVII [Myths and Realities of the Spanish-Japanese Relations in the 16th-17th Centuries]. *BROCAR, 29*(29), 53–75. doi:10.18172/brocar.1680

Reyes Manzano, A. (2014). *La Cruz y la Catana: relaciones entre España y Japón (siglos XVI-XVII) [The Cross and the Catana: Relations between Spain and Japan (16th-17th centuries)]*. Universidad de La Rioja.

Richmond, W. (2013). *The Circassian Genocide*. Rutgers University Press.

Rivers, C. (2017). *The Italian Invasion of Africa: The History of Italian Colonization in Africa and the Rise and Fall of the Italian Empire*. Create Space Independent Publishing Platform.

Rodao, F. (1997). *Españoles en Siam, 1540-1939: una aportación al estudio de la presencia hispana en Asia [Spaniards in Siam, 1540-1939: a contribution to the study of the Hispanic presence in Asia]*. CSIC.

Rodao, F. (2002). *Franco y el imperio japonés. Imágenes y propaganda en tiempos de Guerra [Franco and the Japanese Empire. Images and propaganda in times of war.]*. Plaza & Janés.

Rodrigues, F. C. (2013). A desmobilização dos combatentes africanos das Forças Armadas Portuguesas da Guerra Colonial. *Ler História, 65*(65), 113–128. doi:10.4000/lerhistoria.484

Rodríguez Caparrini, B. (2014). Alumnos españoles en el internado jesuita de Beaumont (Old Windsor, Inglaterra), 1880-1886 [Spanish students at the Jesuit boarding school at Beaumont (Old Windsor, England), 1880-1886.]. *Hispania Sacra, LXVI* (Extra I), 403-452.

Rodríguez Esteban, J. A. (1996). *Geografía y colonialismo. La Sociedad Geográfica de Madrid (1876-1936) [Geography and colonialism. The Geographical Society of Madrid (1876-1936).]*. Universidad Autónoma de Madrid Ediciones.

Rodríguez Esteban, J. A. (1996). *Geografía y colonialismo. La Sociedad Geográfica de Madrid (1876-1936)*. Ediciones de la Universidad Autónoma de Madrid.

Rodríguez González, A. R. (1989). El peligro Amarillo en el pacífico español 1880-1898. [The yellow peril in the Spanish Pacific 1880-1898] In F. Rodao (Ed.), *España y el Pacífico [Spain and the Pacific]*. AECI.

Rodríguez González, A. R. (2016). *Tramas ocultas de la guerra del 98 [Hidden plots of the war of '98]*. Actas.

Rodríguez Jiménez, J. L. (2020). *Historia contemporánea de Japón* [*Contemporary Japanese history*]. Síntesis.

Rojas, R. (2021). *El árbol de las revoluciones. Ideas y poder en América Latina.* Turner.

Romero Morales, Y. (2014). Prensa y literatura en la Guerra de África (1859-1860). Opinión publicada, patriotismo y xenophobia [Press and literature in the African War (1859-1860). Published opinion, patriotism and xenophobia]. *Historia Contemporánea, 49*, 619–644.

Rossi, G. (1974). *Anatomy of a Rebel. Smith of Rhodesia: a biography.* Graham Publishing.

Rotberg, R. (1988). *The founder: Cecil Rhodes and the pursuit of power.* Oxford University Press.

Roth Mitchel, P. (2015). *The Encyclopedia of War Jounalism (1807-2010).* Grey House Publishing.

Rüger, J. (2009). *The Great Naval Game: Britain and Germany in the Age of Empire (Studies in the Social and Cultural History of Modern Warfare).* Cambridge University Press.

Rust, C. (1905). *Krieg und Frieden im Hererolande. Aufzeichnungen aus dem Kriegsjahre 1904* [*War and Peace in Hereroland. Notes from the War Year 1904*]. Kittler.

Saïd, E. W. (2002). *Orientalismo.* Debolsillo.

Sáiz, C. (1974). *Guerrillas en Cuba y en otros países de iberoamerica [Guerrillas in Cuba and other Latin American countries].* Editora Nacional.

Salas, R. (1992). *El Protectorado de España en Marruecos [The Protectorate of Spain in Morocco.].* Mapfre, 1992.

Salazar, A. O. (2016]). Política Ultramarina. In Discursos e Notas Políticas, 1928 a 1966 (1041-1060). Coimbra Editora.

Salazar, A. O. (2016). A política de África e os seus erros. In *Discursos e Notas Políticas, 1928 a 1966 (1101-1107).* Coimbra Editora.

Sánchez Mejía, M. L. (2013). Barbarie y civilización en el discurso nacionalista de la Guerra de África (1859-1860) [Barbarism and civilization in the nationalist discourse of the African War (1859-1860).]. *Revista de Estudios Políticos, 162*, 39–67.

Sánchez Román, J. A. (2021). *La Sociedad de Naciones y la reinvención del imperialismo liberal [The League of Nations and the reinvention of liberal imperialism.].* Marcial Pons Historia.

Santiáñez, N. (2007). De la tropa al tropo: Colonialismo, escritura de guerra y enunciación metafórica en *Diario de un testigo de la guerra de África* [From the troop to the trope: Colonialism, writing of war and metaphorical enunciation *in Diary of a witness to the war in Africa.*]. *Hispanic Review, 76*(1), 71–93. doi:10.1353/hir.2008.0002

Sanz Díaz, C. (2019). Relaciones internacionales y formación para la diplomacia en torno a la Primera Guerra Mundial: un estudio de caso [International relations and training for diplomacy around the First World War: a case study.]. In Lozano Vázquez, A., Sarquís Ramírez, D.J., Villanueva Lira, Jorge, D. ¿Cien años de relaciones internacionales? Disciplinariedad y revisionism [One hundred years of international relations? Disciplinarity and revisionism] (pp. 285–299). Siglo XXI.

Schmidt, B. (2019). Revisando la historia temprana de las relaciones internacionales: imperialismo, colonialismo y raza [Revisiting the early history of international relations: imperialism, colonialism, and race]. In Lozano Vázquez, A., Sarquís Ramírez, D.J., Villanueva Lira, Jorge, D. ¿Cien años de relaciones internacionales? Disciplinariedad y revisionism [One hundred years of international relations? Disciplinarity and revisionism] (pp. 250–264). Siglo XXI.

Schmidt, B. (1998). *The Political discourse of anarchy. A disciplinary history of international relations.* SUNY Press.

Schneider, J. C. (2020). A Non-Western Colonial Power? The Qing Empire in Postcolonial Discourse. *Journal of Asian History*, *54*(2), 311–341. doi:10.13173/jasiahist.54.2.0311

Schöning, J. (1997). *Triviale tropen: exotische reise- und Abenteuerfilme aus Deutschland, 1919-1939. [Trivial tropics: exotic travel and adventure films from Germany, 1919-1939.]* Kritik.

Schulte-Varendorff, U. (2007). Schutztruppe. [Protection Force] In U. Van der Heyden & J. Zeller (Eds.), *Kolonialismus hierzulande: Eine Spurensuche in Deutschland [Colonialism in this country: A search for traces in Germany]* (pp. 386–390). Sutton Verlag.

Schwabe, K. (1899). *Mit Schwert und Pflug in Deutsch-Südwestafrika. Vier Kriegs und Wanderjahre. Mit zahlreichen Karten und Skizzen sowie Abbildungen und Tabellen [With Sword and Plough in German South-West Africa. Four Years of War and Travel. With numerous maps and sketches as well as illustrations and tables].* Berlin, Ernst Siegfried Mittler u. Sohn.

Sèbe, B. (2013). *Heroic imperialists in Africa. The promotion of British and French colonial heroes, 1870-1936.* Manchester University Press.

Sèbe, B. (2013). *Heroic imperialists in Africa. The promotion of British and French colonial heroes, 1870-1939.* Manchester University Press.

Segura Valero, G. (2006). *Ifni. La guerra que silenció Franco*, Ediciones Martínez Roca, S.A.

Serna, A. (2001). *Al sur de Tarifa. Marruecos-España: un malentendido histórico [South of Tarifa. Morocco-Spain: a historical misunderstanding].* Marcial Pons.

Serrallonga Urquidi, J. (1998). La Guerra de África (1850-1860). Una revision [The African War (1850-1860). A review]. *Ayer*, *29*, 139–159.

Shapiro, M. (1997). Violent Cartographies. Mapping Cultures of War: University of Minnesota Press.

Sharman, N. (2021). *Britain's informal empire in Spain, 1830-1950.* Palgrave Macmillan. doi:10.1007/978-3-030-77950-4

Sharp, J. P. (1993). Publishing American identity: Popular geopolitics, myth and the Reader's Digest. *Political Geography*, *12*(6), 491–503. doi:10.1016/0962-6298(93)90001-N

Sharp, J. P. (2000). *Condensing the Cold War. Reader's Digest and American Identity.* University Minnesota Press.

Shaw, M. (2008). *International law.* Cambridge university press. doi:10.1017/CBO9780511841637

Shehadi, K. S. (1993). *Ethnic self-determination and the break-up of states.* The Adelphi Papers. doi:10.1080/05679329308449209

Shehim, K., & Searing, J. (1980). Djibouti and the Question of Afar Nationalism. *African Affairs*, *79*(315), 209–226.

Shelley, F. M. (2013). *Nation Shapes. The story behind the world's borders.* ABC-CLIO.

Shikova, N. (2020). The possibilities and limits of non-territorial autonomy in securing indigenous self-determination. *Philosophy and Society*, *31*(3), 277–444. doi:10.2298/FID2003363S

Shi, Y. (Ed.). (1996). *Zhonghua Minguo Waijiaoshi Cidian [The Dictionary of Diplomatic History of the Republic of China].* Shanghai Ancient Books Press.

Sidaway, J. D. (2003). Iberian geopolitics. In K. Dodds & D. Atkinson (Eds.), *Geopolitical Traditions. A century of geopolitical thought* (pp. 118–149). Routledge.

Simons, O., & Honold, A. (2002). *Kolonialismus als Kultur. Literatur, Medien, Wissenschaften in der deutschen Gründerzeit des Fremden* [Colonialism as a culture. Literature, media, science in the German early days of the foreign.]. Francke Verlag.

Smith, H. W. (1998). The Talk of Genocide, the Rhetoric of Miscegenation: Notes on the Debates in the German Reichstag Concerning Southwest Africa, 1904-14. In S. Friedrischmeyer, S. Lennox, & S. Zantop (Eds.), *The Imperialist Imagination: German Colonialism and Its Legacy* (pp. 107–123). University of Michigan Press.

Smith, P. (2010). *Estados Unidos y América Latina. Hegemony and resistance*. PUV.

Snider, T. (2022) The war in Ukraine is a colonial war. *The New Yorker. s*https://www.newyorker.com/news/essay

Sociedade de Geografía de Lisboa. (1886). Mapa de cor-de-rosa. Lisboa. https://purl.pt/93/1/iconografia/imagens/cc976a/cc976a_3.jpg

Sorrentino, G. (1911). Atraverso il Benadir [Across Benadir]. *Bollettino della Società Africana d'Italia, [Bulletin of the African Society of Italy]*, 225-239. http://digitale.bnc.roma.sbn.it/tecadigitale/giornale/TO0017 9105/1911

Souyri, P. F. (2005). La colonización japonesa: un colonialismo moderno pero no occidental. [Japanese colonisation: a modern but non-Western colonialism] In M. Ferro (Ed.), *El libro negro del colonialismo. Siglos XVI al XXI: del exterminio al arrepentimiento* [*The Black Book of Colonialism. Sixteenth to twenty-first centuries: from extermination to repentance*]. La Esfera de los Libros.

Spillmann, G. (1967). *Du protectorat à l'indépendance: Maroc [From protectorate to independence: Morocco] (1912-1955)*. Plon.

Spottorno, R. (1921). *Consideraciones generales y de carácter histórico acerca de la Diplomacia [General and historical considerations about Diplomacy.]*. Ed. Reus.

Srivastava, N. (2018). *Italian Colonialism and Resistances to Empire, 1930-1970*. Palgrave Macmillan. doi:10.1057/978-1-137-46584-9

Stanard, M. (2011). Afterword. In Mackenzie J. M. (Ed.), European empires and the people: popular responses to imperialism in France, Britain, the Netherlands, Belgium, Germany and Italy (pp. 229-233). Manchester University Press.

Stanley, B. (2007). Djibouti City. In M. R. T. Dumper & B. E. Stanley (Eds.), *Cities of the middle East and North Africa. A historical encyclopaedia* (pp. 132–135). ABC-CLIO.

Statute of the International Court of Justice. (n.d.). *Statute*. ICJ. https://www.icj-cij.org/en/statute

Steinmetz, G. (2005). Von der 'Eingeborenenpolitik' zur Vernichtungsstrategie: Deutsch-Südwestafrika, 1904 [From 'Native Policy' to Extermination Strategy: German South-West Africa, 1904]. *Peripherie, 97/98*, 195–227.

Stucki, A. (2017). *Las guerras de Cuba. Violencia y campos de concentración (1868-1898) [The Cuban wars. Violence and concentration camps (1868-1898).]*. La Esfera de los Libros.

Subtelny Orest. (2009) Ukraine. A History. University of Toronto Press.

Sueiro, S. (2004) La historia de las relaciones internacionales en España [The history of international relations in Spain]. Un balance. Tendencia actuales y perspectivas de future [A balance. Current trends and future prospects.]. In Rémond, R.-Tusell J.-Pellistrandi, B.-Sueiro, S. Hacer la historia del siglo XX [Making 20th century history] (pp. 95-118). Biblioteca Nueva (UNED).

Summers, J. (2007). *Peoples and international law, how nationalism and self-determination shape a contemporary law of nations*. doi:10.1163/ej.9789004154919.i-468

Summers, M. W. (1994). *The Press Gang: Newspapers and Politics 1865–1878*. University of North Carolina Press.

Taddia, I. (1994). Ethiopian source material and colonial rule in the Nineteenth Century: The letter to Menilek (1899) by Blatta Gäbrä Egzi'abeher. *Journal of African History*, *35*(3), 493–516. https://www.jstor.org/stable/pdf/182645.pdf

Tang, J. (Ed.). (2000). *Zhongguo Waijiao Cidian [Dictionary on China's Diplomacy]*. World Affairs Press.

Teixeira, R. A. (2006). Guerra de África: Angola, 1961-1974. QuidNovi

Teshale, T. (1995). *The Making of Modern Ethiopia: 1896-1974*. The Red Sea Press Inc.

The First Historical Archives of China, Peking University, & Macao Polytechnic Institute (Edit.). (2004). The Collection of Sino-foreign Relation Archives of the Ministry of Foreign Affairs in Qing Dynasty, China and Spain. Zhong Hua Book Company.

The Times. (1908). The Fighting in Italian Somaliland. *The Times*. https://www.thetimes.co.uk/archive/article/1908-04-11/5/23.h tml?region=global#start%3D1785-0101%26end%3D1985-%2012-31%26 terms%3DMullah%26back%3D/tto/archive/find/Mullah/w:1785-0101 %7E1985-12-31/8%26prev%3D/%20tto/archive/frame/goto/Mullah/w :1785-01-01%7E1985-1231/79%26next%3D/tto/archive/frame/goto/ Mullah/w:1785-01-01%7E1985-12-31/81

The Times. (1914) The Dervish Danger in Somaliland: Increase of protective forces, *The Times*. https://www.thetimes.co.uk/archive/article/1914-03-17/7/5.ht ml?region=global#start%3D1785-%2001-01%26end%3D1985-12-31%26 terms%3DMullah%26back%3D/tto/archive/find/Mullah/w:1785-01-0 1%7E1985-12-31/7%26prev%3D/tto/archive/frame/goto/Mullah/w:1 785-01-01%7E1985-12-31/66%26next%3D/tto/archive/%20frame/got o/Mullah/w:1785-01-01%7E1985-12-31/68

Thies, C. (2021). Myth, half-truth, reality or strategy? In C. Thies (Ed.), *International relations and the first great debate* (pp. 118–132). Routledge.

Thomas, M. (2005). *The French Empire between the Wars*. Manchester University Press.

Thompson, A. (2014). *Imperial Britain: The Empire in British Politics, 1880-1932*. Routledge. doi:10.4324/9781315840321

Tibebu, T. (1996). Ethiopia. The Anomaly and Paradox of Africa. *Journal of Black Studies*, *26*(4), 414–430.

Togores Sánchez, L. (2019) La defensa de la soberanía española en Filipinas [The defense of Spanish sovereignty in the Philippines]. *Revista de Historia Militar, II Extraordinario [Military History Magazine, Extraordinary II.]*. https://publicaciones.defensa.gob.es/media/downloadable/file s/links/r/h/rhm_extra_ii_2019_.pdf

Togores Sánchez, L. E. (2000). *Japón en el siglo XX. De imperio a potencia económica [Japan in the 20th Century. From Empire to Economic Power]*. Arco Libros S.L.

Togores, L. E. (2006). Guerra cubana de los diez años [Cuban Ten Years' War]. In *Aproximación a la historia ilitary de España [Approach to the military history of Spain]* (pp. 537–556). Ministerio de Defensa.

Togores, L. E., & Neila, J. L. (1993). *La Escuela Diplomática: cincuenta años de servicio al Estado (1942-1992) [The Diplomatic School: fifty years of service to the State (1942-1992).]*. Escuela Diplomática.

Tone, J. L. (2008). *Guerra y genocidio en Cuba [War and genocide in Cuba]*. Turner.

Torikata, Y. (2007). Reexamining de Gaulle's Peace Initiative on the Vietnam War [November]. *Diplomatic History, 31*(5), 5. doi:10.1111/j.1467-7709.2007.00659.x

Torre del Río, R. de la. (1985). El Japón Meiji [Meiji Japan]. *Cuadernos de Historia (Santiago, Chile), 16*(255), 4–16.

Tripodi, P. (1999). *L'eredità coloniale in Somalia [The colonial legacy in Somalia.]*. St. Martin Press. doi:10.1057/9780333982907

Tully, J. (2000). The Struggles of Indigenous Peoples for and of Freedom. In Duncan, I., Patton, P., & Sanders, W. (Eds.), Political theory and the rights of indigenous peoples (pp. 36-60). Cambridge University Press.

Turp, D. (2001). *Qubecs Right to Secessionist Self-determination: The colliding paths of Canadas Clarity Act and Qubecs Fundamental Rights Act*. Unpublished paper.

UK Parliament(1910). Somaliland. *Actas del Parlamento Británico, Cámara de los Comunes [Acts of the British Parliament, Cámara de los Comunes], 16*. https://hansard.parliament.uk/Commons/1910-04-05?showNoDebateMessage=True

UK Parliament. (1920). Successful operations against Mullah, *Actas del Parlamento Británico [Acts of the British Parliment], 125*. https://hansard.parliament.uk/Commons/1920-02-17/debates/0cc406be-0086-41c8-8022-a9c16845e9a5/SuccessfulOperationsAgainstMullah?highlight=mullah#contribution-c81a5a2f-4a19-44e2-91e9-90437b0f2de7

UN. (1957). *Resolution 1012*. UN. http://www.worldlii.org/int/other/UNGA/1957/15.pdf

UN. (1957). *Resolution 1184*. UN. http://www.worldlii.org/int/other/UNGA/1957/127.pdf

UN. (1960). *Resolution 1573*. UN. https://www.noticieroficial.com/Internacional/DIH/ONUAG/ONUAGR1576-1960.pdf

United Nations General Assembly. (1957). *United Nations General Assembly Resolutions*. UN.

United Nations Office of Legal Affairs. (1959). *Article 2 (para. 7); Case N°- 27; The Algerian Question*. UN. https://legal.un.org/repertory/art2/spanish/rep_supp2_vol1_art2_7.pdf

Uoldelul, C. D. (2007). Colonialism and the Construction of National Identities: The Case of Eritrea. *Journal of Eastern African Studies: the Journal of the British Institute in Eastern Africa, 1*(2), 256–276.

Uzoigwe, G. N. (1985). European partition and conquest of Africa: an overview. In A. Adu Bohaen, A. (Ed.), General History of Africa VIII. Africa under colonial domination (1880-1935), (pp. 19-44). UNESCO.

Vaïsse, M (dir). (2014), *De Gaulle et l'Amérique Latine*. Rennes, PUR.

Vaïsse, M. (1998). *La grandeur. Politique étrangère du général de Gaulle*. CNRS Éditions.

Vaïsse, M. (2004). De Gaulle and the Vietnam War. In L. C. Gardner & T. Gittinger (Eds.), *The search for peace in Vietnam (1964-1968)*. Texas A&M University Press.

Vanhanen, T. (2000). A new dataset for measuring democracy, 1810-1998.

Veeser, C., & Bobea, L. (2020). Guerrilla movements in the Dominican Republic. In D. Krujit, E. Rey, & M. Alvarez (Eds.), *Latin American guerrilla movements. Origins, evolution, outcomes*. Routledge.

Velasco de Castro, R. (2012). España ante la «crisis del Trono» alauí: ¿una política de oportunidades perdidas? [Spain in the face of the Alaouite "throne crisis": a policy of missed opportunities?] In *Martínez, L. (coords.): La presencia española en África: del "fecho de Allende" a la crisis de Perejil [The Spanish presence in Africa: from the "Allende date" to the Perejil crisis]* (pp. 131–162). Asociación Veritas.

Velasco de Castro, R. (2013). Objetivos y limitaciones de la política exterior española en Marruecos: La batalla de Tetuán (1859-1860) [Objectives and limitations of Spanish foreign policy in Morocco: The battle of Tetouan (1859-1860).]. *Revista Historia Autónoma, 2,* 93–106.

Villalobos, F. (2004). El sueño colonial. Las guerras de España en Marruecos [The colonial dream. The wars of Spain in Morocco]. *Ariel.*

Villalobos, F. (2004). El sueño colonial: Las guerras de España en Marruecos [The colonial dream: Spain's wars in Morocco]. *Ariel.*

Villanueva, J. R. (2019). El primer gran debate en relaciones internacionales: ¿mito disciplinario? [The first great debate in international relations: disciplinary myth?] In *Lozano Vázquez, A., Sarquís Ramírez, D.J., Villanueva Lira, Jorge, D. ¿Cien años de relaciones internacionales? Disciplinariedad y revisionism [One hundred years of international relations? Disciplinarity and revisionism]* (pp. 195–211). Siglo XXI.

Vitalis, R. (2015). *White world order, black power politics: the birth of American international relations.* Cornell University Press.

VVAA. (1909). Taotai Liu's dimissal causes demostration. *San Francisco Call,* https://cdnc.ucr.edu/cgi-bin/cdnc?a=d&d=SFC19090329.2.21

Wahl, N. (1984), *De Gaulle et le Tiers Monde. Une alliance de raison?* in VV.AA, *De Gaulle et le Tiers Monde.,* Éditions Pedone.

Walker, R. B. J. (1993). *Inside/Outside: International Relations as Political Theory.* Cambridge University Press.

Warren, C., & Higginson, C. (2006). At the Going Down of the Sun, 77-78. Zanj Press.

Weeseling, H. L. (1999). *Divide y vencerás. El reparto de África (1880-1914) [Divide and conquer. The division of Africa (1880-1914).].* Ediciones Península.

Wehler, H.-U. (1969). *Bismarck und der Imperialismus.* [Bismarck and imperialism.] Kiepenheuer u. Witsch.

Wehler, H.-U. (1976). *Bismarck und der Imperialismus [Bismarck and Imperialism].* Deutscher Taschenbuch Verlag.

Wehler, H.-U. (1985). *The German Empire, 1871-1918.* Berg.

Weller, M. (2009). Settling self-determination conflicts: Recent developments. *European Journal of International Law, 20*(1), 111–165. doi:10.1093/ejil/chn078

Wesseling, H. L. (1981). Colonial Wars and Armed Peace, 1870–1914: A Reconnaissance. *Itinerario, 5*(5), 53–73. doi:10.1017/S0165115300007142

Wesseling, H. L. (2013). *The European Colonial Empires, 1815–1919.* Routledge.

Wessels, H. (2015). *A Handful of Hard Men: The SAS and the Battle for Rhodesia.* Casemate.

Westad, O. (2005). *The Global Cold War: Third World Interventions and the Making of Our Times.* Cambridge University Press. doi:10.1017/CBO9780511817991

Westad, O. (2018). *The Cold War. A world history.* Galaxia Gutenberg.

West, O. (2010). Introduction: The United States, the Dominican intervention, and the Cold War. In F. Halliday (Ed.), *Caamaño in London. The exile of a Latin American revolutionary*. University of London.

Weyler y López de Puga, V. (1946). *En el archivo de mi abuelo: biografía del capitán general Weyler [In my grandfather's file: biography of Captain General Weyler]*. Verdad.

Weyler, V. (1910-1911). *Mi mando en Cuba [My command in Cuba.]*. Imp. De Felipe González.

Weyler, V. (2004). *Memorias de un general [Memories of a general]*. Destino.

Wilson, J. (1996). Ethnic groups and the right to self- determination. *Conn. J. Int'l L.*, *11*(3), 433–486.

Wilson, P. (1998). The myth of the first great debate. *Review of International Studies*, *24*(5), 1–13. doi:10.1017/S0260210598000011

Wincler, A. v. (1912). *Im afrikanischen Sonnenbrand [In the African sunburn]*. Verlag Abel & Müller.

Wolf, J. (1994). *Maroc, la vérité sur le protectorat franco-espagnol: l'épopée d'Abd el Khaleq Torres [Morocco, the truth about the Franco-Spanish protectorate: the epic of Abd el Khaleq Torres.]*. Ballànd.

Wood, J. R. (2009). *Counter-strike from the Sky: The Rhodesian All-Arms Fireforce in the War in the Bush, 1974-1980, 30.° SouthPublishers.

Woolf, L. (1935) War and Capitalism. *The New Statesman and Nation*, February 16th.

Woolf, L. (1928/1933). *Imperialism and Civilization*. Hogarth Press.

Wylegala, A., & Glowacka-Grajper, M. (2019). *The Burden of the Past: History, Memory, and Identity in Contemporary Ukraine*. Indiana University Press.

Xiong, Y. (2013). *Zhongguo Jinxiandai Shi Juan [The Chinese Modern History]*. Shanghai Lexicographical Publishing House.

Xu, K., & Mu, Y. (2009). An overview on the Late Ching Government's Commercial Policy towards Spain. In X. Li, & Ch. Li (Ed.), *The Symposium of Conference on "China and Spain during the Ming and Ching Dynasties* (pp. 329-339). Macao Polytechnic Institute.

Yale Law School. (1954). *Lillian Goldman Law Library; The Avalon project; Treaty of Alliance, Political Cooperation, and Mutual Assistance Between the Turkish Republic, the Kingdom of Greece, and the Federal People's Republic of Yugoslavia (Balkan Pact)*. Yale Law School.

Ybarra, M. C. (1993). Acción política española en la independencia de Marruecos (1951-1956) [Spanish political action in the independence of Marruecos (1951-1956).]. In J. Tusell (Eds.), *El Régimen de Franco (1936-1975): política y relaciones exteriores, Tomo II [Franco's Regime (1936-1975): politics and external relations, Tomo II]* (pp. 401–4013). UNED.

Ybarra, M. C. (1998). *España y la descolonización del Magreb. Rivalidad hispano-francesa en Marruecos (1951-1961) []*. UNED.

Yemane, M. (1989). Italian colonialism in Eritrea 1882–1941. *The Scandinavian Economic History Review*, *37*(3), 65–72.

Ylönen, A. (2017). Confronting the 'Arab North': Interpretations of slavery and religion in Southern Sudanese Separatist Resistance. In Taylor, I., João Ramos, M. & Kaarsholm, P. (Eds.) Fluid networks and hegemonic powers in the Western Indian Ocean (pp. 104-129). ISCTE-IUL. .

Yoon, M. (1997, August). Explaining U.S. intervention in Third World internal wars, 1945-1989. *The Journal of Conflict Resolution*, *41*(4), 580–602. doi:10.1177/0022002797041004005

Yusuf Abdi, S. (1977). Independence for the Afars and Issas: Complex Background; Uncertain Future. *Africa Today*, *24*(1), 61–67.

Zantop, S. (1997). *Colonial Fantasies: Conquest, Family, and Nation in Precolonial Germany, 1770-1870*. Duke University Press.

Zarouk, M. (2007). Revisionismo y colonialismo en Marruecos [Revisionism and colonialism in Morocco]. In B. López García and M. Hernando de Larramendi, Historia y memoria de las relaciones hispano-marroquíes [History and memory of Spanish-Moroccan relations] (pp. 45-76). Ediciones de Oriente y del Mediterráneo.

Zewde, B. (2007). Iyasu. In S. Uhlig (Ed.), *Encyclopaedia Aethiopica* (Vol. III, pp. 253–256). Harrasowitz.

Zhaickuan, (Ed.). (1997). *Zhongguo Jiyou Cidian [Diccionario de Filatelia de China]*, vol.2. Beijing Press.

Zhai, Q. (2004). China's response to French peace initiatives. In L. C. Gadner & T. Gittinger (Eds.), *The search for peace in Vietnam (1964-1968)*. Texas A&M University Press.

Zhang, K. (2003). *Historia de las Relaciones Sino-Españolas [History of Sino-Spanish relations]*. Elephant Press.

Ziai, A. (2016). *Development discourse and global history: from colonialism to the sustainable development goals*. Routledge.

Zijderveld, A., den Bol, L., & Zwick, S. (2022). How social media proves to be a vital instrument in times of war in the year 2022. *Shaping Europe. Ideas to bring the European Union forward*. https://shapingeurope.eu/en/

Zimmerer, J. (2011). *Von Windhuk nach Auschwitz: Beiträge zum Verhältnis von Kolonialismus und Holocaust [From Windhoek to Auschwitz: Contributions to the Relationship between Colonialism and the Holocaust]*. LIT Verlag.

About the Contributors

Miguel Madueño Álvarez is a Doctor of Humanities from the Rey Juan Carlos University, with an Extraordinary Prize with a thesis entitled "Falangism during current democracy (1977-2019)". He has a degree in History from the UNED and a specialist in Military History from the IUGM. He is a professor in the Contemporary History Area of the URJC and has taught subjects such as Current World History, Current Spain History, American History, African History and Contemporary Culture. He is the founder and director of the Digital Magazine Guerra Colonial, dedicated to the study of colonial wars, decolonization processes, and neocolonialism.

Alberto Guerrero Martín is PhD in Contemporary History, Master's degree in Strategic Thinking and Global Security and director of the academic journal "Atenea. Revista de la Asociación Española de Historia Militar". Author of several articles and book chapters in the field of military history and strategic studies. Editor of Imperialismo y ejércitos (Editorial de la Universidad de Granada) and Mujeres en la guerra y en los ejércitos (Editorial Los Libros de la Catarata).

***

Julio Alfonso González is a specialist in Military History from the IUGM and has studied for a degree in History with a specialisation in Geography at the UNED. He is a member of the editorial board of the digital magazine Guerra Colonial and his main lines of research are focused on military history, with special attention to colonial wars and armament. He has also published several articles in different specialised journals, including "Tres días de Marzo" in Historia de la Guerra.

Juliia Andriichenko has a PhD in Philological Sciences, Professor of the Department of Romance Philology of the Educational and Scientific Institute of Philology at the Taras Shevchenko National University in kyiv; For 18 years she has been participating in research projects on gender problems in cognitive linguistics and communication strategies; She is the author of more than 60 scientific papers, including monographs, articles, and books.

José Carlos Aránguez Aránguez graduated in History (2013), Interuniversity Master's Degree in Contemporary History (2014) and PhD in Contemporary History (2019) from the Complutense University of Madrid (UCM), he also holds a Master's Degree in Teacher of Compulsory Secondary Education and High School (2021) from the Comillas Pontifical University of Madrid. He is currently professor and coordinator of the Degree in International Relations at the European University of Madrid (UEM), in addition to collaborating with other educational institutions of higher education.

Pablo Arconada Ledesma holds a degree in History (University of Valladolid), a Master's degree in International Relations and African Studies (Autonomous University of Madrid) and a PhD in Contemporary History (University of Valladolid). He is currently Assistant Professor at the University of Valladolid. He is also director of the Observatory of African Studies and member of the African Studies Group (GEA). He has participated in several national and international conferences and has published in indexed journals and several book chapters. His research interests are international relations in the Horn of Africa, Contemporary African History and Cultural Studies.

José Manuel Azcona Pastor professor of Contemporary History at the Universidad Rey Juan Carlos de Madrid (URJC), he teaches the subject History of the Modern World. He is Director of the Ibero-American Chair of Excellence URJC-Santander Presdeia, attached to the Santander Universities Program of Banco Santander. He has been Professor of Contemporary History at the University of Deusto; Professor of Geography at the UNED; and of Economic History at the Official School of the Chamber of Commerce of Bilbao (Center attached to the University of the Basque Country-EHU). He is Master in Cooperation and Security in Ibero-America by CESEDEN (2001) and author of 190 scientific papers published in Spain, Italy, Germany, France, Albania, Bulgaria, United States, Uruguay, Brazil, Mexico, Japan and China on emigration, political violence and terrorism and contemporary political-social movements, in prestigious publishing houses and academic journals with significant impact factor. At the URJC he has been, among other positions, Vice-Dean of Students at the Fuenlabrada Campus, and Director of Social Outreach Activities and Director of Cultural Activities between 2001 and 2013. Since 2019 he has been Director of the Senior University. He is coordinator of the Contemporary History Area of the URJC.

Alfonso Bermúdez Mombiela (Zaragoza, 1992), is a Juan de la Cierva-Formación postdoctoral researcher at the Grup de Recerca en Estats Nacions i Sobiranies (GRENS) of the Pompeu Fabra University of Barcelona, where he was previously a Margarita Salas postdoctoral researcher. He holds a PhD in Contemporary History from the University of Zaragoza, with a thesis entitled: Colonialismo español a principios del siglo XX: el impacto de las Guerras de Marruecos en Zaragoza (1906-1927), for which he has carried out several national and international research stays at the Internationaal Instituut voor Sociale Geschiedenis (IISG) in Amsterdam and Trinity College Dublin. His lines of research focus on the repercussions of the Moroccan Wars in 20th century Spain, the impact of recruitment systems on the Spanish population, and the analysis of colonial discourses in comparative perspective. He has published several articles in scientific journals on these subjects, such as the Revista Universitaria de Historia Militar (RUHM) and the Revista Digital de Guerra Colonial, and has participated in numerous meetings and conferences.

Javier Castro Arcos is director of the Department of History, Universidad Gabriela Mistral, Santiago de Chile. Associate Researcher at the Center for International Studies of the Pontificia Universidad Católica de Chile (CEIUC). Javier holds a PHD in History from the Universidad de los Andes, Santiago de Chile, and a MA in International Studies from the Instituto de Estudios Avanzados of the Universidad de Santiago de Chile. He was Visiting Research Associate at The University of Texas, Austin, USA. He has developed lines of research in the field of international relations and history of international relations, with special emphasis on Latin America. Among his publications are: Guerra en el Vientre: Birth Control, Malthusianism and Cold War in Chile (1960-1970). Santiago, Bicentenario, 2017. With Cristián Garay, Chile and the Korean War. An episode in Chilean foreign policy. Revista de Relaciones Internacionales. Universidad Militar de Nueva Granada, Colombia. Vol. 12, n°1, 2017. Guerra por el Desarrollo: El control de la natalidad en Chile 1960-1970, Revista Complutense de Historia de América, Universidad Complutense de Madrid, Vol. 41, 2015. With Pedro Martínez Lillo "En torno al Orden Internacional del siglo XXI" in Revista Alcores de Historia Contemporánea, N°24, 2020. With Froilán Ramos, Tensiones de la Guerra Fría: Chile y la Primavera de Praga (1968). Perseitas, 10, 216-249, 2022. Finally, the papers: Neomalthusianismo en América Latina: Paradigma de seguridad hemisférica norteamericana durante la Guerra Fría, Revista de Historia y Geografía Núm. 46 (2022), and Neomalthusianismo, Guerra Fría, y redes evangélicas trasnacionales en la guerra contra el hambre, Chile (1960-1970). Secuencia, Journal of History and Social Sciences. Mora Institute, CONACYT. N° 111 (2021) September-December, 2021.

Felipe Debasa Navalpotro is a professor of Contemporary History and Current World at the Rey Juan Carlos University. Director of the official Master in the European Union and China. Secretary of the Area of Contemporary History framed in the Department of Humanities. Among his lines of research are technology, the IV Industrial Revolution and transhumanism. Author of various publications in the field of digital humanities in which he implements technological processes from other disciplines in history and in legal and social sciences.

María Gajate Bajo has a PhD in History from the University of Salamanca (2011) and Extraordinary Doctorate Award (2012), specialising in Contemporary Military History from the University Jaime I (2016). Her lines of research include: the Spanish-Moroccan military campaigns, the attitude of public opinion towards them, intellectual thought and the use of war propaganda. He has published the monograph Las campañas de Marruecos y la opinión pública. El ejemplo de Salamanca y su prensa and is co-editor of Guerra y Tecnología. Interaction from Antiquity to the Present.

César García Andrés holds a degree in History (University of Valladolid), a Master's degree in European Integration (University of Valladolid) and a PhD in Contemporary History (University of Valladolid). He is also treasurer of the Observatory of African Studies and member of the Research Group "Historical Memory, Human Rights and Political Transitions". He has participated in several national and international conferences and has published in indexed journals and several book chapters. His lines of research revolve around European integration and Africa-Europe relations.

Mariano García de las Heras is a historian and political scientist. Pre-doctoral fellow in the Political Science and Administration and International Relations at the Complutense University of Madrid (UCM). Member of the Research Group "Espacio y Poder" and Editorial Secretary of Geopolítica(s). His academic interests are border studies, geopolitical discourses and political violence in the contemporary world.

Luis Illanas García is a graduate in history from the UNED, a specialist in Mediterranean and Middle East Security and International Conflict Resolution from the IUGM, a peace process operator from the EGET and a specialist course on the Balkans and frozen conflicts from the UCM. He is a researcher at the URJC Santander Presdeia Chair and editor of the journal Guerra Colonial. He also collaborates with the international politics magazine Atalayar and with media outlets such as Radio Nacional de España.

Miguel Ángel López de la Asunción (Madrid, 1973) has a degree in English Philology from the Complutense University of Madrid (UCM), where he also studied Romance Philology and obtained the Certificate of Pedagogical Aptitude from its Institute of Education Sciences. He is a member of the Spanish Association of Military History (ASEHISMI), historical adviser to the Blas de Lezo Foundation and adviser to the Spanish Federation of History Associations (FEAH) and an Honorary member of the History Association of the Carlos III University and the Association IV Promotion of the Basic General Academy of NCOs of the Spanish Army. He is co-author of the books Los Últimos de Filipinas: Mito y realidad del sitio de Baler (Actas, 2016) and El Sitio de Baler: La heroica gesta de los Últimos de Filipinas (Actas, 2022), as well as a multitude of articles. In 2020, he was awarded the accreditation diploma at the Ejército Magazine Awards for his article «Claves para la exitosa defensa de la posición de Baler». Likewise, he has been curator of the exhibition Los Últimos de Filipinas: La gesta de Baler (1898-1899), in the city of Guadalajara.

Pedro Martínez Lillo is Chair of University in the Department of Contemporary History at the Universidad Autónoma de Madrid, and Director of the Jesús de Polanco Chair of Ibero-American Studies (UAM-Fundación Santillana). Master in European Communities by the Spanish Ministry of Foreign Affairs. Specialist in History of International Relations, Spanish Foreign Policy and Contemporary Latin America, he has been Visiting Professor at the Colegio de Veracruz (Mexico) as well as Visiting Professor at the Institute of History of the Pontifical Catholic University of Chile, the Center for Latin American Cultural Studies (CECLA) of the University of Chile, the Institute of International Studies (IEI) of Chile, the Institute of Advanced Studies (IDEA) of the University of Santiago de Chile (USACH), and the Diplomatic Academy Andrés Bello of the Ministry of Foreign Affairs of Chile. In recent years he has worked as Visiting Fellow at Sciences Po (CERI-CNRS-Paris), Visiting Fellow at the Institut des Hautes Études de l'Amérique Latine (IHEAL-Paris III), and Visiting Scholar at LLILAS-Benson, University of Texas. His books include Pedro A. Martínez Lillo, Una introducción a las relaciones hispano-francesas (1945-1950), Fundación Juan March, Madrid, 1985; Juan Carlos Pereira and Pedro A. Martínez Lillo, Documentos básicos sobre la historia de las relaciones internacionales (1815-1990), Editorial Complutense, Madrid, 1995; Pedro A. Martínez Lillo and Juan Carlos Pereira, La Organización de las Naciones Unidas, Arco-Libros Madrid, 2001. Pedro A. Martínez Lillo and Pablo Rubio, América Latina actual. Del populismo al giro de izquierdas, La Catarata, Madrid, 2017; and Pedro A. Martínez Lillo and Pablo Rubio, América Latina y Tiempo Presente. Historia y documentos, LOM Editorial, Santiago de Chile, 2015. Pedro A. Martínez Lillo and Joaquín Estefanía (coords.), América Latina: un nuevo contrato social, Marcial Pons, Madrid, 2016. And Pedro A. Martínez Lillo and Juan Carlos Pereira, Historia y Presente de las Relaciones Internacionales. Documentos básicos (1914-2017), Editorial Universitas, Madrid, 2018.

Roberto Muñoz Bolaños has a PhD in Contemporary History from the Universidad Autónoma de Madrid and lecturer at the Universidad del Atlántico Medio, Universidad Camilo José Cela, Universidad Francisco de Vitoria and Universidad Nebrija. He specialises in 20th century military history. He has written more than thirty articles in academic journals, more than twenty chapters in collective books and ten books, including Guernica, una nueva historia: Las claves que no se han contado (Espasa, 2017), Las conspiraciones del 36: Militares y civiles contra el Frente Popular (Espasa, 2019), and El 23-F y los otros golpes de Estado de la Transición (Espasa, 2021). In 2015 he won the Javier Tusell Prize for New Historians for his article "La última trinchera: el poder militar y el problema de la Unión Militar

Democrática durante la transición y la consolidación democrática, 1975-1986" ("The Last Trench: Military Power and the Problem of the Democratic Military Union during the Transition and Democratic Consolidation, 1975-1986").

José Luis Neila Hernández has a PhD in Contemporary History from the Complutense University of Madrid (1994) and Professor of the Department of Contemporary History of the Faculty of Philosophy and Letters of the Autonomous University of Madrid since 2021, the center from which I have carried out my academic activity since 1994. My professional career has been inextricably linked to reference lines of work intertwined from the history of international relations and the history of Spanish foreign policy, from which my research profile, my activity and my teaching training have grown, and a very of the informative activity in the publishing world. A journey in which interest has been aroused towards other historiographical areas, particularly towards the history of the present time and towards cultural history, and the exchange and collaboration with other colleagues from the neighboring social sciences has been intensifying. This is evident in the participation in various research projects in which I have worked on the international dimension of the political transition in Spain, the articulation of a democratic foreign policy, the image of Spain today or more recently Spain, the studies international organizations and intellectual cooperation after the Great War

Guanjie Niu is an associate professor at the History School of the Renmin University of China. His research interests include Qing and modern China history. he wrote several books, such as The Structure of the rulership in China in the mid-19th Century, The Market and Economic Development in China from the 17th Century to 19 Century, and published dozens of papers, such as Historical Writing and the Formation of the Qing Empire's Political Influence: Based on the Manzhou Yuanliu Kao(Central Asiatic Journal), Contracting without contracting institutions: The trusted assistant loan in 19th century China(Journal of Financial Economics)

Pedro Panera Martínez holds a degree in History from the University of León and posses various masters and postgraduate courses in History, Diplomacy and International Relations. Currently hired as full-time predoctoral researcher at IUGM-UNED, he is carrying out his PhD in the field of Military History and International Relations.

Natalia Popova has a PhD in Philological Sciences, Professor of the Department of Romance Philology of the Educational and Scientific Institute of Philology at the Tarás Shevchenko National University of kyiv; a member of the Scientific and Methodological Council of the University. For 22 years she has been participating in research projects on discourse pragmatics, cultural and cognitive linguistics, stylistics and communication strategies; She is the author of more than 75 scientific papers, including monographs, articles, and books.

Raúl Ramírez Ruiz is a profesor Titular de la Universidad Rey Juan Carlos (Madrid) y Director del Grupo de Investigación Consolidado en Relaciones España-China (1864-1931) de la URJC. Fue Investigador del Congreso de los Diputados (2000-2020); Profesor visitante becado por la fundación de investigación "José Castillejo" en el Centro de Estudios de China en el Extranjero de la East China Normal University (ECNU) en 2012; Profesor visitante del "Understanding China of New Sinology Program" 2015. Ha sido invitado a dar conferencias sobre historia china y las relaciones entre China y

España en diversas universidades chinas. Entre su obra de carácter sinológico destacan las monografías China. Historia, pensamiento, arte y cultura (2011) e Historia de China contemporánea. De las Guerras del Opio a nuestros días (2018) y diversos artículos publicados en español, inglés y chino, en: España, Estados Unidos, Costa Rica, México y China.

Jerónimo Ríos Sierra is currently Lecturer in Political Geography at the Faculty of Political Science and Sociology of the Complutense University of Madrid and was previously a Postdoctoral Researcher Fellow in the excellence programme "Attraction of Research Talent 2018" co-funded by the Community of Madrid. He has taught at various universities in Colombia, Spain and Canada and has carried out short research stays in universities such as Granada, Valencia, Coimbra (Portugal) and San Martín de Porres (Peru), as well as being an advisor to the Organization of Ibero-American States in Colombia during the process of dialogue and implementation of the Peace Agreement with the FARC-EP. His main lines of research are political violence and insurgencies in Latin America, with special attention to the cases of Colombia and Peru, and he also investigates critical geopolitics and discourses on violence and security on the Latin American continent.

Natalija Shikova is an Associate Professor at the Faculty of Law, International Balkan University in Skopje, the Republic of North Macedonia. Her main area of interest is International Public law. She is an author of a books, articles, and analyses in the related field. Except for the academic, she has more than 15 years of professional experience in assisting the national and international constituencies as a local and international consultant in the field of EU integration, creation of public policies, human rights protection, confidence-building measures, etc.

Iryna Sitdykova has a PhD in Philology, Head and Professor of the Department of Romance Philology of the Educational and Scientific Institute of Philology at the Taras Shevchenko National University in Kyiv. For 25 years she has participated in research projects on the French language and communication strategies; She is the author of many scientific papers, including monographs, articles, and books.

Index

T

U

W

Y

Z

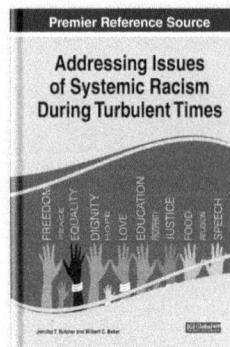

Ingram Content Group UK Ltd.
Milton Keynes UK
UKHW051827120523
421682UK00007B/57

9 781668 470404